PRISONERS OF CLASS

"Of the many Khmer Rouge survivor memoirs that have been published, *Prisoners of Class* stands out as the most raw, immediate, and honest of them all. With prose of sheer poetry, Chan Samoeun takes you on a guided tour of the killing fields. You will never be the same after reading it."

—Craig Etcheson, author of *After the Killing Fields*

"Chan Samoeun's *Prisoners of Class* is among the earliest, most detailed, and most vividly rendered accounts of the Khmer Rouge revolution. Written in the immediate wake of the chaotic and tragic events that it narrates, the memoir details with spare, unfiltered detail the terrors of everyday life under Pol Pot's Panopticon, and the almost miraculous resilience of those forced to endure it. The book, available to English readers for the first time in Matthew Madden's sparkling translation, is a priceless new addition to the testimonial literature on the Khmer Rouge, which sheds new light on one of the greatest tragedies— indeed, crimes—of the twentieth century."

—Sebastian Strangio, author of *Hun Sen's Cambodia*

"*Prisoners of Class* is a poignant and personal journey through a society turned upside down. Through its proximity to the events described, Chan Samoeun's memoir gives a unique and captivating voice to a tragic chapter in Cambodian history shared by so many."

—Lachlan Peters, host and creator of the *In the Shadows of Utopia* podcast

"[*Prisoners of Class*] makes a contribution to documenting the lives of victims of the Khmer Rouge and to preserving a history for later generations of Cambodian to study and prevent such a regime from rising again."

—Chhang Youk, director of the Documentation Center of Cambodia (on the Khmer edition)

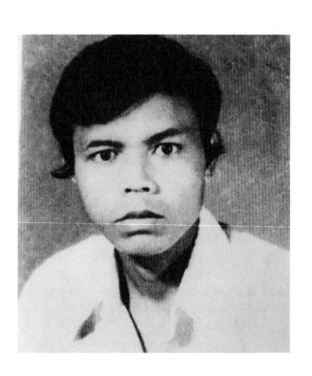

PRISONERS OF CLASS
A Historical Memoir of the Khmer Rouge Revolution

Chan Samoeun

translated from the original Khmer by
Matthew Madden

with a foreword and afterword by the translator

Mekong
River
Press

Behind my back are the rice fields where the grains of rice ripen and turn golden, covering the face of the land. And even further behind me is the land of Phnom Srok district, the place where my younger brother, my cousin, my sisters, my uncle, and my nieces were killed or lost their lives, their bones littering the earth and the woods. My body walks forward, but my feelings run backward, as though pining for the land that took the lives of my family, the place that left me and my brother orphaned and aimless young men. No! I do not pine for that blood-soaked land. But I miss my brother, my sisters, and my uncle...And now I am walking away from them, leaving behind their corpses, victims of unnatural deaths, left in woods without graves, without relatives or friends.

Contents

Poems and Songs

A Brief Historical Note

Cambodia is a small Southeast Asian kingdom, bordered by Vietnam on the east, Thailand on the west and north, and Laos to the north. Its primary religion is Theravada Buddhism. Its main ethnic majority are referred to as Khmers, and the national language is Khmer. The capital city, sitting at the confluence of the Mekong and Sap rivers, is called Phnom Penh.

The kingdom was colonized by France for nearly a century, from 1863 until 1953 when it secured full independence from France under the leadership of King Norodom Sihanouk. Sihanouk abdicated the throne a year later to take a leading role in Cambodian electoral politics, which he dominated for the next fifteen years as a popular and powerful head of state.

On 18 March 1970, Sihanouk was deposed in a parliamentary *coup* by his prime minister, General Lon Nol. This seminal event broke Sihanouk's long and carefully maintained neutrality that had kept Cambodia out of the Vietnam War raging next door, as Lon Nol immediately aligned with the United States against the communists, causing the conflict to spill over into Cambodia.

Thus began a bloody civil war, as Lon Nol founded the Khmer Republic, notoriously corrupt and heavily funded by United States military aid; and the embittered Sihanouk, with Chinese support, publicly allied himself with the Cambodian faction of communists, dubbed (by him) the "Khmer Rouge," in an armed resistance against the new government. Hoping for a return to power, Sihanouk allowed himself to be made the nominal figurehead of this armed resistance, and because he was highly revered by many Cambodians, especially in the countryside, this decision lent tremendous influence and strength to the Khmer Rouge in recruiting large-scale support from the Cambodian populace.

Five years of violent conflict and devastating national division led, ultimately, to an imminent Khmer Rouge victory in mid-April 1975. As Khmer Rouge forces surrounded Phnom Penh for the final battle against disintegrating government forces and prepared to capture the city, the city's population eagerly awaited the end of the war and the return of peace.

Foreword

Chan Samoeun penned the original manuscript for *Prisoners of Class* shortly after the collapse of the Khmer Rouge regime in 1979, in a stack of school composition notebooks, while taking refuge in a village in northern Cambodia. Over the previous four years, as much as a quarter of the country's population had perished under almost unimaginable circumstances, including most of his family, and he labored to capture in writing a detailed and personal account of that devastating period.

Due to circumstances of poverty, instability, and uncertainty, it would be another twenty years before he would publish his manuscript. He published it serially in five parts, in Phnom Penh, between November 1999 and July 2000, under his professional pseudonym, Oum Sambath. Originally titled *1366 Days in Hell*, the memoir was retitled *Prisoners of Class* with the publication of Part Three in February 2000. He explained in the preface to that volume that the original title captured the "duration of the suffering, but not the essence of the book," adding shrewdly that it was also "wordy and cumbersome to say." The new title succinctly captured the essence of the memoir, as a central theme of the book is the relegation of the author's family, along with millions of other city-based Cambodians, to a slave-like, disposable underclass.

The second Khmer edition was published in 2006, this time as a single paperback volume, by the Angkor Book Shop in Phnom Penh.

I first became aware of *Prisoners of Class* in 2001 or 2002 when I came across the first two volumes in a bookseller's stall in Tuol Tumpung Market, in Phnom Penh. They were thin volumes with flimsy paper covers, stark black with the old title in white text, priced somewhere around one US dollar apiece.

I was intrigued by what I had found, and when I began to read, I was captivated. The richly detailed account of the fall of Phnom Penh on 17 April 1975 and the days that followed vividly described familiar settings from my own time coming of age in Phnom Penh in the late 1990's. I was drawn in by the vibrant and meticulous details, the immediacy, and the emotional evocativeness of the narrative. I was impressed that here was a full-length Khmer Rouge survivor memoir written not one or two decades later for a Western audience by a refugee, but very early—almost immediately after the liberation—and in Khmer, by a man who had remained behind while countless others fled to the refugee camps. There is no other work like it. And the writing was, I felt, of a depth and quality belied by the humble state of its publication. The prose, itself often lyrical, was punctuated throughout with original poems. I concluded right away that this remarkable work was a hidden historical treasure that ought to be translated into English and brought to the awareness of the world outside Cambodia, and I aspired to be the person to do this, though I felt insufficiently qualified to do so at the time.

And then time passed, as it does. I married the local Phnom Penh girl I was courting and settled back in the United States, where I am from. Over the years that followed, I worked as a Khmer-English court interpreter and freelance translator. I studied linguistics. I divorced and remarried.

In 2012 I returned to Cambodia to work for the detention program of the International Committee of the Red Cross in Phnom Penh, working with everyone from the lowliest detainee in Cambodian prisons to senior government officials on issues of prison conditions and overcrowding. In the course of that work, I personally met and conversed with senior leaders and architects of the Khmer Rouge revolution in the detention facilities of the UN-backed Khmer Rouge tribunal, including Pol Pot's comrades Khieu Samphan, Nuon Chea, and Ieng Sary, as well as Duch, former commander of the notorious S-21 prison.

Through it all, I kept *Prisoners of Class* simmering on a back burner, returning to the text and translating chapters intermittently over the years. I picked up another volume in a Phnom Penh store in 2002, and I completed the set in 2005 when I found the final two volumes in a bin of books at the Bayon Market in Long Beach, California.

In the meantime, Tomoko Okada, professor of Khmer Literature at Tokyo University of Foreign Studies, reacted to the book much as I had done and in 2004 wrote to ask the author for permission to translate it into Japanese. Her translation was published in Japan in 2007 by the Daido Foundation under the title *1366 Days in Hell*[1] by Oum Sambath.

It wasn't until early 2022, living back in the US a full two decades after my first encounter with the book, that I resolved to dedicate that year to the completion of the English translation, the great unfulfilled ambition of my life, and

---

[1] 地獄の1366日

bring it to print. It's true that I had benefitted from the two intervening decades by maturing and growing in experience as a Khmer speaker and translator; but I feared that perhaps I had delayed too long, and that if I waited any longer, the author would no longer be alive to authorize the project. So, in early 2022 I searched for the author from afar and was pleased to find him, with the help of the Khmer Writers Association, still alive and retired in Phnom Penh at the age of seventy. I sent him a letter asking his blessing to translate and publish his book in English, and told him of my profound appreciation for his work:

> I first read your book *Prisoners of Class* some time ago. I have a strong interest and affinity for the book and a desire to translate it into English for publication...I feel that the world ought to have the opportunity to become acquainted with your harrowing experiences and your eloquent recounting of that period of Cambodian history.
>
> While there are already accounts of the period written in English, virtually every author is a refugee in a foreign country, writing many years after the fact, for a foreign audience in a foreign language. But the world has never seen a memoir written by a Khmer author living in Cambodia, written in Khmer, penned while the events were still so fresh and bright in the memory of the author as *Prisoners of Class* was.
>
> Your book is uniquely special for these reasons; but your writing is also vivid and clear and riveting in its own right, besides. I am moved while reading it. *Prisoners of Class* is filled with many detailed descriptions of such things as the geography...the labor, the illnesses, the modes of travel, the weather, the food, the flora and fauna, etc. of the time, all of which bring the account to life and make *Prisoners of Class* an important historical document with tremendous value. I believe that many foreigners who are interested in Cambodian history would take great interest in this document and your unique perspective, as I have done, if it were to be published in English.

I was delighted to receive a letter back from him right away, in which he wrote, in part,

I want to tell you that it has been my wish to translate *Prisoners of Class* for a very long time....

If *Prisoners of Class* were to be translated into English, it could be shared with the world. I thank you for your perfect appraisal of my memoir. I want to tell you that when preparing the manuscript [for publication], I wrote in my bedroom with the door closed so that my wife and children would not see. I feared that my wife would think I was crazy, as tears flowed down my cheeks while I wrote. There was not a page of that draft manuscript that was not soaked by my tears. Even as I write this letter to you now, my tears fall like raindrops. The suffering, the starvation, the separation from my parents and siblings, the working like cattle without rest, the loss of my beloved—all of these things are imprinted indelibly on my feelings.

I am delighted and pleased to give you permission to translate my book into English as requested.

With his blessing in hand, I set about over the following year to complete my translation. This was achieved with the cooperation and friendship of Chan Samoeun himself, as during that year I returned to Cambodia, where I had the remarkable honor of meeting, befriending, and traveling with him personally, and of visiting many of the sites described in the book. I was fortunate beyond expectation to be able to ask him many questions about the text and speak with him in person about his experiences, after all those years, sometimes in the very settings where the events occurred. Through that process I would learn for myself, on multiple occasions, how truly close to the surface this man's tears lie. An account of those experiences is found in the afterword to this book.

Now it is my great pleasure to present, for the first time in print, the English translation of *Prisoners of Class*.

Matthew Madden, 15 January 2023

Preface

In Cambodian society we have very few articles or books describing the real lives of people who lived in any era of our history. When I was young, my mother often told her children about the difficulty and misery of life during the French colonial era and during the Japanese occupation. But we don't see any books about the real-life stories of people who lived in those times. We don't share in their suffering, and we scarcely remember their bitter experiences. Those events of history have faded away along with the generations of people who lived in those times. For this reason, we see that Cambodian society is a perpetually new society, without the continuity of experience and knowledge from earlier generations passed on to later generations. What documents we do see are mostly compositions or elaborations on the views of some author or a politician; they rarely reflect the true lives of the common people in society.

Apathy toward the bitter lives of our ancestors and forefathers makes us ungrateful people. We are "newcomers on old land." It is a tragedy that we are still ignorant of how to resolve the same problems that our forefathers faced.

Though I had never been a writer, after passing through the dark period under the Pol Pot[1] regime I attempted to compile an account of my family's real-life experiences during that stage of history. True, it is the story of the personal misery of me and my family; but it also reflects the reality that Cambodians in that period faced and experienced, and the awful burden that millions of Cambodians carried on their backs during that unspeakably horrific time.

The piles of bones cannot relate to you the experiences that they went through, the obstacles that they overcame, or the torment that they endured before they quit this life. And the story will remain a mystery if those who shared the stage with them, who have not yet turned to bones, do not attempt to unfold the truth.

My children and my grandchildren will never know the pain of missing my mother and father, my brother, and my sisters. But I still miss them. My tears still fall in sorrowful remembrance. We left the city together, but they did not

---

[1] 1925–1998; general secretary (1962–1981) of the Communist Party of Kampuchea (otherwise known as the Khmer Rouge) and prime minister (1976–1979) of Democratic Kampuchea (the official name of the country under the Khmer Rouge). Note that *Kampuchea* is synonymous with *Cambodia*.

return with me. The city of my birth...yet there are no friends from birth left alive.

I began writing this memoir in October 1979 and finished in early April 1980. But since that time, because circumstances have not permitted it, I have never had a chance to compile it into a book. I feel that now is a good opportunity for this memoir to finally be revealed to the world, to become an aid to the next generation of Cambodians in the search to understand the lives of their parents under the Pol Pot regime, and in studying ways to prevent this bitter history from coming back to haunt Cambodian society again.

Phnom Penh, 20 November 1999
Chan Samoeun

Acknowledgements

I wish to express my gratitude to the people of Prey A village in Kralanh district, and the people of Ta Toy village, Puok district (currently called Angkor Chum district), Siem Reap province, for caring for me and my younger brother after our escape from the Pol Pot regime. This created the ease that allowed me to compile this bitter memoir.

I wish to dedicate any merit that may arise from the writing of this book to the souls of my parents, brother, sisters, uncle, grandparents, and kin who lost their lives in our journey through Hell on Earth.

I wish to also dedicate merit to my foster father Puk Pong, Mea Mil, and my brothers and sisters of Ta Toy who have departed this life. Some of them lost their lives under tremendous suffering. May their souls pass on to Paradise.

Birth Determines History

Under light rain we flee the Viets[1] and take refuge in Prey A
Khmers who love Khmers offer pity I take up a pen and record my history.

A life of suffering and wasting away days and months in a row
left behind as a record as an admonition to endure life.

chorus:
My children, live in happiness heavy labors your father has endured,
swollen and shriveled endure hardship, my children.

Trapeang Thmor is the work of all young, old, men, women, living, dead
Khmers striving to leave a legacy remember till death, Khmer patriots.

penned on 10 October 1979

---

[1] Note that in traditional Khmer poetic forms such as this, couplets continue from left to right across a column break before moving to the next line. This form is followed with all of the poetry in this book.

Part One: Abandoning the City

Introduction

In order to help the reader better understand my story, I wish to relate some of my family's background and history before the events of 17 April 1975.

My father, Pen Doeuk,[1] was born in 1909 in Tuol Ampil village, Koki sub-district, Kien Svay district, Kandal province. He took a wife in Tuol Ampil and had two sons and a daughter with her. Because of marital troubles, my father left when his children were small to become a worker on a commercial boat transporting rice from Battambang province to Vietnam, saying nothing to his mother or sisters. When the Japanese occupied Cambodia,[2] my father took work pedaling a *cyclo*[3] in Phnom Penh.

My mother, Chan It, was born in 1913 in Ampe Tum village, Lumpung subdistrict, Bati district, Takeo province. Her father died when she was only a year old. Afterward, my grandmother took a new husband called Ta Chan and had two sons and another daughter with him. She died when my mother was a teenager. My grandfather then took the four children to live in Phnom Penh, where he worked pulling a rickshaw.

When my mother came of age, she married a man called Neang, who worked pedaling a *cyclo*. She gave birth to two sons named Lon and Leang and a daughter named Ol. When her daughter was only a year old, her husband fell in love with another woman in Prek Ta Pov village, Ta Khmau subdistrict, Kandal Steung district, Kandal province. He asked my mother for a divorce in order to marry his lover. Without bearing a grudge, my mother took her young children to see the wedding of their father to his new wife. She was willing to live life as a divorcee, selling grilled beef at the "Stone Theater" (the Spean Kon Kat Theater)[4] to support her three children.

My mother and father met and married each other during the Japanese occupation. However, my father never told my mother about his past, his place of birth, or his family. My mother often said that my father was a sober man, of few words, but very patient and stern.

---

[1] Cambodian names throughout the book follow the Cambodian custom of surname first, followed by given name.

[2] 1941–45

[3] a classic Cambodian pedicab/trishaw in which the driver pedals behind while the passenger rides in front; pronounced *see-klo;* from the French *cyclopousse;* see photograph on page 508

[4] The location of this theater is uncertain, though the author believes it was likely near Wat Lanka, as his mother lived in that area at the time.

Their first daughter together died at age one. Their second daughter, my older sister Oun, was born later. Then followed their third child, a son, who was me—born in July 1951. But my mother still knew nothing of my father's background. She said that when I was born, I was a chubby baby and that my parents, uncles, aunts, and siblings all fell in love with me and started calling me "A-Tuch."[5] My mother took advantage of these circumstances, when I was just old enough to sit up, by threatening to divorce my father if he continued to insist on hiding his past.

Cornered, my father told my mother about his relatives and friends in his home village; but still he refused to take her to meet her mother-in-law. It wasn't long before my mother was off with her younger sister to my father's home village, toting me along with them.

Leaving the taxi in front of Wat Slaket, my mother walked through the *wat*,[6] through the cemetery behind the *wat*, through the trees at Don Duong Lake, and up to Tuol Ampil. She asked around for the home of Grandmother Ruos and was directed to the house.

Grandmother Ruos was an old woman who sat in her house sucking on betel nut. My mother carried me up the stairs, brought me near my grandmother, and set me down. She got on her knees and raised her hands, palms together, three times toward her mother-in-law. My grandmother was stunned and sat watching her with eyes open wide. My mother lifted me up and handed me to my grandmother.

She said, "Mother, this is A-Tuch, your grandson!" Grandmother reluctantly held out her arms to take me, not understanding what was happening. My mother then told her everything.

It had been more than ten years since my father left his mother and sisters without a word. They had assumed that he was dead, and every year since they had performed ceremonies to ease his soul in the afterlife. On this day she met her grandson in the stead of her son, and she wept with joy and hugged me tightly to her chest. All of the villagers gathered around to look at my mother, delighted to learn that my father was still alive.

---

[5] *Tuch* means "tiny." The prefix *A-* is commonly attached to intimate nicknames and indicates very informal closeness.

[6] a Buddhist monastery and temple (or "pagoda") complex, consisting of the grounds, the temple itself, stupas, monks' dormitories, and other buildings

From that time on my father began to visit his home village, though he never went to see his first wife. A few years later my grandmother passed away.

In those days Phnom Penh was not very crowded, but my mother was unable to buy land to build a hut. She couldn't live outside the city, either, because her occupation required her to be where the population was; so she would always ask to build her hut on the available land of others.

Lon and Leang sold *kantuot*[7] fruit preserves in front of the Stone Theater. One day Leang tripped and spilled all of the preserves. Fearing that my father would beat him, he took Lon to Wat Chak Angre Krom and asked the monks if they could live there. Our grandfather passed away at that time, further reducing the number of family members at home. But still the landlord asked my parents to remove their hut from his land.

In 1953, with the birth of my younger brother Samat, my parents moved their hut from the area behind Wat Langka to the area north of Wat Tuol Tumpung, near the later site of the Raksmei Chantrea Tuol Tumpung Theater. (At the time, the theater was not yet built.) Unable to sell grilled beef, my mother began a new line of work making clay piggy banks. My father continued to pedal his *cyclo*. However, we couldn't stay there for long either, as we had again built our hut on someone else's land.

In 1956, after the birth of their youngest son, Samorn, my family once again moved our residence. By then I was old enough to remember what was happening, and I remember that I, my mother, and my two younger brothers rode on an oxcart with some of the heavier items. My two sisters walked behind the cart with my father and Thom Pen,[8] who carried some of our belongings using shoulder yokes.

We traveled to the area south of Phnom Penh and settled on the west shore of Boeng Trabek lake. There were very few houses there—only the small shacks of some fishermen and a handful of people farming rice on the shore of the lake. There it was easy to find clay for piggy banks and fish to eat, and sometimes my older sister Oun and I would go gather snails, *trakuon*,[9] and water hyacinths

---

[7] *Phyllanthus acidus*

[8] Author's note: "The husband of my mother's cousin. He divorced my mother's cousin when I was still small, but he continued living with my family."

[9] *Ipomoea aquatica*; "bindweed" or "water convolvulus," an edible green plant that grows in still water, very commonly eaten as a vegetable (both cultivated and foraged) in Cambodian cooking

from the lake to sell in Tuol Tumpung market. However, it was difficult for my father to pedal his *cyclo* into the city to work. Perhaps it was for this reason that he changed occupations and became a house-construction carpenter, the final occupation of his life.

Our house[10] was on the second road south of Phsar Daeum Thkov Primary School[11] (currently Street 490). My family lived there until we were evacuated from Phnom Penh.

Within a short time after Lon Nol's *coup d'état*[12] of 18 March 1970, all four of my older siblings had been married:

- Lon was a worker in a cigarette factory in Chak Angre Lue. He had a wife and three children and a house to the east of us. He died from an illness in the middle of 1970.

- Leang had more education than Lon and worked in the Ministry of Commerce. He had five children and a house in the Or Baek K'am neighborhood.

- My oldest sister, Ol, had a husband who worked as a janitor in the Preah Suramarit Dispensary (the Phsar Daeum Thkov clinic).[13] She also worked making clay piggy banks and had a house behind ours. She never had children, but in 1972 she adopted a one-year-old baby girl whom she named Sophal.

- My next-oldest sister, Oun, was married in 1973. Her husband worked building brick-and-cement houses. She made clay piggy banks with my mother and lived in our house. She had a small daughter named A-Lin.

Before the coup, Samat (my younger brother) studied at Yuvachun Sraoch Srong Cheat High School.[14] After the coup, he volunteered for the army and

---

[10] a wooden Khmer-style house raised on stilts

[11] present-day Phsar Daeum Thkov High School

[12] Though this event is usually styled as such, arguably it was not really a *coup d'état*—defined as an *illegal* seizure of power—as the event was carried out by vote of the national assembly using constitutional procedures.

[13] "Preah Suramarit Dispensary" was the official name of this clinic for many years, though it was often colloquially called "the Phsar Daeum Thkov clinic" after the adjacent market; presently the official name is the Phsar Daeum Thkov Health Center

[14] "Youth of National Salvation High School," a state athletics school located on the grounds of the so-called "Old Stadium"

was sent to train at Lam Son, Vietnam, for an entire year while my parents heard nothing of him. My mother was depressed because she missed her son; my father acted like he didn't care, but he silently worried about him.

Samorn (my youngest brother) graduated from Phsar Daeum Thkov Primary School and then quit school to go to work, building brick-and-cement houses to help the family make ends meet.

On multiple occasions, Samorn was surrounded by military police, herded into a truck, and taken to a CI[15] (military training center). Sometimes it was at Kbal Thnal, and sometimes it was as far away as Ampe Phnom. After CI, recruits were sent to a base or to the battlefield. My mother would worry and couldn't sleep, waiting for news of her son. Whenever I got word that he was out of the CI, I would send my mother to liberate him and bring him back home again. On one occasion we went together to rescue Samorn from the Setbo military base south of Ta Khmau.

As a student, I was able to escape the forced military conscriptions. I studied at the Applied High School on the campus of the College of Pedagogy. After I received my *diplôme* certificate,[16] Leang encouraged me to become a military policeman to ease the burden on my parents. But because I was a good student, my parents didn't want me to quit school. They also worried about me going far away from them as my two younger brothers had done.

I studied hard, but I also understood my parents' struggle to put rice in the pot. As a teenager, during breaks from school I would often work as a construction laborer for a wage of twenty or twenty-five riels per day. When I was big enough to steer a *cyclo*, whether I was in school or not, I would often make time in the evenings to pedal a *cyclo* and earn enough money for my mother to buy food.

In high school I never had enough money to buy textbooks—except for Khmer literature textbooks, which were cheap. I was among the last students to use French as the language of education. The children of rich people mostly ordered textbooks from France, such as math, chemistry, and physics books. My studies depended on some old, practically outdated library books and the books of my friends who had enough money to buy them. During days off and evenings, I would ride my bicycle to study with my friends near Wat Tuol

---

[15] French: *Centre d'Instruction*

[16] obtained by passing the junior high school completion exam

Tumpung, especially at the home of my friend Chea An, which was at the pond of foul water north of Wat Tuol Tumpung.

My bicycle was a motorless Solex moped that my brother Leang got from a friend. I never knew what it was like to wear new clothes; I always wore hand-me-downs from my brother Leang and my friends.

My high school was a model high school, and most of the students were children of the wealthy. In that place I was a crow among phoenixes. Because I wore clothes with patches, many of my professors thought that I was a hippie.[17] One day, a grade-four[18] math teacher called me to stand on the platform at the front of the classroom and made me turn around so that my classmates could see the patches on my clothes. That was the day that my friends realized just how poor I was, and afterwards they would bring me their old clothes to wear.

I never participated in any organized fun, like graduation parties, with my classmates and teachers. I always avoided such activities, even when my friends came to my house and brought me new outfits to wear, and my mother begged me to go with them. I was ashamed of my family's poverty.

Where was the fun for me? Since childhood I had watched my mother hunched over clay piggy banks from the time the rooster crowed before dawn until the middle of the night, when, after I had fallen asleep, I would awaken to see that she still had not gone to bed. The routine never varied, and I watched my mother change from youthful to elderly.

I never saw my mother smile; I only saw her shed tears. I never said "I love you" to my mother, though I did greatly pity and love her. Even when I was bigger, when I would come home from school and wouldn't see her—especially on days when she carried her piggy banks on her head to sell at the market and was late returning—I would worry and fret that perhaps she had fainted on the side of the road.

My father never seemed to think much about whether there was food to eat or not. If there was work to do, he would do it; if not, then he didn't care. The older he got the meaner and more cantankerous he became, quarrelling with my mother virtually every single day. Especially after the *coup*, my father was like

---

[17] Author's note: "American youth at the time who liked to wear patched, disheveled clothing." This note's inclusion in the Khmer edition suggests that the term "hippie" was known in Cambodia in the 60's and 70's but had lost cultural currency for younger generations of post-revolution Cambodians.

[18] equivalent of US eighth or UK ninth grade, as the old system in use at that time was patterned after the French system, counting backwards from twelve

a man without hope. Every night he got together with his friends, smoked marijuana, listened to the Khmer-language broadcast from Radio Beijing, and analyzed politics.

Because of the poverty I faced, my secondary education yielded mediocre results. In primary school I often received awards for being first or second in my class. But in my secondary education, I was usually only fifth or sixth in the class. In 1970 I took my junior high school examinations and received a "good" citation.[19] In 1972 I passed my first baccalaureate[20] exam with a "fair" citation. In 1973 I managed to rank second in the class, for a change, in my final mathematics course. But I worked myself too hard studying and fell sick about a month before the exam. I had a fever for almost a week, and afterward I had a constant headache that never let up. The ultimate result was that I completed my *bac double*[21] with an inadequate score. Because of my health problems and financial situation, I was unable to go on to college.

At the end of 1973 I passed the examination to become an officer in the National Police. I didn't enjoy that work very much, but there were no civilian jobs for me to choose from. I studied technical training and law for three months and trained in military tactics for another month at the National Police Academy. After graduation they divided us up among various posts. I was assigned to serve on the Intervention Commando Unit at the National Police Department. It was during this period that I was able to buy new clothes for the first time in my life. It was also the period that I encountered the first love of my youth—a love that ended in tears.

---

[19] Exam results were ranked and (if good enough) also assigned a verbal citation of *passable, fair, good, very good*, or *perfect*.

[20] the first out of two rounds of Cambodian high school completion exams, this one taken after the penultimate year; colloquially called *bac un* (*baccalauréat un*)

[21] *baccalauréat double*, or second baccalaureate exam, taken after the final year of Cambodian high school, conferring the equivalent of a high-school diploma or A-Level

17 April 1975

Seventeen April Seventy-five
Khmer society racked with fear

remember, Khmers, women and men
barbarians controlling the land.

Khmer men, women, rich and poor
joyful and glad to escape the misery

civilian, soldier all with expressions
the country relieved of war.

For five years the Khmer nation
land of abundance laid waste

has known only fighting and bloodshed
Khmer shedding blood of their own.

The war has truly ended
savages expel Khmers under blazing sun

but life grows more alarming
to leave homes without delay.

Tens of thousands leave the city
marching forward without rest

commoners and monks *en masse*
gun barrels pointing the way.

Hopes for peace spoil
wife from husband, grandma from baby

turned to separation, child from father
Khmers facing sadness unimagined.

Inexpressible sorrow
bundling dishes and spoons

devastation for all
abandoning home in tears.

A child in arms, hand grasping hand
some pulling, pushing, carrying

children led along in distress
if too heavy, sharing the load.

The rich have means
transport of all possessions

vehicles sufficient to guarantee
while the poor bear burdens on backs.

On every city boulevard
abandoning the capitol

throngs of people in columns
for unknown destinations.

penned on 10 October 1979

Chapter 1

17 April 1975

Though the fires of war have ravaged the country for five years, the capital Phnom Penh itself has never suffered any significant attacks, aside from the occasional artillery shell or 122-millimeter rocket. But in 1975, the inhabitants of the capital celebrate the dawn of the Year of the Rabbit,[1] 2519 in the Buddhist Era, under heavy shelling from artillery and rockets. Soldiers of the broken government forces desert their units and flee the battlefield. My two younger brothers, Samat and Samorn, showed up back home a week ago. The city's defensive perimeter constricts tighter and tighter around the capital and the sounds of pistol and machine-gun fire are heard resounding and rattling around the city.

Fed up with the five-year war, and especially disgusted with the wide-spread corruption infecting the ranks of the military and government, the people of Phnom Penh are both frightened and relieved by the present state of affairs. They live in fear of danger to their family from a stray shell or bullet; but they rejoice with the hope that the bloodshed between Khmers will end, peace will come, and the old, corrupt regime will be replaced by a new and virtuous one.

17 April 1975

At the first light of dawn, the sounds of small- and heavy-arms fire commence resounding in concert. In a panic, the people in the still-slumbering city send their children to hunker down in trenches. Artillery shells of various sizes rain down from the sky on the outskirts of the city. The sounds of gunfire from the battle raging at Kbal Thnal,[2] the last line of defense on the south end of the city, drift to my house as though right nearby, echoing off the small lake. The routed soldiers[3] can be seen fleeing the battle, abandoning weapons and clothing as they go. The people all huddle in their own trenches, not a soul daring to venture out on any errand.

---

[1] Khmer New Year, the biggest holiday festival of the year, is celebrated in mid-April. In 1975 the holiday fell on the 13th, and celebrations continue for three days.

[2] "Highway Head," a major crossroads and roundabout in the south of the city, source of two national highways and two major city boulevards

[3] i.e., soldiers for the government in Phnom Penh

As the sky grows brighter, the sounds of battle on the south end of the city continue to reverberate. Shells continue to rain haphazardly in the area around my house.

I imagine people caught traveling on the streets, wounded with no one to help them. Whispering together, my younger brothers and I prepare a small bag with cotton, alcohol, iodine, and bandages, ready to go out and save them.

My sixty-two-year-old mother, skinny and frail from years of labor, is frightened and says to me in a trembling voice, "Tuch! Where do you think you are taking your brothers?"

"We're going to help the wounded, Mom!" I reply.

This answer worries her further, and she quickly intervenes to stop us from leaving. "Don't you dare go anywhere! I'm old, and you need to stay with me!"

Our mother's objections persuade us to postpone our plan. Later I will wonder why I entertained such ideas without any thought of the danger that was bound to befall my brothers and me.

We don't leave the house, but out of a mounting anxiety to know and see what is happening, we do not stay in our trench, either. We sit concealed behind a coconut palm tree atop a small mound, where it is easy to keep an eye on the events that unfold around us.

At about seven o'clock the sounds of gunfire diminish to occasional, sporadic bursts. Soon afterward, the sounds die out altogether.

The people in our neighborhood seem relieved as they venture out of their trenches to gossip and chatter in clumps on the side of the road. We speculate about what will happen after the silence.

Two or three soldiers come running through the water and mud and emerge at the road in front of my house. Some throw away maps, and others remove their uniforms and beg the locals for civilian clothes. Oh, the life of the defender! He doesn't know where home lies, where his wife and children are to be found. I have never been near a battlefield, so I have never known this before: that the vanquished in war shake and tremble; that their faces grow pale; and that they open their mouths as if to speak but can hardly utter a word. We pity them, and stare after them until they disappear out of sight down the road.

One of these defeated soldiers just told us that the southern defensive belt has been broken. This news causes some confusion. Are we to rejoice or be afraid? It's impossible to say, but one thing is sure: for now, we are glad. We wave our hands in welcome to the victors who begin to appear. Soldiers dressed all in black make their way northward along the road (Street 430) that connects to the Phsar Daeum Thkov roundabout from the south.

The presence of these latter figures causes us to rejoice and seems to relieve the tension of a war that has burned for five years. Among all of our neighbors, my father is the happiest of all.

My father is a large man, straight and strong. This year he is sixty-six years old, and his hair is white, but the signs of old age have not yet taken their toll on his body. He can still saw, plane, and chisel wood to build houses as he has always done. Lon Nol's *coup* made my father unhappy. Living in a time of war and the shedding of Khmer blood under a corrupt military regime has made him especially fed up and disgusted, and he has waited for the day that this regime will fall.

Now the day that my father has awaited is here. He is very happy, and he calls out to me, "A-Moeun![4] Go and get Samdech's[5] flag and a white cloth and hang them up!"

It doesn't take me long to go into the house, rummage in the bottom of a chest, and return carrying the flag with the three-spired temple[6] and a white cloth, which I tie up in the doorway of the house.

My father grumbles, "Samdech is coming back now.[7] No matter what happens now, it can't be as miserable as living with these traitors."

The opposite of my father, my mother is in a still and quiet mood, as though she has nothing unusual on her mind. Actually, she is also pleased with the change in the situation. As an old person who has lived through many eras, she knows very well in which eras life was easiest and happiest.

As for me and my brothers, we are young and hot-blooded. We are not over-joyed, but we can't sit still either, and we want only to go and see the army up close. After getting permission from my mother, I take my brothers to watch the procession of troops at the Phsar Daeum Thkov roundabout.

Locals—male and female, young and old—living on the roads along which the soldiers now pass come out to greet and congratulate the victors by waving

---

[4] an intimate nickname for *Samoeun*

[5] a Khmer title of high honor, in this case referring to Sihanouk

[6] i.e., Cambodia's former (and present-day) flag, which had been changed under the Khmer Republic

[7] Due to Sihanouk's alliance with the Khmer Rouge, many Cambodians expected their victory would bring him back to power.

white scarves, a sign of peaceful intentions. Some people act as though they know some of the soldiers, and they greet, shake hands, and visit with them. Houses selling soft drinks open bottles for passing soldiers. Young men and teenage boys gather around and follow the soldiers and watch them long and hard, sizing up just who it is that they are meeting.

At about eight o'clock in the morning, another line of troops begins to march down from the upper road[8] down past the roundabout, where they shake hands with the other line of soldiers coming from the south. This column of troops seems to be coming from Boeng Tumpun.

The traffic along the road[9] to Tuol Tumpung is fairly normal, only not so busy. A PC motorbike[10] stops beside me as I am watching the procession, and I turn toward it.

"Oh! A-Neang, where are you coming from?" I ask the driver.

"Just cruising. Come on!" he tempts me. I turn to tell my brothers, then jump onto the back of the motorcycle behind A-Neang.

A-Neang is a friend from my work in the police. He has a wife at home near Cao Dai.[11] He has just spent the night guarding the national police headquarters. Since leaving work he hasn't returned home but has been out watching the soldiers.

We ride his motorcycle toward Tuol Tumpung. The soldiers march quietly along the right side of the road, about five meters apart, each carrying a weapon carefully pointed forward. This road does not have crowds of people standing and congratulating the soldiers like the locals at Phsar Daeum Thkov did.

As we approach the Tuol Tumpung stoplight,[12] A-Neang says to me "A-Moeun! Look up there ahead!"

I stare forward and, in the intersection, the black-shirted figures approach a soldier who is not carrying a weapon. They point their guns at him and order him to remove his clothing and shoes. My stomach turns in fear, until the

---

[8] Author's note: "the Russian Hospital causeway, present-day Royal Cambodian Armed Forces Road"

[9] Street 163

[10] nickname for a Honda PC50 moped

[11] Refers to the neighborhood of the Cao Dai temple located just south of Mao Tse Tung Boulevard near its intersection with Monireth Boulevard. (Cao Dai is a religious sect founded in Vietnam in 1926. The small Phnom Penh temple, still extant, was established in 1927.)

[12] at the intersection of Street 163 and Sereipheap Boulevard

soldier wearing nothing but underpants continues onward, and I feel my chest relax.

A-Neang turns the motorcycle along Sereipheap (Mao Tse Tung)[13] Boulevard toward Daeum Ko Market. This road is quiet, with no soldiers. Even the locals remain quietly in their homes. The traffic is light. As we approach the roundabout[14] at the Chenla Cinema, we see that the cars, motorcycles, and bicycles are stopped as a procession of soldiers passes. We pull up next to them and wait.

On the roundabout stands a black-shirted soldier who appears to be an officer, with a cape of black cloth at his neck covering his shoulders and back and fluttering down to his calves, shaking hands and welcoming the passing army. Here the soldiers walk with long, hurried steps as they shake the hand of this leader. They are coming from the Steung Mean Chey Bridge and heading into the city. Several soldiers run up onto a trio of M113 armored vehicles that have been abandoned in front of the Chenla Cinema and drive off with them toward the Olympic Stadium.

When the procession has passed, traffic is allowed to resume. We drive around the roundabout with the intention of heading back. But we have only gone little more than halfway around the circle when a soldier stands in our path and points the muzzle of his gun toward the Steung Mean Chey Bridge and orders, "Go that way!"

Startled, we stop the motorcycle and plead, "Excuse us comrade, can we go back the way we came?"

"No!" The forceful, clipped answer, along with the muzzle of the rifle now pointing at our chests, causes us to quickly redirect the motorcycle, trembling in fear, in the appointed direction. Having lost our freedom, both of us are filled with worry, and we inch the motorcycle slowly forward, looking for a chance to escape from the flow of traffic.

On the east side of the road the newly arriving troops march into the city. On the west side of the road before us the mass of people which before had been chaotic and disorganized is now beginning to march in an orderly fashion

---

[13] The boulevards known originally (and currently) as Mao Tse Tung and Monivong were renamed for a time under the Lon Nol regime to Sereipheap (Freedom) and Pracheathipatay (Democracy), respectively. (The original names were restored, after further renaming by the communists, in 1994.)

[14] The intersection of Monireth and Sereipheap (Mao Tse Tung) boulevards, near the Chenla Cinema, once featured a traffic roundabout.

toward the bridge, with a wall of soldiers standing at ten-meter intervals super-vising them and permitting no one to veer from the road.

A-Neang is close to his house, but he can't cross the road toward Cao Dai. We are now only 300 meters from being forced across the bridge. Our hope of finding a way out continues to diminish. Just three meters in front of us, an old Chinese man dashes in an arc toward the east side of the road. A soldier standing in front of us yells "No stealing!" but the old Chinese man thinks only of running and the soldier chases after him.

Dear God! A chance for escape! We push the motorcycle down off the road to the right. Fortunately, we go directly down a small side road. We loiter beneath a brick-and-concrete building comprising five or six apartments built on the west side of Monireth Boulevard. On the ground floor there are four or five rooms where people live. About ten other people have taken shelter here already before we arrive.

Feeling uneasy, we pace back and forth, unable to sit still, and beg the owner of the house to claim that we are members of the household. The owner takes our bicycles and motorcycles and hides them in a room. We try to maintain calm demeanors so as not to upset the owner, but our eyes dart about and our ears are tuned to anything unusual.

For over an hour, nothing unusual happens. We begin to feel that the situa-tion is lightening up. But then the owner of the house tells us that we are being expelled.

The confusion begins. We barge into the room and extract our bikes and motorcycles. We push over a barbed-wire fence behind the building to access a back road, then force the lock on the gate of the house behind and push our way into the Boeng Salang neighborhood. The owner of the house tries to stop us, but it is no use, and we push past with our vehicles.

A-Neang swerves back and forth around the small houses on the shore of Boeng Salang lake, crosses Sereipheap Boulevard, and then drives along the north side of Daeum Ko Market and across Monireth Boulevard at the Mekong Cinema. We drive along back roads, avoiding encounters with soldiers. A-Neang drops me off near the archery center in the Arabian Village[15] and heads back to find a way to his house. I am far from home, but I can't compel my

---

[15] the old Arabian quarter of Phnom Penh, around the mosque on Street 173, a block north of Sereipheap (Mao Tse Tung) Boulevard

friend to take me any farther than this. He is worried about his wife, whom he left the night before. But where should I go?

It is nearly eleven o'clock. I walk away from the archery center down the road straight toward Me Phleung.[16] In this neighborhood, it seems like nothing unusual is happening, and the locals are calm. Some people chat in front of their houses in their yards. Some people stand around on the street. Seeing me half-walking, half-running with fear on my face, some of them call out to me and ask, "What's the matter?"

"They're rounding people up!" I answer without stopping. I don't notice whether they believe me or not, whether they are afraid or not, but *I* am afraid, and I run to curb my fear.

When I reach the Raksmei Chantrea Tuol Tumpung Theater, there is a large group of people sitting around listening closely to announcements on the radio. They don't believe me because statements by the Revolutionary Organization[17] ask the people to remain calm and not to panic. I run into my cousin, who used to live in this neighborhood, and who had just moved in with my family a little more than half a year ago. I stop running and say to him, "A-Soeun! They're rounding people up. Why don't you go home?"

"You go ahead, I'm going to butcher a pig first," he replies apathetically. Doesn't anybody believe me? Doesn't anyone understand my alarm? I walk away in a daze and head for the house of my friend An, a classmate from my high school days. His house is north of Wat Tuol Tumpung, about 350 meters from here. On this stretch of road, I don't hurry as much, partly because I am tired and hungry, and partly because my fear is beginning to subside with the general atmosphere of the neighborhood.

An's house is built over a pond of foul water, connected to the road west of the house via a wooden footbridge about forty meters long. The lot directly north of An's house is on dry land with a wooden fence running along beside the wooden footbridge leading to An's house.

---

[16] the area around the intersection of Street 360 and Pracheathipatay (Monivong) Blvd (referring to a prominent substation for the municipal electricity network formerly located here)

[17] *Angkar Pakdevoat;* the label by which the Communist Party of Kampuchea, a.k.a. the Khmer Rouge, usually referred to itself. The shorter and more common version of this was simply *Angkar,* or "the Organization."

From a distance, I had thought that this neighborhood was quiet, but when I draw close my heart begins to race again. The locals are organizing their things to leave. My God! Has An's family already left? Without wasting time to walk around to the start of the footbridge, I cut through the lot in front of An's house, climb the fence, jump down onto the footbridge, and walk to the house.

An's family is surprised at my presence. They put down their packing and surround me to question me about my wanderings.

"Samoeun! Where did you come from? Don't you know that they are evacuating people?"

"A-Moeun! Your mother is surely wondering where you are!"

An's older sister and mother interrogate me mercilessly. Worry beyond worry! Concern beyond concern! I can't think straight anymore. An's family finally calms down when they hear my story. They give me some rice to eat, urging me to relax and then go with them.

As I am eating, a soldier dressed in black clothes and a black cap and holding a pistol in his hand walks by shouting, "Brothers and sisters, mothers and fathers, hurry up and leave your houses! Don't bother taking too much stuff with you! You will only be gone for three days to give the Organization a chance to sweep out the remaining enemies who haven't laid down their weapons!"

At one o'clock in the afternoon, we depart. An's family is a large one, with a total of eighteen members, young and old. They have two PC motorbikes, an improvised cart, and three bicycles. I ride a PC motorbike loaded down with luggage on both the front and back. One of An's older sisters walks alongside and holds the load with her hand. An pushes a bicycle loaded with dishes and pots and sacks of light items. Some of An's siblings carry various objects between them or on their heads, and his young cousins and mother follow behind. We travel along Street 113 up to Sereipheap Boulevard. There I catch a glimpse of my friend A-Neang walking his motorcycle, alone, with a scowl on his face and no belongings. He must not have made it back home.

On Sereipheap (Mao Tse Tung) Boulevard, the people are moving along the south side of the road. The north side of the road is reserved for military traffic. Occasionally, soldiers drive by in a jeep against the flow of the crowd. No one is able to walk in the opposite direction or cross Sereipheap toward the south.

When we reach the Bokkor stoplight,[18] we turn south onto Pracheathipatay (Monivong) Boulevard. There we merge with the flow of people coming from the north, from the Or Roessei and Pet Chen[19] areas. Far away behind our backs, thick black smoke billows into the air, apparently from a burning gas station.

Our progress is extremely slow. At about three o'clock in the afternoon we reach the area in front of the Faculty of Law. Across from Boeng Trabek High School, where Street 484 connects to Pracheathipatay Boulevard from Phsar Daeum Thkov, I can see a crowd of people running back and forth across the road. *What's going on there?* I think to myself. As I draw closer, I understand. A group of people from the Phsar Daeum Thkov neighborhood are crossing the road to take supplies from warehouses in Chamkar Mon.[20] There! My two brothers are pushing their way across the road toward the warehouses.

Incredible! My opportunity has arrived. I hand the motorcycle over to An's sister and make polite with a female soldier who is sitting near the road, guarding the crowds.

"Excuse me, Comrade, can I go to my house?" I ask.

"No, you can't! Once you've left, you can't go back!" she answers sternly.

I back off, but I don't lose courage. I tell An's sister to drive the motorcycle, and I will hold the load for change. I whisper to her that if a good opportunity arises, then I will have to take my leave. The other members of An's family haven't arrived yet, but I won't have many opportunities.

When we reach the mouth of the road where the confusion is, I dash from the motorcycle and run toward home. Like an animal released from its cage, I am overjoyed! I rejoice that fate has allowed me to meet back up with my parents and siblings. I think what good fortune it is that my family and neighbors will be able learn about the evacuation beforehand from me. We will have a chance to get our things ready. I think that when I get home, I will take the wheels off of my bicycle and make a pull-cart that can carry a lot of belongings, and a few smaller wooden carts as well. I will help my mother

---

[18] the intersection of Sereipheap (Mao Tse Tung) and Pracheathipatay (Monivong) boulevards, so called because of the Bokkor Cinema (no longer extant) located nearby

[19] "Chinese Hospital"; the intersection of Preah Sihanouk and Pracheathipatay (Monivong) boulevards, so called because of a prominent hospital (no longer extant) located there

[20] commercial warehouses along the Bassac River east and south of the Chamkar Mon State Palace

decide which thing to take and which to leave behind. Most of all, I think that my parents will be relieved after having lost me for the whole day.

For more than a kilometer, I run with great loping strides, like the soldiers who marched past the roundabout at Phsar Daem Ko earlier this morning. Along the way I call out, "They're evacuating the city! They're evacuating the city! They're evacuating the city!" to people I know, until finally I arrive at home.

I dash into the house and call out, "Dad! Mom! They're forcing everyone out of the city!" But my neighbors and family are busy celebrating peace and the end of the war and the spoils of victory at the hands of the Organization; they are not interested in what I have to say.

I have just spent a day filled with worry and fear. My family has just spent a day celebrating with a happiness that they haven't seen for five years. Everything that I had just imagined to myself was all wrong—especially the reaction of my parents. In fact, my parents haven't worried a bit about my absence. They feel that everything is going wonderfully. They have figured that I was gone all day tasting the joy of the birth of a new Khmer society.

The neighbors who have been going back and forth to gather loot from the Chamkar Mon warehouses know perfectly well that people are being evacuated from the city. But they assume that this matter does not affect *them,* that *they* won't be ordered out by the Organization, because the Organization has allowed them to take freely from the warehouses.

Almost every family goes out to collect loot and stockpiles it in their house. My younger brothers procure three sacks of rice, several cases of beer, two or three mattresses, and large amounts of salt, fish sauce, soy sauce, and soft drinks, and pile them all over the house.

A French proverb says that "a single swallow does not herald the arrival of Spring." I am but a lone swallow, the one person who desires to instill fear and an awareness of what will come. But no one believes me! They only believe in what is plain: that they have become wealthy without the necessity of effort. Let the neighbors refuse to believe, but I must win over my own family. My mother doesn't matter; my father is the one who controls the power in the family.

I attempt to speak with my father about what is on my mind, but he objects, saying, "A-Moeun! You aren't thinking straight. If they have just taken the city, what is the point of forcing us out? Do you remember what happened last year? People in Steung Mean Chey and Boeng Tumpun fell prey to propaganda that they would be forced out, and they fled in the middle of the night all the way to the riverfront by the palace. When they went back home, all of their stuff was gone."

"That was a matter of hysterical propaganda, but what happened this morning is real, Dad!" I reply. But the words have scarcely left my mouth when he cuts me off.

"All right! If it's true, then it only pertains to the people in the heart of the city, where there are a lot of multistory brick-and-cement buildings with a lot of nooks and crannies that are hard to sweep out. But for us here on the outskirts of the city, nothing is going to happen. And if it happens, then Kru Mo's[21] brother in the army will come and tell him first!"

My father is a man who does not easily give ground, who maintains firm control over his family. Only I, the favorite son, would be so bold as to talk back to him. But this is not the time for a son to argue with his father. Unable to win over those around me, I back down.

At five-thirty in the evening, having bathed, I stroll down to the mermaid statue at the Phsar Daeum Thkov roundabout. Here, the locals of the Phsar Daeum Thkov and Boeng Tumpun neighborhoods like to sit around, relax, and enjoy the fresh air in the evening.

The road to Tuol Tumpung is quieter than usual, with very little traffic. I stroll from the mermaid to the Phsar Daeum Thkov clinic, around the clinic to the market.[22] People sell their wares as usual, but it's a bit quieter than most days. I walk back and forth to calm my feelings and forget the day-long nightmare, saying goodbye to the place I have lived peacefully for the past nineteen years.

---

[21] Author's note: "a teacher who lived about thirty meters west of my house"

[22] Phsar Daeum Thkov, or "Thkov Tree Market," namesake for the neighborhood and multiple landmarks in it (school, roundabout, clinic) to this day, though the market itself is no longer extant. *thkov* = *Neolamarckia cadamba*

Fate of the Vanquished

1. Pity Khmer dwellers of country and city   suffering in the fires of war
hearing of peace their faces perk up   Khmers stop shedding Khmer blood.

2. But it's not to be, even the monks   must leave their homes and robes
barbarians expel Khmers sparing none   with suffering like a mountain.

chorus:
Children large and small cry out *wah! wah!*   seeing Mommy, but where is Daddy?
blessed mother cries, distressed   with the agony of losing dear husband.

3. Carry one child, hold the hand of another   children run after dear mother
endure, my child, for your father succumbed   stay alive lest they kill a name.

penned by moonlight on 9 October 1979

CHAPTER 2

The Great Journey

18 April 1975

Last night I slept well without the sounds of gunfire I had endured the night before. But I can't stop thinking about An's family, wondering where they ended up sleeping.

This morning there is nothing noteworthy, nothing to arouse alarm. No one goes to work. We all rest in our houses, with the lone exception of Nho, my oldest sister's husband, who goes to sweep the Phsar Daeum Thkov clinic. He returns with cases of IV solution and medicine because none of the doctors have shown up to work today.

Bored, I lie around in my room looking at photographs of myself taken with classmates and teachers, and a personal photograph of my girlfriend that she gave me as a souvenir when we broke up. After lunch I return to my photographs, looking again and again, without growing tired of them, as if trying to imprint them on my heart. After looking at my photographs, I look at my painting of a Haitian girl bathing topless in the ocean. I copied the painting from a photograph on the cover of a religious magazine sent from America called *La Verite*, from February 1975, which I have hung on my wall by the door.

The Haitian girl is so beautiful! In her beauty she is like a Cambodian girl. She has an oval face with bright eyes guarded by long lashes, rosy-red cheeks, a long and rounded nose to match her face, and lips which are neither full nor thin. Her long black hair is parted to one side and rests on her right shoulder, falling on her round breast, from which roll droplets of water as bright as diamonds from the sunlight on the ocean in the afternoon. She stares at me. She smiles at me as though casting a love spell. The Haitian girl is beautiful, and my painting is good. I drew and painted it without instruction from any teacher. I am pleased with my work and pleased by the beauty of the Haitian girl. I am lost in my thoughts and in the beauty of the girl from a far-off land, when suddenly someone knocks *tok tok* on the door.

"Tuch! Tuch!" my mother calls.

"Yes, Mom?" I answer quickly.

"They are evacuating us!" she replies despondently. Suddenly startled, as though I have been left behind, I jump up and run out onto the road in front of the house. A soldier dressed in black and holding a pistol is walking up the road ordering people to gather their things and leave. It is the same sight that I witnessed yesterday. But today, as I see it again, I am like an ox that has been struck with an ax between the eyes, and I feel the strength drain from me. After my failure to convince the others, I had allowed myself to succumb to the general mood until I no longer thought that there would be an evacuation. Now the thing which I ceased to anticipate is happening, and my mind reels, not knowing what to believe and what to reject.

Like me, my father abandons all expectations, and in despair he sits quietly, waiting for the time to leave. My mother, sisters, and brothers prepare bundles of clothing, mats, pillows, mosquito nets, dishes, pots, and pans and stuff them into rice sacks. Our extended family will all go together. In total, there are twelve of us:

- My family of seven, including Dad, Mom, Oun,[1] Lin (my two-year-old niece), me, Samat, and Samorn.

- My oldest sister Ol, her husband Nho, and Sophal, my five-year-old adopted niece.

- Thom Pen and My-L'et, his fifteen-year-old daughter.

We don't know where to go, but wherever we do go, we will go together. We have no means of transporting our belongings besides my old bicycle, so we have to prepare two or three shoulder yokes.

Lacking means of transportation and believing that we will only be gone for a short time, we leave behind anything that is unnecessary for daily subsistence. The provisions that my brothers spent all day yesterday hauling home are all left behind.

In a daze, I put on a judo tunic and a pair of black trousers without a thought for anything else. My photographs are left scattered on the bed in my room. My mother gathers two or three more changes of clothing and brings them to me. I am convinced that we will only be gone for three days, so taking a lot of stuff will only make returning more difficult.

---

[1] Author's note: "My second oldest sister who had a daughter. Her husband had left and taken another wife."

The sun's searing rays blast the poor creatures whose hearts are already torn from leaving their beloved neighborhoods, homes, parents, children, wives, and husbands, making the misery just that much worse. The neighborhood locals, who just last night made merry in the face of the suffering of others, are now in a state of disorder. On every road, large and small, a single, common activity has begun: abandoning home. We all leave at the same time for fear of being the last ones, lest the Organization accuse us of resisting orders; so whether we have adequately packed our belongings or not, we hurriedly carry the bundles out and place them on the road.

We have to leave the city from the south via Kbal Thnal. From my neighborhood there are only two major routes: the Russian Hospital causeway and Pracheathipatay Boulevard. The causeway (present-day Royal Cambodian Armed Forces Road) is narrow and crowded with people. My family decides on Pracheathipatay Boulevard.

The wealthier people have automobiles, carts, motorcycles, bicycles, and *cyclos* adequate for hauling their possessions and provisions. But what do the poor have? We must carry our belongings, alternating the loads between our heads and our shoulders or carrying them between two people.

We leave home at one o'clock in the afternoon. I push the girl's-frame bicycle with two bags of rice on the book rack and two more on the frame. My brothers carry two yokes loaded with mats, pillows, mosquito nets, clothing, pots and pans, *prahok,*[2] and salt. My oldest sister Ol is small and weak and carries a bundle of her family's bedding and clothes on her head. Her husband Nho also carries a yoke on his shoulders loaded with pots and pans and uncooked rice. Oun, my next-oldest sister, carries her two-year-old daughter on her hip with one arm and holds a bundle on her head with the other. She is as sturdy and strong as the men. My-L'et, the daughter of Thom Pen, balances a bundle of bedding and clothes on her head. Thom Pen is sixty-five years old, and he carries a grass mat on his back and a basket of pots and pans in his hand. My father and mother follow in the rear leading their granddaughter Sophal by the hand.

My two brothers and I are all about the same height, a little over a meter seventy. But Samorn and I are thin while Samat is sturdy, big-boned, strong,

---

[2] a paste made of salted fermented fish, and a key component in Cambodian cooking

and fearless. We take turns pushing the bicycle and carrying the yokes, along with our sister Oun.

When we reach Street 484, our progress turns slow. This is the only route connecting the Phsar Daeum Thkov area and the area south of Tuol Tumpung Market with Pracheathipatay Boulevard.

No one is allowed special consideration to stay home and not leave. Even the patients in the hospital who can't walk are expelled from the city: some of the hospital patients are placed in carts and pushed by their families with bags of IV fluid dangling precariously from poles. Other patients who are separated from family and staying in the hospital alone clutch crutches for support and stumble after the rest.

The sun is blazing hot, and dust rises in clouds from the dirt road whenever the wind blows. Bicycles, motorcycles, cars, carts, and people intermingle on the narrow road. The sounds of children crying mixed with the squawks of chickens and ducks, which some have brought tied to yokes as eventual meals, create a dissonant symphony that pierces the agitated minds of travelers carrying loads on their shoulders and heads, sweat soaking their backs and shirts, without the slightest opportunity to set down their burdens to rest.

Only 150 more meters and my family will reach Pracheathipatay Boulevard. But the road is narrow and crowded and we are unable to move either forward or backward. We can only inch our feet forward a little at a time. We reach this point at three o'clock, but an hour later we have not yet gone fifty meters. Everyone is equally covered in sweat, their faces and backs drenched from the heat and suffocating stuffiness. Even the wealthy sitting in their cars with only their heads poking out the windows wipe sweat and fan themselves constantly.

Not until six o'clock, when the sun is about to set,[3] does my family reach Pracheathipatay Boulevard. Here it is slightly roomier and there is a refreshing breeze mingling with the cool air of sunset. We continue forward another hundred meters until we receive word that traffic over the bridge has been suspended. Everyone begins to leave the road to look for a place to rest. My family crowds into the yard of Boeng Trabek High School to camp.

Tonight the electricity is out and the whole city is covered in blackness. After finding a spot to rest, each family takes out their pots and pans and begins

---

[3] The sun sets at around 6 p.m. year-round at this tropical latitude.

to cook. The scattered lights of candles, oil lamps, and stoves shine in the darkness, creating a black veil punctuated by tiny points of orange light.

The scene is breathtaking and reminds me of the visit of the French president Charles De Gaulle to the Olympic Stadium in the late sixties. For the final act of the program, the electricity was cut, and the stadium plunged into complete darkness. Then each attendee lit a match at the same time, creating countless tiny pinpricks of light peppering a carpet of black. These two scenes are seemingly the same, but with opposite meanings: one born of joy and celebration, the other of affliction.

Tonight my family begins to discuss a long-term journey, no longer believing that we will return quickly. We consider our lack of food provisions and think of the three striped rice sacks that we left back at home. But we don't dare test our luck by returning to retrieve them.

After eating, Samat, Samorn, and Nho take flashlights and go look for rice at the Chamkar Mon warehouses they looted yesterday, and in nearby homes that have been abandoned by their owners. They return with a large three-*tau*[4] sack of rice and some clothing.

Because my younger brothers used to be soldiers, they both lack civilian clothing to wear. Now anything military is thrown away since no one dares to use it or carry it with them. Civilian clothing is a necessity for us.

Tonight we sleep in the fields[5] under the stars. Those of us who are young, exhausted from the day, fall asleep immediately. But the older ones, though truly exhausted, can hardly sleep. Tremendous concerns weigh on their minds.

It is the nature of parents to desire the welfare and happiness of their children. My parents think constantly of their three sons still in their youth, the age of blossoming, the age of clear thought and joy of life, the age of enjoyment. They worry about my personality because I am timid and don't talk or laugh with girls very much. They constantly pity their three sons, who have become grownups during a time of national turmoil, without knowing joy and peace in their lives.

With the end of the war yesterday, my parents rejoiced in the hope that they would open their eyes and see happy, rich lives for their three boys. But all this

---

[4] a unit of dry measure equivalent to about half a bushel (roughly 18 liters or 4 gallons)
[5] the school's football (soccer) fields

has vanished in the space of a single night. My parents despair in the depths of care and worry that no child could understand. Because of the events of this day, it is the blackest day my parents have seen in their lives.

19 April 1975

A rooster crows before dawn, and my mother wakes me.

"Ktuch![6] Ktuch!"

"Yes Mom?" I answer.

"Wake your brothers and get ready to go! If we leave early, it will still be cool, but I can't walk once it gets hot!"

I jump up and wake my brothers to get ready. We imagine that our family will be the first to leave. But it is not so: as we poke our heads outside the wall around Boeng Trabek High School, we see tens of thousands of people already moving slowly forward in silence under the dark veil of night along Pracheathipatay Boulevard. Didn't they sleep last night? What time did they wake up, that they are already swarming on the road at four o'clock in the morning?

Experience teaches people. Yesterday's traveling in the blazing heat in the middle of the day was an experience for all who will travel today and after. Walking in the heat of the day, the sun makes you sweat and dehydrates you, makes you thirsty, and in the hot air it is hard to breathe. If it's a dirt road, then it gets dusty; but if it's a paved road, then the asphalt melts and burns your feet and expels vapors that rise up hotly into your face until you can hardly bear it. Traveling at night avoids the heat of the sun, and the air is cool. We sweat little, and aren't easily exhausted, so we can travel further. Our task, for now, is just to get out of the city, and the faster the better. It is for this very purpose that hordes of people grope anxiously forward in the dark.

From four until eleven o'clock in the morning, we creep forward a distance of only 800 meters, from the gates of Boeng Trabek High School to an "American-style"[7] house on the right-hand side of the road behind the Esso gas

---

[6] an intimate variation on the nickname *Tuch*

[7] "American style" referred colloquially to a style of roof that, rather than being peaked in the middle, featured a steeper rear slope that overhung a lower front slope, with vents in the vertical gap between the two for heat ventilation. (Otherwise, this is clearly a Khmer-style house; see below.)

station.[8] My family crowds into the shade under[9] the house and divides up the tasks of making food. The owners of the house have already been evacuated, and the masses of people sheltering in and below the house are all travelers.

During the heat of the day my parents and Thom Pen, being old, become exhausted and breathless, like chickens at midday in the dry season. My two little nieces also struggle to endure the heat. As for those of us who are younger adults, each of our shoulders become swollen and raw. They are unaccustomed to bearing yokes for very long and aren't callused like the shoulders of people who do it every day, and now we have to carry them for two or three hours at a stretch without setting them down or resting.

Because of the large numbers of people, the soldiers are unable to disperse the crowds and give orders like they did when we were still at home. Faced with flagging strength, we decide to stay here for the night.

20 April 1975

Between dawn and 11 a.m., we are finally able to cross the Monivong Bridge, and we continue beyond to the Chbar Ampov subdistrict headquarters building, where we stop to rest and prepare food. Here there are tamarind trees with cool shade. My brothers and I go to look for water for cooking rice. We figure that drawing water from the river will be easier than searching for well water at local houses. We walk through Chbar Ampov Market (the old market on the south side of the highway) and head for the river.

This is the first time in my life that my eyes have ever witnessed such an awful scene. Only four days ago, this was a battleground, and large brick-and-cement houses have been demolished, with chunks of brick and cement of all sizes, shards of roof tiles, dishes, pots and pans, tables, and chairs littering the ground all over the road. In the gendarmerie post, the body of a woman lies face up on a desk, naked and swollen, maggots perforating her flesh. Along the riverbank lie the bloated corpses of soldiers, some on the banks, others floating half in and half out of the water. Some bob up and down on the water's surface, occasionally washing up against the bank. The water here, which appeared from above to be decent, is in actuality covered in a slick of dark-green foam

---

[8] Author's note: "present-day site of the Mekong River Commission headquarters." (While true as of 2006, this building has since been occupied by a bank, as the MRC has moved its headquarters elsewhere.)

[9] Khmer-style houses are traditionally elevated two or three meters off the ground on stilts or pillars.

mixed with grease from the corpses. The river water is undrinkable, and we return empty-handed.

Even though National Highway One is narrower than Pracheathipatay Boulevard, the traffic here is lighter because the crowd divided itself into two groups back at the Kbal Thnal roundabout. One group headed right toward Ta Khmau, and the other continued over the Monivong Bridge. After crossing the bridge, this latter group divided again into two groups, one turning right along the river toward Prek Pra and Koh Krabei, and the other continuing along Highway One. But today, the 20th, the road to Ta Khmau has been closed, so all who wish to go that way are forced to cross the bridge and then turn right along the other side of the river in the general direction of Ta Khmau.

In the afternoon the sky becomes overcast, and we continue our journey. After leaving the Chbar Ampov subdistrict office and returning to Highway One, we see that dozens of houses along the right side of the highway have been burned to the ground, leaving only pillars sticking up in the air. Some of the pillars are still billowing smoke. Besides some curled-up and burnt pieces of corrugated iron, shards of cement water jars, and cement footings, we see only piles of ash and charcoal covering the ground. Mango, coconut, banana, and areca trees along the side of the road are burned and smoldering, with broken branches and fronds shriveled and drooping to the ground. Some trees have fallen over completely on top of piles of ash, as though having thrown themselves to the ground out of grief for the burnt homes. The houses seem to have just been burned this morning or last night. Why were they burned? Did the Organization burn them because the owners were slow to leave?

As our thoughts drift with the smoke into the sky, suddenly the sound of gunshots pierces the air: *bang! bang! bang!* Startled and shaken, nearly losing my grip on the bicycle handlebars, I look around, worried that someone has just been wounded or killed. I think this because as we rested a little earlier, we heard that this morning a soldier shot and killed two people who took rice from a warehouse on the west side of the river. But I can't see that anything has happened. The crowd continues walking forward. Then a military vehicle comes driving against the flow of foot traffic with two or three black-clad soldiers sitting on the hood. They are the ones who fired the shots, to open the road. We squeeze together on the right side of the road to allow the vehicle to pass.

We have walked another 200 meters when suddenly a mid-*Pisakh*[10] rain shower begins to pour down without the slightest warning. Our bundles of bedding and clothes are soaked. We continue forward in the rain until we are nearly to Wat Niroth before finding shelter.

The locals here have all been evacuated. We take shelter in a wooden house with a corrugated iron roof whose owner was a fisherman. Up in the house, there are still several old fishing nets of various types and sizes. We salvage one small net and one larger net to take with us. We rest at the house for two nights until our bedding and clothes are dry and then continue our journey.

22 April 1975

We depart at dawn. The road is wide and not very crowded, and traveling is easy. People continue to stream out of the city.

All along the column of travelers, people copy each other by tying white cloths to their yokes, handlebars, and car antennae as a sign of peace and surrender. But still we encounter horrific sights, one after another, along the path of evacuation. We see the corpses of civilians shot dead, lying here and there like the bodies of poisoned rats. People from Phnom Penh like me have never seen such sights before. We panic! We tremble! We fear!

At three o'clock in the afternoon, my family reaches Wat Chroy Ampil. Countless numbers of people are congregating here. The monks' dining pavilion and all around the temple are filled with resting travelers. In the grove of sapodilla trees on *wat* land in front of the temple, many people have laid out their mats haphazardly, but there is still room. My family stops here and shelters in the shade of the sapodilla trees. After setting down our belongings and preparing a place to rest, we realize that we are missing a member of the family: my father. After asking around, we figure out that he has only recently disappeared in the vicinity of Prek Eng Market. Without delay, I ride my bicycle back along sideroads to Prek Eng. (We don't dare travel against traffic on the highway).

---

[10] lunar calendar month from roughly mid-April to mid-May (also called *Visakh*). The Cambodian lunar months are based on the Buddhist calendar used widely in the region, based on an old version of the Hindu calendar, with names derived from Pali/Sanskrit.

Starting from Prek Eng, the locals have not been expelled from their homes. A number of the people from Phnom Penh continue their journey beyond to their native villages. Another large number, whether they have family or friends here or not, stop traveling and make camp here, beginning at Prek Eng Market, up to Wat Muny,[11] Wat Champa, and all the way to Wat Kien Svay Krau. They are mostly concentrated along the side roads near the river. They either stay at the homes of locals who are family or friends, or, in the case of those without family or friends, they camp in the banana, sapodilla, and jack-fruit orchards—wherever there is available land. They rest to gather strength, or to watch the road for family members who have been separated. Most especially, they wait for the Organization to allow them to return to Phnom Penh. Locals and people from Phnom Penh who have been here the longest (especially youths) have had time to travel back up to Phnom Penh by boat, or by holding onto banana tree trunks and swimming up the river, to retrieve supplies and provisions from warehouses or abandoned homes.

The side roads bustle with people, bicycles, and motorcycles. There are people buying and selling snacks and food as usual, but at high prices: 500 riels for a bowl of rice porridge, 5,000 riels for a kilogram of *prahok*. My family doesn't have any money to spend as others do; when we left home, my mother carried a total of only 500 riels.

Prek Eng Market is crowded with people. I ride my bicycle back and forth searching for my father. I don't see him anywhere. Suddenly, I hear a female voice call out my name: "Samoeun! Samoeun!"

I stop and look toward the speaker. It is An's older sister. "Hey there! What are you selling?" I ask.

"I'm selling mangoes," she answers.

"Where did you get mangoes from?" I ask.

"I bought them in bulk, and now I'm selling them individually."

"Where are you staying?" I ask.

"At the house of some friends here in this village," she answers, pointing toward the mouth of a small road.

"What day did you guys arrive here?" I ask.

"We've been here since the day you left us," she replies. On the first day, the roads weren't so crowded, and traveling was easy. Besides, An's family also had

---

[11] Wat Muny Sakor

bicycles and motorcycles, which allowed them to travel faster and haul their belongings.

After chatting a bit, I say goodbye and head back to Wat Chroy Ampil along the highway without any word of my father.

The next day Samat and Nho take some medicine and IV solution to sell for tens of thousands of riels. They take the money and buy some *prahok*, saving the rest to spend later. Samorn and I go on foot and ask around looking for wooden boards with which to make a cart, using my bicycle for the wheels. This will help make it easier to carry more stuff than just pushing a load on the bicycle alone.

We linger here for several days—not waiting for word to return to Phnom Penh, but waiting for news of our father. I meet many former classmates from high school who have all stopped to rest near one another in this area. We are glad, in a way, because we are able to see each other, all of us having abandoned our homes and come out here to sleep on the ground. We chat about our families, about where we plan to go, and about the state of the country.

Here we encounter two groups of soldiers with different uniforms: The group operating here on the side roads along the river wear olive-drab uniforms and hats and tie green strips of cloth on the barrels of their guns. The other group, which controls the highway, wears black and uses red strips of cloth as their sign. We don't understand these two conflicting images.

My cousin and her family traveled to Koh Thom and have just returned to Kien Svay. She tells me that at Koh Thom the soldiers were very severe: anyone who used any kind of military equipment, such as hats, boots, canteens, etc., were taken away. Her family became uneasy and came back here.

This news makes us very concerned about our old classmate Bit Khunvilath, who is a first lieutenant. He had come to Chroy Ampil before me and registered with the Organization headquarters in Prek Eng for volunteer service. Yesterday he said goodbye to us and headed back to Phnom Penh. We are very troubled to see the soldiers dividing people up in this way. What will be our fate?

26 April 1975

At ten o'clock in the morning, soldiers clad in olive-drab uniforms walk up and down, informing the people camped in the fields under the trees that they are to prepare to board a river boat that will take them to Prek Po at 5 p.m.

Yesterday the boat took one load of people on a voluntary basis, without compulsion. This morning we are ordered forcefully. We're not sure where we *should* go, but the most critical thing is that we are separated from our father. We decide that we should go to our father's native village first and then decide where to go from there, in case he is waiting for us there.

At three o'clock in the afternoon, we have finished preparing our belongings, and we set out pulling our cart and carrying our belongings along the smaller side roads toward Koki. We have gone about one kilometer when we see a soldier wearing olive drab, with an AK-47 slung over his shoulder and a radio in his hand, walking straight toward us. I pull the cart forward and think to myself that trouble is coming.

The soldier stops and asks, "Where are you going?"

"We are going to Koki, Comrade," I answer.

"No, you're not! Turn around!" he orders.

"Comrade, we have become separated from our father. We request permission to go to his village and meet up with him first," I plead.

"Turn back! What the hell is there to eat in Koki? Go back and board the boat immediately!" he orders firmly. I don't dare plead any more, and I turn my cart around.

The boat is docked at the pier in front of Wat Chroy Ampil at the northern corner. When we arrive back at the pier, the boat is nearly full of people, and there are still many families waiting to board. We line up behind those who have arrived before us.

At five thirty, just before sunset, the boat is full, leaving six families yet to board. How fortunate for us!

The soldiers order us, "Those who haven't boarded, stay the night in the *wat* and wait for the next boat tomorrow! Don't try to escape back toward the highway! We catch up with you, we shoot you!"

The remaining families follow the orders and find a place to rest in the *wat*, crowding in together beneath the monks' dining pavilion, which is elevated only a meter off of the ground.

Dad is on all of our minds. He is old, and in a situation like this, if he is all by himself, he must be miserable. We have to find him. Tonight we sleep little, waiting for the sky to lighten faintly before making our escape.

27 April 1975

At four o'clock we wake each other quietly and slip away. Two or three other families sneak away at the same time. We only dare take the risk because, from listening to the orders, it sounds as though if we make it to the highway, they won't come after us. It seems that this group of soldiers is trying to covertly divert people to their own region, because they only seem to be moving people at night. Thus, our only obstacle is traversing the 200-meter distance from the *wat* to the highway. In only four or five minutes, we have all run from the danger zone, and we continue our journey onward without hindrance.

We arrive at Wat Slaket at nearly noon and stop to rest at the home of Om[12] Mam, our father's cousin. He has a house on Highway One, across the road and north from Wat Slaket. There we are reunited with our father. When we reached Prek Eng, he had met some of his friends, goldsmiths in Phsar Daeum Thkov market. They had pulled up in a car and offered him a ride with them. They had then dropped him off here and continued onward.

We have spent a total of ten days traveling from Phnom Penh to my father's native village, a distance of more than twenty kilometers. We don't know if our journey ends here, or if we are to continue on to somewhere else. We entertain no hope of returning; three days have passed more than three times over, and still the movement of people migrating away from the city continues sporadically. Some city people who have been evacuated along the route appointed by the Organization have to leave a good distance from the city before rerouting toward their native villages. In such cases, some people are forced to travel hundreds of kilometers because they are unable to go against the flow of outbound traffic on the highways, so they have to leave the highway and sneak around via side roads and trails, through small villages. This can take up to a month, and when people run out of food provisions, they are compelled to just stop wherever they are.

---

[12] This word means uncle/aunt (older than one's parents) and is a polite term of address for a man or woman older than one's parents.

CHAPTER 3
Building a New Life on Ancestral Land

Om Mam's house is not very large. It is barely big enough for his own family. Now one of his daughters has just come from Phnom Penh with her family as well, so my family is living under the house. I take apart the handcart and reassemble the bicycle to ride to look for food provisions. We also have no rice supply, so neither sleeping nor eating is an easy matter.

In the morning I get up while it is still dark and take the bicycle to pull yams along with some other people at Neak Loeung. The fields of yams that stretch for hundreds of meters along the west bank of the river opposite Neak Loeung have no owner or caretaker looking after them. The yams are mature and large but are becoming rotten and worm-eaten. Rather than going without, we cut off the good pieces and mix them with rice. But this yields little results, and after two or three days I stop going.

My cousin-in-law (Om Mam's son-in-law) has a large fishing net about thirty meters long. We try our hand as fishermen for a change. Every morning we get up when the rooster crows and ride the bicycle to Prek Yuon. Leaving the bicycle at the home of some locals along the highway, we wade out into the reedy, shallow lake along the right-hand side of the road. The reeds are more than two meters high, and when we walk into them, we can't tell which way is which. But in the middle of the shallow, reedy lake, a bomb crater[1] has created a large pool with lots of fish. As soon as we close the mouth of the net, we are nearly pulled into the water by frantic snakeheads and pikes and can barely gather it in again. Because the way here is difficult, and because we must wade through the tall reeds for a long distance, each day we catch only a single net of fish and keep only the large ones (snakeheads and pikes). In one day, we can catch between twenty and thirty kilograms of fish, but even this is not very productive, as fish trade very cheaply for rice. Currency is now no longer used, and rice and salt have become the crucial items for survival, so they are highly valued in trade.

---

[1] During the war, B-52's from the United States Air Force dropped many thousands of bombs on Cambodia, creating many such craters.

My family's food provisions grow meager, and there is no end in sight to our current situation. We can't continue living like this much longer, without direction, eating and sleeping, eating and sleeping. Besides, these days the Organization has been going around telling those who aren't residents that they must move on. Dad arranges with some of his nieces and nephews for some corn, bean, and vegetable seeds. We decide to go and clear some land for farming in Tuol Ampil, my father's home village.

Tuol Ampil is a village that sits on a long rise of land behind Wat Slaket. This rise is about two kilometers long, parallel with the highway and separated from Wat Mulysovann-Tamol[2] and Wat Slaket by a lake called Don Duong Lake. The northern end of the rise connects with a village called Tuol Tnaot. At the southern end of the rise is another village called Ta Riep. Tuol Ampil is situated right in the middle of the rise, behind Wat Slaket. Behind the village there is another lake that separates it from Don Sar village. Here the ground slopes downward a distance of about 200 meters to the shore of this lake.

At the northern tip of the rise, there is a small stream that serves as the inlet for Don Duong Lake. The land between this stream and Tuol Tnaot is unused land and farmland. The land south of the village is also farmland all the way to Ta Riep.

In the dry season,[3] the lake dries up and villagers can walk from the southern end of the village all the way to Wat Slaket. But in the rainy season, they have to use a boat.

Before the war, this village had about twenty or thirty houses built in a row, spaced far apart from one another, for a distance of 500 meters on the rise along the shore of Don Duong Lake. During the war, Tuol Ampil suffered frequent attacks; the houses were burned, and the villagers were evacuated to the liberated zones.[4] Now, no one has returned yet, and we don't know where my aunt and cousins might be living.

---

[2] Wat Mulysovann, also known as Wat Tamol

[3] There are two seasons in Cambodia, the dry season and the rainy season, and the water level of ponds, lakes, and rivers fluctuates heavily depending on season. The dry season lasts from roughly November through April, and the rainy season is roughly May through October, with the heaviest rains typically in September and October.

[4] refers to the regions secured and administered by the Khmer Rouge during the war, largely rural areas, prior to the capture of Phnom Penh and other cities on 17 April 1975

End of the First Week of May 1975

The Sun rides his chariot over the treetops, casting rays of brilliant red light onto the earth. Three young men, each with a hoe and a *phkeak* knife[5] resting on his shoulder, walk across the grounds of Wat Slaket. Here it is quiet, without people or monks—there are only the abandoned temple, the dormitories, meeting halls, and stupas, with scars of gunfire showing in places. In the area behind a banana orchard, the trees grow thick and unkempt and vines creep unevenly over the monks' dormitory that has been nearly decimated by an explosion. The pond behind the *wat* has become choked by water hyacinths, leaving only a small puddle of open water near the stairs. The surface of Don Duong Lake, shrunken from this year's dry season, is hardly like a lake at all. Bright red water lilies spread beautifully over dark green lily pads hiding quietly beneath. It looks as though a giant carpet has been stretched from the edge of the pond all the way to the lush green hill on the opposite shore.

How breathtaking, how exotic is this scene! It is more beautiful than the carpet of *krachip*[6] flowers spread by Nou Hach upon the rice fields of Battambang province.[7]

The three of us stand on the edge of the pond and gaze at the rise on the other side, looking for the location of the old village. Aside from the occasional sugar palm trees sticking up here and there, and clusters of bamboo that stand restlessly chattering with one another, we see no signs that this rise was once a village, a place where people lived their lives. The opposite shore is a good three or four hundred meters away from this side of the lake. Before, during the rainy season, we could have called to the villagers on the other side, and someone would have come to ferry us across on a boat.

Not knowing the exact distance, we decide to make for the other side. We advance gradually through the tangled jungle growing at the edge of the lake. Because this path has been abandoned for so long, our progress is difficult. We have to clear a path, and sometimes we have to jump over obstacles or veer to the right or left until finally we are clear of the trees along the shore and wade

---

[5] a kind of traditional utility knife used for cutting vegetation, with a long handle meant to be wielded with two hands; see photograph on page 518

[6] *Pentapetes phoenicea*

[7] a reference to *The Wilted Flower* (see page 94)

out into the middle of the shallow lake, where the only obstacles are dead lilies and some grass and vines.

We emerge from the lake in a wide-open space and are suddenly met by the angry sound of birds crying out loudly. They are startled by the presence of people so near their nests. They fly up from their perches, crying out in alarm. They soar together as a flock, first left, then right, finally perching on some bamboo, where they stare warily after us.

These birds live as a flock, their nests hanging from the bamboo branches. Their nests are beautiful! They are small and narrow where they attach to the bamboo, then expand to a bulge in the center. At the bottom there is a slender tube, the entrance to the nest. Each nest actually has a distinctive style and size according to the tastes of its owner. Some have the entrance tunnel underneath, some on the side, and some on top, and each entrance has a protective cover. The nests dance and bounce with the rhythms of the bamboo stalks, which sway in the wind as though endowed with life.

Oh, little birds! You are but beasts; how is it that you know how to make such beautiful and unique homes? How is it that you know how to unite to protect your homes so well? Don't worry about us three brothers; we are but victims, sufferers. We have no desire to cause you harm, to make you part from your family, your friends, or your children as we have done.

Still the birds cry out. Some perch near their nests, others circle in the air. It seems that they don't trust us, not understanding our good intentions. Oh, perhaps they think, *The human animal is a vicious one. It will kill even other humans without restraint, so why should I, a little bird, dare to trust it?*

Yes, this type of bird has never trusted people. If we dare to approach their nests, no doubt they will send out their legions to battle, and then we'll have nowhere to run. And this type of bird often builds its nests where wasps live.

My two younger brothers are not interested in the birds. They have already gone on up the rise ahead of me and are advancing their invasion up there. Soon Samat yells, "A-Tuch!"

I run up the slope, asking, "What is it, Samat?"

"Dead bodies! Dead soldiers!"

We gather around and look at the body of a soldier, shot and lying face down on his rifle, his flesh nearly rotted away, the grass and vines now growing over his body, making it invisible from a distance. We turn, and there is another body. We turn again and see yet another corpse, lying beside an AK-47 and a

30-mm machine gun. This place was a battlefield. There are trenches dug here and there, and palm trees lying crisscrossed on the ground. It appears that this was a post of the Kien Svay district headquarters defensive belt, and that they were surrounded and slaughtered to a man.

We walk about and see nothing but the remains of dead bodies, and none of us can figure out where the location of the old Tuol Ampil village is. Actually, neither of my brothers is very familiar with the place because they have rarely ever come here to visit. Dad usually only brought me along with him. I know the old village better than my brothers, but now even I don't see anything that sparks my memory.

It is almost noon, and we still can't determine the location of the old village. I decide to take my brothers and go back, stopping to gather 30 mm machine gun ammo boxes to take home and use.

When we meet up with Dad again, we figure out that we had gone too far and ended up at the old location of Ta Riep village. Apparently, when we picked our way through the thick jungle at the edge of the lake, we had inadvertently strayed in the direction that was easiest. But now we know the precise location of Tuol Ampil.

Each morning the three of us pack a meal and go clear the land, each one carrying a sickle. When we arrive at the old village site, we first go to cut straight reeds along the lake behind the village and lay them out to dry in the sun, then go back and work to clear the land. When the sun is about to set, we gather the reeds and tie them into bundles and then take them home for our mother and sisters to weave into thatch for the roof of a hut.

Some days we don't go to Tuol Ampil, but instead sneak down to pry off boards and bits of wood from the houses near Koki Market. The people living around Koki Market were evacuated by the Organization, so their houses are now empty, and the Organization is not yet regulating this area.

End of the Second Week of May 1975

The first house constructed on the site of old Tuol Ampil village is born, a four-by-six-meter hut facing east. We make two sleeping platforms[8] about half

---

[8] low platforms attached to hut walls, topped with loosely spaced slats of bamboo strips or wood, used for sleeping on (as well as sitting, eating, or working); Khmer: *rean*

a meter off the ground, one of boards beside the door against the south wall for Mom and Dad, and the other of bamboo strips against the north wall for the four siblings. Thom Pen and Nho build huts to the south of us.

Here we rise to begin working when the rooster crows and continue working until sunset. We plant corn, gourds, eggplants, cucumbers, mint, lemon grass, chili peppers, bananas, and papayas. Nho finds rice seedlings at the Sre Ampil experimental agriculture farm. We start to clear away the water hyacinths in the shallow water at the edge of the lake and divide it into sections to make seedling beds for Mom to transplant[9] the rice. Even though she is old, skinny, and weak, Mom does not sit still. She works hard, hunching over to transplant the rice, teaching her children how this work is done.

Third Week of May 1975

Our food supplies diminish further. We no longer dare cook rice, instead making rice porridge, both morning and evening. This lack of food is not faced by us alone; other evacuated families and some of the locals are facing the same crisis. To alleviate the problem, the Revolutionary Organization distributes rice temporarily at Wat Kien Svay Krau, Wat Champa, and Wat Muny. But there is not enough to go around, and some return home empty handed.

Because there is not much rice distributed each day, and because there are so many people, the contest of fate begins, each person arising in the dark so they can go sit and wait for rice before the others. From Tuol Ampil to Wat Kien Svay Krau is a distance of about four or five kilometers. With the exception of my parents and the two small nieces, who are unable make the journey, everyone in my family always goes to sit quietly and wait for the rice handouts.

Every morning when the rooster crows, we wake each other to go and ask for rice. What fun! On the highway people race each other on bicycles and on foot, making a commotion in the middle of the still night. My old bicycle can hold only two people, so the others have to walk. Even though we have a bicycle, some days when we arrive at the *wat,* the grounds are already completely full of people sitting in lines and we must continue on to Wat Champa or Wat Muny.

Hunger compels people to run back and forth and sit in rows in the dark. Those who live closer have an advantage: they always arrive first, or they sleep

---

[9] In Asian wet-rice cultivation, seeds are first sown in a seedling bed; then later these seedlings are pulled and manually transplanted into another paddy, more spread out, to complete their lifecycle.

there on the ground and wait before the others. Those of us who live far away
are not fortunate enough to arrive first.

One night, Thom Pen and I ride the bicycle to the *wat* and arrive before the
others in the family. Coming into Wat Kien Svay Krau, we sit in line behind the
people who have already arrived. The sky is still dark, but we are disciplined.
There is no chaos; we respect those who have arrived first. No one dares to start
any quarrels over place in line. People continue to arrive gradually, but we can't
see who is who. On some nights, we sit and wait two or three hours before we
see the light of sunrise, and only then can we tell who is kin and who is not. As
the sky becomes light, I can see clearly that my siblings are sitting far from me.
We sit in orderly rows, opening and closing our mouths like baby birds waiting
for food from their mothers. Everyone is like everyone else, their eyes staring at
the sacks of rice standing up on the monks' dining pavilion porch, then turning
to inspect the number of people waiting in line ahead of them, calculating and
analyzing their daily horoscope: *Am I fortunate enough to receive a can[10] of rice
today or not?* Those sitting up front smile with hope, and those who sit in the
back fear that they will go without. As for those somewhere in between, their
stomachs churn with restless anxiety, thinking and fretting, *Will I get any or
not?*

The sun rises at about seven o'clock, and soldiers with guns slung over their
shoulders walk up into the dining pavilion. Some soldiers stand around us to
scrutinize our orderliness and to stop any additional people from coming in
and sitting down to wait. Those who have come later are allowed to wait outside the ring, where they stand folding their arms, stretching their necks to see,
and swallowing their spit, watching those who sit inside the ring waiting to
compete. They are all good people, and they stand praying that those sitting
inside will all receive rice, and that there will be enough left over for them.

The soldiers on the dining pavilion porch begin to untie the mouths of the
rice sacks and order the people to come up and receive their portions. Those
who sit in the front begin to walk forward one at a time. Each of us carries a
krama scarf[11] with one end wrapped around our neck and one end held open
with both hands, waiting to receive the uncooked rice, which they scoop out

---

[10] the standard measure for uncooked rice rations during this period, typically an empty 250 ml (8 fl. oz.)
condensed-milk can

[11] traditional Khmer checked scarf of cotton or silk with many utilitarian and ornamental uses; see photograph on page 517

and dump into each *krama* in rapid succession. We don't use bags because they are too hard to hold open wide; and if we are too slow, the soldiers reprimand us, and all of this can cause grains from our rice portion to fall on the ground as the soldier pours the rice into the bag.

Now we know how to love and recognize the value of a single grain of rice as the birds do. We are so very careful not to allow any rice to spill or dribble over the side. After we have received our can of rice, we carefully tie the corners of our *kramas* and then wrap the *krama* around the bundle and tie it again.

Those who have received their rice descend one set of stairs and those who have yet to receive it ascend another. Sack number one, sack number two, and sack number three have all fallen over empty. But I am not afraid because today the Organization has brought seven sacks, and according to my calculations, my horoscope for today is looking good. Yes, the people in the row on my left are going up one by one, and soon it will be my turn.

Thom Pen and I receive rice from the fourth sack. We don't return home yet, instead waiting anxiously to see the fate of the others in our group. As we left the house in the morning, none of us bothered to walk together, not caring whether ghosts haunted us or not. We each care only about getting to the *wat* quickly. We care only about running out of rice. For this reason, we never sit together in line.

Samat and Samorn receive their rice from the sixth sack. We stand together and await the fate of our sister and cousin. They start on the seventh sack. We count the number of people in front of Oun, my second sister: 10...20...100...140...156 people. Oh no, Oun, you aren't going to get any rice! One sack contains 150 cans of rice, and there are still about 300 people left.

We can hardly stand still. We stand fidgeting, our stomachs churning for fear that there will be no rice left for Oun. We count backwards: 120...110...80...40. Oh! There! The people sitting in Oun's row are going up now, one by one! The rice is nearly gone; the soldier is scraping the can sideways to scoop out the rice. Oh! Don't run out yet, Oun is almost there! The soldier picks up the rice sack and tips it. Oh no! Oun goes up, and the soldier lifts the sack upside down to the side of the can. Oh! There is still one can's worth left in the bag; Oun is the last one to get rice! We are so happy we nearly float off the ground. Oun has come out ahead of a hundred other people, who get nothing. They stand up and brush off their rear ends in despair.

We who have received rice are overjoyed. Those without make sour faces and furrow their brows. They take deep breaths, and their faces look as though they are about to cry. We are accustomed to fending for ourselves, but now we have all become beggars who sit cross legged on the ground, lifting our hands in supplication for alms, uncharitable alms, insincere alms, irregular and unreliable alms, sometimes receiving and sometimes not. Today eight of us have come, and we have received five cans of rice. Some days we receive only two or three cans. Today there were seven sacks of rice; some days there are only four or five.

But no matter how difficult, stressful, or inconstant it is, we always make an effort to come sit and wait to receive our grains of rice each morning because this is the only recourse my family has. Some days Wat Kien Svay Krau, Wat Champa, and Wat Muny have no rice to distribute, and Samorn and I ride the bicycle past Wat Don Sar to go ask for rice at Wat Koh Krabei. But the road is long and difficult, and we are fearful whenever we pass through areas where soldiers live.

In the beginning, my family came to live in nature on the rise of Tuol Ampil alone, like Paul's family in the story *Paul et Virginie*.[12] Now we are not alone any longer. New families come one by one and clear land and trees to build huts. Some build huts to the north of us, and some build to the south. They are not natives of this village. Most of them have relatives living in villages along the highway near Wat Slaket, and it was they who directed them to come here and build shelters on the rise.

The old village site has fertile soil; in only one month our corn is as high as our heads. Our gourds and cucumbers are putting forth shoots and flowering. The chili peppers, eggplants, and lemongrass plants look good. The large rice paddy in front of the hut is beginning to show ears of grain. We are delighted with the growth of our crops. They will help our lives to have some luxury once again.

Late June 1975

People continue to come to live on the land of old Tuol Ampil until it is full. At the same time, the old villagers, who were evacuated to the liberated zones, return to the village as well. The Organization also comes to measure and divide

---

[12] 1788 French short novel by Jacques-Henri Bernardin de Saint-Pierre (1737–1814)

up the land into lots by family, connecting Ta Riep and Tuol Ampil villages. In addition, they start a new village, calling it Phum Thmey,[13] on the vacant land between the old Tuol Ampil and Tuol Tnaot villages. My aunt's family and those of my father's two cousins receive land to build huts in Phum Thmey. The families of four or five other cousins who have come end up over in Don Sar village. They give each family a ten-by-thirty-meter lot.

My large family has now divided into four smaller families in order to receive more land:

1. My family, including my parents, Samat, Samorn, and myself
2. Ol's family, including her husband and her young daughter Sophal
3. Oun's family, including her young daughter A-Lin
4. Thom Pen's family, including his daughter My-L'et

Starting now, a new administrative structure has been put in place: group, then village, then cooperative.[14] All of the leaders are people who had been living in the liberated zones. My group is led by Pu[15] Et. He is in his sixties, dark skinned, skinny, balding in front, with large eyes and curly hair, about a meter sixty in height. He was born here in Tuol Ampil. He has built a hut about seventy meters to the north of mine. The cooperative cadre[16] who has taken charge of Tuol Ampil is called Phal, a man of about thirty-five who used to live at Boeng Trabek near my house and knows my parents very well.

We are a people who no longer have the freedom to move about or eat as we please. We have become workers who labor as we are ordered, in line with the aims of the Organization, at the appointed hours: from six until eleven o'clock in the morning, and from one in the afternoon until five o'clock in the evening. The Organization provides us with the necessities of survival: rice and salt. Occasionally, we receive a small portion of kerosene. We are to go and receive these

---

[13] "New Village"

[14] In this hierarchy, group is the smallest unit, followed by village and then cooperative. Cooperatives were communal resource-sharing constructs established by the Khmer Rouge, in which everyone shared property and resources and later even meals (see page 184). They were typically administered at the level of the subdistrict, a traditional administrative unit containing multiple villages, though individual villages could have cooperative "offices" (cf. page 123).

[15] This word means "uncle" (younger than one's parents) and is a polite term of address for an older man who is younger than one's parents.

[16] This term is used to denote leaders or officials within the communist party. Though often used as a collective noun, referring to a core group or cell of leaders, it can also be used to refer to a single individual, a member of such a group. The word is used in this latter sense throughout this book to refer to individual Khmer Rouge party officials and leaders. Khmer: *kammaphibal*

supplies at the cooperative headquarters in Tuol Tnaot every day when we return from work at noon.

After the land is divided up, our corn ends up on the common land. We are worried that the Organization will confiscate these crops and make them common property.

I ask the cadre who comes to measure and divide the land, "Excuse me Brother, the corn that I planted before—is it still mine?"

"How much corn is it, Comrade?" the cadre asks.

"About twenty by thirty meters, Brother," I answer.

"Oh, that's nothing! You keep it and eat it," the cadre reassures me. We stop fretting and once again our mouths have spit to swallow.

Each day Dad leads his two granddaughters, Sophal and A-Lin, by the hand to go sit and watch the corn so that cows don't eat it. The corn is already starting to produce some ears. The rice that we transplanted with Mom in the water in front of the hut is starting to look nice. One day Pu Et, our group leader, comes to my family and says, "The Organization is taking your corn. Don't touch it!"

This news causes all of us to lose heart and despair, especially my father. He says nothing, and he stops bothering to sit and watch the corn as he used to. One day, as I am going to collect our rice ration at Tuol Tnaot, I ask the advice of the cooperative chairman on the corn problem. He assures me that there is no problem, that we should keep it for the benefit of our own family. His assurance alleviates our anxiety, but with no one to stand guard and protect the corn for a few days, the cows have already eaten nearly half of it.

Pu Et is a very jealous and strict man. He has just arrived from the liberated zones, and he has nothing yet. None of his plants have had time to bear any fruit, so when he sees that others' plants have already borne fruit, he gets jealous and wants them for himself. If we have better food than he does, he is unhappy. If he catches anyone sneaking off to trade things at the villages along the highway for rice, bananas, or yams, he confiscates their spoils and then "builds"[17] them, guiding them in the way of the Revolutionary Organization, forbidding free movement and trade.

---

[17] a term commonly employed by the Khmer Rouge to refer to communist party indoctrination and discipline, usually in the context of correcting incorrect behavior; Khmer: *kasang*

Each day he walks by and pokes his head into our hut at about eight or nine o'clock to see who has what to eat and who hasn't gone out to work. How we despise this attitude! We, all of the "new people,"[18] give him the name "Grandpa Snoopy."[19] When we see him coming from a distance, we call out or whisper to each other, "Here comes Grandpa Snoopy!" Both his wife and his daughter act haughty, as though they, too, are our leaders and supervisors.

One day, about a week after the groups and villages are organized, we receive an order to attend a meeting in Tuol Tnaot at 7 p.m. Each family is to send one representative. When we return from work in the evening, we hurriedly eat dinner and head out for the meeting at the appointed time.

Tonight is a new moon and there is no moonlight. We all sit on the ground in front of a wooden house with a tiled roof beside the highway, near the mouth of the road leading to Wat Don Sar. A small kerosene lamp has been lit and casts a flickering light on the meeting.

A revolutionary cadre dressed in black and wearing a black cap on his head and a *krama* around his neck comes and stands before us to announce the start of the meeting. We don't know his name or his rank, and we can't see his face clearly in the dark. He begins to speak:

"Greetings, fathers and mothers, brothers and sisters, who have just been evacuated from Phnom Penh. The Revolutionary Organization regrets taking so long to get you organized into groups and villages. Our Organization has faced many responsibilities and has been very busy. Now we have gotten you organized, so you ought to understand the political line of the Revolutionary Organization and the way of life in revolutionary society. The Revolutionary Organization has the political aim of annihilating all traces of the regime that ruled the country for sixteen years,[20] as well as the five-year, one-month regime.[21] Therefore, anything in the image or spirit of these two regimes must be obliterated. Fathers and mothers, brothers and sisters who used to live under

---

[18] The Khmer Rouge used the term "new people" to refer to those evacuated from the cities on or after 17 April 1975. The opposite term is "base people," referring to those who already lived in the liberated zones prior to 17 April. The new people constituted the primary class of people targeted for destruction by the Khmer Rouge.

[19] *Ta Aeut (ta* = grandfather, *aeut* = to poke one's head in, or pop in for a visit, i.e., to snoop, in this context)

[20] the Sihanouk regime, 1954 to 1970

[21] the Lon Nol regime, 18 March 1970 to 17 April 1975

these two regimes, you must learn to align, temper, and build yourselves to become suitable as a revolutionary people.

"Cast off the morality of vice! The morality of exploitation! The morality of taking advantage of others! Obey the discipline of the Organization! Don't be free! Don't have your own opinions! Don't be vague in your consciousness!

"Food will be distributed according to your labor. Those comrades who work will receive food. The Organization has no need for the lazy or the worthless!

"The wheel of history rolls forward! No one can stop the wheel of history! Whoever puts forth his arm will lose his arm! Whoever puts forth his leg will lose his leg..."

This is our first lesson. We hear them say nothing about returning to Phnom Penh. We hear only the words "revolution," "annihilate," "temper." Now we see clearly: They don't support Sihanouk's royalist regime as Dad thought. They will squeeze us because we are the people of the two regimes that the Revolutionary Organization must annihilate.

All in the village, except for the elderly and small children, are required to perform the common labor. Every day Samorn and I get up in the dark to turn the soil around the plants in our private garden—gourds, eggplants, cucumbers, peppers, and mint. We water them using shoulder yokes, and then go to perform the common labor.

Samat is very lazy and cares little about helping us. He sleeps until the sun rises and then gets up. But he is diligent when it comes to sneaking a bite to eat. Often, he will furtively pick a cucumber or break off an ear of corn to roast and eat by himself. When Samorn and I catch him now and then, he argues brazenly with us, without any respect for brotherly seniority.

These days Mom, who has had a respiratory illness since we left Phnom Penh, is in bad shape and is unable to walk very far. She stays home and scoots around among the gourds, eggplants, and peppers, picking weeds, turning the soil around the stalks, and picking off worms.

Dad is stronger than Mom. He frequently takes the two little granddaughters to watch the corn patch. Now the rice is also beginning to ripen, and he takes the girls to sit on that side as well.

For the common labor, we clear the jungle, level the land, and pull up tree stumps from the stretch of land that spreads out behind the village. Then we divide it into a grid for rice paddies, and then we dig ditches to bring water into the paddies. We begin our work at the south end of the village next to Ta Riep and work northward.

Every day when we return from work, my brothers and I carry home stumps of *sangkae*[22] and mangrove trees that we have uprooted during our work, one apiece, and save them for firewood. We work hard at our jobs, and we don't dare be careless. Even Samat, who is lazy in his work at home, never misses the common labor.

One day I come down with a fever and am unable to go to work, so I ask to rest at home. I don't know if it's from eating too little and working beyond my strength, or what. I rest without medicine of any kind. When we were camped at Wat Chroy Ampil, my younger brother sold the little bit of medicine that we brought with us to get money to buy *prahok*.

In the morning I still have a fever and chills. Samorn leaves to help with the common labor. Dad has gone to watch the rice at the lake shore. Mom sits turning the soil for the garden. Samat hasn't gone to work yet; he is busy sneaking ears of corn to roast on the cookfire at the neighbors' hut to the north. I have to urinate, so I try to get up and climb down off the sleeping platform. As I reach the ground and lift my foot to walk outside the hut, I feel light, as if I am about to float off of the ground. My head spins. I fall and cry out, "Mom!"

A voice calls out somewhere, weakly piercing my consciousness: "Ktuch! Ktuch! Ktuch!"

I think my mother is calling to me. She seems frightened. I feel as if I am in a dream. I feel as if I am in the most comfortable sleep, and I struggle to open my eyes and respond to my mother's call. But my eyelids, sluggish, refuse to respond. I perceive people crying around me.

I hear the voice again: "Ktuch! Ktuch! Ktuch!"

I try to open my eyes. I try to open my mouth. I am lying sprawled on the earth, my head resting on the lap of my mother, whose hands tug frantically at my hair and ears and slap at my forehead. She is overjoyed when she sees me open my eyes and answer feebly, "Mom?"

---

[22] *Combretum lacriferum*

My siblings suspend their crying. Neighbors, who just a moment ago surrounded me, pounding and massaging my flesh, now look relieved. My mother strokes and wipes my face and says to my two brothers, "M'at![23] M'orn![24] pick up your brother and put him on the sleeping platform!"

Samat and Samorn lift me and set me down on the sleeping platform, and the neighbors all leave. My brothers sit around me, massaging my body. Mom dips a *krama* in some water and wipes my face with it. What happened? I don't seem to have enough strength to open my mouth and ask this question. It is all I can do to open my eyes and stare at what is happening around me.

After I have sufficiently come to my senses, Mom tells me, "You fell backwards and hit your head on the water pot on the cookfire, and you passed out. Samat was scared and crying, and he ran calling for help all over the village."

This news reaches my aunt in Phum Thmey. She comes to see me and tells my parents, "When Samoeun came to the village, he didn't miss his grandmother. Now her ghost is unhappy with him. You need to placate her spirit for him."

Dad has never cared for praying to the dead, and he hates candles and incense. But he does believe in ghosts; he used to always call his kids "*a-khmaoch khpeum!*"[25] because he thinks that "If a ghost loves someone, then it will only bother that person. Whomever the ghost hates is off the hook."

I don't understand. Why would Grandma only bother me when she has four grandchildren? Among my parents' four children, none of us is acquainted with our grandparents' faces. Even though we were all born before Grandma died, we don't know her or even remember her face because we were all too small when she passed away. Then I remember that according to the account of my mother, I am the only grandchild that my grandmother held in her arms, and knew, and loved. Yes, it is just as Dad thinks: whomever a ghost loves, it bothers only them.

After Mom prays for forgiveness from Grandma's ghost, I recover from my illness, my countenance improves, and I am able to go to work with the others as usual.

---

[23] an intimate nickname for *Samat*
[24] an intimate nickname for *Samorn*
[25] "one whom ghosts despise"

For the people in the village, making a living becomes more and more difficult from day to day. We face shortages of all kinds: sewing needles, lighter flints, kerosene, rice, salt, etc. We need needles to patch our torn clothing. We have thrown away all of our lighters because we have no flints for them. We live like people in primitive times, using pieces of iron and tinder cylinders[26] to light fires. The iron strips from soldiers' helmets work well for making sparks. We split apart helmets and divide up the pieces.

Kerosene is not a rationed good. When there is kerosene, the Organization distributes it; but when there is none, we get nothing. Sometimes each family receives half a liter, and sometimes only a *zi*.[27] On nights when the moon is bright, we don't dare to light our lamps, conserving our oil for moonless nights. Sometimes we keep a woodfire burning constantly in the hut.

Rice is a rationed good, provided by the Organization daily. When we return from work each day at 11 a.m., a representative from each family is to go and receive a ration of uncooked rice from the cooperative office[28] in Tuol Tnaot, a distance of more than one kilometer from our house. Sometimes we receive our rations quickly, but sometimes we have to wait until twelve or one o'clock. If we have any rice left over from the day before, then we make porridge first, and there is no problem. But if we have run out and have to wait for the daily ration, then we are late returning to work.

We are not allowed to use collecting our rice rations as an excuse for being late to work, or they lecture us: "If the Organization had been as lazy as you comrades, if they wouldn't fight unless they had eaten, then we never would have beaten the American imperialists. Even when we had nothing to eat, we still fought. It was because we had nothing to eat that we fought—we fought for something to eat!"

The amount of rice that we receive changes from day to day and continues to decline, from one can per person per day, to 250 grams, to 200 grams, to 150

---

[26] hollow pieces of bamboo filled with kapok cotton, for catching sparks from bits of metal scraped together

[27] a small measure of volume of uncertain quantity, perhaps a quarter of a liter; encountered by the author for the first time under the Khmer Rouge

[28] This word *office* (Khmer: *monty*) is used, both here and elsewhere, to mean something like "administrative headquarters" (e.g., for a village or cooperative) and should not be understood to mean anything like a modern office building. It is typically more of a hut- or pavilion-like shelter made of wood, bamboo, and/or thatch, sometimes with an open meeting area (hall) for community meetings (cf. page 139).

grams. Some days we are given a can of dusty, weevil-eaten red corn kernels, or two or three unripe ears of corn, instead of rice.

Once, for nearly a week, we are given another type of grain that I don't recognize. Some say it is wheat. The grains are larger than rice grains, short and fat, and purple colored. We boil it from the morning before we leave for work until we return from work, and still it is not cooked; it has only expanded a little. Our stomachs can't digest it; it comes back out just the way it went in. Nearly all of us get diarrhea. Those who have a grinding mill grind it into flour and make bread instead.

Our biggest problem is salt. The older folks always complain to the young ones, "What the hell, there's no salt for the food?" But now we live without salt. The Organization rations us 300 grams per person per month. This is not enough. Sometimes, when there is no salt, we cook and eat our food bland. Some people in the village gather dead spiny amaranth plants, burn them, and mix the ashes with water to make a kind of salty potash.

When we were still free to move about, we would often go to the villages near the highway and trade for enough rice and tubers to get by, or at the very least a banana tree trunk or papaya tree trunk, which we would shave and then mix the shavings with our rice. The machine-gun ammunition cases that we had salvaged could be traded for two or three cans of rice apiece, as they are used for holding palm sugar. Sometimes my brothers and I would sneak off to pick mangosteens in the orchards of the rich along the highway south of Wat Slaket and bring them home to ripen and then eat them. (Now those orchards have no owners to care for them.) Sometimes I would go to my cousin's house in Chamlak village, and he would give me some uncooked rice, ripe corn, or vegetables to take to my parents.

But when we began to live under the control of the Revolutionary Organization, we hit a dead end. When rice is scarce, when we are each given only two or three ears of corn apiece, the Organization says, "What can we do? Our villages are new; our cooperative is new; we are not yet self-sufficient. The Organization had to borrow two or three carts of corn from the Chamlak cooperative just to give to you..."

Now the sole economic resource for the people of Tuol Ampil is Don Duong Lake. At midday, after we have eaten our rice porridge, we go down to the lake to bathe and pick water lily plants to take home and boil. (Water lily stalks have spongy flesh like taro stalks, only harder and a little bit itchy to eat.)

In the evenings after work, we go to the lake and catch fish by trapping them with baskets or scooping them out with nets and then make soup of them. Every household is the same as every other: everyone eats fish soup instead of rice or porridge. Now it is becoming hard to find *trakuon*, water lilies, spiny amaranth, green amaranth, and purslane as well.

Everyone looks the same. The young look like the old. All are spiritless. All have been transformed in body, mind, and emotions.

Even though we are the children of poor parents, none of my siblings have ever learned to curse or despise one another. My father is very stern. None of us has avoided his rattan cane. His discipline has always been strict, expecting his children to love and respect each other. But now, all of this has departed far from us. Unable to tolerate living apart under the tight food rationing regime, Oun returns home to live and eat with us once again.

Back when we had plenty to eat, we never quarreled. No matter who worked or didn't, no matter who helped find food or not, everyone was allowed to eat freely. But now, it is no longer so. We fight each other for the remnants of hard porridge crust at the bottom of the pot, which we boil for hours to soften up and scrape off with a spoon. To avoid quarrels, the four of us take turns cleaning off the bottom of the pot each day.

We children no longer acknowledge father's prerogative. We measure out the porridge into our bowls equally, one ladleful per person, regardless of who is the father and who is the child. (Mom can't eat porridge, so we boil almost half a can of white rice for her each meal.) If there is any porridge left, then we take a spoon and continue to measure it out until the pot is empty. We are very precise; if we had a scale, no doubt we would use it to weigh and divide up the porridge because the porridge is thinner on top and thicker at the bottom. We measure out the porridge in the presence of all four siblings. We each stare without daring to blink, gauging carefully which ladlefuls are heavier and more brimming than others and which bowl they each end up in. The person who dishes the porridge gets the last bowl.

After we have each taken our bowl of rice porridge, we sit around the pot of soup, which is eaten freely. We eat the soup rapidly, eating two or three spoonfuls of soup followed by a half-spoonful to a whole-spoonful of porridge. Sometimes the soup is all gone and there is still half a bowl of porridge apiece, and then we eat just porridge alone. We hoard the porridge because we don't want to see it gone too quickly.

Because of the food shortages, our family unity has become fractured. Contention between siblings, and between father and children, continues nearly non-stop, night and day. These days Dad, who used to be so quiet after the end of the war for fear of being disciplined by the Organization, is now worse than ever before, grumbling, cursing, and yelling, even in the middle of the night.

Samat, who is used to being lazy, is now lazier than ever. He is not concerned whatsoever with helping me and Samorn catch fish or forage for edible plants to make ends meet. Now he has a shivering fever off and on—hot for a day, then cool again for two or three days at a time.

Oun, who is used to picking and nibbling at everything in sight, is now the subject of great criticism and resentment from the rest of us. There are always fights whenever we catch up with her.

Everyone keeps track of everyone else. Everyone stares at everyone else. Everyone hates everyone else. We hate Samat being lazy to work, we hate Oun always picking and sneaking tastes of the porridge, we hate Dad always grumbling and cursing at Mom and us.

Mom, who used to be so good-natured, is still good-natured, still quiet, nursing her pain in the face of the fracturing of her family.

We don't pay much attention to Dad; we think about Mom much more. When we return from work with crabs or snails, we always roast some and take them to Mom to eat.

Whenever Dad sees Mom eating, he sneaks up close and whispers (for fear that the children will hear and know), "Give me a little bit to eat! Let me have the legs and the pincers!"

So hungry! Dad is so hungry! When he feeds porridge to the grandchildren, he often sneaks some for himself. If he sees any of his children come near, he gets scared, and his hands shake. How he loves the grandchildren! But he is still willing to take from their mouths and put into his.

How hungry is he? Unable to find anything to satisfy this great hunger, Dad becomes aimless, lost, cursing and driving away his children and wife: "Fools! What is there to eat? Only the wife and children have anything to eat! They don't let me have anything to eat! I'm not going to live with all of you anymore!

Take your mother and go! This is my land! My village! I won't let you stay! You children don't know your own father! I'm not afraid to die anymore!"

Some days Dad gets angry and yells, "I'm not going to live with you anymore! I'm going to go and live with my children in Tuol Tnaot!" Dad has three prior children in Tuol Tnaot—two sons and a daughter. They are all married. Dad's first wife is still alive as well. He frequently tries to drop in on them, but they don't seem to be interested in knowing him at all.

Our corn is all gone, but the rice is bearing grain and looking very nice. I don't know how much rice our little twenty-by-forty-meter paddy will produce, but we hope that it will help to alleviate some of the suffering in the family.

Dad's body is swollen all over.[29] He sits in one place and doesn't want to get up because whenever he tries to get up, it is very difficult. He scoots over next to a pillar, one hand propped on his knee and the other hand grasping the pillar, and struggles to raise his body until he is standing straight, then grasps a cane to help him walk.

Each morning Dad takes his cane and makes an effort to lead the two grandchildren (Sophal and A-Lin) to go sit and chase away the birds. But he still can't sit down for very long; he keeps walking back and forth, his mind preoccupied with fear that his children might be giving Mom food to eat behind his back.

Mom is very skinny. Now her legs are beginning to swell from the knees down. It's getting harder for her to walk. She sits still in one place or lies down on the sleeping platform. Between fatigue from trying to perform the common labor and private work for the family and feeling depressed over the fights between my siblings, and between Dad and us children, I can barely even think. Dad is sick, and Mom is sick. I have already traded away the last of my newer clothing[30] and my bicycle to buy enough rice to feed Mom.

We run around looking for roots or bark to make medicine for Dad and Mom to drink, but it doesn't seem to do any good.

The arrival of bad news drives my family nearly mad. Our rice has begun to ripen and has turned the color of a parrot's wings when the group leader tells us

---

[29] Edema, swelling caused by fluid retention in body tissues, is a symptom of severe malnutrition.

[30] Author's note: "a set of khaki-colored nylon shirt and trousers that I had made when I was a policeman"

that the Organization is taking this rice as common property. My God! Why didn't he tell us this when the rice was just sprouting ears? Mom worked hard to transplant it. Dad worked hard, leaning on his cane, walking around all swollen, sitting guard and pulling a string attached to a scarecrow to scare off the birds. Now that it has borne fruit, they say it's common property! Everything is common now—even the single stand of bamboo left as my father's inheritance has been made common property, and we are not to touch it. A sugar palm tree belonging to my father is also made common. Common! Common! Common! What is left for an inheritance?

Mom and Dad have had great hopes for the rice crop because it is the fruit of their own labor. Even when she couldn't walk, sitting around in the hut, Mom has been thinking constantly of her rice, which is beginning to ripen, thinking of fresh pounded, roasted rice grains. She has been thinking that when the rice is ripe, she will teach her children how to pound and roast rice grains. But now, all of her daydreaming turns to despair. Dad has grown increasingly bitter about the idea that when the Khmer Rouge won the war, Sihanouk would return to lead the nation again and it wouldn't be so bad as living with that Lon Nol crowd. Now, not only does he suffer, but he is miserable from hunger. The fruit of his own labor, and someone else reaps the reward. What is left? What property is there? Even our lives are not our own property; they can take them away from us whenever they feel like it.

Dad is extremely bitter about the rice, because he has been sitting and watching it every day, morning and evening, sitting and willing the rice to bear fruit, to grow large, to ripen. Now that it is time to open his mouth, they snatch it away! I can't just let it go, and I go to meet with the cooperative chairman and beg him to leave this rice for my family to help make ends meet because our mother is sick, and our father is sick too.

But he doesn't listen to my pleading, and he even lectures me: "Our cooperative lacks seed rice. We are borrowing it from other cooperatives. Your rice is not very much, but it can help the people in our cooperative. If you eat the seed, then what will be left to eat? You have to think of the collective ahead of yourselves. None of the other villagers have transplanted rice like your family has; how are they supposed to live? They are encountering the same hardships as your family. Waging revolution is bound to encounter hardships and difficulty such as this. If it weren't difficult, if it were easy, why would we even need the Revolution?"

Humph! All I can do is sigh. No matter how much they preach at me, I still can't just let it go and forget about it. I feel so sorry for my parents. At night, after work, I often sneak over and pluck off a handful or two of rice grains and then roast and pound them finely for Dad and Mom to eat.

Quarrelling to live, fighting to eat, is not just a problem for my own family. Other families of Tuol Ampil have the same problems—just in various forms, like the little birds' nests bending and swaying on the ends of the bamboo.

In the family living in the hut to the north of me, the parents are about forty years old. They have four children, about thirteen, ten, eight, and six years old. The parents are able to trade for a bit of rice but don't allow their kids to eat any of it. In the evening they make porridge for the kids to eat. When the kids are asleep, the parents cook rice and eat again. If there is not enough rice to cook, they make porridge and then scoop out the solid parts to eat for themselves and leave their children to sip the thin broth. Sometimes they hit and chase their children away to go and steal other families' vegetable crops to bring home for the parents to eat.

That hut is fairly quiet. We don't hear much quarrelling because there is no one to argue with; all of the contenders are young children, and they are all afraid of the cane. But we often see the parents abusing the children.

As for Don Duong Lake, which I once praised for its natural and striking beauty when first encountered by the three brothers, is there anything marvelous remaining to speak of now? The beauty—the splendor—of the carpet adorned with leaves and water lilies, budding red and spreading thickly across the surface of the water of Don Duong Lake, has now melted away. It has been destroyed by the villagers—utterly laid waste, leaving not so much as a shadow of its former self.

No, it has been sucked up, chewed up, and deposited in our guts. First, we ate the water lilies, the stems with their flowers and fruit; then we ate the leafy plants; and then, finally, we dove down to cut out the stalks and pull out the roots, and we ate those too, ate them all up, ate them until they were extinct. We did not even think of seeds, because they were not made common, and because we were about to starve.

Never mind, don't lament their loss, the damn plants. If we keep them, there is no profit, and if we remove them, there is no loss.[31] If we keep them, then it just makes it harder to catch fish. Behold! Whether noon or night, even in the rain and thunder, as long as we have any free time from the common labor, everyone, old and young, can be found playing in the water. No, we are not playing, we are foraging. We eat, and then we forage some more. Some people catch fish with baskets, some use nets, some look for snails and lily roots. All of us, exposed above the water from the neck up, look like a flock of ducks floating on the surface of the water at sunset.

People invade Don Duong Lake, stirring up the water. The water turns the color of dirt and eventually here and there bits of water hyacinth float up to the surface, roots first. All along the shore, it is the same: bits of algae and water hyacinths, dead and shriveled, piled all over one another in heaps. Oh, Don Duong! Without you, we don't know where we would be!

Behind the village there is another lake, but we never dare wade in. That lake has swampy marshes, it has water taro, and it has leeches. Every now and again we cut out taro roots with fear and trembling to take home and boil.

We used to hear that the Biafrans and the Bangladeshi who were going through famine had skinny, emaciated bodies. Now we have encountered, we know, and we understand what they went through because we are experiencing the same thing. Everyone looks alike, whether old or young, male or female. If they are fat (swollen), their skin seems about to split; and if they are skinny, you see only bones.

Here in Tuol Ampil there are three young siblings who live at the southern end of the village. They seem to be about eleven, nine, and seven years old. They are always naked, with emaciated bodies having almost no flesh, only skin covering bones. Their heads are large, their hair sticks up, their cheeks are sunken, their eye sockets are hollow, and their eyeballs protrude as if they are about to fall out. Their long, skinny necks connect their heads to their bodies, which are composed of protruding bones with large, swollen bellies in front. Their legs are stick-straight from the thighs to the feet, splinted by bulging veins. Their knees are large and protruding, as if someone took lumps of something and lashed them to their legs. Their hands and fingers show only bones and wrig-

---

[31] a saying often used by the Khmer Rouge about the new people; see page 157

gling veins. Because they often bathe in the water, these three children have skin that is black and shiny. Viewed from a distance, one sees only popping white eyes and white teeth surrounded by blackness.

As the day heats up, and waves of heat shimmer in the distance, the villagers all go to work in the fields. But these three children can be found bending and crouching, sifting through the water hyacinths and looking for food to fill their bellies. But no matter how much they try, they are unable to find anything to fill their abnormally large bellies. Still, they continue to walk about, ceaselessly sifting through the mounds of plants along the shore of the lake.

Our daily lives remain the same, scouring the lake, not knowing what else we could possibly find to change anything.

It is night, and the rain begins to fall in large drops, which sting when they hit the skin like someone poking it with a needle. Lightning strikes occasionally, and the surface of the lake is illuminated with perfect clarity. All of the villagers have come up out of the water. Samorn and I, wearing only shorts with naked torsos, remain in the water up to our necks, fishing with nets. At sunset the water was still warm, and the people scattered throughout the lake caused the fish and shrimp to hide. After dark, when there are no people and the water gets cool, the shrimp come out and we manage to catch some large ones. This is why I often take Samorn fishing in the dark. Soaking in the water for a long time, and with the rain on top of that, we become cold.

Samorn persuades me to get out. "It's so cold! Let's stop fishing!"

We come up out of the water. Walking through the rain toward home, we tremble from the cold. (We have been fishing in the lake at the north end of the village, where the water is deep, and there is algae and small fish and shrimp). Dad has not shut up yet. He is still yelling loudly even in the middle of the night in the rain. Oun and Samat bring out the fish pot to collect the fish and take it in the house to boil. They pick out large shrimps and roast them on skewers and then give them to Mom to eat. Mom is lying on the sleeping platform with her arm lying across her forehead, as though oblivious of everything, but then, with effort, she opens her mouth and asks in a quiet voice, "Ktuch, is that you?"

"Yes, Mom!"

"Don't take your brother fishing too late, Son!" Mom says without moving her arms and legs. Her eyes continue to stare at the roof of the hut without blinking, as though there is something unusual up there. No, she is depressed.

Mom is depressed that she has been forced to live in such misery as she does these days.

She misses home, our comfortable house to which she is accustomed, not knowing when she will return. She often asks me about returning home.

She frets over her separation from her eldest son (Leang), not knowing in which direction he was evacuated with his brood of children. Leang is her first child, who is thoughtful of his mother and his younger siblings, who loves his mother.

She misses her grandchildren, whom she used to hold and feed. She doesn't know if they are hungry, if they are quarrelling, if they are fighting over food like their aunts and uncles.

She is depressed because her children constantly quarrel loud enough to be heard all over the village. Samat and Oun, especially, don't listen to her nor pity her.

She is depressed because Dad and the kids fight from morning until evening. Dad startles the whole village swearing and cursing at his children, day and night. His cursing even touches Mom, saying, "You kids are all spoiled because of your mother."

She is depressed because she is used to employing any and all means to support and feed her children, not allowing them to go hungry. Now she is old, she is sick and unable to walk, lying on her grass mat, watching her children fight and quarrel over the lack of food, because of hunger. She is unable to reach forth her hand and resolve the quarrelling, because they fight from hunger, from lack of food. If there were food to eat, to end the hunger, they would fear her, they would listen, and the quarrelling would end.

So all she can do is plug her ears, close her eyes, close her mouth, and clench her teeth. Like yesterday, as we were eating our noon porridge, Oun and Samat were fighting. Mom couldn't stop either of them, and neither of them would listen to her. They were yelling and cursing at each other and wouldn't respect their own siblings. Samat got angry and dumped out all of the soup, then snatched his own porridge bowl and stormed outside the hut. Oun picked up the soup bowl and threw it at Samat. The bowl shattered, cutting Samat's hand, his blood flowing and dripping, in the middle of the day, right in front of Mom.

A French proverb says, "Hungry stomachs have no ears." How true! My siblings don't listen to anything besides the loud demands of their own stomachs.

The two of them are stronger than Samorn and me. (When we were young, even though I was older, I could never beat Samat at wrestling.) But now the two of them seem to be much hungrier than the two of us.

Mom's children torment her, and her husband torments her. Dad grumbles and curses at her without rest. Thoroughly depressed, Mom wants only to be far away from them.

When it is quiet, Mom tells me "Ktuch! Take me to Moat Krasah, son, I want to go live with Kravanh [her cousin]." If you leave me here with your father, A-Mat,[32] and K'Oun,[33] then I will surely die and leave you!" How sad must her heart be for her to make such a decision? I weep and pity my mother, I lament her words, and I feel disappointed that I have no way of easing her suffering.

I am not familiar with Moat Krasah village, Lvea Em district. I only know that it is somewhere on the east bank of the Mekong River. To fulfill my mother's wishes, to help ease her suffering, one evening I travel to Wat Chroy Ampil.

The river water in the middle of *Srapn*[34] has risen nearly to the tops of the banks. I stand on the shore and look at the waters of the Mekong flowing swiftly toward Vietnam. Every so often, I see a boat bobbing up and down with the current of the water flowing determinedly across the land.

I exhale the anxious, restless air from my lungs and take in a cool breath of riverfront air to replace it. But I am able to expel only air; everything else that is not air remains in my chest, causing it to tighten and ache. Staring at the opposite shore I see only black lines and green stripes dividing the sky and the water. Where exactly is Moat Krasah?

I lift my hand to my forehead and peer intently for a long time. But though I stare until my eyes are about to fall from their sockets, still I cannot find Moat Krasah, because I have never been there, and I don't know where it is.

Mom is ill and the current is powerful; how could we possibly get across? I don't know Moat Krasah and I don't know where Aunt Vanh's house is, so how can I find it? We have no rice, so how can we hire a boat to take us across?

---

[32] another intimate nickname for *Samat*

[33] an intimate nickname for *Oun*

[34] lunar calendar month from roughly mid-July to mid-August

I am faced with a dead end. The river current is fast, but my thoughts are sluggish. If this river were as clogged as my mind, and the water as backed-up as my thoughts, it would not be long before the water flooded to my knees, then my waist, my neck, my nose, finally swallowing my whole body. Oh, River! How different are we, you and I? I bid you farewell!

Returning home, I tell Mom "The water is high and fast all along the river. We can't cross the river, Mom."

She takes a deep breath but says nothing. I console her to make her forget her concerns. "Mom, just hang in there a bit more! Just wait and see if they call us back to Phnom Penh."

She takes a deep breath and says dryly, "Humph! I don't dare hope for it, my son."

CHAPTER 4
The Deaths of My Parents

Late August 1975

Mom's feet swell and shrink, swell and shrink, refusing to heal. Now the muscle cramps set in as well. She can no longer do anything but sleep on her mat. Though her body is lying here on the sleeping platform, her thoughts are wandering far away. No matter how much her children quarrel, or how much Dad yells, her body remains motionless.

Every night, after roasting her shrimp, I take out her bowl, fill it with rice, and take it to her. I call, "Mom! Mom!" then shake her arm with my hand. She returns to herself, then sits up and eats, then lies back on the sleeping platform.

When the soup is ready, we dish up some porridge and soup for Dad. Then we siblings sit and eat our porridge quietly. Though we often quarrel, sometimes we can still get along and be friendly with one another. After eating, Samat and Oun go to sleep. Samorn and I sit and massage Mom's arms and legs for a bit and then go to bed too. Sometimes Mom sends us off to bed when the sun sets. She is concerned for the health of her children. She feels that if Samorn or I were to fall, the state of the family would become much worse.

As for Dad, though he is usually grumbling and making noise, when he is alone, he sits lost in thought. When all of the children have gone to sleep, he sits up by himself. I don't know what time he must get up so that when I awake and open my eyes, I find him sitting in the same spot. He has slept very little since coming here to Tuol Ampil. Every night I see him sitting there quietly. When the corn stalks still had ears on them, when he would finish hoeing and watering the plants in the morning, he would roast some corn cobs nice and hot and give one to each child, without us knowing when he ever picked all that corn. Dad loves his children very much, but he has never allowed his children to know his heart. He has never joked or laughed with his children. When his children were scattered far from him, he would miss them, but he would never say so; instead, he would sit alone with his marijuana bong and his wandering thoughts. They say that smoking marijuana makes a person lazy. Not so for Dad; he is assiduous. He has memorized various traditional *chbap*[1] texts, such

---

[1] poems prescribing moral conduct

as *The Chbap of Kram Ngoy*,[2] *Chbap for Boys*,[3] and *Chbap for Girls*,[4] very well. He lectures his children by quoting sayings from these collections and expounding on them. At night he often weaves bamboo into all different kinds of baskets. He constantly quotes, "The craftsman of the night weaves bamboo baskets rather than let the women accuse him of wasting time."[5]

But oh, he is so severe! When we were small, if Dad made direct eye contact with any of the children, there was definitely going to be trouble. He had rattan canes of all sizes secreted in the roof of the house. When we children grew bigger, he stopped hitting us; if any of us made him unhappy, he would just get very loud and swear a lot. Because I never caused my parents much grief, Dad always loved me and spoiled me more than the others. When we were in Phnom Penh, if Dad was fighting with Mom and raising his voice at her, if he saw me come home from school or work, he would lower his voice and stop the argument. He didn't want me to ever feel bad for fear that I would get depressed and have trouble studying.

But now, it has all changed and everything is turned upside down. Even the young seem like old people.

In the face of hunger, people become animals. My family has become a den of animals without parents. The children don't listen to or pity Mom. The children don't listen to Dad or understand him. We make him angry and loud. We only give him food to eat regretfully and begrudgingly. No matter which one of us it is, beloved son or not, we all mistreat him. We fight over nothing but food, and always at mealtimes. Outside of mealtimes, we are quiet, not unlike lazy dogs who lie sprawled before the warm coals with their ears to the ground.

On the sixth day of the waning moon[6] of *Srapn*, the night sky is completely dark after a heavy rain at dusk. Feeling quite anxious, after I finish massaging

---

[2] by Kram Ngoy (1835-1936), Khmer poet

[3] by Moen Mei (ca.1800's), Khmer poet

[4] traditionally attributed to King Ang Duong (1796-1860) but suspected by some scholars to have been authored by Moen Mei

[5] *Chbap for Boys*, verse 39

[6] In the lunar calendar, for the first fifteen days of the lunar month the moon waxes, growing brighter from new to full. After the full moon, during the final fifteen days, the moon wanes, growing darker until the new moon at the end of the month. Lunar dates state a numbered day in either the waxing or waning phase of a lunar month.

Mom, I don't go to bed yet. I go outside the hut and sit beneath a sugar palm tree and lean against the trunk, staring at the stars.

The turbulent state of affairs in the family these days has made me depressed, much like Mom and Dad. The only difference is that I have to go out and work to support the family and serve the Organization. When we work, we forget our cares and push aside our difficulties. This is because we have to be focused on doing our work correctly so that we don't get accused of having an unsound "consciousness" (not being pleased with the Organization's work), and so that we can get the work done. But as soon as I am released from work, my mind fills with cares.

I ask myself, *What is the cause of the daily contention in my family?* It is a question that has an answer, but not a solution.

I can't really say that Dad constantly grumbles too loudly; or say that Oun is constantly sneaking porridge and hiding it from us; or accuse Samat of being lazy and doing nothing but sitting around waiting for food; or accuse myself and Samorn of being too rigid and finding fault with our siblings; because before, when we left Phnom Penh, we never argued with each other at all. We traveled, carrying our stuff with much difficulty. We took turns, helping each other, nobody sitting idly by while another struggled. We even respected and loved Dad. We fled from Wat Chroy Ampil at the peril of our lives to come and find him. None of us were angry or resentful toward Dad, who had traveled on without letting anyone know and left his children to worry. Even Mom never said anything and never protested having to look for him. Back then, my family was cohesive. Even when we came here to Tuol Ampil to clear the land together, we were sweet and kind to each other. When building the hut and planting and tending the crops we were unified, we helped each other! We didn't even turn our backs on Samat when he was a little slow and lazy.

The tension in the family began after the Organization took away our freedoms and pressured us to labor in the fields every day under the hot sun with meager food rations, and we were unable to find anything else to make up the difference. Everyone in my family eats a full ration, so nobody can make up for anybody else. Families with many young children get some relief for the adults because children eat less but receive the same rations as the adults.

I can't compare my family with any other family in Tuol Ampil because most of the families who have come here are from the middle class of society. They have gold, silver, diamonds, valuable goods to trade for rice and supplement the rationed rice from the Organization. Even now, they can still trade. My family has never had silver, gold, or diamonds; even our clothing is scant. We had some nice dishes, glasses, and silverware, but they were too heavy to bring, and Mom buried them back at the house. We have no options. From day to day, the lack of food for our stomachs gets worse and worse, as a logarithmic function.

It is a combination of all of these factors that has made nearly every member of my family cranky, faint, and intolerant. I can't accuse any particular member of my family of being in the wrong because we are all in the shackles of hunger. All of our problems could be resolved if only we had something to ease the hunger. Is there anything? No. There is nothing. We can't resolve it. If we sit and ponder until we turn to stone, still we could not resolve it because we are in bondage, because they are torturing us. Is it our fault that we were born and lived in those former societies?

The moon on this sixth day of the waning moon rises low over the tops of the trees and the roof of the temple, casting its soft rays on the face of Don Duong Lake which has just flooded to the brim. Small waves, reflecting the moonlight like the scales of small white fish, glimmer and chase one another, extinguishing themselves in the grass and *kamphlang*[7] plants at the lake's edge. The tadpoles, crane flies, frogs, and toads all cry out noisily, frolicking happily, glad for the rain. Such fun! The little ones with the little ones, the big ones with the big ones, the young females gathering around the males. Diving, surfacing, jumping, chasing, hugging, riding piggyback with free abandon. None is jealous of any other. Such fun! Such fun! No, not fun—they face an emergency. Villagers carrying lanterns and torches come searching in every direction for frogs and toads.

Oh, unpredictable life! Sometimes we break out in song, and sometimes we break down weeping.

In the sky a nocturnal bird flies slowly, occasionally letting out a cry which sends shivers down my spine.

Now and then the wind blows, and raindrops that have collected on the banana and bamboo leaves catch and scatter the moon's rays, like Indra sprinkling mankind with sacred waters of blessing to release them from

---

[7] *Polygonum tomentosum*

suffering and contention. But now there is no Indra, no Brahma, with the power to save our lives. The wind blows the thatch leaves on the hut's roof back and forth with a grating sound.

In the hut, Dad, with a face so swollen it nearly swallows up his eyes, his cheeks numb, sits quietly across from the small oil lamp, which gives off a weak, flickering light. He clutches the mouth of the marijuana bong tightly under his chin with both hands, blinking his eyes as though lost in thought. He leans the bong against the wall, unties the bag of marijuana, and separates out the individual marijuana stems onto a small round cutting board between himself and the lamp. His right hand clutching a hatchet, his left hand controlling the pile of marijuana, he leans in, tilting his right shoulder forward, making an effort to slowly chop the marijuana. Occasionally he uses the edge of the hatchet to scrape the marijuana bits into a single pile and then continues chopping.

After chopping the marijuana, he gathers it into the center of the cutting board and puts down the hatchet. His left hand clutches the bong, and his right hand removes the bowl of the bong, which is made from a bright brass bullet shell. He places his mouth over the bong's stem and blows to gauge the water level inside the bong. Holding the bong to the ground with his chin and clutching it with his left hand, he takes the bowl in his right hand and pushes it upside down onto the pile of chopped marijuana and then inserts it back onto the stem of the bong. He tips the bong forward, then back toward him, then places his mouth on the mouth of the bong. Then he takes a sliver of bamboo and catches the flame from the lamp and lights the marijuana in the bowl. He inhales the smoke from the bong with a loud gurgling sound, while his right hand continues to press the burning marijuana further into the bowl with the bamboo sliver until it is all gone. He inhales the marijuana like it is very delicious. Removing his mouth from the bong, he exhales the smoke. His eyes watch the smoke stream downward under the force of his breath and then naturally float back up again, as though he is nostalgically reluctant for it to fly away from him.

One bowl, two bowls, three bowls...one last bowl and he exhales the smoke slowly, a little at a time in little puffs which float up into the air. They say of marijuana smokers that their minds are not very connected to their bodies. This is very true. Even though he has stopped smoking, even though the smoke has wafted away, still he clutches his bong and stares wide-eyed as though looking for something he has just lost.

He is thinking. He is thinking about life these days, about the misery through which he is passing, which his children and grandchildren are facing.

While we were still in Phnom Penh, Dad used to smoke only two or three bowls before bed. But now, here, it is one bowl after another, one cutting-board-full after another. It's because he can't sleep.

It's true: troubled souls can't sleep. Mom has been lying in her mosquito net for a while, and still she has not fallen asleep. She turns over and stares at her children returning from catching frogs and toads and asks quietly, "Samat, Samorn, are you back now?"

"Yes, Mom," we answer together. Mom is quiet.

Old, haggard and thin, sick, on rations that are virtually nothing, unable to sleep at night—What will become of the two souls to whom I owe the most?

Early September 1975

At midday, the Organization goes around collecting the names of civil servants, telling them that they will be allowed to return to Phnom Penh to work there. Even though people have little faith in this prospect, still many villagers sign up. Some of them really were civil servants, while others were not but have bluffed and signed up anyway, because they are tired of living here. Tuol Ampil has now become a mound of karmic suffering for their lives.

For my part, I have waited a long time for this day. It is not my house or my job that I miss; it is pleasing my mother, easing her misery. I go to sign up.

"Brother, I wish to sign up."

The revolutionary cadre looks me in the face. "What is your name, Comrade?"

"My name is Samoeun," I answer.

"What was your job?" the cadre asks.

"Officer in the National Police." The cadre writes my name in his list without asking much else.

After I sign up, I tell my mother right away, hoping that she will be glad.

"Mom! They have taken our names to return to Phnom Penh."

Mom is delighted and asks, "Really?"

"Yes, it's true, Mom. I just signed up along with Nho," I relate slowly to my mother. She is quiet and says nothing. I sit and massage her legs and arms in silence. She is thinking—thinking of returning to her nest. She speaks in a soft voice:

"I'm sick and confined to my mat. How can you take me?"

"Don't worry, I'll make you a stretcher like doctors use and Samorn and I will carry you."

She is silent, apparently unhappy, doubtful of ever returning home.

For two months now, Mom's legs have become so swollen that she is unable to walk and can only scoot around in the hut. It has now been a month since she got dysentery on top of that. From then on, she has only been able to sit and lie down on the sleeping platform. I saw a hole in the boards of the sleeping platform at her feet and place an ammunition box beneath it to serve as a chamber pot.

Among her four children who have come to live with her here in Tuol Ampil, only Samorn and I devote attention to watching over and taking care of our mother. Samat and Oun help out occasionally whenever I chastise them severely enough. They just don't have any personal will to serve her.

Ol, Mom's eldest child, and Ol's husband never come around to see how she is doing. They won't come near us because all the people in this hut do is fight like dogs, morning and night. They are ashamed to have a family like us. I never dare tell them anything or invite them over, either. Because she is my older sister, she should know better than I do about the responsibilities of children toward their mother. (My sister is very ignorant; neither she nor her husband are even literate.)

I am mostly the one who watches over and helps lift Mom. Samorn takes turns with me, and also helps wash her clothing and diapers. Sometimes I can get Samat and Oun to help do laundry, but they rarely ever sit and massage her arms and legs.

Aside from roots and tree bark, we have no possibility of finding medicine or a doctor to come and have a look at her. Her condition deteriorates daily.

For nearly a week now, Mom has had a hard time sitting up to relieve herself on her own. Samorn and I take turns each night sleeping in the mosquito net with Mom to help lift her up to relieve herself. She feels sorry for us and doesn't want to be any trouble to us. She always tells us to go to sleep before her so that we will have strength to work the next day.

21 September 1975

Mom's condition is getting worse. After making arrangements with Phal, the cooperative cadre, I am permitted to stay home. Mom is able to eat neither rice nor porridge.

In the morning I make a little bit of porridge for her to eat. I pound flour to make her small *ambaeng*[8] and *baboh* cakes to eat with sugar.

When she relieves herself, she has no strength, and she tells me, "Ktuch! Don't make me a sinner, help me clean my bottom."

She is so weak. I call all of my siblings together and tell them, "Mom is very weak now. It's time for all of you to gather around and hold onto her; she might pass away tonight."

This evening she is unable to eat again. She is fully aware of life's journey, and she tells me, "Ktuch! Call K'ol and K'oun to come and massage me."

She still thinks of her children and has no anger for the ones who never come near, but instead she calls them near. I pass along her message to them. Dad sits quietly and says nothing. Thom Pen often comes by to visit his cousin, usually coming to sit with her at night.

Because of old age, chronic illness, and lack of food, Mom's body is thin, her eyes are hollow, her cheeks are sunken, and her limbs have only recently stopped being swollen but are now stiff, nothing but bones and intertwining veins. Her spine is bumpy, which causes her a lot of difficulty sleeping directly on the wood platform.

Tonight is the first night that all of us sit around Mom and silently massage her. Now and then she speaks:

"Don't massage too hard. It hurts!"

She is restless and can't lie still, telling us to massage her legs, her arms, and her lower back, but not her thighs, because they are too sensitive. Though her health is definitely very poor, and she is very weak, her intellect and her memory are still quite good.

---

[8] a kind of thin pancake

She tells us, "I don't want any of you to sleep tonight in case I fall asleep and you don't know it."

She knows that her life is nearly at an end, but she avoids saying it directly and scaring her children. She calls her children who won't come near to come near. She uses the words "fall asleep" instead of "die" to let them know that the final minute between mother and children is near at hand.

But because of the power of fatigue from laboring all day, my siblings fall one by one. By midnight they have all fallen asleep. Mom closes her eyes silently. I, alone, sit up with her.

Tonight it is quiet and windless. The moonlight on the second night of the waning moon of *Photrabot*[9] shines into the hut through the doorway, which has no curtain of leaves to close it off. The moon is high, and the still, motionless surface of the lake reflects the pale-yellow moonlight as though a great sheet of mirrored glass has been laid down there.

I sit inside the mosquito net beside Mom. I hold a fan and slowly fan her with it, every now and then turning it to fan myself. From the sky outside come the cries of a barn owl,[10] followed by a chorus as a dog howls plaintively from the edge of the village. I start as chills go up my spine and across my scalp, and my arm hairs stand on end with anxiety for Mom. I lean over, place my ear near her nose to listen to her breath, and place my hand gently on her chest to feel for her heartbeat.

No matter how much I have prepared my heart to be brave, I am nevertheless startled and frightened when I hear the cry of the owl, for apart from the moon far off in the sky, I am totally surrounded by lifelessness and death. Even the water of the lake, which normally has ripples, has turned still and motionless.

I am alone to face Death, who is trying to snatch my mother away. Death's servant[11] has come, and soon Death himself will arrive. Then there will be a scene of struggle, and Death will understand the depths of my love for my mother.

---

[9] lunar calendar month from roughly mid-August to mid-September

[10] traditionally a portent of death in Khmer culture

[11] i.e., the owl

The Shadow of Death

1. The night is still, and a fruit bat flies slowly   a scops owl cries in fear of hunger
a barn owl screeches, rending night's veil   a sleeping dog opens its eyes and howls.

2. I sit beside you and care for you   your body is old and worn
fallen ill, abed, without healer   never improving, ever declining.

chorus:
The waning moon drowses not   the barn owl glides and startles with its cry
I tremble and feel your chest   confirming the breath of life.

3. Afraid and relieved, daylight slow to come   grieving you, worrying and thinking
fearing your life will pass   Death draws near as I feel your chest.

The sound of a rooster crowing and the faint red light in the east causes my chest to relax and my worry to subside. It is morning! The darkness of night is replaced by the brightness of sunlight. The fear that has smothered my feelings all night is replaced with gladness: my mother is not dead!

I hurriedly prepare the porridge. When Mom awakens, I wipe her face with a wet *krama*. She can no longer sit up. When the porridge is cooked, I dish it up and let it cool, then spoon-feed it to her. Out of love for her son, she tries hard to eat three more spoonfuls. I rejoice and encourage her to eat more. But instead, she pleads with me, "Don't force me, Ktuch! I can't swallow it, Son."

I think that maybe her strength will recover. I go tell Samorn and tell him to come help feed her. Out of love for her children, she tries hard to eat three more spoonfuls. We rejoice, and it doesn't occur to us that this is an omen of our final parting.

Because Mom's condition is so poor, this morning all of us are permitted to rest.

My family has only one can of uncooked rice left. The sugar for Mom is gone as well. Samat and Samorn swim across the lake to Wat Slaket and take the two remaining ammunition boxes to trade for sugar and rice. I sit with Mom.

She speaks softly: "Ktuch, if you want me to get better you have to find a healer, Son." This moves me to great pity for her. As long as she's been sick, we have never tried to find a healer to come treat her, nor has she ever asked us to do so because she knows that we have nothing to give in exchange. Today she has very little strength left, and she asks us to find a healer.

Though I have nothing, I run to Tuol Tnaot to find a healer as requested. But I find none. There is no one to take pity on us. Even Pu By, Dad's friend, refuses to come see her. I return home in despair. When I tell Mom that I cannot find a healer, she remains silent.

At about nine o'clock in the morning, Ol comes to sit with Mom. Samorn and I take this opportunity to go out into the lake to catch some fish with a net and forage for plants. When we come back, we prepare some porridge and soup.

Later, Oun and Samat return empty-handed. They weren't able to find anything. I dish the porridge into bowls. We sit around our bowls and begin to eat.

Suddenly, Mom calls to me, "Ktuch! Bring your brothers and sisters!"

"Let them eat first!" Dad retorts.

"No! Come quickly," she calls urgently, and we leave our bowls of porridge to go and sit around Mom. She lies on her side with her head pointing east and her face turned to the north. I sit right in front of her face, Samorn next, and Samat at her feet. Oun, Ol, and Nho sit behind her back. We all massage her body. She is very weak. She speaks very softly to me:

"Ktuch, when you see your brother tell him gently. Don't let him be angry, all right Son?"

"Yes, Mom," I answer. She is thinking of her eldest son, Leang, who cannot be with her in her final minutes.

She says to Ol and Nho, "Nho and K'ol, look after your siblings. You are older than them." She struggles to speak deliberately, hoarsely. We all try hard to keep our feelings under control and listen to her sad counsel.

She says to Oun, "K'oun, bring me my skirt and shirt." Oun rises and unties a bundle of clothing and removes a black silk skirt and a white shirt and brings them to Mom.

"Lay them over me, that will do," she tells Oun. "I hurt so much!" she says softly.

"Where do you hurt, so I can massage it for you?" I ask her.

"Oh! I hurt everywhere, Son!" she answers.

"Why does dying have to be so miserable?" she complains.

We massage her gently and quietly, not knowing what to do or say. She begins to recite a mantra: "Lord Buddha! Lord Buddha! Lord Buddha!" We recite the words along with her. She has me lift her head off the pillow with my hand. Her voice no longer makes any sound. She closes her eyes. She makes the death rattle. She is dead. My siblings wail.

She has died peacefully, without convulsing, like the flame of a lamp that has run out of oil.

I gradually remove my hand and place her head on the pillow. She died at one o'clock in the afternoon on 23 September 1975, the third day of the waning moon of *Photrabot*, Year of the Rabbit, at age sixty-two, lying on her side.

I don't cry out. Warm tears roll from my eyes. There's nothing to regret, but I feel sorry for my mother, who was born the daughter of poor parents and died impoverished. Now it is proper for her to go on her way. What does she have to endure for in this miserable, meaningless life?

I pity my mother who, all her life, knew only hardship and tears. My mother, who bore a mountain of grief and swam an ocean of tears for the well-being of her children, while some of her children have not understood the purity of her mother's heart. They have thought only of piling up the mountain of grief for her to bear and digging the ocean of tears for her to swim. Now they make an effort to mourn and wail. What are they crying for? To show their regret?

Actually, all of us loved our mother just as much as anyone else. It's just that this love was manifested in different forms, according to the level of discipline and understanding of each, according to the personal perspective of each. Some ways of showing love brought her peace, and others brought her suffering.

Ever since Mom fell sick and became confined to her sleeping mat, Dad has never said much. He keeps to himself, as though we don't even know each other, or as though we were enemies. Even when she was about to die, he didn't come near.

Ever since I've been old enough to remember, I have seen Mom shedding tears because of Dad's frequent emotional abuse. She often said to me, with tears in her eyes, "Make a prayer offering of a spoon of rice and a string bean that I will never have to meet your father again." Now as soon as she passes, Dad falls sick with a fever. He wraps up in a blanket and sleeps alone, with no child to watch over him.

Now I am the one who must handle everything. I don't know whether to cremate her or bury her. I don't know what to do or how to do it. We resolve to cremate her, but because Tuesday is an unlucky day,[12] we decide to cremate her tomorrow morning. I run to find wood and boards to make into a coffin while Samorn and Samat saw up tree stumps that the three of us had carried home and saved a while ago.

Wednesday 24 September 1975

Yesterday Mom sent me out to find a healer, as though seeking an experienced elder or a wise minister to help her on her way. She died without her minister. Her body has been on display for a night without a minister or any relatives coming to see her apart from my uncle and siblings. Even my aunt and her children have not stopped by since Mom fell sick.

The sun rises above the tops of the trees and Pu Et, our group leader, comes and tells me, "This body cannot be cremated. The revolutionary tradition is that bodies must be buried."

What? The nerve of this group leader! He oppresses in every way possible. The corn we plant, he forbids us to eat. The rice we raise, he takes. Now he's here to forbid us from cremating the body. I run to speak with the cooperative chairman in Tuol Tnaot and receive permission as requested.

As we are chopping down banana trees to make a furnace, Ta Et[13] comes to forbid us again and Nho doesn't dare chop any more. These banana trees represent the sweat and blood of my family. We worked to carry them and plant them. They are on the land which the Organization gave us. I can do whatever I want with them. Because I am not afraid, Ta Et no longer dares stick his nose in and interfere anymore.

Fortunately, this morning the villagers have made a gift of three cans of uncooked rice and Pu By has come to officiate as a minister. As directed by Pu By, we wash the body and place it in the coffin. He explains how to prepare the furnace and stack the firewood. We lift the coffin and place it on the wood with the head pointing east and the body face-down (to stop it from jumping out of the fire). Then Pu By officiates according to tradition.

At about 10 a.m., my brothers and I light the fire to cremate our mother in an atmosphere of mournfulness. Samat doesn't help much because he is too

---

[12] Many Khmers believe that Tuesday is generally an unlucky day and avoid doing certain things on that day, from getting a new haircut or wearing new clothes to getting engaged or cremating the dead.

[13] Pu Et (*Ta* means "grandfather" and is possibly being used sarcastically here to show mild contempt.)

busy crying. At eleven o'clock a villager who has just returned from work comes to join in.

"Brother! Can I help you with the cremation?" he asks.

"Yes, thank you, Brother. My brothers and I have never known how to do this, so we'd be very glad if you could help us," I reply.

"I feel so sorry for her. I've wanted to come since this morning, but Ta Et wouldn't let me. I had to wait for the break."

He assists us nobly and skillfully. At about twelve-thirty the cremation is complete. We begin to gather the cremated remains and wash them in coconut water, then turn them over to Pu By to perform the *prae rup*[14] ceremony.

In gratitude to Pu By and the villagers who helped with the cremation, we collect and cook the rice from our rations, along with the rice donated by the villagers, and eat it together with them.

My mother is dead, but the contention between my siblings remains unresolved. One night, after we finish our evening porridge, I speak with them:

"For almost two months we've been fighting constantly. Oun and Samat, you two especially took no thought or pity for Mom, who was sick. You thought only of fighting with each other. No matter how she counseled or forbade, nobody listened to her. Then she died, and now all of you are weepy and regretful. Weep, weep, weep! You think only of weeping until you can't do anything else. Now she's gone, and we have to reassess, to come together as siblings so that others won't look down on us. Look at Ol: even she looks down on us. She wouldn't come to see Mom because we were so busy ripping each other apart."

They begin to come to their senses and love each other, forgive each other, like they used to. Dad, who used to noisily scold his wife and children, begins to quiet down.

Oh, Dear Mother! Were you the cause of the contention? Is that why as soon as you died, our hut returned to peace and quiet and the crisis melted away? No! It's not so! You were so sweet. You were so patient. You always chose submission and tears in order to end the contention with Dad and with Oun and Samat. Only Samorn and I knew your heart. You often said to me, with tears wetting your knees, "Ktuch, your father hurts me so much!"

---

[14] a traditional ceremony involving the washed bone fragments of a cremated individual

"Ktuch, A-Mat won't listen to me at all!"

"Ktuch, K'oun is causing me trouble again!"

I often used to cry in my bed with pity for my mother. Then one time, I dared to contend with Dad on her behalf. He kicked me out of the house, which made Mom even colder toward him. In order to return and live near Mom, I chose the path of submission. I bought some fruit and snacks and brought them to him, kowtowing to him and asking his forgiveness.

My mother was wonderful. She never swore, she never prophesied evil of her children, she never fought with the neighbors. In this life, she had no bad karma—see with what ease she passed away, almost without rival. She knew clearly when it was time for her to leave this earth and knew she could not be late, could not wait for her children to finish eating their porridge. Now those who sinned against her are sad and regretful. They are penitent.

Dad's swelling has gone down for half a month now. When Mom passed away, Dad became feverish and wrapped himself in a blanket even during the day. The children speculate that Dad didn't want attend to Mom's death and didn't want to go near her body, so he pretended to be feverish.

After Mom's cremation ceremony is over, we pay no attention to Dad. And Dad says nothing, nor does he call any of his children to come near him. So we suppose that he is back to normal. We think only of doing our own work.

Usually, Dad rises from the rooster's crow and sits quietly hugging his marijuana bong. He never rises after his children. As for Samorn, Samat, and I, we usually rise in the dark to till and hoe the earth, to haul water to sprinkle on our private crops before we leave to do the common labor. Concentrating on our work, when we wake up, we each grab our hoes, dirt baskets, buckets, and shoulder yokes and fulfill our labor without daring to engage in idle chatter.

Thursday 2 October 1975

The sun has risen nearly to the tops of the trees and the three of us are watering the vegetables with our shoulder yokes, when suddenly Oun cries out from inside the hut, "Tuch! Samorn! Dad is dead!"

"What? Dad is dead!" I exclaim. We throw down our yokes and run to the hut.

"My God! When did he die?" Dad's arms and legs are stiff and at odd angles and his head has fallen off the pillow. His body has large black splotches. The old folks speculate that it was a toxin. He might have been dead since the middle of the night. Before he passed, he clearly suffered pain and convulsions.

Why didn't he call out for his children to come and help? Or did he die without being conscious beforehand?

This quiet death makes us feel dissatisfied, regretful that we didn't come in time for our father's final breath, did not receive his advice or final words of counsel, did not fulfill our duties as sons and daughters toward our father at the very end of his life.

Unlike Mom, who sorrowed for the tragedies in her family, Dad sorrowed for the tragedies in society. Dad was hurt and regretful about his optimistic attitude and his faith in the Khmer Rouge. He had thought that the victory of the Khmer Rouge would bring happiness to the nation; that it would bring the return of Samdech to govern the country. "The Khmer Rouge would not expel the people from the city," he had said.

But what he experienced after the rain and thunder and lightning subsided was a flood. The Khmer people suffered, and Dad became a pathetic beggar, a man who could barely fill his own stomach to satisfy his needs. His family, his children, and his wife lived in crisis because of the influence of his faith. If Dad had believed me and allowed us to prepare for our journey, we could have brought a lot of food to live on for a long time. (Some of the villagers have still not run out of food provisions.)

These disappointments stirred up his feelings and made him feel ashamed before his children, thinking that they were angry and spiteful toward him. And in the end, he decided to leave this world in silence.

In actuality, his children had no feelings of resentment toward him for misjudging the situation. We loved him and Mom the same, equally, and felt sorry for our elderly parents who had to endure such hardship in these difficult times.

But because Dad caused so much suffering for Mom, we began to feel sorrier for her and began to feel detached from Dad, no longer thinking of him, caring only for Mom, the victim.

Mom died and her daily woes ceased. Then we had an opportunity to turn our care toward Dad for a change. But those nine days were too short to get over our grief for Mom, who was so beloved. Oun and Samat's tears are not even dry yet, and now it is time to shed more of them.

We are so sorry! We are so sad! As children, we have no desire to act as a court to judge our parents, to rule on who was right and who was wrong.

Dad died on the twelfth day of the waning moon of *Photrabot*, Year of the Rabbit, at age sixty-six. We lift his body and lay it out properly, bending his arms and legs into the proper positions. Thom Pen and two neighboring relatives help stand vigil over the body.

Without any firewood, we are forced to bury Dad. Samorn and Samat take care of making a coffin. I head off to inform our aunt and our older siblings, Dad's children from his first marriage in Tuol Tnaot, and to find a minister. But apart from Ta Yu, a minister, nobody else comes near Dad. They did not consider him to be their father or their brother. I don't know why Dad's kin have such attitudes. Before the war, Dad's younger sister and nieces and nephews respected and loved him very much. In contrast, though, their children never really cared much for him even from the beginning.

Dad returned to die in the village of his birth, but none of the people from the village of his birth were there to mourn his passing.

Today my house has no rice left and we get no help from the neighbors as we got when Mom died.

With help from Bong[15] Phal (the cooperative cadre), we obtain a boat to take his body over to be buried at Kor Ko (the graveyard site behind Wat Mulysovann-Tamol) at about one in the afternoon. My brothers and I, along with Bong Phal and the old minister, take Dad's body to the burial site. As we carry the coffin up the bank, the old minister walks about inspecting the site and points to where we should dig the grave. Afterward, we lower the coffin into the grave with the head pointed west. The old minister chants in Pali,[16] then crumbles a dirt clod and sprinkles it on the coffin according to custom, then tells us to push in the loose dirt to finish the job.

In the blink of an eye, my two parents are utterly gone, having left to their four children (my sister Ol does not mourn) only sadness, devastation, and self-pity.

---

[15] This word means "older brother" or "older sister" and is also a polite term of address for someone somewhat older than the speaker.

[16] the scriptural and clerical language of Theravada Buddhism, originating in India

Samat and Oun sit and cry in the still, dark hut. Samorn and I each find our own place outside the hut to sit and express our sadness. We ponder and wonder what will happen to us, we who have now become orphans.

Mom died on the third day of the waning moon, and Dad died on the twelfth day. On the third day, while there was still moonlight in the sky, Mom died having left her final words of counsel for her sons and daughters. On the twelfth day, when the sky was nearly devoid of moonlight, Dad died quietly without any final words at all for his children. Dark, like the thirteenth day of the waning moon, when it is so dark you can't see a thing. When all is indistinct, and the surface of the lake is shrouded in haze. Dark like my feelings, aimless, searching, looking for an outlet, looking for a path. So very dark!

Mom had complained, "Why does dying have to be so miserable?" With these final words she wanted to tell her children that dying is the most difficult thing in the life of man. No difficulty, no obstacle large or small in the journey of life, should be considered insurmountable. You have to endure, overcome, conquer.

This is excellent counsel, and I will cherish it as wisdom for my life in the future. My brothers and sisters do not understand these final words. They think only that their parents are gone, that their lives are truly adrift like boats with broken rudders in the midst of the sea.

Life is Grief

1. When you die, we sit and cry | the hut so quiet without you
when you lived, we clung to strife and conflict | when you're gone, self-pity—Oh Karma!

chorus:
No more crying, we live yet, it's called Grief | from this day on, Grief without respite
like drifting debris with no island or shore | without you, never again free from Grief.

2. Oh, Life! Thoughtless, you appear simple | but by the Lord's Dharma, all is Grief
with flesh comes trouble, with life comes Grief | all is *anichang, tukkhang, anata.*[17]

penned on 5 October 1979

---

[17] Pali: "uncertainty, misery, immateriality"

We don't have time to grieve for long. Other major problems overwhelm us, especially hunger. If we look around, we can see we are not the only ones experiencing loss. There are others like us. Some have lost wives, some have lost husbands, and some have lost children to this great famine of rice. They eat a lot of plants, they swell up, they get skinny, and then they die.

We haven't had even a single grain of rice reserves since the day Dad died. On the day of the *Phchum Ben*[18] festival (October 5th), the Organization distributes uncooked rice-ends,[19] which are almost nothing but chaff ends,[20] fifty grams per person for two meals.

Good Lord! Eat up, little ones! We are so hungry that while walking to the worksite where we build paddy dikes, when we encounter mimosa shrubs, we pick the fruits, even if they are green or old, and fold them into our *kramas*. If we encounter a corn field where all the corn has been picked, we run, tussling, to break off the stalks, which we chew as if they were sugar cane. At the worksite we chat about hunger. Everyone is hungry, only some are a little hungry, some are very hungry, and some are extremely hungry.

Today is the day that Yama[21] releases the damned souls from Hell to come and partake of food with their earthly brethren. But today the earthly damned souls have nothing to eat.

Oh! My parents have just died and today is the day of freedom for their souls, but we have nothing to offer them.

They don't allow us to eat, and they don't allow us to rest, so we work without eating. Everyone cranes his neck to stare at the spire of Wat Tamol (our worksite is at the northern end of Phum Thmey, just behind Wat Tamol), imagining that there is something to eat there,[22] because there still remains the solitary abbot (Kru Achar Seng, who is Dad's uncle, though he never introduced us). We work feebly in a delirium.

---

[18] a traditional festival honoring the spirits of the deceased, who are believed to visit the earth during the festival, during which food offerings are placed out for them

[19] bits of broken rice grains left over from the milling process

[20] small pieces of chaff (rice husk) from where the husk attaches to the base of the rice grain, which remain after the milling process (because they are heavier than the rest of the chaff)

[21] lord of Hell and judge of the dead in Buddhist scripture

[22] *Wats* are traditionally sites of celebration and feasting during the *Phchum Ben* holiday.

Brother Sarun, a former professor of French at Chak Angre High School, a small man perhaps in his early thirties, tells a story of hunger from when he went to help raise the dam at the Sre Ampil worksite.

"You struggle to dig and carry dirt till you're nearly dead and they give you gruel to eat. Then *they* eat rice. One day, after I finished eating my gruel, I walked into the hall of the committee members. They were eating rice.

"I cried out 'Oyoy! Oyoy!'

"One of them walked over to look at me and then asked, 'What's wrong with you, Comrade?'

"I answered loudly, 'I want to eat rice! I want to eat rice so badly, Brother!'

"He glared at me. 'Silence! Just because you want to eat rice, you have to yell about it?'

"The nerve of this guy—Not only am I not allowed to *eat* rice, but he won't even let me holler about *wanting* to?"

We laugh ourselves dry at Brother Sarun's hilarious rice hunger story.

After work we want to get together and go to Wat Tamol, where there used to be food to eat, where the creatures of Hell used to come to get food. But because there are so many of us, and Wat Tamol is in the boundaries of another cooperative, we fear that they will accuse us of the crime of going where we please. So we only swallow our own spit and daydream about the *ansam*[23] cakes of the *Phchum Ben* holiday.

After Dad's death, Bong Phal tells me, "The cooperative plans to appoint you as the leader of the young men in the cooperative!" This news worries me very much because I don't understand what work and duties the young men's leader is to fulfill. I worry especially that this work, this role, will surely drag me into the so-called Organization.

When I see Bong Phal, I often ask him about the work that the cooperative young men's leader is to carry out. He explains to me that "the cooperative young men's leader compiles statistics about all of the young men in the cooperative and manages and allocates these forces in the directions which the Organization hands down. Like during the war, the cooperative young men's

---

[23] a traditional Khmer cake eaten at holidays, made from sticky rice and coconut milk surrounding a filling of banana, beans, or pork, steamed inside banana-leaf wraps; see photograph on page 517

leader was responsible to send youth forces to the front lines of the battlefield as appointed, or to send youth to help with agricultural production."

Undoubtedly the "Organization" who is watching me now is none other than Bong Phal himself. Bong Phal knew my parents, and Bong Phal loves me and wants me to have a role in the Party like he does. If I join the Party, I can live. But my parents have just died because of this party. And this party continues to kill my relatives, my friends, and Khmer society. Would that not be incredible, as a Khmer, to be willing, for my own survival, to partake in serving those who killed my own parents, and who are killing our own race? I can't reject the Organization's appointment, but I have to find a way to get out of it.

After the *Phchum Ben* holiday I fall ill with a shivering fever. Thom Pen chastises me, saying that it's because I sleep on the platform where my parents died that I'm ill, that this place is bad luck, and that we built the hut on an old *memut's*[24] foundation. (My father's older sister kept a *memut* statue. She died during the war.)

My body is so skinny that my bones stick out. My body is so hot that all I want to do is go shirtless. I take advantage of this opportunity to beg Bong Phal when he comes:

"I'm sick. Maybe I can't be the leader of the young men, Bong!"

Bong Phal replies, "That's all right! The cooperative isn't forcing this appointment yet. Tuch, you just wait till you're better and we'll set it up. The Organization also has its eye on another young man, but the comrade cooperative chairman prefers you."

I have no more excuses. Bong Phal really does love me sincerely. He's not a very educated man, and he doesn't see how the Party is hurting his people; or else he does know, but he doesn't know what to do about it. If he knew my heart, he could explain things a bit to help get me out of it. But he doesn't get it, and I can't directly reject his moral support.

---

[24] a kind of witch

Part Two: Prisoners of Class

CHAPTER 5

Journey to Region Five

20 October 1975

At noon when we return from work, Samorn brings me news. "Bong! They are calling us back to Phnom Penh!"

This news makes me very happy. I am sick and tired of living here. For me and my family, it is a camp of sorrow. I fell ill, Samat fell ill, Mom is dead, Dad is dead, and now I'm ill again—all in the space of five months. There is nothing here to support so many human lives. Not to mention that now I'll be able to get out of being appointed as the cooperative young men's leader.

Ta Et, the group leader, taunts us, saying, "Go on! Go ahead and eat the stones of the mountains! Don't expect to eat the bread of Phnom Penh!"

We don't have much hope of going to Phnom Penh, but go we must. At the very least we'll know what the next place has in store for us that could possibly be worse than this one. My thoughts are far away when suddenly Samorn runs up to me again in an attitude of desperation.

"Bong, our names aren't on the list!"

"What about Nho?" I ask.

"Nho's name is there," Samorn replies.

"What? I signed up before Nho, even!" I think for a moment. No, we have to go. If our names aren't on the list, then we'll go with Nho. I ask Samorn, "When do they leave?"

"They leave tomorrow morning, but this evening they're going to spend the night at Koki Market."

"Tell Oun to get everything ready!" I tell Samorn. My siblings all hurry to get packed. Unable to help, I can only give verbal orders. I stand up on the sleeping platform and reach up to retrieve Mom's ashes from the shelf and put them in a small suitcase.

At about three o'clock, my siblings have finished packing. They carry all of our things with shoulder yokes and place them in a pile, then come back to help me walk.

Farewell To Tuol Ampil

1. Tuol Ampil, village of tarnished beauty   today I bid farewell to you
my sad hut, my palm stump used for a pillow   I bid farewell to these sad shores.

2. Mom's ashes wrapped in a thin cloth   held tight in my arm to keep her close
she loved me like the Moon and Rahu[1]   letting go of life in my arms.

chorus:
Farewell Kor Ko, take care of Dad's grave   I am sorry I could not come
my brothers will help me walk, Dad, don't fret   I cannot come, farewell from afar.

3. Protect me with your spirit, Dad   we go to live in another land
this left pain in my breast enough to burst it   we go in hope that comfort awaits.

penned 7 October 1979

21 October 1975

Those with food provisions wake up and cook porridge at first light; in particular, the people who came from around Chamlak village. We don't have so much as a grain of rice or any salt. The rations distributed yesterday were all eaten yesterday. We gather all of the siblings, nieces, and nephews and sit around quietly, pretending we don't even know how to be hungry, waiting to see if the Organization will distribute rice. But there is nothing.

Now it is clear that most people aren't yet as bad off as we are. They still have some fish sauce, garlic, oil, sugar, and MSG. The smell of frying food makes our mouths water. Oun walks around and returns with a bottle of pickled crab sauce that someone has abandoned. To us, it is a priceless treasure.

At about nine o'clock the rains begin as a light drizzle. I don't see the trucks that are to take us, as they apparently have not yet arrived; instead, I see the cooperative chairman walking straight toward me.

"Comrade Tuch! Who said you could come?" he demands.

"My sister's name is on the list, and I request to go with my sister," I plead.

"No! Your name is not on the list to go, Comrade Tuch!"

---

[1] a celestial being in Hindu and Buddhist mythology who causes eclipses by swallowing the moon

"But I'm sick and my sister has already packed all of my things. Please let me go with her!" I beg again.

"No! If you don't return to Tuol Ampil, you can go stay in Tuol Tnaot with me." Saying no more, the cooperative chairman walks away.

My name must have been removed from the list by the cooperative chairman. But why? So that I could be the young men's leader? Maybe so. The day before yesterday, Bong Phal told me that they would put someone else in that position. But I don't really believe it. Maybe it was a trick to stop me from running off and getting on the trucks today. It's fortunate that I didn't go see Bong Phal and say goodbye yesterday. If I had met him, I wouldn't be here now.

Or maybe the cooperative chairman knows the destination of our current evacuation? Like Bong Phal, the cooperative chairman is sympathetic toward my family. Like when we looked for boards to make coffins for my parents' bodies and requested my mother's cremation—he always helped us out.

Oh, where will this journey take us? Are we really going to eat the stones of the mountains, as Ta Et taunted? I can't just get out of it myself and abandon my sisters and uncle. We must live or die together.

Soon after the cooperative chairman walks away, many trucks arrive and turn around to face Phnom Penh before parking. They park in a row on the east side of the highway. They are military trucks manufactured in China. Some have a roof covering them, and some do not. Everybody begins piling their things beside the trucks. The Organization calls people's names by family and village to board the trucks. The rain is still drizzling. I walk behind my sisters and try to hold a plastic sheet over their heads while they carry our bundles and their small children.

Even though our names are not on the list, they still allow us to board a truck. I am so relieved! Now the cooperative chairman won't dare to stop me. They check our bundles. This is the first time that the Organization has done this kind of inspection. My God! They take my school record, dictionary, certificates, and other books and tear them up. I regret the loss of my school record. I have taken care of it and held onto it to keep track of my teachers' evaluations of me all the way from primary school to the end of high school. They rip it up and scatter it all over the ground. None of my books are left intact. They don't see the small suitcase containing Mom's ashes because it is still in my hand under the rain sheet.

After everybody has boarded the trucks, suddenly they open a storehouse on the east side of the road to the south and begin to distribute rice. Samat and Oun get off the truck and run to collect one can of uncooked rice apiece. Because the large numbers of people make it impossible for them to work, they quickly close the storehouse right back up again. Only about twenty people were able to get rice. How truly fortunate for my family! This is a true story which I can never forget. If not for those two cans of rice, we would starve to death on today's journey. I have no idea what would have become of my own life in particular.

At about ten o'clock the raindrops are still falling lightly, and the trucks gradually set off one by one. There are about ten trucks, and I am riding in one without a roof, about sixth or seventh in line. Farewell, Koki! Farewell, Kien Svay!

The trucks drive at a medium speed. The rain stops around Boeng Snao. I stop holding the rain sheet over my head and wrap up in a blanket for a change because the wind is chilling me. This is the first time in my life that I have traveled a long distance by automobile. It's too bad that I can't get a good look at the scenery along the road because my head and face are so averse to the wind and sunlight. But occasionally I open the blanket and peak out at the sights around me.

From inside my blanket, I hear someone say, "We're at Chbar Ampov." I quickly remove the blanket from my head and watch the motion of the trucks in front. The trucks cross the bridge, then drive around the roundabout toward Ta Khmau. It's clear that we won't be entering Phnom Penh. I start to worry— Are they taking us to Koh Thom? I hear that place is Khmer Rouge Central.

It is quiet along both sides of the road. I see that there are some Chinese people living in the Chak Angre area. I wrap up in the blanket again to protect myself from the wind. The trucks drive straight without turning. I hear someone say, "Prek Roessei...Prek Ho." Oh! We're at the place where I used to live as a child. I stop worrying about Koh Thom. The truck turns right. Soon I hear somebody say "Kantuot[2] Market." I lift the blanket and look at the market. The houses are all closed up and abandoned. There are only soldiers sleeping in hammocks, just like at Koki Market.

---

[2] Kampong Kantuot

The sun rises higher, and the trucks keep driving. I remain inside my blanket, my ears tuned to every word the others say: "Chaom Chau...Pochentong...The trucks are stopping in Pochentong to distribute bread!" At this last word, I throw off the blanket. Bread! I haven't seen it for so long, and now my stomach growls. If I get a stick of bread, I'll pick off a little bit at a time and eat it slowly, little by little, to make it last. The truck goes past Pochentong Market without slowing or stopping. Oh Lord! Those last words were just the prayer of a hungry person riding in the truck with me.

Here and there, those who have brought rice along chew on it. Those of us who have none cover our faces with *kramas* and swallow our spit. My two nieces are well-behaved and don't cry or ask for anything, but just make faces like the adults. Damn, it is meant to be the communist era now, and yet we still have rich and poor, full and hungry?

The trucks drive to the Institute of Technology and turn left toward the TV antenna, drive onto the Tuol Kork causeway, continue past the old stadium, turn into Phsar Toch market, and come out onto National Highway Five. There is no longer any doubt that our journey will take us west.

We spent half the morning going clear around Phnom Penh. Why didn't they just drive through Phnom Penh, a distance of less than ten kilometers?

In the afternoon, my fever starts up and I begin to shiver like I'm competing against the truck's engine. Samorn and Samat sit holding me up on each side. I am as hot as fire, but if I open the blanket to the air, it is too cold to bear. My headache throbs every time the truck hits a bump, as though a worm is burrowing into my brain in the middle of my forehead. Oh, how it hurts!

The trucks drive to Kampong Chhnang province, then begin to stop one by one. I don't know where we are because I am unfamiliar with the place. They unload the body of a person who has died on one of the trucks up ahead and carry it off to be buried. We sit quietly in the trucks. After about ten minutes, the trucks drive onward. This event makes me think of my parents: if they had lived to make this journey with us then surely their bones would have wound up abandoned in the woods in the same way. As for myself, I don't know what will become of me. Will I make it to our destination?

The sun is about to set when the trucks pull over one by one, spaced about ten meters apart. They allow us to climb down and find a spot to rest. This place is wide and open, with no trees near the road. Samat and Samorn help me get down, then stand me up. My head spins...spins...

The sky is faintly dark, and I find myself lying on a mat spread beneath a truck. My sister brings me some rice porridge.

"Tuch, try to sip some porridge to get some strength while it's still hot." I try sipping some of the porridge as she asks. But I don't remember when I came to lie under the truck. Where did my sister get water to make porridge? And where did they make it? What happened?

Samat, who is sitting beside me, tells me, "When you got down from the truck you fell and hit your head on the road and passed out. Samorn and I carried you over here and laid you under this truck."

Damn. Fainting again? I feel my head with my hand. There are no goose-eggs or splits. This is the second time that I have fallen, hit my head, and passed out, but my head never has any injuries.

The next day we travel all day again. At about five o'clock in the evening, the truck drops us off in Sampov Meas district[3] (Stueng Toch village, Roleap sub-district), Pursat province, near the spot where the railroad tracks cross the high-way[4] that leads toward Phnom Kravanh district. This time my sisters find a place to spread the mat before my brothers help me down and set me on the ground. They carry our things off to find a resting spot along the train tracks. My two brothers and Nho go off looking for rice.

Here the Organization distributes one can of uncooked rice per person. A family of ten gets ten cans of rice. After Samorn has claimed our rice, Samat returns to claim it again. They give away a lot of rice, so now we have plenty of rice to eat.

We have to sleep here for many days waiting for the train to take us onward. And every day, more Life Slaves[5] continue arriving from Kampong Speu and Takeo provinces. We crowd together to find places to sleep on both sides of the

---

[3] now part of Pursat town

[4] Route 146

[5] With regard to his coined epithets *Life Slaves* (a category which includes the author and his family) and *Life Masters*, the author wrote, in an introduction to Part Three of the first Khmer edition, that "the Khmer Rouge...transformed society into only two classes: the Life Masters (the revolutionary cadres and base people) and the Life Slaves (the people of 17 April)."

train tracks along a causeway about six meters wide. Beyond this there are rice fields full of water and budding rice plants.

My brothers tie up a tarp to make a shade for me to rest under. Some people find thatch panels, sheets of corrugated steel, or boards to make shelters with. In some places there were already temporary shelters when we arrived. I hear that there was already one train evacuation like this one before the *Phchum Ben* holiday. They, too, had slept here for days before moving on.

There are many of us crowding together on a narrow causeway hundreds of meters long, like a worm, or like ants swarming onto a patch of high ground in a flooded field. They won't allow us to rest along the highway, which is spacious, but instead send us to pile into this narrow space. Excrement, urine, and sleeping spots are all practically on top of each other. There is no dry land to squat to relieve ourselves. The water is right beside us. This area is full of strange leeches; as soon as your foot enters the water *plop*, the leeches swim over to latch on immediately.

To the west across from our sleeping spot there is a makeshift latrine concealed with two or three thatch panels. People sit quietly in line to use the latrine, like waiting for rice at Wat Kien Svay Krau. Some people have to go too badly and can't make it, so they squat in the open. The excrement from the latrine is scattered clear from the edge of the tracks down into the water. When the wind blows from the east, I'm lucky, but if it blows from the west then woe is me! What else can I do if I can't walk? I have to lie around smelling excrement.

Every morning at about eight o'clock, a train engine with a single car arrives. This train engine is traveling southward carrying a few Chinese specialists. At about four in the afternoon the engine returns. I hear someone say that the Chinese specialists don't drink well water, as we do, but drink only coconut juice. Every time the engine passes, we have to take down our shelters because the wood and bamboo sticks that we use as poles to hold up our canopies are all fastened or tied to the railroad tracks. That's when we sit there and stare up at the train engine and the plump, white Chinese specialists in black uniforms.

On the evening of our second day here, soldiers come by to check our bundles for gold. These days nobody wears gold or diamonds. If anyone has anything, they have already removed and hidden it. The soldiers aren't looking for gold only; they will take practically anything of value. I have no gold. I have only a parachute cord, which they confiscate for use as a hammock rope.

Even though the Organization gives us enough rice to eat here, and we can find fish for meat (I don't know where they find fish, but my brothers go off and find it somewhere), we want to leave this place. For like pigs hog-tied and led away to be butchered, we are surrounded by our own excrement and urine. These increase daily. On top of that, we are anxious to know where the journey will end. Where are they taking us? We are like pigs who have been bought and led away on leashes. These pigs don't know whether they are being taken to be raised or to be slaughtered, but they happily devour the rice they are fed along the way.

25 October 1975

The sun is about to set when a long train arrives. This is the train that will take us onward. It is a freight train, and none of the cars have seats or windows. We act as if we are thrilled, rushing to take down our shelters. We hurriedly gather our things and board the train. Each car is so full of people that there is scarcely even room to stand; so for me, lying on the floor of the car, it is difficult to even find air to breathe.

Everyone is nervous, worried, scared that they won't make it onto the train, scared that they won't get to go, as though an object of great worth, a priceless treasure, waits for them at the other end. They fill the train, but the train remains still and refuses to move. After a little while, everybody gets back off the train. I am able to breathe and feel the breeze again.

We are like moths that have never seen fire before. We don't know where we're going, but we'll fight each other to get there. We go without even having to be told, without having to be driven. In fact, now we're even worse than moths. Moths are free to choose whether or not to enter the fire, while we have only one path: forward! Behind us is fear. Now we are more like a herd of cattle. The cattle at the rear of the herd suffer the whip, so each animal scurries for the front of the herd or hides in the middle.

The train won't actually leave at night, so we will rest here until morning before leaving. Some of us get off and sleep outside, while others sleep on the roofs of the cars. I stay put and go nowhere.

The sun rises brightly, and the train engine starts up. A sound of *chook! chook! chook!* mixes with the sound of the whistle *woo! woo!* Sluggishly, lazily, the train slowly sets off.

We bid farewell to Pursat which had welcomed us so warmly, where we have slept, eaten, and defecated in one place for four nights and four days.

Lying on my back on the floor of the train car, it is not my fate to be able to see the scenery on either side of the train tracks with my own eyes. I imagine the train journey from Phnom Penh to Battambang of Bunthoeun, the main character in *The Wilted Flower*.[6] Bunthoeun sits at the window with a sad face staring at the fields of rice and grass. As for me, I lie down, listening to the sounds of the train's wheel arms, of the wheels grinding against the rails, of the clacking sound where sections of rail are joined, the whole car lurching and occasionally jolting my whole body into the air.

My siblings sit around me to make sure that no other traveler falls on top of me. My sisters try to fan me constantly, hardly daring to stop.

Sometimes I feel so hopeless without any medicine to treat my illness. Every day when it's time to get the shivers, I get the shivers. My strength gets weaker and weaker. Do I have any hope of survival? If I'm going to die, what's the point of traveling so far to do so? It's even harder for my siblings to care for me now than it was when Mom and Dad were sick. Now they are prisoners not only of the Organization, but of me as well. If I die, it will ease their cares and relieve them of a measure of suffering.

The train stops along the way for the Life Slaves to get out and relieve themselves. Now the train stops again, but this time is different from the others. There seems to be some commotion. Oh! We have arrived at our stop! We hurriedly collect our things and disembark from the train, for the sun is very low now. Normally they arrange it so that we can be settled before the sun sets.

My brothers help me walk and lay me down on the tiles of a fuel station with a sign that reads, "Svay Sisophon[7] Diesel Fuel Station."

A megaphone announces the selection of volunteers to assist the revolutionary movement, especially young men and women. Some of the young men go

---

[6] *Phkar Srapoun*, 1949 classic Khmer novel by author Nou Hach (1916–1975)

[7] This town/district is variously called "Svay Sisophon," "Svay," and "Sisophon," as well as, officially, "Serei Saophoan" (see footnote on page 248). All of these variants are used in this book.

to sign up. They are to be separated from their families, parents, and siblings from henceforth.

The sky is dark when my brothers set me down at a house with bright electric lights and three beds arranged close together. They all leave with our things to find a resting spot.

I am resting at a clinic, but I don't seem to see any patients, only two or three fellow travelers. There is neither doctor nor any other kind of medic. We are all waiting for a doctor to come and treat us, but it's getting late, and still we see no doctor nor anybody else from the Organization to look after us. It's night, and there's no sign of either a doctor or my siblings. I am so hungry!

I fall asleep and wake to the vague sound of a voice near my ear: "Tuch! Tuch!" I open my eyes and my sister is rousing me to eat some porridge. I hungrily sip the porridge.

Late in the night, Samat comes down with a fever and comes to lie ill beside me.

27 October 1975

The sun has risen, and the sky is clear, when a soldier walks into the clinic and hands me two pink fever pills and tells me to go find my siblings and get ready to board the trucks for departure. My God, if Samat hadn't come to lie ill beside me, I would be in trouble, with no idea of where my siblings were sleeping; and being ill and unable to walk, who would have helped carry me? I find a rattan cane in the clinic to help me walk. Samat tries to help me walk even though he is sick himself.

There are too few trucks to take so many people, so we and many others must wait for the next trip.

These days malaria medicine is highly valuable. There are two types: one is pink, and the other is dark red. Some people call the dark red ones "tile rubble." When he deserted the battlefield, Samat had a bottle with 500 of these pills. But while we were staying at Wat Chroy Ampil, we sold them all to get money to buy *prahok*. These pills are very effective, and I stop shivering after taking the two I got from the clinic.

At 10 p.m. a soldier gathers us to depart. There are no trucks; we are to ride on trailers pulled by tractors. Having lost my fever and shivers, I am now able to sit up.

There is a waning moon, and the sky is dark. We see only the broad expanse of the water in the fields along both sides of the road and some woody shrubs growing along the roadside. The tractors drive slowly with a speed of only about fifteen or twenty kilometers per hour. We don't know where they are taking us. At one point the tractors turn left. A fellow passenger who is familiar with the area says that if we had kept going straight, we would have reached Siem Reap province. My siblings, and I especially, have never been so far from home.

At about two o'clock in the morning, the tractors stop at a broad flat area that looks like a rice threshing yard. We get off of the tractor wagons and continue our slumber in the yard.

The sun rises dimly and the sounds of oxen calling *moo*! *moo*! *moo*! mixed with the sound of their wooden bells *clack*! *clack*! *clack*! and metal bells *clang*! *clang*! *clang*! awaken us from sleep. We are surrounded by hundreds of oxcarts pulled by small oxen. Other oxcarts hurriedly approach, churning up clouds of dust behind them. Where have they come from? Have they come to transport us? The answer becomes clear when we are ordered to board the carts and continue our journey onward.

Where are we going? They don't tell us. They are a very secretive bunch. Trucks, trains, tractors—they never tell us where we are going. If we ask the cart drivers, they might as well not answer at all because we don't know the area anyway. But we do know that they are taking us to a place where trucks and tractors can't go. Damn! Maybe we really *are* going to eat the stones of the mountains. No, there are no mountains here. As Life Slaves, we are prepared to accept our fate.

Last night we slept outside some village.[8] Now the oxcarts take us over a wooden bridge across a large canal[9] and into the village. We see a sign reading "Phnom Srok District Primary School." When we arrive in the village, the locals—young and old, male and female—stand around in an orderly fashion

---

[8] actually Phnom Srok town
[9] actually the rectangular moat that surrounds Phnom Srok town

watching us as though waiting to welcome a *kathen tean*[10] parade. Indeed, it's a parade like none they've ever seen: hundreds of oxcarts, one after another.

The carts steer through the village and then back out again. We pass over a sandy road through rice fields and sparse trees. I think of my family moving from our house north of Wat Tuol Tumpung to the shores of Boeng Trabek more than nineteen years ago. We had ridden on an oxcart through fields of *kantraeuy* and *barang*[11] grasses with small *reang* and *trah*[12] trees growing here and there in clumps. At that time, I had ridden the cart with my mother. But now there is no mother on the cart with me.

The small oxen struggle to pull the carts along the sandy road, making me feel particularly sorry for them. I ask the driver, "Father, why are the cows here so small?"

"Nephew, this land can only support small cows like this. We can't use the big ones because there is so little grass here that the cows have to eat *prech* leaves." *Prech* leaves? What are *prech* leaves? I used to know of a novel (or maybe a movie) entitled *The Hunter's Trail, the* Prech *Buds*. *Prech* must be in the jungle, where a hunter goes to hunt animals. This driver's home village must be near the jungle. Are we going to live in his village?

After passing through the fields and forests for a while, we enter a village. It's a fairly small village with dense stands of banana trees, coconut trees, papaya trees, and manioc[13] shrubs growing here and there. But we couldn't even see it from very far away. The villagers are surprised at our presence, and they call out to each other and stand around staring at us.

The people of Phnom Srok[14] had looked at us with familiar gazes, but these villagers look at us with amazement and wonder, as though they've never seen such a thing. Perhaps they're as puzzled as we are, wondering where we are going.

I tap the driver and ask, "Uncle! What village is this?"

---

[10] an annual festival in which clothing is donated to the Buddhist monks

[11] *Chrysopogon aciculatus* and *Urochloa muica*

[12] *Barringtonia acutangula* and *Combretum trifoliatum*

[13] a kind of tuber (*Manihot esculenta*), also known as cassava

[14] There are two administrative entities called *Phnom Srok:* it is the name of the district, as well as the small town and local population center which serves as the district seat. In the text, this small town is generally referred to as simply *Phnom Srok*, as opposed to *Phnom Srok district*.

"This is Boh Sbov village, Nephew," the cart driver replies. None of the cart drivers are soldiers or members of the Organization. They are all locals with oxen and carts who have been gathered from various villages to help transport us. After leaving the village, we again pass through rice fields, then through scattered clumps of trees, then through sparse trees, then through forests so wild they nearly overgrow the cart road, forests with tall thin trees. They are taking us into the jungle! Are they taking us to *live* in the jungle? We drive through a forest with large, tall trees and after a while the carts begin to stop one after the other, about ten or fifteen meters apart.

We unload our things from the carts at nearly midday. Some take up hoes and knives and begin to clear the forest and cut small trees and look for places to put their things. Those without any knives, hoes, or hatchets are in for trouble because our village is the jungle. When we left Tuol Ampil, those who had been living in the liberated zones during the war told us it wasn't necessary to weigh ourselves down with hoes, knives, and hatchets because wherever we went, the Organization would provide them to us there. I gave away a good portion of our tools. If I had given up all of them, I would be weeping now.

The second evacuation of my family ends at about 11 a.m. on 28 October 1975, after traveling by foot, carrying our things on our heads and shoulders, by truck, by train, by tractor, and by oxcart, across four provinces: Kandal, Kampong Chhnang, Pursat, and Battambang, for eight nights and eight days.

Chapter 6

Village in the Jungle

When I set foot in this jungle land, I shave my head and pray to the *neak ta*[1] to be healed from my illness and to have the strength necessary to do my work, especially to build a shelter.

29 October 1975

The sky is bright and clear when the Organization begins to survey the jungle and divide it into lots by group. My three siblings and I register as a single family. Our village lies along a river[2] winding from east to west and north to south. We are forced to build our huts facing each other in rows, with a road in between about eight meters wide. Each lot is ten meters wide across the front, with unspecified depth.

We hack at the jungle to clear our individual lots, mark out the building sites for our huts, cut small trees and bamboo stalks, and harvest thatch grass. In this initial period, we shelter in the shade of the trees, or tie up tarps to protect ourselves from the sun and rain. We each work hard to quickly finish our huts because the rainy season has not ended yet.

On our third day in the jungle, a terrible event occurs. The sun is about to set, and everyone is busy cooking their dinners before darkness falls. Suddenly, a cold wind blows with a loud whooshing sound. Countless leaves are blown from the trees and rain down onto the ground. As if in an instant, the clear sky fills with large black clouds hovering low over the jungle where we live, gradually changing the light from bright to hazy and dark. Cries of alarm are heard throughout the village: "The rain is coming! The rain is coming!"

We rush to gather our things and bundles and move them to sheltered locations. My siblings and I have a tarp tied up to shelter beneath. We put a pole in the center and four smaller poles at the four corners, then tie the corners to stakes in the ground.

Our work is not finished yet when, suddenly, large raindrops begin to fall. The raindrops falling on the newly fallen leaves makes loud *pit-pat! pit-pat!*

---

[1] guardian spirits; ancestral spirits
[2] the Rumduol River

sounds. We continue to fortify our position, and I tell my brothers to dig a trench for the water to flow away from our shelter and use the dirt they dig out to make a dike along the inner banks of the trench. The rain falls harder and harder and the sound is deafening. The sky turns utterly black.

The four of us, plus our young niece and our bundles of clothing, mosquito nets, and mats, all squeeze onto a small patch of dirt about two meters square. I sit on the dirt and lean against a bundle of clothing, supported on the other side by my sister, who holds her daughter in her arms. My two brothers don't sit still but turn left and right, pushing out the puddles of water that collect on the tarp.

The rain is windless and pours down like the sky has been ripped open. Now and then lightning strikes in loud and blinding flashes, briefly revealing what lies outside the shelter. The leaves that fell before the rain began have all floated away on the water. The water gushing from the sky seeks the low points and the river.

The cold air brings gooseflesh, and I sit hugging myself. My butt is wet, and my feet are soaked. Oh! The water has broken through the dike and is flowing into our shelter! We crouch on our heels and my sister puts her daughter on her knees. The water flows over the tops of our feet. Our bundles are soaked. We weren't able to find anything to put under them before the rain started. When the lightning strikes from time to time, we peer outside for logs or branches to sit on, but see nothing but running, foaming water flowing toward us.

We raise our hands and pray to the *neak ta* of the forest and the stones to stop the rain long enough to get some sleep, even if we have to sleep sitting up. We are tired and exhausted, I especially, since my shivering fever broke only four days ago. But it is useless; the rain falls tirelessly.

Oh, the miserable life of a Life Slave! Never mind our fellow men—even the rain, thunder, and lightning of nature take no mercy on us, but torment us ruthlessly.

My two brothers get no rest at all. If they allow too much water to pool, it could rip the tarp or pull down our tent. I sit sleeplessly with my head down, but every now and then I drift off and am awakened by the crashing sound of a thunderbolt.

Oh, Preah Phirun![3]

1. Oh! Pity Khmers defeated in war
pregnant, sick, babies, and newborns

the barbarians expel us immediately
they take no pity, and we suffer.

2. Bodies thin, battered, and wasting
leaving home for the jungle, no mercy

eating forest leaves in place of food
a curse of rain makes sleep impossible.

chorus:

Oh, Preah Phirun, soften thine anger
lives of misfortune without mercy

please take pity and save us
building a new life in a graveyard jungle.

3. Please, all spirits, demons, *neak ta*
take pity on our fearful lives

Indra, Brahma, angelic keepers of the forest
living without meaning, awaiting death.

The sky in the east begins to brighten faintly, but the rain continues to fall without letting up. Then the light grows brighter, the sky begins to clear, and the rain eases up, though the water on the ground continues to flow toward the river without subsiding. The nightmare of the Great Night of Rain has passed. The villagers emerge from their shelters and stretch their backs, then shake out their sodden clothing and hang it to dry.

Suddenly, unit leaders and team leaders come around and announce the Organization's new work plan: they are gathering a mobile workforce. All young men, young women, middle-aged men, and women without small children are to go work at a mobile worksite to harvest rice. Only the sick and old are exempt.

My hut has not even begun to take shape. Though my fever has broken, I am still thin and lacking strength. My sister is burdened with a young child-in-arms. Samat and Samorn leave on the mobile work unit. Do we have any hope of ever having a shelter to live in?

After they have been gone for two days, suddenly Samat reappears. He has a shivering fever, and the Organization has allowed him to come back home. On days when his shivering subsides, Samat and Oun go out to collect bamboo, vines, and thatch grass. On the days when he is shivering with fever, he can't go, and Oun goes alone into the jungle. I watch the site and tend to my niece.

The food rations are one can of uncooked rice per person per day. Compared with the food rations in Tuol Ampil village, Kien Svay district, we con-

---

[3] Varuna, the Hindu god of rain

sider this to be adequate. The Organization's rules are also not as strict: we are allowed to trade food or rice with the locals who come and go in the jungle to collect bamboo and vines. But it is not an easy thing to find fish, meat, or edible plants here. The river behind the village has water, but there are very few fish. Samat sets up two and a half nets and gets only one or two fish each night (which in this area are called "white fish," types of fish with white scales, such as *riel*,[4] *lenh*,[5] *kanhchhet cromoh*, and *kbal lan*). The large-mesh nets catch no fish. Snails and mussels are hard to come by as well.

Because we are new arrivals, we have not yet been able to plant gourds, eggplants, tomatoes, or *phty*,[6] so these days we eat only leaves from the jungle, such as leaves from *t'aeuk* vines,[7] *dangraek* vines (some call them "sand vines"), *thnoeng* vines,[8] *tromung* trees,[9] *lngieng* trees,[10] *trabaek prey* trees,[11] *kralanh* trees,[12] as well as *prasva, anao,* and *mchey* trees,[13] etc.

For seven months, my siblings and I have not known meat or fat. One day villagers from Boh Sbov bring pork to trade. My sister decides to trade one of her sarongs for a kilogram of pork. Unfortunately for me, I am not able to eat this pork; I get the worst diarrhea I have ever had. I defecate all night long until morning and still it does not end. There is no excrement, only jets of water. I have only to stick out my butt or bend over slightly for water to shoot out instantly. After defecating, I lie down and the water rumbles around in my gut. Unable to continue helping me up and down, up and down, Samat digs a hole for me to lie over. My ears plug up and I am no longer able to stand. I lie with my butt over the hole and Samat sits fanning away the mosquitoes.

The sun rises and the sky is clear, but my diarrhea does not go away. I continue to defecate until there is no longer any water rumbling in my intestines. I lie quietly, breathing short, labored breaths, the air wheezing in my ears.

---

[4] *Dangila cuvieri*

[5] *Dangila siamensis*

[6] a category of edible greens including amaranth and purslane

[7] *Merremia hederacea*

[8] *Aganonerion polymorphum*

[9] *Garcinia oliveri*

[10] *Cratoxylon cochinchinensis*

[11] *Lagerstroemia rigina*

[12] *Dialium cochinchinense*

[13] Author's note: "These last three words are not found in any dictionary."

My sister makes thin porridge and dishes it out hot for me to eat. Samat lifts me off the hole and sits me up to spoon-feed me. With effort, I eat a bowl of porridge. With sweat coming from every pore, I go to sleep. I have recovered from the diarrhea without any medicine. I fear that some villager has cast a spell on me, for this illness has been unusually savage. But I have never known any of the villagers. Why would anyone hate me so much?

About one week later, I have enough strength to go to the fields to pick vines and cut thatch grass with my siblings. Suddenly, the Organization gives an order to assemble additional mobile forces to go out and harvest rice. With his fever gone, Samat is sent back to the worksite. I am too thin, and they allow me to stay in the village.

The majority of the Life Slaves who rode the train to Svay and then continued the journey to Phnom Srok district were assigned to live in the jungle along both banks of the Rumduol River.[14] They create a new subdistrict for us: Spean Thom.[15] The Spean Thom subdistrict office is established near the actual Spean Thom bridge.[16]

For nearly half a month we clear the jungle to construct a village to live in. But still the village doesn't have a single finished hut with a roof and proper walls. Most of them are just skeletons made from young trees. Some of them have roofs and sleeping platforms. Most of the sleeping platforms are made from small *prech* bamboo stems woven with *preng*[17] or *yeav*[18] vines. (Now I know what *prech* leaves are: the *prech* leaves that the cattle eat are leaves from the variety of bamboo called *prech* bamboo.[19]) The reason the huts are coming along so slowly is that most of the people in the village are elderly, women with small children, or young men who are sick, like me.

At first, we didn't realize that the jungle where we had come to live had malaria. Aside from Samat and me, who have been malarial since Kien Svay, we

---

[14] labeled on some maps as the Kampong Krasang River

[15] "Large Bridge"

[16] Author's note: "Spean Thom is an ancient bridge built from laterite stone spanning the Rumduol River, connecting the road from Phnom Srok to Spean Sreng subdistrict."

[17] *Derris scandens*

[18] *Nephroia sarmentosa*

[19] a smallish species of wild bamboo

haven't seen anyone else in the village fall ill. But now a shivering-cramping-swelling illness starts to spread. The mobile workers sleep in the fields, but those in the village have to sleep in the jungle. Virtually every family gets the shivering-cramping-swelling illness, young and old.

Lin, my two-year-old niece, gets the shivering fever as well. Each time the shivering begins, my sister and I shed tears of pity for her. Lin burns like fire and lies clenching her fists in her mother's arms. When the shivering subsides, she lapses into a fevered stupor, lying unconscious and scarcely able to open her eyes. We have no medicine to treat her with and can do nothing to ease her suffering. We only clench our teeth and shed tears in pity whenever she starts to shiver. We are no different from wild deer that stand weeping and watching their kin shot down by a hunter.

One day my sister gets a permit from the village chief allowing me to travel to the Spean Thom subdistrict office to find some "social affairs" medicine[20] for my niece. She also wants me to bring along one of Lin's clothing outfits to trade, hoping that I can get a few spoonfuls of sugar to put in her porridge. We have no fish or meat to feed her. Besides rice and salt, the Organization has nothing else to give us.

I leave in the morning, asking people along the way for directions to Spean Thom. For more than half a month, I have never left the hut, other than to go to the river to cut thatch grass with Samat. I am not familiar with the roads to get from village to village.

At about nine o'clock I reach Spean Thom subdistrict's "social affairs office" (a site for making traditional medicine). Inside the building there are five or six older men busily chopping up roots and sticks to make medicine. Many people who have arrived before me sit waiting for their medicine. After chopping up a whole grass mat full of medicine, the men mix it together and distribute it. The first matful after I arrive isn't enough for everybody, and I have to wait for the next one. I have no idea how many matfuls they must have already chopped since this morning to make them complain so much about sore, tired hands, despite the help they receive from some of the supplicants who step in to help them chop. I wait until nearly noon to receive one *krama* of medicine.

_____

[20] i.e., herbal medicine manufactured by the subdistrict's social affairs office

On the way here, I didn't encounter any villages of base people.[21] If I go back the same way I came, I won't be able to trade for sugar. I can't waste this opportunity, since we aren't allowed to walk anywhere without a travel permit. Not knowing the roads, I decide on a new path: I walk down the road heading straight away from Spean Thom. The road is wide and there is jungle along both sides of the road. I walk further and further, but still I don't run into any villages. I come to a bridge made from laterite[22] stone like the Spean Thom bridge, about the same size but shorter.[23] The Spean Thom bridge spans the Rumduol River, but this bridge crosses a smaller watercourse, more like a stream or a brook.[24] Feeling tired, I wash my face in the stream and take a drink before continuing on my way.

It gets later and still I see no village. An oxcart overtakes me, and the driver calls out, "Nephew, where are you going?"

"I'm going to the village!" I answer.

"Where is your village?" the driver asks.

"It's along the river," I answer.

"Oh, this is the wrong way! You'll have to go back. This is the road to Phnom Srok!" the driver tells me.

"Aren't there any local villages on this road, Uncle?" I ask.

"No, Nephew, there are none," the driver replies.

I lose any hope of making a trade and turn back. Overcome with hunger and exhaustion, when I get to Spean Thom, I feel lightheaded, dizzy, and lost. I don't know how to get back to my village. My village doesn't have a name yet, so my permit doesn't have a village name on it, only the name of the village chairman who issued it. How am I supposed to ask someone? Where should I tell them I want to go? I meet a soldier on the road and ask him, showing him my permit, but he doesn't know what village I live in, and he's not familiar with my village chairman (Comrade Hoeun).

I approach the subdistrict office and feel so hungry that I'm tempted to enter and ask the soldiers for some rice, but I don't dare. Seeing me standing hesitantly in the middle of the road in the middle of the day, a soldier calls me

---

[21] local people, as opposed to evacuated new people; see footnote on page 47

[22] a type of porous, reddish stone

[23] Spean Kmeng ("Young Bridge"), about one km west of Spean Thom

[24] called "Spean Kmeng Stream" on some maps

over with a hand gesture. He looks at my permit, and it turns out he knows my village chairman. He shows me the path to take back to the village.

I don't arrive home until the middle of the afternoon. I am now feverish from fatigue and exhaustion. My shivering fever returns.

My niece and I both shiver with fever as though competing against each other. My sister is so overwhelmed she doesn't know what to do. She steeps the social-affairs medicine I obtained in boiling water and gives it to both uncle and niece to drink. However, it seems to have no effect at all. Some of the locals who have been to Phnom Srok tell me about a district hospital. They say that the hospital has modern drugs to treat illnesses and abundant food rations. I bring this news to my sister and ask if I can go stay at the hospital.

My sister's answers me, in a tone of melancholy, "If you go to stay at the hospital, who will keep you company?"

This question leaves me stumped. Every day I start shivering at around nine thirty or ten in the morning. Before the shivering starts, I boil a kettle of water in advance. When the shivering starts, I wrap myself up in a blanket and lie on my side and put a metal bowl of hot water at my feet, one in the middle by my stomach, and one by my face. I raise my head from the pillow and blow on the hot water so that the steam hits me in the face. I blow and drink it so that the hot water runs through my insides. When the water turns lukewarm, I exchange it. My sister boils more water at the cookfire and trades out any of the bowls that aren't very hot anymore. By the time the shivering subsides, I have used up two or three kettles of water. After this I sleep in a feverish stupor until around two thirty or three in the afternoon, when I'm able to sit up and eat some porridge.

At least at home I have my sister to care for me. But what if I go to the hospital? I don't know what to think. On the one hand, if I stay at the hospital, I could have medicine, as someone claimed, and then I could get better. On the other hand, if I stay home sick, nothing will change, except that my strength will deteriorate little by little. Look at me now—I've only been sick for four or five days and I've lost so much strength that I need a cane just to be able to walk!

CHAPTER 7

Phnom Srok District Revolutionary People's Hospital

17 November 1975

In the afternoon, a tractor brings rice to the cooperative. After dropping off the rice, a soldier walks around calling out to the villagers, "Any sick people can ride the tractor to stay in the Phnom Srok Hospital!"

I ask my sister again if I can go stay in the hospital. Faced with such constant misery, my sister gives in and changes her mind. She puts an arm around my back and helps me walk to the tractor. Fearing that the tractor will leave without me, I bring only my cane, a spoon, a small metal bowl, a *krama*, a blanket, and a single set of clothes: knee-length white judo shorts and a white jacket. (This jacket was scavenged by Samat in Chamkar Mon on the night of April 17th.)

My sister promises that tomorrow she will request a travel permit to go to Phnom Srok and bring me some dishes, pots and pans, a water kettle, and some clothing.

At about four o'clock in the afternoon, the tractor arrives with five patients from Kok Prasat[1] at the Phnom Srok hospital. The Phnom Srok District People's Hospital is distributed among various local houses along both sides of the road leading to Prey Moan, as well as the road leading to Trapeang Thmor.[2] They put us in whatever hospital houses have available space. Two hospital children take me and two other male patients to stay in a house on the east side of the road to Prey Moan. It's a house constructed directly on the ground, about seven by twelve meters, with a corrugated metal roof, wooden walls, and large, wide-open doors. It looks like a spacious Chinese *kuy teav*[3] noodle house or odds-and-ends shop, with no other rooms. Behind the house there is a large pond of foul water about a hundred by sixty meters. It is full to the brim, thick with nipa palms, with some water hyacinths growing nearby. Both the hospital houses and the surrounding locals use this pond for their toilet waste.

---

[1] the name later given to the "village in the jungle" where the family first settled; see page 127
[2] i.e., houses clustered around the main crossroads where these two roads meet in the town of Phnom Srok
[3] a kind of rice-noodle soup

Inside the hospital house, there are three or four beds filled with patients. Some patients sleep on the ground, lying on boards or corrugated iron covered with mats. The ground toward the back is wet and spongy.[4] In the corner on the right, a wooden door lies on the ground covered with a piece of corrugated iron, occupied by one of the patients who came with me and who got to it before me. Where am I supposed to lie down? Beside the door there is a sheet of humped corrugated iron on the ground which appears to be available. The ground here isn't wet—so why aren't any of the others sleeping here? I am told that somebody has recently died here, and the medics have just taken his body away to be buried. He died from eating the poisonous leaves from a *treas*[5] tree. (They say that you can use *treas* leaves to roll cigarettes, but they're poisonous to eat.) Beside the corrugated iron, there is a broken teapot in which someone has soaked some peeled green papayas in water for the patients to drink. I have no other choice; I have to sleep where someone has just died. Without a mat, I have to sleep directly on the corrugated iron (a crude piece of roofing metal that the hospital brought in for patients to lie on.)

At about four-thirty, the medics call the patients to go eat porridge. The hospital dining hall is along the road leading to Trapeang Thmor, about sixty meters from my hospital house. I see the others pick up their dishes, pots, and water bowls and walk to the dining hall. What can I use for a bowl? It's not hard to eat salted porridge; I can use my small metal dish as a bowl. But when we eat regular rice, I will have to borrow a bowl from the others for my soup.

All the patients at the hospital are Life Slaves; there are no base people mixed in. Some people have the shivers, some have swelling, some have dysentery, some have skin lesions. These are the types of illnesses common during this so-called revolutionary era. Patients lie moaning and groaning day and night. Some patients with no hope of survival have been abandoned here by their families to lie alone, sick and moaning. Some of them have siblings or a spouse to sit with them, help them relieve themselves, and bring them food or water.

We can't tell who are the medics and who are the soldiers. They all wear the same black clothing and black caps with silk *kramas* around their necks. The medics don't watch the patients. They are at their own place over near the

---

[4] i.e., the house has a dirt floor
[5] *Caesalpinia digyna*

dining hall all the time. At about nine in the morning, three or four of them walk over to poke their heads in and check on us. In the afternoon, at about three o'clock, they come again. If a patient dies in the night, the body lies with us until morning. If a patient dies during the day, only after one of the patients goes to tell the medics will they quickly take the body away to be buried. They have no medical supplies or equipment whatsoever. They don't come by to treat the patients; they only check to see who is close to dying and who is not yet close to dying.

Contrary to what I had heard, there is not much medicine. I have been here for four or five days now and haven't seen so much as a single pill. If there is medicine, it is mostly just "rabbit turd" pills.[6] If liquid medicine, it is mostly clear or reddish-colored medicine in old soft-drink bottles.

Most of the medics are females who seem to have no medical expertise. One day they bring some foreign medicine to administer by injection to patients with shivering fever. They have ampules with the word *QUINOBLEU* written in French on the sides, containing a dark blue intravenous liquid. The female medics give me an injection. I feel excited to be so fortunate to be treated with foreign drugs. They turn my arms back and forth, left and right, forearms, wrists, looking for a vein. One of the female medics gives up and hands the task over to another medic. They trade off back and forth and after ten sticks still can't find a vein. I am sick and just can't take any more of this, and I beg them to stop sticking me. They don't know how to give an injection or how to find a vein. I've lost my chance at the good medicine.

The two other patients who came with me from the village to stay in this hospital house are both gone now. One of the men, about my age, had a shivering fever but was still able to walk. He went back to the village after trying out the hospital for about two days. It's better that he left anyway; if he had stayed, it would only have led to catching some other illness. Like me—when I left the village, I only had a shivering fever, but now I have swelling as well.

As for the other man (about forty years old), who had some swelling when he left the village, after he got to the hospital the swelling got worse. He came from the village alone, like me, without any wife or children accompanying him. He dies after sleeping at the hospital for nearly a week. I'm not able to go back to the village, but if I remain, the outcome is clear.

---

[6] herbal pills that look like rabbit droppings

When my father got the swelling illness and walked about unsteadily with a cane, it made me feel tense. Sometimes I thought that he was being soft. Now it's my turn. I'm only twenty-four years old, but now I'm not much different than my father was when he had the swelling. My body is swollen, my cheeks are puffed out, and my eyes are nearly swollen shut. My limbs are tight. My genitals are especially swollen: my two testicles are each swollen to the size of an orange, and my penis is bloated. There is no flesh on my body that hasn't swollen up.

With a bald head, hair growing in sparse tufts, dressed in white with a *krama* around my neck, my right hand clutching a cane to help me walk, I have a gait not unlike an old mother elephant. My legs are so heavy I have to strain every muscle just to take a step. Before I begin walking, I have to survey the state of the path first. If there are any humps or pits, I have to find a way around them. If there is no way around, I have to sit down on the ground and scoot. I walk cautiously, feeling my way, careful to avoid falling. I walk only when it's time to eat rice or porridge and to fetch water from the well at the hospital house across the road. I never drink pond water as the others do because it's too far to walk. I drink only the flat well water that the patients draw to bathe with.

I lose the shivers, but the dysentery comes back to take its turn. These three things go together, and everyone gets them: shivering, swelling, and dysentery.

Tomorrow has come many times over, and I haven't seen my sister come. Unable to continue borrowing other people's dishes every time I eat, I walk over to dig around behind the houses of the locals near the hospital and find a few old dishes with rusted holes, a broken copper pot, and a few soy sauce and alcohol bottles to use. I use some sand to clean the bottles and scrub the dishes clean. I find some tar to patch the holes in the dishes so they will hold rice. I find some string to tie around the necks of the bottles and use them to hold water and salt. When I go out to fetch water from time to time, I find a long string to attach to the bottle neck and lower the bottle down into the well, which is about two or three meters deep. I have to sit hugging the well pipe, which is about a half-meter tall, lift the bottle, and drop it down into the well several times until I am able to fill the bottle up. These objects aren't beautiful, but they are able to help keep me alive here without having to depend on others. I find a pine crate about forty by fifty centimeters and use it to arrange my bottles, dishes, and pots. This crate is useful to help me hide rice.

The food rations for the patients consists of rice in the morning and porridge in the evening. When I first arrived at the hospital, they made soup to eat along with the rice. But now, both the rice and the porridge are eaten with only salt. The rice is usually cooked well, but the porridge is not cooked well at all. It is part burned and part undercooked (thick porridge) because the cooks have a hard time stirring it properly, and the fire is very hot.

After the morning rice, both I and everyone else secretly stash some rice to eat in the evening. We only eat a little bit of the evening porridge for show and save our single spoonful of salt apiece. For this reason, every evening there is a lot of porridge left over in the pan. The medics are suspicious and begin to clamp down: after morning rice, medics wielding cattle whips check the dishes, pans, and kettles of the patients. If anyone has hidden rice, they are whipped.

Every time we eat rice, I secretly stuff some of my rice into a small metal bowl about ten centimeters in diameter and then hide it in a *krama*. After eating, I put the rice bowl in the middle of the *krama* then wrap the *krama* around my neck with the bowl in front and the ends of the krama hanging over it to cover it up. The medics never pay any attention to me, walking unsteadily with my cane in my right hand and an empty bowl in my left. I have rice for dinner every evening.

There must be a lot of other people getting away with hiding rice, like I am, so that now the medics take new measures. They start bringing the rice to us in the house. After eating, the medics walk around and check the nooks and crannies, the pots and pans, the clothing bundles. But they still don't search me, the guy with no clothing bundle at all. All I have is my little wooden crate holding my bottles and dishes at my feet. Actually, my little metal bowl full of rice is hiding inside the crate, hidden by four or five bottles.

Because I don't walk much, and I hide enough rice to eat both morning and evening, my swelling goes down a bit. Though my swelling gets better, and I feel better, the people around me lie sick and moaning constantly.

This hospital is actually little more than a convenient place to strike up our chorus of moans, a place where we can groan freely without fear of bothering those who must go to work. It is a place to wait for our death day, without any doctors or medicine.

During the nearly one month since I have arrived at this hospital house, nearly fifty patients have died. Some days one person dies, some days two. During this same time, how many additional people have died in the other two or three houses here at this hospital in Srah Chik subdistrict? A patient who is strong enough to help pull the cart to carry the bodies to the gravesite said that the one hectare of land has graves laid out in rows, like rows of yams in a field.

Some of the patients here are very wretched. A girl about ten years old is chronically ill and lies moaning continuously. Her desperate parents have returned to the village and left her here to lie moaning, alone.

The next morning, another young girl of about the same age is brought by her mother to the hospital and left here. The two girls join in a call-and-response of delirious moaning and crying, as though something has come to toy with them, to take them. In the middle of the night both of their delirious cries go silent. They die at the same time, as though they had made an appointment with each other to leave this unfriendly world together.

A man about forty years old, with dysentery, is so skinny it looks as though there is nothing left but skin and bones. He lies completely naked on an iron bedstead with no mat. The man is delirious and shouts curses at his wife, who barely leaves his side. Desperate, the wife finally leaves him there. It is chilly at night, and because the man cries too much, the medics light a fire near his bed to keep him warm. In the middle of the night, the man gets worked up and yells deliriously for someone to wait for him, he wants to go with them. He doesn't lie still but thrashes and rolls off the bed and into the fire. The fire burns one whole side of the man, and in the morning he is dead.

An older man from Po Penh village, Spean Thom subdistrict has a wound on top of his foot from skewering it on a piece of *prech* bamboo. His wife comes to sleep by his side. After a week his wife, who had been well, gets dysentery, and both of them are sick. Now the wife, who had come to keep her husband company, dies before him. To come here is like approaching Death himself, and there is little hope of returning home again.

The social order has changed, but my status in society has not. I am still the poorest of the poor. For the nearly one month that I have been here at the Phnom Srok hospital, I have eaten my rice and porridge with nothing but salt. The local base people have plenty of chicken, duck, fish, and meat to eat. The patients strong enough to walk can sneak off to the houses of the locals away from the hospital and beg for some food to eat. (The medics don't permit the patients to go near the locals' houses.) Some people who have valuables to trade are able to get salty fish paste, *prahok*, duck eggs, and marinated fish to eat. I hear that the locals of Phnom Srok won't take diamonds, only gold. If a gold ring has any diamonds, they pry them out.

At every meal, I salivate to see my neighbors eating salty fish paste, *prahok*, duck eggs, etc. I want some too! I want to eat delicious food like them! I sit watching their mouths eating and it looks so good! What can I do to eat food like them? They have no idea how hungry I am.

I can't stand watching others eat any more. With some effort, I walk around the pond behind the hospital house, hoping to find some kind of creature to eat. I walk to the eastern edge of the pond and sit listening for the sound of fish mouths. The pond has fish, but I don't know how to get them. I find a rattan basket lid about the size of a vegetable colander. I get into the water along the edge of the pond, then put the basket lid under the water hyacinths and lift slowly upward. There are small creatures jumping on the basket lid. I have hope! I have food to eat! Sometimes I come up with small betta fish, sometimes small fresh-water shrimp with transparent bodies. I catch them and put them in an empty milk can. By the time I get tired, I have caught about thirty small fish and shrimp. I wash them, coat them in salt, then wrap them in banana leaves and roast them. It isn't as delicious as the others' food, but it is food that I have found on my own without having to beg.

One day I find two small fishing poles that were stuck into the pond bank and left there long ago. I dig up some earthworms and fasten them to the poles' fishhooks at the edge of the pond. In the morning, there is a catfish the size of a child's forearm on the line. I am delighted and take it to roast and eat without any seasoning. I think of my sister and my niece, sick back in the village. If there were anyone traveling to the village, I would send this fish to my sister and niece. They live in the jungle—surely, they aren't able to find any fish to eat. At least now I'm able to find fish and food for myself.

Even though it has now been a month, and even though a number of my initial difficulties have now been overcome, my thoughts still turn to the village and to my sister. I wonder why she has never come to see me. She promised that the next day she would bring me a mosquito net and some clothing. But it has now been many days, and I still haven't seen so much as a shadow of my sister.

I have been walking around in this one set of clothes for a month now. The thin cotton judo shorts dry very quickly and can be washed occasionally by wearing a *krama* around my waist and waiting for my shorts to dry before putting them back on. But the jacket is thick and doesn't dry easily, and I can't go shirtless because I get too cold, so it never gets washed.

Sometimes I think of my niece who is sick back in the village. Sometimes I feel sorry for myself, sick and lonely without any nearby relatives to come see me. That's when the tears begin to slowly flow. My sister must have abandoned me! She must think I am dead!

When I see a strange woman walk up to the hospital holding some stuff, I feel excited that it must be my sister coming to visit me. When I realize that it isn't her, my feelings turn sad. All I see are other people's siblings. Where are mine?

Now I understand the love between siblings. I miss my sister. I want to see her and tell her about my troubles.

In the middle of December, my sister finally appears. I am so excited to see her, but at the same time I feel agitated and want to tell her off for abandoning me for so long. But both my joy and my agitation pass instantly when I hear my sister's sad news.

"I couldn't get a permit, and besides, Lin was so sick and crying so much I couldn't even put her down."

"Is Lin better now?" I ask my sister.

At this question, her countenance changes, and she struggles to speak. "No, she is dead." My sister weeps with pain and sorrow for her beloved little daughter. She struggles to control her emotions and tears as she tells me about the death of my two-year old niece.

"I had nothing to treat her with. I had no way to ease her suffering other than holding her and hugging her when she got the shivers, and then I would sit crying when she passed out from the fever. Yesterday she cried and clenched her fists and pulled her hair until she died right in my arms."

This news makes me feel such sorrow and sympathy for my poor niece! She had barely seen sunlight when her father condemned her to fatherlessness. She had just learned to say *mom*, *grandma*, *grandpa*, and *uncle* when she lost her life, without even knowing yet what life is. What fault could such a small child have that she should be punished with death?

During the one month that I have been away at the hospital, Lin was not the only one to die. Sophal, my five-year-old niece, also got sick and died. Thom Pen, my uncle, also died. My family lost another three members.

The presence of my sister makes me feel happy that I can see her face, but it also makes me sad for such unfortunate news. I feel so bad for my two nieces whom I used to hold and play with. I feel so sorry for my uncle, who used to hold me and my brothers and sisters when we were little. In these difficult circumstances, he fought to travel with his nieces and nephews, and he died with his nieces and nephews. (In fact, he wasn't even supposed to come here at all.) But I wasn't anywhere near him, I wasn't there to be with him in his final minutes. And we have lost all contact with his daughter, who left on the mobile work unit when we first arrived at Kok Prasat.

My sister has brought me a change of clothes, two dishes, and a mosquito net. She brought my father's five-seam silk pants to trade with the locals for some duck eggs, salty fish paste, and *prahok* for me to eat.

This evening, after porridge, I get the news that more Life Slaves have been evacuated to Phnom Srok. They have just been dropped off at the field outside the village where we once slept. I hear that there are villagers from Moat Krasah village, Lvea Em district, Kandal province. I take my crutch and walk to the place where they are staying to look for my aunt. I see my aunt there and invite her to live in the village with me.

I also meet a friend who used to work with me in the police. He warns me to hide my history, telling me, "My father, when he went to his home village in Moat Krasah, when they found out he had been a policeman, they took him away to be killed immediately!" This news makes me afraid after-the-fact, from when I registered in Tuol Ampil. Why didn't they take me to be killed then? Did the village chairman cover it up out of love and pity for me? Many people have been killed only from being *suspected* of having done this or that. I myself have already *confessed* and they still haven't taken me to be killed yet. Is this fate, or just chance?

Regardless, I understand that the good feelings of Bong Phal and the comrade cooperative chairman in Tuol Ampil are important factors in my survival. Both of them loved me and they must have protected me. On the day when we boarded the trucks at Koki, the cooperative chairman tried to stop me from leaving. If I had listened to him, I would not be so miserable now. But if I had not left and had continued living in Tuol Ampil, I'm not so sure I would have kept on living once they reviewed my personal history. I am very fortunate that they sent people away without sending their documents along with them!

Because my sister has to take my aunt back to the village with her, she is unable to stay with me. After staying with me for one night, she leaves in the morning to return to the cooperative.

One week later, my younger brother Samat passes through the town of Phnom Srok with his mobile unit on their way to harvest rice at the Prey Moan worksite. We haven't seen each other for more than a month. He breaks ranks and comes to find me in the hospital house. We don't have much time to visit. He leaves a small pot for cooking and then says goodbye right away. He has to run to catch up with the others. I stand with my crutch and watch him go.

It's the harvest season, and the harvested rice is piled all over the fields and is overflowing in the threshing yards and granaries, yet they reduce the food rations. The patients now have to eat porridge both morning and evening. The medics are relieved of having to monitor the hiding of rice. They also stop bringing us our porridge at the house.

Being one of the senior patients, by now all of the medics know me. Though my swelling has subsided, I am still not cured. I still have difficulty walking to eat porridge in the morning and evenings. The medics allow me to move to a hospital house down the road adjacent to the dining hall on the north side. It's a wooden house about six by fifteen meters, with a corrugated iron roof and wooden floors about a meter off the ground. There are doors on both sides (west and east) and proper brick stairs. The wooden walls have proper windows that open and close. It's a new house, nicer than the other one.

When there was rice to eat, the medics had given us salt both morning and evening. Now that there is only porridge, they make soup to eat in the mornings, and in the evenings they give us salt, as usual. The usual soups are sour soup with water lilies, *kantolet*[7] grass, and pumpkin vine. Every now and then they also boil turnips. The patients lie sick without any medics paying at-

---

[7] a kind of edible aquatic grass (scientific name unknown)

tention to them as they lie groaning, crying, or dying. But when it's time to eat porridge, suddenly there are plenty of medics to watch over us. Two or three hospital youth stand with whips in hand inspecting the patients eating their porridge. One of the kids is called Chan, a child of people who came from Takeo province. Now that his parents are dead, the Organization has sent Chan to live with the medics. Having become a child of the Revolution, Chan forgets his origins and beats the patients without restraint.

In the dining hall there are two long wooden tables running east to west with wooden benches on both sides for the patients to sit on. On each table there are two large dishes of porridge placed at each end. Each morning the patients dish up their porridge then sit around the table waiting for the medics to serve the soup. But there is no order or consistency in how they serve the soup. Sometimes they serve it away from the tables, and sometimes they serve it at the tables. When they serve it away from the tables, the patients leave the tables and run jostling each other to pass their soup bowls to the cook. When this happens, the hospital children invariably beat the patients with their whips. Some patients drop their soup bowls on the ground when they are whipped. I don't dare to jostle for position because I am swollen and unsteady and I am terrified of the whips. So, often, I don't get any soup, but the medics give me salt instead. This kind of thing happens almost every day.

One day a strange thing happens: The soup pot is on the fire and the cook has not yet scooped the soup into a metal pot to bring over and serve the patients. Some of the patients hand their soup bowls to the medics to dish up soup for them. Some of the others see this and run to surround the pan. I try to follow suit because when I do it the proper way and remain passive, I end up with no soup almost every time. Some pass their bowls to the medics to fill, while some come right up to the pan and scoop up the soup directly with their bowls. Some people reach in through the window and lean on the side of the pan and the pan tips over spilling the soup everywhere so that nobody gets to eat any more. What the hell! Hungry people are such a nuisance, fighting for food like dogs!

Woe Is Me

1. Oh my soul, woe is me   chest-splitting anxiety and stupor of mind
if I think too much, I'll cry   parents gone, children far from home
living in agony once more in the jungle.

2. Disease-riddled, no time for rest   cared for by family many days
many months, not daring to part   oh, Death, why don't you take me
what point to keep living, with only illness and no respite?

chorus:
Hospitalized but even more anxious   nothing but suffering and pain
swollen round, shivering and trembling   alone in my peril without kin
people die continually, one soul, two souls, some crying in distress.

3. No medicine, porridge raw and burnt   tears are the blood of the stomach,
shriveled, eating white fish eggs   beaten, whipped, kicked, porridge spilt
crying and pleading, entreating: Indra, Brahma, angels.

penned on 10 October 1979

CHAPTER 8
The Wise Sage

At the beginning of January 1976, in Phnom Srok district, a new thing occurs: the mistreatment of the people by the Organization makes the people of Phnom Srok district so miserable that an escape plot is hatched. More than ten men and boys run away into the jungle. This includes two or three hospital patients. The Organization takes measures for retaliation.

9 January 1976

After eating the morning porridge, at about ten o'clock (today they have called us to eat porridge in the morning), the Organization expels all male patients from the hospital without giving any reason.

We all leave the hospital and go our separate ways to our own villages. When I first came to the hospital, I rode a tractor, but now I return on foot. I look for rope with which to make a shoulder yoke, with my clothes, blanket, and mosquito net in a bundle on one side and my wooden crate with dishes and three or four bottles on the other. I don't abandon these items because such things are not to be found in our jungle village. Fortunately, I run into Comrade Saran,[1] a young man who comes from my village and who also used to live in Tuol Ampil with me. He has the shivering fever, but he is still stronger than I am. We travel together back to the village.

My body is still swollen, the sun is hot, the road is sandy, and I can't walk very far. Every eighty or a hundred meters I have to sit down. Saran has a hard time waiting for me. We stop and go so many times that it is evening before we make it to the village.

My village is quiet and empty of people. It has been almost two months since I was last here, but it looks like nothing has changed or progressed. Many huts still have no roofs or walls, and my own hut still has yet to be finished.

Only the Chinese people[2] have large huts, properly enclosed, with vegetables such as gourds, winter melons, cabbage, and eggplants to eat and trade for rice with the Khmers. They don't get sick much and don't go out on mobile duty because they have enough possessions with which to bribe the unit com-

---

[1] Author's note: "currently a doctor at the city maternity hospital in Phnom Penh"
[2] Cambodians of Chinese ancestry (typically the merchant class in the cities)

manders and village chairman, such as sugar, garlic, MSG, needles and thread, and mentholated balm. They have it easy. Some of them even raise chickens and ducks for food.

The Khmers, on the other hand, are all away from the village. They don't return until nighttime. They don't even have time to find thatch grass to roof their huts with, let alone time to plant vegetables. So we often wrap up some uncooked rice to take and trade for vegetables with the Chinese, one gourd for four cans of rice, or a head of cabbage for four or five cans of rice. People with material possessions are still of value to the Organization.

The cooperative chairman allows my family to move to a hut that already has a roof and walls with decent coverage. The occupants of the hut met some family members who had just been evacuated from elsewhere, and they asked the Organization if they could leave the village to be with them.

Now the Organization gives us rations of paddy rice[3] instead of milled rice. This is not distributed at the cooperative office in the village. We have to go and get it from the Spean Thom subdistrict office about three kilometers away by road.

Each evening after eating, the villagers usually walk as a group to collect their paddy rice, whether by moonlight or in darkness. After returning they pound, sift, and winnow in the dark beside campfires. We don't have many winnowing baskets, so we use shallow metal rice bowls to winnow and clean the rice grains. The rations now are barely enough; the Organization distributes two cans of rice per person. Those who go out to harvest rice often furtively pick some extra grains to put in their pockets when they return home.

I'm not able to go out and work. Every day I watch the house, sitting and roasting paddy rice grains (I eat them directly without pounding them first). A person staying still and not working is always hungry—so hungry! I can't eat enough. I've roasted and eaten up all the paddy rice that my sister saved since the harvesting began.

It's the cool season,[4] and the cicadas' song fills the forest from the *phdiek, trach, kakah, tbaeng,* and *chambak*[5] trees. Some come to sing near me, perching

---

[3] unmilled rice with the chaff still on the kernel

[4] roughly late November through January

[5] *Anisoptera scaphula, Dipterocarpus intricatus, Sindora cochinchinensis, Dipterocarpus obtusifolius,* and *Irvingia malayana*

on the small *trach, sokram,*[6] and *lngieng* trees. I ever-so-sneakily catch them and toss them onto the coals, then dig them back out, blow off the ashes, and plop them into my mouth. The cicadas are a little bit larger than flies, and not very tasty, but hunger doesn't compel one to seek out only the delicious!

My swelling has subsided completely, but I'm not yet able to walk very well, and my knees are still weak. Maybe in another week I'll be able to walk, but for now I don't yet have enough strength to go out and harvest with the others.

Late January 1976

Misfortune befalls my sister. She gets the shivering fever, off and on, shivering one day, not the next. On the days when she isn't shivering, she is able to do some work, but she can't go harvest rice because she is too weak.

With my sister sick, the household duties fall to me for a change. We can't depend on our aunt because she is sixty-five years old, and besides, she is a skilled midwife and never home, always busy giving massages and delivering babies for others.

I have to go and fetch water from the river, wade out and look for snails, and set the nets. Some nights we don't collect our paddy rice rations from Spean Thom because there is nobody to go and get them. It's too far and the rice is too heavy, and nobody will collect it for us. I have to force myself to go and collect our paddy rice along with everyone else.

How long will my recent months of chronic sickness allow me to work so hard at these chores?

Early February 1976

After doing the house chores for more than a week, the shivering fever returns to my ravaged body for the third time. This time it is worse than the other times.

My sister and I shiver as though in competition, and neither is able to help the other. We can't place our hopes in our aunt; she couldn't care less about whether we are well or ill. She disappears each morning and returns each evening. We call her "mother," but she is no longer the aunt she was back when our mother was still alive.

---

[6] *Xylia xylocarpa*

Fortunately, after shivering for half a month, my sister gets better. She hasn't lost much weight and her strength returns quickly.

I start shivering at about nine in the morning and get steadily worse from there. Having had chronic fever for so long, I know very well all of the signs that the shivering is about to start, and what time the shivering will begin each day. Before it starts, I boil a kettle of water in preparation.

First, my lower back begins to get goosebumps and ache terribly. This aching rises gradually along my spine to the back of my neck. Then my whole body begins to tremble and shiver all over.

When my lower back begins to ache, I start to pour the boiling water into three metal bowls. I take all three bowls and lay them out on the sleeping platform, then lie wrapped in a blanket. I lie on my side and place one bowl by my feet, one by my stomach, and one by my face. I blow on the hot water to make the hot steam rise into my face. The heat of the water helps me to somewhat endure the shivering that originates from within my body. When the water gets cool, I have to change it out with fresh water boiling on the cookfire. When my sister had the shivers too, I lay curled on the ground beside the cookfire to make it easier to change out the water by myself. Now that my sister is better, she is in charge of tending the fire and changing the water for me. Each time I get the shivers, I have to change out the water four or five times before nighttime.

On the days when I'm not able to boil the water in time, I have to wrap up in my blanket and lie shivering in the sunshine in front of the hut. When her shivers passed, my sister was able to eat rice and drink water and do some work, while I, on the other hand, am completely the opposite. When the shivering subsides, I'm still as hot as a furnace, burning hot, my eyes half open and drowsy, wanting to sleep constantly without eating. Sometimes I go all day without eating before sitting up to eat something in the evening, then I lie burning and restless and headachy until the middle of the night before I cool off again. In the morning it starts all over again with the shivering. The shivering gives me no days off. Every day there is only shivering.

There are no medicines, no roots, stems, or leaves that can stop me from shivering. My aunt brings some wads of kapok fiber and lights them on my thumbs and big toes,[7] but it doesn't stop the shivering, it only makes sores on my hands and feet. I feel frightened each time the shivers start. After shivering for more than a month, my body is completely emaciated and boney. My butt has no meat, only hollow skin stretched over my tailbone and pelvis. I am skinnier than my mother was when she died. My brothers Samat and Samorn send three striped jute grain sacks to spread under me over the bamboo lattice, but still it feels sensitive and painful to lie down. In a twenty-four-hour day, I probably spend twenty hours lying on those sacks.

My parents used to tell me how in the French colonial times, the people were so poor that they wore grain sacks for clothing and nearly everybody had lice. Now I am experiencing the same things they did more than thirty years ago.

One morning, when I raise myself up from the ground, I see white lice, translucent like shrimp, crawling on my stomach. They are the same size and shape as the black lice that crawl on our heads, only transparent-white.

I want to get better, but I hardly eat anything because every day the only food we have to eat is snails, clams, crabs, and weaver ants. My sister chastises me for eating so little food besides salt so that I have no strength. Feeling sorry for me, fearing I won't live, one day she boils a chicken for me to eat. The chicken tastes good, but it's no cure for the shivering fever.

My hut is directly across from the cooperative office, built right in the center of the village. The villagers pass by frequently whenever they collect their rations or have any other business.

The village's remaining old men who are unable to walk very far are brought by the Organization to sit and weave rattan fibers and twist rope to make *bangky*[8] baskets, whittle bamboo, and weave *kanhcheu*[9] and *chang'er*[10] baskets.

Om Sok is a sixty-year-old man whom my siblings and I met back when we were waiting for the train in Sampov Meas district, Pursat province. At that time, we camped beside one another. He was traveling alone with just his wife. One day, as he was catching fish in the water, a leech swam into the end of his penis. My brothers helped him pull the leech out. Because of this experience,

---

[7] a folk remedy

[8] a kind of scoop-shaped earth-moving basket with handle loops on two sides, used primarily by attaching to the two ends of a shoulder yoke for scooping, hauling, and dumping dirt; see photograph on page 517

[9] a medium-sized round basket

[10] a type of large, flat basket used for winnowing rice

my family and Om Sok became close friends. When we arrived at the village, he was sent to live at the southern end of the village. Whenever he would come to the cooperative office, he would stop by to say hello. We, on the other hand, rarely stopped by to visit him, as we had no other business to take us to the south end of the village. The Organization has since brought Om Sok to work in the cooperative office.

One day at about noon, not having boiled water in time, I am wrapped up in a blanket and shivering in front of the house in the sun. As he is leaving the cooperative office, Om Sok sees me shivering and comes to visit.

"Have you had the shivering fever for long?"

"Yes. A month and a half now, Om," I answer.

"Wow, that's a long time. Why didn't you come find me?"

"We didn't know you knew anything about making medicine, Om."

"My medicine will stop the shivering of a mild case with just one batch. But if you've been shivering this long, I don't know whether it will stop it or not," Om Sok says without much hope.

I plead, "Please help me, Om, if you don't mind!"

He remains silent, saying nothing. He takes my hand, feels my face, thinks for a bit, and then says slowly, "All right, sure. I can make you a batch and we'll give it a try. I can't do it by tomorrow, but the day after tomorrow, I'll bring it by."

"Thank you, Om!"

Two days later, Om Sok brings me the medicine, as promised. The medicine is made from many different ingredients, from all kinds of unknown tree roots and other plants. When I ask, he won't tell me what. He dumps the medicine into a kettle, chants some Pali words, blows on it, pours in some water, then tells me to boil and drink it.

The medicine is very powerful. I get steadily better each day. After only one week the medicine is depleted, and my fever is completely gone. I have nothing to give him in return because the rations have grown so sparse.

Om Sok is a great sage who has come to save my life. After I get better, he disappears and stops coming to weave baskets at the cooperative. He falls sick and passes away within a week.

This is my great fortune. If I hadn't run into Om Sok, I surely would have died.

I am cured of malaria in early March 1976.

CHAPTER 9

Spean Thom Subdistrict

Early March 1976

After resting for a month, my body has recovered its strength somewhat.

My unit leader assigns me to work with the older women who dig and till the soil to make a vegetable patch in the village. They don't make me do any hard work, only pick weeds, collect and discard the weeds, and break up dirt clods with a stick. We are the feeble and infirm ones, unable to mobilize to the front.[1] This work helps me to recover, and I get to know the older folks in the village.

The deprived sit around talking about deprivation. About hunger. Especially those recovering from an illness, like me. I am starving. My eyes are always scanning for something that can be chewed or eaten. Scarcely any living creature that crosses my path gets away alive. I snatch them up and eat them all. As we dig and break up the dirt, we uncover writhing white worms the size of chopsticks. I'm told they are edible, so I collect them to roast and eat. Tiny mice the size of my thumbs, scratching in the dirt for corn kernels or beans we have planted, don't survive for long with me around. I catch them, coat them in ashes, remove their fur, gut them, salt them, roast them, and eat them with rice.

Our labor bears little fruit, but doing nothing would not be beneficial at all. We chat while we work. One day an older woman asks me, "How old are you?"

"Going on twenty-six,[2] now," I answer.

"Oh, how wonderful! The time is ripe to find a wife!" she replies with surprise and delight.

"No, being sick all the time like this makes it too hard to find a wife," I answer without giving it much thought.

"Hey, if you had a wife, you would have someone to take care of you," she explains, trying to persuade me.

I smile bashfully and reply, "I don't want to get married yet."

---

[1] The Khmer Rouge frequently used martial terminology and imagery to describe communal labor during this time, e.g. "front," "offensive," "brigade," "battle," "attack," etc.

[2] In Khmer culture, one's age is calculated starting from one at birth and incrementing every Khmer New Year, rather than on one's birthday. (Thus he will turn twenty-six at the Khmer New Year a month hence.) Because of this, stated ages are one to two years higher than if they were calculated strictly based on number of birthdays elapsed after birth, as in the West.

Under this regime they divide people into various labor units: the children's units, the middle-aged units, and the elderly units.

The children's units are divided into young children and youth. The young children mainly work in the village with the old people. The youth mostly work in mobile units and are rarely in the village as the younger children are.

The youth units are the elite units. They never have the chance to work in the village. They are constantly being moved from one worksite to another. Very rarely do they have a chance to stop by to visit their families in the village. Only when the worksite happens to be near the village, or when they have to travel through the village, do they get a chance to see the faces of their parents or relatives. These are the units that endure the most hardships.

The middle-aged unit (or general-population unit) consists of those who are married. This unit mostly works in the village or subdistrict. They don't usually go very far, and have time to be near their parents, children, and wives.

The old people feel sorry for their sons and daughters who are still "youth." They feel cold, separated from their children and living alone in the village. Because of this system of dividing up the work responsibilities, the older people want their children to get married so that they can come back and work in the village near them. But this is only in their minds; the reality cannot be so.

I have nothing that can be called a life, nor a passion for living. Why do I even want to go on living? Because I'm afraid to die! I'm afraid of that which I cannot see or anticipate. I don't know if it's good or bad, misery or bliss. Nobody who has died before me, my father or my mother, has returned to tell me about it. According to Buddhist doctrine, after death people receive the fruits of what they did while alive. If they did good deeds, they are reborn in a paradise, like Heaven. If they have done evil, they are reborn in a place of suffering, like Hell.

I want to live so badly! To live to do good, to know what will happen in the future. I want to see this thing of which the Organization boasts: the Abundance and Glory of the Revolution.

I don't believe the deceptions of these dark beings, yet I yearn to see tomorrow. Will I have the good fortune to see the sun rise tomorrow? Though I am fine today, it's not at all certain that I will be fine tomorrow. Some people aren't even sick today, and yet they will not see tomorrow. There is nothing that can be called "life." Nearly all is death. Our souls are already hung on the line in the hall of Death. Without life, how can we possibly have *passion* for life?

Having a spouse only brings more worry. When the husband is sick, the wife has no ability to obtain medicine or to take care of him, to massage him and bring him hot or cold water. If the wife is sick, it's the same. So each only bears his or her own suffering and feels pity for the other. If the husband or wife is taken away to be clubbed[3] to death, the survivor knows only tears, left to live spiritless, like a plant waving in the wind.

No. If we persist in this revolution of destruction, starving and dying like this, I will not take a wife. I will live alone and die alone.

I have only just now become acquainted with the place where I live, where the Life Slaves were brought to live: my village is named Kok Prasat, on the west banks of the Rumduol River. North of Kok Prasat along the river is Spean Thom village. These two villages are separated by a small stream. South of Kok Prasat along the river is Chhleuy village. On the east side of the river across from Chhleuy is Chambak Thom village, and across from Kok Prasat is Khla Krohoem village. Past Spean Thom about a half a kilometer is a village called Po Penh.

All of these villages form a new subdistrict in Phnom Srok district called Spean Thom. Kok Prasat is the name of an ancient village located on the high ground east of Boh Sbov. I hear that there is an ancient temple ruin there. The villagers of Boh Sbov tell us that where we are is highly malarial. In older times, people tried settling in this area, but they failed no matter how many music offerings and pig sacrifices they offered up to the local spirits each year. That's why Kok Prasat was abandoned, leaving only a name. On the high ground of the old village site, we villagers till the ground to plant crops. As we dig and till and remove tree stumps, we constantly come across old earthen jars, pots, and betel nut boxes left over from the old village.

As for malaria, among the six villages of Spean Thom subdistrict, Po Penh is the clear winner for the greatest number of deaths. That village has practically gone extinct and silent.

---

[3] The most common method of execution by the Khmer Rouge was to strike the victim at the base of the skill with a blunt object, typically the back of a heavy iron hoe blade.

Among the families of the dead, the family of the old man called Tan Tonghan is in the lead. I hear that Tan Tonghan was a former high-level official in the national Ministry of Education under Sihanouk. Before coming here, he lived in Tuol Ampil just as my family had done. His family had more than ten members, including beautiful young daughters. Now all of their bones have been abandoned in Po Penh. The villagers call Po Penh "the Tan Tonghan cooperative."

Chapter 10

My Younger Brother Is Killed

After the harvest, the mobile units don't come back to the village. Samat and Samorn, my younger brothers, are sent to haul dirt to build a levee along a stream connecting Kok Prasat with Spean Thom. This worksite is called "The Children's Levee." As the work is completed before for the start of the Year of the Dragon, as planned, at New Year[1] my two brothers are permitted to visit the village.

For those of us living in misery, New Year may as well not even be New Year. There is nothing special, nothing pleasurable. The food rations are steadily decreasing. Family gatherings only create a shared atmosphere of worry. We have no ability to prepare food adequate as offerings to the souls of our grandparents, parents, siblings, and kin who have departed this world for the other side, for now we also are creatures of Hell, suffering and starving. And it is a suffering not mentioned in the teachings of Lord Buddha, so we don't know what virtuous deeds to perform to alleviate it.

Before New Year, my sister[2] got married and went off to live with her new husband about eighty meters to the south of my hut.

After New Year, both of my brothers receive orders to return to the Kok Rumchek camp. There they will participate in digging the Kok Rumchek Canal. I remain at home alone with my aunt.

A week after New Year, I receive orders to go harvest thatch grass on the banks of the Sreng River, in Spean Sreng subdistrict, with fifteen men and women from the village.

We rise in the dark to boil and package our rice, then walk about ten kilometers along the road. This is my first long walk under this regime. We cut thatch grass in the fields along the west bank of the Sreng. In the evening we carry the grass on our heads and walk back to the cooperative.

At the place where we cut grass, we encounter the stunted posts of thatch-grass drying platforms, deteriorated thatch panels, old hut pillars, piles of ashes, shards of dishes, bottles, and old metal rice bowls abandoned in the dirt, buried in the grass, covered by the long grass growing over them. This was the site of a

---

[1] Khmer New Year (mid-April)
[2] Oun

village of Life Slaves called Kum Phneang. The cow herders tell us that this place is highly malarial, that the villagers died off to virtual extinction, and that the Organization permitted them to relocate to a village of base people.

Because here there is not so much thatch grass, we harvest for a few days and then are unable to find any more. The Organization issues orders for us to cross the Sreng River and harvest in Kralanh district, Siem Reap province, which is in the Northern Zone, while Phnom Srok district is in Region Five of the Northwestern Zone.

In the dry season the waters of the Sreng River get very low, in some places up to the neck, in some up to the waist, the thighs, or even the knees. The banks are high and steep. If we stand on the top of the banks and look down at the water below, we feel dizzy.

Because it is a long way, and crossing the river is difficult, the Organization tells us to set up our camp by the side of a lake about a kilometer past the river.

Presently, the food rations in the village have fallen to their lowest point. Some days they get only half a can of uncooked rice per person; some days they get only one can for four people; and some days it gets to the point where they use a spoon to measure out two or three spoonfuls of rice per person. For us, the Organization gives one can of rice per person per day. This is not sufficient for people working in the heat of the sun, sleeping in the rain and the dew. All of us fends for ourselves. We pick *trakuon, kamping puoy,*[3] *snao*[4] shoots, *skun,*[5] and water lilies[6] and mix them with rice and boil them to make *phek*[7] porridge. Our porridge has more plants than rice. In earlier times it would have been called "pig-slop porridge." Besides porridge mixed with tree leaves, we eat soup consisting only of boiled plants with salt, and occasionally we also dip raw plants in the salty water.

Every evening after returning from cutting the grass, we walk around foraging for plants to eat. At sunset we drag for fish in the lake with nets until about eight or nine o'clock, then get out of the water and cook the fish. We each cook and eat on our own, as we are able.

---

[3] *Ludwigia adscendens*

[4] *Sesbania javanica*

[5] *Limnanthemum hydrophyllum*

[6] These are all edible aquatic plants.

[7] Author's note: "This word is not found in the dictionary, but we used it in those days."

In the first month of the new year, the rain begins to fall steadily. We have no proper camp for shelter, as our task is not very long. Some nights it rains, and we are unable to sleep. We sit holding plastic sheets to cover our heads and protect the campfires from going out.

One night nearly all of us have stomachaches from eating too much raw *sdau*[8] leaves, and the weather is cold because a heavy rain falls in the middle of the night. In the morning we are unable to work, and the Organization allows us to return to the cooperative after having worked here for half a month.

Fifteen days away from the village feels like a long time, as everything in the village has changed rapidly: many have died, and many huts are empty.

At first, Kok Prasat had more than fifty groups, each group having ten families. Currently there are only about forty groups left, each with about five to seven families.

Upon returning to the village, I am devastated by horrific news: Samat, my younger brother, was taken away and clubbed to death. We just recently saw each other at New Year. We've only been apart for twenty days, and now we will never see each other again.

Before they took him away to be killed, Samat was digging the canal with Samorn at Kok Rumchek. Because the shivering fever had returned, Samat had requested to be treated at the Phnom Srok Revolutionary People's Hospital. Then, all of a sudden, the soldiers took him away from the hospital to be killed.

Taking people away to be killed is just a normal thing for these murderers. But the loss of our brother is a tremendous sorrow for us. He was barely twenty-four years old, he was sturdy and strong, and he was healthier than me. He was fit. He should not have been killed! He should not have died! I am the one who is weak. I am the one who is fit to leave this hateful world. We mourn our brother, but all we can do at this time is stay quiet, holding our sorrow within us, nursing our deep suffering.

So far, over the past year, among the twelve members of my family who left together from Phnom Penh, six have died. Samat is the first family member to be directly executed. And we have lost all contact with My-L'et, my uncle's daughter, and don't know if she is alive or dead. So there are only five of us

---

[8] *Azadirachta indica;* a type of tree

remaining. Five people sitting in the maw of Death. Who of us will be fortunate enough to escape?

CHAPTER 11

Prisoner

These days, the shivering, swelling, and cramping sickness does not spread as strongly as it had the previous month. But a new illness begins to spread around the village: yaws.

Most people get it on the tops of their feet, their shins, and their calves. The sores burrow down into their nerves and muscles, down to the bones. Some are fairly small, while some are as large as your palm. The sores ooze fluid and pus. Some are bright red like the embers of a fire, while others are bumpy and covered with pus and scabs.

There is no medicine to treat it. Everyone fends for themselves, searching for their own remedies. Some boil *thnoeng* and *lngieng* leaves, soaking and cleaning their sores. Some take rags and fabric from old clothes and tie them onto the sores to protect them from flies. Some take strips of copper and make a lot of holes like the holes in a noodle mold and then bandage them over the sores to treat them. We don't know if it works or not, but we do a lot of these types of things.

Most people with yaws are unable to walk and can only get around by scooting their bottoms forward or backward on the ground while resting on their arms. Some use a cane to walk gingerly.

When I return from harvesting thatch grass, I notice a small lump under the knob of my left ankle. This lump bursts and oozes a clear liquid and has a small hole burrowing down into my flesh. I don't think much of it; I suppose it is just a regular lump. Each day the small hole grows larger and deeper and becomes an oozing, purulent sore with an opening about the size of my thumb. Once again, I become an unwell person, unable to go to work.

Due to the fracturing of the human economy, people quarrel. My aunt receives the rations that the Organization distributes, as well as fees from serving as a midwife and masseuse for other people. She cooks separately from me with my sparse rations. Soon she goes to live with Ol, my oldest sister. I am left alone and can walk only a little, with great effort, by leaning on a cane. Every day, with great effort, I make just one trip down to the river and fetch a single kettle of water for cooking and drinking.

My body, after having regained some weight, now begins to waste away again. Because of the cold air at night, my sore aches and I am unable to sleep, and the ration regime gets even tighter.

After the harvest season, the Organization stops distributing paddy rice and begins to distribute milled rice again, bringing it on bicycles to distribute to the cooperative. Every day two tall, black bikes, manufactured in China, bring rice to be distributed. These two bikes carry all of the rice rations for all of the villages in Spean Thom district.

The villagers are all old or infirm and unable to work much, so the Organization takes no interest in providing much food for us. At eleven o'clock the villagers, whether well or sick, come bearing their bowls and sit in the shade of a large *chambak* tree in front of the cooperative office, waiting for the rice bikes to arrive. We all glance nervously about, unable to stand, unable to sit still, watching the road for the bikes with the rice. The sound of a bicycle bell causes our stomachs to lurch as we hurry frantically forward to help hold up the bikes and untie the mouths of the bags. Sometimes the rice bikes go past us and head for Chhleuy, and we have to wait for the next trip. The rice is never as much as appointed by the Organization, with excuses such as impassable roads and a lack of means of transportation. (The Children's levee, connecting Kok Prasat and Spean Thom villages, was breached by the force of the water of the stream flowing into the river.) Some days we receive our rice at twelve, one, or two o'clock. Some days we return to our huts empty-handed, without so much as a grain of rice.

These days I am more miserable than when I was staying at the Phnom Srok hospital. In the hospital I could eat rice and porridge freely. Now the food rations are very sparse, and I live alone, unable to walk around foraging for something to fill my stomach. Every day I sit quietly by the cookfire boiling *lngieng* leaves to put on my sore and clean it. I can't leave it alone. I just want to keep looking at it and picking at it. Sometimes I clean it too hard and the pain shoots so intensely that I writhe about. I cup my ankle in both hands and carefully lift it up, clenching my teeth so hard to withstand the pain that I can hardly breathe.

I want to get better quickly; I don't want to be sick in bed. These days the Organization hates sick people. They think that the sick are just people who are too lazy to work, whose "consciousness" is not pleased by revolutionary work. They always say, "Shivering fever, shaking fever; car fever, tractor fever, rice fever; consciousness fever." The Organization does not bother to visit the sick to ask how they are doing. Only the leaders of the group and the unit, who are all Life Slaves, take the effort to look in on the sick to report back to the co-operative.

After working diligently to clean the pus from my sore using water from *Ingieng* leaves, with some occasional salt as well, my ankle begins to grow some tender red skin and the sore begins to shrink gradually.

Late June 1976

My sore has shrunk down to a small hole and the pain has subsided. I am able to walk comfortably without the aid of a cane. When I first got the sore, I shaved my head bald to avoid lice. These days my hair is starting to grow back. I am hopeful that I will be completely better in another week. But I am a man who cannot escape karma.

After returning to the village from the hospital, my sister found a male chick for me to raise. Afterward, my aunt brought me a female chick to help her raise as well. Now it is a hen about to start laying eggs. Having gone to live with my sister, and being unhappy with me for some reason, my aunt comes to tell me that she will no longer allow me to help raise the hen, and that she will catch it and take it to someone else to raise.

This news makes me very angry. When I was sick, my aunt was willing to abandon me to go live somewhere else. I was the one who raised the hen from a chick, and now that my work is about to bear fruit, she will turn around and take it to someone else to raise. Without saying anything, I catch the hen in the night and cook it. I boil the head, organs, wings, and feet, and eat them. The rest of the meat I salt and stuff into a dish with a lid, then dig a hole under the sleeping platform and bury it, covered with a small board over the top. I'm not worried that my aunt will find out because she is far away, and I don't think any neighbors have seen either. This is a mistake that gets me into serious trouble.

The next evening, my aunt goes out to check on her hen and catch it while it is sleeping. Unable to find it, she comes and asks me, as I am sitting cleaning my sore, wearing only shorts and no shirt, "A-Tuch! Have you seen my chicken?"

"No, I haven't, Mother. Maybe it has gone off somewhere foraging for food," I tell her, feeling nervous.

My aunt leaves the hut and searches some more. A short while later she returns and walks right up to the spot where the meat was buried and begins to lift the board covering it. I panic and lunge forward to grab her and beg her not to make a scene. She doesn't listen. She has no mercy, but cries out loudly, "A-Tuch stole and ate my chicken! A-Tuch stole and ate my chicken!"

She takes the dish with the chicken meat and flings it out onto the road in front of the cooperative office, and continues yelling, "My compatriots, please help me! That insolent Tuch stole my chicken to eat!"

I am terrified and trembling, cowering behind her, not knowing what to do. The villagers stand about watching, both men and women. My two sisters run forward and plead with my aunt, promising to give her two chickens if she will not make a scene, if she will not be angry with me. But she does not listen and continues to yell loudly.

The comrade cooperative chairman, the unit leader, and the cooperative *chhlop*,[1] with a cow tether in his hand, walks up to me. What am I to think? What am I to do? I'm a prisoner now. Now they will surely tie me up!

"What did you do?" the cooperative chairman asks.

"I cooked her chicken, Brother," I answer gently.

"Tie him up," the cooperative chairman says.

The *chhlop* grabs my arms and ties them behind my back. Oun wails loudly. They walk me into the hut and sit me down on the sleeping platform.

"Why did you cook and eat her chicken?" the cooperative chairman asks me.

"Brother, she brought me that chicken to help raise since it was a chick. The other day she told me that she was going to catch it and bring it to someone else to raise. I was angry and cooked the chicken last night."

As soon as I have spoken, the hand of the cooperative chairman strikes me on the cheek repeatedly, *whap! whap! whap!* "You are guilty of malice against others! There is no malice under the Revolution! Go! Take him away!"

The *chhlop* jerks me out of the hut. My bonds feel even tighter than before, with my elbows touching. Outside the hut, they begin to kick me. Because I am as skinny as a rail and my arms are bound, even moderate kicks cause me to

---

[1] A combination of intelligence officer and enforcer. The word literally means "spy," though they were not necessarily clandestine as is often implied by that term, as their role was often transparent to the community. They were usually loyal young Khmer Rouge, often even children, who dressed in the standard uniform of Khmer Rouge soldiers and cadres (black clothes, cap, *krama*) and were responsible for monitoring community members for revolutionary loyalty and correctness, identifying and reporting offenders, and carrying out discipline, including executions. See pages 198, 318.

stumble and fall. They kick and pull, walking me toward the cooperative office. My two sisters weep before the hut behind me. Many villagers stand around watching, and I am so ashamed I don't dare raise my eyes.

Once inside the cooperative office, they untie me and then re-tie me with my back against a pillar in the cooperative meeting hall. They leave me there. I sink down and sit with my legs bent on the ground.

The sun sets and darkness surrounds my body and my heart. I believe I can hear the sobbing of my sisters. Yes, both of my sisters are weeping and fretting. One brother has been killed already, and now another brother is facing the death penalty.

The flame of a kerosene lamp begins to burn inside the cooperative hall. This light moves slowly toward me, then comes to rest on a bed.[2] This faint light shines on me. The cooperative president and the *chhlop* prepare to eat a meal on the bed. I salivate with hunger, seeing them eat.

"Have you eaten yet, Comrade?" the cooperative chairman asks me.

"No, Brother," I reply.

"Well, that's not necessary, is it!"

They bend their heads over the food, and I crane my neck salivating. A cloud of mosquitoes swarms around me, biting me and sucking my blood freely. I try to collect my emotions and ignore them, paying no attention to the suffering of my body. I try to sit perfectly still, in despair, without hope of seeing tomorrow. I feel regret—regret for hobbling with a cane to find my aunt when they evacuated her to Phnom Srok, regret for bringing her to live with us. If not for that, I would not be tied up right now. Now she has become Yama to judge me. Even as I am tied up, even as I am about to be taken away to be killed, she continues to make a scene, condemning me non-stop.

My eyes watch the actions of the *chhlop* without daring to blink. Right now, my life is in his hands. No matter how hard I try to not be afraid, my feelings are overwhelmed, panicked, as I see the *chhlop* pick up a hoe and place it quietly near the bed.

---

[2] This would have been an object much like a sleeping platform (see footnote on page 40) in form and function, i.e. a low, simple wood frame topped with wood or bamboo slats, only freestanding and portable rather than built-in. Like a sleeping platform, these are often used for other purposes in addition to sleeping, including sitting, eating, etc.

Oh, my fate! I'm no different from my brother! Soon my body will surely be lying on the earth. My youngest brother will surely cry for me, and my two sisters will waste away with pity for their brother.

A Brother's Farewell at Sunset

1. The sun lies on the hills and the owl cries you cry and wail behind me — Oh cruel Karma! Your brother bound they are taking me away to be killed.

2. Sick these many months you cared for me without mercy, they beat and strike me — now I pray, I suffer and wretched pain fills my heart.

3. My body is skin over bones arms bound with cords pulled tight — thin and frail with tattered trousers my body covered in scars.

4. My sisters, my sisters, I suffer to die for the glorious nation — prepared to die for the land now I die by Khmer killing Khmer.

5. The sun enters his hole and hides his light cry out throughout the jungle — the owls and creatures of the night claiming my existence, Oh Sisters!

The sun sets and I bid you farewell! I leave you to die!

penned on 11 October 1979

I am overcome by the sorrow of my final minutes, when suddenly a person's voice speaks to me. "Who has sinned against you?" the cooperative chairman asks me.

"Nobody has sinned against me. I have sinned against myself," I reply to his question, acknowledging my errors with the intent of persuading him to spare my life.

He stops speaking and walks away. Is this the question he always asks the prisoners before they are executed?

Perhaps all captives have the same idea as me: to confess in hopes of being spared. I ate a chicken that I had raised from a chick. I, too, was part owner of that chicken. If they were looking for an excuse, to find justice for me, they would not have bound me. But these days justice is the back of a hoe blade. If the man with his hands bound says he did no wrong, it means that those who bound him are wrong, and he is placing blame on them. It is the nature of an ignorant man to desire to be respected, to be praised, to be flattered. To object, to oppose, is certain danger.

Outside of the cooperative office, my aunt still has not shut her mouth. I never imagined I could inflict such suffering on her. She is so hurt that she no longer cares for the life of a formerly beloved nephew. Now my life has less value than the life of her chicken.

Oh! If my mother were still alive and could see her son in bonds like this, how devastated would she be? Especially in bonds because of her cousin, whom she had attempted to cross the river and go live with, the sister she had hoped would love and care for her children as she herself would.

This is the influence of the current social atmosphere, of social pressure. It causes the character, the hearts, and the feelings of people to transform completely from what they used to be.

The horizon in the east grows faintly red, but my feelings, my heart, are still dark and in great turmoil. How I fret, fearing that I will not see tomorrow, for the final minute of my life draws very near. Very near indeed!

The comrade cooperative chairman orders the *chhlop,* "Summon the old woman!" These few words contract my heart and cause it to skip a beat. I am terrified! My stomach churns!

A while later my aunt enters the office weeping profusely. The *chhlop* orders her to sit near the bed. The cooperative chairman begins to question her: "Grandmother, would you like him taken away?"

As though she didn't hear the cooperative chairman's question, my aunt continues to cry. I listen carefully to hear her answer. At this moment whether I live or die depends on the motion of her tongue. I think of the spirits of my grandparents and parents, asking them to put the words in her heart, to say, "Spare him." But she continues crying and says nothing.

The cooperative chairman asks again, "Grandmother! Did you not hear my question? Shall they take him away or not?"

My aunt stops crying and answers with emotion, "No, my son! Though from the anger of my heart I would have you take him away. He has so much contempt for me. Look what you have driven me to!"

"Grandmother, why do you talk so much?"

"Never mind. Spare him!" my aunt replies reluctantly, as though she does not want to answer. These four words loosen my chest and give me hope.

They untie me and bring me to sit beside the bed. The cooperative chairman lectures and "builds" me: "Comrade, you and this grandmother should not have such animosity toward one another. You should not be quarrelling with her! But if there are quarrels again in the future, you must take responsibility, Comrade."

"Yes, Brother!" I answer.

The cooperative chairman continues, saying, "You two cannot live together! Go! Go find some food and water!"

"Yes, Brother!"

Tonight is the first or second night of the waning moon, and the moon rises over the treetops and shines her soft light down on the forest, as though blessing me in congratulation for escaping death. I walk slowly away from the cooperative office.

My aunt walks up to me and says, "You're going to catch me a chicken, and I'm going to cook and eat it!"

Good Lord! When we begged her for mercy, she refused. She let them tie me up and take me off to be killed. Now that I have not died, she comes and demands the chicken that my sisters and I promised when we were begging her.

To end the conflict, I catch my rooster and give it to her. Neither of my sisters wants me to catch it, because they are angry over my aunt's ill treatment of me. After getting one chicken, she is unsatisfied and carries on hollering at me to get another one. I only had the one chicken, and my sister Ol had promised another, but now she refuses to give it, since my release was not conditioned on two chickens.

The yelling and carrying-on reverberate through the village in the middle of the night. The cooperative chief calls me to the office again and demands, "Comrade, what are you fighting about now?"

"She is demanding repayment with two chickens. I only had one, and I gave it to her, but she is not satisfied and is demanding another."

The cooperative chairman bellows, "Who told you to repay her! There is no repaying in the Revolution! Damn, but this woman is a pain! Comrade, go back and tell her to come and see me!" My aunt is "built" by the cooperative chairman and returns quietly to her house.

Everyone in the village, old and young, male and female, feel sorry for me. They are thrilled to see that I have been released from captivity. My sisters are especially happy. Since she got remarried, Oun has not been around me much. But when I was tied up, she was scared that they would kill me.

The next morning, Oun takes this news to Samorn at the Kok Rumchek worksite and brings him to visit the village. My sisters and brother are overjoyed that my life was spared. It is very rare that someone escapes the way I have. In the evening we eat our porridge together as a family, and we are all afraid that someone else in our family will lose their life.

CHAPTER 12

Fertilizer Unit Number One

One week later (the beginning of July), in the village, they organize Fertilizer Unit Number One. All members of the unit are group leaders, some with illnesses or sores which prevent them from being able to leave the village. Because there are not enough group leaders to make a full fifteen people, Bong Sae, my group leader, asks that I be added to the fertilizer unit.

We build a fertilizer shed, about four by six meters, out of young trees, roofed with thatch grass, in the jungle about 200 meters west of the cooperative office. Near the shed we clear and level the dirt to make a yard for drying excrement and mixing fertilizer.

Up until now, we have not built latrines for relieving ourselves, but have just been going in the woods behind the huts. The Organization gives orders for each family to dig a pit about seventy to eighty centimeters deep to use as a latrine, hidden only by screens of thatch grass or *prech* bamboo about sixty centimeters high, to make it easy to scoop out the excrement.

As a first step in making fertilizer, we use *bangky* baskets on shoulder yokes to gather dried excrement and spread it out to dry near the fertilizer shed. Then we haul ashes left over from burning the trees at the cooperative farm at the edge of Kok Prasat out on the rise of the old village. (Back in March, the villagers had cleared the forest and cut down trees to make a field for planting corn, watermelons, cucumbers, bananas, and potatoes. I was down sick, so I did not participate in this work.) We mix these ashes with the excrement. Finally, we break up the clumps of excrement into a powder, mix it with the ash, and then scoop it into sacks.

When the dry excrement is gone, we begin to scoop up fresh excrement from the latrines, layering *trach* leaves on the bottom of the *bangky* baskets, then scooping the excrement on top and carrying it on shoulder yokes to be spread out and dried. The scoopers just scoop, while the dryers turn over the excrement and level it with boards to make it dry quickly. Then in the evenings we mix and bag it.

Under the meager food rationing, life is very difficult. Every morning we awake while it is still dark and go into the forest to find mushrooms. We pick all of the mushrooms considered edible, such as *kanhcheak sla* mushrooms, *kanhchou* mushrooms, *krangaok* mushrooms, *choar* mushrooms, etc. Some people are not very familiar with these and eat *anlung kong* mushrooms (some call them *chungkung kreal* mushrooms) and become very ill, vomiting and convulsing.

After eating our noontime porridge, we take our pots, hoes, knives, and sacks and scatter into the forest without anyone taking the time to nap and gather their strength, except for the sick who can't walk. (In malarial areas they say you're not supposed to nap during the day). Some go in search of pools of water to catch fish, shrimp, tadpoles, crabs, or snails. We take the tadpoles and boil, roast, and eat them. If we get a lot, we make them into *ph'ak*.[1]

Kingkuok[2] and *hing*[3] toads are a rare catch, except for when it rains now and then. The female toads are a light maroon color (the color of *teal*[4] tree wood) and about the size of my big toe. The male toads are yellow and smaller than the females. When it rains, it's beautiful to see them embrace each other and float out on the surface of the water in pairs, yellow and red.

In this area there are *kreat* toads with coloration and form like a *hing* toad, but small and thin like a tadpole. They're excellent jumpers and croak very loudly. This animal doesn't live in groups, and they hop very rapidly, so we've never caught one to eat. These days skinks, centipedes, tarantulas, scorpions, tokay geckoes, *cheas*[5] lizards, *bangkuoy* lizards, *kanhchanh chek* tree frogs, and *achko* frogs are all food for us. As for the *kanhchanh chek* frogs, we eat both the ones on land and the ones in the water.

Duong[6] worms are another food that we seek out frequently. We often look for them under dead fallen trees, especially trees that have been cut down and abandoned at the cooperative farm. We cut off the heads and tails, squeeze out the excrement, cover them in salt, fry them until they turn greasy, and eat them with porridge or rice.

Knhyong beetles have hard wings and are dark red like a *kanhchae* beetle, but they are as small as my pinky finger. This insect comes out and eats the leaves of

---

[1] a kind of seasoned, fermented fish kept in earthen jars
[2] *Bufo melanosticus*
[3] *Callula pulchra*
[4] *Dipterocarpus alatus*
[5] *Acanthosaura*
[6] *Calandra palmarum*

young trees at night, and then during the day it hides in its hole near the base of the tree. We dig them up, roast them, and eat them.

Large weaver ants are the easiest food of all to find. We eat both the eggs and the ants. Sometimes we boil them, salt them, and bottle them to keep and eat for days.

Some people walk around picking leaves which can be used as vegetables or eaten raw, such as the leaves of trees like *sdau, anao, tromung, lngieng, trabaek prey, mchey*, and *lngieng*, as well as spiny amaranth, etc. We take the *mchey* and *lngieng* leaves and eat them raw or pickle them.

Some people go looking for wild bamboo to dig out the shoots or cut them off with a shovel level with the ground. We take the bamboo shoots and slice them thinly, then simmer them for a long time. Then we squeeze out the water and store them in earthen jars or stuff them into bottles and then boil salt water and pour it in to make pickled bamboo shoots.

Some people walk around picking wild fruit such as *phdiek, sdoksdol, kralanh, pring,*[7] *chambak, poun,*[8] *kakah,* and *tromung* to eat.

We walk about scrutinizing the jungle for anything which can be eaten, which can help fill our stomachs in the place of rice or porridge, but these things are ultimately too meager to satisfy the demands of our stomachs.

One day at the end of July, while climbing a *pring bay*[9] tree to cut down a branch, my *phkeak* knife slips and cuts my left kneecap. I struggle to shimmy down the tree and drop onto the dirt, then tear my shirt and tie it on to hold my patella bone in place, which is trying to find a pretense to slip out. I cut a tree branch with a crotch in it to use as a crutch and walk back to the house. This injury lays me out for another half a month.

With orders to do my assigned work, I am not able to rest my leg until it has healed completely. Once the wound has closed up enough that I'm able to walk, I return to work.

The piles of ash on the farm are all used up now. The fertilizer unit makes its own ashes to mix with the excrement. Making ashes is not an easy task; we

---

[7] *Syzygium jambos*
[8] *Spondias*
[9] *Syzygium cinereum*

must fell large trees, saw them into pieces, carry them and place them into piles, and then light fires to burn them. Now the fertilizer unit has been divided into three teams: the ash makers, the excrement carriers, and the fertilizer mixers.

I and Bong Sae, my group leader (a former teacher in Kampong Speu province), who both have similar wounds, are placed in the excrement carrying team. This team has four people: Bong Sae, Bong Phon, Bong Him, and me. We stop using *bangky* baskets to carry the excrement because we find two wooden buckets, each attached to a board. We carry one bucket between two people. It's very difficult because we can't breathe without taking in the stench, but our labor is not as rigorous as that of the ash makers.

Each morning we carry the buckets from the fertilizer shed and scoop the excrement out of the latrines from one end of the village to the other and then back again. In the morning, we must carry four buckets, and another four buckets in the evening. At first, we are reluctant out of sheer disgust. Then after doing it every day, our noses get tighter, and we grow accustomed to the stench. After scooping the excrement into the buckets, those who smoke sit and have a smoke to gather their strength. I'm not a smoker, so I walk around and look at the villagers' huts, observing the lives of each family. Only we, the excrement carriers, have the possibility of becoming so intimately familiar with the real lives of the villagers.

We go from one latrine to the next, from one hut to the next. The shit from this latrine is like the shit from that one, their shit is like my shit. All of it is dark green colored like the leaves of trees, different from animal droppings only in that ours smells worse. Before we had latrines, we relieved ourselves in the fields. When they encountered our excrement now and then, the base people would say, "human tracks, but animal shit." Only the excrement of the cadres, the *chhlops*, the cooperative chief, and the soldiers has a natural color. If any of the people's latrines has fresh excrement with a color like that of an animal, it is certain that last night they had rice or corn to eat. If they didn't trade for it, then they must have stolen some corn from someone's field.

Some latrines have a decent amount of excrement, while others hardly have anything at all to scoop out—even if we only come by once a week. It's because the owner is down sick and has no leaves to eat, so there's not much excrement to produce. At each hut we see illness and suffering. Tears, pus, blood, clear fluid from sores, all flowing and mixing together. When I never saw anybody besides myself, I used to think that I suffered the worst. But after seeing others around me, I am surprised. Most of the people in the village are suffering as badly as I am. Some even have it worse than I do: they have no family, but are left to suffer in illness, all alone.

Some days, the excrement carriers postpone scooping excrement for a while to help carry a dead body to be buried. We cut wild bamboo and split it into strips about a meter-eighty in length, then we use *dah kun*,[10] *yeav*, or *preng* vines to weave the strips into a lattice to wrap the corpse in (instead of a coffin) and carry it to be buried. Some corpses have grass mats to be wrapped in, while other corpses have nothing at all but these bamboo lattices. The four of us don't know any proper religious rites, so we simply bury the corpses straight, like we would any other thing. And we are not afraid of the corpses either, for we have become the village corpse buriers, and we are as accustomed to this work as we are to the smell of excrement.

Those with strength are sent out on mobile assignments away from the village, and those who are ill nearby have no strength to carry the corpses to be buried. So it falls to the excrement carriers. Every two or three days we have a body to carry off and bury.

There is no special place for burying bodies. We usually bury them in the forest behind the houses of the dead, a distance of only about 100 or 150 meters.

Because the fertilizer unit does demanding work, the cooperative chief gives the unit plenty of rice and salt to cook and eat in the mornings at our worksite in the forest. In the evenings, we eat at our individual huts according to the Organization's regular rations. The excrement-carrying team cooks and eats our rice near the fertilizer shed. With rice to eat, we lack only food to go with it. During the midday break, Bong Him is in charge of cooking the rice. As for Bong Sae, Bong Phon, and I, we go looking for food.

Our daily food consists of large weaver ants because they are easy to find. Bong Phon is experienced at finding these ants. We walk around and look for their nests up in trees. If we suspect that there are eggs or *me smel* ants,[11] Phon takes his hatchet and strikes the tree trunk *pok! pok! pok!* If red ants[12] emerge

---

[10] *Tetracera scandens*

[11] princess ants; large, green, winged proto-queens, considered edible like the eggs

[12] female workers, wingless and much smaller than the princesses; not eaten

and surround a red nest, then that nest surely has eggs. If a moderate number of red ants come out along with some *me smel* ants, then there are definitely some *me smel* ants along with eggs. But if the red ants don't come out, or only a few of them come out mixed with black ants,[13] then there is nothing. Sometimes we get nothing but weaver ant eggs to boil with salt and eat. Sometimes we get nothing but *me smel* ants, which we roast until they are fragrant like a coconut.

With plenty of rice to eat for lunch, my body gains weight, and the wound on my knee heals up. This can be considered my good fortune for having joined the fertilizer unit. I scoop and carry excrement, I carry and bury corpses, but I have rice to eat while the villagers struggle in vain with their dwindling rations.

End of August 1976

The excrement carriers are eating lunch together at midday when a young man with a bald head and a tall figure so thin it appears as if the wind will knock him over comes walking out of the forest to the west of the village, straight toward us, carrying a hammock tied to a stick over his shoulder. He walks slowly, as though he is exhausted. My God! It's my youngest brother Samorn! He is so skinny! He is so thin he can barely even walk. I run out to greet him and help him to sit down. He is extremely exhausted.

"M'orn! What's wrong with you?" I ask him.

"I'm just so exhausted all the time, Bong," my brother responds, hoarsely and with great effort. I can't force him to speak, because he is just too exhausted, too weak. I ask the others if my brother can eat with us.

Samorn doesn't have any illnesses, but because he has worked almost without rest and on very little food, he is wasting away and losing all strength. From day to day he has grown thinner and thinner, weaker and weaker. Without any obvious sickness, the district's mobile committee won't allow him to convalesce in the hospital as requested. Unable to continue working, my brother has decided to run away back to the village. Running away from the mobile unit could lose him his life if the cooperative is strict and refuses to allow him to stay and sends him back to the unit. But after seeing the state of him, the group leader, unit leader, and cooperative chairman take pity on him and help hide him so that he can rest for a time in the village.

---

[13] winged male drones; not eaten

The youth mobile units work constantly on the offensive without any time to rest. The food rations are divided up as bowls of cooked rice or porridge. The discipline is very strict, so they are not allowed to go around picking plants or foraging for supplementary food. Those with parents and families in the village who can plant corn and tubers, or who have things to trade, receive assistance from the village, such as corn, tubers, fish, meat, etc. As for my brother, we never have anything to send him, and he lives solely on the food rations provided by the Organization.

Now my brother is very hungry because the rations in the village are even less than the mobile unit's rations. But he is able to get some rest and avoid labor. I can't take the rice rations of the excrement carrying team to share with my brother because all of us have similar problems back at our huts. All three of the others have children and wives with mouths open wide like baby birds. If we take the rice home, the Organization will stop allowing us to have the rice. So we live with our eyes closed, betraying our brothers, children, and wives, eating our fill alone.

My brother is so very hungry! He can't sit still, but walks around very slowly, looking for something to put in his mouth. The two leather cords that he used to use for tying his sleeping hammock he now cuts off one piece at a time, burns and pounds the pieces, and chews them until they dissolve, without even boiling them to soften them first.

When September comes, the rain falls nearly every day. The latrines fill with water, and we are unable to scoop out the excrement, so the fertilizer unit disbands. We cease to know rice any longer. As Bong Sae and I both live next door to one another across from the cooperative office, the cooperative chief asks us to help strip the ripe corn kernels from the cobs at the granary in the office, along with a number of women.

The old folks say, "A hen nesting in the paddy will eat the rice." We, sitting on the corn and picking off the kernels, are not unlike the proverbial hen. We chew on raw kernels of corn while we pick the kernels from the cobs. On the first day, it is kind of hard to chew because the kernels are so hard. After two or three days, our teeth are used to the feel of ripe corn kernels and it is no longer difficult, and the flavor of the raw kernels grows more delicious. It is red corn, which we pick with our own hands. The *chhlops* never check up on us after leaving the granary. This laxity gives all of us the same notion to steal corn kernels.

Every time we go to pick the corn kernels, each person has his or her own personal method for theft. I usually wear the white jacket with pockets inside. Each time I return to my hut, I scoop up two or three handfuls of corn and put it into the pockets. Aside from the corn pickers, nobody knows that we are stealing corn. And nobody suspects it, either, because the corn granary is large, and there are only five or six of us stealing, and only two or three handfuls apiece.

These stolen corn kernels help to alleviate my brother's hunger, to a degree.

CHAPTER 13

Paoy Char Subdistrict

Mid-September 1976

The sky fills with dark clouds and rain falls almost incessantly. The river rises to its banks. The river crests the banks and the water flows through the village. The road is submerged. Our sleeping platforms are submerged.

All of the villages in Spean Thom subdistrict are flooded up to the knees or thighs. The Organization has not yet given any directions, but we take our things and look for higher ground. All food rations are cut off. Not until the third day after the flooding begins does the Organization give orders to abandon the village.

We scatter without regard to groups, units, or leaders. All information and orders we receive are just passed along by word of mouth, vaguely and uncertainly. All I know is that the Organization wants us to leave the village, but I don't know where to go. We just follow the crowd toward Phnom Srok. We have no food, so we pull maniocs from the flooded farm to boil and eat. But the flooded tubers have a sour, stinky smell and are very difficult to eat.

My family is all together now except for my younger cousin (my uncle's daughter).[1] We have lost all contact with her and don't know if she is dead or alive. But we don't have much hope that she is alive, because my brother has never seen her nor heard her name at the district mobile unit.

The lowlands south of the town of Phnom Srok are all flooded. We carry bundles of mats, mosquito nets, dishes, and pots and wade through the water. Our bundles are not so heavy now, as they continue to shrink smaller and smaller.

At midday we arrive at the town of Phnom Srok. Here we receive word that the Organization wants us to travel to Paoy Char and Ponley subdistricts. These two subdistricts are completely new to us. We have never heard of them. We travel along the red gravel road leaving due west from Phnom Srok. This road is not flooded, but about 400 meters outside of Phnom Srok the road is cut by flowing water for a stretch of about twenty meters. Crossing the water

---

[1] My L'et

here is a bit difficult because the current is strong, and the ground is starting to be hollowed out into pits.

My family and a number of villagers are traveling behind all the others, and we are afraid of going the wrong way because we rarely receive any information. Some people left way back on the second day of the flooding. A large number of them went to Ponley subdistrict, while a number of them stayed in Paoy Char subdistrict.

At about three o'clock in the afternoon, my family enters a village of base people called Paoy Snuol. The sky is dark and threatening to rain. We go to the cooperative office to ask for food and directions to Ponley subdistrict. The cooperative committee provides rice rations and asks us to stay in that village. Because the way to Ponley is far, and has to pass through water, and the sky is threatening rain, we decide to stay in the village.

Paoy Snuol village is about three and a half kilometers from the town of Phnom Srok. The road from Phnom Srok, when it reaches the south end of Paoy Snuol, turns due north. The six villages of Paoy Char subdistrict are Paoy Snuol, Paoy Char, Trapeang Thmor, Paoy Ta Ong, Sambuor, and Pongro, all of which lie along this road, which stretches for about seven kilometers.

In Paoy Snuol, most of the locals' houses lie along the west side of the road. We are led to a house on the west side of the road, facing east, with a fence all the way around it except for a gap where a small path leads in on the south side. It is roofed with terracotta tiles, with plank floors, plank walls, and rounded pillars, raised about three and a half meters off the ground. The house is about ten by ten meters in size.

The owners of the house are called Father Suk, a small man about sixty years old, and Mother Lam, a large and sturdy woman also about sixty years old. The family has a total of six people, all adults. Mother Lam raises silkworms and spins silk. Their land, which is about twenty-five by thirty meters, is planted in mulberry bushes on the north side and in front of the house, with *saku* plants[2] (which the locals call *sakhu*) crowded beneath them.

Our family of five people rests beneath the house on a pile of lumber and boards on the north side. There is no wall to shelter us, so at night if it rains and

---

[2] arrowroot (*Maranta arundinacea*)

the wind blows from the north, we have to get up and gather our bedding. The south side is where the owner ties up his cattle.

Paoy Char subdistrict has new people who came to live here even before us. They are the people who arrived on the first train journey, and they arrived in this area before the Phchum season.[3] They live in the houses along with the base people and have a comfortable living, like the base people. They don't get sick and die as much as we do. They have normal, healthy bodies and are unacquainted with anything that can be called *starvation*. This is because their rations are adequate—they have plenty of pork, beef, and sugar to eat. They have farmland on which they plant vegetables, corn, and tubers, just like the base people.

My family are the unfortunate ones. We were evacuated the first time to a place with nothing, and the second time to a place of death. Now we are being evacuated for the third time to live in a place which is just beginning to get difficult because the road has been cut by floods and it is difficult to transport food to the village.

The food rations decrease to half a can of uncooked rice per person. For the villagers, this is not very serious; but for us, the new arrivals, it is very difficult. All we have are the spiny amaranth and green amaranth plants that we are able to forage. Aside from these, everything belongs to someone else, and we can't touch it. Even the papaya trees that have fallen over and been abandoned, when we ask if we can take the trunks to mix with our rice, they ask for something in trade. If we have nothing to trade, we get nothing.

When we first arrive in the village, I give my personal history as a widower[4] separated from his wife, hoping to be able to stay in the village and have the possibility of planting some food to send to my brother, who is required to go to the front lines (in the youth mobile unit). However, quite the contrary, in this village we have no possessions whatsoever. We are only temporary people. Even the place where we sleep is temporary.

---

[3] i.e., before the *Phchum Ben* holiday in October (1975)

[4] used herein by the author to refer to a married man living without his wife, whether because of death or otherwise

The owners of the house stare at us like we are creatures of Hell risen up to dwell beside them. They loathe us. They never invite us up into the house to visit.

On the day of our arrival, it just so happens that there is a large rainstorm, so *kingkuok* toads come out here and there to catch food. The toads in this area are strangely large, even larger than toads in the river country. We catch the toads for food. The owners of the house find this very odd, and Mother Lam says to us, "Damn, you children eat such awful food! The people who came before you never ate such things as you folks. It's disgusting! Hey! Bury the skins far away, don't throw them into my mulberry bushes!"

Indeed, the people of this area are very clean. Never mind the toads—they won't even eat little frogs caught in the village. They will only eat frogs caught out in the rice fields. But we are filthy people, eating anything. Some even go so far as to eat earthworms. The earthworms in this place are also strangely large, as thick as my pinky and as long as twenty-five to thirty centimeters. They call them *traok* earthworms.

After leaving the jungle, we thought we had escaped from worry. But after coming to live with the base people, we have emotional issues, trouble sleeping, trouble eating, trouble relieving ourselves. Having just arrived, we do not yet know the proper order of things, and we don't know where to find a latrine, so we dig holes and defecate among the mulberry bushes. They scold us so loudly it can be heard throughout the village, and then they take us to the cooperative chairman to be "built." Have we no shame!? The jungle people come into society and can't do anything right—not even shit.

We arrive in the evening, and the very next morning they send us to transplant rice seedlings right away. The half-can rice rations must be made into porridge and brought to sip in the fields for lunch and must be saved for dinner as well. My body had begun to fill out while working for the fertilizer unit, but now it begins to steadily lose weight again. Every day we work soaking in the paddy from early in the morning until after sundown before returning to the house. Some days we work in the rain all day long. When the rooster crows, we rise and cook our porridge and put it into a mess kit then walk to the fields about three kilometers from the village. There's no time to look for *kakah*, *kralanh*, or *pring* fruits to fill our stomachs as we used to do back in Kok Prasat.

Every day we see only the *slap chravar*,[5] *chrach*,[6] water lily, *skun,* and *kamping puoy* plants[7] that grow in the rice paddies.

Back when we lived in the jungle with other people of the same "ministerial"[8] class as ourselves, when we all got full or starved together, we never suffered emotional hurt. But coming to live with the "capitalist"[9] class is emotionally painful. We collect our rice rations at the appointed rate of half a can apiece, while they collect a different amount. We bring bowls to collect the rice, while they bring baskets. They eat rice for every meal, while we eat only *phek* porridge (porridge mixed with leaves).

When we fall sick with a fever and ask to rest, they say it is "consciousness sickness,"[10] and they taunt us, saying that it is because we are so lazy that we can't find anything to eat. The others can get sick as often as they like, and when they do, they are tasked with fishing with nets. We are the only ones they send out on mobile units, while the others cool their heels back at the village. Only a week after arriving at this village, my younger brother Samorn is once again assigned to the district's young men's mobile unit at the Kok Rumchek worksite.

One evening, as we are busy transplanting rice seedlings, we are suddenly sent back to the village to prepare for departure on a mobile work detail. We are not led by any of the base people, but are instead driven off like cattle, without a grain of rice or salt for rations. They tell us that clothing, shoes, and rice have already been prepared for us in Phnom Srok. At dusk we enter Phnom Srok and have no idea where to find clothing, shoes, or rice. It's not until very late at night that we finally get some uncooked rice to make porridge with. In the morning we are sent away again with no directions and no assignment.

The poor starve, while the rich are stuffed. Our path to the rice fields passes through a field of manioc. We ask to go in and pick the scraps that are left, and they refuse. I sneak in and cut off the stumps of the manioc tubers where they had been connected to the stalks that are piled up and left in the field. I take

---

[5] *Ottelia alismoides*

[6] *Monochoria vaginalis*

[7] all edible aquatic plants

[8] *kongsey,* from the French *conseil,* the old colonial term for ministers in the French colonial administration (implying that they are city people)

[9] figuratively, the base people (i.e., privileged, but separate from the *kongsey* class, or new people)

[10] The Khmer Rouge frequently used this phrase to imply sickness that is only in the mind, psychosomatic (or even faked) illness caused by an unrevolutionary mindset or by dwelling excessively on the past.

these and peel off the skin, which is hard like wood, leaving only a small starchy core about the size of my thumb, which I save to mix with my porridge.

In the story *Les Misérables*[11] the character Jean Valjean loses the right to live in society because he steals a loaf of bread to fill his stomach. These days some are sentenced to death for stealing a tuber or two. Why would somebody sell their life for such a small price? As for me, I would never make such an inequitable trade. I was arrested before because I was shortsighted, because I did not yet know the revolutionary discipline of the Organization. Their discipline says that if you steal, you die; if you are immoral (engage in secret romantic affairs), you die; if you run away from the unit, you die. In short, if you make them unhappy, you must die. (Speaking of immorality: The unit leader in Kok Prasat called Ienh, aged thirty-something, a former military policeman, was taken away and killed a week before we abandoned the village because he had a secret affair with a widow. The woman was not executed.)

Therefore we must not give them any pretense to arrest and kill us. Oh, how they enjoy killing us! How they love to kill us! They recite a doctrine which says, "To keep you is no gain; to remove you is no loss." If I am hungry, I ask them for food; and if they say no, I swallow my spit and walk away. I walk about and collect anything that they have thrown away that I perceive has having value for my life.

If I see somebody eating some tuber or arrowroot, and they throw away a crumb along the road, I stare at it, look left, look right, reach down, and snatch it up, then take my hand and brush it off and blow on it *puff puff* and toss it into my mouth *plop*. I don't really want to do this, but I am hungry. I am so hungry! I live without dignity, but my life is not cheap.

I am hungry because I have nothing. The base people eat and throw away leftovers, while we have nothing to eat. At *Phchum Ben* time they make confections, which they quietly eat by themselves. We swallow our own spit and dream, sit and dream, walk and dream, sleep and dream, dream only of the rice and soup, and the *kom*,[12] *bot*,[13] and *ansam* cakes of the *Phchum Ben* holiday. Is there any difference between the wretched beasts of Hell and us?

---

[11] 1862, by Victor Hugo (1802-1885)

[12] a type of pyramidal cake with rice flour and a filling of sweetened coconut

[13] a type of cake made from sticky rice flour and salted mung beans, wrapped in banana leaves

If you want to eat some arrowroot or a tuber, then you have to take some clothing to trade for it. Good Lord! If you take nothing and trade it for nothing, what do you get? Nothing! Nothing but your own spit.

End of October 1976

The road from Paoy Char to Phnom Srok is cut increasingly worse by the heavy flood waters. It becomes harder and harder to transport food supplies. The Paoy Char subdistrict committee assembles forces to dam off the water and fix the road. What do we have with which to stop water flowing so heavily? They knock down the temple in Wat Trapeang Thmor and then take the icons and bits of rubble and use them as fill to shore up the road.

Except for six or seven cadres, who cast silk *kramas* around their necks and stand around pointing and yelling orders at us, we are all new people. About a hundred of us are gathered from the six villages of Paoy Char subdistrict. The base people will not stoop to lifting, hauling, and carrying with the likes of us.

We wage constant battle with no rest. This work continues for three or four days. In the evening, they boil yams or sticky rice for the workers to eat to drive the work forward. One day they make sweet yams with a sugar syrup. The word *sugar* alone causes our mouths to water. As soon as they say the words *yams in sugar syrup*, we run to grab our bowls and surround the server. They give us each one ladleful, but some are able to sneak an extra ladleful. These beasts of Hell eat repulsively, running and jostling each other at the sight of food, and in an instant two large metal bowls of yams are gone. Some fight over who gets to clean the metal bowls, to lick them clean. How can they *not* lick the bottom of the bowls? We have gone without sugar for so long that the idea of cleaning them out with water is just too sad.

The supervisors are very orderly. They stand and watch us as we eat, then they begin to eat themselves. The six or seven of them do not even finish their basketful of yams.

After eating the yams, Ta[14] Lam, an older man of about fifty-something, short, fat, with a large protruding stomach, large eyes, and a large forehead, chairman of Paoy Char subdistrict, makes some remarks:

---

[14] This word means "grandfather," but it is also a polite term of address for an older man, and it was an honorific, egalitarian term of address for senior cadres under the Khmer Rouge.

"The Revolutionary Organization is not unaware that you comrades are lacking food. The Organization knows! The Organization supports us in all things. But as you comrades have all seen, the road is cut in many places and we are not yet able to produce enough to sustain ourselves. In the future, we will be raising frogs and eels; planting water lilies, even planting *kantolet* grass. If you comrades are able to produce anything on your own, go ahead and eat it! Eat three times a day, even four times, as long as you work! As long as you work hard!

"The Revolution has no schools with classrooms, with first and second baccalaureate diplomas. We have only the School of the Broken Hoe and Broken Plow,[15] under the sky in the middle of these fields! It's not hard; anyone can attend the School of the Revolution, but you must strive. You must not be slothful or lazy. The Revolution has no need of such people!"

All of us sit with open mouths, listening to Ta Lam teach revolutionary doctrine, without daring to move. This is our first lesson since coming to live in Paoy Char subdistrict.

---

[15] This is a clever play on words in Khmer. The colloquial designations for the two levels of secondary education attainment in Cambodia, used here, are *bac un* and *bac double* (from French *baccalauréat un* and *baccalauréat double);* see page 9. The word *bac* sounds, and is spelled in Khmer script, identical to the Khmer word meaning "broken."

CHAPTER 14

The Or Roessei Canal

12 November 1976

My family is given orders to go mobile for the second time. We don't know how many of the villagers will be going with us, or what we will be doing, or where. Comrade Hoeung, the unit leader, only tells us to gather at Phnom Srok. The Organization will be waiting to receive us there, and we will be gone for only four days. They issue us one hoe and one set of shoulder yokes and *bangky* baskets apiece and force us to leave in the middle of the day. None of the base people come with us. They don't know how to sleep on the ground in the woods as we do.

At about one o'clock in the afternoon, we arrive in Phnom Srok. There is nobody there to receive us. We wander all over the village. Some walk around looking for the house of their godmother or godfather. Some wander around foraging for plants to eat. When the sun is about to set, finally the district committee chairman comes and gathers us together to count heads and issues rations of one can of uncooked rice per person and tells us to spend the night in Wat Kandal. He tells us nothing. In the morning, some of us leave the *wat* to forage for food. When we return, everyone else has already left. There is nowhere to ask directions. We walk along the Phnom Srok–Prey Moan road toward Kok Tonsay and Kok Reach[1] villages but learn nothing. We go back and then head toward Boh Sbov and Kok Prasat. In the evening we finally meet up with the others in Chhleuy.

We dig a canal from the Rumduol River at Chhleuy to a spot behind Kok Tonsay. This canal has a depth of one meter, a bottom width of one meter, a top width of three meters, and a total length of 2,800 meters. It is a district project in which all five subdistricts must participate: Srah Chik, Spean Sreng, Nam Tau, Ponley, and Paoy Char.

---

[1] Kok Ta Reach

The work is divided up among the cooperatives (subdistricts). We are divided into teams of ten. Every day, each team must dig a single section with a length of four meters and build levees along the top on both sides.

The Paoy Char cooperative has twenty-two people divided into two teams. Two people without a team are to go hunting for food and cook. As we have no base people, the Organization appoints Comrade Chuoy, a unit leader from Ponley subdistrict, to oversee the Paoy Char mobile unit. But because he is busy with the affairs of his own unit, Comrade Chuoy appoints me as the deputy unit leader to lead in his place, and the female comrade Dary as my deputy, to oversee the work of the women. I am not pleased with this responsibility, but I cannot object.

The worksite is in a semi-forested wilderness area. There are no structures to sleep in. We pitch camp near the place where we work. Some people sweep the ground and lay their mats out beneath some unruly trees near a termite mound. Some tie up hammocks made from striped rice sacks sewn with a length of bamboo inserted at each end, which is more comfortable than sleeping on the ground.

The winds of *Katdek*[2] have arrived, and cool-season winds blow from the northwest and rustle the leaves in the trees with a loud whooshing sound. The cool weather has brought along with it fog, and wetness covers the area where we sleep at night. Our fingers, toes, noses, and ears get cold. We make fires at our feet or near the hammocks where we sleep. The fires help to relieve the cold a bit, but moisture collects on the leaves of the trees and drips onto our faces and bodies whenever the wind blows, chilling us and waking us up. Camping like this in a forested area with such cool weather may be delightful for tourists on leisure, but not for workers who have to work every day with no time for rest, as we are unable to stay asleep easily, and do not get enough sleep. We have to keep getting up to add firewood and tend the fires, or we are awakened by drops of water falling on us.

Our work here is exclusive by plot. If any team finishes their planned daily quota, they can rest. If not, you have to keep working, into the night if necessary. But we rarely finish our work before resting time at five o'clock because this place is not exactly an open field. Sometimes we run into thickets of woody

---

[2] lunar calendar month from roughly mid-October to mid-November

shrubs or small trees that must be felled and dug out. Sometimes we hit puddles that must be drained of water and mud before we can dig through them. For these reasons, the Organization does not allow us to take charge of our own work schedules.

Red sunlight spreads across the sky in the east, and the sound of a bell wakes us from slumber. All of us, who have been snoozing and hiding from the chill of early morning, arise quickly. We hurriedly wash our faces and grab our hoes and baskets. The moment the sun peaks over the tops of the trees, the second bell sounds. We hoist our tools onto our shoulders and march out of the scrub and head for our own appointed plots of land. Hundreds of hoes compete, rising and falling, breaking the earth into pieces, fine and close, like woodpeckers making holes in trees, the sounds of *bok bok* filling the forest. The ground in this area is not particularly easy; in fact, it is quite hard. We scrape the dirt into baskets and toss them from person to person and pile up the dirt one meter away from the edge of the canal on either side. There, two of us use hoes to spread it level and pack it down to form small levees.

We work hurriedly so that the heat of our muscles can resist the coldness of the early morning, to quickly finish our daily work quotas, and especially so that the Organization does not identify us as someone suffering from consciousness sickness. There is not much tension in our chatter and joking to pass the time, as we are all new people and all middle-aged. Telling jokes and laughing helps us to forget our fatigue and the hardships that we are all enduring.

At eleven o'clock, the sound of the "chicken bell" (a Chicken-brand hoe) is heard again. We set aside the hoes and baskets at the worksite and come up to eat porridge. Eating does not take long; we take our bowls to get a single ladleful of soup from the unit's economy team[3] and eat this with the rice porridge that we have left to simmer since the previous evening. (After eating our evening porridge, we always start the porridge for the next day's lunch cooking.) We eat for only ten or fifteen minutes, as we must hurry to the forest. There we forage for crabs, snails, fish, wild plants, tokay geckos, and *cheas* lizards, or dig for wild

---

[3] mess unit; the Khmer Rouge term for a team tasked with supplying communal food and water (cooking the food and managing supplies) for a unit or cooperative

yams. But each of our minds is on the work, fearing that we will be late returning to work, constantly looking up at the sky and the sun. (We have no wrist-
watches to wear. Those of us who did have traded them away to the cadres. If
they were not traded, the cadres would have taken them anyway. They love a
good Orient TriStar wristwatch; one of those can be traded for a dog or two
chickens.) As the sun passes overhead a little bit, we move gradually closer
toward the worksite.

At one o'clock the bell rings again. We walk to our plots, set aside the things
we were able to forage, and resume our work. Nobody is lazy or slow, for the
Organization has eyes like a pineapple.[4] The Organization is relentless and un-
forgiving.

As the Organization is very pleased with our efforts, they increase our
rations of uncooked rice from one can to one and a half cans apiece, and then
to two cans apiece. But even this much is insufficient for our stomachs, which
have for so long been expanded by foraged wild leaves and plants to sate our
hunger. We continue to forage in the forest every day.

One day I dig up enough wild yams to fill half a sandbag (a small American
nylon sack for filling with sand to build bunkers, each one able to hold a *tau* of
rice). I take my family's aluminum cooking pot to Boh Sbov to trade for five
cans of rice. When I finish work in the evening, I boil a can of rice to make
porridge, mixed with half a pot (Crocodile brand #18) of wild yams. I eat the
entire pot of thick porridge, then start another one for tomorrow. When that
one is done, I start picking at the yams and then I go overboard and eat the
whole second pot of porridge. Having eaten two full pots of thick porridge and
wild yams, I start to cook yet another pot. My stomach is getting tight, but my
mouth wants to keep going. I keep going and eat the third pot as well, but
about halfway through I can't get any more down. I lie down on the hammock,
tied up near the cooking fire, and keep eating. The third pot is cleaned to the
bottom. This evening I ate three full pots of porridge, including three cans of
rice and half a sandbag of wild yams. Amazing! Such incredible hunger! If I had

---

[4] a common Khmer Rouge slogan; see page 318

any more, I probably would have kept eating till I was full up to the throat, until my stomach burst like old Jujaka.[5]

My registering as a widower separated from his wife puzzles my two older sisters, who do not understand my thinking or my resolve. They are worried that I will be unable to take a wife. The revolutionary discipline does not permit the taking of second wives. If you are separated from your wife, you may not marry a new wife. My sisters want me to find a wife so that I can live with her, which is preferable to living alone. They are very pleased with the female comrade who is the deputy leader of my unit. They like to sit and chat with her in the evenings after work, and perhaps they have told her about my own background.

My sisters have also told me about her background, hoping that I would request her hand in marriage. Dary is a widow with one child. Her husband had been an army officer for the Lon Nol regime and was taken away by the Organization for "reeducation" in 1975. She comes from a wealthy family in a village near Wat Slaket, Koki subdistrict, Kien Svay district. She was evacuated and sent to live in Spean Thom subdistrict, and her child died there. These days she lives in Sambuor village, Paoy Char subdistrict.

Dary is the only young widow in my unit. She is about twenty-two years old, and even though she lives in a state of suffering, she still has her beauty. Her soft demeanor and her beauty capture my interest. And through my sisters, she must have learned a lot about my own life. She stares at me with interest.

Even though I like Dary and have warm feelings toward her, I still think this is not a good time to start a family. Firm in my resolve, I give my sisters the excuse that because I am registered as a widower, I am not permitted to take a new wife.

People differ in that some are ignorant, while others are knowledgeable; some are thoughtful, while others are thoughtless. Those who are knowledgeable and thoughtful are mindful of circumstances, and of the manner of living required by each circumstance. They know how to avoid or cut off all passions. The ignorant and thoughtless do not consider the flexibility of the social environment, are not mindful of circumstances, do not analyze the consequences

---

[5] a greedy Brahman from the *Vessantra Jataka*, a Theravada Buddhist legend

of their own actions. They allow themselves to be led along by their own passions, always acting upon the commands of those passions.

The passion which we all face now is hunger. It weighs upon all of the new people. But some people know how to resist, how to be long-suffering. Some others allow themselves to become slaves of hunger to the point that they no longer think about their own lives. What does one gain by being full today and dead immediately after?

Under my leadership, the people in my unit are enthusiastic about the business of trading work for rice, and for life. If we work well, they are pleased, they give us rice, and they keep us alive to see the sunrise tomorrow. But if not, an evil fortune will befall us, and they will take us away to be killed immediately.

Being united in agreement, we fulfill our labor with good results and are encouraged by the district cadres. Unfortunately, however, a small number of people are unaware of the value of their own sacrifice, leading to inactivity, which hurts the reputation of the unit.

Nearly every day, in my unit there are disappearances of dishes, spoons, knives, hatchets, rice, salt, porridge, etc. Some people open their eyes to find that half a pot of porridge has disappeared. Some lose the whole pot of porridge and find the empty pot in the bushes. This phenomenon leads to a rumor that my unit is a thief unit. The district committee is displeased, and Comrade Chuoy cracks down. He begins to spy on the activities of those in the unit who are suspected.

Early December 1976

Comrade Khek, a base person from Paoy Char subdistrict (and a former teacher), brings an additional force of workers. I make a request to combine our strength under his leadership, but Comrade Khek is unable to make such a decision because the district committee has already given this responsibility to Comrade Chuoy. He can only help me resolve issues involving the district or subdistrict committees.

One day, at about four o'clock in the afternoon, I go to collect my rice rations at the district mobile office with Comrade Khek when suddenly a soldier says, "Your unit has already collected its rations!"

This information surprises and concerns me. I tell the district chairman, "Om, I am the only person in my unit who can collect the rations on Comrade

Chuoy's behalf. And this evening all of the members of my unit are still working on our plot, and nobody is unaccounted for."

"Not so! Somebody from your unit has collected the rations and taken them away. I have no more rice to issue you. You will have to resolve this yourself! You must find out who has secretly collected your rice!"

Good Lord! He is the one who has issued our rice to a thief, and now he wants me to be responsible for catching the thief!

All of the other unit leaders have already collected their rice and departed. I am stumped, unable to think of what to do, unsure of whether this is a trick by the district committee chairman to frighten me. I am surely just waiting to die. If they are displeased, they can revoke my life at any time. Forty-four cans of rice is a lot of rice; nobody in my unit would dare to step forward to deceitfully collect the rations. Nobody who is not authorized to be at the office dares to come even near it. Comrade Khek stays beside me and keeps me company and helps to keep me from panicking.

Then suddenly, the next moment the district chairman decides to issue my rations and lectures me, saying, "Comrade, I hear that your unit has endless conflict. Now this news has spread to my office. Whose fault is this? It is your fault! You are not able to lead the work, to follow closely and keep tabs on the troublemakers! Don't conspire with them! Beware of danger to your own life!"

My life at this moment is like a drop of water on a lotus leaf. It is uncertain how long it can remain intact. I am trying to do well, but if people in my unit are doing bad things, then I will not be held blameless. Every time I attend a leadership meeting, I seem to receive threats and pressure. If the work moves ahead rapidly, then I am free; but if it moves slowly, then I am criticized and scolded.

The phenomenon of stealing is not limited only to my own unit. Other units are facing this problem as well.

The rice in the fields is starting to ripen. A number of villages surrounding our worksite have reported to the district chairman that someone has been secretly stripping rice grains from the stalks in the fields. This news makes the chairman's ears burn even hotter.

I hold a meeting in the unit and report on what has been going on around all of the district's mobile units, and in our unit, and lecture the members of the unit about being more careful. Up until now, everyone has been well aware of the punishment that we might face. Whether a big mistake or a small one, there is only one punishment: execution.

One day, after eating lunch, a member of the unit named Comrade On asks to travel to Boh Sbov to find tobacco. As soon as Comrade On departs, there is an uproar in the unit that two small knives have disappeared. Everyone suspects Comrade On and asks me to resolve it. How am I supposed to resolve it if the person has gone, and there is no evidence?

For us, at this point, everything which can be eliminated or sacrificed has already been traded for survival. What few items remain stay on our persons— the things essential for life, that we cannot do without. Knives and hatchets are very valuable to us at this time, and losing them is like losing a hand or a foot. If we go into the forest without a knife or a hatchet, what can we possibly accomplish?

At one o'clock it is time to go back to work, and I have not seen Comrade On return. At five o'clock, as I am measuring out the rice rations for the unit members, Comrade On arrives. He has brought a packet of tobacco and two or three *nonoung*[6] gourds with him. The members of the unit gang up and confront Comrade On. Comrade On objects and makes excuses against the accusations of the knife owners. They are not satisfied and ask me to report to Comrade Khek because they feel that Comrade On does not respect my leadership. They think that the things that have been lost will never be recovered, while the things which have not been lost yet will continue to go missing if troublemakers are not exposed and punished. I beg them to calm down because we have no evidence, and the discipline, the punishment, that is handed down by the higher-ups is execution. Are we willing for them to take away a person who lives with us to be killed? If this matter can be resolved quietly, then we will not have to lose anyone from our unit. But if we cannot keep quiet, the danger will come in one of two different avenues:

1. If I report it, then Comrade On will disappear.
2. If I do not report it, I will disappear, and Comrade On will surely go with me.

What should I do?

---

[6] *Luffa*

Because the people in my unit like me and are sympathetic to me, they agree to calm their anger and end the conflict. I feel a measure of relief in my chest, but I am still worried that such a thing will happen again.

We adjourn and get the pots ready to cook the porridge. A short time later, suddenly a man appears and asks for Comrade On. I ask who he is, and he says his name is Thach, from Srah Chik's mobile unit, and that Comrade On is his friend, that they've known each other since the *Sangkum*[7] days. Comrade Thach is holding half a bag of uncooked rice in his hand. Comrade On hears that his friend Thach is looking for him, and he comes to meet him and hands him a hatchet. The members of the unit are suspicious, and after asking some questions, they learn that he is trading a hatchet for six cans of rice. This hatchet belongs to the villagers for cutting down trees and cutting wood and has just been sharpened. It appears that Comrade On stole the villagers' hatchet and hid it in the woods when he came back to the unit. The two of them must have met and discussed it in advance, and now Comrade Thach has brought the rice to give to Comrade On in exchange for the hatchet. It is becoming increasingly clear to the members of the unit that Comrade On is a nasty sneak who is stealing from the units and trading in the village and stealing from the village and trading in the units. This matter involves other mobile units outside my authority; I cannot keep it hidden. If I hide it, it will bring danger upon myself. I report the matter to Comrade Khek.

So far, we have moved camp three times. Each time, we have set up camp near the plots where we are digging the canal. When we finish one section, we pick up and move to a new spot and pitch a new camp. There is nothing difficult about moving, as we have no structures. We just clear the foliage, sweep the dirt, and tie up our hammocks. The last time we pitched camp, we did it in a wild bamboo grove beside the river at Chhleuy. Our work has reached the end.

Because of the tension during the day, after eating our evening porridge, I assemble the members of the unit to clear our feelings and firm up our work plan for the final phase so that we don't swamp the boat in sight of the pier.

Tonight there is a waning moon, and the stars shine boastfully in their abundant ranks on a black sky. Our campsite is covered by a veil of

---

[7] *Sangkum Reastr Niyum* ("Popular Socialist Community"), Sihanouk's political movement that held power from 1955 to 1970.

impenetrable darkness. An evening breeze blows a wet chill over us. The mist from the river, along with the campfire in the middle of the circle, help to take the edge off the chill. Cries of nocturnal owls resonate in the jungle.

The light of a flashlight oscillates in the distance, sometimes visible and other times not. The light creeps closer and closer to us, but we can't tell who it is. The flashlight bearer calls my name: "Comrade Tuch!"

It is the voice of Comrade Chuoy. I answer quickly, "Yes, Bong!"

I rise and go to meet him. Comrade Chuoy leads me away from the unit, then asks quietly, "Is Comrade On here?"

"Yes, he's here," I reply.

"And where does the man with the rice live?" asks Comrade Chuoy.

"In Srah Chik," I reply.

"What is his name?" asks Comrade Chuoy.

"His name is Thach," I say.

"Come with me for a moment to find him."

I follow Comrade Chuoy without telling the members of my unit where I am going. It seems like there might be people following behind me at a distance, but I don't dare to turn around to look, lest I arouse suspicion.

Along the way Comrade Chuoy tells me, "If the Srah Chik unit leader asks, tell him that Om [the district committee chairman] has asked for Thach to go see him. Don't say anything else, in case the unit leader tells his guy to run."

My God! Run? This is serious. Oh, this is why Comrade Chuoy asked me to follow him: he is worried that I would tell Comrade On to run. The people following behind me must be soldiers. My stomach churns, my chest flutters, and my heart pounds. I am terrified of what is about to happen.

When we arrive at the Srah Chik camp, Comrade Chuoy asks for Comrade Thach. The unit leader calls for Comrade Thach to come and speak with Comrade Chuoy, who then leads him back to my unit. Being completely unaware, Comrade Trach follows readily and without hesitation.

As we approach my unit, Comrade Chuoy tells me, "Comrade Tuch, you go and tell Comrade On to come and see me."

I follow his order without daring to say anything. Suspecting nothing, Comrade On follows Comrade Chuoy without even putting on a shirt first. Knowing that the two men will certainly die tonight, my feelings are in turmoil, fear mixed with regret. Nobody in the unit is worried, as they suppose he is being called out for questioning and "building."

It is late and quiet, about nine o'clock, and nobody has gone to bed yet. They are all sitting around waiting for Comrade On to return. While it's true that we are not happy with Comrade On's wayward behavior, still none of us want him to go away. He is good at coming up with funny things to joke and laugh about, to lighten the mood while we are working hard. He knows how to make some fun to help us forget our worries.

A shadowy figure approaches. The members of the unit rejoice at the appearance of this figure, supposing it to be Comrade On returning. But their relief turns to disappointment when the firelight shines on the face of the figure: Comrade Chuoy.

I ask him quickly, "What are you looking for?"

"I'm looking for a shirt to bring to On," Comrade Chuoy replies.

At that instant, Comrade On's wife wails, understanding that her husband will surely be killed tonight. She gets up and goes to retrieve an old shirt and a bit of mosquito netting which Comrade On often wraps around his neck in place of a *krama* and sends them for her husband. Comrade Chuoy leaves again, and a devastating depression settles over the unit members. Comrade Dary, my sisters, and the other women comfort Comrade On's wife and encourage her to forget her sorrow.

Comrade On was young, only about twenty-three or twenty-four years old. His wife is only about twenty. They have never had any children, and they seem to have been very poor. Belonging to the lower classes, like my own family, causes such tremendous hardship. Everything is a dead end, and there is never anything to trade with anyone. Now we are all starving, but the degree of starvation is not equal. Those who had been wealthy still have gold and diamonds and new clothing, so they are still able to trade. They are somewhat hungry. Those who had been poor to begin with are ears-ringing hungry; drooling hungry; guts-about-to-rupture hungry. It is this intense hunger that caused Comrade On to forget himself and the death that was so near at hand.

It has been nearly a month and a half since we left the village and pitched a work camp in the woods. The canal has been dug, but we do not have any clear instructions about whether to return to the village or go somewhere else.

Comrade Khek tells us that perhaps the Paoy Char subdistrict mobile unit will be sent to harvest rice in the *roneam*[8] (along the shore of the Tonle Sap lake).

Even though we have been away from the village for so many days, and the work has been so much more grueling than the work in the village, sleeping under the sky, exposed to the wind, we have no desire to return to the village. For us, the village is a place of suffering. In the village we had no home and had to sleep under somebody else's house. Sometimes they would sweep dirt onto our heads, or spit on our heads. They were prejudiced in the distinction between base people and new people. The villagers had food to cook and eat, but we would return from work empty-handed, watching their mouths as they ate. The rice rations in the village were worse than the rations in the mobile unit. We are willing to endure hardship so long as we can get full!

25 December 1976

We receive instructions to eat our porridge in the morning then pack our things, our tools, hoes, *bangky* baskets, and yokes, and then meet up at the district's mobile committee office. We assemble at 9 a.m. There they hold a ceremony to marry three new couples.

The three couples rise, hold hands, and commit themselves to each other as husband and wife before all of us, with a sound of applause and congratulations. The district chairman (Om Oem) stands and shares some remarks and gives advice to the new couples to take each other's hands and fulfill their revolutionary work victoriously. He declares the closing of the canal worksite and asks each of us to return to our own cooperatives.

We depart from the Or Roessei canal with a sense of loss for the two who were killed there. My siblings and I return to the village with hesitant hearts and unhappy feelings.

---

[8] a region of seasonally-flooded forest along the shore of the great lake of the Tonle Sap, which expands and contracts with the seasonal monsoon cycle

CHAPTER 15

Pulling Carts Like Cattle

For those of us who are new people, the process of returning to the village is much easier than that of leaving the village on a mobile deployment. When we are leaving the village on mobile deployment, the unit leaders and village chairman don't dare come near us or speak to us. They are afraid that we will ask for rice, sugar, potatoes, tobacco. On the other hand, as soon as they know that we are returning to the village, they rush to greet us and call us to work right away, not giving us even the smallest chance for rest.

My two sisters and their husbands are sent by the village Organization to harvest rice. As for me, I am assigned to push over rice stalks. I am unfamiliar with this job. The rice plants in this area are large and tall—some as high as a person's chest. In some fields the wind has blown the rice stalks over flat. In some fields the rice is still standing up straight, which makes it hard to cut. So before they harvest the rice, it has to be pushed over so that it lies flat to one side.

Pushing over rice is as exhausting as playing basketball. Two of us hold the two ends of a length of wild bamboo and then fall over simultaneously, pushing the rice stalks down level along with us. Then we raise the bamboo and do it again. We fall into the water and stand back up, over and over again, pushing down the rice stalks in a rapid fashion. It is not very long before we are gasping for breath and have to sit down to rest.

After working to flatten the rice stalks for three days, they reassign me to help transplant rice instead. After that they assign me to clean and level the threshing yard to prepare to trample[1] the rice.

No matter how difficult the work is, we always manage to get it done. But we are helpless in the face of hunger and thirst. Everywhere is the same: the overwhelming problem is food. We are skinny from lack of food, we are sick from lack of food, and they take us away to be killed over food.

In the village the uncooked rice rations are only one can apiece, and we are not able to find wild yams to mix with our porridge as we did when we were mobile, in the woods. And our work is done together with the local base people, who do get enough to eat. We are exhausted and starving, while they are

---

[1] part of the process of threshing, by which the rice grains are separated from the stalks

not exhausted and not starving. If we dare to take a rest, they chastise us, they "build" us, calling us sluggish. If you have two engines the same size, and one of them has only a little bit of fuel while the other has a lot, can they really race against one another?

We are much more exhausted than when we were mobile. If you don't have to know, to hear and see, it's not so bad; but when we have to see others eating bananas, sugar cane, sugar, arrowroot, and tubers, our mouths water, our stomachs churn, and our eyes follow without blinking, barely able to refrain from lunging to take the food from them. Standing around looking at others eating food like this, back in the old days, adults would scold children and say, "Hey, no-manners boy! Can't you see someone eating something without standing around gawping at them?" Now we have become the no-manners boys, walking around looking for leftover bits of tuber, sugarcane, or corn, eating them without any thought for hygiene or health.

Every evening when returning from the harvest, the base people strip off enough grains from the rice stalks with their hands to fill up a *chan srak*[2] or a mess kit to take back home. We, the new people, can't conceal it anywhere. Even if the girls try to hide it in the folds of their skirts or their brassieres, the young *chhlop* children will search them and take away every last grain. And then they will "build" us, saying that we are betraying the collective. If we do manage to smuggle a small amount back to the house, we can't do anything with it other than roast it and chew it. When the masters of the house have finished pounding their own rice, they take the pestle away and hide it so that we can't use it to pound anything.

Damn, hunger is a powerful thing! Every day and every night we sit and think, lie and think, walk and think—think about how we can get enough to eat.

Early January 1977

They assign me to kick and trample straw on the threshing floor. We work there day and night, trampling the rice stalks until nine or ten at night. But they give us free rations. They cook rice to for us to eat both morning and evening. There is fish soup with plenty of fish. The work is not too difficult compared

---

[2] a set of stacking, cylindrical metal dishes for carrying meals; see photograph on page 518

with the harvesting work, when we were constantly bending over and standing up, making our backs ache.

After being skinny, eating nothing but porridge for months (even when the uncooked rice rations were two cans per day on the mobile unit, I still only ate porridge), and then suddenly getting free rice rations, with soup and plain fish dipped in salty *ph'ak*, after just one week I have become a fat person. I am swollen—what the old folks call "rice-swollen." They stop allowing me to work on the threshing floor and send me to the team in charge of transporting and stacking the rice straw.

My unit's threshing floor is set up in a rice field west of the village. We have to take the straw to be piled up at the south end of the village. We carry the straw in an oxcart, pulled by humans. The straw team has five members: two older men who are base people, age fifty-something; two middle-aged new people; and me. The three younger men get into the harnesses and pull the cart, while the two older men help push from behind. This job sounds difficult, but for me, in my swollen state, it is a little easier than kicking straw because I have some opportunities to sit and rest. When kicking straw, I had to stand kicking the straw around with my feet, turning the straw over until it was sufficiently trampled, and then I had to gather it up and take it away, then lay out new bundles of rice, and I was standing constantly.

Now I know that my previous assumption was not entirely correct: not all of the base people are bad. Father Lun and Father Pov are appointed to lead our work. They are older and have good hearts, follow Buddhism, know the difference between good works and sin, and are kind to us. They criticize the inhumane behavior of some of the leaders. (The leaders in this cooperative are all base people.)

Once, we are sitting around chatting and they tell me, "Just you wait, Tuch. Those who do good deeds get good in return, while those who do evil will receive evil. Those who kill others cannot avoid someday being killed themselves. There is a saying of the Buddha: *sokatao sokata*, which means 'give comfort to others, receive comfort in return.'" I keep this saying in my heart and remember it because I agree with this philosophy.

They tell me their history, how in the days of Samdech[3] they sold cattle and had money. They were accused of being *Khmer Serei,*[4] and then they didn't dare return home, opting to sleep in the forest, and in stupas and tombs. Now, those who had falsely accused them are all dead. And they, who never did anything wrong, are still alive to this day. They tell me that from Trapeang Thmor to the Thai border is only a journey of a day and a half or two days on foot. They know all of the roads and paths. If they were single like me, they would have fled to Thailand already rather than tolerate living in misery like this.

To be seen to agree with Father Lun and Father Pov's views, I always say that I don't know the roads, and if I were to try and flee, I'm afraid I would get lost or fall into danger. But in reality, my views are different from theirs. As a Khmer, I am determined to live and die in Cambodia. I must be acquainted with the Khmer race, the Khmer nation, the Khmer homeland, the Khmer story, the sufferings of the Khmer people. Especially in such difficult circumstances as these. I have to know what is happening in Cambodia, what miseries are being faced by the Khmer people in this so-called revolutionary era. If I am not able to make it through this revolutionary era alive, then so be it. Dying is a normal part of a human life. I will have died as a Khmer who yearns to be acquainted with the real lives of the Khmer people. And if I don't die, then someday I will surely be remembered as a Khmer man who successfully endured all the myriad obstacles and dangers that came about during these times. Then I will possess sufficient answers for my children when they ask, "What was it like when the Khmer Rouge ruled the country?"

---

[3] Sihanouk

[4] the "Free Khmer," a dissident guerrilla movement led by nationalist Son Ngoc Thanh that opposed both communism and the monarchy through the late 50's and 60's

CHAPTER 16
The Camp at Phnom Veng

In mid-January 1977, the Revolutionary Organization of Phnom Srok district requests workers from the various cooperatives to join a mobile work unit to collect bat guano from the mountains for fertilizer. Some workers have already departed, but the Paoy Char cooperative has not yet sent enough people to satisfy the Organization's orders.

Because this work is being done near the Cambodia-Thai border, the Organization requests that only base people participate because they are afraid that the new people will flee. But the base people who have been appointed refuse to go, so they end up turning to the new people anyway. It is a matter of routine, by now, that the new people must serve the base people and stand in for them. My swelling has gone down, and once again I become the target of mobile deployment.

25 January 1977

I am appointed to join the mobile work unit deployed to the mountains along with two others, also new people: Comrade Tha and Comrade Sat.

The cooperatives of Phnom Srok district normally issue rice, sugar, tobacco, clothing, and *kramas* to the people leaving on a mobile deployment. The Paoy Char cooperative, on the other hand, has never done any such thing. Paoy Snuol, especially, has never given us any rice to eat. They usually inform us in the morning as we are working, telling us to go home and get our things together and leave immediately, that rice and water will be given to us on the other end when we get there. This time they send the three of us to eat rice at the Trapeang Thmor cooperative, which is where we are to gather before leaving. In fact, it is all deception: there is no rice for the three of us. Everybody else already ate their rice in their own villages before leaving.

At two o'clock, fifteen of us gather along with two elephants for transporting rice. We start out walking behind the elephants. When we reach Paoy Ta Ong, we see two or three tractors leveling the plain west of the village. Poles with red flags waving on the ends of them have been set out in rows: the initial survey for the Trapeang Thmor Reservoir worksite.

The elephants walk much faster than we do and get almost out of sight ahead of us as we cross the plain to the west of Paoy Ta Ong heading northwest.

We try to keep up with the elephants, each of us carrying a small bundle on our backs and a jute-sack hammock at our sides. Comrade Sok, a twenty-seven-year-old base person from Trapeang Thmor and a former law-school student, is our leader.

We cross the plain and enter the forest. At about four thirty we arrive at Chhouk Ang, a farm near the forest where older men plant crops and raise animals, where mobile units often come to pitch camp to cut thatch grass and bamboo. We rest and recover our strength here for a while, then the soldiers take us back into the forest.

As the sun is setting, its last rays touching the treetops, we arrive at a military camp in the forest, which they call Svay Chuh. We must stay the night here. The soldiers cook rice and a dish of wild boar meat to receive us. We bathe in a pond and wash our bodies before eating.

As we are soaking in the cool water, I cough and suddenly two or three clots of blood fall from my mouth. Comrade Sok sees this and takes me to report to the soldier in charge.

The soldier says, "Why didn't you say anything at the village? Now that you're out in the jungle, where will we find the strength to exchange for you? We can only exchange you in the bushes!"

These words frighten me, and I don't dare say anything more about not feeling well.

In the morning we rise and take some rice. The sun casts its crimson rays through the leaves of the trees and we head out again. Where are we going? Nobody knows for certain where we are headed. The soldiers only tell us to follow the cart track continually without turning aside at all; they will come along on the elephants a little later.

All around us is forest, with tall trees and short trees. Sometimes we encounter sparse woods with *phchoek*,[1] *khlong*,[2] *thaeng*, and *kakah* trees spaced far apart with meadows of grass and stands of *prech* bamboo growing beneath them, where we can clearly see the sun and the sky between the trees. At other times we walk under a canopy of leaves that shuts out the sun and the sky, leaving us in a nice cool shade.

---

[1] *Shorea obtusa*
[2] *Dipterocarpus tuberculatus*

At about ten o'clock, we arrive at Tuol Thmenh Trey, a place where mobile units have camped previously to cut thatch grass. We rest under an abandoned shelter. The elephants carrying the food catch up to us, and the soldiers collect our clothing bundles and place them on the elephants before continuing on. A soldier uses a lighter to ignite a bundle of kapok fibers and drops it on the ground to set the grass on fire. The elephants are afraid of the fire and run ahead without looking back.

We follow the old track. Sometimes the elephants leave their droppings scattered along the path to help us recognize the way. We all walk without carrying anything, and yet it doesn't seem light at all because we grow increasingly weary and exhausted. We begin to get thirsty. Having never walked in the mountains before, and because the soldiers didn't say anything about it, nobody brought water along. Along the way we don't see any source of water. We walk and rest, walk and rest. The old folks in the village used to tell me that if you're walking in the mountains and get thirsty, you should look for *chhveng*[3] vines. This kind of vine clings to trees in a spiral from left to right and has the shape of a tube. If you cut the vine up high and then again down low, water will flow out of it. I watch for this type of vine but see none.

We come across a low area with fresh green grass growing on the ground. We all leave the path and head for this spot. But there is not even a little bit of water there; it has all dried up. Desperate, we sit down to rest, but because it is already about two o'clock, we don't dare rest for long and soon resume our journey.

We continue straight, veering left a little up a slope, and suddenly we come upon the place where the people who came earlier have pitched camp. Their camp has been set up under the trees along the side of a mountain stream. We are up on a mountain; we have climbed a mountain without even realizing it. Just a little while ago, all we could see was jungle, and now we see mountain after mountain rising one after another to the west. We rest for a while and then get into the stream, whose water is very cool.

At about three o'clock, the people who had arrived before us finish cooking some rice. The soldiers tell us to prepare some rice as well. The two economy workers in charge of fishing arrive carrying a large narrow-bottomed basket full of fish. We don't understand—are they preparing breakfast, or dinner? It seems awfully early for dinner, as it seems too bright. But as soon as we finish eating,

---

[3] Khmer for "left"

we barely even have time to find a place to sleep before darkness covers the jungle.

At the mountain near this camp, all of the fertilizer has been collected by those who came before. Tomorrow morning we will have to move camp to find fertilizer at another mountain. Now we number about thirty workers, plus seven soldiers.

The next morning, after eating our breakfast, the soldiers lead us onward again. We cross the stream across large slabs of stone, climb the mountain, and descend again. In some spots there are large stands of *prech* bamboo on both sides of the path, higher than our heads. The soldiers point out various mountains that we see along the way: Phnom Kambaor, Phnom Changkran Yeak, and so on. Along the way we come across a camp of soldiers that appears to be a guard post, set up at a place where a mountain stream flows.

At about eleven o'clock we encounter a camp of soldiers from Thmor Puok district, pitched along the stream, with about seven or eight soldiers living in it. We cross the stream to the other side to make our camp along the same stream, but about half a kilometer from the soldiers' camp. We prepare camp beneath the trees on a rise beside the stream.

We are to collect fertilizer at Phnom Veng, a mountain about three kilometers from here. Because there is no water source there, we cannot camp there. The trail to the mountain is small and narrow and overgrown with jungle, so it is more difficult than the trail from the village. Every morning at about five o'clock, the economy team wakes and cooks rice in the dark. Because the jungle is so high and thick, we are not able to see the sunrise here.

When the sky over our heads turns a faint red color, we eat our breakfast and then prepare our hoes, shovels, *bangky* baskets, bags, and leather straps and head out to hike up the mountain, which is about 200 meters high.

When it is fully bright, we arrive at the top of the mountain. Around and on top of the mountain is sparse forest with meadows, thickets of tall grass, and trees growing far apart. This mountain stretches from east to west. In the distance, about ten kilometers north of the mountain, stretches a range of mountains. The soldiers instruct us not to go to these mountains because they are dangerous, and it is a forbidden area. We suppose that this must be the Thai border.[4]

Our task is to scoop up the bat guano in the caves of the mountain and collect it into bags, which will be sent down and piled up at the foot of the mountain. An oxcart or tractor will come to collect them and take them away.

There are three different caves where we collect the guano:

The first cave is on top of the mountain. The mouth of the cave is large and has the aspect of a regular downward-sloping path with large stones along either side. We descend this path about fifteen meters to a fairly level spot and then turn right. Here we have to climb a large boulder about two meters high. After that we squeeze through a narrow opening about a meter across and then descend in stages about three meters to a spot where it levels off, where we can then walk directly into where the fertilizer is to be collected. This cave is low and narrow, and when we go inside, the bats are startled and fly very closely past us, looking for the exit. Inside the cave it is pitch dark, and we light an oil lamp to light the path and the place where we are to scoop up the bat guano.

The bat guano is not very heavy, so we fill the sacks nearly halfway, twist up the top, and then pass them from person to person to the mouth of the cave. This cave does not have very much guano, and after only two days it is all gone.

The second cave is reached by walking up the mountain from the south. From the top of the mountain, we walk down the north side about fifty meters to the mouth of a cave. The cave is large and spacious and descends in a straight shaft to a depth of about thirty meters. This is where a pulley is placed to lift the bags up. In order to go down into this cave, we must feel our way, bent over, into a small tunnel east of this one about twenty meters. Then we arrive at the mouth of another passage that goes straight down. But because it is dark, we can't see anything, and it's not too unnerving. We descend on a ladder, made of tree branches, about ten meters tall. The person holding the lamp goes down first and then places the lamp on the ground below so we can see the steps of the ladder. After descending the ladder, we walk down a sloping path about another ten meters to the spot below the pulley. We must then descend further past this point along a fairly steep slope into the darkness. The sunlight coming

---

[4] These are likely the Dangrek mountains, which do indeed form the frontier with Thailand, but are more like thirty or forty kilometers away.

in through the pulley shaft does not penetrate this far. Inside the cave it is pitch black, and we hear only the cries of the bats on the roof of the cavern high overhead, echoing and resounding. This cave is large and spacious and tall, but it smells a bit of bat urine and guano.

This cave has a lot of bat guano. Nobody knows how many years they have been defecating here or how many meters deep it is. When we dig with our hoes, we hear loud *plok plok* sounds, and we collect only the freshest guano.

We divide our strength into three teams: One group sits up top and pulls the bags up with the pulley. Another team carries the bags on their shoulders and piles them in one spot. These two teams take turns trading roles because pulling the rope chafes one's hands quickly. The third team collects the guano in the cave. I work on this third team. We spend more than a week in this second cave and then turn to the third cave.

The third cave is reached by walking down from the top of the mountain, keeping close to the mouth of the second cave, until we reach the middle of the mountainside, then skirting the length of the mountain eastward for about a hundred meters. Then we turn back up the mountain for about twenty meters to the mouth of a shaft that descends about fifty meters. We set up a pulley here. In order to get into the cave, we have to walk along the length of the hillside another hundred meters. Along this path we encounter loose limestone scattered about. We reach another cave opening and walk into the darkness through a gap in the stone and descend along a ladder made of tree branches. We feel our way forward a bit at a time, sometimes bending over, sometimes bending sideways, sometimes having to slide down from a stone drop off. We emerge into sunlight. The floor of the cavern is level and above there is a shaft going straight up so that you can see the sky, with a square opening about four meters across. Through this opening we can see the sun only at noon. We must pass under this shaft and go another twenty meters to reach the place where the pulley is fixed, with leaves and branches covering the opening above. To reach the place with the guano, we turn left and go further in. In some places we have to bend over, and in some places we have to waddle. Because the passage is low, we have to drag our bags until we reach a high place and can pick them up once again.

This cavern is even more spacious than the previous one. Hundreds of people could fit in this cavern. There is even a little bit of sunlight allowing us to see dimly. Inside the cave it is cool like an air-conditioned room. Working here, we don't feel very tired, we don't sweat, and we don't get thirsty. Because we can't see the sun, we don't know the time.

These three caves where we collect guano are places where people used to collect fertilizer in eras gone by. This makes it easy for us, as there are old ladders and places to tie pulleys.

At about two-thirty or three o'clock in the afternoon, the people up top call us out of the cave. When we emerge from the mouth of the cave and hit the creeping heat on the outside, it makes us think of food. We gather together for a head count and then hurry down the mountain for camp.

At about four o'clock, we return to camp and bathe in the stream. This stream flows down from the mountain and in the rainy season it has a depth of about seven meters, a span of about thirty meters, and a bottom of solid stone. Right now, it is the dry season, and the stream has shrunk, the water gathering into pools only as deep as your calf or thigh, or perhaps your waist. The water is crystal clear so that you can see the bottom, and it trickles lightly from stone shelf to stone shelf, each lower than the last by about thirty or forty centimeters to half a meter. On the bottom are loose stones and pebbles with dark green moss growing on them. Schools and schools of *kanh, andaeng,*[5] and *riel* fish swim from rock to rock. Some leap up against the current *plik-plok! plik-plok!* We can reach out and catch fish with our hands when they swim into narrow gaps in the rocks. But because we have so much food to eat, we don't bother much with catching these fish. The *andaeng* fish are very small, the largest only as big as your big toe. The stream is very cool, and when we bathe, we don't want to get out again. We scrub our bodies and wash our clothing and *kramas,* which are covered with light red bat guano. We are not able to spend as much time in the water as we would like, as here in the mountain jungles with large trees, it gets dark quite early, and we must hurry to eat our dinner while it is still light.

Our food rations during this time are unlimited. Every morning two econo-omy workers and one soldier ride an elephant to find fish. Because there are so many fish, they have only to dam the stream on three or four upper shelves, and then they can clear the water from the lower shelves with their hands and grab

---

[5] *Clarias batracius*

the fish. In the time it takes for the water to fill and overflow the three or four upper shelves, they have caught enough fish. When these two men and the soldier return to camp, they have enough fish to fill a three-*tau* rice sack anywhere from half full to nearly full.

There are no edible plants in the jungle, so we eat boiled fish with salt for nearly every meal. Some days the cooks make an effort to grill some fish for us to eat. As we enter February, the *prich*[6] plants begin to bud and flower. We eat soup made from fish and *prich* shoots and blossoms. It is so delicious! The soup is sweet and cool.

The clarity of the water does not guarantee that it has no impurities. At first, we drank water from the stream without thinking; but now, we drink only water that has been boiled first. Stream water that has been boiled and left to cool forms a scale of bright white residue on the bottom of the pot. This phenomenon worries us. But because we have no other choice, we continue to boil rice and cook with the stream water.

Even though we are exhausted from our work during the day, we rarely go to sleep right after dusk. Though it is dark by the time we finish our dinner, the sun still has not set over the horizon. We usually finish dinner at about five o'clock, and then we make a campfire and sit around chatting, or lie around in jute-sack hammocks, which we tie up close together. There are not many mosquitos here in this jungle.

On evenings when the moon is waning, our camp is covered with a curtain of blackness that no eye can penetrate. When the moon waxes again, moonlight parts the leaves and casts its light to the ground. We can see flying squirrels, which throw themselves from tree to tree. Sometimes they eat fruits and drop them on us.

Whether the moon is waxing or waning, we always listen to the same beautiful symphony of nature: the stream flowing from shelf to shelf, *chor! chor!* Fish jumping over stones and splashing down *plik-plok!* The evening breeze blowing *woo! woo!* Leaves falling *raok-rak! prek-prok!* Grasshoppers and crickets crying *chrek! chrek!* Now and then a wild fowl cries *kok-kae-kut! kok-kae-kut!* Sometimes an owl perches nearby and hoots *tituy! tituy! tituy!* This makes us sleepy, and we fall asleep to the listless cries of these nocturnal birds.

---

[6] a type of wild edible plant (scientific name unknown)

The pleasantness of the mountains, combined with work that is not very taxing, calms and soothes our mood. We forget all about the cares of before, and we don't think about what will happen in the future. We are just over ten kilometers away from the border and freedom. But none of us thinks about that. We have children and wives who bind us here. And even though I myself have neither children nor wife, I have never considered such a solution. But the soldiers who lead our work feel differently; they are worried that we will want to flee.

One night after eating dinner, we sit around with the soldiers under a waxing moon. The soldiers urge us to focus on our revolutionary labors and not to have frivolous thoughts. The leader of the squad of soldiers tells us, "Some of our people fled into Thailand and met up with the In Tam[7] faction. Those guys are having a revolution like us, and they are also raising dams and digging canals. Because they were unable to endure the hardships, they fled back to Cambodia. The Organization arrested them and clubbed them all to death. With such people, too keep them is no gain, and to remove them is no loss."

Whether this is true or not, it causes me to ponder. Avoiding the obstacles of life is the philosophy of a desperate person. A desperate person is always dodging, constantly avoiding obstacles, an attitude that debases a person. Some people are unable to endure the labors of the mobile work units, and they flee to the cooperatives and beg to be hidden. And the cooperatives can push them wherever they like, do whatever they like to them. If you make them unhappy, they will send you right back to the mobile unit. And now you face the risk of losing your life. A number of the new people have been taken away and killed in such cases.

Because we work hard to fulfill our task, the soldiers lose their initial concerns about us. They are all young, between the ages of twenty and thirty years old. They have a trust and closeness with us, much more so than the mobile cadres, who are base people. The soldiers eat rice with us and chat with us. Sometimes they take the elephants to a village in Thmor Puok district and bring us back sugarcane and bananas to eat. At first we worried about having

---

[7] a Cambodian politician (1916–2006), briefly prime minister of the Khmer Republic (6 May 1973 to 9 December 1973), who led a short-lived rebellion against the Khmer Rouge from Thai border areas

armed men in charge of our work party; but now we see that they don't have an arrogant attitude, as the cadres back in the cooperatives do.

15 February 1977

We receive orders to return to the cooperatives after having carried out our work for more than twenty days in the mountains, where the weather is cool, and the air is fresh. All thirty of us return safely to our villages at dusk on 16 February 1977.

CHAPTER 17

Communal Meals

The wheel of history rolls forward without stopping. We pass from the Red Revolution to the Revolution of Democratic Kampuchea[1] and on to Socialism. The Organization of the Great Leap Forward declares that in 1977, Cambodia has passed into Socialism. The people must cast off all private property and take their meals collectively.

At Phnom Srok, they began to eat meals collectively back on the 30th of January. In my village they are constructing dining pavilions for each unit. (Paoy Snuol has been divided into multiple units, each one with thirty families.)

My second older sister, Oun, and her husband, who have sturdy bodies, were deployed on a mobile work unit to the Trapeang Thmor Reservoir dam construction site in the beginning of February. As for my oldest sister Ol, who has a small frame and little strength, she continues to work in the village with her husband.

Because of the new plan for common meals, my bundle with my clothing, spoon, knife, and hatchet, my inheritance from my parents, were collected and given away to my unit while I was away working in the mountains. All I have left are a rice bowl, a soup bowl, a spoon, and a metal dish which I had carried with me. Actually, the base people did not have their possessions gathered up and taken away as we new people did; their cupboards are still as full as before.

Because I return to the village after they have already gathered forces to raise the dam, I am destined to work in the village. At first, I participate in building the unit's dining pavilion, which is going up in my village just west of the hut where I live. After that, they assign me to fish for the unit along with Father Lun and Father Pov, my former leaders on the straw team.

Every morning Father Lun and Father Pov carry one fishing net apiece on their backs and lead the way. I follow behind with a cage and a bundle of rice on my back. We cast our nets into the natural ponds in the plain west of the village. It is a large plain, stretching as far as the eye can see, with no trees growing on it.

---

[1] *Democratic Kampuchea* was the official English name of Cambodia under the Khmer Rouge. (The word *Cambodia* is simply the common Anglicized form of the Khmer word *Kampuchea*, the latter form being preferred by the Khmer Rouge regime.)

They may be old, but these two men are very fast. Sometimes I have to run to keep up with them.

Fishing with nets in this region is quite different from fishing in the river country. They cast the nets without holding on to an attached rope. Then they sit in the water and press down the edges of the net, then lie down side-by-side in the water and grab fish. Because there are too many people living in this area, fish are hard to find.

In the dry season, the natural ponds dry up and are only knee-deep or so. The water is cloudy because so many people are casting nets, chasing fish, and hooking *chhlonh*[2] fish. We leave one pond and look for another one about two or three kilometers away. We search for fish from the morning until about three o'clock, and then return to the village.

After returning from the mountains, I am plumper than I have ever been before. My thighs bulge and rub together, which makes it hard to walk. Every day we walk about fifteen to twenty kilometers. After walking like this for a week, my thighs are rubbed raw and painful, and I am not able to keep up with the older men. I ask to take a break from fishing.

I receive a new job: building and maintaining dikes in the rice paddies west of the village. I work with my oldest sister and her husband. I meet a young childless widow. Her husband, who had been a military officer, was taken away by the Organization for reeducation and disappeared. Her name is A-Mum, the daughter of Dr. Keo Chea. About twenty years old, A-Mum has a lovely figure and appearance. Unlike Dary, who is a sober girl, A-Mum has a carefree disposition. She likes to joke around and laugh. Sometimes she sings while she works; this is her natural personality. A-Mum likes to sing the song "*Aimer Bong Teuo*,"[3] and with this habit she is able to dispel all the worries that she faces. My sister feels sorry for and likes A-Mum, and she pushes me to request her hand in marriage. I also pity and fancy A-Mum. However, it is not my desire to have a wife and children under these circumstances.

During this time, I meet educated people experiencing deprivation for the first time. No matter how much we like or respect one another, we very rarely

---

[2] *Macrognathus siamensis*

[3] "*Aimer* [French: Love] Me," a 1973 pop song written by Voy Hor and sung by Meas Samon

dare to ask each other anything, or to directly disclose that "I used to do this or that," or "I have such-and-such an education." This is a matter of life and death. Instead, we get to know each other by chatting, analyzing some problem or idea. As the French proverb says, *"Dis-moi qui tu hantes, je te dirai qui tu es!"*[4]

Bong Det, a man in his forties, is a former professor at Lycée Descartes.[5] His wife, Teacher Malis, was also a professor. Bong Det had been sent by the Organization to a reeducation camp. He works soberly and diligently. He might be under observation by the Organization.

Bong Det and his wife are sent by the Organization to be reeducated again in the middle of 1977, leaving behind two small children with their grandmother, after they find out that Teacher Malis's younger sister, Makara, was a former military police officer by means of a name tag and a pay stub. They execute Makara at a canal worksite in Spean Sreng subdistrict, then arrest Bong Det and his wife afterward.

The life of an intellectual, especially those who had worked in the Old Society, is very precarious. No matter how dumb or deaf, no matter how much they forge themselves and work hard, they are still labeled as an exploiter and a member of the exploiting class. I am unable to understand the ideas behind this revolution. The Organization boasts that they have done so much with their bare hands. The Glorious and Enlightened Organization, the Great Leap Forward. They can say whatever they like because we, the listeners, don't dare to ask questions or object. Now the Organization is taking automobile and motorcycle engines and turning them into water pumps. The Organization is truly very clever!

---

[4] "Tell me who you haunt, I'll tell you who you are!"
[5] a prominent French-language *lycée* (high school) in Phnom Penh

Part Three: Trapeang Thmor Reservoir

CHAPTER 18

Trapeang Thmor Reservoir

West of Paoy Char subdistrict, there is a vast, treeless plain of rice fields. This plain stretches westward to Ta Sok and Ta Vong villages of Ponley subdistrict. It extends northward to the forest around Phnom Kon Khlaeng.

Father Lun and Father Pov have told me that this plain is a large drainage basin for the Tonle Sap Lake. Some years, they would travel to Ta Phraya (in Thailand), and the ground would be completely dry. Then two or three days later, on their return, they would be wading through water up to their knees. The water flows down from the mountains and mixes here on this plain. When the water would flow down from time to time, foaming white, the villagers would rush to fetch their cattle, carts, plows, and harrows to dry land and barely make it in time.

Last year, when I came to Paoy Snuol, I was sent to transplant rice seedlings at Ta Kuy.[1] One evening we were plowing and harrowing and transplanting seedlings in water that was ankle deep. In the morning, the fields were completely full of water, covering the seedlings. Comrade Khan (a base person from Paoy Char village) and I were directed to take a boat to collect the seedling bundles which had floated away and washed up against the Ta Vong causeway. The water was up to our knees, and in some places above our knees. The Ta Vong causeway was flooded over in some spots. The flooding happened while the villagers were fast asleep.

In the rainy season, Paoy Char subdistrict has a lot of water, but in the dry season it is very dry. Water is found only in natural ponds far out in the fields, or in man-made ponds near the village containing small amounts of water, not guaranteed to be suitable for use. The ground here is stony and hard to dig wells in, and if you do manage to dig one, it dries up in the dry season.

Because there is a lack of water every dry season, the locals have a custom of digging "pound wells": The water in the natural ponds is shallow and muddy and can't be used, so the villagers dig small holes near the edges of a pond about the size of a sugar jar, or a little larger. Then they scoop up some water and fill the holes between halfway and nearly full. Then they stand and pound the

---

[1] Author's note: "The rice fields west of Paoy Char and north of the Ta Vong causeway (a road crossing the fields, connecting Paoy Char and Ta Vong villages)."

water two or three times with a wooden post about the size of a rice pestle. They let the water settle for a while, and then they scoop it out and use it. West of Paoy Snuol there is a natural pond called "Pound Well Pond."

The soil in this plain has lost its fertility because the water flows through it every year. After digging only one or two strokes with a hoe, we see dirt mixed with fine gravel. If this situation continues for another twenty or thirty years, this plain will no longer be able to support crops.

Now the solution to natural erosion and the lack of water has arrived: the Organization lays out a plan to build the Trapeang Thmor Reservoir. Constructing the dams for the Trapeang Thmor Reservoir is now the major project for Region Five of the Northwestern Zone.

As the terrain slopes downward from west to east, and from north to south, the dams must be built east-west and north-south. The two dams are to meet at a place called Spean Reap, located about a kilometer west of Paoy Char subdistrict, between Trapeang Thmor and Paoy Ta Ong villages.

The east-west dam is to be built along an ancient road, with laterite stone slabs from a stone railing tipped over and lying about in places. This dam terminates at Ponley village, Ponley subdistrict. Spean Reap is an ancient, collapsed bridge built from laterite stone. The old folks say that this ancient road connected the Banteay Chhmar temple in Thmor Puok district with the temples at Angkor. Why are they erasing this ancient road?

The north-south dam is to be constructed nearly a kilometer behind Paoy Ta Ong, Sambuor, Pongro, and Suong villages (I have never been to this last village) terminating at Phnom Kon Khlaeng.[2] The size of the dams will depend on the lay of the land. At the junction, the dams will curve, especially the east-west dam, which is to have a base about sixty to a hundred meters wide, a top about fifteen meters wide, and about seven meters tall.

There are to be three water gates (which during this time are called *bridges*): the first water gate, second water gate, and third water gate. These gates are to be built into the east-west dam about three kilometers apart. Coming from the three gates will be three canals to deliver the water to irrigate the fields in

---

[2] Though this is the name of an actual hill (see page 216) somewhat distant from the northern end of the dam, the forested wilderness surrounding the hill for some distance was also colloquially dubbed Phnom Kon Khlaeng. This is the sense in which the term is primarily used in this book, referring to the wilderness region and not necessarily the hill itself.

Phnom Srok and Preah Netr Preah districts. These canals will have bottoms three meters wide, tops fifteen meters wide, and depths of one meter. According to the plan, the reservoir can hold about 300 million cubic meters of water. This project is planned to span three years: 1977, 1978, and 1979. (The details of the plan are written in white paint on a large green chalkboard displayed above the office of the regional mobile committee.)

More than 30,000 people from the four districts of Region Five (Phnom Srok, Preah Netr Preah, Thmor Puok, and Svay Sisophon) participate in the project. Numerous shelters, covered with palm fronds or thatch grass, about thirty-by-five meters in size, are constructed in rows south of the ancient road, about 150 meters from where the dam is to be raised, and in the plain west of Paoy Ta Ong. These structures have roof awnings protruding about a meter above the ground. In the shelters there are two rows of sleeping platforms raised about forty centimeters above the ground along the length of the shelter, and a walkway down the middle about a meter wide. These platforms are topped with strips of wood or bamboo. There are walls only at the ends. The shelters are all aligned east-to-west.

The worksite begins operation on the 15th of February. But the workforce is traveling and arriving in waves. Some arrive on foot, and others on trucks or trailers pulled by tractors. Each worker has his or her own set of work equipment: one hoe for digging, one shoulder yoke pole, and one pair of *bangky* baskets. Each district and each subdistrict is responsible for supplies to construct shelters. The regional Organization provides rice, salt, dried fish, *prahok*, sugar, Chinese-made Chicken-brand hoe blades, and, occasionally, to-bacco or cigarettes.

The regional mobile committee's office is located near Spean Reap. In the first phase, the work begins near this office, where the dam turns, and proceeds along the east-west part of the dam, the most crucial part.

The workforce participating in this project includes:

The regional mobile brigade: Divided into the young men's unit, young women's unit, and children's unit, the regional mobile brigade is an orderly unit with strict discipline. The members of this brigade never have the opportunity to visit their parents in the villages. They are the spearhead unit, always sent into any worksite where a large-scale offensive has been launched in Region Five. This brigade wears all-black uniforms, has abundant food rations, and has quality medicines for treating illness. The people in this brigade have robust health.

The regional mobile brigade is led by a cadre about forty years old, of medium height, with a thin frame, called Ta Val. Ta Val is a man who is very focused on the work, and the members of the brigade adore and respect him greatly. They often call these units "Ta Val's brigade" or "Ta Val's mobile brigade."

District mobile units: These are divided into a young men's mobile unit, a young women's mobile unit, and a middle-aged mobile unit.

The youth mobile units are also orderly units, but they are under the direct supervision of the district Organization and fulfill their work under the auspices of the district. They have fairly strict discipline as well, and also offer little opportunity to visit the villages. They have black uniforms, but not a lot of clothing. As for food rations and health, they are not as well cared for as the regional mobile units. My younger brother Samorn is a member of Phnom Srok district's young men's mobile unit. We have never seen him since we first moved to Paoy Snuol.

The middle-aged mobile unit is composed of people with spouses, or who are widows or widowers, but who are not yet elderly. This is not an orderly force. When there is a project, they are assembled and sent out on mobile duty; and when the work is done, they return to the villages. They are disorganized and not very disciplined, with mixed-color clothing, carrying pots and kettles around with them, clanking and clacking wherever they go. I am a member of this unit. The Organization does not issue black clothing to this unit. If clothes are provided, they are a white shirt and white pants. Sometimes they distribute two-meter-long sheets of white cloth for making into *kramas* or blankets, which is always rough cloth. Not everybody gets a full set of clothes; some get a shirt, some get trousers, and others get the white cloth. So that the clothes do not wear out too quickly, we strip pieces of bark from trees such as *pring*, *mchey*, or *kandaol*[3] and boil them, then soak the clothes in the water and hang them to dry three or four times, finally trampling them in mud. They're not

---

[3] *Careya sphaerica*

black, but rather a dark reddish-brown, and the cloth is thick from the resin of the trees. I love the black uniforms because the cloth is thin and light, mostly fine cotton or mixed-synthetic fabric, but it is not my fate to wear such clothes.

Uniquely, Phnom Srok district, for the occasion of launching the offensive to build the reservoir, selects people from the middle-aged unit with sturdy frames and solid strength for the creation of another unit called the *special unit*. The special unit of Phnom Srok district is led by a cadre who is a base person from Paoy Char village, called Pov. He is a sturdy man of medium height, about forty years old. People refer to the special unit as "Mea[4] Pov's Unit." This unit wages battle fiercely and has strict discipline. They wear black clothing like the district's youth mobile units.

In the regular middle-aged units, the men must dig and haul three cubic meters of dirt per person per day, and the women must dig and haul two cubic meters per person per day. Meanwhile, in the special unit, the men must do four cubic meters per day and the women three. My sister[5] and her husband, who are both strong and sturdy, are in the special unit.

The chairman in command of the site is usually referred to as Bong Yon, but I have never seen his face. Phnom Srok district, especially Paoy Char subdistrict, are the owners of the reservoir, so a large portion of the workforce is gathered from there.

29 March 1977

Ta Lam, chairman of the Paoy Char subdistrict committee, gives orders to gather more supplementary forces from the subdistrict to help build the reservoir. This time, they gather everyone of sound body, men and women, old and young, except for those base people who work on the economy team or who have small children. (The new people have no small children. If they had children, they have died by now; and if they don't have any yet, now they can't.)

Now it is my turn to go mobile again. From all of Paoy Char subdistrict they have assembled sixty people, young and old. At nine o'clock in the morning we

---

[4] This word means the same thing as Pu (Uncle), and was also an honorific, egalitarian term of address for mid-level cadres under the Khmer Rouge.

[5] Oun

gather in an open field near the cart road west of Paoy Char village to take instructions from Ta Lam before going to the battlefield.

Ta Lam boasts of building a hydroelectric dam and turning this region into
a city. He concludes by saying that our force is the core force, a select unit, and
that even when the dams and reservoir are completed, we will not be disbanded
back to the village.

The new supplementary forces assembled from all of Phnom Srok district
are not combined with the old forces, but remain separate under the command
of Ta Lam, both in labor and in distribution of food. Ta Lam also personally
leads the supplementary unit from Paoy Char subdistrict. That's why my unit's
camp is the food distribution site for all of the supplementary forces of Phnom
Srok district.

In my unit there are twenty men and young men. Subtracting four for transporting equipment and distributing food, with one to lead the children's team,
that leaves only sixteen men to wage the battle. The children's unit has seventeen children. There are twenty-six women and young women. We work separately, not combined as when we dug the Or Roessei canal: the men and young
men, the women and young women, and the children.

The Organization divides the length of the dam into sections and assigns
them to each district and to Ta Val's mobile brigade. The districts further sub-
divide their sections into subsections for each unit.

Ta Val's brigade is the spearhead force in charge of the area around Spean
Reap, where the east-west and north-south dams connect, and where the first
bridge (the first water gate) is to be constructed. Continuing westward from Ta
Val's brigade (along the east-west dam) are the forces of Phnom Srok, Preah
Netr Preah, Svay Sisophon, and Thmor Puok districts. Continuing northward
from Ta Val's brigade (along the north-south dam) are the supplementary
forces of Phnom Srok district.

On this occasion, I run into a girl from my high school class named But
Bunroat. Her family had twelve members and was a well-off family in Phnom
Penh. Since then, her parents and ten of her siblings all died in the Tan Tonghan

cooperative.[6] These days she and her youngest brother are the only ones left and are living with locals in Paoy Char village.

When she was still in school, Bunroat had a warm brown skin tone, and was thin and lovely, attracting the eyes of her male classmates and other fellow high-school students. Now, a young woman in her twenties, Bunroat has the body of an old woman, so thin the wind can almost knock her over. Her health is poor, yet the cooperative sent her to haul dirt along with her younger brother. Bunroat works here for a brief time, and then requests to go rest at the hospital. She dies there not long after.

Because my unit arrives at the worksite just as they are launching the offensive of the Great Leap Forward,[7] we have no opportunity to collect materials to build shelters. We have only an economy shed for storing food supplies and for cooking. The workers, both male and female, sleep out in the open. We work exposed to the heat of the day, eat in the heat of the day, and sleep in the dew.

Taking small opportunities during the rest hour, we divide up and go searching for small trees and fronds to craft a shelter for shade. Even coconut fronds are hard to find these days. We build a shelter with a form like a trellis for growing gourds, with only tree branches and leaves crisscrossed on top for cover. We have shade for eating our meals, and posts for tying hammocks, but there isn't a roof for sheltering from the rain.

One night, after eating our evening meal, the wind blows *woo! woo!*, the lightning strikes *crack! crack!*, and the thunder rumbles *boom! boom!* A mid-dry-season rainstorm begins to drop large raindrops. We are not unlike monkeys (after all, the locals do call us "hooters"[8]), as we have a shelter but cannot escape the rain. We hug our bundles tightly and scatter our separate ways to find places to take shelter. Three or four children who have poor night vision walk clinging to me. We enter a sleeping shelter belonging to some young women, when suddenly a young cadre, who has tied his nylon hammock in the

---

[6] see page 128

[7] The Great Leap Forward was the name of the party's aggressive four-year plan to triple national rice production to three tons per hectare, focusing heavily on the Northwestern Zone. (Large irrigation projects like this one were a key part of this overambitious plan.)

[8] Khmer *a-voch*, which refers to the hooting sounds made by monkeys

walkway through the middle of the shelter and is now resting there, chases us away.

"Hey! This is a young women's shelter! You can't take shelter here, it's *immoral!* Get out of here!"

My God! He accuses us of being immoral just for seeking shelter from the rain!

What exactly is this *morality*? He is a young man lying in his hammock and chatting away with the girls in the young women's sleeping shelter, and this is moral! We have only requested to take shelter on a spot of ground near the doorway, and this is immoral!

Oh, Morality! Why must you be so picky? *No, you may not, the penalty for immorality is death, and you must leave!* If we go here: *immoral*, there: *immoral!* By the time we find a proper place to take shelter, our clothing bundles and hammocks have become completely soaked with rain.

It rains for two hours before stopping. We sleep soaking wet, and in the morning we have to go to work as usual, the same as those who managed a decent night's sleep.

CHAPTER 19

Sixteen Hour Days

In the beginning, not having organized a proper management system yet, and lacking experience, the Organization divides up the work by individual allotment: each man must dig and haul three cubic meters of dirt per day, while the women and children do two cubic meters apiece per day. Whatever unit completes its allotment is allowed to rest. The women's and children's units, as well as the men's units, wage fierce battle and are usually able to rest by sundown. At night we resume work together, without individual allotments, from seven to ten o'clock. The workers then have adequate time left over to rest, stretch out their backs, and get some sleep.

But then we reach the Great Leap Forward offensive, and the mode of working changes. When the work first began, only Ta Val's brigade and the district young men's and young women's units kept working twenty-four hours per day. They would take shifts both day and night, one unit up and another down. But starting in early April, all of the units begin to work both day and night, and there are no more individual allotments.

We eat three times per day:

- At six o'clock in the morning we eat in the dirt pit. The economy team carries our rice and soup to us on shoulder yokes. We take a break for about fifteen minutes to eat our meal. (We take our break when the economy team arrives; there is no rule that we must stop at exactly six o'clock.) After eating, those who smoke have an opportunity to roll a cigarette and smoke it, while those who do not must return to work.

- At midday we come up out of the pit to eat in the camp. The schedule does not dictate whether we stop at eleven or twelve o'clock, but the allotted time is one hour. After that we must return to the pit.

- In the evening we return to eat at the camp for an hour, the same as midday. After that we must return to the pit to work according to the nighttime duty schedule.

In one day and night there are three shifts. In my unit, the men and women take turns working at night. Because of this, the working hours are not the same. The men start work at six o'clock in the morning and continue until eleven or noon, then take a lunch break. In the afternoon we work from twelve or one o'clock and take a dinner break at six o'clock. At night we work from ten o'clock until three in the morning. We have two chances to sleep at night, from seven to nine thirty, and again from three thirty to five thirty in the morning. In total, in one day and one night, the men work for sixteen hours and sleep for four and a half hours.

The women begin work at four o'clock in the morning and work until eleven o'clock or noon. In the afternoon they work from noon or one o'clock until six o'clock. At night they work from seven to ten o'clock. The women sleep only once per night, from ten thirty at night until three thirty in the morning. In total, in one day and one night the women work for sixteen hours and sleep for five hours.

The Sun opens his hood in the east and spits his bright red venom to heat the earth. The birds startle and chatter loudly, flying in pairs, swarming in flocks, with joy at the stunning beauty of the spring sunrise. At the same time, the workers at the Trapeang Thmor Reservoir worksite are not joyful, and they are not startled at the beauty of the scene created by the sun's rays this morning. This remarkable scene makes us worried, afraid, fearful of the power of the heat that will scorch our skin in the middle of the day and the afternoon. With such a clear sunrise, the heat is bound to be intense. The circumstances of such intense sunlight instill in us fear and hatred, as though we were ghosts or vampires who dread the sun. But we cannot escape, we cannot get away from it. We think only of digging dirt, hauling dirt, without thought of darkness or light. Even in the darkness we do not sleep , and even in the light we don't rest. Day and night! Night and day! It's only a change of time, but our work remains, digging and carrying dirt, without change.

In the dark of night while the sun slumbers, the worksite teems with activity. Tens of thousands of hoes chop and break up the surface of the earth. Countless workers, like ants or termites, don't shrink from the darkness of night, but bend their backs to carry dirt and pile it onto dams.

Faint, clear light along the eastern horizon is only a sign to us that the sun will soon rise, that it *is* rising, but it does *not* tell us that our breasts will soon be clear of worry, or that our bodies will be freed from the miserable, grueling toil!

When the sky is bright and clear, the economy team (cooks) carry rice and water to us at the edge of the pit. During the transplanting season, we were so hungry for rice. We wanted to eat rice so badly! The word *rice* would make our mouths water like dogs that have seen a piece of meat. But now, the word *rice* has a different meaning, a bitter flavor. If they weren't afraid that we wouldn't have the strength to dig and haul dirt, we wouldn't have rice to eat. Now they give us abundant rice. Leftover rice is thrown out because the economy team doesn't even have time to dry it.[1]

But it isn't rice for which we hunger now, it is sleep. We can't get enough sleep. But nothing is up to us to decide. We have neither time nor rights to think about anything. The Revolutionary Organization is the one who does the thinking, who resolves everything. We have only our strength to do the labor, and that is sufficient for them; they are content with that.

We drop our hoes, baskets, and yoke poles in one spot, and then we each untie our own bags and take out our bowls and spoons, dish up our rice, and sit around the soup pot and try to swallow, try to chew, but without heart, and without daring to prolong the moment.

We can barely finish eating the rice before we must rush to pick up our hoes and baskets and get back to work right away. The Organization tells us, "People can rest, but the hoes, *bangky* baskets, and yokes must never rest!" Dear God! Each person has one hoe, one yoke pole, and one set of *bangky* baskets. If a person rests, how is the equipment supposed to keep moving? This kind of language makes us all shrink in fear, not daring to rest or take time to eat.

It's not only the unit cadres who watch over us personally and supervise our work activities; clandestine *chhlops* from the region work among our units as well. Their presence intimidates us, and we work hard without daring to converse with one another. They come to assess our mentality toward the work and toward the leadership of the Party. Every thoughtless utterance which they perceive to be an objection to the Revolution is a danger to our lives. They can take you away without even telling you what you have done wrong. They take you away secretly. Only the people in your unit will know that you have been taken away to be killed; other units will have no idea.

How many people have already been taken away and killed at this worksite? Nobody knows. My older sister tells me to be cautious. A few people have already died in the special unit just for saying, "Gee, this rice looks a bit spoiled."

---

[1] Leftover rice is commonly spread out to dry for use as animal feed.

They were dragged away immediately and clubbed to death beside the base of the dam.

The economy unit rises to cook the rice in the middle of the night. They cook a pot and dump it into a large basket, then another and another. Because the earlier rice and the later rice are all piled together, sometimes this causes it to take on a sour, spoiled smell. Saying that the rice is spoiled means that you are not pleased with the Party, that you are hindering the work of the Revolution.

The fragility of life fills us all with terror! Each of us works to appease Yama so that he will spare us to live another day.

We divide the strength of our unit into two teams: the team that digs the dirt and scrapes it into *bangky* baskets, and the team that hauls the dirt with shoulder yokes to dump it onto the dam. The diggers try to dig and fill the baskets quickly enough to keep up with the haulers so that they are not left standing and waiting. The haulers run in single file to keep up with the diggers so that there are no leftover baskets. Sometimes we haul yokes with two baskets of dirt per side, and sometimes three. My unit works beside Ta Val's young women's unit. Men working beside women are especially strong. We race them in hauling the dirt, and Ta Val's women work so mightily they can hold their own against the young men. We haul the dirt running, single file, as though we don't know how to be tired. In fact, we are tired, but we have to do it this way. If we don't run, we hinder the momentum of others, and if we don't run it's difficult to make it up the slope from the base of the dam.

We take turns being the digging team and the hauling team. The digging team strain their hands and chest, while the hauling team strain their legs and shoulders. The dirt here in the Trapeang Thmor area is not easy to dig, as it is full of small bits of gravel. If you swing your hoe and strike with all your might, the head only bites in about halfway. Our hands on both sides are calloused and raw from struggling against the hoe handle. With each stroke the hoe vibrates you all the way to your chest, and your chest hurts. Everybody has a sore chest. The haulers don't get their chests jarred and don't get calluses on their hands, but their calves and thighs ache, and their shoulders are raw, and their knees hurt. We frequently switch our yokes between our left and right shoulders. But a shoulder that is unaccustomed to a yoke has difficulty, as the pole doesn't quite fit snugly on the shoulder as it does on one which is accustomed. I am used to carrying a yoke only on my left shoulder, so I am not as strong when using my right shoulder.

We haul at a run, both going and coming. There is no strolling to count blades of grass here, and nobody slackens their activity. Those who smoke are allowed to take some breaks to roll and smoke cigarettes, but those who don't smoke have no excuse for stopping or standing around. Nobody stands around with their chins resting on their yoke pole or their hoe handle. If the diggers can't move the dirt fast enough, the haulers can't just stand still and wait; they must help scrape the dirt into the baskets in order to quickly haul it away. If a *chhlop* ever stares right into your face, you get very worried.

Even if we have to relieve ourselves, we don't dare to spend much time on it. The latrines are built near the sleeping shelters way over yonder, and the work-site has no latrines. We all defecate and urinate in the open area on the interior of the reservoir. The young women, men, women, and children all stick their butts out and defecate here and there, with *preet proot* sounds all mingling together. Nobody dares to look at anybody else, nobody laughs at anybody, and nobody is ashamed of anybody. We are all the same beasts of Hell. If you feel shame, then you have to walk far away. If you walk far away and take a long time to poo, or poo often, then you come under suspicion, and the Organization will say that you have "consciousness" issues, that you are too lazy to work. If you are too lazy to work, the Organization says, "To keep you is no gain, to remove you is no loss," and the Organization will take you away and club you to death. Actually, we Life Slaves don't dare be lazy, as we are afraid to die. We do whatever they want us to, so long as they don't kill us.

At noon they call us up from the pit to eat. At lunch and dinner we have to eat at camp. We each collect our baskets, yokes, and hoes and carry them over our shoulders toward camp. Actually, after eating we will have to come back and work in the same spot, but we don't dare leave our equipment behind, as we fear it will be stolen, either for keeps or for trading.

Hoes with sharp blades and flexible handles help to conserve your strength when digging. A flexible yoke pole helps to ease the weight and makes it easier to run while hauling. A nice *bangky* basket and a good set of *bangky* ropes help you to work quickly. The most valuable objects for our lives at this time are hoes, *bangky* baskets, and yoke poles. We care for them as a soldier cares for his rifle. When we sleep, we place them near our bodies. If you lose them, you lose your life. The Organization will accuse you of "hindering the progress of the Revolution," and then your life is over.

As soon as we reach the camp and stash our hoes and baskets, we grab our bowls and spoons and go to eat our meal right away. There is nothing delicious, I assure you! We come from work huffing and puffing, soaked in sweat, soiled with dirt, to eat our rice in the middle of the heat of the day, without washing our faces or our hands and feet. Water is very scarce! Water is found only in a pond in the *wat* and at the Trapeang Thmor brick-kiln pond. The distance from my camp to there is about two kilometers. Back when we worked by the cubic meter, we could take an opportunity to go and bathe from time to time. Now, though, it is rough. Very rough! There isn't even water to splash on your face when you rise from sleep in the morning. The Organization transports water for distribution, two jerrycans per unit, to use for washing vegetables, cooking, and drinking for twenty-four hours.

For more than a week, we don't see any water for washing ourselves. We sleep dirty, we eat dirty, we eat in the heat of the day, we eat competing with the flies. The latrines are forty or fifty meters from camp. In the hot months, the flies are everywhere! Flies with red heads, flies that swarm the shit, then swarm our soup, black and thick like a queen bee. If you fan them away and you fan too hard, the flies fall into the rice and soup bowls.

Our daily food is boiled dried fish with *phty* greens, collard greens, or cabbage. Sometimes there are no vegetables, or no fish, and there is broth made of *prahok* and salt. This food is not difficult for the economy team to cook: a ladleful of *prahok* and a ladleful of salt boiled in a large pot of water.

When we ate porridge, we dreamed of rice. We thought rice with salt would be so delicious. But now that we eat rice every day, three times per day, we start to dream of the food to go with it. Without the food we can barely swallow the rice. We can't just eat rice with a lump of salt like we used to before because now we expend tremendous amounts of energy every day. We need soup broth to relax our throats and ease our swallowing. We need fish and meat to replenish the energy that we lose working.

But even when there *is* beef or dried fish, there is really nothing special. When we eat our meals, we stick our spoons into the soup dish and stir around, but rarely encounter a piece of meat or fish. The economy team members hoard it all to support themselves and the cadres, and they send it back to their own families in the villages.

It's true: if a chicken nests in the paddy, it will eat the rice!

In the meeting held to celebrate the second anniversary of the April 17th victory and the anniversary of Democratic Kampuchea, held at the Trapeang Thmor worksite on 17 April 1977, Om Mul Sambath, chairman of the Northwestern Zone committee, gives a speech:

"The senior leaders of the Organization are very mindful of how the people are living here, brothers and sisters. The Organization has provided food, clothing, and equipment to distribute to you all in turn. But the lower Organization leaders, such as the cooperative chairmen, the unit leaders, and the economy team leaders, have been embezzling them, hiding them for their own use and that of their own families. Comrades, do not hesitate to expose these people and pull them down from their positions.

"...Kapok[2] pods and kapok cotton are very valuable, comrades. As a foreign export, kapok cotton has a higher price than anything else! Everybody, plant kapok trees!"[3]

Who would dare protest this guidance? The Life Masters have tremendous power. Whomever they choose to arrest can be taken away and killed. They instruct us to expose the embezzlers, but then they tell us to plant kapok trees. Which of these instructions should we take as our focus?

When we work, we sweat. When we eat, we sweat. Sweat soaks our clothes until they become stiff. The rice has barely left our mouths before we stretch out and try to catch a couple winks of sleep.

The day grows so hot that the air appears to smoke. If you look at the fields in the distance, you see the Sun walking her children.[4] The wind blows now and then and stirs up the dust into the air. The birds fly off looking for shade in the trees, and the oxen and water buffalo raise their heads and look off into the distance and head off to find pond water to drink and wallow in. The chickens, ducks, dogs, and cats all nap in the villages. Oddest of all are the human ani-

---

[2] a tree with pods filled with fluffy white fibers similar to cotton, used to make cloth and as filling for pillows and mattresses (among other things)

[3] "Plant a kapok tree" was a common saying during this time with a double meaning. The Khmer word for kapok, *ko*, also means "mute" so that planting a kapok tree is a euphemism for keeping one's mouth shut.

[4] a Khmer idiom referring to visible heat waves in the distance on a hot day

mals, the Life Slaves, assembled together with their hoes and yokes over their shoulders, filing in orderly rows toward the steaming hot worksite, which they have only left an hour before.

Only Ta Val's brigade and the district young women's and young men's units wear uniforms consisting of a matching set of a long-sleeved black shirt and a pair of long-legged black trousers. As for our "hooter" (monkey) unit, we wear mixed clothing cobbled together as we are able. Some people have both trousers and a shirt, and others wear only long trousers or shorts with a bare torso. If you wear a shirt, the yoke will quickly wear through the shoulder of the shirt and rip it.

The sloping base of the dam on the inside of the reservoir slopes gradually for a long distance, so that we can haul dirt and run up it to the top of the dam. The slope on the other side is very steep, and it is not easy to haul dirt up it to the top of the dam. We haul the dirt for a distance of only about fifty or sixty meters from the pit to the base of the dam. When we climb up the dam, we have to walk carefully and slowly, step by step. We make stairs from small logs laid crossways along the side of the dam and haul the dirt up one step at a time or dig the dirt itself into narrow stairs up the side of the dam. Hiking up a mountain with just yourself is already difficult enough; so how much more difficult is it to haul a whole yoke full of dirt up a steep slope like this? Our *bangky* baskets are all large enough that twelve or thirteen yokes yields about a cubic meter of dirt. We never dare to fill our baskets less than completely full. Rather, we fill them all the way and then tamp the dirt down tight so that it doesn't spill out along the path. But because we do this every day, and we build the height a little at a time, from low to seven meters tall, we gradually become used to it, and we are able to do it, however difficult.

The muscles and tendons in our heels, arms, and shoulders are tight and firm and pop out from our flesh. Our muscles grow hard and sweat covers our faces, soaks our backs, and shines brightly in the sunshine. Our toes and knees work hard to support the weight and push our bodies, which are bent over supporting the yokes of dirt, up the slope to the top. They are so heavy! And it is so hot we feel like we are about to suffocate! As we reach the top of the dam, our chests relax, and we stand taking deep breaths to take in the breeze that blows from afar, filling our lungs with it, and then we run back down again.

On this outer slope, once the dam grows tall, I no longer dare to haul double basket loads. Nobody else dares to try it either, except for one man whom everyone calls Ta Thang Cheng. Ta Thang Cheng is a man over thirty years old, a member of the middle-aged supplementary mobile unit from Srah Chik sub-district in Phnom Srok district. He has dark skin and a stocky build, a small head, and large arms and legs covered with muscles, with a large, thick neck and thick shoulders. He mostly wears a pair of shorts and no shirt. He is the sole person who carries the largest yoke on the worksite, with a volume of about half a cubic meter per yoke. (Some people in the special unit carry yokes with a volume of a quarter of a cubic meter per yoke.) When the dam reaches a height of seven meters, he also starts to relax his load and doesn't pack it so tight. But we keep making bets with him. If he can carry a yoke with full baskets, packed tight, to the top of the dam, he gets a cigarette. (The Organization distributes a pack of cigarettes to each person.) Ta Thang Cheng is not afraid to make a bet with someone; he lets them trample the dirt down and pack it as tightly as they like. However packed it gets, he still always manages to haul the dirt to the top of the dam without so much as a pause halfway. When he reaches the top, we applaud and cheer and give him cigarettes to smoke.

Constantly sweating under the heat of the blazing *Chetr*[5] sun makes us very thirsty. We need to drink water frequently. But unfortunately, drinking water is not plentiful. Water transported by truck to Phnom Srok or Spean Thom is saved for cooking; water for drinking at the worksite has to be managed on our own. Every unit appoints one person to go and haul drinking water. At the Trapeang Thmor brick-kiln pond can be seen a crowd of black heads lining up to fetch a yoke full of water. It takes an hour to an hour-and-a-half to haul a single yoke full of water to the worksite. Only the women's units are able to get a full two buckets of water to the pit because the men don't take any from them. As for the men's or young men's units, by the time the water arrives at the worksite, the buckets are only half full. People along the road constantly run up and ask for a drink, and the hauler can't get away.

Our work is hardest from about one o'clock to four o'clock in the afternoon. Our stomachs are still busy digesting our food, the sun is at maximum heat, and the air is still and nearly windless. After that, the heat of the sun

---

[5] lunar calendar month from roughly mid-March to mid-April

begins to diminish as the light slowly fades and a light refreshing breeze drifts in, helping to revive the energy of the workers who are starting to weaken, giving them the ability to fight on until evening when they finish their daily labor.

The moment the sun sets, we walk to camp, where dinner is waiting for us. It is nice to have food waiting as soon as you leave work, but it's just a bit difficult to eat. On nights when the moon is bright, we are fortunate, as we can see our rice bowls and the soup bowl; but on moonless nights, we hear only the sound of spoons hitting against the sides of the soup bowl. We don't dish it up right away, but rather stir our spoons around a bit, in case we have the good fortune to encounter a morsel of meat or fish. We fight over these, as each of us casts our net into a pond with very few fish.

It's true that the temperature at night is much cooler than in the day, but your body is still hot and muggy, itchy with dried sweat sticking to your skin, patches of dirt stuck here and there. As soon as they finish eating, the women and girls grab their hoes and baskets again and head back out to the worksite. As for we men and boys, we each find our own spot to lie down and sleep. Some of us have rice-sack hammocks to sleep on, while others have not made any such preparations. The women, especially, lay out mats or tarps and sleep right on the ground. The Organization was very thoughtful to provide shelters and sleeping platforms, except that the supplementary units, where I am, are not fortunate enough to have a shelter, and we must sleep on the ground. Actually, it's not even a big deal for us these days. We can sleep anywhere—on the dirt, on the grass, in the pit; so long as we can lie down, we fall asleep immediately. The only hard thing about it is that we don't have time to sleep.

Our eyes are closed, and we are sound asleep, when the unit leader walks around waking us to go back to work. At 9:30 p.m. we hurry to collect our equipment and depart. The unit leader carries a flashlight and walks in front, and we follow behind in a line. At night we work in a different location: we go to work in the area behind Pongro village. The distance from Paoy Ta Ong to Pongro is fairly far, nearly three kilometers. We work in the same pit as the women from our unit. When we arrive at the pit, the women head back to get some sleep. Some of us walk in a daze, sleepwalking, and only when we reach the pit do we wake up and become bright-eyed. The night is very dark, and we work under electric lights placed on poles spaced about twenty meters apart along the top of the dam, along the path down into the pit, and inside the pit. They are all fluorescent tubes sixty centimeters or a meter long.

Because it is so hot working in the middle of the day, some people get night blindness and can't see in the dark. To determine whether someone is truly night blind, on a dark night the unit leader will poke his fingers at their eyes or take them by the hand and walk them into the pit. Despite being blind, it is not their fate to be able to rest from the night labor. The Organization collects all of the night-blind people into a single team. Back when we worked by the cubic meter, the night-blind team had to work from dawn until dusk without any break. The economy team would carry their food out to them in the pit both morning and noon, as these people did not work with the others at night. But once we reach the offensive phase, the night blind have no right to rest, and must work at night along with the others. They are required to haul dirt while holding hands in a line. Their eyes may be blind, but their arms and legs and shoulders are not blind. If they were allowed to rest, how could their labor be exploited? Whether a little or a lot, fast or slow, it is better than letting them rest. These people are not able to run while hauling dirt, as those who can see do, but must take small careful steps, and sometimes if they take a wrong step out of rhythm, their feet get tangled up and the whole line falls over. Whatever you do, don't get night blindness, as there's no profit in it!

As the land behind Pongro is high, the dam here is not so tall and large as it is back at Spean Reap. In the evening the air is cool, and we don't sweat so much when we work, and we don't get so tired. But the darkness and the exhaustion and weariness from the daytime make our eyes heavy and sleepy and want to close. Your heart doesn't want to, but your eyes stop taking orders, and sometimes you fall asleep for a moment even as your feet are moving forward. When we leave camp, the economy unit is asleep and we usually take two or three bamboo tubes full of water to share for drinking, and for splashing on our faces to combat the sleepiness. But the coolness of the water only helps wake up our eyes for a brief moment. The electric lights are far enough apart that they can't illuminate the entire worksite clearly. So the muscles of our eyes have to strain much harder than in the day to see everything clearly. This is what makes our eyes get tired so quickly and want to close.

When cornered, a person, like an animal, stops thinking of death. Some nights, a number of unit leaders sneak away to take a nap. It's a good opportunity, as there is little close supervision, for the rest of us to take turns having a nap as well. The pit is about a meter deep, and you can hide in a dark corner without anyone being able to see from a distance. We sleep one or two at a time for about twenty or thirty minutes at a stretch. The diggers and the haulers keep watch to protect the sleepers.

However, we do not get good opportunities like this all the time. Some nights, a sturdy female soldier, dressed in black or sometimes olive drab, comes to help haul dirt in our unit. We have never seen her before, and we all speculate. Some say she is from Phnom Srok, while others say she is from Svay. But wherever she comes from, we must understand that this woman is our Yama.

The female soldier runs while hauling dirt and we try to keep up with her, run to keep her company, run to please her. Sweating at night, our lazy, sleepy eyes that don't want to open suddenly don't dare close, for if they close now, they will surely close forever!

The female soldier works alongside us to stop us from getting sleepy until the shift is over, when she takes her leave. We anxiously await the hour of separation, but when will it be three o'clock? The cock crows weakly in the village, which brings a surge of relief, but it's not clear that we are free yet. Every night we watch for the constellation Libra, which rises in the south. The sound of the whistle releasing us from work always sounds when the scales' arm rises above the horizon.

Whether carrying dirt or digging, we frequently look up and watch for the scales of Libra, begging the stars to rise quickly. No natural object has any consideration or compassion for us! But even if Libra were to somehow rise before the appointed time, the unit leader's wristwatch still wouldn't be as fast as the scales. In actual fact, Libra can only help indicate that the time of temporary respite from our suffering is near at hand; only the sound of the whistle piercing the veil of darkness can release us. We gather our hoes and baskets, sling them over our shoulders, and head back to camp.

We are totally worn out. If we will work at the same site again after sunrise, we lie down on top of the dam, not bothering to walk the kilometers back to camp. However fast we walk, it will take us at least half an hour to get back to camp. The economy teams are rising to cook, and the women and girls are rising to travel to their worksites. Right now, only we have the right to sleep.

At five thirty the unit leader walks around rousing us to return to work. Oh, my poor eyes! You only just closed little over an hour ago, and now you have to open again!

This daily routine repeats itself day and night, like the Earth spinning without tiring, and continues to do so for two weeks. Those with flesh on their bones like me become skinny. Those who are already skinny get even skinnier still, and their eyes become sunken.

CHAPTER 20
The Skilled Physician

In carrying out this massive endeavor, are there any sick people? Are there measures to treat the sick? The Dharma of the Buddha states *cheatek, chorea, pyeathik, moranak,* which means "birth, old age, illness, death." Is there any living creature that can escape these four forms of suffering? There are none. Therefore, there must surely be sick people, and the Organization takes care of this as well.

In the units there are medics to treat the sick and those who are unwell each day. Any cases of serious illness are sent by the Organization to the Paoy Ta Ong hospital, or to the hospital in Wat Trapeang Thmor. These two hospitals are regional hospitals, recently created at the initiation of the Trapeang Thmor Reservoir worksite. But the word *hospital* during this period of so-called revolution does not signify the treating of sick people.

A principle of the communist regime is to eliminate the parasites and those who eat but don't work. Children, the elderly, and the sick are people who are not productive, so there is little attempt to care for them. Otherwise, the sick are considered by the Organization to be lazy people, people suffering from consciousness sickness. Such people constitute about half of the people laboring here.

Patients who go to the hospital suffer torture. The food rations are reduced, there is no medicine, or only rabbit-turd medicine. You can only walk within the perimeter of the hospital, and if you leave to bathe now and then, you have to go in groups, and the medics follow and watch you like prisoners. If your sickness is mild, you'd rather endure going to work, or you ask to rest in the unit and beg not to be sent to the hospital. But now it's not like before; they don't easily send you to the hospital, unless you can't even get up to go to work, because they need your labor.

For more than the first week of work at the site, my body has not yet wasted away, and I still have a plump figure. Because the food is unsanitary, and the drinking water is unclean, one day I get diarrhea. I have diarrhea for two days straight and am unable to work, so I ask to remain at camp. I am very depressed as everyone else goes to work, and I am left to lie on a hammock tied beneath our gourd-trellis shelter, without walls, and anybody can see me.

On the second day, the diarrhea gets somewhat better, but my body is weak and devoid of strength, my ears ring, and I am confined to the hammock. Ta Lam walks by and sees me and calls out to Bong Yong, the economy team leader, "Yong! What's wrong with this fatso sleeping on the hammock?"

"He has diarrhea, Father!" Bong Yong replies to Ta Lam.

"Gee! That fat, and still sick?" Ta Lam blurts out in a mocking tone.

I shrink and lie still in the hammock and close my eyes, listening, feeling sorry for myself for having worked hard to the point of sickness, and then to be considered at fault. As for himself, he is chubby, and when he complains of sickness, it is somehow proper, it is fitting. He says he has high blood pressure. Oh well, my life is merely that of a sheep, just waiting to be found in error.

On the third day, the diarrhea is gone, but I still have no strength and my ears still ring and I cannot yet get up or walk straight without staggering. The economy team has gone to take the morning rice to the worksite and has not yet returned. The sick are left to eat last. The unit leaders walk about collecting the sick from every shelter and brings us to a meeting in a field. There are about sixty or so of us. The Organization has us sit in two separate groups, the men and the women.

We sit quietly for a while, and then Ta Lam and a female medic appear, headed toward us. I think to myself that maybe they have some actual scientific medicine to give us.

When they reach us, Ta Lam stands in front of us and asks, "All of you comrades are sick, correct?"

"Yes, Father," we all answer in unison.

Ta Lam continues: "For a while now, you have all been a bit neglected, as both I and the medics in the units have not given much attention to you comrades who are sick in the shelters, as we are busy at the worksite. You comrades lack medicine and depend on the economy teams, who have only rice and soup to treat you with.

"Today you comrades are all very fortunate, as a very Skilled Physician has come to help treat you, a doctor from the region. She can only come once every four or five days. She will divide the patients into a mild group and a serious group to make it easier to distribute the medicine. Each of you comrades will tell her your name, your unit, and your sickness so that she can write them down, and then she will treat you afterwards!"

Ta Lam finishes his introduction and then turns to speak with the unit leaders. The female medic holds a book and calls each of us one by one and writes down our names. We are all overjoyed to have a physician to treat our sicknesses. Lying still without a medic to treat us, we fear that the Organization will say that we have consciousness sickness. Each of us tells the medic our symptoms in detail. Most of us have shivering fevers, cramps, or diarrhea. Many of the women have lost their periods. After writing this in her book, the medic calls our names again and confirms our sickness. We each stand and show our face, while Ta Lam stands watching and points for us to go sit in a new spot. After calling all of our names, we are sitting in the same two groups as before, the men and the women. All except for one man who has dislocated his hip, who is sitting apart from the other groups. The unit leaders arrive with work equipment—hoes, baskets, and yokes.

Ta Lam begins to speak. "Now the division of the sick by mild and serious cases is complete. The man with the dislocated hip will return to the shelter, and for the rest of you, here is your medicine!" Ta Lam points at the hoes, baskets, and yokes and then continues speaking.

"The unit leaders will organize you into teams, appoint leaders of the sick teams to take responsibility, and lead you to measure some ground to divide up by teams for you to dig! You won't get better easily lying still!"

Good Lord! He boasted that she was a Skilled Physician, and yet she didn't examine anyone or give out any pills, but instead collected the sick to go to work.

My unit has three sick people: myself; Comrade Sae, a skinny man with a shivering fever; and Comrade Run, a plump man like me, who this morning had asked to rest and get coined,[1] but when he heard that a doctor had come to treat the sick, he came along with us.

The unit leaders divide up the ground into plots for the sick teams to work on, at a new spot beside some other workers. Those with enough strength try to raise their hoes and bring them down on the dirt and scrape the dirt into the baskets. Those who don't have enough strength carry the dirt to be dumped in pairs, one person carrying a handle on either side of a single basket. We work

---

[1] Coining is a common traditional remedy (for dizziness, headaches, fatigue, insomnia, stomachaches, and all manner of ailments) in which the patient's skin is scraped with a coin, producing dark red stripes of subcutaneous blood, on which ointment (if available) may be applied.

hard to do something, however small, as this is better than sitting still; for if we stay still, the Organization will accuse us of thwarting the path of the Revolution.

Nine o'clock passes, then ten, and the economy unit still has not brought our breakfast to us. As our stomachs are accustomed to digesting food at regular hours, when there is no food, they get upset and make us feel sick. Sick, with no food, and performing labor as well—Can we even do it? I am totally exhausted and can no longer stand, so I sit down, and a moment later I am lying down. A number of others are like me: we can't go forward; we have no more effort to expend. Even if they were to bring rice, I still wouldn't be able to work as normal. I sit looking at the ground under the hot sun, occasionally standing to help someone else carry a basket of dirt.

The unit leaders who were put in charge of us know very well that we are actually sick, but they cannot resist orders from the Organization, so they pitch in. They don't just stand there watching or bossing us around.

At about nine o'clock, something happens at the worksite which has not happened before: many people in the special unit fall on the ground and begin convulsing because of contaminated water. These people are carried away at a run, past us, to the shelters. Because water is increasingly scarce, those who have gone to fetch water have not been careful enough. They have fetched any water they could find.

We are sick, but they gather us up and make us haul dirt, while those in the special unit who are sick get carried off to sleep in the shelters. How are we different? No, no, they are sick, they are convulsing, but we are not openly convulsing, so we are faking it. It is very fortunate that the Organization has not chosen to implement its doctrine of "to keep you is no benefit, to remove you is no loss" on us. But when the end does come, we will not be afraid, and we will accept it. We, the Life Slaves, work hard to preserve our lives. But when it reaches a point where you have no more effort to expend, no more ability to fight, you slip into a pit of despair and lay down your body in surrender. At that point, if they take you away to be clubbed to death, you will no longer feel sorrow, you will no longer demand that they spare your life, for your ability to fight has fallen to zero.

At noon, the other units go to eat their lunch one by one, while the sick receive no orders, so we continue to work as we are able, sitting and standing, sitting and standing.

At nearly one o'clock, they finally allow the sick unit to come up out of the pit. When we first arrived at the pit, Comrade Run ran away to work in his regular unit. So the only ones left to carry on the fight in the sick unit are me and Comrade Sae. I am plump, but I cannot walk, and Comrade Sae is skinny, but he can walk, so he helps me walk out of the pit with an arm around my back. Afraid that we will disperse, and to stop us from returning to camp, they lead us to rest in the shade of a Bodhi tree to the south of camp about fifty meters. Comrade Sae lays me down, and I sprawl out on the ground.

Despite my plump flesh, having diarrhea for the past two days has made my body lose all of its strength. Now they lead me back to dry in the sun again, but what does my body have left to fight with? I feel sorry for myself and lie staring at the small clouds that drift across the sky and then suddenly begin to fade away a little at a time, going who knows where. How like the life of someone passing through this so-called revolutionary era. Some people have lost themselves, both body and shadow, and their names as well. As for those who still live, it is not certain that they will continue to live either. Sooner or later, they will all fade away just the same. Why do we have to hurt each other and kill each other like this?

When I turn to look at the reservoir dams taking shape and showing off their lofty forms, towering over the earth, my feelings turn to elation, and I feel pride for the accomplishment, for the thing that my own hands have achieved as a single worker among the tens of thousands of workers who have brought about this feat.

Apart from two or three small grading machines, which crawl back and forth seemingly tirelessly on the top of the dam, all of this work has come from the sweat of human beings. Perhaps it is because of this tremendous sacrifice that the Organization has relaxed. Even though they think we are merely suffering from consciousness sickness, they don't take us away to be clubbed to death but inflict this mild torture on us instead.

I have never suffered from consciousness sickness, as I value my life, and fear the loss of my life, so I always adopt a mindset in my heart that says, *Life is suffering, but the results of your work will be a benefit to your nation and your motherland.* I always consider every challenge to be merely a barrier, a trap designed to assess man's ability to strive, to fight. The final words of my mother are a great path to guide my life at this time: "Why does dying have to be so miserable, my son?" Meaning that the hardships of living are not as hard as the passage from the world of the living to the world of the dead. A similar phenomenon exists in the laws of nature, where spacecraft must accelerate to reach an escape velocity to leave the gravity of the earth and reach outer space.

After the workers in the other units finish eating, the economy team brings us some rice to eat. As soon as we finish eating, it is time to return to the pit.

The sun is hot, like a bolt of lightning scorching the grass and the earth, but a hot sun and hot dirt are normal things for us Life Slaves. The workers, men and women, carry their hoes, baskets, and yokes over their shoulders and return to the worksite. Comrade Sae lifts me and helps me walk back to the pit with an arm around my back. At the same time, Comrade Chuop, a team leader, and Comrade Mat, a team member, come up and smile at me, and Comrade Chuop calls out, "How's it going there, Tuch?"

"Do you think it's right that I'm sick, and you're laughing?" Tears fall from my eyes to accompany the words that have escaped automatically from my lips. Comrade Chuop and Comrade Mat quickly apologize and walk on past.

In fact, the two of them had left their ranks with the intent to come ask how I was doing, and to help ease my suffering, but I went and scolded them instead. Why did I do this? Did they act improperly toward me? It's truly as the old timers say, "Angry at the cow, smite the plow." Right now, I am suffering the most profound emotional pain. I try to work hard, making me a favorite of my friends and my unit leaders, to the point that they made me a deputy team leader. But now that I have fallen sick, I am made to suffer this torture. The Organization considers me to be unclean, a bad example to others.

The men and women workers who see us, who see me lying on the dirt, looking so different from the others—What is their perception? How are they looking at me? How do they disapprove? I feel so ashamed! I want to yell at the Organization and tell them that they are unfairly torturing us, torturing me, but I don't dare. I wouldn't dare to criticize or to imply that this so-called glorious Organization is crazy. So when I saw my friends laughing at me, in my heart I saw an organization that *didn't* have the right to kill me, at whom I *could* yell. This is a law of nature: the big animals eat the little animals, and the strong oppress the weak. Before a lion, a wolf is as a lamb; but before the lamb, the wolf is king of the lions.

My friend puts his arm around my back and helps me walk to the worksite, but will I be able to work? Surely not, but I have to go and accept the punishment that the Organization has meted out to me. For we are the lowliest slaves of the Organization. Oh, Life! You are truly a thousand, ten thousand times more brutal than a play on a stage! On the stage, the protagonist of the story dies, but the actor does not. But in the play of life, the actor certainly does die and cannot get back up to perform again. This is what makes us, the actors, so frightened. We are afraid of dying and never performing again.

We walk to the worksite, where those who are able to work do so, and those who are not sit down, lie down, lie in the middle of the field under the sun, hot from above, hot from below. I lie flat out on the ground with the sounds of the hoes chopping dirt resounding in my ears. If they take me away to kill me now, then I will just die because I have no more ability to expend any additional effort. If I die now, I would be counted among those who took part in building the nation to the very last moment of life. I can't work, so I lie and keep them company, as an example to others: Comrades, try hard to overcome weakness, and don't fall ill like me, as it is pure misery! Erase *pyeathik*, and let *cheatek, chorea,* and *moranak* suffice.

The sun is very hot, and the activity of the units across the entire worksite is warming up. As for the sick teams, some are sitting, some lying down, no longer afraid of dying, no longer wanting to live, sprawled out around the pit. Seeing this scene, the Organization believes that these people are truly ill, so ill they can no longer rise and work, lying flat on the ground in the middle of the heat of the day, no longer afraid of being grabbed by the neck and dragged off to be clubbed to death. At about three o'clock, the Organization finally allows the sick teams to return to rest at camp.

I lie sick for three more days before I gain the strength to resume the battle of labor.

This is the Revolutionary Organization's method of examining patients. No need to use a stethoscope or thermometer. Both those who have met her before and those who have not all pray that they never have to meet the Skilled Physician.

CHAPTER 21

The Camp at Phnom Kon Khlaeng

A hill called Phnom Kon Khlaeng[1] sits north-northwest of Paoy Char sub-district. This is a very low hill that cannot be seen from Trapeang Thmor; only forest is visible. The old folks in Paoy Snuol relate that long, long ago, the men and women made a bet with one another to raise mounds of dirt into hills. The men raised Phnom Kon Khlaeng, while the women raised another nearby hill (whose name I don't recall). The men were so busy going to spy on the women playing *chap kon khlaeng*[2] that they didn't do much work, which made them fail to finish their hill and lose to the women, and they named the failed hill Phnom Kon Khlaeng.[3]

The work at Trapeang Thmor comes to an end, with only a handful of tasks remaining, which are left for the district youth units and Ta Val's brigade to complete. The middle-aged mobile units are given orders to resume work at Phnom Kon Khlaeng,[4] at the far side of Trapeang Thmor Reservoir. About a week ago, Ta Lam sent some forces to prepare shelters there for the Phnom Srok district mobile units. On the night of the 19th of April, we are given permission to take a break from our labor and make preparations to depart.

20 April 1977

The cock crows at first light and we awake, rise, eat our breakfast, and then prepare our personal effects: our hoes, *bangky* baskets, yoke poles, hammocks, and clothing bundles. When the sky is bright and clear, we help organize and load the economy team's supplies, like sacks of rice, *prahok* jars, dried fish, salt, and water cans, onto an oxcart. A quantity of additional supplies is divided up to be carried by individuals. The men take down the shelters to recover the thatch grass. Each of us is to carry three thatch panels per person for thatching the shelters, skeletons of which have already been erected by some of the advanced forces.

---

[1] "Kite Hill"
[2] the name of a traditional game meaning "catch the kite"
[3] Very similar legends are told to explain pairs of hills in multiple location in Cambodia.
[4] i.e., the wilderness area surrounding the hill, not the hill itself. See footnote on page 189.

The sun rises over the tops of the trees, and nearly 20,000 workers depart from the Trapeang Thmor Reservoir worksite. We march single file along the top of the recently built dam until we reach the area behind Pongro, then turn left and descend from the dam top and follow an oxcart trail which is about wide enough to drive an automobile down, across fields of grass, shrubs, and sparse trees, toward the north. Even though the work is hard and tiring, and even though we all must sleep on the ground and in the woods, each person seems to be feeling glad-hearted right now, for we are excited about the thing that we have accomplished: lofty dams which obscure the villages and the countryside beyond, rising up behind our backs. They were born of the efforts of all of us, from all of our sweat and blood. Even though the project is not complete, the primary bulk of the project is done, and what concern is there for the secondary parts that remain?

We walk in a long, stretched-out, single-file column that extends for kilometers. The head of the column has already disappeared into the forest, but the tail still hasn't left the dam, and it looks like an army from the time of swords and spears, surrounding a foe. At intervals among the column of people are ox carts carrying jerrycans and clanking, clacking pots and dishes. Some people celebrate by playing a drum, or bowing a *tro*,[5] and dancing comical dances to forget their sorrows and cast off their worries. For the moment, they are free, with nobody to lead them or forbid them from doing anything as when we are working. But as the old folks say, "Joy turns to sorrow!" This kind of glad rejoicing will be silenced in a very short time, like a *maong dop* flower[6] that blooms in the sunshine but is wilted and shrunken by that same sunlight.

As we do not know the destination of our journey, nor the geography of the area, we did not hurry to depart early in the morning, and we walk casually, dancing and singing, like the monkey racing the turtle.[7] The journey grows longer and longer, and the sun grows hotter and hotter. At noon we have walked about ten kilometers and our bodies are soaked with sweat and caked with dust that is kicked up along the path. We begin to get thirsty, as the small quantities of water that we have carried on our persons have all been drunk. We are in an open plain with sparse trees, where the trees are mostly trunks with

---

[5] a traditional Khmer string instrument with one string, played with a bow
[6] "ten-o'clock flower"; *Portulaca grandiflora*
[7] refers to a traditional Khmer fable, *The Monkey and the Turtle* (very similar to *The Tortoise and the Hare*)

treeless branches and no shade in which to take shelter. We begin to break ranks and run off to seek shade and water to drink. We drop the things we are carrying and begin craning our necks, looking left and right, ahead and behind, looking for a puddle of water or a natural pond, but in this plain there is no water at all. We see a *snao* plant with tender, flexible stalks and we hope that there is water, but actually it is a dried-up pond. We try to dig into the bottom of the pond to a depth of about half a meter but find no water. We walk about searching for sour leaves or fruits to chew on to produce saliva. We sit in ranks beneath the trees along the roadside, which have few leaves and little shade.

The *Chetr* sun scorches us with its heat, and a gentle breeze blows hot fumes and dust against us, which makes our throats even drier. We look like chickens that are overheated, panting, their throats contracting and short of breath, opening their beaks to suck in air. The people walking on the road are ex-hausted and tired, walking slowly, dragging their feet, dragging their thatch panels, producing thick clouds of dust. We stare, looking for something to save us.

Far off to the south, the wind blows a swirling whirlwind of dust toward us. A small black lump moves ahead of the dusty whirlwind and grows steadily larger. No! It's not a whirlwind, it's a truck! The water truck is coming! The water truck is coming! We are overjoyed that help has arrived when we need it and anxiously await it. Supposing that the water truck will surely not stop to distribute water along the road, we get up and resume walking rapidly in order to reach the camp quickly. As we walk, we keep looking back, fearing that the water truck will veer off into the forest rather than follow the road we are on. The truck gets closer and closer, and we can see it more and more clearly! It is so clear now!

Oh Lord! It's not a water truck, it's a food truck. Our hopes evaporate along with the blowing dust that covers us and obscures the shadow of the truck, which zooms off into the forest. Why is that truck driving so fast? Is somebody starving in that forest? We become very irritated with the food truck, which has increased our stress to another level by making us choke on dust. We walk forward and stop bothering to look behind us, stop bothering to believe, stop bothering to trust in anything that is not plainly manifest.

Ahead of us, the roofs of a camp begin to appear slightly in the gaps between the trees. This sight gives us hope and each of us picks up the pace, when suddenly the sound of a truck horn sounds *pom pom pom,* causing us to startle and quickly move out of the road. A water truck zooms toward us with its horn blowing nonstop.

We are so excited and happy we shed tears and get so choked up we can't speak. We run after the water truck, which drives past us and turns in to stop beside the camp. Crowds of people surge out of the shade from every direction to surround the water truck, like bees surrounding the hive in an emergency. We all squeeze in tightly, stepping on one another's feet without fear, young and old, men and women, hands clutching bowls and dishes, raised straight up in the air. Unable to open the valve to release the water through the pipe on the back of the truck, the driver climbs up on top of the truck and opens the lid to scoop water out. This water has been sent for distribution to the units for cooking and drinking, not for the masses. But now we are so thirsty!

We lose all sense of order and cannot wait any longer. They pass buckets of water from hand to hand to be carried and poured into the economy team barrels. We stand staring at the buckets of water with tremendous thirst. We thirsted, we walked toward water, we found water, but we cannot drink the water! Only we who are so desperate and dizzy from thirst can know the true value of water. We step back and wait to sneak a dip from the water that is being carried toward the economy team's shed. The short people have a hard time, but tall people like me have it easier. An oxcart driver carries a bucket and asks for water for the oxen to drink, and the driver scoops it full and hands it back to him immediately. Good Lord! The oxen are more fortunate than the people! The oxen get to drink without having to fight for it.

Seizing the opportunity, I jump forward and dip my bowl full of water from the oxen's water ration, and suddenly I am surrounded by children crying out, "Uncle Tuch, give me some! Uncle Tuch, give me some!" The children are not fortunate to have snatched any water to drink at this time. I give them the water to share, then take my bowl and return to find another chance to snatch another bowlful.

My group is all middle-aged people who are fed up with the children's chaos. I am the only one, the single young man in disguise living among them, who is friendly and understanding toward the children. That's why they love me, and when I go to the village, if they have snacks, they often come and share them with me. The Organization asked me to lead the children when we first got to the worksite, but because of regrets over my time leading the canal-digging team at Chhleuy, I objected and declined this responsibility. The leader of the children's unit does not pay much attention to easing the work for kids who are only twelve or thirteen years old, so they follow me. (Only the children of the new people are sent to the worksite; the children of the base people are tasked with collecting cow patties to make fertilizer in the villages.)

The place where we fight over the water is the mobile camp of Preah Netr Preah district. Our camp is another two kilometers further into the forest. After getting some water to drink, we continue our journey onward and reach camp at about three o'clock in the afternoon.

CHAPTER 22

Criticism

Communist doctrine states that "wherever there is oppression, there will be revolt." Does reality follow this doctrine?

Our lives these days, if compared against our lives in 1976, are very different. We no longer eat rice porridge, but now eat rice three meals per day. Rice is abundant, and we eat meat, with a rice crust leftover in the pot, which we leave for the oxen to eat. And when regular rice is left over, the economy unit doesn't even have enough time to bother drying it out, but just throws it away instead. There are multiple sacks of rice left over in the units from the rice rations, and the economy team sends them back to the cooperative.

A comparison between the districts in Region Five that have deployed their mobile units at this time reveals that Phnom Srok district is the poorest one. The cooperatives do not provide as much food rations to their mobile units as in the other three districts. The other districts have desserts, with leftovers; they eat beef, pork, vegetables, and sugar; they send tobacco, clothing, and *kramas* regularly. As for Phnom Srok district, especially Paoy Char subdistrict, things are extremely rough; apart from vegetables, the subdistrict doesn't send anything to its mobile units. If the mobile units make requests now and then, they can only get them answered with difficulty. They make excuses that we are under the control of the regional Organization, so all supplies are the responsibility of the region, and the cooperative is concerned only with the forces in the village itself.

Compared with other nearby units, I can see that things are very rough for my unit. We receive support from the regional Organization like the others, so why are we so different? Because of embezzlement! Supplies, clothing, food, sugar, and cigarettes, which the Organization provides to our unit, by the time they reach the hands of us workers, are at a bare minimum: one small disk of palm sugar to divide between four people. Supplies that are very scarce, like clothing, *kramas*, and blankets, are barely enough to supply the economy team, and then only if there is any surplus does it overflow to the rest of us. These days we think very little of things that cannot be eaten, so if they don't provide them then so be it. Every day we work shirtless in both hot sunlight and rain. But we are in dire need of things which can be eaten! We want them badly! For it is only by eating that we can have strength to wage the battle, while working in the heat and the cold, without faltering. Dried fish, *prahok*, sugar, fat, and soybean oil are all provided regularly, especially the dried fish and the *prahok*. But the soup has very little fish meat in it; it is mostly broth and vegetables, which we call "cloud soup." Whenever we eat it, we stir around with our spoons searching for bits of fish to share, and around swirls the broth, but the bowl is as devoid of fish as a pond in the dry season. If now and then we are able to get thickened, steamed *prahok* to eat, it is our great fortune, as normally we eat only black-colored boiled *prahok* that looks more like a marinade for actual fish. Other units get discs of hard palm sugar to share around and eat in the dirt pit, while our economy team says that they will save them for the soup and does not distribute them for eating.

Whenever we see the economy team members eating meals, we swallow our spit and stare and wish we could eat with them. For the four or five of them they have two or three dried fish, with chopped roasted *prahok* giving off a nice pungent odor. Whenever beef or pork is distributed from time to time, the economy workers fry it, *kho*[1] it, or roast it for themselves, while we can stir our soup bowl until it tips over and still not encounter a single piece of meat. We see only bones; we gnaw on bones like dogs.

Some of the dried fish, sugar, *prahok*, and fat are divided amongst the economy unit members and secretly sent to their families back in the villages. We know about it but don't dare say anything because Ta Lam takes meals in our unit, and we are afraid of bumping up against him and dying for it.

About a week before we pulled back our lines, Ta Lam left to prepare the camp at Phnom Kon Khlaeng, while in the unit we received a lot of pork rations. The economy unit made a large pot of pork *kho* for themselves to eat, and what small amount of meat was left over they made into soup for us for a single meal, and then after that they went back to *prahok* soup for every meal.

One day, after a rain when the air was cold, some children came into the economy shed to get warm by the fire and opened a pot lid to look inside, when suddenly a woman on the economy team threatened them: "Hey, that belongs to Bong Yong, don't touch it!"

---

[1] to cook meat in a kind of dark stew, itself also called *kho*, with caramelized sugar, soy sauce, and spices

Gee! Belongs to Bong Yong, you say? A man who has never lifted so much as a single basket of dirt gets an entire pot of pork *kho* all to himself? Oh, right! He's the chief of the economy team, so shut your mouth!

As we were preparing to depart for Phnom Kon Khlaeng, the economy unit sent a whole *tong* (a large square oil tin) full of sugar back to the village, while we couldn't find so much as a morsel of sugar to lick. Before departing, they boiled a whole big pot of sweet pumpkin dessert just for themselves. And then they couldn't even eat all of it and saved the leftovers to enjoy along the way. Oh! Because they have important jobs, they get to eat better food than we do.

When we arrive at Phnom Kon Khlaeng, our biggest problem is drinking water. We lack drinking water, so we have to use the water that is meant for washing pots and dishes for drinking. But Bong Yong sneakily bathes and washes his clothes at night while we are away working in the pit. Amazing! If you have to die, then go ahead and die, so long as I can live comfortably! Bong Yong is a new person who managed to get a good position, so he ought to have pity on us, fellow new people, who are exhausted and miserable. But instead, Bong Yong is so afraid he won't get to live a life of pleasures beyond his fate that he can't even see our suffering and hunger. Perhaps he thinks of us as mere animals. We grumble and groan in contempt for this arrogant and inconsiderate attitude, but we don't dare to openly criticize him for fear that he will raise a mountain (Ta Lam) to block our way, for fear that we will become the insolent egg who dared to butt heads with a stone. So instead, we merely make insinuating comments to the economy women who bring us our rice.

Sitting around grumbling, talking bad about others, talking behind people's back, are all violations of the revolutionary path. The Organization instructs us to engage in open criticism, in meetings. Talking behind people's backs is considered something that stirs up negativity, and you can be taken away and clubbed to death immediately for this.

I encourage the others to be bold and raise all of the inappropriate things that they have seen in a criticism meeting. But each of them shrinks and is afraid they will only raise Ta Lam and place him before us. I explain to them that they should only raise issues which don't directly impact Ta Lam, and I promise to be the spokesman who rises to speak first. They agree to this idea, and each of them promises to stand and criticize the economy workers for the things that they have clear knowledge of. We ask the unit leader to hold a meeting with the economy team.

On the third day of camping at Phnom Kon Khlaeng, Ta Lam returns to Paoy Char subdistrict, which is a good opportunity for us. After eating dinner, we hold a meeting with the economy team. Bong Yong is so very important! Bong Yong does not attend the meeting. He assigns Comrade Raeu, a female base person with responsibility for leading the cooking work, to attend on his behalf.

After the unit leader announces the opening of the meeting, I stand and make my remarks: "I express my respect for the comrade unit leader! I express my respect for the comrade sister representing the economy team, other comrade brothers, comrade sisters, and our brother and sister children in attendance. For a while now, we have waged constant battle in our labors and have had no time to rest, so we never meet with the economy workers, which is why we have grown apart. And at the same time, various indications have come to light that the economy team has been secretly embezzling the property of the collective and eating on a level that is not equal with the other members of the unit. For this reason, we wish to raise those points of shortcoming for your information and ask that the comrade sister representing the economy team explain those points in order to eliminate suspicion!"

I finish my remarks and sit down, the members of the unit applaud, and then Comrade Raeu stands up and responds, "I express my respect to the assembly! And I wish to respond and explain the economy team's issues regarding food. As all of you comrades have seen, Father Lam is the cadre who represents the district in leading the work, and he eats in our unit, so the economy team has to make special food for him to eat, and we eat whatever is left over from him. Do you comrades want Father Lam to eat the same as you? I understand that if you die, you will not be equal, so don't desire to be equal with the leadership!"

Comrade Raeu finishes her explanation by simply picking up the mountain and setting it down smack in our way, which is why everyone is stunned and buries their own opinions and loses their courage and nobody dares to stand and ask any questions. The meeting is silent, which puts me in an emergency as I am the one who initiated the meeting, and nobody dares to step forward and support me. They are so cowardly that they can only grumble and shove when they're outside the boxing ring.

Unable to delay for long, I stand back up and make additional remarks. "I appreciate the response from the comrade sister representing the economy team. In fact, I have the same perception, that the food issues of the economy team have to do with Father Lam. But I keep hearing rumors of this or that, some saying that in Father Lam's absence the economy team took sugar back to keep in the village, that the economy workers take nighttime showers while the rest of us can't even find water to drink, and so on.

"But now, here in the meeting, it appears that none of my comrades will stand to express their concerns. This demonstrates that all of these rumors must be untrue, unclear, or vaguely overheard by word of mouth, which may be a cause for the economy team to feel unappreciated and discouraged in fulfilling their work of service to the collective. For this reason, from now on, I ask that all of you comrades put to rest your doubts about the economy team, and strive to fulfill your revolutionary duties, to achieve one hundred percent victory!"

The sound of applause resounds. The unit leader announces the adjournment of the meeting, which only exposed the issues but featured no discussion to resolve anything.

Tonight I feel very worried and regret my courage to stand and raise the issues by myself, with nobody to back me up. But because all of the issues I raised are true, the economy team members are also worried about themselves, and afraid to cause any more trouble. For instance, in the matter of taking the sugar back to the village, the oxcart driver witnessed it clearly, so it cannot be denied.

We applied the wrong medicine to the wrong ailment! From now on, Bong Yong becomes unhappy and spiteful toward the dirt haulers, especially me, and takes revenge by further oppressing us. If anybody has a headache or dizziness and can't work, and asks the unit leader to rest in camp, Bong Yong refers them to the hospital to sip porridge, whether they are a middle-aged adult or a child. Bong Yong is even stingy with the drinking water and looks for excuses to restrict it, saying that the dirt haulers are not allowed to take any with them to drink at the worksite.

CHAPTER 23

Water Is Life

The dam at Phnom Kon Khlaeng is not very large, only about one meter high, with a bottom six meters across and a top three meters across. This worksite is in a sparse forest with close-set, small-to-large trees and stands of wild bamboo providing shade, which makes the work more pleasant than at Trapeang Thmor. The work here is done by allotment, with plots of land divided among the units. If any unit finishes their daily allotment, they can rest. When we first arrive, the moon is bright, and we work at night. But after two or three days, the waning moon grows darker, and we can no longer work at night. The work is light, but living here is challenging and miserable to a degree that most people never encounter in their lives.

The value of all things change with time: water is important when you are thirsty, sleep is important when you are sleepy, money is important when it is spent, rice is important when you are hungry, and soldiers are important in a battle.

At Trapeang Thmor, we did not bathe because there was no time to go bathe. At Phnom Kon Khlaeng, we don't drink water because there is no water to drink. We arrive here in the middle of the dry season when the weather is hot and dry, the ponds are dried up, the earth is cracked, and the grass is wilted and dead and lying limp on the ground. There is no water within a radius of ten kilometers from our camp. If we leave at dawn and return at twelve o'clock, we can find enough water to fill only a single bamboo cylinder apiece, as there is not much water for us to find. The economy team's oxcart drives off to find water at two or three o'clock in the middle of the night and returns at one or two o'clock in the afternoon and is only able to get one jerrycan full of water. Water for cooking and drinking is supplied entirely by water truck, with each district getting only two water trucks per day. Divided up by individual, this comes out to about six liters per person. The human body needs five liters of water per day, so six liters for washing vegetables, washing dishes, cooking, washing faces, and drinking is not sufficient. But if you do get that much, you can get by somewhat, as the economy oxcarts of each unit never dare to stop searching for water.

But angels above! Some days you get one water truck, and some days you get nothing until seven or eight o'clock at night. The rice ration is enough to make porridge, but if the water ration decreases, what can we do? Dry-swallow uncooked rice? No! Nobody complaining of hunger wants to dry-swallow uncooked rice. Everybody needs water; everybody is thirsty for water!

Every day after eating our meals, we lick our spoons and bowls clean instead of washing them with water. We ask the economy team for the leftover dishwater to drink. Whatever, it's like drinking soup broth, a bit salty. But some days we can't even find enough water to wash the dishes. The dishes and pots remain stowed face down, the uncooked rice remains uncooked, there is no water for cooking, and everyone sits around with their mouths open. When we come back from work, we always discreetly send somebody to go and look for water to drink in addition to the water rations that the economy team gives us.

One evening, every unit is completely out of water, and when we return from work, all of the rice pots and soup pots are face down. Today we received only a single water truck in the morning. We lie prostrate, panting and motionless, our thoughts wandering to the nooks and crannies of the forests and hills, to the stony places, to any place where there might be drinkable water, but without hope! The veil of night covers the camp in darkness, when suddenly a cadre walks up to call us to a meeting to watch a film. Nobody dares avoid it. We all go and sit with our mouths open, watching a film with dry, sticky throats and churning stomachs. This is the first time that I have watched a film since being evacuated from Phnom Penh.

The film describes the progress achieved during this revolutionary era, which in the *Sangkum* era they would have called an "update." We see crisscrossing grids of salt-evaporation marshes, where salt farmers wield wooden rakes to push the salt into piles that rise above the surface of the salt marshes, which appear shiny and smooth like sheets of glass. There are grids of paddy dikes and newly dug canals through which water flows, splashing onto lush green fields of transplanted rice. We see a team of doctors in white coats working in a room in a hospital in Phnom Penh, then turning on water faucets to wash their hands in a sink...

This evening the Organization has brought water to pour all over our feelings though the film, which makes us even more thirsty, more desirous of water; and then we get irritated at the doctors, who turn on the water to wash their hands without conserving or thinking that there are tens of thousands of people whose bodies are hollowed out, who don't have enough water to so much as moisten their throats. Even though there is abundant water in the scenes of the film, in real, actual life, our stomachs are withering for lack of water. It's about 8 p.m. now, but water still refuses to flow from the canals and into the barrels of the economy team. Oh, it can't! There are no canals here!

Our eyes stare at the white sheet, but our dry throats send our minds fleeing secretly to find water in every crack and cranny. The sweet, lovely words of the film's narrator being amplified by the speakers until they fill the forest cannot pull our thoughts away from the anxiety of our thirsty lives.

Our ears strain for the sound of a water truck rather than listening to the film's narration. Here in the forest we can't see the headlights of the truck, but the rumbling of a vehicle engine lets us know that a truck is approaching our camp; it must be a water truck! Soon light from the truck's headlamps turns to shine directly on us where we sit with our heads down at the mouth of the road. It's like we have seen Lord Indra himself coming down to redeem mankind. We jump up and dash toward the water truck, which is now driving toward the spot where the economy teams' barrels have been left waiting for so long.

Oh, Master Water! How we have missed you! We love you so! No matter how much we fear the Organization, which has gathered us to sit and watch a film, when we see you, we lose all fear and stop thinking of that tremendous power.

We encounter the bitterness of waterlessness nearly every day that we work in Phnom Kon Khlaeng. It's just that some days we have no water in the morning, and some days we have no water in the evening. It's because the Organization doesn't have enough water trucks. They have only a single gasoline tanker truck, with a volume of 3000 liters in a long oval cylinder, to transport water for all of the mobile units in the entirety of Trapeang Thmor. And the Organization lacks water pumps, having to depend instead on the strength of six or seven people to haul water up in buckets to fill the truck. Actually, these things are not really adequate in a case of such great lack, but this is a great era for using human strength, an era of heating, hammering, and quenching (tempering). They consider a human being to be a piece of iron in the tongs of a blacksmith, to be heated and hammered, heated and hammered, and then finally quenched in water. If they are good and useful iron, they are kept; but if they are poor iron, they are thrown away.

One day we run out of water while working in the morning. The sun rises and casts his raw red light through the gaps in the large and small trees. In the pit the workers, men and women, strive to haul dirt with great effort, unit racing against unit, subdistrict against subdistrict. The work is not so difficult for us, as we are used to waging battle to raise great dams, and now we are raising a small dam; and besides, the dirt at Phnom Kon Khlaeng is looser than the dirt at Trapeang Thmor. The diggers think only of digging and placing the baskets, while the haulers run with six or eight baskets at a time on their yokes. Here the men and women work face to face, each raising one opposing side of the dam. As Phnom Kon Khlaeng has a history of men losing in competition with women, the men work hard to stamp out the traces of the old history.

For both the men and the women, working close to one another seems to fill them with a strength and a courage greater than normal. The men haul six or eight *bangky* baskets of dirt at a time, while the women, undeterred, haul four or six baskets. We are able to do this because the distance we have to haul the dirt is not far—only about ten meters.

Ta Lam walks along the top of the dam supervising the work, and when he reaches our unit and sees people hauling so many baskets at a time, he scolds us. "Hey, Comrade! Why are you hauling dirt so greedily? You are not waging a one-day revolution, you know! Comrade, you have to do this for many more days to come. If you hurt yourself and can't haul dirt for one or two days, will you profit, or lose? What if you break your yoke, comrade, will you profit or lose? Beware lest the Great Leap becomes the Great Destruction!"

After being smitten by the club of Ta Lam, we all lose our will. For someone like me, a single young man working beside girls and women, there is a degree of showing off, boasting that you are strong. But what about the men who are married? Why are they showing off? And the women and girls, why are they trying so hard? In fact, we want the work to be finished quickly and the project to be complete so that we can quickly retreat from this waterless place.

Through vigorous work, we start sweating first thing in the morning. Sweat flows like water and then dries many times during the day, forming a hard crust, as if we'd never known water before, and our skin grows tough. After the sweat dries, we feel exhausted and thirsty. Every day the work progresses, but in the mornings the weather is cool, and we are not very thirsty. Later in the day, it is hot and the pace falls off and becomes plodding due to exhaustion and, especially, thirst. But every morning there is a little bit of water left over in the economy team's barrel, which we can scoop out and divide up for drinking. However, this morning none of the units have any water remaining to wash their faces with because yesterday the water truck made only one trip in the morning; but in the evening we didn't see so much as even the shadow of a truck. In addition to the lack of water, yesterday evening my unit ate rice with salty *prahok* soup, still stuck in our throats until this morning because there is no water to wash away the taste.

Damn! Why does this have to be so hard? We have already abandoned anything that could be called a substantial possession, so that all I have left is two changes of clothes, sour and stinky from sweating morning until evening without any water to wash them; two meters of white cloth, which the Organization distributed for use as a blanket; an old rice sack used as a beloved hammock; a bowl; a spoon; a metal dish; and a bottle of salt. We don't even have hair combs. Is this not sufficient to qualify us to wage the Revolution with them? The regional cadres drink coconut juice, while we drink only pond and bog water, and they don't even bring us enough of that to drink our fill. If our throats are dry from thirst, what can anyone do?

We drop our dirt baskets and wander aimlessly looking for water in places where there is no water. Nobody has even a drop of water, and there isn't anyone who isn't thirsty right now. We are thirsty to the point of weak limbs, all at the same time, at about eight o'clock in the morning.

Now the doctrine that "people can rest, so long as the hoes and *bangky* baskets never rest" has lost its effectiveness. The people are resting, as are the hoes, baskets, and yokes, without directions or orders; just resting by themselves. The hoes, baskets, and yokes are resting together in the pit, while the people rest here and there in the shade of large trees along the dam. Some people sit with their backs resting against a tree trunk, while some break off leaves for a bed and lie flat on their backs on the ground. The cadres have all disappeared, so we see nobody coming to drive us back to work. They are also suffering the effects of this thirst; all of their limbs are weak like ours. Truly, only when it gets hard for everyone does it get easier. We need water! We are so thirsty! My sweat has dried to a sticky crust all over my body.

The sun is very hot, and water vapor rises from under the layer of dead leaves up into the sky, so that you can see the hazy waves. The sky is cloudy, and the air is still, and we each feel like suffocating. Now and then, someone gets dizzy and passes out, so everybody is pulling hair and pinching skin.[1]

We wait expectantly for the people we secretly sent out looking for water, who don't return until at least noon, and for the water truck whose shadow is nowhere to be seen. Oh, holy angels above, why such bad karma? If they want to kill us, why don't they just kill us quickly? Why leave us to suffer such drawn-out agony? If they spare us in order to work, why don't they provide adequate rice and water? As for food, when they starved us to the point of measuring and distributing dry rice with a spoon, we still worked hard, following the directions and the rules of the Revolution without daring to do anything that could be called a reaction against the Organization's leadership.

Now we see clearly what is the thing which can make us forget about work and the Organization's disciplinary line; what can make us forget death from failing to obey the Organization's orders. We don't want to die, but we are all dying, dying from despair of living.

If we endure working even another hour, we will pass out and fall over dead, one by one. If we stop working and rest, we can live for another three or four hours waiting for the water truck. If the water truck shows up within this time, we will live! But if they take us away to kill us while waiting for help, what of that? No, nobody can take us away to be killed now, as the unit leaders and soldiers are all as thirsty as we are; and even if they weren't thirsty, the twenty or thirty of them don't have the ability to kill the tens of thousands of us in the space of just two or three hours.

Right now, the unity of our unit is equal to when we were raising the dams at Trapeang Thmor. We are all united in sitting down and lying down and watching the road for the water truck. Ever since we started to live in this revolutionary society, many people have been taken away to be killed because of hunger, from daring to steal paddy rice, milled rice, corn, or tubers; but nobody has dared to put up any resistance. Now people do dare: they dare to go on strike and refuse to work, a strike without any preparation and no leader.

---

[1] Hair pulling and pinching, along with squeezing, massaging, and coining (see page 211), are all traditional interventions for dizziness and fainting in Khmer culture.

No, this strike actually does have clear leadership. The leader, who is as strong as life itself, is Thirst. Water has blocked the wheel of history from rolling forward for an hour now. Water is powerful! More powerful than human life! More powerful than the Revolution!

Nine o'clock, ten o'clock, ten-thirty, and still no water truck has arrived. The worksite is silent and still. Apart from the rustling of leaves on the trees and bamboo when the wind stirs them from time to time, we hear no sounds. This makes it very easy for us to listen carefully for the sound of the water truck.

At nearly eleven o'clock, the sound of a truck engine drifts through the layers of leaves and trees and touches all of our senses. The anxiety and desire to live boils up as if driven by the winds of a storm, and we all jump up and run noisily toward camp to grab our metal water dishes and then run toward the place where the water truck stops each day. The economy workers bring their buckets on yokes and lay them out in an orderly row.

The truck has not even arrived yet, but people are waiting to welcome it in a thick crowd. There! The top of the truck appears above a clump of wild bamboo, and now it is turning toward us. Joy, anxiety, and fear of being unable to fight for water all mix together inside of each of us. The truck slows down and then stops suddenly, and people flock to surround the truck in a tight crowd, pushing and shoving all over the place. Children squeeze in under the truck to wait to catch the water that falls down from the mouth of the pipe. Because of the chaotic struggle, water spills all over the ground. The unit leaders and soldiers intervene to push the crowd back away from the water pipe. But it is useless; we shove one another and push our way forward, reaching out to scoop up water, to catch the water pouring into the economy team's buckets, without fear or restraint. As the crowd pushes from one side and clumps up on the other, a soldier gets his nose bent out of shape and fires his AK-47 rifle to warn the crowd, *bang! bang! bang!*

Though faced with death, because of thirst, people don't think of death by any other means. We don't back off, our thoughts thinking only of water! Water! Water! Rather, it is the sound of water flowing into buckets *glug glug glug* that draws our attention and moves our feelings; the sound of gunfire has lost all meaning. Because firing warning shots had no effect, the soldier who fired the shots stands and angrily stares down the damned souls of Hell. A soldier grabs a rifle barrel with two hands, raises the rifle, and begins to club the head of the person nearest the water barrel before him, *thud! thud! thud!* Ouch!

The unlucky victim drops his metal bowl and raises his arms to protect his head, which is now bleeding profusely and soaking his head and face, and runs to get out of the crowd. The person with the split head backs off, but those whose heads are still intact press forward toward the water. This is the only place that has water, that has life.

In the face of death, people don't fear death. There is no power that can constrain the fear of death. If a soldier beats you, you raise one arm to protect your head, while the other arm holds your metal bowl and reaches for the water.

Out of options, the soldiers stop shooting and clubbing and start a new campaign: they stand around the water barrel in a ring facing outwards, holding their guns, preventing anyone from coming near. One water barrel fills up and is handed off to one unit, and then they stand to protect the next barrel. In this way, we are unable to get close to the water barrels, so we turn to trying to snatch scoops of water from the buckets that the economy teams carry on yokes toward their own units.

Fighting for water is a daily occurrence, but only on this day do we suffer the risk of having our heads broken. Those who participate in building the dam for the Trapeang Thmor Reservoir at Phnom Kon Khlaeng will surely never forget this bitter memory.

30 April 1977

At first light we pull our lines back from Phnom Kon Khlaeng and return to Trapeang Thmor, after having fulfilled our work building a dam in this wilderness place for nine days. We travel in haste and in joy that we can finally leave this place so inhospitable to life. But unfortunately, two workers from the special unit do not return with us. They were clubbed to death, their bodies lying on the ground, swollen and rotten in the middle of the jungle.

At about four o'clock in the afternoon we reach Kok Krasang, a *kok*[2] west of the southern end of Paoy Snuol, a distance of about one kilometer from the village.

---

[2] a spot of relative high ground, usually with trees, in the plains of rice fields, which stays dry during flooding; see page 260

CHAPTER 24

The Hanged Corpse

As of now, the Trapeang Thmor Reservoir basin has been all but completed for the 1977 phase of the project. The remaining work of finishing things up is the task of Ta Val's mobile brigade and Phnom Srok district's youth units. The middle-aged units of each district are given the task of digging canals to carry the water from the three water gates. Phnom Srok district is assigned the task of digging the canal from the first water gate, across the rice fields west of Paoy Char subdistrict, then straight to the large canal that follows the Phnom Srok–Prey Moan road, connecting to this canal near Kok Kraol village.

This canal is fifteen meters wide across the top and three meters wide across the bottom, with a depth of one meter and a length of more than ten kilometers. The extracted dirt is piled to form two levees along the canal banks on both sides, to a height of one meter. The length of the canal is divided into sections to be completed one phase at a time, then further subdivided into subsections for each subdistrict.

The entire middle-aged mobile unit of Phnom Srok district sets up camp at the south end of Paoy Snuol to make it easy to supply water and food. The camp is about three to five kilometers away from the worksite.

The natural ponds in the fields are all dried up, so the water truck has to bring water to the camps as well as the worksites. At the *phnom*,[1] we could walk for half a day and not see a puddle or a pond, so there were constant interruptions in the water supply; so now, as we have come to camp three or four kilometers away from a water source, are they not afraid that we will have water shortages? Some days we see the truck come, and other days we don't, as it is busy transporting gasoline.

Independence and Self Reliance is the doctrine we must follow. We lack supplies. Two or three pairs of buckets are saved for the economy team to carry rice, water, and soup with shoulder yokes. We use bamboo cylinders, bottles, and kettles to carry drinking water to the worksite. People steadily come and go fetching water from the pond west of Paoy Snuol. If you look from a distance, you see a black line of many people, as though hauling dirt at a dam. While

---

[1] the Phnom Kon Khlaeng camp

water here is not abundant, at least it is not completely lacking as it had been at Phnom Kon Khlaeng.

The work of digging the canal is not particularly difficult, but it is not easy either. The sections are divided up by unit. The Organization is making a Great Leap Forward, the discipline is flexible, and the mode of work adapts. If we finish our section first, we have to help the women with theirs. But if not, then what is the reason? Ta Lam and the district *chhlops* patrol with guns, supervising the work from one end of the worksite to the other, back and forth, until resting time. Nobody would dare to stop or stand around or go on any kind of strike anymore, for we have rice, and we have water.

The economy team carries our rice and water to us on shoulder yokes to the worksite, so we don't have to bother walking back to camp. Cambodia abounds in fish: freshwater fish, saltwater fish, dried fish, smoked fish, chopped fermented fish, *prahok*; but it is not our fate at this time to be acquainted with anything that you could call "abundance." In the morning we eat boiled *prahok*, and in the evening we eat boiled *prahok*. Sometimes it is bitter, and sometimes it smells so bad you can barely swallow it. There is very little dried fish or smoked fish; these are reserved for the higher-level officials.

We take our midday rest at eleven o'clock and return to work at one o'clock. After eating lunch, all of us, young and old, women and men, spread out all over the fields with our hoes over our shoulders to dig rat holes under the blazing sun. When we return a bit later, each group has a half to a full *bangky* basket of rats, which we skin, salt, and then fry or roast. We eat all of them, from the smallest ones whose eyes haven't opened yet to the fattest ones. Apart from some of the Muslim Khmers, who practice their religion faithfully, there isn't anybody who doesn't eat rats. Whoever says they don't know how to eat rats is not much different from rich people who used to say before the Revolution that they didn't know how to sleep on the ground. Now even if you don't know how, you have to do it anyway. It's like the old timers say, "Desperation trumps principle."

We are fortunate to be able to sleep in our shelters, which we labored to construct, for only two nights. Starting on the third night, we sleep at the worksite, at the place where we dig. At first, the moon is bright, and we work until ten or eleven o'clock at night. Then as the moon waxes, we go to sleep at dusk and then wake up at three or three thirty in the morning. Only the economy team gets to sleep in a shelter, while the unit leaders have come back to their home village, so they sleep at their own houses. We can't even go to the shelters, let alone go visit home. And as for me, I don't even have a home to visit. At the locals' house that we used to sleep beneath, they have now removed all the wood. I have no house and no possessions, so what point is there to go into the village? Apart from my rice sack and my change or two of shabby clothing, I have nothing else for my life. I can spread the sack over me to sleep, or spread it under me to sleep, under the sky on the ground, out in the open, exposed to the wind and the dew—all reasons to be glad.

With what light there is in the sky at night on the plain, we can see everything, without exception. The plain is vast: south all the way to the horizon; north all the way to Trapeang Thmor Reservoir's dam; west to the sparse forest far off in the distance; and east to the smattering of coconut palms, sugar palms, and scattered camps that divide the sky and the earth.

On a full-moon night, we sit chatting contentedly and breathing in the cool air, which blows gently and cleanses our souls, weary from working hard during the day. We gaze at the moon rising from the black horizon, and we make bets with each other.

"Can any of you eat an entire bunch of chicken-egg bananas?"[2]

"Eat how?"

"When the moon starts to rise, you start to eat, and when the moon has cleared the horizon, you have to stop."

"I can eat the whole thing!"

"You can't eat the whole thing. It's been tried before, and they couldn't eat the whole thing, so don't bet on it!"

"They couldn't eat the whole thing, but I can. Bring it here and watch me do it!"

All because of hunger! We think only of eating. We make bets about eating. Sometimes we make bets about eating a whole pot of rice made from four cans of uncooked rice. Sometimes we make bets about eating a *kor*[3] cake a handspan square and a handspan high. Nobody objects that they can't eat it because we

---

[2] a variety of very small, sweet bananas
[3] a kind of rice-flour dessert

are hungry, because the one making the bet is hungry—and the fact is we don't have any of it.

A soft reddish light rises up from under the earth and touches the clouds drifting across the sky like a spotlight. The light gets redder and clearer, and grows larger and larger, more and more rays spreading out and upward and to the sides. There! A reddish circle is rising! The moon appears little by little from a black line, peeking out a little from the treetops, her light running to touch the leaves on the trees, which flutter and flash in the currents of light flung from within the dark black curtain that hides our sorrows and sadness. The moon floats slowly upward, higher and higher, past the tops of the trees, her clear bright light shining down upon the earth, allowing us to see everything around us.

We never allow such a splendid sight as this to pass before our eyes without savoring the flavor and imprinting its image on our feelings. But we don't have time to gaze or be carried away on the waves of the moon's cool light for as long as we would like. Because now the moon has become the enemy of our peace. The moonrise is an omen of fatigue and sweating. We pick up our hoes, *bangky* baskets, and yoke poles automatically, without hesitating or waiting for a command from anyone. Oh, lovely Moon! Now you have a notorious name! You are still beautiful, still the moon of love, but in the hearts of the workers you are a devil, a devil which makes us fearful, afraid to meet you, praying that you be buried forever in the far-off horizon until we can escape our misery.

On nights when the moon rises early, we barely get to rest at all after dinner. If the moon rises late, we have time to rest in the early evening, but then we have to work until nearly the middle of the night.

At the new moon there is impenetrable darkness, and we cannot work at all. After dinner we all lie on the earth, side by side in ranks beneath the vast sky, our eyes gazing at the stars shining brightly and spread thickly above, adorning the black sky, turning it into a cover studded brilliantly with twinkling points of light. We point out to one another and name the constellations that the old ones called The Chick,[4] The Turtle, The Horse, and The Plow Handle,[5] shining above us, while The Crocodile[6] rises in the north. Some nights we see

---

[4] the Pleiades
[5] Orion
[6] Ursa Major

lights, sometimes white, sometimes yellow, blue, or red, shooting across the sky, flaring brightly and then disappearing in a brief moment. The old folks tell us that these are "field lights" and that they have always seen them.

Some nights, while watching the bright, twinkling stars, we see a star drifting lazily through the other stars. No, not a star, a spacecraft! A spacecraft passes overhead! We point it out to one another and rejoice, following it with our eyes until the light is buried in the sky, as though wishing we could send it messages:

"Oh, Spacecraft! Please pass a message to the people living outside of Cambodia. Tell the Khmers living abroad that we, the Khmers back home, suffer terribly! Please, look down on us! The shelters are abandoned near the village, and people sleep in scattered rows, men, women, and children, out here in the middle of the fields, on top of a levee, beside this pit in the ground.

"People sleep in the fields while the corpses sleep in the woods. Paoy Trach, a thinly forested patch of high ground south of our shelters, is covered with corpses. Corpses lie piled on top of one another, rotting and crumbling, bright white bones scattered among the trees. Those of us living in Phnom Srok district, if we do anything wrong, they arrest us and take us there to kill us. Samat, my younger brother, was taken there and killed. If you don't see it, if you don't believe us, come down and see it for yourself. You will see it clearly, as we describe, and even more. We live in fear, we live in terror, not knowing what day they will come and take us from the fields to lie still in those woods. However tiring and grueling the work, however cold or hot the weather, we don't shrink from it; we fear only dying, we fear being taken away to be killed, we fear death so much!

"Please, Spacecraft, carry our pleas and tell the rest of humanity so they can come to our aid, come and deliver us from the cruel, tormenting manacles of this Hell on Earth! Please, don't forget us, all right? Please help us!"

During *Pisakh,* at the start of the new year, the rain begins to fall intermittently, and water begins to collect somewhat in the puddles, ponds, and canals. On days when it rains hard in the afternoon, the ground becomes wet and swollen, and we can't sleep on it, so the Organization lets us go spend the night in our shelters. But if it rains in the morning or at midday, by evening the ground is partially dried out, and we are not allowed to spend the night at camp. So then, what if it rains at night?

The sun is about to set and the workers, men and women, rush to finish hauling the extracted dirt. The economy teams of each unit have brought rice, soup, and water on shoulder yokes to the worksite. The shrieks of the whistle releasing us from work sound long and piercing. We gather our work supplies and emerge from the canal and pile them up by unit and by team near our sleeping spots, then grab our bowls and spoons and head for the economy site to eat our meal.

After dinner we each look for a place to lay out our rice sacks or thatch grass and sleep in rows by unit and by team, women and men, young and old, some on top of the levees that were just built, some among the rice stubble on either side of the canal. Those who are able to sleep simply lay their bodies down and begin to snore, while those who have a harder time falling asleep chat with one another, watching the sky and the stars, listening to the sounds of the nocturnal creatures, listening to the sounds of nature's night music.

Tonight is a moonless night, the sky almost completely dark. In the sky above, the countless scattered stars shine brightly and twinkle, like fireflies criss-crossing through the veil of night at the start of the cool season.

Over at Trapeang Thmor Reservoir, the electric lights cast their pale light in a line. Whether the sky is dark and moonless or bright with moonlight, the work there never ceases. The Region Five mobile brigade of Ta Val and Phnom Srok district's youth mobile units have joined forces to construct the water gate of reinforced concrete.

A night breeze blows cool and refreshing, making those who are asleep fall into even more pleasant sleep, while those who have not fallen asleep yet begin to nod off little by little. But those of us whose thoughts are still far away, watching the sky and counting the stars, begin to wonder. Some of the stars have disappeared from the sky. Now nearly all of the stars have disappeared, and the sky has grown pitch black. At the same time, the wind begins to blow harder, blowing dust on us, mixed now with large drops of water falling steadily. No longer wondering, we jump up and cry out in alarm and wake those who are asleep: "It's raining! It's raining!"

Thus begins the late-night pandemonium. Those who were asleep jump up in a daze and snatch up their rice sacks, men removing their shirts and rolling them up and handing them to people with tarps to help protect them from the rain.

The wind dies down, but the rain begins to come down like it is being poured out, like someone has torn open the sky. It is so cold! So cold! Those of us who are shirtless sit hugging ourselves, shivering and huddled together out in the open, exposed to the rain. Should we head for camp? No, we don't dare because we have not been ordered! The important unit leaders are asleep at their houses in the village, while the lesser leaders don't dare make a decision, awaiting directions from above. Easy enough! Afraid to die, not daring to run for shelter, they'd rather sit hugging themselves, their faces down, shivering, awaiting orders. Who will bring us orders? Nobody! We see nobody coming to tell us to stay or go. Before the rain started, nobody dared to go because they feared it wouldn't rain. When the rain comes, water starts to flood the road and the fields, and still they won't let us go because there has been no order. If the rain stops, and we still have no orders to go sleep at camp, will we even be able to sleep in this water?

Now and then lightning strikes *crack! crack!* And the thunder roars *boom! boom!* For nearly half an hour we bathe in the rain, cleansing our bodies of long-accumulated and stiff crusts of dirt. We mostly feel sorry for the women and children who shiver and shake, their teeth chattering, some of their fingers and toes going numb.

Unable to endure any longer myself, I cry out in the midst of the rain, "Who will go and get orders? It is so damn cold!"

"Who will go and get orders, dammit!" others cry out in refrain.

Who should go? Who dares to go? Only the unit leader can decide it; the lesser leaders fear the power of the unit leader, so they all endure the shivering along with the rest of us. In the light from the flashes of lightning, we see a man carrying a flashlight walking away from the worksite and heading toward the camp south of Paoy Snuol, a distance of about three kilometers. All of us sit with heads bent, anxiously awaiting orders, eyes fixed in the direction of the camp.

After a long while, we see the light from the flashlight twinkling in the direction we have been watching, coming slowly toward us. The unit leader must have given orders! Will he tell us to go, or stay? Nobody dares to speculate, as our suffering is of no concern to the Organization. Nevertheless, the sight of this light causes our mood to change, to lighten, to have hope.

We have sat with our heads down in the rain for an hour, waiting for the order from the Organization, which now gives us permission to return to sleep in the camp. Water is pooling all over the fields, in the canal, swelling the dirt, the dikes in the rice paddies becoming slippery, the mud sticking to our feet. We march single file, groping our way across the fields, across the canals, up onto the dikes in the rice paddies in the darkness.

Sometimes we slip and fall down in a jumbled heap, the whole line of us, especially those with night blindness. We reach camp at about ten o'clock. The rain has slackened but continues to fall.

Early in the morning, when the moon rises faintly at about four o'clock, they wake us and send us back to the worksite. If there is no rain, we prefer to sleep at the worksite because if we sleep at the camp, we have to walk back and forth and spend our strength and waste our sleeping time.

Despite the work being difficult, despite the struggle to temper ourselves to such a high degree, our lives are in a precarious state. Can we yet avoid being taken away, tied up, and clubbed to death? Nobody knows; nobody can say definitively or predict it. Neither those who have been taken away to be killed already nor those who still await the day of their death can know for sure what their crimes are, or what the crimes of their friends or siblings were. It is this not knowing our true crimes that causes us all to live in a state of trembling and fear, not knowing when it will be our turn.

The crimes that we all know about are immorality (men and women secretly making love) and theft; whether big or small, a lot or a little, it all carries the same penalty. But a number of people have been taken away to be killed without having stolen or committed immorality, and for what?

These days this infectious disease has spread to the cooperative. The villagers all have sober, sad faces, men and women, new and old. All is still in the evenings at the village. The villagers, men and women, young and old, stay quietly each in their own house, nobody daring to visit anyone else's house. They extinguish their fires and their lamps soon after dusk. If now and then you hear the sound of a dog howling or barking, that is the sound of the executioner going to wake a villager, tying up a man and marching him to be killed at

Paoy Trach. Some victims are covered with dirt, while some are left for wild dogs[7] to gnaw on.

Terror covers all of our feelings. Those in the mobile units are afraid to go and visit their families in the village. And the villagers don't dare visit their children in the mobile units.

The work in the cooperative is a bit easier than the mobile work, but their food rations are much more diminished than ours. And abductions and executions are much more serious there than in the mobile units. In each round, there are ten to twenty victims. The chief executioner in Paoy Char subdistrict is Comrade Chhin. Comrade Chhin is over thirty years old, about a meter sixty-five in height, with a medium frame. He is the deputy chairman of the subdistrict under Ta Lam. Comrade Chhin has never gone mobile but is tasked with leading the work in the subdistrict. He is the most dictatorial and cruel man. Before killing someone, Comrade Chhin asks questions and hands them a cigarette to smoke before tying them up and taking them away. Some say that Comrade Chhin eats human livers and swallows human gallbladders. His eyes are red like the eyes of a crow pheasant. This man travels everywhere on a racing cart pulled by the finest, fastest oxen, with decorated collars and dozens of small bells that make a loud noise whenever he drives by at a gallop from time to time.

The viciousness of Comrade Chhin makes everybody in the cooperative tremble in fear, especially women. Nobody dares to look Comrade Chhin in the face when he walks about inspecting the work in the fields.

In the mobile unit, we have yet to encounter this degree of fear, terror, and dread. Only occasionally do we lose somebody, quietly. But now, suddenly a strange new thing happens in our mobile unit.

End of the First Week of May 1977

Our front lines that started work at the first water gate reach the end of their section. Srah Chik subdistrict finishes their work first, and then starts a new section continuing on from that of Paoy Char subdistrict, the unit working on the last section in this first phase. The work of the Paoy Char cooperative is not yet completely finished because we are still cleaning up the levees and the banks of the canal in some places where it bulges or slants in an uneven way.

---

[7] *Cuon alpinus*

At four o'clock in the morning, we awake and resume work to finish our jobs. I dislocated my shoulder the previous evening and am unable to work, so I sit watching the road for the unit leader to return from the village so I can ask permission from him to go and recover at camp.

Because today all of the cooperatives will be moving their lines, some people have been allowed to return to camp to collect equipment, hoes, and baskets, or to bring bundles of things to stow there. For this reason, there are a lot of people traveling back and forth to the camp starting from first light. But nobody brings any news to those of us working at the worksite. Suddenly, when the sun has fully risen, a horrifying piece of news drifts to us: "Somebody has been hanged at Kok Krasang!"

We are all very surprised and puzzled by this news. In the old society, people would commit suicide by jumping into water, hanging themselves, taking poison, or jumping in front of a train because of a romantic crisis, because of family conflict, or because of being ruined in business. During this revolutionary era, on the other hand, despite living under stresses far more miserable than that of any such person, everybody strives doggedly and determinedly to the utmost to survive. We have never heard of anyone resorting to suicide to remove themselves from this oppressive and dictatorial society. People want to live, and they don't dare do anything careless which could cause death. In particular, everybody seems to have this thought: *Better to die because I am killed than to die because I failed to fight to live.* Stealing tubers, sugar cane, corn, or paddy rice to support life, if you end up being arrested, your life is over; but people still take the risk in order to survive. Even when they come to tie you up and take you away to be killed, most people turn themselves over to be quietly bound without any reaction at all. Because people want to live, because they think that meekness can lead to mercy, that they might be released. But nobody who is tied up has ever been seen to return. When I think about this, I feel sinking dread in the pit of my stomach to think back on my own fate, when I myself had been released from bonds.

People try to think of every possible means to survive; people fear to die— they don't want to die, so why would anyone hang themselves? Did they do it to demonstrate to the Revolutionary Organization their suffering while living under the exploitation and oppression of this totalitarian regime, to demand freedom for their family and friends who still live? Is it a man or a woman, a young person or an old person? Each of us is panic-stricken wanting to know, wanting to see it clearly with our own eyes, yet nobody dares to set aside their work and run off to see.

Seeing our agitation, Ta Lam says, "Keep working hard! Don't think about other people's affairs. This person didn't want to engage in the Revolution, he didn't want to live, so that's why he hanged himself!"

But we still feel just as agitated. I can barely sit still, watching the road for the unit leader, when at about 7 a.m. the unit leader arrives at the worksite and agrees to let me convalesce at camp as requested.

Kok Krasang is a low *kok* with close-set sugar palms and *krasang*[8] trees growing on it, without any smaller vegetation apart from grass growing beneath the trees. Because it is the dry season, and the grass has all withered and died on the *kok*, it is empty and clear. The *kok* is nearly a kilometer from the worksite. Every day, after eating lunch, those who don't go foraging for food often come here to nap and recover their strength.

This morning people pass through Kok Krasang one after another, but nobody tarries long or stands looking at the hanged corpse; they look only briefly and then continue on their way, for fear that the Organization will take note. Looking from afar, I see about ten people standing with their faces looking upward into a *krasang* tree about seven meters tall. The hanged man must be there, but I can't see him. Then as I draw closer, I can clearly see the corpse of a young man about twenty years old, wearing shorts, with a bare torso, his shirt having been removed to tie his hands behind his back, his neck encircled with an ox rope, hanging from a limb of the *krasang* tree about five meters above the ground. The others and I watch the corpse, which sways slightly, with solemnity and horror. Then the sound of a woman weeping reaches us. She is the older sister of the dead man, a young worker from the mobile unit of Srah Chik subdistrict, Phnom Srok district. She weeps as she runs toward Kok Krasang with a number of women running after her.

When she can clearly see her brother, she stomps on the ground and sobs even more loudly. She keens loudly and cries, "Why did you hang yourself? No, he didn't hang himself! They killed him! They killed my brother! What did my brother do wrong?"

---

[8] *Feroniella lucida*

At the same time, three or four cadres dressed in black arrive, and one of the cadres climbs the *krasang* tree and cuts the rope, dropping the body to the ground, *thud,* like dropping a coconut. The women who have come with her lead the sister of the dead man back to the worksite, comforting her, urging her not to cry here. And we walk away silently.

Workers at Trapeang Thmor Reservoir have been killed one after another, but we have never known when it was happening; they took them away quietly. This is the first time that the Organization has hung a corpse for all of us to see. What does the Organization intend by this? Neither the sister of the deceased nor any of the rest of us know what sin this young man committed. We only know that this was a threat against all of us.

This sight imprints itself on all of our minds and makes us pity the victim, causes us to worry about our own future fates, and causes us to further fear the power of the Organization.

At the beginning of the rainy season, the rain falls regularly—sometimes during the day, sometimes at night—but our work goes forward continuously, despite rain and thunder, cold, or mud. When it rains hard, the water pools in the pit, and we bail the water out as we dig. When it rains, the cadres lead the unit leaders away to take shelter at camp, while we work in the rain. We work even more actively, running quickly, calling out to one another from unit to unit to help our bodies endure the cold. If the rain stops before the day's work has ended, we continue working until our bodies and clothing are dry. After the rain, the work becomes difficult, as the dirt is not quite water and not quite earth, sticky and clinging to our hoes and baskets.

Some days the rain falls at mealtime, and we eat our rice and sip our *prahok* water mixed with rainwater. Some days it rains in the middle of the night and our sleep is interrupted as we walk kilometers to sleep back at camp.

After about three weeks, the work of digging the canal from Trapeang Thmor Reservoir to Kok Kraol is completed. Apart from the forces of the special unit, who are to move their lines to Kok Rumchek, the rest of the forces are to go and dig a medium-sized canal from the banks of the Rumduol River at Kok Prasat to the area east of Phnom Srok, passing through Boh Sbov.

The old folks claim that Phnom Srok's original name was *Phnom Srot*.[9] Because of how the terrain is situated, we can see that this claim is plausible. East of Phnom Srok the land rises gradually. And in the forest north of Boh Sbov, we encounter large, flat slabs of mountain stone and laterite rock scattered unevenly about.

Starting from the fields east of Phnom Srok to the west side of Boh Sbov, the ground is normal and easy to dig. Starting from Boh Sbov to the river, it is a harsher battlefield than we have encountered before. The large Chicken-brand[10] hoes with thin, sharp blades, our special weapon in many battlefields, are now set aside as they are of no effect here. Only the Elephant-brand hoes, which are small and thick, with short blades (nearly worn away) and short handles, which we were about to throw away, are effective in gnawing away at this dirt mixed with laterite gravel that has nearly turned into stone itself. If we use the Chicken hoes, if the blades don't just break apart, then they split, or their handles snap, or the handles become so loose you can hardly pound them back in place. The teams that use Elephant hoes take turns using them to dig, and they are in constant use without any rest.

It is truly difficult! When the earth was loose, people loved to use only the Chickens; but when the earth becomes hard, their love turns to the Elephants. They attack the earth without mercy, using Elephants to battle the stones.

We swing with all our might and the sharp hoe blade penetrates only a finger's width into the ground. The hoe blade strikes stones and sparks fly, the hoe handle jarring all the way up to our chests. We rub spit on our palms to stop them from becoming hot from rubbing against the hoe handles as we clutch them tightly and swing them hard against the ground. Even though all of our hands are calloused, they still hurt, and our shoulders and chests become sore.

In some places, there are big slabs of stone that even Elephant hoes are unable to resist. They don't budge. We attack with a new strategy, carrying fire-wood to pile up and burn on top of the stone. The stone absorbs intense heat and cracks somewhat, and then we use metal pry bars and chisels to gradually break it up. Because of the obstacles of the stone slabs, we are unable to dig a nice canal as we had done in the flatlands. Our canal has an appearance more

---

[9] "sunken mountain"

[10] *Chicken* and *Elephant* refer to actual brands stamped on Chinese-manufactured hoes

like a natural waterway, winding and turning through the gaps between large slabs of stone.

Because of the complexity, the thick forests, the gravelly dirt, and the large slabs of stone, our work here proceeds only during the day. We finish our work at the end of May after having waged a fierce battle for exactly one week. On the last day of the offensive, the Organization kills an ox and makes a meal for us. Even though it's not much, meager fare, it provides us with an unusually delicious flavor that we have not experienced for a long time.

The next day we strike camp and move our front lines to a new destination: the Kok Rumchek worksite.

CHAPTER 25

The Kok Rumchek Threshing Yard Worksite

We may have finished our tasks at one worksite, but the work of the Revolution has no end, and there is no time for rest. To rest from revolutionary labor is to rest from eating; that is, to die. So long as we still live, there is revolutionary labor for us to perform at all times. The people in the cooperative villages are no different from those of us in the mobile units. When one assignment ends, another assignment begins: plowing; transplanting; harvesting; threshing; clearing land to make fields; planting tubers, taro, sugar cane, corn, and beans; building paddy dikes; digging canals; sowing; transplanting...

The old men who cannot walk far, lacking in strength, plant tobacco and vegetables; raise chickens, ducks, and pigs; watch fields; weave *kanhchraeng, kanhcheu, chang'er, l'ey,* and *bangky* baskets; and repair and make oxcarts, plows, and harrows.

The old women watch small children, raise silkworms, weed and care for mulberry orchards, weave silk, card silk, spin silk, weave *kramas,*[1] etc. Everywhere is like everywhere else: there is no end to activities, and nobody ever complains that there is not enough work or that they have nothing to do.

Even though the work at Trapeang Thmor Reservoir has ended, and the season of rice farming has arrived, the forces that left the cooperatives to be workers for the Trapeang Thmor Reservoir remain at large in the plains. Especially the forces from Phnom Srok district (except for the children, who are given permission to return to the villages after completing the digging of the canal from Trapeang Thmor to Kok Kraol). Ta Lam calls this force the "assembled force" and says that nobody will return to the villages.

The forces of Serei Saophoan[2] district return to their own district. The forces of Preah Netr Preah district, the middle-aged unit anyway, return to their own district, while the young men and young women are assigned to the Kok Lvieng collection worksite, located along the Phnom Srok–Prey Moan road, south of Kok Rumchek. As for the forces of Thmor Puok district, like Preah Netr Preah district, the young men and young women units remain behind at

---

[1] a traditional cottage industry in this area

[2] Sisophon. *Serei Saophoan* is the official Khmer name of the district/town, of which *Sisophon* is the common Thai-derived pronunciation (as the region was formerly under Thai control).

the Kok Roessei collection worksite, located south of Kok Krakhop (a local village just south of Kok Kraol).

Kok Rumchek is a worksite that gathers the young men and young women mobile units from Phnom Srok district, located on the west side of the road to Prey Moan, a distance of about eight kilometers from the town of Phnom Srok.

An east-west causeway about eight meters wide, one meter tall, and more than ten kilometers long, coming from the Sreng River at Char Kok Team village and extending to Tean Kam subdistrict, passing immediately south of the Kok Rumchek collection worksite, was completed in 1976 by the Phnom Srok district young men's and young women's units. This causeway constitutes the border between Phnom Srok and Preah Netr Preah districts.

1976 was a period of harsh oppression in terms of revolutionary work and discipline. The Revolutionary Army was busily engaged in activity at the worksites. The *chhlop* units would collect intelligence at nighttime to get a feel for the mentality, stance, and viewpoint of the young men and young women toward the Revolution. Many young men and women from the mobile units were taken away to be clubbed to death at night, near the base of the causeway, just for reminiscing about songs from the old society, being perceived as resistant to revolutionary labor, not respecting the Organization's appointments, etc.

It was also in 1976 that my next younger brother Samat was taken from the hospital and killed. Friends who used to work with him think, some of them, that my brother was killed because of viewpoints incompatible with the cadres in charge, while others think that my brother was killed for taking something that belonged to somebody else. Which of these opinions is true? It's all very unclear, all speculation. The truth, the plain reality, is that my brother was arrested, his arms tied behind him, and marched away to be killed. These circumstances, dying by being taken away and clubbed to death, is the legacy of all Life Slaves. Nobody laughs at anyone, and nobody sneers at anyone. Each person thinks only of working to redeem his own life.

The men's section of Phnom Srok district's special unit, which was separated from us after completing the canal from Trapeang Thmor to Kok Kraol, comes to build an automobile parking lot directly east of Phnom Srok–Prey Moan road, across from the Kok Rumchek worksite. These men rest at the Kok Rumchek worksite with the young men's and young women's mobile units. As for we who have arrived last, we have to camp at the Kok Kakah worksite, which is about a kilometer north of Kok Rumchek. Kok Kakah is the camp site for Phnom Srok district's middle-aged unit.

Our task now is to construct a threshing yard about 400 meters east of Kok Rumchek. This threshing yard is adjacent to the Kok Rumchek–Char Kok Team causeway along the south side, with a height of one meter, a length of 300 meters, and a width of 100 meters. It is divided into lots according to sub-district, cooperative, and unit. The pit for extracting the dirt is about ten meters south of the yard.

Even though the worksite is just over a kilometer away from the campsite, we get acquainted with Kok Kakah for only the one night of our arrival. On subsequent nights we sleep at the worksite, near the edge of the digging pit. Because it is now the rainy season, we are allowed to take a quantity of branches and thatch grass and build small huts for each team to take shelter in at night.

Our food rations decrease to two cans of uncooked rice per person per day. We lose breakfast, and lunch and dinner are diminished as well. The free rations have been replaced with careful measurement. But our labor remains grueling and intense, both day and night. Electric lights are arranged around the pit and at the threshing yard construction site to provide illumination on moonless nights.

Our work is more heavily supervised than before. Higher level Organization officials from the district and the region, with whom we are not familiar and whom we have never seen before, walk about monitoring our work activities. They are assessing our mentalities toward the Revolutionary Organization now that the rations have been reduced. Actually, our feelings are stable and have not changed; we have never dared to place conditions on the Organization. On the contrary, we have only strived to work hard to please the revolutionary cadres, to please the Organization, not daring to offend.

Some days two or three soldiers dressed in black uniforms and carrying guns walk about watching us work. This is a new situation for our little infantry unit; this kind of situation usually only happened at the special unit, when the Organization had to arrest somebody and take them to be clubbed to death. Fear and worry consume us all: *Today who will receive an evil fate like that of the people in the special unit?*

Sometimes the soldiers put their guns down and pick up hoes to dig. The fear doubles. Our mouths taste sweet with fear, the muscles in our hands and feet twitch and tremble, and we don't dare to speak, each of us meditating on despair. Paralyzing remorse oppresses our minds, each of us pouring over every error and failing we have ever committed, each with a melancholy, sober face, staring at one another in silence as if wishing to impart our last words.

The fear and confusion in our feelings is relieved when the soldiers leave our unit. Though the presence of soldiers was terrifying, no evil thing befell any member of our unit. It is our fate to have survived to continue to carry out the revolutionary labor.

We have worked for more than half a month and finished about fifty percent of the project when suddenly orders come down for us to suspend the work and move our front lines again, to go and dig out and deepen the bottom of the canal at Smach village, where water from the Rumduol River is sent to Kok Rumchek for dry-season rice farming. We work in the water and the mud for three days and then finish, and our whole force returns to Kok Kakah.

CHAPTER 26

Journey to Spean Sreng

All of the workers return to the camp, but we are not allowed to stay there for very many days. We meet just to say goodbye again, as we receive new directions to move our lines to dig a canal in Spean Sreng subdistrict.

Spean Sreng subdistrict is located southeast of Phnom Srok. There is a whole string of villages along the Sreng River, the river that divides Battambang and Siem Reap provinces.[1] This subdistrict shares a border on the north with Nam Tau subdistrict, on the west with Spean Thom and Srah Chik subdistricts, and on the south with Teuk Chor subdistrict of Preah Netr Preah district, while the eastern border is marked by the Sreng River.

9 June 1977

At first light all of the workers in the Kok Rumchek and Kok Kakah camps arise and prepare to depart. As is custom when moving the front lines, we disassemble the camp for materials, especially thatch grass, to use for building the new camp.

The sun rises high above the treetops and thousands of workers are on the move from Kok Rumchek and Kok Kakah camps, forming a massive marching column, extending as far as the eye can see.

Is there any other scene as lively and moving to the observer as watching the scenes of the Play of Life? Scenes of a play performed on a stage, scenes of a film projected onto a white screen—these are only vignettes in imitation of the Play of Life, adapted and enhanced with artistry to make the audience lose themselves in the scenes. But the fact is, they are still not real nor authentic. The Play of Life, on the other hand, features all the things that occur in real life: rejoicing, sorrow, devastation, arrest, torment, kicking and hitting, clubbing to death, etc.

In reality, right now, all of the Khmer people on the stage of Cambodia are united in performing the Play of Life in the scene of "The Great Tragedy." Everywhere one looks—in the center of the stage, on the edges of the stage, in the corners of the stage—all one sees is suffering, sorrow, devastation, and misery! And now today we, the members of the cast, perform the scene of "The

---

[1] Since then, Battambang has been split into Battambang and Banteay Mean Chey provinces, with Phnom Srok now falling in Banteay Mean Chey.

Journey to Move the Front Lines," in the style of people living in the age of slavery. The only difference is that the slaves in the age of slavery were usually put in chains and manacles when marched to work, while we walk freely. But this does not prove that our fate is superior to that of slaves back then. In fact, it shows quite clearly that, presently, Cambodian society has only two distinct classes: the Life Masters (cadres), and the Life Slaves (the Khmer people).

Slave masters feared that their slaves would run away, so they bound the slaves or placed them in chains. That's because in a society with many classes, there are many layers of many different kinds of people, which can make it easy for slaves to get away, to escape from the oppression of being enslaved by others. As for the Life Masters, they have no such concerns. They have no fear at all, so they don't need to put chains or manacles on their slaves. For in this society, there are no intermediate classes whatsoever on whom the Life Slaves can depend to help them hide or disguise themselves.

Slave masters used clubs and whips to beat and abuse their slaves, to motivate and compel them to work, or to suppress any individual who resisted, who was lazy, or who was not diligent in their work. This meant that, at times, there would inevitably be slaves who dared to rise up in rebellion or opposition. As for the Life Masters, they have only to walk about inspecting the work, without any hitting, kicking, or abuse. But we who are the Life Slaves strive to work hard, without slackening. Nobody dares to complain or resist because these people have the right to take our lives at any moment, without remorse.

Slaves had solemn and somber faces all the time, for they had the right to demonstrate the truth, to show their hearts to others in society, so that others could feel sorry for them, take pity on them, and help them escape from slavery. As for us, we work hard to hide our suffering and sorrow, keeping them in our breasts, not daring to let others see our shriveled hearts. Our outward appearances are unfaithful to our true feelings and disguise our hearts. We act as if we are happy, glad for our fate to have become slaves with lives beholden to the Revolutionary Organization. If we hurt, we dare not say that we hurt; if we worry, we dare not express worry. These are the rights of the Life Slaves.

We are living in a society that has not been seen in the history of humankind, a society where everybody lives awaiting the day of their death, the day when they will be killed without even daring to show a reaction. Instead, we try to manifest mannerisms and facial expressions to be seen as someone without concern, without any frivolous feelings, so that they will indulge us in sparing our lives for a while. Such is the case today, when we play the roles of pathetic characters with cheerful faces, smiling happily.

Here is today's cast of characters:

Some members of Ta Val's mobile brigade, costumed in matching black uniforms with few possessions, carrying their hoes and *bangky* baskets over their shoulders, with only a small bag of clothing on their backs.

Next are the Kok Rumchek[2] young men's and young women's mobile units, including Samorn, my younger brother. These are mostly costumed in black, with a medium number of possessions, with rice-sack hammocks, which is one thing more than the young men and women of Ta Val's brigade have. (Members of Ta Val's brigade, like soldiers, carry nylon hammocks, which can be folded and rolled up and placed into their clothing bags.)

Next is the special unit from Phnom Srok district, costumed more or less like the Kok Rumchek mobile units. My second oldest sister and her husband are in the special unit.

Next come the central characters of our story: the middle-aged mobile infantry unit from Phnom Srok district, headquartered at Kok Kakah. These have a wardrobe that is liberal, deficient, pants dyed, shirts dyed, some a pale reddish color, some a dark reddish color, some a muddy whitish color, covered in dirt and mud, torn and tattered beyond recognition. Some wear only shorts down to their mid-thighs, with bare, black-skinned torsos, sweat flowing and sparkling in the sunlight. Some wear hats made from sugar palm leaves to protect them from the heat. These have the most abundant and the heaviest possessions: the *bangky* basket on one side of the shoulder yoke holds a hoe, a bottle of salt, a bamboo cylinder or teapot full of water, and pots and dishes; the other *bangky* basket holds a bundle of clothing rolled up in a rice-sack hammock with pieces of bamboo inserted at both ends and wrapped up with a cord made from a sugar palm frond or a *dah kun* vine. Besides all these supplies, we each carry two or three thatch panels. Most members of this Phnom Srok district infantry unit are married, some deployed alone, others deployed together as a couple, having abandoned their homes and shelters so that they also have to carry with them a few supplies for family life. That's why we carry so much stuff sticking out everywhere, unlike the others.

---

[2] i.e., from Phnom Srok district, but camped at Kok Rumchek

We march single file by unit and by team. Each unit holds up a bright red flag flapping in the breeze, with one or two star characters dressed in black with silk *kramas* of mixed red, green, and yellow around their necks, wearing brand-new shiny-black rubber sandals, walking outside the column and watching us: the Life Masters. We, the Life Slaves of the middle-aged unit, have few shoes or sandals to wear. Most of us walk barefoot. Rationed sandals are rare; only the Life Masters get them. In Ta Val's brigade, and in the young men's and young women's units, they mostly wear rationed shoes, or sandals made from automobile tires. Samorn, my brother, has an old pair of tire sandals that are still wearable, but I am barefoot.

The people of Char and Smach villages, both young and old, women and men, who are deployed in district mobile units farming dry-season rice[3] east of Smach, stand watching our column pass with great interest. Noon is their resting time, so they are permitted to view our play on the stage without objection. The villagers rest and take their food and water, but we must keep marching forward; our road is still far to travel.

It's now the rainy season, and in the sky there are great masses of thick clouds drifting aimlessly, helping to amplify the heat from the sun, making it even hotter. The heat from the sun pours down from above and waves of heat rise up from below, engulfing our bodies in an atmosphere of intense heat. We sweat until we are soaked. If the soles of our feet were not thickly callused from being accustomed to walking barefoot, they would surely blister and sting, making us unable to walk due to this intense heat. We walk along the top of the causeway, which has no tree shade whatsoever. The sweat flows until we are depleted, and we begin to get thirsty, we begin to be exhausted and tired, dragging our feet step by step. Some units break ranks and leave the causeway, going down into the rice fields and along the paddy dikes in the fields, seeking shade in which to take shelter and recover their strength. Some units press forward, as the shade from small trees and shrubs beside the road are not sufficient shelter for recovering their strength anyway.

The afternoon grows later, and a sizable portion of our force has now entered Char Kok Team on the banks of the Sreng River. This village has mango, jackfruit, orange, banana, and coconut trees growing here and there, with deep,

---

[3] rice planted in the dry season (though it has now become the rainy season)

refreshing shade. We drop our baskets, yokes, and bundles and sit down to rest in the shade of the trees along the river.

Is there anything more joyful than being thirsty and finding water, or missing someone and seeing their face? We can scarcely drop our things fast enough as we race to throw ourselves into the water *splash splash* with our clothes still on, not caring about being wet. We drink the water, and we soak in the water to cool our bodies, burning up with heat from the rays of the sun. We soak in the water until it is time to continue our journey.

We have traveled for nearly ten kilometers, and there are still many kilometers which we must endure to reach our destination. For this reason, we can't rest in the water of the river as long as we would like to. We follow a path northward across fields and through scattered trees. After a while, our wet clothing has become dry, and we come to a spot of land where there are trees with nice cool shade. We stop and rest again.

Five small stone temples built of large slabs of sandstone, each weighing tons and placed atop one another, hide themselves in the shade of the trees. The villagers call this place Prasat Pram.[4] The spire of each small temple has collapsed to the ground. The stone slabs that formed a wall around the perimeter of the temples have been carved with beautiful designs that float above the surface of the stone. I climb up onto one of the temples and sit on the highest slab of stone and breath in the cool air that blows off the river, and carefully observe with awe and excitement the handiwork of my Khmer forefathers. At the northeast corner of the temples is a large pond crowded with water hyacinths, mingled with the occasional lotus. Some say that Prasat Pram was built on a stretch of an ancient road built from Banteay Chhmar to Angkor, apparently as a rest stop.

At about four o'clock in the afternoon, we stop and rest to end our long journey just west of Pongro,[5] a village about two kilometers north of Prasat Pram, also on the Sreng River like Char Kok Team. Dropping my baskets and yoke immediately, I run to jump into the river to soak my body and scrub myself again, then climb back out to find a place to rest. Meanwhile, the unit

---

[4] "Five Temples"

[5] a different Pongro village from the one in Paoy Char subdistrict (this one located in Spean Sreng subdistrict)

leaders go to a field westward to make measurements and divide the land into plots for us to work on.

Digging a canal is fast-paced work which requires relocating our resting place many times over a short period. For this reason, it is not expedient to construct any sort of large camp; we just clear the forest and the bushes to make a resting spot. Some people sleep directly on the ground, while others tie up hammocks beneath mango, orange, and jackfruit trees. The thatch grass that we have all so diligently carried along is for roofing a kitchen shed for the economy team, and for roofing a small hut for each unit in which to store our clothing bundles when it rains.

The canal that we are to dig at this time is medium sized, with a top three meters wide, a bottom a meter wide, and a depth of one meter, for taking water from the Sreng River to irrigate the fields west of the villages of Spean Sreng subdistrict. This canal leaves the river in the region near Rok village, then turns straight south toward the fields west of Prasat Pram.

10 June 1977

At first light, we begin work on digging the Spean Sreng subdistrict canal. The ground in this area is much harder than the ground at Trapeang Thmor and Phnom Kon Khlaeng. We are not able to dig it up in large chunks or slabs of earth. As our hoe blades strike the ground, they make loud *bung bung bung* sounds that hurt the ears. But however difficult and grueling it is, we must be resolved to fulfill the revolutionary work, victoriously, in all places. On the first day of our campaign, I and everyone else strive with all our might to smash the surface of the earth with fortitude, without retreating. We take turns wielding the hoes to break up the earth with frequent, hurried strokes, sparing no strength.

At about nine o'clock in the morning, the sun casts its golden rays onto the earth. I am bent over, swinging the hoe handle to break up the surface of the ground, when suddenly a feeling of vertigo and fainting comes over me. I put my hoe on the ground and lean on it to keep from falling over, then call out for help. The people standing near me drop their hoes and run to hold me up, then carry me away from the pit and place me on the ground, my legs sprawled out before me, as they pound and squeeze my shoulders and back, tug my armpits, rub my face, pull my hair, squeeze my arms and legs, and then lay me down flat to rest. But I still feel dizzy and faint, my lips pale. Seeing me in this state, the unit leader allows my friends to help me walk back to camp.

Two or three women, who have been allowed to rest to patch clothing, help to coin and pinch my skin until I am bruised all over. I feel better, and my dizziness has passed, but I am unable to keep anything in my stomach, whether rice, porridge, or water. As soon as I swallow it, I vomit it back up immediately with the bitter taste of bile in my mouth.

Tonight I am unable to sleep, my stomach churning, and I have four or five bouts of diarrhea. Comrade Chuop, the unit leader, ties his hammock up next to mine. He is the one to help me get up each time I have diarrhea, occasionally digging a hole for me near the hammocks.

My sister and brother are working to the south of me about four or five hundred meters. I ask my friends to send a message to them, but nobody has the time to take sympathy on me. I plead with the unit leader to take a message to them, but I encounter only silence, not seeing either of my siblings coming to check on me. They must not know that I am ill. During the day everybody leaves to work while I lie sick and alone.

Although the work has been grueling for a while now, my body has not become overly thin, but has remained strong enough to work at full speed like the others. But being ill for two days, without any rice or porridge entering my stomach, without medicine, my body begins to shed weight, becoming exhausted, ears ringing, almost unable to stand up or walk. The Organization decides to send me back to convalesce at the field hospital in Kok Kakah.

12 June 1977

At first light a friend puts his arm around my back and helps me walk to and lie down in an oxcart, which takes me to the hospital. Another patient goes along with me, but his condition is not as serious as mine; he is able to sit up. It is Bong Yong, the former leader of my unit's economy team.

Ever since I criticized the economy team while building the dam at Phnom Kon Khlaeng, Bong Yong, the economy leader at the time, has not spoken to me. I have thought very little about whether he speaks to me or not. Now we are both sick and heading to the hospital together. Bong Yong seems to have softened his heart, and he speaks with me on friendly terms once again. As soon as we reach Kok Kakah, both Bong Yong and I seem to feel better and are able to drink water and eat porridge, without taking any medicine. I think to myself that I must have fallen victim to the land of Spean Sreng subdistrict, especially the water of the river that I had soaked in twice while my body was overheated.

For the Life Slaves, a hospital is a place of torture, a place for treating illnesses of the mind, where patients who are lazy must be subdued until they flee back to the worksites. The porridge is thick and burnt, dark brown like soy sauce, with a scorched flavor so strong you can barely swallow it, but now and then with raw lumps. They measure out one bowlful for each patient, with a pinch of salt. Dried fish, smoked fish, and solid rice are only for the medics, who think only of hunting animals and guarding the patients so that they don't try to run home or wander off looking for something to eat.

The medics know Bong Yong, as he used to be in charge of the district economy team, so they bring him scientific medicines to take. As for the other patients, they give us the rabbit-turd pills. The patients who are in serious shape are sent along to the district hospital that has now been established at Wat Chey (in the town of Phnom Srok).

As the porridge in the field hospital is so hard to eat, the economy team at the Kok Kakah farm makes pots of small-batch porridge and roasts dried fish and brings these to Bong Yong to eat for every meal. I, too, get nice food to eat at every meal because of him.

With scientific medicine to treat him and with porridge and dried fish to eat regularly, after resting only three days at the hospital, Bong Yong recovers and leaves to work on the Kok Kakah farm. I, with only rabbit-turd medicine and a more serious illness than Bong Yong, have to continue my ordeal of living in the hospital. But none of the patients are itching to stay at the hospital; we are eager to say goodbye as soon as we are better. A week later, I ask to leave the hospital and am assigned to work on the Kok Kakah farm. But after a little more than a week, I turn right around and return to the hospital.

This time I resolve to endure eating the porridge and salt in the hospital until I am truly recovered and have adequate strength before I ask to leave. I stay for another half month exactly.

CHAPTER 27

The Kok Kakah Farm

In former times, Phnom Srok district was an area that flooded during the rainy season. Only spots of relative high ground escaped the flooding, where the people would build their homes and form villages. The locals refer to such a place of high ground as a *kok* or *paoy*.[1] Along the Prey Moan–Phnom Srok road, there are many of these spots of dry land, some with villages of locals, and some with cemetery woods where the dead are buried, such as Kok Kraol, Kok Krakhop, Kok Tonsay, Kok Lvieng, Kok Roessei, Kok Reach, Kok Kakah, Kok Rumchek, etc.

Kok Kakah is a cemetery wood, located between Kok Rumchek and Kok Roessei, a distance of about seven kilometers from Phnom Srok, and one kilometer from Kok Rumchek. This *kok* has a long east-west shape, with a width of about 200 meters and a length of about 500 meters, and an area of about ten hectares, with dense thickets of *kakah*, *thnuong*,[2] *trach*, *lveang*,[3] and *trabaek prey* trees. It is a place of burial where the cart drivers are afraid to stop to rest.

After the completion of the first phase in the campaign to build Trapeang Thmor Reservoir, the district Organization appointed this place as the campsite for the mobile units of Phnom Srok district. And Kok Roessei, which is located about a kilometer north of Kok Kakah, was appointed the campsite for the mobile units of Thmor Puok district. Kok Rumchek, Kok Kakah, and Kok Roessei are situated on the west side of the Phnom Srok–Prey Moan road.

When we first arrive at Kok Kakah, two or three long shelters aligned east to west, thirty meters by five meters, have already been constructed near the road. Construction continues steadily for the thousands of people coming to stay here as the mobile units gather to work on the paddy dikes in the area. In total, there are thirteen structures assembled in a row at the front end of the *kok*:

---

[1] *kok* means simply "dry land" in the standard Khmer dialect; *paoy* possibly comes from Thai

[2] *Pterocarpus cambodianus* or *Pterocarpus pedatus*

[3] *Rhamnus tinctorius*

- A wooden structure roofed with thatch grass, four by fifty meters, with downward-slanting awnings, built parallel to the road (north-south) at the entrance to the *kok*—a dining pavilion for the mobile units.

- An economy kitchen, five by eight meters, built from wood with a thatch-grass roof, located at the southwest corner of the dining pavilion.

- A cadre's office built from wood, thatched with grass, four by six meters, on the west side and right in the middle of the dining pavilion.

- Three rows of shelters for the mobile units, each shelter five by thirty meters, built east-west, with three shelters per row. The first row is immediately south of the economy kitchen; the second is immediately north of the economy kitchen; and the third row is separated from the others, about forty meters farther to the north. These shelters are made from small trees, with roofs and walls of thatch grass, and partitioned into small rooms with sleeping platforms made with slats of *prech* bamboo or small trees.

- The field hospital, made from small trees, roofed and walled with fronds, about four by ten meters, located north of the second shelter in the third row.

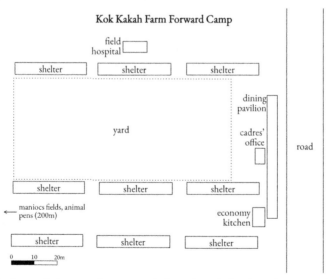

Kok Kakah Farm Forward Camp

Though the mobile units have now left Kok Kakah, this place is no longer a wilderness. Apart from the patients staying ate field hospital, there remain some forces working to clear land here. Some of them are the older men and women with flagging strength who have a hard time following the mobile units, and a fair number of people who are patients released from the Kok Kakah field hospital, but who don't yet have enough strength to be sent back to the mobile units, such as Bong Yong and myself.

The work here is divided among four objectives: one team clears land and cuts down trees; one team removes large tree stump and burns them to help clear the land; one team digs ponds; and one team tills the ground and plants tubers and sugarcane (with two yokes of oxen for plowing).

Ta Lam is in charge of this work, with two or three *chhlops* as assistants and three base people leading teams: Mea Lik (a base person from Trapeang Thmor village); Ta Yoeum (a base person from Paoy Char village); and Bong Tith (a base person from Paoy Snuol village). Mea Lik and Mea Yoeum are both about forty years old, and Bong Tith is about thirty-five.

Immediately after leaving the hospital, I join the team clearing trees with some motherly women, and then I join the team that removes and clears stumps.

About a third of the land area has been fully cleared already, and the remaining land has already been cleared of the dense forest so that you can see from one end of the *kok* to the other, except for the far west end of the *kok* where they have left about half a hectare uncleared.

At the west end of the *kok*, the young men are digging a pond for holding water to use in the dry season, as wells dug here do not produce water.

After working on teams with motherly women for about four or five days, the Organization removes me and sends me to haul dirt with a shoulder yoke for the team digging the pond. The work here is not terribly difficult compared with the work of the others engaged in the offensive in Spean Sreng subdistrict. We have tree shade in the heat of the day, shelters, and platforms for sleeping on. But unfortunately, after hauling dirt for only three days, I come down with cramping diarrhea and am unable to work. Not wasting any time allowing me to rest and continue eating rice like the other workers, the Organization sends me to the field hospital immediately.

From one day to the next, the graveyard wood of Kok Kakah slowly transforms into a farm, with vegetable crops beginning to grow, then sprouting leaves, lovely and fresh. The Organization creates a place to raise animals at the western end of the *kok*, and they hand responsibility for this over to Bong Yong. The site for raising animals is adjacent to the trees that still remain on the western end of the *kok* about 200 meters from the forward camp. It is very quiet there at night.

When I leave the Kok Kakah hospital for the third time, Bong Yong asks Ta Lam if can go there to help him with his work, and to have someone to keep him company while he sleeps at night.

In the beginning, the site for raising animals is not very large. There is only a small hut built from small trees and roofed with leaves, about three and a half by six meters, facing west, with a short awning in the front about chest high, so that we have to bend our heads down whenever we enter or leave it, and another overhang in the back about one meter above the ground. This hut is divided into two rooms of the same size. The south room is a pen for chickens and ducks, with a door on the south. The north room is a sleeping room, with two sleeping platforms made of bamboo slats about a meter twenty by a meter eighty each, parallel with one another, one along the north wall and the other along the south wall, with a space in between about sixty centimeters wide, and another platform connecting to the other two at the back wall. This room's doorway faces west, open, without any leaves or door to cover it. Bong Yong sleeps on the left-hand[4] platform against the chicken pen, while I sleep on the right-hand one. This hut is built near some termite mounds and a large *kakah* tree with a broken-off top producing nice cool shade, at the northwest corner.

When I arrive, with help from two other young men, we build a pig pen by cutting down a tree with a trunk about the size of a human thigh, cutting it into sections, and embedding these in the ground to make fenceposts for the pen, about thirty meters south of the chicken pen.

The animals we raise here include four pigs, four *angkam* ducks, and thirty chickens. The vegetables and animals raised here at Kok Kakah are for supplying the mobile units from Phnom Srok district waging offensives at various worksites. Even though there is little production capacity, it helps to supplement the diet of the workers on the front lines to some degree.

---

[4] while facing the doorway from the inside

CHAPTER 28

Disappearance

A Buddhist proverb says,[1] *attahek attanao neathao*, meaning "one must be self-reliant." Some Buddhists follow Buddhism vaguely, with unclear understanding of the scriptures, Dharma, and discipline, which leads them to stray from the path of the Buddha's words. The Buddha was a man, not God. He instructed man to live after the manner of man—that is, one must be self-reliant and not be dependent on others. Being dependent on others makes you lose your balance, your footing, your independence, your supremacy. This Buddhist proverb has proper and good meaning for any individual who desires to build themself into a true person, a winner, an athlete. This proverb is especially good as a path to guide one's life in the circumstances of this so-called revolution. The Organization creates a new motto for use in their time, but with an old meaning, which says, "Independent Self-Reliance: He Who Works, Eats." This motto has the same meaning as the Buddhist proverb *attahek attanao neathao*. It is very clear! We all no longer have parents, siblings, or children. The children live on their own, mother lives on her own, each with their own regime, nobody helping anybody, nobody depending on anybody.

The Buddha engaged in a revolution, transforming Brahmanism to create a new religion. He engaged in mortification of the flesh, eating only two balls of rice, eating only one ball of rice, not eating at all, sitting motionless in meditation. The Revolutionary Organization wants us to temper ourselves, eating only two ladlefuls of porridge, one ladleful of porridge, or no porridge at all; but they force us to work hard, to strive, in the hope of living to see the Glory of the Revolution.

What is the magnitude of our struggle at this time?

Some people don't understand the value of their own sacrifice and struggle. They don't have faith in the dharma of the Buddha which says *attahek*

---

[1] in Pali

attanao neathao. They don't understand the motto "Independent Self-Reliance: Whose Hair, His Head"[2] and they live in dependence on others, relying on those others, like Bong Yong. At thirty-nine years old, Bong Yong is slender, of clear complexion, with a height of about a meter sixty or so. He is a new person who was given high responsibility, which other new people rarely ever have the fate to receive: he was appointed as the leader of the district's economy team back when we came out to build the Trapeang Thmor Reservoir. Bong Yong never knew digging, hauling dirt, or hauling sacks of rice and food. He had light labor and lived easily to the point that he seemed to no longer be aware of the suffering of the rest of us, the other new people in his own unit. He ate good food, he slept comfortably, and he acquired an exploitative mentality, which added yet additional burden on the rest of our lives. Some of the supplies and rations the Organization provided for us found their way back to the cooperative through Bong Yong and the rest of the economy team because their siblings, children, and wives back in the villages were not getting full enough. Nobody dared to clear their throats at Bong Yong because Lord Lam was his patron, and Bong Yong pampered Lord Lam. The rest of us suffered intensely because of the opportunism of him and his clique, to the point that we dared to call a meeting to criticize the economy team while building the dam in the forest at Phnom Kon Khlaeng. We didn't hate Bong Yong, but we loathed his exploitative behavior. Through this criticism, Ta Lam became aware of Bong Yong's misdeeds, and he ordered that a large tin of sugar that was hidden in the village be returned to the unit.

Bong Yong came under scrutiny. Dependent on the patronage of Lord Lam, with his round belly, Bong Yong felt no concern, and continued to exploit the rest of us. If we got sugar, beef, or pork, Bong Yong secretly sent it to his house, every time. His status declined, and he continued to make mistakes: When we moved the front lines from Phnom Srok to Kok Kakah, he was demoted from the economy team for the whole district to the economy team for the unit. When the front lines were moved to Spean Sreng, he was demoted from unit economy team leader to an assistant to the district's economy team leader. Now that he has left the Kok Kakah field hospital, he is no longer on the economy

---

[2] "Whose hair, his head" or "Whoever's hair it is, that's whose head it is" is an idiom that means something like, "Whoever does something bears the responsibility for that thing."

team at all, and the Organization has assigned him to raise animals for a change, apart from everyone else, where he is easy to keep an eye on.

The pig pen has been completed, and in addition to hauling pig feed and feeding the pigs, Ta Lam also assigns me the task of collecting unused hoe heads from the mobile units' shelters, sharpening them, attaching handles, and providing them to the people digging the pond and removing stumps to clear the land. The two young men who helped us build the pig pen return to digging the pond, but they still come back to sleep with us each night.

The food rations decline to one can per person. We eat porridge both morning and evening. Every evening the two young men and I set deadfall snares and usually have two or three rats every morning. We each collect our own porridge ration at our own subdistrict's economy kitchen and then bring it to eat together at the chicken pen.

One day a young man, a base person about twenty years old, comes to sleep at the chicken pen with us. Some days he goes to help haul dirt, some days he strolls about here and there, and some days he just lies around at the chicken pen.

Who is this young man? Why is he sleeping here with us? The other two young men and I are worried, thinking that this comrade must be a spy who is keeping an eye on our activities.

But Bong Yong doesn't think so. He believes Ta Lam, and Ta Lam has told him, "That comrade is so lazy! The Organization reassigned him from the army to an art-performance unit, and then reassigned him from the performance unit to be a medic, and now they have reassigned him from the hospital to haul dirt. Yong, you should keep an eye on him while he sleeps at the chicken pen. I don't want such a lazy person near me!"

Because he has such unwavering faith in his patron, Bong Yong has only contempt, but no concern, for the presence of this young base person, considering this comrade to be a person whom the Organization has cast off, whom the Organization does not trust or esteem.

The chickens become sick and lethargic, two or three of them die, and Bong Yong takes the dead chickens to show Ta Lam. Ta Lam gives him guidance: "Next time if any chickens become lethargic, bring them here right away before they die!"

When chickens become lethargic, Bong Yong catches them and takes them to Ta Lam, as instructed. Ta Lam takes them and has them cooked just for him and the other cadres and four or five *chhlops* to eat. Bong Yong becomes resentful.

One day the young base person entices him, saying, "Father! We should consider slaughtering a chicken and eat it. If we take a sick chicken to Ta Lam, he never lets us eat any of it."

"No, I don't dare," Bong Yong objects.

One night, the two young men and I attend a meeting in the forward camp. When we return to the chicken pen, suddenly Bong Yong sends me to go and bury some chicken feathers. We are surprised by this, and worried that something bad will come of it. An exploitative mentality resides in Bong Yong's heart continually. Having roasted a chicken, he produces half of it to eat with us, and hides the other half, supposing that because it is dark, we can't see it. But both we and the young base person are well aware that he has hidden the other half of the chicken.

The next night, Bong Yong complains that he doesn't know how to eat porridge with boiled *prahok*, then grabs a handful of salt and leaves the circle to go off by himself and eat the chicken. Starting from that day onward, the young base person no longer comes to sleep with us very much, and soon afterward he disappears altogether. Bong Yong gets bolder and bolder, sometimes slaughtering and eating a chicken all by himself, not even sharing any with the rest of us. We don't demand any, and we don't envy him because we are afraid to die. We catch rats every day, which does not cause us anxiety like stealing and eating a communal chicken would. Feeling uneasy, the two young men return to sleep with their own unit.

Should we believe some of the traditions of the local villagers?

My father used to tell his children, "If you travel in the highlands, in the hills and forests, if you encounter a *neak ta* statue, if somebody jokes and smacks the statue on the head or pokes the statue in the belly, you should not laugh. If you laugh, the *neak ta* will make you ill."

In some places people believe that if a barn owl cries in the village, it is an omen that somebody will die. So if a barn owl cries in the village at night, they take a piece of firewood with burning coals and throw it at the owl to chase it away.

Some people believe that encountering a *kray* snake[3] is an omen of death, etc.

One morning, none of my deadfalls has caught any rats, but one has caught a snake instead: a large *kray* snake about as thick around as my wrist, and about a meter long. It isn't round but has a triangular shape (an isosceles triangle), with black and yellow markings in alternating stripes: black, yellow, black, yellow.[4] Some people don't call this snake a *kray*, as it is an omen of misfortune, but they call it a *thnang ampov*[5] snake instead.

Nothing is more powerful than hunger: I try not to think too much about this and put it out of my mind, taking the snake back to the chicken pen to eat it.

When Bong Yong sees me carrying the snake, he asks me, surprised, "Hey Tuch! Where did you get that snake?"

"It was caught in my snare, Bong," I answer.

"Tuch, do you know what kind of snake that is?" Bong Yong asks me with a note of concern.

"I don't, Bong."

This reply makes Bong Yong more anxious, and he feels reluctantly compelled to explain to me, "Listen, that snake is called a *kray*, and it is very unlucky, Tuch! If two brothers see one, one of the brothers will die! How could you dare eat it? Damn, you don't know anything!" After saying this, Bong Yong walks away.

I played dumb because I was hungry, but now that Bong Yong has explained it to me, it would be impertinent of me if I pressed on out of hunger. I decide not to eat the snake, but I regret the loss of its meat, so I take it and give it to the young men digging the pond.

---

[3] krait (*Bungarus*), a genus of highly venomous snake
[4] likely a banded krait (*Bungarus fasciatus*)
[5] "sugarcane joint"

I begin to feel worried, thinking of my younger brother who is working at the Kok Rumchek worksite. Why did I find this snake? Will misfortune befall me?

One Week Later, *19 July 1977*

Tonight there is a common meeting at the farm. It is a moonless night, and a completely dark sky blankets the world of suffering. In the darkness, we make a roaring campfire beneath the *kakah* tree in front of the hut for light and protection from animals. A *chhlop* comes and summons me to attend the meeting and tells Bong Yong to stay and watch the hut.

At this time, a number of the mobile forces have returned to the farm, increasing the number of people living here. A large crowd of us, gathered from each unit and subdistrict, sits around a kerosene lamp in the yard between the second and third row of shelters. Ta Lam is dressed in black with a silk *krama* scarf around his neck, standing in the middle of the circle, leading the meeting. The topic of the meeting is reorganization of the units to include additional strength that has just arrived, to divide up the objectives of the work, to organize the leadership, and to assign the responsibilities of each unit.

The meeting is long, so that some members of the assembly have to turn around backward and cover their mouths with both hands to suppress yawns *hom! hom!*

After organizing the units, Ta Lam asks after me: "Where is the comrade who lives at the chicken pen with Yong? Is he at the meeting?"

I jump up and answer, "Here I am, Father!"

"What is your name, Comrade?" Ta Lam asks.

"My name is Tuch, Father!" I answer.

"Ah, yes, Comrade Tuch. You are to be responsible for raising the chickens, ducks, and pigs, all right? Take care of them, give them food and water, and find ways to prevent them from getting sick. Let's find an older person to go and sleep there with you so don't get frightened," Ta Lam instructs me.

"Yes, Father!" I answer, accepting the assignment, and then sit back down.

The meeting is adjourned at about ten o'clock, in an atmosphere of great drowsiness. There are many questions in my mind, but because I am so sleepy, I climb straight into my mosquito net and go to sleep.

Every morning I arise while it is still dark to sweep the yard in front of the
hut and around the chicken pen, carry water on a yoke to water the vegetables,
the *trakuon,* cabbages, peppers, eggplants, and tomatoes planted behind the
hut, and clean the manger and set out water for the chickens and ducks to
drink. Bong Yong has never risen so early in the morning as I do.

This morning I open my eyes to see that Bong Yong's blanket is crumpled
up on his sleeping platform, and I don't know where its owner has gone. Where
would Bong Yong have gone so early in the morning? I don't think much of it,
thinking that perhaps Bong Yong has gone to the forward camp. I fill the watering cans and finish watering the garden, but I still haven't seen Bong Yong
return. No longer wondering, I begin to understand the new instructions that
Ta Lam gave me. Bong Yong must have been taken away to be killed last night.

The sun rises above the treetops. I put the chickens and ducks out of their
pen and give them their food. Then I take some hoe blades and sit to sharpen
them under the *kakah* tree, as usual.

Every day, Ta Lam walks about with an AK-47 slung over his shoulder, supervising the people clearing the woods on the north side of the *kok* and the
people digging the pond at the western end. At about nine thirty or ten, he
comes to the chicken pen and then returns to the forward camp.

Today Ta Lam arrives at the chicken pen very early and asks me, "Comrade
Tuch! Where are Yong's things?"

"They're inside, Father!" Having prepared myself in advance for this, I
respond without hesitation, then stand up and walk into the hut.

Ta Lam walks in behind me, then sits down on the platform where I sleep.
Yong did not have very many things: a red wool blanket, a rice sack to hold stuff,
a small pot, a dish, and a rice spoon. I gather these things and hand them to Ta
Lam.

He says, "I sent Yong back to Spean Sreng. What the hell, why would he
leave alone without bringing his things? Huh, well, Comrade Tuch, you go
ahead and keep them and use them. If the owner comes for them, you can
return them, but don't give them to anyone else!"

"Yes, Father," I answer.

Ta Lam leaves the hut and walks over to look at the pigs. He tells me to
compile figures on the animals and turn them in to him, then he goes off to
observe the digging of the pond.

Even though Ta Lam tried to throw me off, I have no more doubts. Bong Yong left for Spean Sreng at night with only a single pair of shorts and a *krama*? Two or three days later, we find out that Ta Lam gave orders to Bong Tith, who is in charge of the *chhlops* at the farm, along with two *chhlops*, to take Bong Yong away and kill him while I was at the meeting. That night, Bong Yong's wife, the former wife of an army major, who had just given birth at the cooperative, was also taken away.

They accused Bong Yong of being a former lieutenant in the Lon Nol regime. This is only a pretense, as normally if they want to kill some dog, they simply shout that the dog is rabid, and it's done. Like when they rounded people up from the cooperative and executed them at Paoy Trach a month before, they buried the bodies with both hands protruding above the ground and placed handwritten signs that said "stole" and "traded." (A villager who herds cattle told me this; I never went there.)

Bong Yong lost his life because of carelessness, from relying on Ta Lam, pampering him, supposing that this revolutionary loved him, when, on the contrary, Ta Lam was the one to end his life.

We had lived together in harmony like brothers. However bad he was, we made a lot of memories together these last days. The killing of Bong Yong makes me feel panic and concern about my own future fate. He is the second person to be taken from me to be killed, after Comrade On.

CHAPTER 29

Revolution

The Spean Sreng canal is complete. The middle-aged women have been allowed to return to the cooperative to farm rice. The middle-aged men and the young men and women of Kok Rumchek are sent to complete the Kok Rumchek threshing yard, and then to be stationed at the Trapeang Thmor Reservoir worksite with Ta Val's mobile brigade.

As we enter August 1977, revolutionary cadres from the Southwestern Zone come to take charge of the work here in the Northwestern Zone. The purging of the Northwestern Zone cadres commences. The regional committee chairman for Region Five (Ta Hoeung), the mobile chairman for the region (Ta Val), and the mobile chairman for the district (Ta Lam) are each arrested and taken away to be executed, one after the other.

Now that Ta Lam is gone, Bong Tith is given temporary responsibility for leading the work at the Kok Kakah farm. The work is reorganized all over again: the young men and women are sent to the Trapeang Thmor Reservoir worksite to farm rice, while the middle-aged men and women are sent back to the co-operatives. The farm now becomes the farm for the regional mobile units, and no longer serves the district mobile units. The crops of corn, beans, melons, watermelons, manioc, yams, peppers, eggplants, tomatoes, pumpkins, *khlouk*[1] gourds, winter melons, *nonoung* gourds, *trakuon*, cabbage, and tobacco are picked and distributed to the worksites in turn. The strength which remains stationed at the farm consists of thirty people: twenty women and ten men (including cadres and *chhlops*), who eat meals together in a single dining pavilion.

Mid-September 1977

The Kok Kakah farm receives a new leader appointed by the Organization to take the place of Ta Lam. Bong Tith's role is merely that of assistant to the new leader. He is a man called Ta Moeun, about fifty years old, small framed, about a meter sixty in height, his hairline receding a little bit, wavy haired, very talkative, with hair growing on his chest, seemingly a harsh man. He is a base person from Spean Sreng subdistrict, perhaps the subdistrict chief, but this

---

[1] *Lagenaria siceraria*

man rides a bicycle everywhere he goes, though he doesn't have a *nirasar*[2] with an AK-47 slung over his shoulder following on a bicycle behind him as Ta Lam used to have.

For more than two years now, I have been engaged in this Revolution under a pall of darkness, without understanding, reluctantly, under compulsion from the Organization. Now I am beginning to understand a little bit about this word *revolution*. The Organization often uses their motto "Temper, Conserve, Innovate, Take Active Initiative" to exhort us. Through this motto, combined with my mother's last words to me, "Why does dying have to be so miserable?" I understand that I can find a life of light and happiness, with a desire to continue living, not weary of the obstacles, large and small, that continuously stand in my way during this period. On the contrary, if life is dark and degraded, living in despair, people will cry out for death.

This type of revolution is a new thing that Khmer society has never encountered before. A Khmer proverb says, "Enter the river according to the bend." If we live with the Revolution, we must engage in the Revolution. The Organization says that "if you do not engage in the Revolution, the wheel of history will grind you up!" In order to survive, we have to go with the flow. Whether this revolution will build the nation or destroy the nation, I don't know; but in order to live, I have to adapt myself and engage in the Revolution with open eyes and awareness; I have to engage in a revolution to build myself. Every individual can work toward building the nation only so long as they first know how to build themselves. Building the nation is building oneself, and not building oneself is not building the nation. If you don't know how to love yourself, or your family, then you don't know how to love the nation.

Through this revolution of personal growth, I am able to live with greater ease (unobstructive) within *their* revolution. I fulfill my work with attentive care, wanting to learn and to understand. Apart from the duties that the Organization assigns to me, I take opportunities to do extra work, planting supplementary vegetables like eggplants, tomatoes, *trakuon*, and cabbage around the hut. In my free time, I learn to sew palm-frond hats. I sew them beautifully, some with regular corners and some with a round, conical shape. I help repair

---

[2] Author's note: "This word is not found in the dictionary but was used in this period to mean something like a bodyguard." This word, coined by the Khmer Rouge, is sometimes rendered as "messenger," and delivering messages was also a typical function of this role.

the leaky shoulder-yoke watering cans for watering the crops on the farm or construct new watering cans. I make hoe handles, sharpen knives and hatchets, etc.

It is true that you are born naked and pure, with nothing, and your value as a human being depends on what value you construct for yourself, while others only appraise that value. If you build little value for yourself, others will appraise you cheaply; but if you build much value for yourself, they will appraise you dearly. Your own value is knowledge; if you know a lot, and are skilled, people will value you highly.

But this is not enough. These days, they have arrested many of the educated and those with advanced learning and taken them away to be clubbed to death. If you have knowledge, but you don't know how to survive, then you will not make it. You have to know how to assess the circumstances, the social environment, to humble yourself lower than the cadres who supervise you, most of whom are ignorant and poorly educated. Hence the importance of the word *morality* during this time. If you don't know how to make them love you, you better at least not make them hate you.

Because I know how to adapt myself, everyone at the farm—the men and women, the new people and the cadres—love and esteem me. The cadres come to me to sew palm-frond hats for them to wear. When Bong Tith gets vertigo and dizziness from time to time, he comes to me to coin him and massage him. They are small tasks, but all of these things make the cadres feel that I am a person who is valuable to keep, and a loss to remove.

When I took over the responsibilities from Bong Yong, there were only ten chickens left: seven hens and three roosters. But over the next three months, they multiply to fill the pen. I build another large, spacious pen about nine by three meters, north to south, in front of the old pen. I do the work myself, after I get help to assemble the ridgepole, rafters, and crossbeams.

Every day I rise at dawn and haul water to water the crops, then I sweep the pens, let out the chickens and ducks, scatter hay, and put down feed for them to eat. I scoop the chicken droppings from the pen and pile them for the people planting vegetables to take and put on the garlic, then I put a sack over my shoulder and go hunting for spiny amaranth and *puk bangkang*[3] grass to

---

[3] "lobster beard"; possibly *Alternanthera sessilis*

simmer for the pigs to eat. The four pigs are very large now, each one about fifty kilograms. Later in the day, I haul water on a shoulder yoke to bathe them, and pour some on the ground for them to wallow in. Late in the afternoon, I go to the economy kitchen and haul back rice slop, for the second time, for the pigs to eat, and then I haul water for the evening crop watering. At dusk I round up the chickens and ducks into the pen.

At the farm they ring the bell for the evening meal at about five thirty. I never go to eat with the others, as the chickens and ducks have not gone back into the pen yet. At about six or six thirty, I am finally able to take a pause to have my dinner. Because I eat after the others, some days I end up eating with the *chhlops* and cadres, who get special food.

There are five ducks: four hens and one drake. Every day they lay three or four eggs, and I have collected about seventy of them now. Bong Tith gives me orders to hatch ducklings, which I do by placing the duck eggs in hay inside an old gasoline can, and I light an oil lamp for warmth at night. In the daytime I place the eggs in the sunshine for warmth. Neither I nor Bong Tith have ever hatched duck eggs before, but we experiment according to his notions. Bong Tith wants to send me to learn how to hatch duck eggs in Svay Sisophon, the headquarters for Region Five, because there they raise thousands of ducks and there are people who know how to hatch ducklings. But Ta Moeun rejects this idea because he thinks that our farm is small and does not require an expert of this kind.

Phnom Srok is a district with vast and abundant rice fields, as far as the eye can see. During the *Sangkum Reastr Niyum* era, this district produced rice so abundantly that there was rice left over for export abroad. And now, even during this revolutionary era, rice productivity is higher than in the *Sangkum Reastr Niyum* era because there is less threat from floodwaters in the fields around Trapeang Thmor Reservoir, and now we have additional capacity for dry-season rice farming as well. But despite this, during this revolutionary era Phnom Srok district is in dire poverty in every area, more so even than the other three districts in Region Five (Thmor Puok, Sisophon, and Preah Netr Preah).

The people eat rice only during the season of harvesting, trampling, threshing, and gathering the rice into the granges. After the rice has been col-lected into the granges, the food rations begin to decline again, little by little, until there is only the occasional grain of rice in the porridge, which is simmered with bits of tuber. This rainy season, the people in the cooperative are going through a period of intense tempering, more grueling than any other time before. In the regional mobile units, whose needs are supplied by the Organization, food rations have fallen to one can of uncooked rice per person per day. Those of us at the farm have supplementary vegetables, corn, and tubers to fill the gaps. But for the mobile units at the worksites, these rations are not sufficient for the labor that they carry out each day.

The rations decrease, but the discipline of the work gets stricter and more oppressive. After finishing the work to dig the canal in Spean Sreng subdistrict, Oun (my second-oldest sister) is sent by the Organization back to the cooperative. As for myself, ever since being deployed on the mobile unit to help construct Trapeang Thmor Reservoir, I have never set foot back in the village, and I don't know where in the village my two sisters live.

Mid-October 1977

Bong Phan, a somewhat aged widow and a cook for the farm, used to live in the village with me. She used to work with my siblings and me when we dug the Or Roessei canal last year.

One day, I am hauling the buckets of pig slop on a shoulder yoke in the morning, and Bong Phan calls out to me, "Hey, Tuch! Come here, and I'll tell you something!" She waves her hand signaling for me to come close.

"Sure, what is it, Bong?" I ask.

She signals for me not to talk so loudly, and then says, softly, "Your Oun is sick back in the village, Tuch. She has been unable to transplant rice for two or three days now."

"You saw her?" I ask.

"That's right, I saw her. She told me to tell you to go and visit her," Bong Phan says with a grim face.

"Yes, thank you Bong. Oh! I forgot: What house does my sister live in?"

"Oun is in a newly built hut at the south end of the village, along the south side of the road to Phnom Srok, the fifth house from the corner."

"Thank you, Bong!"

This news rattles my emotions and makes me think of my sister. I ponder as I carry the slop to the pigs, and I continue to ponder as I feed the pigs. I ponder what I can take to my sister. But I can't think of anything, and I'm afraid to ask permission to visit the village, as the pens are full of pigs, chickens, and ducks, and I am the only one to watch them with nobody to fill in for me. Everyone else has their own duties; and besides, every day there are hatching chicks and ducklings that have to be taken and dried out.

One day goes by, then two. On the morning of the third day, I resolve to ask Bong Tith for permission to visit my sister.

"Bong, I would like permission to make a visit to the village."

"Gee, you want to go visit the village? What for?" Bong Tith asks me, in an attitude of surprise.

"I want to go visit my sick sister, Bong."

Bong Tith remains quiet as though thinking, and then questions me further. "Tuch, if you go, then who will feed and water the chickens, ducks, and pigs, and who will gather them back into their pens?"

"I will only be gone for the morning, and I will come back in the after-noon."

"All right, go ahead! Ask Bong Phan to give you a rice ration of one scoop."

"All right, thank you Bong!" I answer excitedly.

Bong Tith has a lot of sentimental feeling toward me. The appointed ration is only one can of uncooked rice per person, but he is giving me one scoop (two cans) for one meal. If it were Ta Moeun, I would never dare to even ask.

After setting the chickens, ducks, and pigs in order, at about nine-thirty in the morning I leave the farm walking along the paddy dikes, cutting straight across toward Paoy Snuol. Feeling elated, I half walk, half run, wanting to reach the house quickly in order to see my sister and have time to visit with her for a while.

It's the rainy season, and the paddies are full of water. The road is flooded in sections, some places with water shallow enough to wade through, but in other places up to my waist. At about ten thirty, I reach the village, a distance of about eight kilometers from Kok Kakah. The village is dead quiet without many people around, including children and old people, as there usually is.

The huts of the new people, though newly built, are dilapidated and falling apart. Lacking roofs, lacking walls, some patched with three or four thatch panels mixed with tattered sleeping mats, some with roofs of thatch grass with-out a ridge pole, some of the thatch peeling away or fallen to the ground. They are built on columns made of small tree trunks, high up off the ground. The dilapidated state of the houses reflects to the observer the form and shape of the lives lived by the owners inside. The village of the new people is spacious and open, and beside the ramshackle huts, there are no vegetable gardens as in the villages of the base people. I walk along the outskirts of the village, my eyes scanning for my sister's house according to the description given by Bong Phan.

My elation at having been permitted to visit the village is transformed in an instant to pained alarm when my eyes fall on the form of my sister, sitting in the doorway, her eyes watching the road in front of her hut almost without blinking. She must be watching the road for her brother, for me. This woman who used to have such a sturdy frame, thirty years old, who could work as hard as the men, now has the emaciated body of an elderly woman.

As soon as she sees me, my sister becomes excited and tries to speak to me in a soft voice, painstakingly, in the manner of a person who has no strength left: "Tuch! Come on up." She scoots out of the doorway to make way for me to enter the house.

The hut is about three meters by five meters, divided into two small rooms, with a floor of thin wooden slats, eaten by termites until pieces have fallen off so that it's hard to find a place to sit down. I sit with my legs outstretched and my back against the side of the doorframe, which is wide open with nothing to cover it, my eyes looking up at the sky through a hole in the grass roof, which is falling apart.

My sister is silent from joy, and I am silent from the turmoil in my heart, from seeing things that I could not have imagined. Ever since leaving Phnom Penh, I have been the one to suffer chronic and debilitating illness. Even when my sister caught malaria, she never wasted away to a state of such skinniness. I feel such pity for her that I can barely open my mouth to speak.

Seeing me sitting silently and sighing, she begins to ask me questions. "Bong Phan told you?"

"Yes, but because there was nobody to take over my work, it was hard for me to get permission to come. What's wrong?" I ask.

My sister lifts her sarong up a little above her knees and shows me her right leg, which is swollen from the ankle all the way to the kneecap, and says, "This leg is so swollen and burns so badly I can't walk. I don't know what happened to it."

I examine her leg, which is swollen and shiny beyond recognition. I don't know what illness this is, and there is no medicine to treat it.

To turn my feelings away from despair and anxiety, I ask my sister, "Where have Ol and Nho gone?"

"They leave to transplant before dawn and return at dusk."

We speak slowly, each with our own concerns, each of us wondering to ourselves what to do in the face of such a state of affairs.

The sound of the village's dining-hall bell peals *mung! mung! mung!* The elderly and small children carry their bowls and dishes, one apiece, toward the sound of the bell, then return each with a dish filled with two ladlefuls of thin porridge apiece. My sister remains still, as though she didn't hear the bell. Has she asked someone else to bring her food to her? No, it doesn't appear that she has told anyone to do anything.

Stillness. Nobody else can be seen returning from the dining pavilion anymore. Still filled with uncertainty, I ask her, "Oun, you're not going to collect your rations?"

"No. When we returned from being deployed on the mobile unit, they told us to transplant rice. Our porridge was distributed by the economy team at the Bodhi tree west of the village. Every day My Yon, in the house just west of here, would collect rations for me. Starting from yesterday, they cut off my rations because I have been ill for more than three days. They told me to go to the hospital, but I didn't know who could take me there, so I decided to just rest at home without rations..."

My sister tries to speak but chokes up, and her eyes well up with tears.

Oh, the life of the poor! Poor, and wretched besides. Sick, and without food rations to boot. Where is her husband? Does he know that his wife is suffering?

"Where does Bong Khloeng work?" I ask her.

"Your brother-in-law hauls dirt at Paoy Ta Ong. Every evening, when he collects his rice, he bundles it up and brings it home to eat with me. As for Ol and Nho, they collect small rations that are barely enough for themselves!"

At a dead end, we sit silently, not speaking, but my mind races, trying to think of how I can help my sister. Bong Tith gave me a scoop of rice. When I left the farm, I thought I would cook it and have a meal with my sister for a change, then sit and visit until the afternoon, when I have to return. But now I see that this was the wrong idea entirely, that this scoop of uncooked rice has tremendous value for my sister's life. She can live for two or three days on it.

And the four cans of rice dust[4] that I saved by pilfering from the pigs can allow her to rest at home for another two or three days. I will miss my midday meal ration, but this evening I will eat again.

I take the package of rice and rice dust and pass it to my sister. "Oun, take this rice and broken rice ends and eat it! I have to go back now!"

She takes it and says, "Tuch, come to visit me often, all right?"

"Of course!" I walk away from her with my head spinning, full of pity for my sister.

At midday the water in the fields is getting hot. Tiny crabs about the size of my big toe, red, purple, and white, emerge from the clusters of rice plants and hide in the spaces between clumps of grass along the water's edge by the paddy dikes. I remove my trousers and don my *krama* scarf around my loins, then tie off the legs of my trousers to make a bag to hold crabs. As I walk, I catch crabs and put them into the legs of my trousers. Today I will eat these crabs in place of porridge for my lunch.

At about one thirty I return to the farm. Feeling famished, I waste no time in putting the crabs on to boil, then I eat them with Comrade Sambath, the young man who keeps the oxen on the farm, whom I had asked to come and watch the chicken pen. After eating, Comrade Sambath returns to work, and I place the duck eggs out to sun on the gourd trellis and then lie down and go to sleep.

As if in a dream, faint cries reach me and wake me from my sleep: "Tuch! Tuch! Crows are taking the duck eggs!"

Trembling with fear, I jump up and head for the gourd trellis. Good Lord! Crows are carrying away the eggs! They have taken ten eggs, and I am in big trouble! I take the egg basket into the hut and then run off in search of the eggs the crows have carried off behind the hut.

Suddenly I hear the cries of Comrade Sambath again: "Tuch! The crows have entered the hut!"

In fear, I turn around and go back. A pair of black crows circles the hut. Oh...No, I *did* hide the egg basket.

---

[4] dust produced as a by-product of the rice polishing process, often used as animal feed

If not for the girls and Comrade Sambath (who were weeding the corn north of the *kok*) noticing in time, this pair of black crows would have taken all the eggs from the basket. Comrade Sambath runs to look for the eggs where he saw the crows had flown off to perch. We climb the trees, we search near the termite mound, but we don't see any of the eggs. In despair, I walk back and come across a duck egg that the crows have pecked open and left on the ground behind the hut.

Damn, how could I be so unlucky? Just as I am worrying about my sister, now I am caught in another emergency. Ten eggs are a lot; I can't find eggs to replace them anywhere, and besides, everyone on the farm knows about it, so I can't hide it. I try to collect my thoughts and think of a solution, but there is only one option: prepare myself for punishment. At about four o'clock, I carry the shoulder yoke with buckets to go fetch the pig slop, and I take with me the egg that was pecked open by the crows to report to Bong Tith about what happened.

Bong Tith and Ta Moeun are sitting together in the cadre office. I approach Bong Tith and say, "Bong, the crows have taken ten of the duck eggs!"

I have barely finished speaking when Ta Moeun cuts me off abruptly. "Crows have taken the eggs? You mean two-legged wingless crows, right?" Ta Moeun suspects that it was people and not crows that stole the eggs.

"It really was crows, Father! Comrade Sambath and the girls helped me chase them."

I make excuses, but it's no use. Ta Moeun still doesn't believe me and says, "I've never seen crows here!"

No longer daring to speak, I hang my head and stand frozen in fear. Bong Tith begins to ask questions. "Where did you leave the duck eggs, Tuch?"

"I left them out to sun on top of the gourd trellis like every other time, Bong!"

"If you weren't there, why did you leave the eggs out to sun?"

"I just barely set them out after returning from the village, Bong!"

"Why did this never happen before? You can see clearly why. The reason is that you went home. I understand that you are alone without a wife or siblings, and that's why I gave you this responsibility, Tuch; and now suddenly you have siblings! Siblings must be set aside for now; now is the time for revolution. If people are busy thinking about siblings, like you, Tuch, they can't possibly wage revolution. If someone is ill, there is a hospital. Did you think that they don't know how to wage revolution, that the hospital doesn't know how to treat illness, so you would go and visit your sister yourself? Now, because you went to see your sister, has she gotten better? You don't yet know how to wage revolution, Tuch. You are not yet fully committed to the Revolution."

Bong Tith stops speaking, appearing to think about something. I am ashamed of my error and afraid that I will pay with my life, and I stand there stunned and unable to look up.

Suddenly Bong Tith says sternly, "Go! Go on back! Try to build yourself and don't make this mistake again!"

"Yes, Bong!" I respond with relief that I have received a reprieve. My head is tight and very heavy, heavy with the words of revolutionary doctrine that Bong Tith has sprinkled over me. But I also understand that this was a clever method which Bong Tith chose to save me; if he had not intervened to speak, and left Ta Moeun to resolve the matter, I might not have escaped with my life, as Ta Moeun thinks that I stole the eggs and brought them home.

However, I still don't understand what they're even waging the Revolution for, if the Revolution does not allow children to know their parents, or for a brother to know his own sister.

After taking my leave from my sister, I had thought to ask permission to visit her again in three or four days to bring her more rice dust. Now my wishes have melted away, and I no longer dare ask to visit my sister. Instead, I must learn to wage revolution like the others, wage a revolution to forget about my siblings, to not care about them. Whether I am able to do it or not, I must conform myself in order to survive.

Part Four: Love in Hell

CHAPTER 30

Condemned to Death

November 1977

The rice being farmed by the regional mobile units stationed at Kok Roessei and Kok Rumchek, in the fields on the east side of the Prey Moan–Phnom Srok road, stretching from Kok Tonsay to Kok Lvieng, begins to ripen throughout the fields. The rice at the cooperatives—in particular the cooperative of Paoy Char subdistrict—has begun to turn as green as a parrot's wing. At the same time, the food rations grow exceptionally meager.

It is not only the people in the cooperatives who are suffering from hunger; the regional mobile units working at the entire Trapeang Thmor Reservoir worksite, who work almost without rest, are starving too. Some days they get rice porridge to sip in the morning, but nothing in the evening. Some days they get nothing at all from morning till evening, and then they get a small amount of uncooked rice to make into porridge and divide amongst themselves.

This lack of food is caused by disruptions in transportation. Some days a truck transporting rice comes to Phnom Srok from Svay Sisophon. Some days we don't see so much as the shadow of a truck.

In the face of these disruptions, the Organization allows the cooperative of Paoy Char subdistrict and some of the regional mobile units to pitch in to harvest some rice and provide it to the cooperatives and the regional mobile units working at various worksites.

Both the regional mobile units and the cooperative mobile units involved are mostly young women and middle-aged women. 600 of them have come to stay at Kok Kakah to harvest and thresh the rice crop. My sister Oun is among them. These women, especially the young women of the regional mobile units, have emaciated bodies, pale and thin like stalks of rice, walking feebly, in a state of weakness from doing labor that is too strenuous for women, while eating insufficient food for the needs of their bodies. These mobile women eat in the dining pavilion along with those of us stationed at the farm.

Because the mobile units have no means of transportation, such as oxcarts, every day when they return from harvesting rice, each member of the mobile units carries a bundle of harvested rice stalks on her head and leaves it in the yard between the second and third row of shelters. Some days they don't harvest at all, but spend the day carrying all of the rice in from the fields on their heads.

Despite all the harvesting, the rice rations remain constant and unchanged, except that no meals are skipped. The starvation continues for people who have gone without for a long time now. When returning from the harvest, everybody sneaks a handful or two of paddy rice to roast and eat. At the midday and evening breaks, we hear the constant sound of paddy rice grains popping *snap pop snap pop* at every fire in every shelter. Everyone walks around munching on popped rice grains. At night they sit around chewing on popped rice grains, like oxen chewing their cud, until they go to sleep.

The Organization at the farm gives orders to stop the roasting of rice grains. Everyone who is permanently stationed at the farm is authorized to confiscate any pot, dish, pan, or other equipment used for roasting paddy rice. It is quieter than before, but some people continue to do it. They roast the rice in pots, kettles, or cans covered with a lid so that the popping can't be heard from very far away.

Whenever they see anyone stationed at the farm coming near, they panic, sometimes picking up the pot or kettle they are using to roast and running away, sometimes abandoning it and saving themselves. I don't make any effort to suppress this activity, for I know hunger the same as they do. Sometimes I sneak some paddy rice from stalks whose grains are still young and tender and chew on them. Sometimes I sneak grains of rice that have just sprouted on the rice stalks and chew them; sometimes I chew grains of ripe paddy rice raw; and sometimes I chew grains of milled rice or kernels of ripe corn I come across at the economy kitchen.

But some people take no pity on others, especially the young men who keep the oxen for trampling the rice at the threshing yard (the farm personnel help trample the rice that the mobile young women bring in). They act macho, walking around confiscating other people's equipment to show off. *They* steal, *they* roast, but there is no one to catch them, for they are the catchers.

Now there is nobody who does not steal. Everybody steals according to their own abilities and opportunities. Some steal a little, others steal a lot; some steal secretly, while others steal openly.

The cadres steal a lot, and openly. They steal from the mobile units to bring back to the cooperatives. Nobody dares to see them stealing, and they don't bother to hide it. They steal it openly, and the economy team prepares it for them.

As for myself, I steal secretly, and I steal "legally" (though of course there's no such a thing as legal stealing) without anybody knowing that I am stealing. I appear to be very proper, when in fact I am a secret thief, stealing from the pigs. Some of the finer rice dust is eaten by the pigs, and some is eaten by me. Sometimes I roast it, and sometimes I eat it raw. As for the courser bits, before I pour the rice dust into the manger, I mix it with water in a bucket, then take my hand and stir its so that the broken rice ends and chaff ends settle to the bottom of the bucket, then pour out only the rice dust and water mixture into the manger. The rice ends are for me; I wash these many times with water to remove the chaff ends and cook them in the small pot left to me by the late Bong Yong. So long as there are any course rice ends in the rice dust, I get some rice ends to eat every meal. The pigs don't know that I'm stealing from them, as they are animals; they are ignorant; they are stupid. They only thank me and love me for bringing them rice to eat every meal and for hauling water for them to bathe in. But if they did know, they wouldn't dare object, for I am their cadre. I have the right to beat them, to deprive them of food, to cut off their rations.

Some days I sneak a chicken egg and the hen doesn't dare squawk at me, as I am her master. But if there are other chickens with her, even if I am standing right there, she will chase *them* all over, pecking and attacking them mercilessly. Perhaps this is a case of "being angry at the cow and smiting the plow."[1]

Oh, how nice to be a cadre! Even if only the cadre of the chickens, ducks, and pigs—still it is a great way to live.

In summary, apart from the chickens, ducks, and pigs, everybody is a thief. So why is it necessary to catch people stealing, if you are also a thief? Some people want to catch others to hide their own deeds, to improve their own ability to steal.

But it is hunger that has taught people to fight for survival. The higher-ups give orders to confiscate equipment used to roast rice grains, and a number of dishes, pots, and kettles are taken away by them. But the stomachs remain hungry as before, unchanged.

How great is this hunger? Very great! So great that a sated person could never understand or even imagine it!

---

[1] a common Khmer idiom referring to misdirected anger

Even without dishes or pots, people sit around the fire, take out the paddy rice grains they have hidden in their pockets, and place them on the ashes of the fire with small coals hiding beneath. The roasting grains pop and fly onto the dirt, and they pick them up one by one, place them on the palms of their hands, and clean them off by blowing on them *puff puff* and then plop them into their mouths.

Is this not the behavior of a hungry person? And is this not stealing? Why not come and confiscate the coals as well?

The middle-aged mobile units from the cooperatives are not much different from the regional mobile units, except that they supplement their rations with private food, which the regional mobile units are not allowed to do. They can take time to go look for crabs and snails and pick leaves from the forest to boil with their porridge and the food that the economy team cooks and distributes. In the evening when they return to camp, when the sun has set, they collect their porridge and soup rations, but nobody eats it yet. First, they prepare and light their private cookfires and make their own private soup, the lights of these fires twinkling out across the fields. Some people stay and cook in the camp.

During the harvest offensive, all the women of the regional mobile units sleep in the third-row[2] shelters, while the middle-aged women of the Paoy Char cooperative sleep in the second-row shelters. The shelters in the first row are used to house the people stationed at the farm and the economy kitchen.

Every evening I eat later than the others because I am busy gathering the chickens into their pen. Tonight, after eating my evening rice, the sky is pitch dark during the waning moon of *Katdek*, and across the sky stars twinkle. As I am returning to the chicken pen, I run into Comrade Sambath and two or three female comrades at the end of the first row of shelters, and I stop to stand and chat with them. Suddenly, the women who sleep in the second row of shelters run from their shelters heading in our direction.

Puzzled, I call out, "What's wrong? What's going on?"

"I don't know!" the runners reply. Without knowing why, they are running, running with their clothing bundles, scattering everywhere.

---

[2] northernmost

I run in the opposite direction toward the first[3] shelter in the row. I ask the people who come running out behind the others, "Why is everybody running?"

"The shelter is on fire!" they reply.

Not seeing any flames, I shout, "Which shelter?"

"One of the cooperative mobile units' shelters!"

I don't see any flames, but people are pouring out of the first[4] shelter in the second row. I toss aside the spoon I am holding in my hand and run into the east end of the shelter.

My God! Fire is consuming the thatch grass wall that divides the shelter into two rooms down the middle, and the fire is spreading to the roof.

The shouts are deafening. Some women shout for me to grab their clothing bundles for them, and some shout for a man to put out the fire. The cadres for the cooperative mobile units and the oxcart drivers are all men, but they all seem to be stunned and don't come to help. By myself, I cannot put out this raging fire. I must cut off the fire to stop it from spreading westward toward the second shelter. Fighting the fire empty-handed, I yank on the thatch panels, but they don't budge. Changing tactics, I hold onto a wooden beam with both hands and hang, kicking the thatch panels with both feet as hard as I can. Thatch grass comes raining down, opening the wall wide so that people can see me from outside.

Bong Tith sees me struggling by myself and runs to help me. The two of us stand facing in opposite directions and kick down the roof thatch, one side apiece. In the blink of an eye, the fire's westward motion is stopped. Bong Tith leaps outside, while I remain and continue my defense.

The fire rages. Red flames leap and dance, blown by the air currents of the evening breeze coming from the north, as though possessed by a seething anger kept inside for a long time. Roiling black smoke rises into the sky carrying raw red sparks with it, casting them into the black veil of night like a dragon breathing fire.

We stand with our arms folded, watching the fire devour the shelter, with sadness, as though the smoke of death were devouring the body of a compan-

---

[3] easternmost

[4] closest to the road; easternmost

ion, taking them from this earth. Suddenly we hear a panicked cry: "The economy shed is on fire! The economy shed is on fire!"

This voice wrenches my attention toward the new emergency, and my feet automatically start moving toward the source. Unfortunately, my right foot treads on a gap in the platform slats and my leg falls in up to my thigh, and I fall forward, striking my chest on the crosspiece at the end of the platform. Ouch! My chest is in agony, and I can't get up. I hold still and wait for the pain to dissipate then push myself up with both hands and stand up straight, extricating my leg from the gap in the platform and removing myself from danger.

The economy kitchen shed is in danger because the wind is blowing the flames from north to south. But it is saved by three or four young men who climb up on the roof and douse it with buckets of water so that the thatch grass cannot easily catch fire.

I sit down in pain and stare at the flames that continue to mercilessly devour the shelter of people who are already suffering. The flames completely consume the thatch grass and the small slats and crosspieces. The fire loses strength little by little, while the pillars and the posts of the platforms that remain upright amidst the piles of glowing red coals continue to burn...

My sister and a number of the middle-aged women who sleep in the shelter that burned down were able to remove their clothing bundles in time, but some people's things burned in the fire. The fire is extinguished, and the danger is past, but fear and worry surely continue to oppress the feelings of some individual, as the question "Who started the fire?" is asked around.

After mealtime, the unit leader calls a meeting of the unit to ask questions about how the fire started. Fault usually ends up with those who are low and weak. The base women[5] accuse a woman named Bong Yon, a new person and widow about thirty-something years old, of having lit her cooking fire inside the shelter, causing the fire to spread to the wall. After a confession, the cadre "builds" the person at fault, then compiles a detailed report of the individuals who suffered losses from the fire.

A day and a night pass without anything noteworthy happening, either to the person at fault or to the rest of us, who feel sorry for her.

---

[5] i.e., female base people

This evening a refreshing winter breeze blows from the north. Large dark clouds roll in and cover the face of the Moon, who has been trying to peer down and follow the events of yesterday evening's fire and the fate of the unfortunate soul who took the blame. The sky is dark and threatens rain.

After eating the evening meal, all the mobile units retire to their sleeping places to rest. The leader of the cooperative mobile units summons both Bong Yon and Bong Lang to a meeting. Where are they going? They will be taken to Ta Moeun to be "built." Bong Lang was not involved in starting the fire, so why build her?

After dark, at about eight o'clock, after putting her five-year-old child to sleep, Bong Yon goes to meet Ta Moeun with Bong Lang. Two armed soldiers stationed at Kok Rumchek sit waiting for the suspects together with Ta Moeun. The moment the two women arrive, the *chhlops* arrest them and tie them up immediately and then silently march them away without saying a word. The women disappear without a trace into the dark veil of night of the waning moon of *Katdek*.

Oh, small child, not old enough to understand! How will you cry when you awake from sleep and can't find your beloved mother?

We are puzzled about why they arrested Bong Lang and took her to be killed. Two or three days later, my sister tells me that when they compiled a report about the individuals who lost their possessions and clothing in the fire, Bong Lang put her name down with the rest. In fact, Bong Lang was staying in the shelter at the west end of the row. Feeling suspicious, the cadre asked to check her clothing bundle and found her husband's pass for collecting his gendarmerie salary. It goes without saying that Bong Lang was an enemy of the Revolution who had to be destroyed by the Organization.

Bong Lang was about thirty years old. Her husband was a former agent of the gendarmerie in the Lon Nol regime, who was sent away for reeducation by the Organization at the end of 1975, after his family was evacuated to Paoy Char subdistrict, and never returned. Bong Lang had retained her husband's identification badge as a memento to remember him by. Now it has become instrumental in taking her life. I knew her during the transplanting season of 1976, when my siblings and I transplanted rice with her in the fields west of Paoy Char subdistrict. I never knew Bong Yon.

CHAPTER 31

Stealing Because of Hunger

After completing the region's rice harvest, all of the forces return to their respective cooperatives and units. The lack of food faced by the Paoy Char subdistrict and the regional mobile units has been resolved. But Spean Sreng subdistrict, which suffered flooding at the end of the rainy season (October), causing nearly all of their rice to be spoiled, begins to face the prospect of famine. To resolve this crisis, the Organization decides to have the people of Spean Sreng subdistrict participate in harvesting the rice of Srah Chik subdistrict, which takes place in the rice fields west of Kok Kakah.

For this harvest, the mobile forces of Srah Chik pitch their camp on Kok Kon Sat, about a half kilometer west of Kok Kakah. The mobile forces of Spean Sreng pitch their camp on the western tip of Kok Kakah, about a hundred meters from the chicken pen. Between the end of the *kok* and the chicken pen is a stretch of uncleared woods.

On the land of Kok Kakah, the crops are growing and bearing fruit. There are fifty or sixty rows of yams, thirty meters long, along the north side of the *kok*. Hundreds of manioc shrubs are growing higher than my head between the chicken pen and the forward camp, their tubers cleaving the soil. The winter melons and watermelons planted north of the chicken pen are bearing fruit.

Every night people from the cooperative mobile units sneak onto the farm and dig out or pull up tubers and pick winter melons and watermelons to eat, sometimes four or five plants, and sometimes ten to twenty plants. Ta Moeun issues orders forbidding any cooperative mobile unit member from entering or passing through the land of Kok Kakah and requires all the males stationed on Kok Kakah, except for me, to guard and patrol at night.

Hunger and thirst follow no schedule; sometimes people come and steal food at night, but sometimes they risk sneaking a tuber in the middle of the day. When the guards catch them from time to time, a cry goes up, to the west, the east, the north, the south, like a pack of hunting dogs chasing down and barking at a wild animal. "Thief in the yams! Thief in the maniocs! Thief! Thief!"

I feel sorry for the thieves, as they steal to survive, not because they are trying to secretly hoard these things to become rich, or to accumulate more than others. They steal only to fulfill the immediate demands of hunger. When compared with the greedy feeding and embezzlement of every cadre, their offenses are minor indeed. But it doesn't occur to any cadre that they themselves are a thief or a gangster. They are the ones leading the nation and killing the people, causing the people to suffer and starve until they are forced to steal just to live; is this not the fault of the revolutionary cadres? The people don't have enough to eat, and they steal. The cadres eat their fill and also steal. Which is the unforgivable sin? There are no scales; there is no weighing or balancing, so long as those in power, the cadres, hold the authority to kill the people.

Behold! Even now, they are chasing someone who has stolen because he is hungry. I never enter the fields, so I'm not very familiar with the paths that the thief is taking, running back and forth, up and down, to the west, to the east, to the north, and finally to the south.

"Tuch! Straight toward you, Tuch!" the voice of Mea Lik calls out to me.

The thief is running toward me? Can I act like I didn't see or hear anything? No, I definitely can't get away with it. I stand up and move to block the path of the thief. Hopeless of getting away, no longer able to run, sweating profusely, his mouth open, panting heavily, trembling and shaking and gasping like a water buffalo struggling to pull a cart through sand in the middle of a searing-hot day, the pathetic figure walks straight toward me. He is an older man.

He lifts his hands, palms together toward me, and pleads with me, "Please don't hurt me, Brother! I am so scared!"

"I won't hurt you, Brother. But why did you dare to steal in broad daylight like that?" I ask him.

"I was too hungry, Brother. Please help me!" the pathetic figure pleads with me.

"I can't help you! Look, here comes a cadre, plead with *him*!" I respond.

No matter how humane one is, one would never dare to respond to such a plea by just letting someone go, for we are not cadres. We are not the Life Masters. Mea Lik arrives and takes the man and hands him over to Ta Moeun.

The man who climbs the tree only picks the fruit, but the man who takes the fruit and cuts it open eats his fill. A thief can only manage to pull a single plant or pick a single tuber. It is the guards who catch them who eat their fill. They enjoy the fruits of theft legitimately. The thief becomes the provider for the guards and the cadres, who are already full, so that they become even more full.

If a thief comes to steal a tuber, the guards and cadres get to enjoy a treat. Some nights they manage to catch a tuber, but not a thief; some nights they might pull up a plant on their own and yell that a thief stole it. But if there really is a thief, they would certainly never spare them or let them go. They chase them until they catch them, as justification for their own deeds, to collect all the offenses *they* have accumulated and place them upon this individual, to take advantage of an opportunity to hide the evil that they themselves have committed. For even though the workers on the farm are the ones who labored to produce the fruits, they have no right to pull a manioc or yam or pick a winter melon or watermelon to eat as they please. Not unless they are ordered to do so by a cadre.

Every human action is committed under the orders of either the stomach or the passions. In a prosperous, democratic society, the rule of law reins-in human actions to a level that is acceptable by society. But what about a lawless society like this one? What guardrail is there to restrain human action? Especially for people who possess authority, people who are cadres? When human passions are combined with boundless authority, a human becomes a tyrant.

One morning at dawn, a refreshing breeze blows in from the fields and stirs the leaves of the trees on the *kok*, making a whooshing sound. The roosters beat their wings and cry out to one another in a call-and-response between Kok Kakah and Kok Kon Sat. The exceptional figure is the human curled up in a ball, snoozing and sheltering from the cold *Mikaser*[1] breeze.

Suddenly the sound of faint cries, one after another, rise from the yam fields at the north edge of the *kok*: "Thief! Thief! Thief!"

This cry wrenches me from my slumber and I am instantly alert, as I jump up and run out of the hut. I think, *The night guards are all hot-blooded youths, caught up in showing off how well they can thoughtlessly execute orders. Whenever they catch a thief, they beat them mercilessly.* I cannot remain unconcerned; I have to intervene.

---

[1] lunar calendar month from roughly mid-November to mid-December

I run in the direction of the cries, which drift through the trees, toward the rice fields west of the *kok*. When I emerge into the fields, there is a faint light in the sky, but all has gone quiet.

Suddenly the cries resume loudly amid the still-unharvested rice about a hundred meters in front of me. "What, are you going to try to fight back? You dare to fight back against *me*?"

Mouths continue to shout as hands and feet continue to pummel and kick with a steady *thud thud thud* sound. Three young men are surrounding and beating a thief sitting in shin-deep water, like wild dogs tearing apart a lamb.

Call them base youths, and say that they delight in beating new people to boast of their current power; but what about Comrade Savuth, who himself is a new person? Why does he not take pity on his own kind? He shouts energetically and beats the unfortunate soul, a fellow new person, as though exercising a long-held resentment.

"It's because of *you* that I have not been able to sleep for many nights now!" He pummels as he speaks, pummels until he has had his fill. Having gotten plenty to eat and plenty of rest with the cadres, Comrade Savuth has forgotten his own birth.

Having just arrived, I cry out to stop him, "Stop! Stop hitting him! That's enough!"

"No! This one is very hardheaded, Bong Tuch! He dares to fight back against us!" Comrade Savuth replies.

"Stop hitting him! That's enough! Hand him over to me!"

As I speak, I reach out my hand to raise the unfortunate figure to his feet. These boys are still very young, about twenty years old or thereabouts, and they respect and listen to me. Even though I have no authority in this matter, they stop the beating as I request.

Comrade Savuth says, "Tie him up, Bong Tuch!" He yanks on the *krama* tied around the unfortunate man's waist.

"It's all right! No need to tie him up. He won't run if I march him."

Holding onto the man's arm, I lead him out of the rice with the three youths framing us on either side and behind. The Spean Sreng mobile units, who were awakened by the cries of the youths chasing the thief, stand around watching in orderly ranks. Some blurt out, "Hey! It's Comrade Khan, the team leader!"

"Don't imitate me, brothers and sisters! I did wrong!" Comrade Khan says, tears flowing from his eyes, to the brethren and comrades of his team and his village. A younger man who, like me, is hiding among the general middle-aged population, he is about the same height and age as me and seems to be a man of learning.

Comrade Khan says, "I was wrong, Brother! I will build myself, firm up my foundation. I have been educating my brethren not to break discipline, not to deviate from the Revolutionary path."

"Why did you make this mistake, Comrade?" I ask.

"Last night I was too hungry, Brother! I had diarrhea twice and was totally exhausted and couldn't fall asleep. I couldn't take it any longer and I made up my mind to get up and steal a yam!"

Comrade Khan speaks hesitantly, remorsefully. I feel sorry for him, concerned for the plight of this comrade who is about to face an unpredictable fate. When we have marched Comrade Khan to the cadres' office, Ta Moeun, who is sitting beside the fire, stands up quickly and moves to take down his hammock and uses the chord to tie the man's hands behind his back, then kneels him down on the dirt and ties him to a pillar of the hall. Then he kicks him and lifts his foot to stomp him in the head and the face. Unable to keep my eyes open to witness the torture, I withdraw and return to the chicken pen feeling upset.

Normally, neither the mobile units nor the cooperatives have authority to rule on the fate of any criminal who is not under their jurisdiction, meaning they aren't allowed to take them away to be killed.

At about nine o'clock in the morning, the chairman of the Spean Sreng mobile units comes to meet Ta Moeun and asks that Comrade Khan be released to return with him. We don't know whether the cooperative's response will be to build (reprimand) Comrade Khan, or something else.

CHAPTER 32

Morality

Governance in this regime of so-called Democratic Kampuchea has no reference documents. Every work direction, plan, or order comes down to the Life Slaves from mouth to mouth, without any written documentation. Whatever the cadres tell us to do, that is law. Any deviation from this guidance is considered a violation of law and is subject to penalties: "building" or death.

The word which the cadres use over and over without tiring is *morality*. This word, *morality*, can mean orders, the party line, or rules, such as in the phrase "The Revolutionary's Twelve Principles of Morality," outlining twelve activities in which a revolutionary may and may not engage. (Because I have no intention of becoming a revolutionary, I cannot remember all twelve of these moral precepts.)

For those of us who are Life Slaves, there is no clearly defined morality by which we must live. And the word *morality* seems to focus heavily on relationships between men and women. If a man and woman fall in love and secretly make love, they are accused of immorality. The penalty for this error is execution. Sometimes, in some places, it is only the man who is executed; the woman is released after being "built." Sometimes, in some places, both members of the couple are executed and their bodies are dumped together into the same pit.[1]

During construction of the Or Roessei canal, orders from the Organization strictly forbade a male and a female from walking together to forage for wild tubers or dig for crabs and frogs in the forest, even if they were brother and sister or husband and wife. Anything contrary to this was considered a violation of morality. A young man and young woman could not converse together apart from the others. A young man could not visit a young women's shelter, and a young woman could not visit a young men's shelter.

While digging the Trapeang Thmor Reservoir, when we were completely soaked by the rain and tried to take refuge in a young women's shelter, we were expelled because this was "immoral." And yet the cadre himself, a young man, was allowed to tie his own hammock up and sleep inside the young women's shelter.

---

[1] Author's note: "Kok Key village, Teuk Chor subdistrict, Preah Netr Preah district, October 1978"

Because the word *morality* has an imprecise definition, changing according to time and place, we are all constantly afraid and worried about committing some violation, each sex trying to protect the other.

Samorn, my younger brother, will later recount an anecdote to me: In the rice-growing season of 1976, when returning from transplanting rice to the Kok Rumchek camp in the evening, a unit of young women were wading across the canal that runs along the side of the road. By chance, a young woman walked over an underwater well that had been dug in the bottom of the canal during the dry season and sank down into the water. Her fellow young women did not dare try to save her because they didn't know how to swim, and the young men who were standing on the road nearby didn't dare try to save her for fear of violating "morality." This unfortunate young woman drowned under the gaze of hundreds of people.

Does simply catching or holding up a member of the opposite sex to save them count as a violation of morality?

The twenty women assigned to plant vegetables at the Kok Kakah farm are mostly women in their twenties, some of whom are the widows of former government officials in the Lon Nol era, and some who are young women hiding among the middle-aged women. Among these women, Comrade Tha is a widow of part-Chinese descent, big-boned, with a clear white complexion. Comrade Tha is not very able to endure hard labor or work in the sun because she suffers from degenerative heart weakness. She occasionally suffers heart palpitations when performing difficult, exhausting labor, or when very frightened. Both the cadres and her friends working alongside her often take pity on her, not daring to make her perform work as demanding as the others.

While harvesting rice for the region, the cooperative mobile units and the regional mobile units engage in competition over their respective output. Because of this, they mostly harvest the prime rice—rice that stood up straight, rice in flat open places—while the rice that is lying down or in ponds is left unharvested.

After all the harvesting units have withdrawn, the regional Organization issues orders for the forces stationed at the farm to go out and harvest the rice that remains.

Some ponds are virtually dried up, while others have water up to my knees. The last pond has water up to our waists and has large leeches about the size of our thumbs, and the rice plants are thick and heavy with grain, falling over and lying across one another. The twenty women under the leadership of Bong Ny (a widow), as well as the female medics, are out harvesting. There are six men: Ta Moeun, Mea Lik, Mea Yoeum, Comrade Sarik (a base person who is an ox-cart driver), Comrade Sambath, and me. (This is not my responsibility, but because of a lull in my own duties, I have come to help.)

The men wear trousers with the legs, whether short or long, tied tightly at the bottom to protect against leeches. The women don't wear trousers, but wear either a sarong or a skirt, and don't dare to tie it up into a *kben*[2] out of shyness.

For fear of leeches, the women harvest beside the men so that we can help to pick leeches off them. We harvest rice starting in the shallow ponds and progressing to deeper ponds, up to our hips. Leeches continually latch on, and we pick them off and place them into a pail to soak in water with tobacco.[3] As we harvest, we converse to distract the women from fear. Comrade Tha is harvesting to my left. We are each bent over harvesting rice when suddenly Comrade Tha cries out, "Bong Ny, a leech!" and then goes silent as she falls over. I reach out my left arm to catch her, as she has fainted. Bong Ny rushes to assist, helping to carry her up onto dry land. A female medic comes to help remove the leech, to help keep her heart beating, and to help her regain consciousness.

My action was done automatically, without any thought. As I continue to harvest, I begin to fear that I have committed a violation of morality, while at the same time the women who are afraid of leeches draw closer and closer to me.

Unlike the previous incident, in which simply asking to take shelter from the rain in a young women's shelter triggered accusations of immorality, now everyone on the farm loves me and the word *morality* has no influence over my reaction in catching Comrade Tha. I saved the life of a woman without any danger to my own life.

---

[2] a skirt or sarong worn passed between the legs and tucked in at the waist on the other side to make a sort of rudimentary short trousers
[3] because tobacco kills leeches

This is a very important point: As long as we can get the low-level cadres in charge of us to like us, then our lives will be spared. But if we make them hate or dislike us, we will die before very long. It seems that these people have the authority to kill Life Slaves without having to get permission from their higher-ups, so long as they report to them (perhaps verbally) that the individual committed some violation.

However, with regard to other base people who are fellow cadres, it is not easy to attempt to have them killed.

The women assigned to the farm are divided into two teams. One team, led by a man named Mea Lik (a base person from Trapeang Thmor village), carries out the work of planting *phty* greens, *trakuon*, cabbage, and tomatoes. The other team, composed of ten women who are all young, led by a man named Mea Yoeum (a base person from Paoy Char village), carries out the work of digging up stumps and clearing termite mounds that remain, and of planting tubers, gourds, wax melons, cucumbers, pumpkins, and watermelons.

All the cadres and *chhlops* stationed here are base people from Paoy Char subdistrict, except for Ta Moeun, who is a base person from Spean Sreng subdistrict.

Because of a disagreement over leadership, one day Ta Moeun reports to Comrade Chhin (the chairman of Paoy Char subdistrict) that Mea Yoeum has committed immorality. One night, when Ta Moeun is absent from the farm, a *chhlop* from Paoy Char subdistrict comes and requests to arrest Mea Yoeum. Bong Tith refuses to authorize the arrest because nobody knows anything about the matter. With which woman has Mea Yoeum committed immorality?

The following day, Bong Tith goes to meet Ta Ry, chairman of Paoy Char subdistrict's *chhlop* unit, and finds out that Ta Moeun has made a slanderous report against Mea Yoeum. Ta Ry summons Ta Moeun to question him in front of Bong Tith, and Ta Moeun confesses and requests to withdraw his exaggerated report.

Amazing! If this had happened to a Life Slave, it would have all been over.

CHAPTER 33

A Young Man Separated from His Wife

During the Lon Nol era people used to say, "Young men are the pillars of the Republican Revolution!"

During this era of the Red Revolution, youth remain the premier revolutionary force for building the nation. Young men and young women are gathered from every district, village, and cooperative into the mobile units of every district and region throughout the country.

Most of the young men and young women who volunteered for mobile revolutionary units back when we disembarked from the trains at Svay Sisophon were incorporated into Ta Val's regional mobile brigade, which has been deployed all over Region Five. This is an elite unit, an example mobile unit with the strictest discipline, and nobody is allowed to visit home. And most of them didn't even know where their parents, siblings, and families were ultimately sent to live.

The majority of the Life Slaves who were evacuated to Region Five were sent to live in the district of Phnom Srok, followed by Preah Netr Preah, Thmor Puok, and Svay Sisophon (Serei Saophoan).

The young men and young women who went to live in the cooperatives were then gathered into district mobile units assigned to various worksites. This category of young men and young women can visit home once or twice per year, depending on the strictness or leniency of the cadre in charge.

People everywhere work, and working on a youth mobile unit is preferable to remaining in the cooperative. We are able to become acquainted with various districts and villages, forests, mountains and hills, fields and plains, the sky, the stars, heat, coolness, cold, all kinds of weariness and difficulties, as experiences for our future lives.

But humans are not beasts of burden; humans have sentiments, thoughts, and feelings that turn toward family, parents, and siblings. Especially in times of hardship and poverty such as these, nobody wants to be parted from their families or parents. Whether with or without food, in whatever manner of suffering or sorrow, we want to be together. For older parents, it is good to have a young son or daughter living with them to help prepare the hot and cool water in the mornings and evenings, during bouts of trembling chills or burning fever, and to help pick up their slack around the house. But apart from the base people, nobody is allowed to keep a young son or daughter at home in the cooperative.

Among the Life Slaves, couples and individuals have various methods for keeping a young son or daughter at home in the village and cooperative. There are generally two common solutions to this problem: creating a false personal history and forming a new marriage.

1. Creating a False Personal History

Because the evacuating of people from region to region and place to place was done without a document trail, this created a gap that made it easy to alter one's personal history. Most secret young men and young women are registered as widowers and widows. And nearly all young men and young women who have falsified their personal history in this way have claimed that their husband or wife is dead. In these cases, the young man or young woman has the right to ask for a new spouse whenever they feel the desire to do so.

As for cases of a personal history involving separation from a husband or wife, the Organization does not permit the formation of a new marriage until clear confirmation has been received of the death of the former husband or wife. But this solution can prevent being forced into something by the Organization. This is a risk because the Organization has a rule that says, "Any young man or young woman from the Revolutionary Armed Forces who has been wounded and lost an arm or leg shall have the right to point to any young woman or young man they please and request them as wife or husband, and the young woman or young man so chosen shall have no right to refuse." (Even though this special case exists, people rarely apply the formula, as they are afraid of getting themselves entangled in something.)

2. Forming a New Marriage

A large number of people resolve the issue by fully involving themselves in the affairs of life; that is, by creating a new family in these uncertain times. This method is not really a solution to the problem, but rather creates more problems and causes stress.

For the Life Slaves, our manner of living at this time is not conducive to married life as husband and wife, whether long wed or recently wed:

The inadequate food and lack of sufficient nutrition for the needs of the body causes people's bodies to become emaciated, worn out, exhausted, and drained of strength. This problem is especially pronounced for men, who perform heavy labor. The women seem less affected by this problem.

The excessive strenuousness of the daily labor places an additional strain on a body which is already under strain from the food regimen. This problem is especially pronounced for women, who are the weaker sex. Most of the young women suffer from loss of their menstrual cycle, their bodies wasting away little by little until they eventually lose their lives.

Most husband-and-wife couples do not live together but are required to go their own separate ways based on their individual work assignments, separated by several kilometers for three or four months at a time before being allowed to see one another again. Husband and wife live apart, so if they get sick at night, neither is able to help the other. Each lies awake worrying and anxious about the other. Sometimes a husband makes a mistake and is taken away to be killed, and his wife doesn't even find out. Sometimes a wife will fall ill and pass away without her husband ever being allowed to visit her or take care of her.

Women very rarely become pregnant, and among those who do, most of them miscarry. If a mother has no food, her baby has no milk to drink, and many babies pass away two or three days after being born. Any baby fated to survive is a monster child, shriveled and wilted, barely able to even open its eyes. Emaciated parents have babies who are born emaciated. Can such an infant grow up to become a person fit to build society?

Most newlywed couples do not get along, the wife refusing to live with her husband, refusing to sleep with her husband—and why? Because it is a marriage of convenience, a marriage of desperation. Their parents, who did not want their son or daughter to be taken away from them, have compelled their son or daughter to take a wife or a husband.

Bong Meng is a thirty-year-old young man from Paoy Snuol who asked for the hand of Huoy, a young woman in the village, and they were married in early 1976. In the nearly two years since their wedding, Huoy has never once allowed Bong Meng to touch her, despite interventions from the village, cooperative, and subdistrict cadres. Bong Meng lives in a state of emotional stress and has requested a divorce, but Ta Lam refused to authorize it, as the Revolutionary Line forbids it.

Does this constitute family bliss, or the essence of married life?

Despite having no attachments (my parents having passed away) and preferring the mobile life to life in the cooperative, I nevertheless declined that option in order to live in the cooperative when we first came to live in Paoy Snuol in late 1976.

The mobile life is satisfying only in having opportunities to become acquainted with new lands and villages, sleeping on the ground out in the open, and watching the sky and stars; but not with regard to food rations beyond basic rice or porridge with a broth of *prahok* or salt. The mobile units don't have access to sweet or savory snacks—fruit, melons, papayas, bananas, sugar cane, or beans—the way those in the cooperative do. People with parents or siblings living in the cooperative can often get supplementary food sent to them. When they visit home now and then, they often get tubers, sugar cane, or a cob of corn to gnaw on. But those without parents or siblings in the cooperative have nothing extra to eat as the others do.

When we first arrived in Paoy Snuol, my youngest brother, Samorn, and I registered as a single family. Feeling sorry for my brother, who was deployed on a mobile unit without any other support from the village, I registered myself as a widower separated from his wife so that I could be allowed to live in the village and plant some vegetables and other crops to provide to my brother on the mobile unit. But being in such unfortunate circumstances, living in Paoy Snuol beneath somebody else's house, on top of a lumber pile, without house or land, what did I have with which to produce anything? And because I was a separated widower without children or attachments, I was not destined to remain in the village as I had intended.

Young men and young women are mostly in separate units, doing separate work, and rarely have opportunities to mingle. As a separated widower, I was assigned to a mobile unit with other married people: the middle-aged unit. This unit was mixed, with men and women living together and working near one another—sometimes working together directly. In my mobile deployments I often get to know young widows and young-women-in-hiding. I usually seem to receive friendship, closeness, affability, trust, pity, and affection from them.

Perhaps this is just my natural propensity, as other young-men-in-hiding who work in the same unit as I do don't tend to have the same fate. Some ask women to marry them, and they agree, but then when the Day of Ceremony[1] (wedding) draws near, they change their minds and refuse.

Regarding marriage, the revolutionary line is as follows:

– Young men and young women have the right to choose their own partners. That is, a young man can request a young woman, and a young woman can request a young man with whom they are pleased.

– A young man or young woman who has been requested to be somebody's spouse three times and still refuses can then be compelled to accept.

A story is told: On the Phnom Kambaor[2] regional mobile unit, there were three young women who loved each other like sisters. They promised each other that they would each only marry if the other two also married. Young men often asked for one of these three young women but were refused, as one or more in the trio was not asked. The cadres know the weakness of these three young women. One day all three of them were requested at the same time. As agreed, they all accepted. On the Day of Ceremony, three old men arose to take the hands of these three young women for their wives.

Their partners were karmic partners, given to them as a legacy by the Revolutionary Organization. Apparently the three young women had not known the faces of the men who had requested to marry them in advance; but as this was their last chance, they had to accept whether they were pleased or not.

I, my own tears scarcely dried from a failed romance,[3] am well familiar with the cool sweetness, the bitterness, the pain, and heartache which are the unique features of such an experience. I have learned lessons, and I am wary of forming a new romantic relationship. But true love is not something that can be willed into being, that we can create. It is something that appears on its own, born of

---

[1] This euphemism for a wedding, in particular a mass wedding of many couples, was an innovation by the Khmer Rouge.
[2] in Preah Netr Preah district, immediately south of Phnom Srok district
[3] a reference to a pre-revolution relationship; see page 9 and page 23

its own accord without compulsion. And as it spreads and grows, it scorches the lovers who fall headlong under its hypnotic spell.

No! Love is not something to be feared. It is an elixir of immortality that distills cool mists upon the souls of the lovers. It is a powerful force which pulls on the emotions of the lovers and weaves and twists them together into a single cord, a single heart. If you are in love, then you understand the depths of love, the sentiments of lovers, and you have a desire for everyone to have love, for the entire world to be filled with love. The first sign of love is a smile. A smile generates joy and hope. The beauty of a smile can take a heart of pure steel and turn it into a sponge, thoroughly punctured with small holes, as soft as cotton.

If a person is in love, they know how to have compassion, to love others, to love nature, to love human society, to love mankind.

But now we are in the clutches of people without love, beastly people, people who don't know the value of a human being, the value of themselves, the value of love. They separate lovers, sometimes killing one, sometimes killing both and casting them into a single grave. They are revolutionaries bent on destroying the Khmer race, effacing the soul of the Khmer nation. And to what end?

Should we desire to sample the sweet, cool taste of love during this time? No. This is what led me to concoct a personal history as a "widower separated from his wife." I thought that the words *separated from his wife* would bind me and prevent me from desiring a wife. And that they would bind the women I would meet in my journey through this hellish life, preventing them from harboring tenderness, sympathy, or love toward me, as I am a man who is bound, whose feelings are confined to his wife.

But these are all thoughts that I have kept hidden in my own mind. My two sisters know nothing about my intentions, and they struggle with such an insane decision. Oun, especially, wants me to find a wife. She thinks that I am old already, and that if I fall ill, she will not be able to care for me as she used to, as she has a husband now and lives with him. That is why whenever she is deployed with me on a mobile unit, or near me, she often whispers to people around her about my true history. Like now, as we harvest the rice around Kok Kakah in November, she preaches this good news to the women stationed on the farm. In fact, they already knew all of this through Bong Phan, the head cook. But it was fraught with doubt and uncertainty, as they were hesitant to fully believe the words of Bong Phan. But when they hear it from the mouth of my own sister, the doubt and uncertainty melt away and are replaced by sympathy and secret crushes.

It is not only the women who pry into my true personal history. Bong Tith also follows this matter closely. Since the disappearance of Bong Yong, Bong Tith often comes to sit and chat with me and ask me questions about my true history.

"Tuch! Have you ever been married?"

"Yes, Bong," I answer.

"How many children do you have?"

"I don't have any. We were only together for half a year before we were separated," I answer.

"What was your job during the *Sangkum* era?" Bong Tith asks.

"I pedaled a *cyclo*," I answer.

"So how did you become separated from your wife?"

"On the day the Revolutionary Army entered Phnom Penh, I was pedaling my *cyclo*, and my wife was at home. The Organization began to evacuate the people right away. Because the roads were blocked and I couldn't get home, I left along with the crowds, but fortunately I met up with my parents and siblings. I have been separated from my wife ever since."

Bong Tith ponders silently, then continues to ask, "Have you ever heard any word of your wife?"

"No, not at all. Here in Region Five, I have asked around and found nothing. I found a cousin living in Preah Netr Preah district, but they didn't know anything."

"So here in Phnom Srok, is there anyone who used to live near you in Phnom Penh?" Bong Tith asks.

"No, there isn't, Bong. When we were evacuated from Phnom Penh, we all went to our respective home districts, and then the Organization evacuated us again from there to Region Five," I answer.

"So not everyone from Phnom Penh was evacuated here to Region Five?"

"No, Bong. The people evacuated to Region Five by the Organization were mostly people who went to live in Kandal, Takeo, and Kampong Speu provinces," I clarify.

Bong Tith repeatedly asks me questions like these, which makes me very suspicious. Sometimes I try to find other topics to distract him with and lead him off the trail. But sometimes I am afraid that perhaps he knows about my true history, as he is a fellow resident of Paoy Snuol, and I am tempted to confess the truth.

Back in September, Bong Tith raised questions about my personal history yet again. Finally, he said, "Would you like to find a new wife, Tuch?"

This question was difficult to answer. I was living on the farm, and the daily living was a bit easier, not so strenuous as it had been when I first decided not to seek a wife. But for now, I had to maintain my original stance.

"No, Bong," I replied.

"What if somebody requests *you,* Tuch?" Bong Tith asked.

I smiled, thinking that he was joking.

"Hey, you know, Tuch, somebody actually did request you," Bong Tith clarified.

These last words surprised me, and I quickly asked him, "Who? Are they on a mobile unit, or stationed on our farm?"

"Somebody here on the farm. Go ahead and guess!"

Damn. Which woman could it be? What should I answer? Here on the farm, Comrade Khom and Comrade Pov were the two women who were closest to me. They were both around twenty-two or twenty-three years old and appeared to be flowers-in-hiding.[4] I never dared to ask them about their personal histories, so they would not think that I was harboring some intention. Both women paid a lot of attention to me. If they ever had any kind of extra food to eat, they would often bring some to me at my hut. Their eyes were full of mystery, and even though I tried to act like I had no idea, in fact I understood their intentions perfectly well. Their mouths were full of the words "Bong[5] Tuch! Bong Tuch!" Comrade Khom would often glare at me and labeled me "the man with mean eyes and a mean heart." Comrade Pov liked to frolic and tease and always called me the person that she could never verbally defeat.

Among the two of them, which one requested me? I did not dare guess. Because I refused to guess, Bong Tith told me the name of the person who had requested me. It was a third person whom I had not thought of. She was a big-

---

[4] i.e., young women posing as widows

[5] Besides being a polite term of address for slightly older people, this word is also an affectionate term of address for a romantic male partner, with amorous implications. Thus its usage here is easily interpreted to be flirtatious, though ambiguously so.

boned widow about the age of my older sister. In fact, I only wanted to know who it was, but my decision remained the same regardless. I made an excuse that I was not over my wife and wanted to continue waiting for news of her.

When the cooperative mobile units came to the farm to carry out the regional rice harvest and camped at Kok Kakah, I ran into a young woman who was one of my former high school classmates. When we were in school, we were not close, as I was from a poor family and quite shy and did not dare to chat with the girls. But we were both excited to meet one another under these impoverished circumstances. Her name is Sadet, and lives in Sambuor village, Paoy Char subdistrict. We met on the evening of the fire in camp. The next morning Bong Khek (cadre for the Paoy Char cooperative) took Sadet and four or five other women away to make *prahok* at the *roneam*[6] on the shores of Tonle Sap Lake.

Now, the mystery of my true personal history is fully uncovered and my intentions of curbing any attraction or interest from women fail, as there are now people who both openly and secretly fancy me, including someone who has even requested me.

Should I continue to encourage these games of disappointment and heartache? No. If I have a wife, other girls will stop staring at me and they will not have to face the heartache of unrequited love.

Whom should I request? Comrade Khom and Comrade Pov both seem to feel equally strongly toward me, and I feel some compassion and affection for them as well. I often joke and flirt with them, which further fans the flames of affection.

Both those who are hiding their affection and those who are openly displaying it watch and wait for my decision. If I request one woman, the others will be saddened, offended, and heartbroken. Whom should I choose?

One day, when Bong Tith comes to inspect the chickens and ducks, I ask for his opinion.

"Bong! Can you help me with something?"

"What is it, Tuch?" Bong Tith asks.

"Would you please request a wife for me?"

---

[6] ideal for *prahok* production due to the abundance of fish there

"Request a wife? I thought you were waiting for news of your wife?" he says, smiling, as though he has caught me at something.

I smile back and say, "I seem to be out of hope."

"All right, that's up to you, but make sure you're sure. Who are you thinking of asking?" he asks.

"A young woman on a cooperative mobile unit," I reply.

"What? Why don't you choose somebody closer?"

"We went to school together," I answer.

"All right, fine, I will ask the chairman for you. What cooperative is she in?"

"The Paoy Char cooperative, Bong. But now she has gone to make *prahok* at the *roneam*."

"Oh! That will not be easy. It's difficult to communicate that far. With one of you on a regional mobile unit and the other on a district mobile unit, it will be very difficult for you to attend the Day of Ceremony!"

"That's all right, Brother. Will you help me make the request?"

"No problem."

In fact, Sadet and I feel only compassion for one another, having studied at school together, but we don't have love for one another, as we have scarcely seen one another at all. And the one time we did meet was only for about an hour. We chatted about how each other's family was doing without touching on anything that would draw us together. I have made this decision all on my own. It is a good option I have chosen. The women on the farm are not resentful toward one another because of me. They are not disappointed or hostile toward me and continue to be on friendly terms with me, as I tell them that the girl I requested is an old friend who satisfies the wishes of my sister.

CHAPTER 34

Supernatural Beliefs

Every aspect of faith—religion, *neak ta*, ghosts, demons—has been erased. The monks have all been defrocked and forced out of the priesthood to live as laymen. All *wats* and temples have been abandoned and converted into pig farms, warehouses, and granaries, or torn down completely in some cases, like the temple in Wat Trapeang Thmor.

But some temples possess great power and cause peril for those who tear them down. I hear that this was the case when the Organization ordered the tearing down of the temple in Wat Chey in the town of Phnom Srok.

A story is told: One day Comrade Hat, the chairman of Phnom Srok district, ordered someone to tear down a *neak ta* shrine. The man was hesitant because he had known the power of the *neak ta*, but he did not dare to argue with the decision of the Organization. Perceiving the reticence of the man, Comrade Hat secretly followed him and spied on his activities. Carrying a hatchet and a crowbar, the man walked to the *neak ta* shrine, knelt down, placed his palms together and reverenced the *neak ta*, and said out loud, "Comrade Hat has ordered me to take down your shrine. If you are displeased, please take it out on him!"

Understanding the mindset of the people, Comrade Hat showed himself before the *neak ta* and stopped the man from tearing down the shrine.

In fact, during the war, the Khmer Rouge soldiers all followed gurus and carried protective magic amulets such as *chae kach*, *khnay tan*, *katha* necklaces, *yoant*[1] scarves, etc. That is to say, they also believed in and reverenced supernatural objects. Now the senior levels of the Organization have given them orders to erase these beliefs, and they have to comply, but in their feelings they are still uneasy, still frightened, especially when they hear that the people who follow their orders place the responsibility for it on them.

---

[1] a small elephant tusk left embedded in a tree; a wild boar's tusk; a rolled-up gold or silver scroll with an inscribed prayer; and a magical drawing inscribed on paper, cloth, or skin, respectively

Kok Kakah used to be a cemetery wood where the dead were buried, famous among the locals as a place of ghosts and spirits, where they were afraid to stop and rest overnight, or even for a midday break. Even though the trees have all been cleared except for a handful of large trees, and it has become a farm, a place where people live, the power of supernatural things has not yet been erased.

Some nights, a ghost possesses a young woman from a mobile unit who is camping here, making her cry out, thrashing her arms and legs, angry that people have come to invade and exploit its home. Fortunately, ghosts mostly only possess young female base people.

Seeing these things happen right in front of them, the cadres believe in them, and they often pray and make offerings for the ghosts to depart quickly so that people will not be afflicted. These things continue to happen now and then, especially when newcomers come to stay here.

Some of the locals say that in the *Sangkum* era (before the Revolution) during the season of plowing and sowing rice, the villagers would often park their oxen and carts at the western end of the *kok*, but they couldn't sleep well there because the ghosts would press and harass anyone who didn't believe.

As for the matter of ghost-pressing,[2] I have often experienced this myself since childhood. Doctors did not believe in this, and they would often explain that it was some problem with my heart, like a heart palpitation. But for me, having experienced this frequently, I understand that being pressed by a ghost has nothing to do with the heart, but it does have something to do with breathing. When a ghost presses you, you can't breathe until you manage to break free, and only then are you able to breathe again.

My mother used to tell me, "If a ghost presses you, you have to move your big toe, and then you can break free." This was the only way I was able to break free whenever a ghost pressed me.

While I have previously experienced ghost-pressing, I have never encountered anything like this on Kok Kakah, and neither has anybody else, apart from the occasional spirit possession. Since the disappearance of Bong Yong, I have lived alone in the small hut in the shade of the stunted *kakah* tree, separated from the forward camp by the maniocs, which now sprout bushes higher than my head.

---

[2] *khmaoch sangkot*, the Khmer term for the phenomenon of sleep paralysis

At night my hut has a very lonely aspect, solitary and forlorn in a world of darkness. This gives me goosebumps and makes me feel frightened sometimes, especially during the waning moon. In the darkness, light can dispel fear, so each dark night I carry a stump or log over and build a campfire in front of the hut beneath the stunted *kakah* tree.

The cool season arrives, the rice is golden colored throughout the fields, and the wind blowing from the north makes a whooshing sound and dries up the water that has collected in puddles and ponds in the rice fields. At night, packs of wild dogs come out to hunt for food in the fields and howl loudly to one another throughout the fields *awoo! awoo! awoo!* Sometimes they come quite close to my hut. The cold does not bother me much because I have the woolen blanket left by the late Bong Yong to wrap up in. I do, however, suffer from an inability to sleep well.

One night, in the middle of the night, I have a dream in which Comrade Sambath stands in front of my hut, and he reaches up and grabs onto a branch of the *kakah* tree and says to me, "Hey Tuch! Beneath this *kakah* tree is the grave of a widow with a baby, you know."

As soon as Comrade Sambath stops speaking, suddenly a weight presses down on me and I am unable to move. I wake up and lie still until I can't breathe, and then I move my big toe and can move again. I am able to break free, but my eyelids are very heavy and want nothing but to fall back asleep. When I let myself succumb to sleep, the ghost begins to press me again. I am not in a rush to break free quickly, for if I do the ghost will only press me again immediately. If I can endure until it becomes a struggle to breathe, the ghost will back off and not press me again immediately.

From then on, the widow with the baby comes to press me once every third night, and on each occasion she presses me two or three times. One night, as the ghost is pressing me, I feel as though my body, which is lying flat, is floating up and out of the hut through the doorway. When I have cleared the awning of the hut, I see the sky strewn with stars. Then my body floats through a gap between large trees, as though I am in a mountain forest with a bright, clear light, like the moon. I lie perfectly still, wanting to know where the ghost will take me. But now I cannot breathe, so I move my big toe and try to move my body. Every time I try to move my body, I become completely exhausted.

One day, when I am due for another round of ghost-pressing, at the evening meal I talk about it with the older folks staying in the forward camp. The women listening to my story are frightened. They believe me because I never tell tall tales. Bong Pen, a man of about thirty or so who used to be a monk at a *wat* in Muk Kampul district, Kandal province (his wife is called Bong Mon, a cook at the farm), promises to help me.

"It's all right, Tuch! Let me come and sprinkle some water and cast out the ghost for you."

After eating, Bong Pen comes to the chicken pen with me. He carries a metal bowl full of water, walking and chanting in Pali, stirring the water and sprinkling it onto the hut where I sleep. Tonight I sleep soundly, without any disturbances.

In the morning Bong Pen asks me, "Well Tuch, how was it?"

"It was fine, Bong. I slept well!" I reply.

"But *I* did *not* sleep well last night," he says. "The woman brought her baby in her arms and sat grumbling at my feet. 'I was at peace, and you came to disturb me! I was at peace, and you came to disturb me!' she said. She sat with her head down until the sun was about to rise and then got up and walked out with her baby in her arms. This ghost is unusually polite, but whether we have triumphed or not we will find out within three nights."

Before, the ghost only seemed to be toying with me. She would press me only two or three times for only a half hour or an hour and then stop, and then take a break for a few days. But then one day, after Bong Pen sprinkles the water, she stops toying with me and begins to outright harass me.

Every night, when the ghost presses me (at about two o'clock in the morning), I wake up, but I feel drugged, like I can hardly keep my eyes open. When she is ready to press me, my senses perceive a loud scream as of some furious creature, causing me to break out in gooseflesh and get shivers down my spine, and then the ghost begins to press. She presses again and again, many times, stopping only when dawn approaches. I am utterly exhausted from trying to break free.

My body has become someone else's battlefield. The ghost refuses to yield to Bong Pen, and Bong Pen wants to gain victory over the ghost. Bong Pen makes me an *ambah changkeh*[3] to wear around my waist for protection, telling me that if the ghost cannot press me for three days, then she has lost, and she will not dare to press me ever again.

On the first night, wearing the *ambah changkeh*, the ghost can't do anything to me. She tries many times, but the *ambah changkeh* only twitches around my waist, while I lie still hoping for results. Losing this round, the ghost withdraws, and I sleep soundly until morning.

On the second night, the ghost has the same difficulty, but after trying for one and then two tries, suddenly she succeeds by trying a new strategy: pressing me only from the waist up. I struggle to breathe just the same as when the ghost presses my whole body.

Everyone on the farm, men and women, follows the progress of my battle. Ta Moeun and Bong Tith suppose that I must be scared, so they assign Bong Chhuor, a man more than thirty years old, to come and sleep in the hut with me at night. In fact, Bong Chhuor is afraid of ghosts, but he does not dare argue with an order from the Organization. He sleeps near me on the platform where Bong Yong used to sleep.

One night, around the time when the ghost would normally come to press me, suddenly I hear Bong Chhuor struggling to move with short gasping *uh uh uh* sounds. After a short while he kicks the wall with a loud *bang! bang!* and I lie there smiling, thinking that the ghost must be harassing Bong Chhuor for a change.

I am right. In the morning Bong Chhuor says to me, "I saw her holding her baby, standing at my feet, and she opened the mosquito net with one hand and asked to leave her baby with me, and then she suddenly began to press me. I was scared and tried to move, and when I was finally able, I raised my leg to kick her and ended up kicking the wall instead!"

However, the ghost only presses Bong Chhuor that one night, and after that she resumes harassing me. One night, Comrade Bon, a young man who keeps the oxen on the farm, comes to sleep with me because he is curious about this phenomenon of ghost-pressing. The two of us share a mosquito net. Tonight the ghost does not press me, but instead harasses Comrade Bon all night long

---

[3] literally "waist thread," a traditional protective amulet made from cotton string or thread worn tied around the waist

so that he can't sleep. Comrade Bon runs away and no longer dares to sleep with me.

Bong Pen tries to think of every way possible to defeat the Ghost with the Baby. He makes an additional *ambah* to tie around my neck. But it's no different from the *ambah changkeh* at my waist. On the first night, the ghost fails to press me; the *ambah* only trembles around my neck. On the second night, the ghost presses me from my neck down to my toes.

Finally, Bong Pen gives me some "thumb-and-toe" *poat seima*[4] Pali incantations to memorize, to recite by myself before going to bed. But there is just no method that can defeat the Ghost with the Baby. I am still harassed every night, starting from around midnight until dawn. For a month I grow skinny from lack of sleep, and exhausted from trying to break free of the ghost.

Bong Pen is out of options, and Mea Lik takes a shot at helping me for a change. He is a base person who used to be a monk for many years at Wat Trapeang Thmor.

One night Mea Lik comes to perform *poat seima* around my hut for seven circuits. He thinks that the ghost is coming into the hut from outside. I am reassured, thinking that at least I will be able to sleep for one night. But after midnight, suddenly the ghost presses me again, as usual, as if there were no talismans nor enchanted boundary at all. Thinking about the first time that Bong Pen sprinkled water and then chanted incantations around the boundary, I think that I must be sleeping directly over the ghost's grave.

Unable to stand being pressed by the ghost in my sleep any longer, I sit up. I reach into Bong Chhuor's mosquito net to wake him so he can sit up to talk with me. "Bong Chhuor! Bong Chhuor, sit up!" I say, but he will not sit up.

"Damn, Tuch! I don't know what you're doing. Why are you up in the middle of the night?"

Because he has been sleeping well, without any harassment from the ghost, Bong Chhuor does not understand my struggle and has no compassion for me,

---

[4] Typically, *poat seima* refers to a protective ritual in which someone (normally a monk) recites Pali incantations while walking a prescribed number of circuits around the boundary of something, e.g. a house, often with a string. In this case, this "thumb-and-toe" version of *poat seima* meant that he was to recite the incantations himself a prescribed number of times and then mark, in turn, each of his thumbs and big toes with a + sign, using a piece of charcoal, to signify completion.

pressed by the ghost until I have grown thin from lack of sleep. He thinks only of closing his eyes and enjoying his rest.

I sit alone in the darkness of the night. Out in the fields the wild dogs howl faintly, while inside the hut the ghost keeps me awake. What good is it to just sit here? To keep Bong Chhuor company and stop him from being scared? No, what is the use of looking out for someone who is dead to the world anyway?

No longer able to continue to sit here alone in the middle of the night, I grab my blanket and leave the hut and walk through the manioc field to sleep with the young men in the forward camp.

After I leave the hut, the ghost tries to find a way out of the hut, but she is trapped by the enchanted boundary and cannot get out, so she moves back and forth along the outside wall of the hut, brushing against the thatch panels, making a loud rustling sound, sometimes brushing against the trough of corrugated iron I've placed for the chickens to drink from beneath the awning, making a ringing metallic sound, waking Bong Chhuor and making it hard for him to sleep.

Supposing that it is just me, having gotten up, Bong Chhuor shouts "Tuch! What the hell are you doing in the middle of the night?"

Not hearing a reply, and still hearing the sounds, Bong Chhuor becomes more puzzled and puts his arm into my mosquito net looking for me. Now he is sure it's the ghost brushing against the walls and making the rustling sound, and he starts to get scared and dashes out of the hut at a run, his feet barely touching the ground.

In the morning, the cadres are startled to see that I have come to sleep in the forward camp, and they all laugh, and Mea Lik teases me, "How's it going, Tuch? Did the wild dogs bother you last night, so you abandoned your hut?"

"I couldn't stand it, Mea. We did *poat seima* for seven circuits, and she still came to harass me!" I reply.

Because we can't defeat the Ghost with the Baby, Ta Moeun, Bong Tith, and Mea Lik come to inspect the location of the hut. They think the hut is "yoking" termite mounds.[5] They inspect the ground to look for a suitable place

---

[5] i.e., the hut is situated between two termite mounds, like the two burdens on either end of a shoulder yoke. Termite mounds are sometimes associated with malicious spirits or ghosts in Khmer traditional belief.

to rebuild the hut and decide that I should build a new hut in the fields about thirty meters south of the old one.

I build the new hut three by four meters, nice and tall, with a front awning higher than my head, facing to the north, with only a single sleeping platform topped with wooden slats along the eastern wall of the hut about a meter off the ground. The frond walls are closed on three sides, and the front wall is a short wall only a meter-fifty high, without any shutters on top. The doorway is wide open like the old hut.

Immediately north of the hut, an east-west cart track runs along the south side of the *kok* and then turns north onto the *kok* in front of my hut and goes up to the west end of the *kok* before making a crooked turn northward toward Kok Roessei.

Bong Chhuor abandons me, and there is nobody else left to sleep with me, so I am all alone. But in this new hut there are no more disturbances, and I am able to sleep soundly until morning.

CHAPTER 35

Arrest

The Lord Buddha taught that the fruits of good and bad deeds will be received by man in future incarnations. This is the Buddhist doctrine that the old folks call the Law of the Buddha. As for the worldly realm, the fruits of one's bad deeds are received in the current incarnation. Who oversees the deeds of man? Religions describe beings like gods, angels, Indra, Brahma, Yama. These beings have divine sight and hearing, and there is no evil deed or good work of man hidden from their eyes and ears.

In our worldly realm, when we were a modern society, an advanced society with laws to govern the country, a democratic society, every human activity was subject to oversight and governance under the Ministry of Security.

For us, now, living in a society with neither religious faith nor laws to govern the country, a primitive society, who is it that oversees human activities?

There are certainly overseers for us, the Life Slaves; everything is tracked. If we do anything, if we get anything whatsoever to eat, swallow, or chew on, someone is tracking it, always: the cadres and the *chhlops*. The *chhlops* include old people and young children. They constantly remind us that "the Organization has eyes like a pineapple!" That is, the Organization has hundreds and thousands of eyes, and if anybody does anything, the Organization knows about it. If we do anything that can be considered a violation of their discipline, or against any one of them as individuals, they take our lives immediately.

However, their own activities have not been subject to the oversight of anything. This is what has enticed them to nurture murderous hearts, eating livers and swallowing gall bladders, without any reticence or compassion, without even the slightest recognition that "this is my brother" or "this is my own race."

All human actions and actions arising from nature (natural phenomena) have causes and effects. Whoever splashes water into the wind will receive a rain shower as a result. In other words, there is no action without consequences. Sooner or later, there are always consequences. Father Lun and Father Pov were not wrong when they said, "Whoever kills today will be killed tomorrow." Now tomorrow has arrived for the drinkers of our blood and the gnawers of our bones. Cadres, leaders, and *chhlops* who were once strong and vicious are now disappearing steadily, one after another.

Bong Tith is a base person from Paoy Snuol, about thirty-five years old, with a slender frame. He used to be chairman of Paoy Char subdistrict's *chhlop* unit. I hear it whispered that when Bong Tith was the chairman of the *chhlop* unit, he would kill people viciously and without compassion. When he rode a horse to chase down people who were fleeing toward Thailand, he beat them to death immediately with the stalk of a rifle. Anyone who was labeled as having done something wrong would be taken away and clubbed to death immediately by Bong Tith. Many people lost their lives, leaving behind wives and children, at the hands of Bong Tith.

Presently, Bong Tith seems to have awakened to an awareness of his deplorable deeds, and has adopted the persona of a gentle leader, understanding of those who work with him, recognizing our weariness and hardship. If he catches somebody stealing tubers or other crops on the farm, he takes little interest in beating or punishing them. He wants to build himself into a good person to cleanse himself of the sins that he committed before. But Bong Tith has run out of time to cleanse himself of bad deeds. The curse of the horrible suffering of those he killed—and of their families, children, and wives who live in misery—catches up with Bong Tith, damning and ensnaring him by the neck and casting him down into Hell with his eyes wide open.

27 January 1978

At about 4 p.m., a Paoy Char subdistrict *chhlop* comes to find Bong Tith and tells him to return to the village, saying that his wife is sick. An old hand experienced in the work of the *chhlop* unit, Bong Tith is suspicious of the facial expression of the *chhlop*, one of his former minions. He tells him to go on ahead, promising to follow along after.

When the *chhlop* has gone, Bong Tith sends Mea Lik to collect intelligence in the village: Is his wife really sick?

In fact, it is a ruse by the *chhlop* to arrest Bong Tith. Three members of the *chhlop* unit who have come from the cooperative—including Ta Ry, the new chairman of Paoy Char subdistrict's *chhlop* unit, who had been Bong Tith's deputy, plus one other *chhlop*—wait for Bong Tith in Phnom Srok. When they do not see Bong Tith going as promised, at nightfall Ta Ry takes his underlings and returns to the cooperative.

28 January 1978

The eastern sky is beginning to lighten faintly when Bong Tith arrives at my hut. He lies down on my sleeping platform and tells me to coin him, as last night he was upset and unable to sleep. He forbids me from telling people on the farm that he is hiding in my hut. He closes his eyes to try and sleep.

Mea Lik and Ta Moeun leave before dawn to Trapeang Thmor to contact the chairman of the regional mobile committee to arrange protection for Bong Tith.

Because my new hut is in the open and exposed, you can see it from every direction, and everyone knows anything I do. Young child *chhlops* ride bicycles in and out of the farm along the cart track in front of my hut. Unable to sleep, Bong Tith tells me to monitor their activities and to take a jute sack and hang it over the wide-open doorway.

Just before noon, when I return from eating, I bring some uncooked rice from Bong Phan (the cook), hidden inside some rice dust, to cook for Bong Tith. I boil a duck egg and pick a watermelon for him to eat, and then I go to sit in front of the old hut and watch in case any strange people come around.

Nothing out of the ordinary occurs. After he finishes eating, Bong Tith sits leaning against the short wall at the head of the sleeping platform, smoking a cigarette and blowing long streams of smoke. I go into the hut and collect and tidy the dishes, then stand eating half of the watermelon which Bong Tith left for me at the end of the sleeping platform.

Bong Tith says to me, dryly, "They're definitely coming to arrest me today, Tuch."

"So why don't you run?" I ask him.

"I'm not running anywhere, Tuch. I don't know what I've done wrong!" Bong Tith struggles to speak with a tight, despair-filled chest. He goes silent for a while and then resumes speaking.

"Huh! If they're going to arrest me, Ta Moeun and Ta Lik could at least come back first...They've been gone for so long! It's noon already and they haven't even come back yet!"

He exhales his cigarette smoke gently and then says slowly, "I just don't get it, Tuch. I don't understand why the Organization is doing this, arresting people who haven't done anything wrong, without any consideration. I have strived to wage revolution, to serve the Revolution faithfully for many years, and still I can't avoid being arrested. If the Organization does this, nobody is going to want to keep struggling to wage revolution with them anymore!"

Bong Tith stops speaking and pulls a long draft of the cigarette smoke into his lungs. What kinds of things should I say to him to ease his anxiety? I have never had to prepare myself to await execution like this. It is true that I have been arrested before, but I was bound suddenly and without expectation or warning, so I didn't have to endure the long panic of anticipation. I begin to ask him, "Have you ever made any mistakes?"

"No! I don't know what I've done wrong, Tuch...Oh, there was something. When I was head of the *chhlop* unit I objected to a decision by the Organization once." He pauses for a moment and then continues. "One day we caught someone who had run for Thailand. When we interrogated him, he answered against four fertilizer makers in the cooperative, saying that they wanted to run away with him as well. The Organization ordered me to arrest those four people and have them killed as well. I defended them because there was no evidence or attempted follow-up to confirm. If someone has only to answer against someone else for them to be arrested and killed like that, without any further consideration, we will soon run out of people to carry out the Revolution. They accused me of disobeying orders from the Revolutionary Organization, and they removed me from my office as chairman of the *chhlop* unit and made me mobile ever since."

Bong Tith is silent, and then he takes a big breath and continues. "Huh! I'm in trouble for protecting someone else. It's like what happened recently—you saw it! They came to arrest Yoeum without any verification. If I had not defended him, Yoeum would be dead now."

Bong Tith stops talking and raises his cigarette to his lips, then strikes the lighter and re-lights it, sucking in the smoke and then blowing it upward, nostalgically. Then he turns to me and asks, "Tuch?"

"Yes?" I reply.

"Did you know Yong before?" Bong Tith asks.

"No, I didn't know him," I answer.

"So why did Yong say that he used to know you? Yong said that during the *Sangkum* era you had a higher job than anyone," Bong Tith asks.

"No, Bong! During the *Sangkum* era I never knew Bong Yong, and I didn't have a job. I met him for the first time when I came to take part in constructing Trapeang Thmor Reservoir in 1977!"

I am not afraid to deny the accusations of Bong Yong because, other than my own siblings, nobody knows what I did during the *Sangkum* era.

Bong Tith starts to spill the beans to me. "After they took away Bong Yong to be killed, the Organization gave me orders to follow you, Tuch."

"Oh, I remember. Bong Yong must have harbored resentment toward me because I once criticized the economy team when we were building Trapeang Thmor Reservoir at Phnom Kon Khlaeng. At that time he was the head of the economy team."

I recount to Bong Tith the matter involving Bong Yong. Today I finally understand why Bong Tith kept prying and asking questions about my personal history so many times, asking about my job and how I got separated from my wife.

"It's because I love you faithfully, Tuch, that I'm willing to tell you this now. If it isn't true, then don't worry about running away. Work hard, engage in the Revolution, and build yourself well!" Bong Tith instructs me.

"Yes, Bong. Thank you for making me aware of it."

I do not ask Bong Tith what job Bong Yong accused me of having previously held so that Bong Tith will not think that I'm feeling worried or guilty about it.

We are busy conversing and forget to think of the imminent danger that threatens Bong Tith, of being surrounded by enemies. Bong Tith, who is sitting and leaning his back against the short wall, glances to the west along the cart track and suddenly trembles in fear, jumping down from the platform to hide in the corner beside my jerrycan, where I have placed some rice plants in the back corner on the east side, and whispers to me, "Tuch! Soldiers!"

I drop my spoon and stop eating the watermelon and push aside the jute sack to go outside. I stand and stare westward along the silent cart track, then to the north and east, but see nothing. Where did Bong Tith see soldiers? I walk over to the chicken pen and run into Comrade Soem[1] coming out of the old

---

[1] Author's note: "a young *chhlop*, about seventeen years old, who used to live at Kok Kakah when Ta Lam was still alive"

hut straight toward me. Without hesitation, I quickly smile welcomingly at him and call out, "Where are you headed?"

Comrade Soem smiles and replies, "I'm headed to find a drink of water!" and without hesitation he walks right past me and straight toward the new hut. He enters the hut before I do and sees the watermelon, then turns to me and asks, "Who did you pick that for?"

"Oh, just for myself," I answer quickly.

"So I can have a little bit, then."

"Sure!"

Almost before I can finish answering, he has picked up the spoon and shoveled a bite of watermelon into his mouth and out of the corner of his eye sees the corner where Bong Tith is cowering and hiding. Comrade Soem walks out of the hut. I follow him out.

Coming out of the chicken pen and walking straight toward the new hut is an older man of about forty with a stocky frame, a firm face, and sharp eyes: the chairman of Paoy Char subdistrict's *chhlop* unit, Ta Ry. I receive him with a smile and say politely, "Please, come in, Uncle!"

Without answering a word, Ta Ry pulls aside the sack covering the doorway of the hut and walks straight to where Bong Tith is hiding. Seeing Ta Ry, Bong Tith trembles with fear like a soaking wet baby sparrow and raises his two palms together before him and pleads, "Don't hurt me, Brother!"

"Who is hurting you?" Ta Ry menaces.

"Are you arresting me?" Bong Tith asks.

"Yes! Stand up!" Ta Ry menaces.

Holding his rationed sandals in his hand, Bong Tith stands up and walks out of the hut as ordered. Ta Ry and Comrade Soem follow behind him. I walk out of the hut.

Dear Lord! Two large female soldiers dressed in black, with bandoliers of bullets crisscrossed on their torsos and holding AK-47 rifles in ready positions, show themselves on the cart track near a bush west of my hut. It must have been these two female soldiers whom Bong Tith saw.

Now it is not just Bong Tith who is trembling with fear. Now *I* am shaking with fear and about to have a heart attack. Should I stay with the hut, or should I follow the others? No, I don't dare stay behind! I will follow the others. I am very afraid of these female soldiers. I lengthen my steps to catch up to Ta Ry and Comrade Soem, who are marching Bong Tith toward the forward camp. I am not following Bong Tith so much as I am looking for aid, for someone to help me. I am so scared! I feel weary and my limbs are weak.

They march Bong Tith to the cadres' office, and I dart into one of the female shelters and lie down to hide. The women are taking a midday rest and don't know what is going on, and they are puzzled by my demeanor, lying prone and panting heavily in their shelter. They surround me and ask questions.

"What's going on, Bong Tuch? What's wrong?"

I am struggling for breath and can barely speak. "They arrested...they arrested Bong Tith!"

Hearing just these few words, all the women are stricken with fear, opening their eyes wide. They all thought that Bong Tith had already run away from the farm, and they didn't know that he was hiding out at my hut. Bong Phan is overcome by fear and starts to shake and faint and asks for people to help coin and pinch her. We all feel afraid and sorry for Bong Tith. Here on the farm, Bong Tith is a gentle cadre who does not speak harshly like Ta Moeun does. He is understanding toward all of us, and that is why we were all stunned when we saw the chairman of Paoy Char subdistrict's *chhlop* unit, a former comrade of Bong Tith, come to arrest him.

After walking to the cadres' office, one of the female soldiers removes a hammock string coiled at her waist and ties Bong Tith's arms together behind him and sets him down on the floor. They call Bong Mon (a female cook) to bring food and water for them to eat. After finishing their meal, they march Bong Tith away northward along the cart track toward Kok Roessei, laying a *krama* over his back to cover his bound arms. Soon after, Comrade Soem returns to look for the Orient TriStar wristwatch that Bong Tith had secretly removed and tossed aside onto the top of a mosquito net to hide it.

Today at the cooperative, Bong Dith, Bong Tith's older brother and a cadre in Paoy Snuol, is also arrested and taken to be killed.

Oh, Life! Now can anybody be certain in their heart that they can avoid death, or know when they will be arrested and taken away to be killed? Now it is not only we, the Life Slaves, whom they kill. Even their own, those who have lived with them and eaten and slept with them, are killed by them without hesitation, as soon as they are no longer useful to them, when they are no longer a benefit to the Party. They take no thought for the struggles or past merits of such individuals on behalf of the Party. Instead, Bong Tith, who had served the

Party for many years, did not truly understand the position of the Party and thought that the Party would be understanding toward him, who had voluntarily served them, to the point that he refused to run away and hide, but was instead willing to give himself up to the Party, who arrested him and killed him so easily.

Bong Tith lost the trust of the Party by defending and demanding justice in an unjust society. He defended the fertilizer workers and Mea Yoeum, which constituted standing up to his superiors. The fertilizer workers were not killed, and neither was Mea Yoeum, so Bong Tith had to be killed in their stead.

Bong Tith had an awakening, became jaded by all the killing, and wanted to remove himself far away from such things. He understood that the Party had done wrong, killing only their own people, their own compatriots, an activity that he ought no longer to pursue. He was satisfied to accept the loss of his own life rather than continue living only to kill his own compatriots on behalf of others.

It is true that he had made mistakes, but his final decisions surely had great value for his reputation, and for the Khmer nation. For if he still lived, he would have to serve the Party, to kill Khmers on behalf of the Party. And the next person to be killed would certainly have been me.

About a week after Bong Tith's arrest, on 2 February 1978, the regional Organization issues orders for us to retreat from the Kok Kakah farm and return to the cooperatives.

CHAPTER 36

The Death of My Sister

Before the harvest season, as a result of sipping only thin porridge with a few grains of rice mixed with bits of manioc and *phty* greens or boiled *trakuon*, without salt, nearly everyone with a weak constitution, especially children and the elderly, becomes afflicted with swelling.

Ol, my oldest sister, though only thirty-eight years old, has a very weak constitution and has suffered from swelling for nearly two months now, but I have not dared to ask permission to go visit her. When we retreat from the Kok Kakah farm, we pass through Paoy Snuol, and I take advantage of this opportunity to visit her. A friend and two girls who adore me go along with me.

We find a sight so upsetting and disturbing that it is hard to endure: My sister's body is completely swollen, her eyes so sunken she can barely open them. She is lying flat on a ragged rice sack spread out on the wooden floor slats in place of a sleeping mat, groaning *uh... uh...* like the cooing of a dove. Now and then she cries out, "Oi! Oi! It hurts so much! Mama, help me!"

Ol is delirious and has lost all lucidity. Nho, her husband, and Oun can do nothing to please her. They have tried all kinds of remedies to treat her, one after another, but she has not improved at all.

Because this chronic illness has gone on for months, the two of them are exhausted and hopeless of making her better, and they sit silently and glance at each other, occasionally bowing their heads, hugging their knees, and sighing in despair. We, who have only observed this for a few minutes, also sink into despair, mixed with intense, tight-chested pity. What should we do? Can we possibly help to ease so much suffering?

We are each like a person stunned by a heart attack, unable to do anything, unable to speak, looking at the patient who sometimes groans and sometimes cries out for relief from the agony in her body.

My sister's eyes are open, but she cannot see or discern who is around her. I scoot near and bend down close to her and ask, "Ol! Ol! Ol, do you know who I am?"

Her eyes do not recognize me, but her ears still remember my voice. She stops groaning and whispers, "Who is that? Is that A-Tuch?"

"Yes, it's me! How are you doing?" I ask.

As if she doesn't want to answer the question, my sister continues to cry out, "Oi! Oi! It hurts so much! It hurts everywhere! Mama, help me!"

My mother died quietly, so that we would hardly have suspected that she was experiencing pain at all. On the contrary, my sister is facing the most prolonged and miserable agony. When Mom was still alive and sick, Ol never bothered to give her attention or care. Now, as she faces the Angel of Death, Ol's mind turns to Mom, and she calls out for her.

Oh, children! Do you know how much your mother has done for you? Should you be angry at your mother, or hate her, or forget what she has done for you? You should not; whenever you encounter a struggle in life, your thoughts will turn to her first.

Unable to sit listening to my sister's cries of agony and watch her delirium in her final minutes of life, we abandon her after only fifteen minutes of watching her suffer, taking away with us a feeling of somberness and melancholy. In my heart I plead with the Angel of Death to come and take my sister's life soon, to quickly relieve her of her suffering on this earth.

On the night of the 7th of February, I dream of my sister's death. The next day, after taking the midday meal, I take the opportunity to go and visit her house. Ol's groans have fallen silent, replaced with stillness. Ol passed away two days ago. This death released Oun and Nho from their protracted anguish.

My younger brother Samorn pulled back his front lines from the *roneam* to Trapeang Thmor on the 2nd of February, the same as me. But because he didn't know her house, and because he was not allowed to break ranks, he couldn't visit our sister before she died.

We have lost yet another sibling. Now, of the twelve who left Phnom Penh together, there are only four left. Of me and my siblings, only three remain.

These days the death of a person has become as commonplace as the death of a rat, a cockroach, a dog, or a cat. Apart from family members who come to surround the deceased, to smell the corpse, and to mourn the dead, nobody else can be bothered about it. And in some cases, even family members don't dare come and pay their final respects if the death was ordained by the Organization, as the Organization thinks that "to keep you is no gain, to remove you is no loss."

They are humans, and they kill humans without pity. They are Khmers, and they kill Khmers without any regrets. What do they do it for?

Wild tigers are famous for being vicious, but even tigers don't wipe out their own kind. The numbers of wild tigers have declined as a result of the work of humans, but the tigers are not themselves to blame for their own decline.

So why does the Organization have poorer reasoning capacity than that of a wild tiger, massacring their own kind, without any self-remorse as fellow Khmers?

CHAPTER 37

The Penalty for Desertion

The forces that withdraw from Kok Kakah now disperse to their own subdistricts. Those middle-aged people with wives and children are allowed to return to their cooperatives. Otherwise, among the forces of Paoy Char subdistrict, those without husbands, wives, or children are assigned by the Organization to join the region's youth mobile units.

Comrade Savuth and I are ordered to work with the region's Third Mobile Brigade, in the young men's unit, led by Comrade Sariep and Comrade Hul. This is the brigade formerly known as Ta Val's brigade. Currently this brigade is assigned to haul dirt with shoulder yokes to shore up the dams at Trapeang Thmor Reservoir and to do dry-season rice farming along with the region's young women's brigade, led by Comrade Sister Sov and Comrade Sister Chhom. The young men's unit that hauls dirt makes camp near the second bridge (water gate) and take their meals there. The young men's unit working on dry-season rice farming takes their meals with the young women in the dining pavilion near the Trapeang Thmor brick-kiln pond.

Comrade Savuth, who had been in charge of the oxen, is assigned to drive an oxcart to transport the brigade's supplies. I am assigned to help lead the brigade's vegetable farming team, which is currently led by Comrade Chey and has three other members: Comrade Sieng and the boys Chhong and Nhes.

Wat Trapeang Thmor is in Trapeang Thmor village, on the east side of the subdistrict's main road that connects all the villages from south to north. Directly behind[1] the *wat* there is a side road that branches to the west, a dead-end road about 300 meters long and about eight meters wide. At the end of this road are the rice fields. The Trapeang Thmor brick kiln is on the south side of this road, about 200 meters from the *wat*.

Immediately west of the brick kiln is a pond about thirty-by-thirty meters in size. At the north end of this pond is a large Bodhi tree. The dining pavilion for the young women of Comrade Sov's brigade is built east-to-west in between

---

[1] Though this road is directly across from the main entrance of the *wat*, relative directions with respect to a *wat* are expressed based on the direction of the temple in the *wat* rather than the location of the main entrance. Because the temple in a *wat* always faces east, west is "behind" the *wat*.

the pond and the Bodhi tree, about five by fifteen meters. Across from this pavilion (on the other side of the road) there is a rice machine-milling shed.

East of the brick kiln is a long shed built north-to-south, about five by thirty meters, for making bricks and roof tiles. Adjacent to this shed, to the east, is a shelter for the young women of Comrade Tum's unit, of Comrade Sov's brigade, about five by thirty meters. More than thirty young women live in this shelter. The young women from other units of Comrade Sov's brigade live at a camp inside Wat Trapeang Thmor.

Immediately east of the young women's camp is the Third Brigade's vegetable field, about fifty meters square. The vegetable team has built a sleeping shelter, about three by five meters, against the eaves of the women's shelter. The vegetable team, like the young men tasked with farming rice, take their meals with the women in the dining pavilion by the pond.

On the first day we arrive here, before we have found our supervisors, Comrade Savuth and I go to eat in the dark, after everyone else has eaten. The cooks are base women, but they are very friendly and receive us warmly. One young woman asks us, "I heard that you just came from Kok Kakah, is that right?"

"Yes, we did just come from Kok Kakah," I reply.

"How many of you are there?"

"Just the two of us," I reply.

The young women lead us to a long dining table and makes themselves busy preparing some rice and soup for us to eat. While we eat, we answer the questions of two young women from the economy team, who sit across from us.

"What did you do at Kok Kakah?" one of them asks.

"I kept the oxen for plowing and pulling carts," Comrade Savuth answers.

"What about you, Bong?" she asks me.

"I raised the pigs, chickens, and ducks," I answer.

"Oh, so you were at the west end of the *kok*, right?"

"Yes, that's right," I reply.

"So did you ever see us?"

I think for a moment, then reply, "No, I'm sorry, I don't recall. Have you been to Kok Kakah?"

"Yes, during the last rainy season, we farmed rice in that area and stayed at the Kok Roessei camp. We would sometimes rest in the shade by the chicken pen," one of the young women recounts.

That's right, some base women used to come stand around at my place, but I never dared to look any of them in the face because most of the base women have an attitude and don't want to talk with new people.

"Oh, I remember. But forgive me if I don't remember you, Comrades," I reply.

The attention and questions of these two young women make us feel very shy, as there are just the two of us young men eating our meal in the light of a single kerosene lamp. We scarcely dare to raise our eyes to look them in the faces, but they seem to want to get to know us, and don't seem to grow tired of it.

"So have the two of you already received work assignments here in Comrade Sariep's brigade?" one of the young women asks.

"Yes, Comrade Savuth is in charge of the oxen and driving the cart, and I am on the vegetable team," I reply.

"Oh, then you will take your meals with us, while you, oxcart driver, will go stay at the second bridge."

Our little vegetable field is positively crowded with vegetables: gourds, mint, *trakuon*, eggplants, lemongrass, cabbage, peppers, tomatoes, etc. We are responsible for picking these vegetables and sending them to the forces at the second bridge, where Comrade An, the head of the economy team for the brigade, receives them, and some to the women's dining pavilion at the brick-kiln pond as well.

Because of how crowded and small our vegetable field is, I contact the cooperative to request another field, about fifty meters square, immediately south of the pond, to expand our vegetable garden. There, we plant many more rows of corn, pumpkins, wax melons, winter melons, *phty*, and *trakuon*. We build a small hut there to use for watching the field.

Our work is entirely in our own hands, so there is no clearly defined work schedule. In the morning, we get up and carry watering cans on shoulder yokes to water the vegetables until about seven thirty or eight o'clock. Then we care for the vegetables by turning the soil, picking weeds, picking worms, and building up mounds at the bases of the eggplant, tomato, and pepper plants. We are continuously busy until about 4 p.m., and then we fetch water with shoulder yokes and water the vegetables again until sunset. But compared to the work of people who haul dirt, our jobs are easier.

As a leader of the team, I can come and go from the cooperative to look for vegetable seeds, corn, and beans to store for planting. Coming and going from the village, one day I meet a former classmate, Comrade Ty Chihuot.[2] Chihuot was my classmate at the Applied High School in Phnom Penh. Due to heartbreak from a romance that he had cultivated since he was a student at Ang Chan I (a.k.a. Bak Tuk) Primary School, he dropped out of high school and went off adventuring, working as a *cyclo* driver, and then later made a living writing novels.

Ty Chihuot was evacuated here to Region Five on the first railroad wave with his wife and children and shared a house with some base people in Paoy Char village. Because he knew how to cut hair like his father, who was a barber, Chihuot was assigned by the Organization to be a barber in the village, and to perform secondary jobs like twisting ropes and weaving *bangky* baskets. We are both mutually delighted to meet an old classmate we haven't seen in nearly ten years.

Because I have a good relationship with the cooperative, Comrade An, Comrade Sariep, and Comrade Hul often use me for tasks other than vegetable farming, such as arranging for repairs to oxcarts and bicycles, fixing flat tires, etc.

One day, at about 2 p.m., Comrade Sariep sends Chhong and me to take his bicycle to have a flat tire patched at the mechanic's shed at the cooperative office in Paoy Char village. There, we find a large assembly of people equipped with hoes, *bangky* baskets, yoke poles, and clothing bundles, as though about to depart on a mobile deployment.

Suddenly, Comrade Savuth comes running up to greet me. "Where are you going, Comrade Tuch?" Comrade Savuth asks me.

"I'm bringing Comrade Sariep's bicycle to be patched. What about you, Comrade Savuth, where are you coming from?" I ask.

"I'm being deployed with the middle-aged mobile unit to construct the reservoir dam at Ansang Neav."

---

[2] 1952–1987; Cambodian novelist and writer

"Oh, have you returned to the village, Vuth?" I ask.

"Yes, I returned to the village a week ago," Comrade Savuth replies.

"Where is Ansang Neav, Vuth?" I ask.

"I don't know either. I'm just going along with the others."

"So when are they leaving?" I ask.

"We're waiting until everyone gets here. They said we'll depart at three o'clock."

Comrade Savuth ran away from the regional mobile unit to come back to the cooperative, but now the cooperative is sending him out on a mobile unit just the same. Because he missed me, he ran over to chat with me, not thinking that this act would bring danger to himself.

After the tire has been patched, I return to the brick kiln. Chhong had stood by and listened to the conversation between me and Comrade Savuth, and on his return he reports it to Comrade Sariep, who is sitting and waiting for his bicycle. Without delay, Comrade Sariep takes Chhong out to find Comrade Savuth.

When he sees Comrade Sariep coming, Comrade Savuth gets scared and runs off to hide in a manioc field. Comrade Sariep goes to see the cooperative chairman and requests to take Comrade Savuth back to the regional mobile brigade. The comrade cooperative chairman can't harbor members of the regional mobile brigade, so he summons Comrade Savuth to come and meet Comrade Sariep. Cornered, Comrade Savuth has to follow Comrade Sariep back to Brigade Three and is taken to be executed that evening.

The crime of Comrade Savuth was deserting the regional mobile brigade and going back to live in the cooperative. But his penalty was execution.

Oh, Life! Why must you be so fragile?

Comrade Savuth is the fourth person to be taken away from me and executed, after Comrade On, Bong Yong, and Bong Tith.

Chapter 38
A Budding Romance

In our first meeting under the dark veil of evening, under the flickering light of a kerosene lamp, I didn't think to observe the beauty of the two economy girls who practically pinned me down and questioned me. I only got the feeling that they were extraordinarily friendly compared to other base women, who tend to be haughty and snobbish and don't like to speak to young men who are new people. This strangeness kindled a question in my mind, as I wondered and worried if this was their customary behavior, or was this a special case?

Living nearby allows me to get to know them better, both their beauty and their kindness. They are the two beautiful roses of Comrade Sov's young women's brigade, desired by all the worker bees.

They go everywhere together as a pair. One is called Comrade Dy, with a round face and wavy shoulder-length hair. The other is called Comrade Ly, with an oval face and long black hair down nearly to her waist, which she usually wears draped over her right shoulder and hanging free over her front. She is about as beautiful as the Haitian girl whose photograph I painted a copy of and hung over my bedroom doorway back in Phnom Penh. Both girls have a clear complexion, curvy figure, height over a meter sixty, and age about twenty years old. They have generally generous and friendly dispositions.

My politeness, gentleness, and friendliness lead most of the young women in Comrade Tum's unit, both the new people and the base people, to like me and feel friendly toward me. Comrade Dy and Comrade Ly are the closest of them all, and Comrade Ly, especially, takes a noteworthy interest in me.

Every day, I haul water past the front of the young women's shelter. In the evenings, when she is finished with her cooking, Comrade Ly usually takes time to stand at the edge of the pond watching me fill the watering cans on my yoke and smiling at me. Sometimes I force myself to stand and chat with her, with the yoke on my shoulder, to satisfy her interest. Every time she asks for vegetables to cook with, Comrade Ly goes along with me to help pick them; even if I go under the gourd trellis, she crawls in after me.

Carrying my watering cans back and forth in front of the young women, I can't go shirtless as I had done when hauling dirt to build the dams. My white jacket is made from thick cloth and helps ease the pain on my shoulder from hauling the water, but the sleeves get in the way badly when tipping the cans to water the vegetables. I consider removing the two sleeves and turning it into a vest. In the young women's shelter there is a sewing machine.

One afternoon I approach Comrade Ly and ask to use the sewing machine to sew my jacket. All the young women are out in the rice fields, with only the economy girls left behind at the kitchen. Comrade Ly is the only person in the entire sleeping shelter. I have now become a young man who can enter the young women's shelter without violating morality. Even when just the two of us, a young man and a young woman, are alone together in this spacious shelter. Comrade Ly looks for a shuttle and a needle and inserts them into the sewing machine, then turns to me.

"Bong Tuch, let me sew it for you!"

"That's all-right Comrade Ly, I can do it." I am not accustomed to imposing on others.

"Do you even know how to sew with a machine?" she asks me.

"I've known how since I was young. When my clothes ripped, if my mom didn't patch them for me, I would patch them myself. When I lived with my sister, she had a sewing machine, and I learned to patch my clothes with a machine."

I bend my head to my work and speak with Comrade Ly while I sew. Comrade Ly watches me sew very attentively. She says to me, "Bong Tuch, look how good you are at sewing! And you push the treadle with only your right foot, just like me."

I pull my foot back and smile up at her. "Comrade Ly, you praise me too much!" I say, as she smiles back.

"No, really! You know how to sew like a girl. Where are you from, originally?"

"I'm from Phnom Penh."

"If you're from Phnom Penh you've probably had a lot of education. What grade did you study to?"

"I studied all the way to the last grade."

"You are very educated. My parents and older brothers only like educated people."

These words give me greater insight into her motivations. I think I should ask some questions about her life as well so that she doesn't feel let down.

"Comrade Ly, are you from Phnom Srok district?"

"No, we are from Thmor Puok district." Comrade Ly's expression changes, and she speaks slowly.

"So Comrade Ly, have you been with the regional mobile brigade for long?"

"Yes, we've been mobile for a long time. Because our homes were so far away, we boarded at Svay Sisophon Junior High School. A-Dy, A-Top, and I were all in grade four in the 'modern system.'[1] When the Revolutionary Army entered Svay, they conscripted us into the mobile unit right away, without allowing us to even return to our home village." Comrade Ly recounts this story with a sad expression. My question has made her feel downcast.

I stop the machine, raise my face, look straight into hers, smile dryly, and say slowly, "Comrade Ly, have you ever gone back home to visit?"

"No, never. For the last three and a half years, none of us has ever seen our parents' faces. Because our work is so busy, we are constantly moving our front lines from place to place, and the Organization has never given us permission to go visit our home village."

"Have you ever heard any news from them?"

"Yes, some. During the offensive to build the reservoir last year, we had opportunities to meet siblings who came to take part."

Comrade Ly has a sad countenance, and her mood has descended into a deep melancholy. As a girl far away from her parents and family for years, she must surely feel cold and desolate.

To ease the tension I say to her, "Hey, what can you do, Comrade Ly? We all have our sorrows, but your fate is better than mine. There is still a future day when you can see the people who have done so much for you, but for me that day does not exist."

As if suddenly snapping out of something, Comrade Ly says to me, "Your parents are both dead, aren't they, Bong?"

"Yes, it's true. Both of my parents died within the space of just ten days, before the Organization evacuated me here to Region Five."

"How many siblings are in your family?" Comrade Ly asks me.

"There were seven of us, but some of us have been separated, and some have died, and some have been killed, and now there are only three of us left: my

---

[1] i.e., the French system in place at the time, counting backward from twelve; see footnote on page 8

older sister, my youngest brother, and me. And we are constantly separated by mobile deployments."

My family's history helps Comrade Ly disconnect from her own personal problems and makes her realize that there is someone suffering from greater, more pitiful hardships than hers. And that pitiful person is helping her to forget her own troubles born of long separation from family.

Comrade Ly feels better, but she is wallowing in her problems.

One week after coming to live with the Third Brigade, the young men's unit that is farming rice with the young women of Comrade Sov's brigade is pulled back to the dirt-hauling worksite. From now on, the vegetable team no longer takes our meals with the women's unit; we start to make our own meals. Then nearly a month later, Comrade Chey is removed from the vegetable team and sent back to the dirt-hauling unit.

One evening, when a dry-season storm has come and rained in the afternoon, we don't have to water the crops, so we are able cook and eat while it is still light out. We start eating at five o'clock. Suddenly Comrade Ly and Comrade Dy show up at our hut and Comrade Ly calls out to me, "Bong Tuch! Can I [*oun*]² borrow a pair of watering cans?"

I raise my head and smile at her and ask, acting as though I hadn't heard her clearly the first time, "What did you say, Comrade Ly?"

"I said let me [*oun*] borrow a pair of your watering cans."

"Come! Have some dinner with us first, Comrade Ly, Comrade Dy!"

"All right, thank you Bong!" they both answer in unison.

"What will you use the watering cans for, Comrade Ly and Comrade Dy?" I ask.

"I [*oun*] will use them to haul uncooked rice, Bong!" Comrade Ly replies.

"Chhong, bring a pair of cans for Comrade Ly!" I say to Chhong.

Now I, who not long ago was trying to figure out how to flee from romance and remove myself from the path of love, am causing a young woman to fall in

---

² Significantly, this pronominal term, a diminutive form of the word *p'oun* ("younger sibling"), is also an affectionate term of address, both in the first and second person, for a romantic female partner, so it has significant romantic or intimate overtones when used in a context like this. Comrade Ly's use of it here is an important signal of romantic intention, which is noticed by her audience.

love with me. No, it is not intentional. I am not trying to attract her interest or draw her to me.

I am not afraid to acknowledge the truth; I must have done something to attract her eye and her feelings. But whatever it was, it was not intentional on my part. After coming to Trapeang Thmor, I searched for the house of Sadet, my former high-school classmate, whom I had met at Kok Kakah and asked Bong Tith to contact for me. I met Sadet's parents in Sambuor and brought my older sister to meet them to discuss the possibility of engagement.

Now I have to face emotional confusion all over again. I agonize over how to manage the current developments. In fact, Comrade Ly is the girl who is in my heart. But at first, I never imagined that I could possibly snare the heart of such a beautiful woman who is also a base person; and besides, I was worried about other problems I was facing, so I was determined not to get involved. But everything I have done was incompatible with that determination, like chatting with just the two of them beside the pond, looking her right in the face and smiling at her, and especially sitting, sewing, and chatting alone with her in the spacious and silent shelter.

And now, it is even harder to stick to that determination because I have caused a girl, whom I consider to be very loveable, to fall headlong in love with me. All the young women in Comrade Tum's unit call me "Bong Tuch," but only Comrade Ly uses both *oun* and *bong* with me. She must have much greater feelings for me than I had imagined.

The old timers say that "it is better to live with someone who loves you than with someone you love." It is now my fate to have met someone I love, and who loves me exceedingly. Does it make sense to be reluctant?

Sadet and I have no emotional bond. And up until now, I have become increasingly aware of obstacles that will keep us apart: we are in mobile units camped far away from one another, dozens of kilometers, and are unable to even contact one another. The Day of Ceremony for the mobile units usually happens very suddenly, without any advanced preparation or foreknowledge.

23 March 1978

Through Comrade Nang, Ta Lam's former *nirasar*, I receive a letter from Comrade Sarann, a former friend of Comrade Sadet. She used to live at the Kok

Kakah farm with me, and currently she lives in Nam Tau subdistrict. The contents of this letter are as follows:

> *To Comrade Tuch [back of the letter]*
>
> > *Dear Missed Comrade of the Highest Revolution,*
>
> > *Comrade! Ever since I parted from you, I have been missing you greatly. When will we live in the same unit again? The memories that we shared together pull on my heart and make me feel sad, missing you so much. Anyway, I don't need to say any more than that, as you certainly understand the pure amity between friends. These days you are on the vegetable-planting unit; how are you doing? We are doing fine, as usual. We have returned to live in the cooperative. I have been wondering about the relationship between you and my friend. How is that going? Please send me a message and let me know, and I will await this news always. If you meet A-Det[3] personally, please tell her that I miss her very much, and to write me a letter. If you have time, please write me letters often, as we never see each other anymore. If you can send a letter, please send it via Comrade Nang, who often comes and goes.*
>
> > *Before I end, I want to ask your forgiveness for writing this in red ink due to a lack of options, and I wish you the greatest well-being.*
>
> > > > *From a comrade,*
> > > > *Rann*

The introduction of this letter confirms her sadness in having parted from me, and about how much she misses me. At the end of the letter, she wishes me well-being, and not for me to be reunited with her friend. Her sentiments are only for me.

People can hide anything, but they can't hide love. Even though they may desire to hide it from others, they can't help but want to show it to the object of their affection. In fact, I perceived the feelings of Comrade Sarann toward

---

[3] Sadet

me when we lived at Kok Kakah, where she was the most mysterious of them all.

I write a letter replying to Sarann, detailing the relationship between myself and Sadet, and confirming how much I miss her in return.

At this time I am not much different from the character Tum,[4] who caused upset among the women in Tbong Khmum. When I left the women at the Kok Kakah farm and passed over to the women at the brick-kiln camp, I had no intention of stirring up their feelings, nor do I understand why it is happening.

"Tum was well-spoken and wise besides, with a youthful voice and appearance."[5] These are the qualities of the character Nen Tum, as praised by Bhikkhu Som, and are what caused the young women of Tbong Khmum to become agitated and drawn to him. As for me, I don't seem to have any of those qualities.

Thinking that Comrade Chey had been in charge of the brick-kiln vegetable farm for a long time, I feel sorry for him, and I make a request to Comrade Sariep that Comrade Chey be sent back to help with the work on the farm as our crops in the field south of the pond are flourishing more and more. Comrade Sariep agrees and sends Comrade Chey back to the farm, after having hauled dirt for half a month.

This is one of my worst ideas as Comrade Chey is greedy, stingy, and mean, and he doesn't get along with anybody else. When Comrade Chey oversaw the work here, the young women in Comrade Tum's unit never came to the vegetable field, except for the economy women. Now that I am in charge of the work, especially since Comrade Chey went away to haul dirt, the young women often come to visit and check on the growth and progress of the crops. Sometimes they ask for a pepper, or a few sprigs of mint, or a few lemongrass leaves.

Upon his return to the farm, and seeing that the situation has changed, Comrade Chey is unhappy and turns merit into fault, scolding me. "Bong Tuch, you are too generous! Before you came here, all these girls would never dare to enter the vegetable area and ask for vegetables or ask to borrow watering cans!"

---

[4] a reference to main character of the traditional folk tale *Tum Teav*; specifically, the classic 1915 Khmer poetic-novel rendition by Bhikkhu Nguon Som (1853-1932)

[5] *Tum Teav*, verse 34

"I don't think that a few leaves of lemongrass or a few peppers or tomatoes is a significant loss, and borrowing watering cans to fetch water for bathing is also harmless. They are girls coming to ask for a favor, with hopes of getting it, and if I turn around and refuse them and say 'no' it would be very embarrassing for them! I can't be like you, Comrade Chey."

"Bong Tuch, if you don't dare answer 'no' when they come looking then send them to me!" Comrade Chey yells back at me.

Damn! Comrade Chey is back in charge of me. I can't understand the heart of this man. He is young, about twenty years old, with very little education, but he acts arrogant and tough, and fights against me without any gratitude.

The Revolutionary Organization says that "it is better to kill a person in error than to release a person in error." I saved a person in error. I saved a crocodile, and now that crocodile is turning to bite me. I decide to distance myself from him.

"Don't worry about it, Comrade Chey. In that case, you stay and tend the vegetables here with Chhong. Comrade Sieng and I, with Nhes, will go and tend the field south of the pond."

Comrade Chey accepts this solution with gladness.

CHAPTER 39

The Killing of Comrade Ran

In approximately early March, we observe the presence of two young men who come and go at the young women's unit and my farm. We don't know exactly where they stay, though perhaps it is at the cadres' office for the regional mobile units. They are former soldiers who have been relieved from Svay (or so I hear it said). One is called Comrade Bor, and I don't recall the name of the other.

When we stopped taking meals with the young women, the fertilizer team for the Third Brigade also began to collect its own rice rations and make its own meals like the vegetable farming team. Comrade Ran, the head of the fertilizer team, collects his rations and then cooks and eats them along with the vegetable farming team, and also sleeps with us at the vegetable field south of the pond.

Comrade Ran is a young man with a large, sturdy frame, about a meter seventy tall, about thirty years old. He is a former *bhikkhu*[1] who graduated with a diploma from Preah Suramarit Buddhist High School in Phnom Penh.

These days Comrade Ran acts like a man who is half crazy: During the two weeks of the waxing moon, his personality is that of an outgoing person who speaks like an intellectual, gesticulating with his arms and legs; unconcerned with his responsibilities; thinking only of expounding on the implementation of socialist revolution, and about Buddhism; and helping other people with their work, especially older folks, both night and day. He is a man who is well spoken and wise, and nobody can trip him up with questioning. He has a document that speaks of the dissolution of Buddhism in Cambodia for a period of five years: the Years of the Tiger, Rabbit, Dragon, Snake, and Horse,[2] followed by its rebirth, and about the practices of Buddhists necessary to live through this period of Buddhism's dissolution. Comrade Ran often uses the document to expound to the old folks and ties it all in with the Revolution so they won't feel hopeless. He often explains that "it is because of the Revolution that Comrade Ran is thirty years old and doesn't have a wife yet."

---

[1] senior monk

[2] 1974–1979

The full moon is when Comrade Ran becomes very manic, forgetting his duties and his meals, forgetting everything and listening to nobody. He walks around all day and all night from place to place. Whether they want his help or not, Ran always triumphs in helping others with their work. Whether it is carrying bags of paddy rice or milling the rice, he is never still.

During the two weeks of the waning moon, Comrade Ran is a sober man, gentle and non-vocal, sitting alone and lost in thought. The chairman of the brigade and his friends understand about Comrade Ran's idiosyncrasies, and they are not easily bothered by him. I am the only person who can interrupt Comrade Ran now and then, as we sleep together and take our meals together.

Sometimes, Comrade Ran dresses in black pants and a black shirt and cap like a soldier and goes about taking people's bicycles and riding all over the cooperative or stopping military vehicles and asking them friendly questions.

One afternoon, Comrade Ran tells me, "Ta Tuch! This morning some soldiers invited me to ride in their truck with them out to Paoy Trach! But I didn't go because I would miss you too much, Ta Tuch. If I went, who else would chat with you?"

"Yeah, you ought to be cautious. If you think only of wandering about and sharing your wisdom, watch out they don't take you to Paoy Trach for real one of these times, all right?" I scold Comrade Ran, but he doesn't reply, and heads toward the village with his knife over his shoulder.

Then a short while later Comrade Bor comes to ask me, "Ta Tuch! Did you see where Ta Ran wandered off to?"

"Gee, I don't know where he went. He walked off with a *khvaev*[3] knife over his shoulder a while ago," I reply.

"This evening we're going to have some fun and tie up Ta Ran for a change!"

Comrade Bor says this and then walks away. I think they will tie up Comrade Ran for a lark and don't think much else of it. Then the next morning we find out they had taken Comrade Ran away and clubbed him to death, on accusations that he had attempted to set fire to the rice machine-milling shed.

---

[3] a long-handled knife similar to a *phkeak*; see photograph on page 518

Amazing! Killing a human being is so easy! It's as easy as killing a dog. In fact, Comrade Ran had no such intentions at all. He would often walk around explaining and encouraging people to love the Revolution. What benefit would he gain from burning down the rice machine-milling shed?

There is nothing special about the life of a Life Slave. A Life Master can revoke it whenever he feels like it. Like a rooster kept in a pen, who flaps his wings and crows to waken the master every morning, thinking that his master loves him and will allow him to continue living, to continue his beautiful crowing, but cannot avoid someday being caught and having his throat cut.

Comrade Ran is the fifth person living close to me to be taken away and executed.

CHAPTER 40

Obstacles to Love

Early April 1978

One morning at about nine o'clock, Comrade An, head of the brigade's economy team, Comrade Bor, and Comrade Hul (deputy chairman of the Third Brigade) come to my hut with cheerful expressions. Comrade An calls out to me as I am weeding the pumpkins, "Ta Tuch!"

"Yes, Brother?" I reply.

"Ta Tuch, come here for a moment!" Comrade An calls out to me again.

I drop my hoe and then walk over to receive them.

"What is it, Brothers?" I ask them.

"Ta Tuch, would you please help me write a Family[1] Request Letter for a minute?" Comrade An says.

"Oh, my goodness, my handwriting is not attractive, Bong!" I say with a smile.

"So who carved the words '*Chan Tuch Nhep*[2] on your spoon?" Comrade An asks me.

"I carved them, Brother. But my normal handwriting is not attractive," I demure.

"Attractive or not, it's better than our handwriting!" Comrade Bor says.

I smile at Comrade An and ask, "Who are you going to request, Comrade An?"

"I'm going to request to marry Comrade Ly, from Comrade Tum's unit," Comrade An replies.

Good Lord! He is going to request the woman I love!

"And I will request Comrade Dy!" Comrade Bor says.

Unable to object, I have to satisfy their request.

"What should I write? I have never written a Family Request Letter before," I ask.

"Go ahead and write and I'll tell you what to say," Comrade An says.

---

[1] During this period, the Khmer Rouge promoted use of the word "family" to mean "spouse."

[2] "Teeny Tiny Moon"; a fanciful nickname based on his surname (*chan* is a homophone with "moon") and nickname (*tuch* means tiny)

I lie face down on the sleeping platform and write according to the instructions of Comrade An.

Family Request Letter

> I, Comrade An, head of the economy team for the regional young men's mobile unit of the Third Brigade, hereby request to take Comrade Ly, from Comrade Tum's regional mobile unit in Comrade Sov's brigade, as my family.

> If this request is denied, though the waters of Trapeang Thmor Reservoir should dry up, I will continue to request Comrade Ly as my partner until I am successful.

> Trapeang Thmor, 3 April 1978
>
> Comrade An

Comrade Bor's letter is about the same. They are very pleased with my meticulous efforts at handwriting.

Three days later, the letters reach the hands of the intended recipients. The young women of Comrade Tum's unit read the letters and analyze them. They don't believe that they are in the handwriting of Comrade An or Comrade Bor, as at the beginning of each line I wrote using a larger script, similar to the writing that I had engraved on my rice spoon.

The sun is preparing to set and casting its red light upon the western sky. I am tilling the ground and placing fertilizer on the rows of *trakuon* when suddenly the boy Nhes comes and whispers to me, "Bong Tuch! Bong Ly is waiting to see you by the side of the pond."

"Did Comrade Ly tell you what she wanted?" I ask.

"No, Bong," Nhes replies.

"Then you finish this task while I go and see her for a minute."

I hurry to wash and dry my hands and then go to meet her. Two young women are sitting on the grass at the side of the pond: Comrade Ly and Comrade Dy. I sit down in front of them, and they smile at me quietly. I ask, "What is it, Comrade Ly, Comrade Dy?"

"I [*oun*] have something I want to ask you," Comrade Ly replies.

"Whatever it is, go ahead and ask!"

I smile at her and act as though I don't know what she will ask me about. Comrade Ly spreads out the letter she is holding in her hand, then hands it to me.

"This letter was written by you, was it not?" Comrade Ly says slowly.

"Yes, it was. Comrade An asked me to write it for him," I say softly.

Comrade Ly and Comrade Dy are quiet, saying nothing, as though wanting to ask me, *What should we do? How should we answer?*

I ask another question. "Comrade Ly, have you agreed to this request?"

She lowers her face, fraught with tension and shyness, and then speaks slowly, "No, Bong. Oun..." She has difficulty saying this last word.

"In that case, Comrade Ly, go ahead and answer, 'I don't want to yet.'"

She is quiet, and then says slowly and without hope, "He will continue to ask me."

"That's all right. No matter how many times a particular individual asks, they consider it only one request," I explain to her carefully. This notion makes Comrade Ly feel a degree of relief.

"What about you, Comrade Dy? What is your decision?" I ask Comrade Dy.

"I feel the same as A-Ly, Bong."

"Thank you, Bong," Comrade Ly says.

The two of them smile dryly, their smiles filled with worry. We bid one another farewell with heavy hearts.

Every time I meet Comrade Ly, I try to hide any behavior that might reveal that I love her. I feel compassion for her, and I don't want to add any firewood to the flames of love that might scorch the budding heart of this girl, and yet I continue to desire to sound the depths of the love that she has for me. This is what reveals my heart to her, a heart roiling with flames of love. Now I have become the young man in whom she places all her hope and trust, her Prince Charming. Can I possibly fill this lofty role?

It's a risky adventure that I am undertaking, jumping headlong into matters of romance, for the Life Masters are even more powerful than Archun Moen Nguon in the age of Tum Teav:

| Archun is too powerful | most beneath the sky are lower than the mountains |
| while he has unchecked might | hacking, stabbing, and smiting without mercy.[3] |

| The mighty Life Masters | kill whomever without fear |
| without court to judge | killing all they snare on sight.[4] |

My hut is a place where the leaders of the brigade come to sit and chat with each other whenever they come to the brick kiln. They are always talking about the girls they are interested in, the girls they desire. Comrade Ly and Comrade Dy are their first and second choices. This is an obstacle that has me very concerned.

It would be very imprudent to try and compete with these Life Masters. But it would be even more imprudent to pretend that I didn't know what is happening in the heart of Comrade Ly. A girl choosing to use the words *oun* and *bong* to converse with a young man—Is this not a testament to love, arising from the depths of her pure heart?

It is a love that arose because of my presence, because I permitted the love spell to charm her heart and influence her feelings. If I were to abandon her, it would mean that I am a criminal, a scoundrel, a vampire of love.

Although it is true that my feelings are in turmoil and disarray, thinking constantly of my beloved, I am not able to come forward and request her at this time.

The simultaneous rejection by both Comrade Ly and Comrade Dy is a nuclear explosion among the Life Masters. They are thoroughly disgraced. It is something they had not imagined. No doubt they will investigate to discover the reason, to eliminate any uncertainty, to restore the situation, for they have a clear plan: if any comrade fails, a new comrade will step forward to press the matter.

11 April 1978

At 11 a.m. Comrade Sieng and I are given orders by Comrade Hul, the deputy chairman of the brigade, to leave the brick-kiln camp immediately and report to the second bridge to plant vegetables there with Comrade Lim and Comrade Phal, who are also vegetable farmers for the Third Brigade.

---

[3] *Tum Teav*, verse 378
[4] This first stanza is quoted from *Tum Teav*, and the following one is improvised by the author.

After eating lunch, we prepare our supplies, seeds, watering cans, and clothing bundles and get ready to leave. Suddenly, the boy Chhong comes to my hut to stop me. "Hold on, Bong Tuch! Bong Chey sent me to search you first."

Good Lord, they have set themselves as my enemies!

"Search me for what, Chhong? Go ahead and check!"

Chhong unties our bundles and inspects them, then forbids me, saying, "Bong Tuch, you must not take the watering cans or the vegetable seeds with you!"

"I was ordered to go plant vegetables, not to haul dirt. All these supplies are necessary for the work. We each have our own sets of watering cans, and I am the one who searched out these vegetable seeds, so I have to take them with me," I reply slowly.

"But these are the orders of Bong An!" Chhong clarifies.

"I received my orders from Comrade Hul, the deputy chairman of the brigade, not from the head of the economy team," I reply.

"You were very good at finding them in the first place, Bong Tuch. Go find some more!" Chhong says emphatically.

"Back off, Chhong. You're acting like I'm a thief or someone deserting the unit! I received orders to perform duties at a different location in the very same unit, all right?" I respond forcefully.

Because I'm not listening to him, Chhong stands there stock-still with a red face. We take our supplies and leave at noon, walking along the paddy dikes west of the brick kiln, up to the top of the dam and then toward the camp of the Third Brigade about a hundred meters east of the second bridge.

13 April 1978

Comrade Sieng and I receive new orders from Comrade Hul to live apart from the others and clear land at the base of the dam to plant our own separate vegetable plot. We prepare a new vegetable plot about a hundred meters east of Comrade Lim's plot. We walk around and collect small branches and old left-over thatch grass from around the brigade's camp and use them to build a hut.

15 April 1978

At two in the afternoon I am pulled away, alone, as I am busy building the hut. They send me back to the brick kiln to join the young men tasked with hauling dirt, who are preparing to depart to Spean Sreng subdistrict.

Unbelievable! This is truly a Great Leap Forward! In the space of only five days, I have received three different work assignments. These people are spinning me around like an *apaong*[5] die. I don't know a soul in this new unit.

Because it is the New Year holiday, the Organization allows the mobile units to take a break from their work. We haven't departed for Spean Sreng yet, so we come to stay in the brickmaking shed located immediately west of the young women's shelter of Comrade Tum's unit.

The young men and young women get together and play the popular games *bah angkunh*[6] and *leak kansaeng*,[7] laughing and singing and having fun. I tie up my rice-sack hammock and nap alone in the large and spacious brickmaking shed, allowing my thoughts to drift aimlessly. Pulling me away to go plant vegetables elsewhere is a normal thing because Comrade Sieng was also removed and sent along with me. But taking just me away and sending me to join the young men's dirt-hauling unit alone is *not* normal.

It's no use wondering; this is the result of my actions. When it came to my work, they were well satisfied with me, to the point that they decided to remove Comrade Chey and leave me to lead the work alone. Not only that, but they were willing to fulfill my request to let Comrade Chey come back to farm vegetables. But in matters of romance, I am a sharp thorn in their eye. They have to pull that thorn out and smash it under their foot.

Most people at the brick-kiln camp know something about the amorous feelings between me and Comrade Ly, and Chhong and Comrade Chey in particular know a lot. They are the ones who already harbored a grudge against me, and they must have reported it to Comrade An and Comrade Hul. Now this is a good opportunity to fulfill their intention to get rid of me. Now they have achieved victory, as I have landed far away from them.

---

[5] a gambling game in which a die is spun and covered with a coconut shell before making bets

[6] a traditional game ("toss the *angkunh* seed") in which the large, woody seeds of the *angkunh* vine are placed in a triangle and players attempt to knock them down by tossing other *angkunh* seeds

[7] a traditional game ("hide the handkerchief") involving hiding a handkerchief behind one of several players in a circle

The fury of the young Life Masters (they are all younger than I am) and their limited knowledge could be very life-threatening if I remain under their control. If I go to Spean Sreng, they can easily find some pretense to have me taken away and executed. But if I desert my unit, I will meet the evil fate of Comrade Savuth.

Now I am caught in a dilemma. What should I do? The others are resting and laughing and having fun, while I lie here agonizing, worrying, and thinking. The young women of Comrade Tum's unit are playing *bah angkunh*, *chaol chhung*,[8] and *leak kansaeng* in the shade beneath the Bodhi tree near the dining pavilion.

Is Comrade Ly having fun with the others, or is she lying around agonizing like I am? My sudden absence, without any notice, must be causing her to worry and lose sleep. I don't want her to find out about me, especially about the reasons for their removing me, because it will make her even more upset and make her feel even more sorry for me and sadden her even more. I curl up like a pangolin, pulling the hammock cloth down over my head so nobody can see my face.

At dusk I meet Comrade Sariep, chairman of the Third Brigade, who has come to the brick kiln. I tell him, "Bong, I would like to request to go to the Fourth Brigade."

"Why do you want to leave my brigade, Tuch? Have I used forceful authority to oppress you, or something?"

"No, Bong! You've never used any kind of forceful authority, but Fourth Brigade is my old unit,[9] where I used to live before going to the Kok Kakah farm. And there I can be with my brother-in-law, and we can help each other out when we're sick," I give as an excuse.

---

[8] a traditional game ("throw the cushion") involving two sides (typically boys vs. girls) singing songs and throwing a cushion back and forth at one another until one side has eliminated the other

[9] See page 388. Men from Paoy Char subdistrict who belonged to Phnom Srok district's special unit, middle-aged unit (the author's former unit), and young men's unit were reorganized after the conclusion of work at Trapeang Thmor Reservoir in late 1977 into a new region-level brigade called the Fourth Brigade, under the leadership of the former head of the special unit, Mea Pov. So while this is a regional brigade, it is composed of recent members of the author's former district-level unit, all from Paoy Char subdistrict.

"So why didn't you want to go before? Then when I remove you from the vegetable farm, you suddenly want to go? Might you be suffering from consciousness sickness in this matter?" Comrade Sariep asks.

"No, Bong. Vegetable farming is work, hauling dirt is work, it is all revolutionary work. But when I worked at the vegetable farm, I had a defined location, and my sister coming from the cooperative knew where to find me, and my brother-in-law coming in from mobile deployment could find me; but now, if I go on mobile deployment to Spean Sreng, I will be taken far away from my family," I complain to Comrade Sariep.

"No worries, I will ask Bong Yon, chairman of the regional mobile committee. If he agrees, then I'm willing to let you go," Comrade Sariep replies.

"Thank you, Brother! Could you please ask him soon?"

"Sure," Comrade Sariep replies.

The 16th passes quietly, with no word.

On the 17th, by the evening I still haven't heard anything from Comrade Sariep. In the morning the mobile unit will depart for Spean Sreng subdistrict. Comrade Sariep must have lied to me. This evening I must make an unavoidable choice between one of two deaths (boiled or roasted?) :

If I go to Spean Sreng, these people will certainly not spare my life, and my sister will have no word of my death.

If I run to the Fourth Brigade, they can track me there, arrest me, and bring me back to be executed like Comrade Savuth; but if I die at Trapeang Thmor, at least my sister could be made aware.

At dusk I bundle my clothing and hammock and slip away from the brick-kiln camp silently, without anybody knowing, and head off to find the Fourth Brigade, who are staying among the locals' homes at Paoy Ta Ong.

CHAPTER 41

Love in Hell

The Fourth Brigade is led by Comrade Ron (a young man) and Mea Pov. This brigade is a mixture of young men and middle-aged men. I join the middle-aged unit with my brother-in-law.

Now we have entered the dry season, and the water level[1] in the reservoir is below the tops of the water gates. The Fourth Brigade is tasked with cutting through the dam at a point between the first and second bridges and building a large concrete pipe to release water from the reservoir at a height lower than both the first and second water gates.

To facilitate the work, about two days after I join them, the Fourth Brigade pulls out from Paoy Ta Ong village and pitches camp at the base of the dam near the pipe worksite. Here, I am tasked with transporting cement by boat from the regional mobile committee office, just east of the first bridge, and dropping it off at the pipe worksite with Comrade Chuch, who is from Chamlak village, Koki subdistrict, Kien Svay district, Kandal province. I am also tasked with helping to dig a canal to channel water away from the mouth of the pipe. Comrade Chuch rows the boat, while I load the bags of cement. When we leave the worksite and head for the first bridge, we ride the boat together; but on the return trip, to avoid overburdening the boat, I usually walk along the dam.

Since leaving Phnom Penh, I have been recording the dates of important events, such as changes in my residence and the work I am doing at each phase, using a pencil and a sheet of notebook paper. All memories of facts and events can be retained and recalled if they are tied to concrete objects, such as villages, houses, ponds, lakes, people, animals, and plants. But dates are not easy to recall and are easily forgotten or confused, so you have to write them down clearly in order not to forget them.

But it is very hard for me to hide the notebook paper, as my superiors constantly look for paper to roll cigarettes, and this could capture their interest and trigger suspicion. Now I take some paper from a bag of cement and use it to replace the notebook paper, folding it several times and keeping it in my cloth-

---

[1] The new reservoir has since filled with water in the 1977 rainy season.

ing bundle. This cement-bag paper allows me to write down a lot of things and calms my feelings and stops me from worrying about it being found in a search, as they don't recognize the value of such thick, dark-colored paper.

A week or so after I rejoin the Fourth Brigade, the food rations fall from one-and-a-half cans to one can per day of uncooked rice. Cooked rice rations turn to thick porridge, both morning and evening. Here there are no supplementary edible plants to find. After eating the midday porridge, the workers silently leave camp and go out to catch fish, dig for crabs and frogs, and search for clams and snails to bring back and boil into soup for extra food. The clams are found by swimming out into the middle of the reservoir, which is vast and fraught with danger. Because the bottom of the reservoir slopes downward from north to south, if you swim far out you can reach places where the water is only up to your neck or chest.

Some days, the wind and rain blow so hard that it causes people to go under and choke on water. I never go out to look for snails and clams because the energy gained doesn't seem to be worth the energy expended.

One evening I go out with some others to fish with nets far out from the second bridge, toward the far side. Here, the water is up to my waist or my thighs. We fish by forming a circle and chasing the fish inward, then casting our nets inward toward one another. I step on the thorn of a *krumpuk* tree branch that had been cut and tossed in the water, and this thorn goes all the way into my foot. When I pull it out, the end of the thorn breaks off, buried in my flesh.

My foot swells up and I can't walk or work for four or five days. Eventually, the end of the thorn works its way upward and emerges from the top of my foot in the space between my toe bones, and then the swelling goes down and the wound heals. This is an experience to remember. The old folks often say that thorns in the flesh will creep, that they don't stay still.

Late April 1978

One evening I run into two young women from Comrade Tum's unit: Comrade Thom and Comrade Khom. They are both surprised to see me. "Oh, Bong Tuch!" they both exclaim at the same time.

"Hey, where are you coming from, Comrade Thom and Comrade Khom?" I ask.

"We're coming from transplanting rice. Where are you living now, Bong Tuch? Why have you become so thin?" Comrade Thom asks.

"I'm in the Fourth Brigade hauling cement by boat and digging a canal near the second bridge," I reply.

"So you're not in the cooperative?" Comrade Khom asks.

"No, I'm right here with the regional mobile unit," I reply.

"When we didn't see you watering the vegetables anymore, we wondered where you had gone. We asked Comrade Chey, and he said you had requested a family in the cooperative, and when the regional Organization didn't approve it, you ran off to the cooperative, stealing the seeds and watering cans and taking them with you," Comrade Khom says.

I smile and ask them, "Comrade Khom and Comrade Thom, did you believe him?"

"No, we didn't believe him, but nobody knew where you had gone. Comrade Ly misses you and is very worried," Comrade Khom says.

"I also miss Comrade Ly, and I miss all of you very much too. But I never have free time, and I'm embarrassed to see Comrade Chey, so I don't dare go to the brick kiln for fear of running into him," I say.

"Why? Are you and Comrade Chey in a quarrel?" Comrade Thom asks.

"No, but Comrade Chey had bad feelings toward me after I requested that he be brought back to help farm the vegetables. Perhaps he thought that I was the reason he was removed and sent to haul dirt in the first place?"

"But you're the one who made the request for him to come back!" Comrade Thom says.

"He must not have believed it," I say.

"So why did Comrade Chey have to lie to us and say that you went to take a wife in the cooperative?" Comrade Thom asks.

"Maybe he was just guessing because Comrade Chey didn't know for sure where I was. Anyway, let him think what he wants! Are Comrade Ly and Comrade Dy still working on the economy team these days?" I ask.

"They have quit that. The economy team is a new team, now. Bong Dy and Bong Ly are also transplanting rice, but they work in a different paddy from us," Comrade Khom replies.

"Thank you. So long, Comrade Thom and Comrade Khom. Please let Comrade Ly and Comrade Dy know I miss them, and that I'm doing fine!"

"Sure, Bong!" Comrade Thom and Comrade Khom reply.

1 May 1978

With the concrete pouring completed, we take a rest at about ten o'clock in the morning. After eating porridge, I ask permission from the unit leader to go visit Sambuor to inform Sadet's parents about our difficulties and our lack of hope that the regional and cooperative mobile units will ever meet up, and to tell them not to cause Sadet any more difficulty by pointlessly waiting for me, and that she has the right to choose another partner.

At almost eleven o'clock, I leave camp and walk along the top of the dam. About 500 meters east of camp, I see a small shelter roofed with grass, shaped like a tent, with a low roof, the walls closed on all sides with only an open doorway on the west side, built on top of the dam along the south side. I don't know whose unit this shelter belongs to, as it is newly built, and I have never met the people who live here. As I approach the small shelter, a young woman from the economy team arrives carrying porridge and soup on a shoulder yoke, which she sets down in the shade of a *snuol*[2] tree. The economy girl stands waiting for the workers, who have not yet returned from the rice fields. As I draw near, I recognize her as a member of Comrade Tum's unit.

We smile at one another and I open my mouth about to speak when suddenly I hear the lovely voice of a young woman coming from inside the small hut: "Bong Tuch! Look, my [*oun*'s] cheek is bruised!"

It's a voice I know, the voice of the person I miss, the person I long to see. As though commanded by God, I turn toward the doorway, bend down, and enter the hut. Comrade Ly is lying flat on the ground against the side of the hut, with her head pointed east, and with a tarp spread beneath her. She receives me with a smile.

"Have a seat, Bong!"

My heart leaps with delighted excitement, as well as concern. I sit down as commended by my beloved, directly beside her to the south. Comrade Ly sits up. We both sit with our legs folded to one side, facing one another, staring into one another's face, in complete silence, as though meditating. Neither of us had

---

[2] *Dalbergia nigrescens*

imagined that we would meet, and we are experiencing feelings of excited joy, of worry, and of deep hurt. I ask her, speaking slowly, "A-Ly, what's wrong, Oun?"

It is a new word that has just emerged from the depths of my heart, a word that she has waited to hear for a long time. This word causes the wound in her heart to knit, giving her hope, hope that the young man whom she dreams about, whom she loves, understands her heart and feels compassion for her.

Comrade Ly speaks slowly and carefully, almost like a lonely wife recounting her sorrows to a beloved husband after a long separation. "I[3] had a bicycle accident, Bong. Last evening, I was riding a bicycle down the dam along the steep path near the first bridge. When I was nearly to the bottom the brakes snapped and the handlebars started to shake and then I crashed."

"Was it serious?" I ask her.

"It wasn't too serious, Bong. But my body is sore, and my cheek is bruised." She takes her hand and pulls her hair back from her left cheek, turning it for me to inspect. There is a dark bruise beneath the corner of her left eye, but the skin is not broken or abraded.

This is the first time in my life I have ever inspected the cheek of a woman so closely. I feel a strong desire to raise my hand and gently caress the cheek of my beloved. She must desire this response herself, but something holds me back, compelling me to remain still.

At this moment, my life and the life of my beloved are in my hands. She has given her life to me. If I lead her to death, she will die. A young man and a young woman being alone together in a small hut like this is against revolutionary morality. But we are still at a point where others can help cover for us and protect us. If I touch her, the violation becomes more serious, and we will lead each other ever closer to the dwelling place of the Angel of Death.

What would be gained by sharing intimate affection with one another now, only to be taken afterwards and killed and buried together in a pit?

Oh, my Soul! My chest is so tight! I don't dare satisfy the affectionate desires of my heart toward you! We must not die now!

Comrade Ly puts her hand down, allowing her hair to fall back over her cheek, and she turns to look at me and says slowly, "You are so thin and bluer

---

[3] Throughout this dialog, and in all subsequent dialog by her, Comrade Ly routinely refers to herself in Khmer with the pronominal *oun*, signaling clear romantic intent (see footnote on page 337).

[she means blacker][4] than before! A-Thom and A-Khom whispered to me that they met you here on top of the dam. I wanted to see you! I miss you! I miss you so much!"

Oun Misses Bong!

1. Not seeing you, your darling is sad   where did you go? no word at all
    I fret, lying awake thinking   how are you, my dear?

2. Hearing word of you, my worry recedes   my heart trembles to see you
    to see your face, to utter words   to tell you how *Oun* misses *Bong*!

chorus:
The tale of Brick-Kiln Pond is true   the sun moves from day to evening
    I remain true, you remain constant   the sun rises and sets, and still I wait.

3. I wait only to be united with you   rain or thunder, still I wait
    though now we suffer torment   still I wait, wait for you always.

A-Ly! I know your heart! You love me, you miss me. I miss you; I love you; I love only you.

Bong Loves Only Oun

1. High noon and my heart spins in love   you alone I desire to care for and coddle
    caress your cheek, your skin so fair   indulge my wishes, give me your heart.

2. Your words so lovely and sweet   "Bong Tuch, see my bruised cheek"
    my heart sinks, desiring to hold you   hapless, you and I, bound in Hell on Earth.

chorus:
Thmor Puok Girl, Frontier Flower   I love you truly, ten-thousand waves as witness
    Trapeang Thmor waters clear and blue   if I betray you, no mercy, my life is forfeit.

3. But now I surely dare not   if I ask your hand, I confront the foe
    their power mighty, their hearts cruel   you and I would surely die like Tum and Teav.

---

[4] both the odd word choice and the parenthetical clarification are found in the original text

Comrade Ly stares into my face without turning away. Her eyes photograph my face and store it in the box of her heart.

I say to her, "It's not good for you to sleep here, Oun! In the daytime the sun is hot from above, and at night the heat will rise up from the ground below. You should ask permission to go rest at the brick-kiln camp and ask for some betel leaf from Father Kun [a villager near the vegetable farm]. Heat it up on the flame of a lamp and then hold it on your cheek, and in a few days the bruising will be gone."

She smiles at me and says, "You know so much, Bong! I will do what you say."

It is noon and the girls will come back up soon to eat their porridge. I can't remain sitting here and conversing any longer.

"A-Ly, I have to say goodbye now, all right?"

"All right. Come to see me often!"

I stand up and walk out, and my beloved arises and walks out after me. Outside the hut, I turn around and smile at her. "Goodbye!"

"Yes, goodbye, Bong!"

She drags out these words as though she is loath for me to leave her. I walk back toward camp, and behind me she stands holding onto the roof of the hut, staring after me as I go, her heart tense, not ready to let go.

I intended to travel to Sambuor, about five kilometers away. But after seeing Comrade Ly, my heart is wounded, like a snake crushed by an oxcart, and my limbs are so weak I can't go on, so I turn back.

I keep asking myself, *Was it fate, or was it arranged by somebody, that Comrade Ly and I were able to meet at this time?*

Comrade Ly had her bicycle accident near the first bridge, so she should have gone to recuperate at the brick-kiln camp. True, it's farther than coming to the small hut on top of the dam, but it would have been more comfortable there. But instead, she came to rest in the small hut; she must have intended to meet me and hoped that she could if she settled for resting there. As I approached the hut, the economy girl must have told her, and that's why she was able to lie there and call out to me just as I drew close enough to hear.

Damn, but love is a sickness! A wondering sickness. A thinking sickness. A pondering sickness. Asking and responding, asking and responding, all alone, and without resolution. Wondering: Does she love me? Does she miss me? Is she faithful to me? Is she committed to me? Every answer is an analysis and a speculation.

It is true that love does not reside on the lips, on claims, or on promises. All these things are merely instruments of romantic deception.

Some profess their love with oaths. But this is only the cooing of a decoy dove.

"I love you faithfully my darling"	but her body attained, he abandons her.
The nation suffers from faithless love	the girl robbed of beauty, resigned to tears.
Great love, but really false love	she sits weeping, devastated
her family divided and broken	patriotism so great they tear and consume her.[5]

Now we are all in the clutches of a deception, a ruse of hateful love, a vampiric love, a love that murders lovers. They say that they have compassion, that they love us, that they have liberated us:

On April 17th, Kampuchea is liberated	cries of victory are heard in all directions
the black clouds dissipate	a bright light shines on a glorious view....[6]

Yes, they liberated us. They liberated us from freedom, and now they crush us, cook us, scorch us, and ultimately, annihilate us.

This is the profoundly bitter experience which every young man and young woman should remember and ponder before giving their hearts, their love, to any individual. Is it true love or fraudulent love, the love of deceit?

For true love is concealed by a curtain. The heart is the master of the actions of love. It directs the performances of love. It is the repository both of hatred and of love. The sentiments of love are manifest through the eyes and through words, and through actions that reside in secret and obscurity, though real and deep. Lovers should strive to understand, to analyze, to ponder, and to synthesize all the phenomena of love, and only then will it take the form of true love.

For in true love, lovers are stingy, hoarding all of their love, loath to spend it haphazardly. They give it up, they share it, only with someone who is equally as

---

[5] This short song was composed by the author as a high-school student in 1972, during the depths of the Cambodian Civil War. The Cambodian nation is personified as the beautiful girl, and professed patriots as the insincere and exploitative romantic suitor.

[6] a paraphrase of the opening lines to a Khmer Rouge anthem entitled "Determined to Learn of The Heroism of Our Glorious Comrade Soldiers"

stingy as they are, for they perceive that that person will conserve it, will care for that love as they do. For this reason, they are very selective in choosing a romantic partner; they are cautious, secretive, tentative in manifesting their feelings of love to the object of their love. For then if they are mistaken in their love, it is easy to retract it, to summon it back and re-hide it in the box of the heart. Their love grows slowly, expands gradually in stages. The stronger it grows, the more they are troubled, the more they worry. The more such a one understands that love, the more anxious they become, the tighter their breast, and the more they long to be with their beloved.

And, furthermore, should you encounter obstacles in love, as I am now, it is even harder to bear. I am troubled even more, I am anxious, I can't sleep, I can't lie still, I toss and turn in my hammock until it quakes, disturbing those whose hammocks are tied to the same pillar as mine.

In the still of night, the others sleep, but I think anxiously of Comrade Ly, seeing her before my face. No matter how much I am determined to close my eyes, my eyes won't close. Because now my eyes are under the command of my heart, and they no longer receive orders from my brain as they have always done before.

Unable to lie still, I arise from my hammock in the middle of the night and walk up onto the dam to sit beside the reservoir. Here, the wind blows gently and refreshingly, unlike the still, muggy air of the camp at the base of the dam. Cool night mists settle about. The water of the reservoir stretches out vastly, decorated with tiny waves that reflect the moonlight, sparkling and flashing as they chase one another from a distance and cast themselves against the dam, creating a pleasant sound. This motion is unceasing, untiring, like the activities of the humans who worked hard to haul the dirt and piled it up to form this dam, transforming a plain into a lake of vast extent.

This reservoir is the work of humans. It is a manifestation of human capability, but it is also embedded with incalculable human suffering, sorrow, and death.

Now all these things—the suffering, the death—have been replaced by the precious vista of the water's surface, cool and vast and reflecting the light of the sun at dawn and at dusk, creating a scene of great beauty appreciable by all lovers. In particular, if such lovers were to come here at night, in the quiet under the light of the moon, no doubt they would comprehend the vast coolness of nature on the shore of this reservoir where love was built, which would bind them together until they better comprehend the nectar of faithful affection, of pity, of love; and then they would take one another's hand and build a human society filled with mercy and compassion.

But my love, the first love of this reservoir, does not have the fortune to receive the ratification of nature by night. My beloved is not at the small hut where we sat gazing into one another's face earlier today. Even if she were, we would not be allowed to come and sit together beneath the moonlight.

Oh, Love! Why must you be so beset with obstacles?

I, the son of poor parents, pathetic and miserable all my life since birth, not having been spoiled by my parents like the children of the rich, now desire attention and comfort from a mate. Now I have found the love that I imagined, but I am not able to clutch that love to me as my own.

As soon as he received the scarf of Teav, Tum was sleepless and anxious, and he bid farewell to his master and ran off to find his beloved. So I—having sat and conversed sweetly with my beloved in sweet words of *oun* and *bong*—are my feelings to be calm? No! I miss her. I miss her terribly. I want to see her! I want to bring her to sit with me here, but I cannot. The Angel of Death stands with a sharp sword blocking my path, forbidding me from going to meet her.

Oh, Love! Love in Hell!

Love in Hell

1. The reservoir where our love was forged
waves march over the face of the water

the dews of night cover the earth
the moonlight clear and bright.

2. Nature at night is gentle and sweet
the hateful regime extinguishes all rights

our loves turn withered
to live as humans, as lovers.

chorus:
Great love, but mere negotiation
without right to cuddle or care

twisting chords of devotion with our eyes
instead, a torrent of love in our hearts.

3. Our love is true, my Heart
Mara[7] comes to interrupt and divide

from within our breasts, a love divine
detaining me far from my beloved.

---

[7] the Buddha's demonic enemy; the Destroyer

CHAPTER 42

Revolutionary Marriage

Love is the natural heritage of the animal kingdom. Ants, dogs, cats—they all have the same kind of love. Human animals have a different kind of love. Couples live together as husband and wife, as a family that makes a living and cares for one another, having children, governing and teaching their sons and daughters to grow up to be of use to their family and to their nation and society.

But some people are not human animals, they are animal humans (beastly humans), who make love only to satisfy their arousal, and then abandon their partners like animals. It is the sleaziest kind of behavior, bringing suffering to other people and to society. With cattle, the moment their calves are born, they can walk and run, and before long they can graze and eat on their own as well. Are human children anything like calves? When they are born, they can only lie there. They turn over, they scoot, they crawl, and they demand care and attention from their parents for a very long time.

During the Revolution, morality is pure. There is no living like animal humans, there is no secret love making. Whoever dares will have their flesh torn asunder. Whoever dares will be annihilated. Sexual relations are permitted without fault only if two people are married as husband and wife.

Amazing! This is truly remarkable. No longer will people live like animals. No longer will there be babies without fathers, abandoned by their mothers along the side of the road or in garbage cans. No longer will there be babies victimized because of the passions of animal humans. No longer will there be homeless orphans. May such a beautiful morality become immortal in Khmer society!

But is it true? Is it truly so pure and unsullied?

Young men and young women have equal rights in selecting a partner, without regard to any kind of station or class. This is the party line of the Revolutionary Organization. But up until now, I have never seen young men or young women among the base people marry young women or young men from among the new people.

If anybody wishes to marry, they must satisfy the procedures for requesting a family. If their request meets with agreement, the requested partner (fiancé) must wait for an opportunity to hold a Day of Ceremony (that is, a wedding).

A Day of Ceremony to marry many "families" is held after the completion of some phase of work, such as building the reservoir, finishing the rice transplanting, or finishing the harvest. But they don't inform the parties involved of the exact time until only one or two days before the Day of Ceremony is to be held. At each Day of Ceremony for the regional mobile units, they marry twenty to thirty couples at a time, or even as many as seventy or eighty couples.

In 1975 and 1976, Day of Ceremony weddings were held with a feast, and the Organization would gift the newlyweds clothing and *kramas*. These days, the new couples merely stand and take one another by the hand before the collective under the presiding authority of some leader representing higher levels of the Organization.

For the people in the cooperative, such ceremonies are nicer than in the mobile units. They have chickens, ducks, pigs, and cows for making food. They have clothing or *kramas* woven in the cooperative. And most importantly, they have houses or suitable locations for the newlywed couple to spend their honeymoon night alone together.

In August 1977, after the offensive to build Trapeang Thmor Reservoir and dig the canals was completed, the regional Organization prepared a Ceremony to marry more than seventy families from the regional mobile units at the regional mobile committee office near the first bridge. Young men and young women who had already requested a family, who were working at various worksites like Kok Rumchek, Kok Kakah, and Kok Roessei, were allowed by the Organization to rest from their labors for half a day (in the afternoon) on the Day of Ceremony, in order to get ready to make the journey to Trapeang Thmor Reservoir. Each of them ran around borrowing black clothing and *kramas* from their friends to adorn themselves for when they would stand to clasp hands.

The matter of sleeping arrangements for the first night was something that the Organization had to attend to. The regional Organization gave orders to build shelters in the field west of Paoy Ta Ong with a sleeping platform raised off the ground at about knee height, with slats interwoven with *Ingieng* saplings, *trach* saplings, and *phneang* (*phnom phneng*)[1] shrubs, and divided into small rooms (two meters square), with walls consisting of three or four thatch grass panels, as places for the new couples to sleep together.

---

[1] *Hymenocardia wallichii*

It was a festive time. After the hand-clasping ceremony before the collective in the regional mobile committee office, all the newlywed couples walked carrying their sacks and sleeping mats in a throng toward the Hall of Victory for their honeymoon night. Comrade Rithy, an oxcart driver in the Third Brigade and a cousin-in-law of Sadet, told me that on his first night he and his wife didn't do anything, as they were too busy listening to the neighbors.

Amazing! Remarkable! A mass wedding and a mass honeymoon night, all competing and mingling together.

Early May 1978

All of the work at the Trapeang Thmor Reservoir site—dirt hauling to shore up the dam, water pipe construction, and dry-season rice farming—comes to a conclusion. There is news of an impending Day of Ceremony to marry new families. Young men rush to request young women for fear that there is not enough time. But nobody knows on what day or at what time the Day of Ceremony will be held.

9 May 1978

The leadership committees of every mobile unit and brigade assemble to receive new work orders from the regional mobile committee at the office near the first bridge at 4 p.m. At about six o'clock, they return to camp and inform everyone who has requested a family to prepare to attend the Ceremony at the regional mobile committee office. The pandemonium begins as the affected young men and women run around in a rush to get ready and contact their fiancés. For the young women, most of whom are working here at the Trapeang Thmor worksite, this is not a problem; but for some of the young men carrying out tasks far away from the camp, like scooping sand at Spean Sreng or fishing at Suong, what are they supposed to do?

The couples and their friends and relatives all assemble at the regional mobile committee office near the first bridge. Young men and young women who are from Trapeang Thmor have older women—their mothers—in attendance at the Ceremony to watch their children join hands.

The Ceremony begins at 10 p.m. in the wooden hall with plank floorboards, roofed with thatch grass, about seven by fifteen meters, raised about forty centimeters off the ground, with no walls and only a railing clear around the hall like a *sala chhortean*[2]. The regional mobile committee members all sit directly on the floorboards on the east side of the hall beside a table on which are lists of the names of the brides and grooms to be married this evening. On this side there is a gas-mantle lamp hung in the center of the hall to illuminate the attendees.

A revolutionary cadre rises and stands near the table and opens the list and calls out the names of the pairs of young men and young women to stand at the podium, take one another by the hand, and accept one another as husband and wife, and then to sit down with their legs bent to the side in parallel rows before the leadership, about three meters from the table. For some of the couples, only the man is present, and the woman is absent; and for some, the woman is present, but the man is absent, and the cadre calls their names once, twice:

"The young man Sophal, paired with the young woman Chantha!"

Sophal stands and appears at the podium, but Chantha is nowhere to be found. The cadre calls Chantha's name again. Somebody calls out from outside the hall, "Comrade Chantha is sick at the hospital in Wat Trapeang Thmor!"

The cadre holding the list says, "Can she make it? If she can make it, somebody go and fetch her here! There aren't many chances to hold a Ceremony! Go and find her!"

Sophal looks down at the floor and walks down from the podium, and the cadre calls the next names. Those whose partners are present rise and clasp hands and smile under the sound of applause from their friends. Those whose partners are absent stand shyly aside, not daring to look up. Now and then they encounter another case of a missing partner:

"Comrade Ny is partnered with Female Comrade Sinat!"

Female Comrade Sinat walks up to the podium and stands before the collective, but there is no sign of her partner Comrade Ny. The cadre calls out for Comrade Ny, "Where is Comrade Ny? Comrade Sinat has been standing here waiting for a while now!"

A comrade who is a member of the Fourth Brigade speaks up, "Comrade Ny is camping out at Suong to collect fish, Comrade!"

"Ah, in that case, wait until next time!" the cadre cries.

The names of those who are absent are called repeatedly by the cadre but still fail to appear, as they are in some distant place fulfilling some task, like Svay

---

[2] a traditional, open-sided, pavilion-like structure used for distributing alms

Sar, Svay Khmau, Suong, Spean Sreng, etc. Thirty-one couples are present, and six more couples must wait for the next Ceremony due to absence.

The calling of the names comes to an end and Comrade Yon, representing the regional mobile committee, stands beside the table to make some remarks. After paying respects to the assembly, Comrade Yon, a man of about forty, begins to speak:

"You mothers who have joined the Ceremony have seen clearly that marriage in the age of the Revolution and marriage in the age of capitalism and feudalism are very different. In the previous age, they would only allow you to get married if you got permission and paid taxes to the state authorities.

"Parents would fuss over preparing their homes and communities, invite relatives, and spend exorbitant amounts of money, which they had worked hard to earn and save for a long time. Some would go into debt over a wedding, until by the time they have one or two children, they're no longer able to pay it off, for the sake of pointlessly wasteful feasting and dancing.

"In the Revolutionary Age, we marry without having to spend anything at all. Both young men and young women are allowed to choose their life partners freely, without pressure or compulsion from anybody, without any regard for class, poverty, high status, or low status.

"We can get married any time without the trouble of finding a suitably auspicious day,[3] or worrying about the wet season or dry season, as long as there is a respite from work. Right now, for instance: some of you parents didn't even know that your child was to be married tonight, so you didn't have to go to the trouble of planning anything. The Organization has taken responsibility for the wedding in your stead.

"That's how easy marriage is in the age of the Revolution. You can get married today, or tomorrow, without having to ask permission or pay taxes. In the old times, you had to pay taxes when you were born, you had to pay taxes when you got married, you had to pay taxes when you were buried. Now the authority of the state is in the hands of the people, of the proletariat, and now all of us are responsible for the fate of our nation.

"All you comrades who have clasped hands as families tonight, don't be sluggish and forgetful of your duties. Don't think that now that you have a

---

[3] Traditionally, in Khmer culture great care is paid to identifying days and times for momentous events, especially weddings and funerals, that are suitably providential and auspicious based on notions of numerology, astrology, and other factors.

family, your duty to the nation has diminished. Not so! In fact, comrades, your duties have expanded to encompass an additional and important duty: the building of the population. Strive with all your might, in a Great Leap Forward, to fulfill the plan to expand the population of the Party, to achieve within ten to fifteen years a population of thirty million.[4]

"But don't forget your other duties, either! Don't be complacent. If you are only a little bit unwell, don't rest. You must help each other to pull. If your wife is sick, husbands, don't you be sick too; it's not so easy as that!

"Finally, on behalf of the Revolutionary Organization, I bestow upon all of you comrades who have clasped hands to create a new family this evening a blessing of wellbeing and happiness at all times, to partake in building and defending the nation, to partake in the people's authority of state, to defend our Revolution and keep it strong forever!"

The sound of applause roars and pierces the dark veil of night (a moonless night). Then the female leadership and the male leadership rise in turn to make remarks and give advice, to shore up the revolutionary philosophy, stance, and mindset of the thirty-one new couples.

Finally, one new couple representing all the thirty-one couples stands and clasps hands before the collective and expresses gratitude to the Party for organizing the Ceremony and marrying them tonight, and then they shout their resolutions:

"Resolved to be undeviatingly faithful to the Party! Resolved! Resolved! Resolved!

"Resolved to increase rice productivity from three tons to seven tons per hectare, without fail! Without fail! Without fail! Without fail!

"Resolved to increase the population within ten to fifteen years to twenty to thirty million, without fail! Without fail! Without fail! Without fail!"

These slogans are repeated in a roaring shout by the other thirty couples sitting behind them.

The Ceremony is adjourned at about 11 p.m. Both the guests and friends, as well as the brides and grooms, drift from the gathering in search of their own camps. Those couples who are children of base people and have relatives with houses in nearby villages are able to find places to enjoy the romance of their honeymoon night. As for the new people, those who came from far away, they

---

[4] The population was only around six million (and rapidly declining) at the time.

are able only to clasp hands and acknowledge one another as husband and wife, and then go their separate ways, each to their own resting place, as this time the Organization has made no preparations for a special shelter to accommodate them.

Revolutionary Wedding

1. Oh, what day is this?	Oh, Mother	your daughter is getting married
married without parents	Oh, Mother	without parents to tie our hands.[5]
2. Married *en masse*	Oh, Mother	like cattle
without kin	Oh, Mother	to shower with flowers.
3. They bow in unison	Oh, Mother	relatives smiling in congratulation
I stand with them	Oh, Mother	stand and shout resolutions.
4. We stand clasping hands	Oh, Mother	tight-chested
before the Organization	Oh, Mother	without parents to bless us.
5. A revolutionary wedding	Oh, Mother	a new revolution
no kin or crowds	Oh, Mother	no gong or cymbal.

---

[5] Traditional Khmer weddings feature a ceremonial tying-together of the couple's hands.

CHAPTER 43
Final Farewell

The food rations decreased from one and a half cans to one can per day more than a week ago. We no longer know cooked rice, but instead eat porridge morning and evening. For the women, the weaker sex, the decrease in food rations has a lesser effect. But for the men, this change causes a decline in energy and makes our bodies waste away.

Facing this scarcity of food, each person strives to the best of their ability to find extra food to fill their stomachs. Those with family in the villages can arrange for tubers, corn, sugar cane, or bananas to supplement their diet. Some people spread out over the fields hunting for fish, crabs, snails, and frogs. Some people take advantage of the darkness at night to sneak into the cooperative's fields and pick tubers.

As for me, I have no support from the village. My sister has only been back in the village for about half a month since construction work on the dam at Ansang Neav was completed. Besides, I don't dare engage in sneaking and stealing as some do. However, my brother-in-law often gets his hands on tubers, and sometimes some small tuber, or a piece of one, overflows to me, which I hide and eat quietly.

10 May 1978

Very early in the morning, around dawn, we receive the news that the front lines will be pulling back from the Trapeang Thmor Reservoir worksite. Everyone is busy packing their clothing bundles, their hammocks, and their supplies, preparing to depart.

Because last night was a Night of Ceremony, most of the workers slept overnight in the village, and then woke up in the dark and returned to camp. My brother-in-law[1] has just returned from his house, and he smiles at me and asks, "A-Tuch! Have you been married yet?"

"No, Bong, my fiancée is at the *roneam*."

"Is that so? If you request a wife so far away, I don't know when you will ever get married."

"When you were in the village did you get to see Oun?"

---

[1] Khloeng

"No. She has been out here digging a canal near the reservoir since yesterday."

"Oh, maybe they are the unit taking over our digging, near the Bodhi tree south of here."

After this brief chat, my brother-in-law goes on his way to pack his things.

The Sun rises over the treetops in the east and shows his raw, red face, and then begins to roast the world of men. The workers of the Fourth Brigade are busy taking down camp.

Along the top of the reservoir's dam, a cooperative *chhlop* who used to live at the Kok Kakah farm with me rides a bicycle and stops near the small hut belonging to the chairman of the Fourth Brigade. This *chhlop* is carrying a passenger who is weak and struggling to dismount from the bicycle. Those of us taking down camp at the base of the dam glance up at this man, and we are all moved with pity as we realize that he is a member of our unit. It is Bong Lo, a man of about forty. He is unable to stand, and he scoots along the ground on his bottom.

The *chhlop* enters the hut to talk with the brigade chairman. I run up on top of the dam to see Bong Lo and find out what has happened.

My God! Bong Lo's face and limbs are covered with scars and marks, swollen and bruised from being beaten. I ask him in a whisper, "What happened, Bong?"

"I made a mistake, Tuch! Last night I snuck into the field to steal a tuber and got caught."

Hearing this one sentence, my heart sinks in cold panic and pity for Bong Lo, and I am afraid to be seen speaking with him. I withdraw, as now Bong Lo is a prisoner of the Organization.

They summon my brother-in-law and another comrade to the hut of the brigade chairman. Both are tied up and marched away with Bong Lo. My brother-in-law must have stolen tubers with Bong Lo last night!

The brigade's unit leaders collect the clothing bundles of these three men and pick through them, shaking them out and dividing up the items. They are very cheerful whenever any of the Life Slaves is taken off to be executed, as this is a chance for them to divide up their inheritance.

I am filled with terror and pity for my brother-in-law. My feelings are in turmoil, as we parted without saying goodbye or even looking into one another's face.

Should I try to send news of this tragic event to my sister?

We finish eating our morning porridge. The time to depart draws nearer. I decide that I must go see my sister and say goodbye before I leave.

I run across the rice fields, jumping over the paddy dikes, running straight toward the crowd of workers digging the canal near the Bodhi tree south of the reservoir, near the Ta Vong causeway. I run for more than a kilometer without stopping. As I approach the site where they are digging the canal, I slow down, gasping and trying to catch my breath. A villager who knows me calls out, "Tuch! Where are you going?"

"I'm looking for my sister. Have you seen my sister?" I struggle to say between gasps of breath.

"Over there! Oun is digging over there, to the south," he says, pointing.

Out of breath, I stop running. I approach the unit leader and ask to see my sister. He allows my sister to come up out of the pit to see me. Her facial expression is frightened, seeing that I have been running to the point of breathlessness, and she asks me right away, "What is it, Tuch? Is something wrong, that you ran here?"

"Hold on...Give me a second...I'm so tired..."

I sit down on the ground, putting both hands back behind me and leaning back, so exhausted I am unable to speak. I ran this far thinking that I would tell my sister about the terrible thing that just happened to her husband, but now I realize that I should say nothing about it because it will make her panic and despair and weep, and it will cause a disturbance among the unit digging the canal. Never mind, she will find out another day.

Catching my breath, I tell my sister, "My unit is pulling back its lines to Spean Sreng, Oun. Right now!"

This news surprises my sister, and she quickly asks, "They're going to Spean Sreng? Are you going too?"

"Yes. We're all going."

"How can I see him? I traded for a little bit of tobacco to give him, and I thought I would bring it to him at the midday work break. Tuch, why don't you take it and give it to him."

"Sure, Oun, bring it to me."

I have to accept the package to avoid any suspicion. She walks over and unties her clothing bundle and retrieves the tobacco. Oh! How would my sister feel if she knew that the recipient of this tobacco has already been taken away?

She comes back and asks me, "Tuch, have you ever heard any word from A-M'orn?" referring to our youngest brother.

"No, I haven't seen him for a long time. When I returned from Kok Kakah, I saw him briefly near Wat Trapeang Thmor. They were coming back from harvesting rice at the *roneam*. They only stayed in Trapeang Thmor for one night, and then the Organization sent them off again to harvest rattan in Siem Reap province. At New Year I wrote a letter to him, but I never got a reply."

"Huh. It's been almost a year since I've seen my little brother's face," my sister says, slowly and with great sadness, missing her baby brother. But time is short; we don't have time to say much.

I say, "Oh! Oun, can you help me with something?"

"What is it, Tuch?"

"Can you take a message to A-Det's mother?"

"What's this about?"

"Well, I don't have any hope of us ever being together. We are always mobile and deployed far apart from one other, dozens of kilometers apart. Besides, the regional Organization won't let us take a spouse in the cooperative."

"In that cause, you should request a girl in your own regional mobile brigade," my sister opines.

"But we should notify A-Det first."

"Tuch, do you have your eye on any particular girl?"

"Yes, I do. I'm in love with a base person."

"A base person! You don't think that will work, do you? Does she love you?"

"Yes. We're in love with each other!"

"Oh, then if you're both in agreement, you should request her. Don't wait too long because you are getting old!"

As she speaks, my sister unties a bundled *krama* and removes a package of tobacco for me. "Here is the tobacco, and here is some crushed sour *krasang* fruit."

"No, you keep that and eat it yourself!"

"Take it! You take it and eat it, Tuch. When you're mobile it isn't so easy to find *krasang* fruit as when you're in the village."

My sister has nothing to give me besides this one small package of crushed sour *krasang* fruit. The old folks often say that when saying goodbye to someone, you should never give a present of guava because it is an omen of permanent separation.[2] So what about crushed sour *krasang* fruit? Could it be a symbol of a final farewell?

In earlier times, newlywed couples were allowed to take three days off from work. Now, not only is there not a shelter provided to sleep together, but the newlyweds don't even get a chance to take a break, as nearly all the regional mobile units are pulling back from the Trapeang Thmor worksite this morning: four young men's mobile brigades and two young women's mobile brigades.

What are we going to Spean Sreng to do? Build a dam? Dig a canal? Nobody knows. Hoes and *bangky* baskets remain the equipment we are expected to carry with us. But in addition, we receive more than twenty yoke of cattle per brigade, with accompanying equipment: plows and harrows.

We set out from the Trapeang Thmor Reservoir worksite at about nine in the morning. As usual, aside from some modest belongings in a small bag and our work equipment, we are each required to carry three thatch panels apiece. Some people are given charge of equipment for managing the oxen instead of hoes and baskets.

I am put in charge of a yoke of oxen and a plow. It is a new duty, which pleases me because I want to learn how to do a lot of things. I want to know how to care for oxen, and I want to know how to plow rice fields. Digging dirt and hauling dirt has left my hands and shoulders callused, and there is no variety. It's just the same thing over and over, and I'm tired of it.

We walk with the oxen, dragging the plows and harrows alongside the canal from the first bridge to Kok Kraol. From there, we travel along the Phnom Srok–Prey Moan road as far as Kok Rumchek, where we turn and head east along the causeway from Kok Rumchek toward Char Kok Team.

The early rainy-season sun takes no pity on us; its heat is intense. We move without stopping to take breaks in the shade along the way. My brigade is the last group in the procession, and at dusk we arrive at Char and Smach villages, on the Rumduol River. We are to rest here temporarily for one night. The

---

[2] "Guava" in Khmer is *trabaek*, while *baek* means "to be separated."

young women's units are to rest at Wat Smach, about 200 meters down a side road to the left. The young men rest in the cooperative's dining pavilion and beneath villagers' houses. The cattle units also camp at Wat Smach, as it has a yard for tying up the cattle.

The sun sinks beneath the horizon, leaving only a red light to paint the clouds. The sky begins to change color to darker, duller hues. Because we are all exhausted, both the oxen and the humans take slow, plodding steps, dragging our feet toward Wat Smach. Ahead of us about ten women dressed in black and wearing black caps with silk *kramas* around their necks walk in a line in the opposite direction from us, apparently leaders of some base young women. As a habit, I don't normally look into the faces of the base young women. They walk past us, and suddenly the voice of a young woman calls my name with joy: "Bong Tuch!"

I raise my face to look at the owner of the voice. Good Lord! It is Comrade Ly, the queen of my heart! Is there anything more delightful than seeing the person you are in love with? Comrade Ly and Comrade Dy stop walking, and I tug on the lead to stop the oxen, and we stand conversing.

"A-Ly! Where are you coming from?" I ask slowly, with a feeling of joy and a welcoming smile.

"I'm coming from a meeting in Wat Smach, Bong! Did you just arrive?"

"Yes, I just arrived. So have you and Comrade Dy been here long?"

"We arrived five days ago."

"So what is your team doing, and where are you camped?"

"We are soaking rice seedlings for transplanting, and we are staying in a camp constructed along the causeway to Char Kok Team about a kilometer from here. Where are you staying?"

"I don't know yet, but tonight they sent us to stay in Wat Smach."

Comrade Ly's countenance wilts and she says to me in a whiny voice, like a small child who wants something, "Bong, I miss my parents so much. A-Dy and I are thinking of running away back to the village."

These words move me, and I feel compassion for my beloved. I also have a feeling of fear that I will be separated from her.

I comfort her, saying, "A-Ly, don't go yet. Wait a little while longer."

I say to Comrade Dy, "Comrade Dy, don't go back to your village, all right?"

"Yes, Bong," they both say together.

Comrade Ly continues, "But you have to visit me often, all right?"

"Of course! Whenever I am free, I will go to visit you." I smile at her in encouragement.

It's true, when you are a child, you demand comfort and attention from your parents. But when you become an adult, it is the comfort and attention of a romantic companion that is essential. After hearing my pleas and comforting words, Comrade Ly's face is filled with life again, and she is willing to abandon her thoughts of running away to her village.

The sky grows darker and the light fades, and Comrade Ly and Comrade Dy go on their way, leaving me with a feeling of longing, of sadness from parting from my beloved. I stand watching her until she fades into the veil of darkness.

Oh, Love! All you have done is make my heart ache with longing, compassion, and affection, and make us wilt from despair!

Oh, Love! You make my heart groan. The joy of meeting has turned into the sorrow of parting within only a few minutes.

Oh, My Love! Why do you flicker so briefly, like the flame of a floating lantern? One moment you are bright, and dark the next; one moment glad, and afraid the next.

Oh, Gods! Why are you so cruel?

Our possessions are not our own.

Our bodies are not our own.

And our love is not our own.

Love in Chains

1. A shadow swallowed into darkness   my heart longs for you to stay
I watch your silhouette, like an orphan   feeling cold without you, Darling.

2. My love is larger than the earth   my love turns to sorrow
a star in the sky I fear cannot be kept   a star falls nearby, but I cannot grasp it.

chorus:
My arms long to hold you   to care for you, my darling
I want to tell you my breast won't rest   if I can't have you nearby.

3. Powers of Wat Smach, help me   to meet her, my pinnacle, my foundation
to unite our fates, our paths and pillows   to rest from sorrow, this Hell on Earth.

Tonight we tie up the oxen and buffalo and set up our hammocks in the front yard of Wat Smach. Most of the young women's units go to sleep inside the temple, leaving only a handful outside. Here I meet Comrade Khom and Comrade Pov, with whom I used to work at Kok Kakah. Now they, too, have been sent to wage battle on the same battlefield as me.

The cadres in charge of the brigade travel to Phnom Liep in the night to receive orders for our work plan.

Part Five: The Last Camp

CHAPTER 44

Veal Saen Khyal, Or Ta Phal, Phnom Tralok

11 May 1978

This morning the Fourth Brigade is reorganized into new units: the paddy dike construction unit, the fertilizer unit, and the plowing unit. Through this reorganization we are informed that our task at this time is to increase rice production.

I have often heard people speak of a Prophecy of the Buddha[1] which says that we all must cross three plains. I don't know what the plains are, but I remember hearing that the final plain is Veal Sen Khyal,[2] Or Ta Phal,[3] and Phnom Tralok.[4] Now we have arrived at this final plain.

The east-west causeway with a canal running alongside it from the Kok Rumchek worksite to the Sreng River is the border between Phnom Srok district and Preah Netr Preah district. From Char-Smach to Char Kok Team on the Sreng River, this causeway divides the vast plain of rice fields into two parts:

- The part north of the causeway consists of the rice fields of Spean Sreng subdistrict.

- The part south of the causeway consists of the rice fields of Teuk Chor subdistrict.

The rice fields of Teuk Chor subdistrict are vast and wide, extending from north to south for many kilometers. Throughout this plain are Bodhi trees growing here and there at distant intervals. At the southern extent of the plain, you can see patches of trees growing along National Highway Six, and you can see three mountains that appear to be connected: Phnom Liep, Phnom Trayong, and Phnom Tralok. At the eastern and western extents of the plain are villages of locals along the Rumduol and Sreng rivers, kilometers apart. In the middle of this plain are low areas where water collects in many twists and bends

---

[1] In Khmer lore, these are prophecies passed via word of mouth or found documents. The prophecy mentioned here is remembered by the author as something he heard orally, and it is not known whether this prophecy, or any similar to it, is recorded anywhere in writing.

[2] "Plain of Great Wind"

[3] "Grandfather Phal's Stream"

[4] "Tralok Mountain"

in a shape like a stream, with one end emptying into the Rumduol River at Kok Key Bridge. This plain is called Veal Sen Khyal; the flooded area is called Or Ta Phal; and the mountain at the southernmost extent of the plain is Phnom Tralok.

This area is a flood plain during the rainy season, where the locals used to sow floating rice[5] in the old society. Our task now is to make a system of paddy dikes and canals to transform the plain into dry-season rice fields and seedling beds and increase rice productivity here.

The camp of each brigade is constructed in the open plain, strung in a line along the length of the plain from north to south, each about a kilometer from the last. My brigade's camp is the northernmost camp, about half a kilometer from the Smach causeway (the east-west causeway) in a place that the local villagers call Or Kambot. West of our camps, along the Rumduol River, are the villages of Ta Khek, Kok Key, Lao Te, and Bat Trang.

The ground here is sandy clay that sticks to the plow blades when wet, and quickly becomes hard and unyielding to seedlings if it is plowed while wet and then left too long before transplanting.

In the early rainy season, it rains occasionally, and in low-lying areas the water pools, and the ground becomes wet and sticky and mixed with old rice stubble, which sticks to the plow blades until they become nearly impossible for the oxen to pull. After plowing for one or two circuits, we have to stop the oxen and clean off the mud and debris. Spots of higher ground remain dry, and the ground is hard, so that we have to push down hard on the plow handles with both hands to make it bite deep and form a furrow. In some places, tractors have made a pass to turn the soil over, and there we have an easy time of it, as all we have to do is plow the soil to mix it up a bit.

The plowing work is divided between three teams led by Bong Bor, Comrade Dy, and Comrade Mang. I am on Comrade Dy's team. Each team has six or seven plows and is expected to plow one hectare per day. Some days we encounter loose soil that is easily plowable, and we are able to fill the quota. Some days we encounter soil that is hard and sticky, and we can barely plow it,

---

[5] a variety of rice that grows well in flooded conditions

and we work until eleven or twelve at night before the Organization finally permits us to rest the oxen and water buffalo.

My team has three yokes of water buffalo for pulling harrows, kept by Comrade Chuch, Comrade Ly,[6] and Ta Sau (an older man over forty years old).

Apart from the plowing unit, the fertilizer unit, and the young women of Comrade Tum's unit—who are tasked with soaking and sowing the seeds—all the other young men and young women units are tasked with constructing a system of paddy dikes in a grid, dividing the plain into large and small rice paddies, either fifty meters square or a hundred meters square, depending on the topography, and digging ditches to channel water into the paddies. Together with supplementary forces from the cooperatives of Phnom Srok and Preah Netr Preah districts, these units dig a north-south canal ten meters wide across the top that connects to the canal running between Char-Smach and Char Kok Team and cuts across the plain to Phnom Liep to provide water for rice farming.

This canal divides the rice fields of Teuk Chor subdistrict into two parts:

- East of the canal is the territory of the cooperative of Teuk Chor subdistrict.

- West of the canal is the territory that the regional mobile units are to attack.

In little over half a month, this plain that was wild and overgrown with bushes and small trees, grass, and stubble is transformed into lush rice fields covered with beautiful, green rice seedlings.

After completing the large north-south canal, the regional mobile units pull back to work on productivity. The young women are tasked with pulling and transplanting seedlings, while the units in charge of the paddy dikes are tasked with carrying the seedlings on yokes to be laid out in the fields for the young women to transplant. The cattle team must work hard, whipping the oxen and water buffalo and splashing water on them, just to fulfill the daily quota, to make sure that the others have ground ready to transplant the seedlings in. If we don't finish the quota in the morning, then in the evening we must gather the oxen and water buffalo and finish it.

---

[6] Author's Note: "currently a police officer in the Ministry of Interior"

We have some fun competing against one another: those who pull the seedlings and those who transport them race against the transplanters, while the transplanters race against the plowmen, and the plowmen push the oxen and water buffalo without fear of tiring them and without pity. But the moment we glance at the food rations, we lose all our vigor and spirit. The daily rations are one can of uncooked rice per person. In the morning we get a small dish of thick rice porridge, and in the evening we get a small dish of cooked rice. (They don't give us porridge both morning and evening as at Trapeang Thmor Reservoir.)

Can this much food possibly make up for the energy that we expend in our labor, running after the oxen and water buffalo all morning without stopping?

Those of us who are plowmen each carry a small bag tied at our waist or tied to the plow handle. With our right hand, we hold the plow handle against our waist, and our left hand holds a whip, raising and lowering it to whip the cattle so that they pull urgently to keep up with the plowman in front. All the while our eyes scan the turbulent, muddy water churned up in the wake of the oxen's hooves in case a crab or snail floats up. Our eyes are as keen as those of an egret watching for a fish to surface. We bend down and snatch up every crab and snail that floats up and put it straight into our bag. Our hands are as fast as the talons of a hawk snatching a chick, but occasionally we can't grab it in time, and then we feel so much regret! We feel regret for the lost food that has escaped our mouths. We can't slow the oxen because if we lose the pace, the plow of the person behind us will hit us in the back.

If we catch larger crabs, we put them into our bags to season and boil later. But if we catch tiny crabs, about the size of our thumb or big toe, we mostly just plop them straight into our mouths and chew them up straight away, not wasting any time because we are so exhausted!

Chapter 45

Resistance

The cattle unit[1] is a strong unit. Only those with sound bodies and plenty of strength are chosen for the cattle unit. But this is a group of people trapped in a prison *within* a prison.

It is true that the oxen and water buffalo are the ones who pull the plows and harrows, but there are always people in bondage running along behind them. They can sit and catch their breath or roll a cigarette to smoke only when they rest the cattle's legs. Some days they work hard from the morning until they finally stop plowing, without any chances for rest, and by then both the cattle and the humans gasp for air, taking short, grating breaths, almost unable to catch their breath.

Discipline is very strict. Whoever whips an ox with a whip—made from a piece of bamboo, a stick, or tree branch—and leaves marks, is "built." Whoever puts away the cattle, or lets them out, without dousing or rinsing them with water, is built. When we return to camp, we are scarcely able to sip our porridge before the unit and brigade leaders come looking for us.

"Hey! Eat quickly. How long does it take to prepare a little bowl of porridge? The sun is already high in the sky, and you've tied up and left the cattle. Don't they need to eat just like you do?"

Every ox and water buffalo must be herded and tended to. If they don't eat enough, we get built. If they escape at night and eat the cooperative's rice or crops, we get built. If we lose a plowshare or break the moldboard tip,[2] we get built. (The plowshares are mostly lost while dragging the plow, while the moldboard tips break off when the plow strikes a tree stump hidden in the dirt.) The plowmen's minds are on the oxen and water buffalo every second of the day. Whenever there is a break for a holiday or meeting, those of us in charge of the cattle don't stop to rest or join the meetings as the others do.

The cattle unit is a strong unit, but the Organization takes no care to feed the unit well. During the offensive to dig the north-south canal, the dirt haulers had their rations increased to a can and a half per day, and they got cooked rice

---

[1] used synonymously with "plowing unit" (as the cattle are used for plowing)

[2] i.e., the point where the metal plowshare is attached to the wooden moldboard

both morning and evening. Meanwhile, the cattle unit remained at one can per person, as before, sipping our porridge with loud *slurp! slurp!* sounds. (We usually collect our porridge ration then mix in water and recook it to increase the volume, sometimes adding plants.)

Other units have opportunities to go out and forage for frogs, crabs, and snails, or wild plants like *phty* greens, *trakuon*, or bamboo shoots for extra food. But the plowmen are stuck with the oxen and water buffalo and can't go very far, as we don't dare abandon our animals.

To solve the problem of hunger, each plowing team quietly combines their cattle into a common herd and appoints two people to watch them. The others split up and go hunt for crabs, snails, and frogs; fish with nets; and forage for edible plants, while some go and pick *preal*[3] shrubs to make into cattle rope.

After eating our midday porridge, we drive the cattle back out of camp, and we go with them, each to our own appointed field. Among the three plowing teams of the cattle unit, only Comrade Mang's team enjoys reasonable concord in assigning tasks for finding food to cook. They have a fishing net, and they pick bundles of *trakuon* and bring them back to cook every day, and they won't tell the other teams where they pick this *trakuon*.

Meanwhile, my team and Comrade Bor's team struggle without any fishing equipment. We go out and catch *achko* frogs in the rice fields and collect weaver ants or hunt for clams and snails to cook with spiny amaranth or purslane.

Living among the general population is quite different from living in the society of young people. The youth are not very heavily influenced by the corruption of the old society. They are purer and more in harmony with one another. In general-population society, everything that used to happen in the old society still happens, and it is vicious. The youth engage in the Revolution for the sake of the Revolution, while the general population engage in the Revolution to get away with things. Oppression, extortion, and exploitation, the soul of a corrupt regime, occur in the general population from the top down to the bottom. The cadres don't just exercise their influence over us to fulfill our revolutionary work; they dominate us even in the petty things of this rice-by-the-can life, and we live without freedom. Although, as for those who have little fear

---

[3] *Columbia auriculata*. The bark of this shrub is used to make rope.

of death; who are willing to react, willing to object and resist; who are stubborn and defiant of procedure: they don't dare to oppress or compel them as much.

Comrade Mol is a young-man-in-hiding, like me. He is older and more knowledgeable than me. He is a man of few words, and always accepts every task the group leader gives him without question, complaint, or objection. We are on Comrade Dy's team together. Comrade Mol once tells me, "Anybody who doesn't steal from me can live with me."

We have similar sentiments, but I have a different philosophy from Comrade Mol's: I can live with any type of person, but it is rare to find a person who can live with me.

Because we talk little and carry out our tasks diligently, Comrade Mol and I are instructed by the team leader to mind the oxen nearly every day, whether it is our turn or not. The others spend only an hour or two fishing and foraging for frogs, crabs, and edible plants, and then return to camp to take a nap. We cowherds, on the other hand, can only sit or walk around collecting and counting the oxen, protecting them from getting lost, and preventing them from mixing with other herds or eating cooperative crops—without ever daring to take a rest or lie down for a nap or even close our eyes a moment, from noon until near sunset, when we have to collect the oxen and herd them back into camp.

While it's true that I am a man of few words like Comrade Mol, unlike him I am a person who tends to react. I try to control myself and suppress my emotions to avoid pain, turmoil, and a preoccupation with the worthlessness of living.

Oh, my eyes! Don't see anything that is crudeness or exploitation or oppression!

Oh, my ears! Don't hear anything that is disdain, contempt, or reproach.

Oh, my heart! Remain neutral and don't give in to feelings of hatred, love, sorrow, or joy. If you can't restrain yourself, if you can't take it, if your chest is too tight, then go head and explode; explode now, while out herding the oxen, while far away from everyone else. Explode in the fields, under the sky. No matter how upset you feel, however agitated by hatred toward this person, or in love with that person, you are completely free to unfurl it and release it from your head and your chest. All of nature will never condemn you, nor hold these things against you, nor use them to stir up trouble with anybody else.

But the Lord Buddha was able to exercise tolerance and strove to build virtue, resolving to disengage his feelings from the tainted things of men, because he abandoned this tainted society and went to live alone in the silent wilderness. I, on the other hand, am among the masses; with people who are in misery, who are enduring the most horrible torments, who are fighting to live in the face of death, flailing their arms in search of anything they can grasp to pull themselves out of the pit of death.

Can I resolve to disengage my own feelings from such suffering if I myself am but a lone individual, caught in the endless and miserable cycle of life, death, and rebirth?

Comrade Dy provokes me terribly! Whenever he doesn't feel like herding the oxen, he makes me do it in his stead. On the days when he goes herding with me, he leaves me to watch the oxen alone while he goes to hunt for *achko* frogs and pick wild plants to cook and eat all by himself. Boasting himself as the team leader, he bans the members of his team from private cooking, yet he can do it. It's true: the laws that the powerful create have dominion only over the weak.

One night there is a common meeting among the plowing unit, and I ask the unit leader if I can make some remarks.

"First, I would like to pay my respects to the comrade unit leader, the comrade team leaders, and all of my comrade unit members who love the Most Exalted Revolution! I wish to speak at this time, to ask the comrade unit leader to help resolve a personal problem. I can't bear to live on Comrade Dy's team any longer, and I implore the comrade unit leader to allow me to leave this team and join a different one."

Comrade Dy is shocked. He never imagined that I would challenge my oppression, and he threatens me: "If you can't endure the Revolution, better that you die instead, Comrade!"

I reply to Comrade Dy slowly and clearly, "Excuse me. Comrade Dy, listen to my words carefully, and don't try to misconstrue them to deceive the collective and push me into a pit! I want to say that I cannot endure your exploitation and oppression of me, as a team leader; *not* that I cannot endure the Revolution. Make no mistake!"

Once I have made my point clearly, Comrade Dy no longer dares to confront me or demand answers about how I consider him to be exploiting me.

Comrade Cham, leader of the plowing unit, agrees to let me leave Comrade Dy's team as requested and appoints me to Comrade Mang's team instead.

CHAPTER 46
The Fourth Brigade

Am I the only person suffering oppression? Is Comrade Dy the only oppressor?

After the offensive to raise the dams and dig the canals for Trapeang Thmor Reservoir for the 1977 plan, life for the general-population units[1] changed. The men were separated into men's units, and the women into women's units. They were no longer mixed as they had been previously. And the men's and women's units were mostly deployed on mobile assignments far apart from one another.

My unit is a brigade with unusual structure and characteristics among all the brigades of the men's regional mobile units. This brigade is commanded by Comrade Ron, a young man, along with Mea Pov and Mea Chout, who are middle-aged men. These three cadres are base people from Paoy Char subdistrict. This brigade is divided into two regiments: the young men's regiment and the general-population regiment. (Other brigades do not have these sub-units.)

Mea Pov is the former head of Phnom Srok district's special unit, which was the strongest unit during the Trapeang Thmor Reservoir offensive. This was a unit of middle-aged men and women with robust health, distilled from the mobile units of all the subdistricts in Phnom Srok district. In late 1977, the regional Organization permitted the special unit to break ranks and return to live with their families in the cooperatives. Unwilling to relinquish his position or his influence, Mea Pov would not allow the middle-aged men from Paoy Char subdistrict to return to their villages, but instead combined them with the young men's mobile unit of Paoy Char subdistrict to create the Fourth Brigade, a.k.a. Bong Ron's and Mea Pov's Brigade.

In his leadership of the special unit, Mea Pov was very mean and strict, which made that unit the most productive unit in terms of both labor and of killing people. The unit members feared Mea Pov, not daring to look him in the face or displease him. If anyone dared to say that the rice was sour or too raw, they would certainly end up stinking themselves, as a vulture played the flute.[2]

---

[1] generally synonymous with "middle-aged units"
[2] a Khmer euphemism for death

These days, Mea Pov is not as mean or strict as he once was, but he is still feared by the members of his unit. Mea Pov uses his old influence to create a manner of living that I would call exploitative, oppressive, and a betrayal of the people. Life for the valueless class (the evacuees),[3] both in the cooperatives as well as the mobile units, must remain under the dominion of the base people, who are the class of Life Masters. These base people, especially those who were born to be cadres, exploit us and oppress us until we scarcely have room to move, like slaves and masters.

After the revolutionary cadres from the Southwestern and Western Zones came to take control and lead the work here in the Northwestern Zone, they largely reined in and put an end to the excessive killings. This was a wake-up call for those cadres who survived, and they made some changes to their behavior. When that happened, life for us was like a dead leaf being exposed to morning dew, and things got a little bit better. In most cooperatives and mobile units there was now a cadre from the Southwestern or the Western Zone serving as either a counselor or a direct leader. Unfortunately, my brigade remained an un-affected unit, without any of those cadres in positions of leadership. So the things that had happened before began to happen again, and worse than before, like a sickness that was treated with the wrong medicine.

Not many base people are required to join mobile units. In my brigade, in both the young men's as well as the general-population units, the base people are given positions as cadres, and senior ones at that, from regimental leader on up. If they are given roles as oxcart drivers to transport rice and vegetables, or rope makers, whistling as they lounge about, then they are given the title *Big Brother*, leaders of units without members, leaders of ghost units. All of these Big Brothers have power and copious salaries (rations), daily, monthly, and yearly. We are given wages of porridge or one small dish of rice apiece, plus a large dish of soup per team each meal. Meanwhile, the rations of one Big Brother are equal to the rations of two or three of the rest of us when the rations are more lenient, and three or four of us when the rations are tight. High tide is no different from low tide for them, as their flesh remains plump regardless. Never mind, close your eyes. They dine amongst themselves, and never with the rest of us. The more you see and hear, the more upset you get.

---

[3] i.e., the new people

But you can't help but see. One day the cattle unit plows both morning and evening at the south end of the plain, about nine kilometers from the camp. At noon an economy worker brings porridge on a shoulder yoke for us to eat in the field. Taking a break from plowing, we are covered in sweat and our clothing is soaked with water, and we release the cattle into a stand of sparse trees and then head straight for the porridge dishes that the economy worker has already dished up and set out, one for each member of the plowing unit. If we were at camp, we could take time to pick some leaves to boil along with some small frogs, crabs, or snails that we had caught in the wake of the plow or harrow while plowing or harrowing. Out here in the rice field, we can't cook soup, so we light a fire and roast our catches to eat with the porridge, which is gone after just two or three sips. Today there are two dishes of porridge left over, as two members of the plowing unit were allowed to take a plow back to camp to be repaired. We sit staring at the two leftover porridge dishes with longing.

Every day, Mea Pov normally returns to camp to eat his porridge, so the economy workers never bring his porridge. Today he has decided not to go back to camp, and he sits down to eat his porridge. The economy workers give both dishes of porridge to Mea Pov in front of the rest of us, who sit there swallowing our own spit. There is no mystery here, as this is something we have all known about, but today we see it firsthand. We can't help but feal jealousy toward a leader who has only to walk about and raise a hand to point left and right without performing any strenuous labor like the rest of us, but who nevertheless receives abundant food rations. No longer able to just sit there swallowing his spit, Bong Pav grabs a spoon and begins eating porridge along with Mea Pov and says, pretending to joke around, "I'm just gonna go ahead and help Big Brother eat his porridge since he got more than we did."

The general-population regiment contains 125 men, who eat separately from the young men's unit. In this general-population unit there are ten Big Brothers. Not only do they support themselves, but their families, wives, and children back at the cooperative must also grow fat. A portion of the rations of food, uncooked rice, fish, meat, salt, *prahok*, and kerosene find their way to the cooperative through these men. They divide up the spoils and take turns visiting their families: one Big Brother comes, and another goes.

Because of this, the rations for the rest of us are short, much different from the rations given to members of other brigades. On days when we eat our midday meal in a rice paddy near the young women transplanting rice, or other young men units, we nudge each other and watch their rice rations, which are more abundant than ours. Even the food is different: smoked fish, dried fish, duck eggs, and oil are given only to the Big Brothers and consumed only by the Big Brothers, while the rest of us only sip boiled *prahok* or cloud soup to which is added some sour flavoring and some slightly wormy *prahok*.

When we are given clothing rations from time to time, we receive either a shirt with no trousers or trousers with no shirt. They write down our names to remember to complete the outfit next time. As for the Big Brothers, each of them gets one or two complete outfits, and they select the nicest ones. There is no mistaking them: if you see someone with a black shirt, black pants, and a silk *krama* around his neck, it must be one of the Big Brothers.

The economy team belongs to the Big Brothers and supplies the Big Brothers. The rest of us have a saying: "If it's small, it's for the people. If it's heavy, it's for the cooks. And if it's as big as your thigh,[4] it's for the Big Brothers." They surround the economy kitchen with barbed wire so no one can enter besides the economy workers and the Big Brothers. They are afraid we will sneak in and take salt, *prahok*, rice crusts, or rice water. If anybody dares to enter the economy shed, they will write down his name and give it to Mea Pov to summon him for censuring and "building." In fact, they don't want us to see or know about their arrangements.

After cooking, the economy team dishes up the rice or porridge into large dishes set aside for the ten Big Brothers, and then divide the rest up for the battalions (the plowing unit, the fertilizer unit, and the paddy-dike-maintenance and canal-digging unit). It is the same with the other food, as the boiled and roasted fish are set aside for the Big Brothers. When taking a break from work, the Big Brothers all go into the economy shed to eat so they don't have to sully themselves by condescending to eat with the little people in their units.

The economy workers are the ones who give rations belonging to the people to the Big Brothers to take back to their homes, and they are the ones who arrange transport for the Big Brothers.

The Big Brothers eat their fill and have plump flesh and plenty of strength, and they come around to exhort the rest of us, who don't get enough to eat, to

---

[4] In Khmer language and culture, it is customary to indicate the relative size of objects using body parts for comparison, especially limbs and digits, with the thigh being the largest of all.

work hard. All they do is carry a hoe on their shoulder and open or close a paddy dike to let water in or out of the paddy when we plow. If there is a women's unit working nearby, only then will they actively work the plows themselves, driving the oxen and water buffalo without restraint. Those of us who are feeble and weak struggle to run after these men, who are strong, until eleven thirty or twelve o'clock before taking a break. Then we are so exhausted we can hardly keep from falling over.

Asking for permission to go home to visit your wife and children is exceedingly difficult. Back when we were digging through the dam to install the large pipe between the first and second bridges, more than twenty men ran off to visit their wives who were on a mobile detail in Spean Sreng subdistrict after not having seen them for many months. There, they lay low and worked hauling dirt alongside their wives. Mea Pov reached out through his contacts and asked for these men to return. Then he took them all to meet the chairman of the regional mobile committee. It was very fortunate for them that the regional mobile committee chairman was sympathetic after having received the same response repeatedly: the men had abandoned their unit because they missed their families. The cadre ordered Mea Pov to be lenient toward those with families and allow them to visit twice a month. But these directions were followed only while working at Trapeang Thmor Reservoir. Ever since moving the front lines to Veal Saen Khyal, this is no longer enforced, as we are far from their homes. Meanwhile, the Big Brothers take turns going back and forth like snails to visit their own wives.

We, the lowly members of the unit who are the victims of this exploitation and extortion, are all miserable and unhappy, and we react to it. But by reacting, we push ourselves into a pit. Nobody dares to openly object to or criticize the Big Brothers and say that they are cheating us, or that they are stealing from the collective. So we react in a way that is essentially being angry at the cow but smiting the plow: when the vegetable cart arrives at camp (usually in the evening), some members of the unit surround the cart, and some of them reach out and snatch a bit of this or that and then fight over their spoils right in front of the cadres.

The cadres do not suppress this behavior, but instead act like they aren't aware of it and allow the theft to go on. This is because these people steal only a little bit—two or three stalks of *trakuon* or water hyacinth, or a tomato or cucumber—and because this behavior facilitates their own theft.

When a bit of sugar or half a bag or a full bag of yams arrives by request from the cooperative, at night the economy team will boil it up and then go out to collect the Big Brothers for a "work" meeting. In the morning they will announce that some of the yams were stolen by thieves, and there are too few left to distribute to members of the unit, so they will be mixed with the porridge or cooked with the soup. All of us know very well who the thieves are but would never dare to raise our hand and point to their faces. The cadres have no interest in serving the people or solving their problems. They think only of the comfort and good eating of their own group.

The cadres give orders to shut down all private cooking because private cooking causes delays in going back out to work. They walk about and confiscate fishing nets, fishing poles, gill nets, and nylon mosquito nets and make them common property, then assign economy workers to catch fish for the unit. But the fish they catch are only for the Big Brothers, who enjoy roasted fish and small-pot soup dishes, while the rest of us continue to eat sour soup with *prahok* and no fish.

Following the example from above, without anything being said, we resume private cooking as before. Mea Pov gets very angry and calls us to a meeting where he announces that he will confiscate dishes and pots if he sees anybody doing private cooking. Is this a solution to the problem? We don't get enough of the collective rations to get full, and when we forage for wild edible plants and leaves to cook and eat, this is condemned as wrong. If he says that midday cooking impacts returning to work, then what is wrong with doing it in the evening?

Though we say nothing, we are all very upset. For each of us listening to these so-called revolutionary lectures, it's like pouring water on a duck's back. They encourage us to wage fierce battle, but don't allow us to get full. I ask permission to express my opinion.

"Pardon me, Mea, but if you shut down private cooking, whether in the regiments or the teams, then I suggest that you ask the economy team to increase the large-pot soup. If the large-pot soup continues to be broth without fish or vegetables, as it is now, this restriction will surely be ineffective, and the small-pot cooking will return as before."

The collective applauds my opinion. Mea Pov agrees to adapt. But it is only a reply of convenience. They cook water hyacinths and tomatoes for us to eat using the whole plants, including stems and roots, because we asked for more vegetables.

The rules are written for us only, while they continue to eat roasted fish and small-pot dishes. Nobody dares to react or protest this. Each of us balls our fists and folds our arms and goes our separate ways to forage for food and engage in secret theft. The cadres steal from the people, and the people steal from each other, stealing clothing, shoes, knives, hatchets, dishes, and spoons to take and trade in the villages.

Some people, unable to endure living in the dark world of this inexpressible Hell, run away to the cooperative or to join another unit. After living and working in Veal Sean Khyal for a month, Bong Bo runs away and abandons both the unit and his wife back in the cooperative, who is nine months pregnant. He runs away into the forest, telling close friends, "I can't take it! If I have to endure living here any longer, either they or I will have to die!"

The number of people in the unit diminishes little by little because of people either being clubbed to death, running away from the unit for another unit, or running away back to the cooperative.

During a meeting in Char Kok Team in the middle of June, the regional chairman poses a question that nobody dares to answer: "Why do people keep abandoning the unit?"

Because my responsibilities don't permit it, I rarely attend large meetings, so I am not as acquainted with the region or zone chairmen as some of the others. When they hold the meeting in Char Kok Team, once again I don't have an opportunity to attend because I am busy herding oxen. Many people have died. Many people are engaging in actions that will lead to yet-unknown deaths in the future by creating extraordinary suffering. How many more people will be victimized by this factor (suffering caused by leadership)? Those who die no longer suffer; it is the survivors—their children, their parents—who waste away in misery. If I had been in the meeting, I definitely would have stood to respond to the regional chairman's question so that the senior levels of the Organization could have a clear knowledge of the reasons why people are becoming fed up with the Revolution, to put an end to this protracted calamity. Go ahead and let them kill just me! I have no wife and no children. The sorrow and misery of my parents is already in the past.

I become resolved that if there is another meeting, then I will sneak off to attend it to give my opinion to the senior levels of the Organization. But I don't see any more meetings called. I begin to write a secret report to hand over personally to a representative from the regional committee. But when I have finished writing it, I suddenly fall ill.

CHAPTER 47

Overworked

The work is extremely strenuous and difficult, and there is no time nor day when it lets up or when we can rest. The cattle unit struggles especially hard, more than any other unit, to farm rice here. Now that the rainy season has begun, the rains soak the fields, and the soil becomes soft and easy to plow; but wading through the water is so taxing and so exhausting that it's worse than plowing dry land. We have to plow and turn the soil and drag the plows from paddy to paddy and from place to place, unrelentingly.

Though the oxen and buffalo have unlimited rations, they nevertheless become very thin, and if you whip or goad them, it seems as though they scarcely feel pain anymore. They struggle to lift their hooves and drag the plows and harrows under duress, with faces so wilted that you feel sorry for them. They have only two or three hours per day to rest from plowing and to graze. Meanwhile, grass is hard to come by, and then only by plucking it along the dikes in neighboring paddies to where we are plowing. The plain has been completely transformed into rice fields. If we were to lead them to graze in groves of trees one or two kilometers away, by the time we lead them there and back, wending our way left and right over paddy dikes and around ditches and canals, it would be time to go back to work plowing, and there would be no time for the grazing itself.

Like the animals, ever since the transplanting began more than a month ago, we, the plowmen, never eat our midday porridge back at camp as the other units do. Our battle plan entails plowing both morning and evening, so that the economy workers have to bring our food to us in the fields.

At eleven thirty or twelve o'clock, we stop plowing and harrowing and bathe the cattle with water and tie them up in one place. We clean our own bodies, our hands and feet and clothing, which are soiled with mud, and each grabs a dish of porridge to eat right away. When we have finished, we lead each ox and water buffalo to graze along the paddy dikes, then sit and rest directly in the sun until two or three o'clock before leading the cattle back into the field to resume plowing and harrowing. Then at five thirty or six o'clock, we stop plowing and lead the cattle back to camp. The people are given evening food rations, but the cattle get no grass at night. We tie them up together and leave them.

On days when there is no rain, our trousers get soaked only up to the knees or thighs. But on days when it rains, we have to wear water-soaked clothing all day long. With daily rations of one can of uncooked rice per person, after embezzlement by the cadres, we each get one small dish of porridge per person per meal. We lick our bowls and spoons until there is no porridge left, which makes it easy to keep them clean. Are rations like these sufficient to sustain our bodies and keep them strong enough for such grueling labor? The cadres can't even finish all their porridge, while we can't even get enough to fill our stomachs halfway. How great is our misery and our resentment? Those who engage in stealing and trading and those with parents, siblings, wives, and children in the cooperative can often get their hands on snacks, sugared yams, uncooked rice, or dried rice to supplement the meager rations and support their health and keep their bodies from wasting away.

As for me, I have nothing to trade. Every four or five months I am issued a shirt or a pair of trousers. If I were to take these to a village, I could trade with the locals for half a kilogram or a kilogram of tubers, but I would have to do it secretively so that neither the cooperative *chhlops* nor the unit leader caught me at it. Several among us are willing to endure wearing ragged, torn clothing and take the clothes they are issued to trade. I think that such a small quantity of tubers is not worth the value of the rationed clothing, and the trading is as difficult to hide as stealing.

And stealing? No way! My life is far too valuable for that. If I were to steal something, it would have only the value of the thing being stolen: one or two shrubs worth of tubers.

I don't trade, and I don't steal. I have no family members living permanently in the cooperative. I live like a monk, eating only the small bowl of porridge with a handful of boiled plants that I'm able to find while herding the cattle. Day by day my dietary deficit grows and grows.

As it is, even those *with* access to supplementary food are growing thin; so what about me? I don't really see myself, but I know that my trousers are loose, and my shirt is loose. And people who have known me, especially girls from Kok Kakah and from the Trapeang Thmor brick kiln, are surprised whenever they see me. "Bong Tuch, you're so skinny! Are you sick?"

Actually, I haven't had any sickness that would stop me from doing my job, but I am aware that I am getting weaker and skinnier. It's true! I am very skinny. My arms are nothing but bones, and my ribs stand out on my chest. I am starving! I am tired! I am so very exhausted! When I finish plowing, I can scarcely even herd the cattle back to camp. Every time I try to sit down, I feel like I will fall over completely. Every time I stand up, I get dizzy, and I have to bend over with my hands on my knees and my eyes closed, or stand holding onto something for a moment, until the dizziness subsides and I can take a step, my ears wheezing. My ears are so plugged up I can hardly hear anything. When I walk back to camp, I try to avoid meeting any young women for fear that they will ask me something and I won't be able to understand them or talk to them, and because I feel so tired whenever I open my mouth to speak. By now, I've become so worn out that I'm not unlike my brother Samorn when he became exhausted from overwork and ran away from the Kok Rumchek worksite to Kok Prasat in late 1976.

I am so tired! I am so exhausted! I am scarcely able to wade through the water behind the ox anymore. Bong Kop,[1] a Khmer Muslim who is on the plowing team with me, gives me a suggestion. "Tuch, you need to ask permission to rest, and then find some kaffir lime leaves and lemon grass to boil and inhale the vapors so you can get better."

I convey Bong Kop's suggestion to Comrade Cham, head of the plowing unit, and ask him if I could rest for a time. Comrade Cham replies with contempt, "Comrade Tuch, don't just inhale herbal vapors. You'll never get better that way. Boil it in a pot and then climb on in for a soak; that's easier."

Despite these terrible words, both the unit leader and the brigade leader agree to let me rest in camp starting on 1 July 1978, for the reason that I am too thin and no longer able to work.

Our sleeping shelter here is constructed north-to-south, with low eaves and no walls and no sleeping platforms. Those with rice-sack hammocks drive poles into the ground and tie them up, while those without hammocks lay down rice sacks or tarps and sleep on the ground. We all crowd in and sleep side-by-side. Those with wives also working on mobile units nearby in Veal Saen Khyal construct small huts and sleep apart from the others. This is because their wives can get permission to leave their units and sleep with their husbands two or three times per month. The cadres' shelter and the economy kitchen shelter are constructed west of our sleeping shelter about ten meters.

---

[1] Author's Note: "currently residing behind the old Chbar Ampov Cinema" (in Phnom Penh)

During work hours, everyone is gone, and the camp is silent. Only two or three sick persons remain, plus the cooks for the economy team and some of the Big Brothers, who lounge about.

I am the only person from the cattle unit who is out sick. The fertilizer unit has Comrade Sok, who is younger than I am, about twenty years old, and part Chinese. Apparently, Comrade Sok has no siblings or parents, and he is sick almost all the time. He is as thin as I am, and mostly wears trousers with no shirt, and walks aimlessly around the economy kitchen shed holding a metal bowl.

Generally, sick people have their rights and freedoms restricted. Their rations are also reduced to half of what those who work receive. Freedom to leave camp is taken away. The sick are not allowed to go out into the fields to forage for plants or hunt for crabs or frogs. Engaging in discussions about work assignments or chatting with friends, as well as reading revolutionary newspapers or magazines, is forbidden.

Because I am unfamiliar with the local villages, and because my freedom of movement is restricted, I can't find any kaffir lime leaves or lemongrass to vaporize as recommended by Bong Kop. I do nothing but rest in camp.

But because of hunger, my eyes and those of Comrade Sok, whether we are lying down or sitting up, are continuously drawn in a single direction: toward the economy kitchen. These days our sole source of survival is in that place. No activity of the economy team—washing pots, cooking porridge, cooking soup, cooking rice, draining rice water, stirring rice—escapes the gaze of the two skinny spies. Every now and then, we glance toward the cadre shelter. If nobody is there, that is a good opportunity for us. We grab our bowls and go sit and watch the economy workers. We hold our bowls and ask for rice water or ask permission to clean out the bottom of the porridge pot, but the economy workers never allow it. This is because they are also under pressure by orders from leadership. People are not allowed to loiter around the economy kitchen, especially sick people. Regarding the rice water, even if we didn't loiter, but merely left our bowls for them to drain rice water into, this is also not allowed, as they save this water to be drunk by the oxen that pull the cart.

But even though we know we can't have it, still we continuously try to find opportunities to sit and watch the economy workers, not caring if they curse us. We do it because we are so hungry, because we realize that even though these days nobody has any right to give us anything, if we can manage to snatch something without them seeing, or which they are too reluctant to take back from us, then we can have it. But these opportunities are very rare. Comrade Kun, head of economy, has no personal quality that could be called "sympathetic." So sometimes all we do is walk around the economy kitchen swallowing our own spit, like foxes circling the chicken pen.

I can only sit quietly and not go anywhere outside camp, but I become very bored and am unable to keep my mouth shut and not speak to anyone. Especially since I can't work, all I want to do is read or talk to someone to fight the boredom. The unit leader "builds" me, saying, "If you are sick then don't talk. Lie down and rest and be quiet! What illness have you got that makes 'doctrine' come tumbling out of your mouth to irritate other people?"

It's true! I do talk a lot now. Lying around seeing and knowing things makes me ever more discontent, more so even than when I was working. I see things I haven't seen before. When the porridge is ready, I see the Big Brothers going into the economy kitchen to roast and fry fish and eat porridge. Sometimes they tell the economy workers to make small pots of rice for them to eat. After eating their fill, they lie around and sing songs and horse around with each other and have a good time in their shelter.

This is completely contrary to the revolutionary doctrine found in the revolutionary newspapers and magazines: "The collective socialist regime is pure and just, without poor and rich, without exploited persons, without those who are full and those who are not. All are generally equal..." They forbid me from reading the newspapers and magazines because this will allow me to see and understand their improper practices. But I continue to be curious, wanting to understand more clearly about what the doctrines are, and what is actual practice. When I was working, I had no opportunities to read; now that I am resting, I have to try to gain some understanding of the philosophy of their Revolution. In reality, the doctrine is completely opposite from practice. The doctrine speaks of doing good, purity, and justice; but the actual reality is that we are a people living in a pit of suffering, in a pool of blood.

Doctrine of Deceit

1. They say the Old Society exploited   while the New Society is equal
no rich, no poor, no high, no low   they have leveled all to a single class.

2. They kill without sparing or pity   old, young, men, women die and rot
the survivors' hearts quake in terror   afraid, worried, and weeping.

3. Social doctrine is a deceit   while practice is plain to see
killing to make men fear   their own flesh and blood, bones litter the woods.

4. The people suffer with pained faces   without pity they are killed at will
these are but foes, their lives worthless   let them sleep in the dirt, fertilizer for the fields.

5. Magnificent: the socialism of murder   left unchecked, the Khmer race will die out
no more territory to inherit   called no more "Khmer," but "Finished."

CHAPTER 48

The Sorrow of Love Lost

At sunset on the 10th of May was the last time I saw Comrade Ly, near Wat Smach. At that time, she admonished me to frequently visit her at the place where she is stationed. I feel great compassion for her, and I love her very much; but I have not complied with her request at all. There is no young man who does not miss or dream about his beloved. There is no young man who doesn't desire to see his girl's face or engage in flirtatious chatter with her. But I am not destined to do the things that lovers do.

For the first half a month plowing here, we were only able to rest from plowing in the evenings. I should have had time to go visit my beloved; but instead, my team leader sidetracked me into herding cattle with no free time at all. Comrade Ly's camp was little more than half a kilometer from my camp, but I had no excuse to drive the oxen to graze in that direction, as her camp is in the middle of fields where there is nothing but seedling beds and irrigation systems.

I tried to get out from under the oppression of my team leader to find an opportunity to visit my girlfriend; but unfortunately, we moved into the transplanting phase, and the cattle team became busy with plowing both morning and evening, and during the rest hours we now have to lead each of the oxen to graze along the paddy dikes.

During this transplanting season, I often meet women from Comrade Tum's unit, some of whom are transplanting rice in the fields near where I am plowing; but I have not had any occasion to meet Comrade Ly, as she is tasked with soaking and sowing the seeds and caring for the seedlings, all of which is done near her camp. The work of plowing and harrowing to maintain the seedling beds is the task of the cattle teams in the Third Brigade—the brigade of Comrade Sariep and Comrade Hul, my former brigade when farming vegetables at the Trapeang Thmor brick kiln.

I love Comrade Ly and I want her for my life partner, but I am not yet resolved to make an official request, as I perceive that there are still many obstacles on the path along which I wish to travel:

> – My most dangerous rivals in this matter—Comrade An, Comrade Hul, and Comrade Sariep—are currently stationed near Comrade Ly. I

consider the fact that they did not track me down and bring me back to be executed when I left their brigade and came to live with the Fourth Brigade to be an indulgence on their part. Recently I learned from women in Comrade Tum's unit that Comrade Sieng, the young man who had planted vegetables with me at the Trapeang Thmor brick kiln, was taken by Comrade Sariep and clubbed to death here at the Veal Saen Khyal worksite because Comrade Sieng ran away to be with his parents in the Spean Sreng cooperative. Would it be prudent for me to risk confronting these people?

– Comrade Khom and Comrade Pov are also working at the Veal Saen Khyal worksite. Both of them still harbor feelings of affection for me, and they often watch me. It is true that I can't forbid young women from fancying me, but I can do what is necessary to make sure that their hearts are not burned because of me. When I requested Comrade Sadet, I used the pretense that we were old high-school classmates, and that it was to fulfill my sister's wishes. It was for this reason that neither of them was overly heartbroken; they could understand the difficulty of my decision. But now, if I request Comrade Ly, a base person, then certainly they will perceive that I don't pity or care for them. This is a problem about which I am having difficulty making a decision. To resolve the problem, I am trying to wait until they are married first, and then I will take a wife afterward. Now I hear that Comrade Phat, a member of my brigade, has requested Comrade Khom. This news makes me happy, and I pray that they can come together successfully.

– These days I am no longer the Comrade Tuch who farmed vegetables at the Trapeang Thmor brick kiln. Then, I had meat on my bones, and I was Comrade Ly's Prince Charming. But now, I am only a scrawny cowherd. In such a feeble state, what creature would think of loving me?

There is no joy in my heart as my life approaches the end. If I continue to decline, is there anything of value left for my life? Now I am in the same emotional state as when I had just recovered from my illness at the end of 1975. I think, *Live alone, die alone, cause no trouble for anyone else.* But the situation now is different than it was then. Despite my resolution not to make anybody suffer because of me, I am aware that somebody is already suffering because of me, and it is the person I long to meet the most. But I keep asking myself, *While you are in such a scrawny, shaky state, should you allow your girlfriend to see you like this?* I think that I should not because it would cause her to worry twice as much. Though she is a base person, her home village is far from here, and she has no capacity to help me. What is the point of bringing sorrow to the one I love?

But lying still makes me restless, and all I can do is lie around thinking, pondering, and imagining. I miss my sister, I miss my brother, and I miss Comrade Ly, who is right under my nose, so it's a shame not to seek her out. I recall the time when I sat and sewed with her, the times when we stood chatting on the side of the pond, the time when she raised her hand and parted her hair to show me her bruised cheek, the time when she told me, "Come to visit me often, all right?" Comrade Ly must be eager to see me. She must be watching the road for me! No, I have to go visit her! Despite not wanting her to see my unsightly appearance, I still need her to see the affection that I have for her.

Though I only rest, without medicine, my health nevertheless improves little by little, as my strenuous daily labor has been suspended.

On the 10th of July, my unit leader tells me, "Tuch, tomorrow you must return to plowing!"

After eating my midday porridge, I carry a small hatchet and head out for Comrade Ly's camp. The camp is quiet, as many of the women have gone to transplant rice in the field to the south. Here, there are just over ten women, working on planting seedlings. They appear to have just finished eating their porridge. I pass along the causeway in front of the women's shelter toward the east side, trying to get a look into the shelter. I have difficulty recognizing who is sitting and chatting inside the shelter. I walk past the women's shelter without being able to tell which of them is Comrade Ly. I keep walking a short distance and then turn back and walk past the shelter for another pass. A young woman has come out and is standing outside the shelter; Comrade Ly must have seen me, and she is standing and waiting for me! No, it is not Comrade Ly, and it is not Comrade Dy either. Oh, it's Comrade Top!

She smiles at me and exclaims, "Comrade Tuch! Why are you so thin? Are you sick?"

"Yes, I've been sick," I reply to her, slowly.

"What's wrong?" Comrade Top asks me.

"I just have no energy!"

"Where are you headed now?"

"I am headed to pick some *preal* to make a cattle rope, and I took a detour this way. Is Comrade Ly here, Comrade Top?" I ask her.

Comrade Top acts tentative and hesitant and then says, slowly, "Comrade Ly and Comrade Dy ran away back to their village a week ago, Bong."

As if struck by a tornado, I feel dizzy and frantic and almost unable to breathe. Comrade Ly has left me! She has no compassion for me. She doesn't understand the feelings I have for her.

In a stupor and a daze, I say, slowly and quietly, without hope, "A-Ly doesn't pity me."

Comrade Top quickly responds, "That's not how it is, Bong! A-Ly had an unsolvable predicament, and she wanted to meet you, and she sent someone to bring a message to you. But for the past week, we haven't seen you in the rice fields at all!"

Comrade top speaks slowly and painfully, and then falls silent with tension. I was wrong. I was mistaken about my beloved.

"Was something wrong with A-Ly, Comrade Top?"

"Yes. Comrade Sariep requested her, and he was forcing her to decide." She falls silent, and then continues, "We tried to help her think it through, but she didn't know what to do. She lay on her bed and cried and watched the road for you, but she had no hope. She decided to run back to her village. She ran away with tears in her eyes. She told me that if I saw you, to tell you that she said goodbye."

A Tearful Farewell

1. Bong, I am going far away
worse than Teav, taken by the king

such pain cannot be assuaged, my dear
a lady in waiting, parted from Tum, her love.

2. Accused an enemy of the Revolution
refusing to accept as a husband

fighting the Organization's line
a man with the people's blood on his hands.

chorus:
Trapeang Thmor Reservoir, brick-kiln pond
at Wat Smach I swore to love you always

birth of a love unsullied
and you would love only me.

3. Ta Khek, Kok Key, *koks* of evil karma
you watched the road for me till sunset

they made you fear and tremble
then resolved to flee, tears in your eyes.

God only knows the depth of my sorrow. The Lord[1] taught that the suffering caused by losing something you love is equal to the love you had for that thing.

It is true! Only those who have lost their parents know how valuable their parents were in their lives. Before they have lost their parents, some people make an effort to care for them so that harm will not come to them. But others don't understand and are only irritated by those to whom they owe so much. When they have lost them both, then they weep with regret, then they understand how tragic it is to lose them! Then they light incense and prostrate themselves before their graves to show their grief as great as a mountain for those to whom they owe so much.

It is true, we don't know what we have not experienced, or we know it insufficiently. Only those who have experienced being separated from someone they love can understand the level of pain and anguish caused by such a tragedy. Not long ago, I thought that my life was nearly over, and that there was nothing of importance left for it. But now, in the face of this tragedy, with the loss of my beloved, I finally understand how great the pain of such a loss truly is. How great is my regret? Now I understand that it is not only rice and porridge which sustain life, which instill it with beauty; but that I also require my heart, a heart of love. I need love! Now my love has drifted away from me! My love is gone!

The Sorrow of Love Lost

1. My darling, I miss you so
my body so thin and wasting away

I lie in my hammock and think of you
but my heart longs only to meet you, my dear.

2. Night and day I think only of you
left for me in desperation

now you are gone, only your words remain
what meaning, without you?

chorus:
Hateful Mara, you've taken my love
I live in sorrow and sadness

Oh, Indra and Brahma, why not take my life
my heart wounded by the loss of my love.

3. Oh Preah Phirun, please rain down
annihilate all those with loveless hearts

withhold not, flood the earth, destroy the crops
to cleanse the world of sadness.

---

[1] Buddha

CHAPTER 49

Grief

About one hundred meters east of the Fourth Brigade's camp, the mobile units dig another canal running north-to-south, connecting to the canal that runs between Smach and Char Kok Team, and running parallel to the large canal that runs straight to Phnom Liep. But this is a smaller canal, three meters across the top, one meter deep, and one meter wide across the bottom. Up until now, we have farmed rice on land east of this small canal. All of the rice fields within one or two kilometers of camp have been plowed, harrowed, and transplanted. Now we have to drag our plows and harrows to plow and harrow fields to the south, a distance of up to three or four kilometers from camp. Traveling such long distances, leading the oxen and water buffalo along the paddy dikes and across canals, is difficult and causes delays in our work. The brigade chairman authorizes the plowing unit to withdraw from the camp at Or Kambot and make camp on the banks of Or Ta Phal stream starting on 8 July 1978. On the evening of the 10th of July, I go to stay with the plowing unit at the Or Ta Phal camp to resume work.

At Or Ta Phal, the thirty of us crowd together in a sleeping shelter built north-to-south, near Or Ta Phal on the northern bank, along with the young men's battalion tasked with reinforcing the paddy dikes. It is a shelter roofed with fronds, without walls, twenty meters by three-and-a-half meters. The Or Ta Phal camp is east-southeast of the Or Kambot camp. From the Or Kambot camp to the Or Ta Phal camp is about three kilometers. From the Or Ta Phal camp to the large north-south canal east of camp is about half a kilometer. But the topography of the land east of camp is mostly irregular, and we abandon this land, making no effort to settle it. The rice fields that the cattle unit is to plow and harrow are south of the Or Ta Phal camp about one or two kilometers. At noon the economy team brings porridge on shoulder yokes out to us in the paddy. In the evening they bring our food to the Or Ta Phal camp.

The Organization gives directions that "we must increase rice production from three-and-a-half tons to seven tons per hectare. To achieve this goal, the cattle unit must plow quickly and plow well, uniformly and deep, and harrow thoroughly." Everything is based on the dictates of the Organization. As workers, we have only one duty: to be resolved to carry out the plan of the

Organization one hundred percent, and more. At all times we are confronted with words like "attack," "offensive," and "relentless." We have to leave camp while there is faint red light on the eastern horizon and return to camp when this red light returns to show itself again on the western horizon.

Or Ta Phal has a width of twenty meters and is deep. In some spots, the water comes up to my armpits, and in some it is over my head. Every day the cattle unit has to cross Or Ta Phal twice. There is no raft for crossing; we have to cross by swimming. We have a severe shortage of clothing, especially *kramas*. Each of us can hardly even find a *krama* to wipe our face with. The cooperative does not supply them to us because we are a regional mobile unit and must receive our supplies of clothing and food from the regional mobile Organization. We are not fortunate enough to be supplied with clothing regularly from the regional mobile Organization because we are a general-population unit, composed entirely of new people with no base people whatsoever (apart from the leadership). We take great care of our clothing, lest it quickly become tattered and torn and we are no longer able to wear it. As we are far from the eyes of women, and to be extra conservative, when we swim with the cattle across Or Tal Phal, we take off all our clothes and hold them over our heads out of the water and swim across naked. When we reach dry land on the other side, we put them back on.

Because this area has a lot of grassy fields, we get some respite. After eating our midday porridge, we can make time for a nap, assigning shifts of only two or three people per day to herd the cattle. At one-thirty or two o'clock, the cowherds drive the cattle back to the fields to continue our plowing and harrowing.

Early August 1978

After nearly a month, our work at Or Ta Phal comes to an end. The cattle unit is given orders to return to the Or Kambot camp. We are to plow and harrow rice fields east of Kok Key.

Ever since leaving Trapeang Thmor and coming to work the rice fields in Veal Saen Khyal three months ago, I have never once lain eyes on Trapeang Thmor. And I have never received a single bit of news from my sister. People regularly return to the village to visit their wives and children, but they never bring any news to the people back in camp, as they are afraid the Organization will accuse them of "inciting a movement." So they don't dare take any messages from the unit to people living in the cooperative, nor do they dare bring messages from the cooperative to people living in the mobile units. If some message or news from the cooperative is essential, a person returning from the village doesn't dare tell the recipient of the message right away upon returning to camp. They sit on it for five or six days before stealthily passing it to the recipient in secret.

Bong Choar is a middle-aged man residing in Paoy Snuol who went to collect bat guano for fertilizer at Phnom Veng with me. As he was part of the first wave of migration, he went to live with the base people in the village. Currently we work together on the plowing unit, on Comrade Mang's team. Before pulling back our lines from the Or Ta Phal camp, Bong Choar asked permission to visit his sick wife in the village. He has been back at camp for nearly a week now.

This evening we plow for only two hours before running out of land to plow. Not yet having received new orders to plow another location, our unit leader allows us to put away the cattle at about 4 p.m. We lead the cattle to be rinsed and bathed and then lead them to graze along the paddy dikes before taking them back to camp.

Bong Choar approaches me and says, "Tuch! Come sit here with me for a moment."

"Sure, Bong."

I twist up some grass for making into an ox rope and then go sit beside Bong Choar. He says to me, "Tuch, have you ever asked permission to go visit the village?"

"No Bong, I haven't. I haven't dared to ask."

"Have you ever heard any news of your sister Oun?"

"No, I have never had any news from her at all. I don't know whether she is on a mobile deployment or in the cooperative. When you went to the village did you see my sister?"

Bong Choar remains silent and says nothing, glancing around. Then he says quietly, "Tuch, don't tell anybody, all right?"

"Of course."

"When I returned to the village, your sister was working digging tubers in the cooperative. When she saw me, she said that when I return to camp, I should let her know and she would send some dried tubers back for you."

This news makes me salivate, and I quickly ask Bong Choar, "So did you bring some tubers back? I'm so hungry for some tubers!"

"No. I never met Oun again."

This response puzzles me. "Where did she go? Did she go back out on mobile deployment?"

Bong Choar remains silent and lets out a long sigh. He looks me in the face and says softly, "Oun has disappeared."

This answer fills me with dread. "Is this true, Bong? Has my sister been disappeared? Is my sister dead?"

In a state of delirium, drained of strength, my mind spinning, about to faint, I bend over and stare at the grass. Bong Choar places his left arm on my shoulder and says, gently, "It's true. Oun has disappeared. But I don't know what happened. You should ask permission to visit home so you can find out for sure. But don't let them know that I told you!"

"Of course. Thank you, Bong."

I just recently ran into my youngest brother Samorn. We had been apart for more than seven months. He returned from harvesting rattan and came to work here at this worksite. He is staying at the young men's camp far off to the south of my camp. I just met my brother again, and now I have been parted from my sister. Oh, my fate!

At dusk, after leading the oxen back to camp and tying them up for the evening, I walk over to see Mea Chout to ask permission to visit the village. I approach him and say softly, "Mea, may I have permission to visit home?"

Surprised, Mea Chout says forcefully, "Go home? Hell no! You can't. They are waging a transplanting offensive, and we haven't finished plowing land for them to transplant on. Look, today we put the cattle away early, and meanwhile tomorrow they have no land ready to transplant!"

Mea Chout turns around and calls out to us, who are busy tying up our oxen and water buffalo in their respective places, "Tomorrow the plowing unit will rise in the dark and pull the plows over to plow at Ta Khek! If not, then we will hold up the work of others! Today you barely plowed anything before wrapping up for the day. Nobody listened, and nobody asked anybody. If you had no more land to plow, then why didn't you ask me? Tomorrow, if you haven't plowed enough land to enable them to transplant, then don't put away your plows until you have!"

Mea Chout stops speaking, and then I plead with him again, "Mea! I'm asking you to go home just this once, Mea! I will only ask you this once and I'll never ask you again!"

"Damn, are you deaf, Tuch? You have no wife or children, so I have no idea why you're asking to visit the village."

"I have very important business there."

"What business could be more important than your revolutionary labor?"

He should not be so strict with me. I have worked with great diligence and have never once asked to visit the village. If I don't tell him the truth, he will not understand my concern, and will not give me permission to go.

"My sister has disappeared, Mea."

"If she has disappeared, then will you find her there?"

Either Mea Chout has answered without thinking, or he doesn't understand the great pain of someone whose sibling has been taken away to be killed. I am in anguish with regret for my sister's loss, and I am in anguish over being reprimanded. Tears begin to roll down my cheeks. I look down and clench my teeth and keep my mouth closed, not responding.

My tears have made Mea Chout aware of what is boiling up inside of my breast, and of his own inappropriate words. He says slowly, "How did you find out about this, Tuch?"

"A comrade in the south camp just returned from the cooperative and he told me when I was herding oxen, Mea."

"Perhaps he was lying to you?"

"No, Mea."

"So what do you want to go for, Tuch?"

"To take care of her things left behind at the house, Mea."

Mea Chout stands there thinking, and then says, "All right. Tomorrow you can go for one day. Give your ox to the team leader so he can find someone to plow in your place, all right?

"Yes, thank you Mea!"

Tonight I don't sleep at all. While I believe the words of Bong Choar, I still feel like my sister is not dead, and I still harbor some hope that tomorrow I will see her face.

For good or ill, my sister is my sister. We were both born from the womb of the same mother. We used to play and fight with one another like all children do. When we were small, we used to go down to pick *trakuon* and water hyacinth flowers and hunt for snails in Boeng Trabek lake, then carry them on our heads to sell at Steung Mean Chey Market and Tuol Tumpung Market, just the two of us.

One day as we were walking back home, I stepped on a pile of ashes that someone selling roasted bananas had dumped out. Hot coals burned blisters all over the sole of my foot, and I couldn't walk. My sister carried me on her back from Tuol Tumpung Market to our house.

When her little brothers went to school, my sister sat making clay piggy banks with Mom and never got to go to school like other children. She sacrificed for the education of her little brothers, the same as my parents did. Even during this time, my sister has tried to do everything for her brothers, to protect her brothers, for the lives of her brothers.

No! My sister is not dead! My sister is not dead! We just parted from one another not very long ago! She gave me crushed sour *krasang* fruit. She stood watching me run across the rice fields…

Though I got permission to visit the village, the brigade chairman never issues letters of passage (travel documents) to us. We have to run and slither and dodge all on our own, traveling in constant worry that *chhlops* stationed along the road will arrest us.

At 9 a.m., after the porridge is cooked and I have finished eating, I depart. The distance by road from the Or Kambot camp to my village is nearly twenty kilometers, and there are many *chhlop* stations along the way. I carry an ox's throat harness and cattle rope on my left shoulder and carry a whip in my right hand and take long, rapid strides. After passing through Smach, I leave the road and walk along the paddy dikes across rice fields that have yet to be plowed or transplanted, to reduce the distance and avoid being detained.

The vast plain of rice fields stretches out before me. Along the length of the road from Prey Moan to Phnom Srok, roofs of mobile camp shelters and locals' houses appear indistinctly and sporadically between the green treetops: the Kok Rumchek camp, the Kok Kakah camp, the Kok Roessei camp, Kok Krakhop, Kok Reach, Kok Kraol. I have to cut across the fields at an angle toward Kok Kraol, and then travel along the levee road beside the canal that connects from Trapeang Thmor Reservoir.

Pooled rainwater covers the fields. Some paddies have already been transplanted, while others are in the process of being plowed, harrowed, and transplanted, one by one. Flocks of herons and egrets come down and spread out over the fields, walking around in the water looking for fish, crabs, and snails. When they see me coming near, they startle and take flight, great white flocks scattering into the sky, which makes me worried that somebody will take notice of my hasty journey.

Sometimes I have to avoid a paddy where rice farmers are busy working, bent over, intent on their work transplanting rice; or paddies where oxen or water buffalo charge through the field, splashing water.

My journey to the village encounters many dangers and fears. I have never taken the risk to pass through so many obstacles before; but now, no matter how daunting the impediments, I have to press on, move forward, and reach home! I have to see my sister's face!

But the truth remains the truth, even though I doggedly think that my sister has not died, has not disappeared; that I am destined to find her sitting in the doorway of the house, staring out at me, calling me up into the house, as when I came to visit her last year. The power of hope, born of imagination, helps me to reach the house quickly. But the collapse of my emotions when I encounter the hopeless truth makes my arms and legs go weak and the strength drain from my body, and I collapse in the doorway of the hut.

There is nothing left in the house for me to take care of.[1] But I wanted to visit the hut, to see the place where my sister was arrested and taken away to be killed, to make certain that she really is dead, that I am now truly bereft of my big sister. Is there anything left for me? For my life?

In only the blink of an eye, the members of my large family have died or been killed until we are nearly extinct! Is this fate, or sins, or crimes of injustice? What sins did my little brother or my big sister commit, that they were so easily taken away to be killed? What did my sister do wrong? Was it so serious that it

---

[1] The small suitcase containing his mother's ashes (see pages 86, 88), previously kept in this hut by his sister, was no longer there. The ashes were never seen again.

could not be forgiven, that the Organization had to arrest and execute a woman in this way?

This broken-down little hut, with a broken, dilapidated roof, abandoned by its owners (Bong Nho is away on mobile deployment) can tell me nothing. And there are hardly any people in the village. Those with any strength have all gone out to work in the rice fields. Those who remain are old or disabled and unable to work. They are reluctant to tell me what happened to my sister. Nevertheless, I am able to learn some things. I learn enough to piece together the sordid story:

Comrade Sambath is not a base person from this district. But because he often came and went on business in Paoy Char subdistrict during the old society, he has many friends in this area. After being evacuated here, because of his connections to the area, the Organization came to consider him a cadre, like a base person.

Currently, Comrade Sambath is the deputy head of the fertilizer unit in the Fourth Brigade, with me. His wife lives in the village with other evacuees, and her house is east of my sister's. As the wife of a cadre, she has never been required to go on mobile work details and is allowed to plant vegetables near her house.

One evening, as my sister returned from transplanting rice, she picked a handful of Comrade Sambath's wife's *trakuon* (the owner was not home) to take and munch on. Then she grabbed a yoke of watering cans and went to fetch water from the pond west of the village. When Comrade Sambath's wife came home, she noticed that somebody had picked her *trakuon,* and she cursed and vilified the culprit and reported it to the village *chhlops.* The *chhlops* pay careful attention to the wife of a cadre. When my sister returned to the house with her water, the *chhlops* arrested her and tied her up and marched her away to the Paoy Char subdistrict office. They next day they took my sister away and killed her.

This news fills me with sorrow and regret for the life of my sister. I remain dissatisfied and continue to think that they should not have killed my sister for such a small fault. Though I don't wail, I am devastated, pained in my breast, like the young woman who keened and wept before the body of her younger brother whose body was hung from the *krasang* tree. I imagine my sister helping me onto the tractor; my sister visiting me at the Phnom Srok district hospital; my sister weeping and wailing when the Organization arrested and tied me up, kicking me and dragging me into the office. My sister startled the whole village with her wailing. She was upset and afraid that they would kill her little brother. But when they came to arrest her, neither of her two brothers knew about it, did not feel fear or concern, did not weep or wail. My sister died alone without any of her family knowing, a solitary, lonely figure.

How did they torture my sister before they killed her? How did she suffer when they tied her up and deprived her of food at the Paoy Char cooperative? What method did they use to kill my sister? Normally they hit people with a hoe blade or a piece of bamboo. How much pain did my sister endure? How did she convulse before the life left her body? She must have suffered, and she must have called out for her brothers, to tell us of her suffering before she died...

Grief

Tuch! M'orn! I hurt so much, my brothers!

1. A handful of *trakuon* for my life
they tie me up without thought

I never imagined such a heavy price
they bind my body in pain and torment.

2. Bound and starved and famished
tied tightly, body swollen

however thirsty, no mercy
mosquitoes biting my flesh all night.

chorus:
The Paoy Char cooperative kills me
sweat pouring like blood, such agony

ties and curses me and leaves me in the sun
ashamed of those who pass on the road.

3. At night owls cry, bees enter the hive
to Paoy Trach, the blood-red *kok* of death

while I am lead away
my brothers, there lies my corpse.

Chapter 50

The Black Night

We live like frogs in a well. Apart from some revolutionary magazines distributed to cadres, which boastfully describe the accomplishments that the Revolutionary Organization has achieved in some model cooperatives, we have no access to any kind of information at all. We live in a world of darkness, without light of any kind, apart from the daily rising and setting of the sun. No good news or information reaches us. On the contrary, the only news we ever receive is alarming news, frightful news, sad news.

Who are the leaders in charge of the country these days? We have never known. What are they doing this for? To where are they leading us? Nobody knows. All we know is that the Revolutionary Organization instructs us to work hard, to temper ourselves and struggle in our labors, and to properly follow the revolutionary path in hopes that we might be spared and live to the see Glory of the Revolution. And what is the Glory of the Revolution? Nobody knows, nobody understands, and nobody dares ask them to explain exactly what it is they call the "Glory of the Revolution."

As I sit holding the end of the ox's lead rope while it grazes, I often ponder to myself: Can the Organization possibly lead the country to prosper and become strong by torturing its own people like this? I often see young soldiers whom the Organization has released from the army returning to the cooperatives. If they do this, what happens if we are invaded by a neighboring country? Where will they find the strength to repel them? If this were to happen, I think that we would be cornered, and that we are only awaiting the day of our destruction. But these complex thoughts belong to me alone, as those around me don't take their thoughts to such delirious extremes. They think only of what they are facing right now, today, and that is the fear of losing their lives.

A Khmer proverb says, "life lived, things obtained," which means that only if you have life can you have all else. If you lose your life, can you expect to support and defend the life of the nation? But even if we were to be released from the life-and-death struggles of society and the nation, we would still be in a state of being doubted and mistrusted by the Revolutionary Organization.

Late August 1978

Lately the Organization has been conducting many propaganda meetings to inform us of the campaign to purge the enemies of the Revolution. The targets of this purge are the CIA, the KGB, and agents of Vietnam.

CIA is a term that we are all familiar with, but *KGB* is a new term that we have never heard before, and we don't know what it is. But we all sit with our mouths closed, listening quietly, filled with worry, imagining some inexorable peril about to come upon us. The Organization instructs us to come forward and confess if any of us are involved with any of these three entities. Those who confess will be pardoned by the Organization. But nobody comes forward to confess. Everyone is in a state of shock and paralysis. We have never imagined that such a thing could happen at this time. Because all those who have been suspected or known by the Organization to be a danger to the Revolution have already been arrested one-by-one and taken away by the Organization to be killed long ago, ever since the first evacuation.

As for the Vietnamese, they are not to be found on Cambodian territory. During the time of the Khmer Republic, Lon Nol arranged with South Vietnam to send all the Vietnamese back to their country.

This open announcement by the Organization makes all of us feel panicked and anxious, not knowing who will be taken away and killed by the Organization on the pretense that they are a secret enemy.

We hear that the fertilizer unit is digging large pits east of Ta Khek to make fertilizer. Is this just preparation for a mass execution?

This purge campaign is being carried out generally, both in the cooperatives and in the mobile units. But they begin the purge primarily in the cooperatives first, as there it is easier to flee than in the mobile units.

Bong Heng was born in Kampuchea Kraom.[1] He is about forty years old, and a member of the Fourth Brigade's fertilizer unit. Bong Heng, as well as other people from Kampuchea Kraom, are all very worried right now. Their minds are on their wives and children living back in the village.

---

[1] the name (meaning "Lower Cambodia") of a region in southern Vietnam, around the Mekong Delta, that once belonged to Cambodia and is still heavily populated by ethnic Khmers

One day, Bong Heng gets permission to go visit his wife and children in Paoy Snuol. This is the day the Organization begins the purge of the cooperative, the day of death for his family.

After dark, after eating dinner with his children and wife, Bong Heng extinguishes the lantern and goes to bed, like the other villagers, all of whom are in a state of dread and worry. It is a night of a waning moon, and the sky is devoid of light. Though they lie in bed, the villagers cannot sleep, as their ears listen for any strange sounds or footfalls in the night. At nine o'clock, they hear the footfalls of a large group of people walking through the village. It is the thing they dread, as the *chhlops* walk through the village and knock on the door of any villager the Organization has targeted for destruction.

Somebody knocks on Bong Heng's door. Every member of the family is bound by the *chhlops* and marched to the execution site with other villagers, all of them bound. The bonds at Bong Heng's hands are not very tight; while he walks along in the procession, he loosens the knot little by little. When they reach the pit where they are to be killed, the knot comes loose. Because the night is so dark, the *chhlops* cannot tell. When they sit down, Bong Heng throws himself down flat on the ground and begins to slither away and hide himself behind some tall grass. Bong Heng escapes, while his wife and children are all clubbed and tossed into the pit.

The next day at about noon, Bong Heng returns to the camp at Or Kambot and recounts this horrifying tale to the brigade leadership, asking them to hide him. Mea Pov agrees to help protect him.

The rest of us, who learn about this through whispers passed along, are terrified and sorry for Bong Heng, and we regret that he came and showed himself in the tiger's lair. But there is nothing we can do, there is nowhere we can crawl away to. Death is near us and among us. If there were a place to run to, we would certainly run. Now we are all like cattle being led to the slaughterhouse: death is before the cattle and they bow their heads and shed tears as they file quietly toward death, without startling, and without frolicking as they had once done when they cavorted and grazed in the fields. For the cattle understand that there is no point and no hope in resisting now.

One week later, this dreadful terror comes to the mobile units farming rice in Veal Saen Khyal.

Most of us who keep the cattle don't know how to twist cattle ropes. On my team, Comrade Chuch is the one who makes all the cattle ropes we use. Those of us who don't know how to twist the ropes walk around and collect the bark from *preal* shrubs while we herd the cattle, and we bring this to Comrade Chuch to twist into ropes for us. This evening, Comrade Chuch has twisted two new cattle ropes for me, and he brings them to me to replace my old shabby one.

After we eat the evening meal, the sky grows dark and threatens to rain. Each of us seeks out our own sleeping spot. We lie conversing and chatting about this and that, and some people start to snore. At about eight o'clock we suddenly hear word that the rain is causing heavy flooding, and some of the paddies are filling with water so deep it is covering the newly transplanted seedlings, which could cause the rice to spoil. The brigade leader wakes the fertilizer unit and the paddy-dike unit to go out and work in the middle of the night.

The cattle unit has no obligation to go with them, but we can't sleep. We feel uneasy, as going out to work in the pitch-black dark of night does not seem very plausible. Our minds dwell heavily on the Organization's purge campaign.

Only certain people are assigned by the Organization to go out and work. Bong Kae is from Kampuchea Kraom, about thirty years old or so, with a large sturdy frame, and slightly wavy hair. He is a man who is unusually good at enduring heat. When they distribute porridge, Bong Kae collects his porridge and mixes it with water and then simmers it in a powdered milk can (*Guigo* brand). When the porridge comes to a slow boil, he alternates between taking sips from the can and putting it back to simmer. Bong Kae keeps cattle on Bong No's team, and he is also assigned by the Organization to go out and work tonight.

Before the meeting has ended, Comrade Mang, my team leader, comes into the shelter, which is lit by a small kerosene lamp. He walks up to my hammock and asks me quietly, "Tuch! Do you still have your old cattle rope?"

"Yes," I answer quickly.

"All right, give it to me!"

I reach up and remove the cattle rope coiled and hanging above the head of my hammock and hand it to Comrade Mang immediately. He walks away, and my heart pounds and races. I am so frightened I get goosebumps and chills up my spine. He must be taking my rope to tie up a human being tonight. I don't dare get up from my hammock and go outside the shelter, as I am petrified, and I understand clearly that those going out to work are certainly being taken to be killed tonight.

At about nine o'clock, the brigade chairman and several unit leaders lead the work team through the darkness heading south. I don't know how many people have left tonight, and nobody knows for sure. We don't dare ask each other, as each of us is silent, his heart pounding, unable to open his mouth, fearing for the very existence of his friends.

Three or four days later, we find out that on that Black Night, in each brigade, approximately ten people were taken away and killed. They killed them all at once so that nobody would know or suspect it beforehand. Bong Heng, who had escaped being killed with his wife and children at the cooperative, was also taken away and killed that night.

It is true: nobody can escape death! We are fish trapped in a bamboo cage. Now nobody dares to show compassion or disobey the Organization's orders.

The dead are free from worry while the living are shaken, their hearts broken, living in sorrow for the loss of their companions. Comrade Hean was a plowman on my team. He had just gotten married half a month ago. His wife was born in Kampuchea Kraom. Comrade Hean had built a little hut to live in apart from the rest of us, but his wife couldn't come and stay overnight with him regularly because they had separate jobs. She lived with the women's brigade camped near Kok Key. Every three or four days she was allowed to come and spend the night with her husband.

A brand-new couple, the lovers head-over-heels in love, enjoying the sweet nectar of romance. This is the birthright of nature, the desire of all lovers.

Every evening that she was allowed to come spend the night with her husband, Comrade Hean's wife would wrap up her rice ration and bring it to eat with him. She would save more for her husband than for herself. It is a remarkable act for any wife to sacrifice for her husband during this time. Comrade Hean loved his wife very much. He was always cheerful and smiling as he would get ready and watch the road for his wife at dusk whenever they had a date to meet.

But after the Black Night, Comrade Hean never again saw so much as a shadow of his wife coming at sunset. Her shadow had been consumed by the darkness on that night of death.

How deep is Comrade Hean's anguish? I only recently suffered from the loss of my beloved, but my love had only reached a mutual understanding and had not progressed to cohabitation and physical affection. It was a love that had not yet been consummated, and my sorrow is surely not as great as that of Comrade Hean.

Comrade Hean is deep in sadness, like a man who has lost his soul, oblivious, not speaking, like a crazy person. Who would not weep, who would not sorrow, if his beloved wife, held close to his breast, was dragged away from him and killed? We all feel great compassion for Comrade Hean. Even the brigade chairman and the unit leaders, the ones who wielded the clubs to kill the victims, are unable to keep themselves from feeling compassion for Comrade Hean.

Comrade Hean goes crazy and becomes lost in his own mind, no longer thinking, no longer afraid of dying. One day, after eating the midday meal, Comrade Hean leaves his oxen with a friend to watch and then disappears from camp. At about two o'clock in the afternoon, Comrade Hean suddenly reappears in camp dragging a chain around his ankles, dust rising up behind him. He runs to the brigade chairman and begs him to help. Mea Pov tells a man who had been a clock repairman to remove Comrade Hean's chain. A half hour later, suddenly two *chhlops* from Ta Khek come into camp riding on horses and asking for Comrade Hean. They have followed his trail and found that it ended here at the camp. But Mea Pov denies having seen him or knowing anything about it. The cooperative *chhlops* are furious, and they gallop away frustrated.

When he left camp, Comrade Hean had gone and stolen a fish from one of Ta Khek village's fish traps in the middle of the day and was caught by the village *chhlops*. As he was part of the mobile force, the village only had the right to punish him. The *chhlops* took a chain and attached it to both ankles and then locked the end of the chain around a pole about three meters tall in the sunlight in front of the *chhlop* office. Taking advantage of the *chhlops* napping, Comrade Hean climbed the pole, pulling after him the end of the chain that was locked around the pole, removed it at the top, then ran away back to camp.

After being released from his chain, Comrade Hean seems to come back to his senses, and the sorrow and anguish from the loss of his beloved wife subsides.

In the middle of September, the cattle unit withdraws from the Or Kambot camp again and goes to stay in a camp east of Kok Key, about three kilometers south of the Or Kambot camp.

CHAPTER 51

Manioc Peels

Our daily food rations are thick porridge in the morning and cooked rice in the evening. These are the only flavors our tongues have known since coming to work at the Veal Saen Khyal worksite. We have no familiarity with any kind of snacks, fruit, dessert, etc. The food rations are insufficient, and the nutritional content is unvarying, and this causes me to fantasize about other kinds of flavors and foods. I especially crave foods that my eyes see but that my tongue is not destined to touch. I constantly salivate like a dog that has seen a piece of meat. My heart yearns for these things, while my body walks away filled with regret.

The food that other people eat most often to supplement the rations of rice and porridge from the Organization, which my eyes often see, and my nose often smells, is maniocs. I don't know where they get them from, but I often see some people eating them. Before I fell sick from overexertion, I would often encounter base young women sitting in groups of two or three eating roasted maniocs on the paddy dike when I would return from plowing at midday. I would stare shamelessly at their mouths chewing the tubers. I would stare at the manioc peels that they had discarded nearby on the paddy dikes. I felt not unlike a beggar who sits quietly biding his time, waiting for restaurant guests to get up and leave their table before moving in to collect the leftover food scraps. But I am not fortunate enough to be able to sit and wait for these guests to leave like the beggar. I regret the loss of those manioc peels, I want those manioc peels, I want to open my mouth and ask for them, I want to reach out my hand and pick them up. But something in me restrains me and tells me to curb my impulse, and I swallow my spit and keep walking past them with regret.

I feel so ashamed! I am afraid the base women will ridicule me and say that "this evacuee young man is so hungry he'll pick up discarded manioc peels and eat them!" In fact, I *am* hungry, very hungry, actually *that* hungry, and if they were to so ridicule me, they would not be wrong. But my shame covers up the truth, restrains me from doing something that my scruples find inappropriate.

If I don't see them, I don't really think much about them, and I don't crave them very much. But if I see somebody eating a manioc, I can hardly restrain my cravings and it takes significant effort to control myself.

One evening, before eating my evening rice at the Or Kambot camp, I see Comrade Chuop holding and eating boiled manioc. I want it so badly! Unable to stand it anymore, I decide to divide my rice in half down the middle of the dish and plead with Comrade Chuop to trade me a manioc. Comrade Chuop agrees to trade me a boiled manioc about the size of a young child's wrist. It does not satisfy my craving, but it does alleviate it to some degree.

Before we moved to the camp east of Kok Key village, the Organization permitted the plowing unit to tie our cattle up near Kok Key, leaving only two people behind to sleep overnight and guard them for the night, while the others walked back to spend the night at the Or Kambot camp. Those whose turn it was to spend the night with the cattle were able to eat their rice earlier than the others, at about three thirty or four, and then come collect the cattle when we had finished plowing and harrowing.

One evening it was my turn to spend the night watching the cattle, along with Bong Son.[1] Though the work is difficult, Bong Son has a healthy body and has not gotten very skinny. He normally wears a long-sleeve white shirt, shorts down to his knees, and a sugar-palm-frond hat. At about four o'clock, we met up at the shelter east of Kok Key. Bong Son had an ox's throat harness and tether rope on his right shoulder, held a rattan whip in his left hand, and held a little old teapot in his right hand. We chatted, and then Bong Son took the teapot and place it front of him, opened the lid, took out a manioc, and said, "Here is a boiled manioc. Tuch, go ahead and have some!" handing it to me.

Dear Lord! Something I had not imagined would happen, happened. During these times nobody has ever shared their food with me. Bong Son was the first person to offer me a morsel of food in these circumstances of tremendous hunger. I accepted the manioc with excitement and said to him softly, "Bong, where did you get maniocs from?"

"Go ahead and eat, and then I'll tell you."

We ate maniocs in silence, and then a bit later Bong Song asked me, "Tuch, have you ever gone to steel maniocs?"

"No, I never have. I've never dared! I've never even dared enter the locals' villages, and I am unfamiliar with them."

---

[1] Author's note: "Mr. Roat Saroeun, former professor at the School of Fine Arts and current president of a branch of the Cambodian company Khmer Chamnan"

"I could see that you are a gentle person, and I thought you probably hadn't stolen maniocs, so I boiled these and brought them to share with you. The people in our unit mostly steal maniocs from the cooperative's field on the west bank of the river. They go in groups of two or three and get from half a sack to almost a full sack each time. They hide them in the woods and eat on them for more than a week."

"Gee, I never knew about this, Bong!"

"Everyone hides it so that others won't find out, for fear that they will report them."

When we were at Or Kambot, one day I was wading across the north-south canal near the camp, and I stepped on a manioc peel. Now I understand: the people who steal maniocs throw the peels into the water so nobody else will know.

"Where did you get these maniocs? Did you steal them?"

"Yes, I went and stole them out of the cooperative's field at Kok Key."

"You went and risked your life and brought these maniocs to share with me. How can I thank you? I will remember this day always!"

"I've only gone stealing twice, Tuch. Last night I had a dream that my father scolded me, and I think I won't go stealing anymore."

"I've been tied up before, and I'm afraid of being killed, so I don't dare steal!"

"Now I'm afraid like you, Tuch."

I was thrilled by Bong Son's kindness and thanked him for telling me the truth about what is going on in the brigade. That is why I so often see people carrying teapots with them when they herd oxen or go into the forest. Maybe that is why they have been able to endure the arduous labor without wasting away and becoming severely, chronically fatigued as I have.

Living in the camp east of Kok Key, things are a bit easier for the cattle unit, as we are spared from walking several kilometers back and forth. An economy team member carries porridge and rice out to us at Kok Key with a shoulder yoke both morning and evening. But I am still struggling, as my body has not had any opportunities to become well fed as others have, and constant exhaustion and fatigue begin to plague me again. It is because I have no supplementary food to eat as the others do. Now I start to think about the cooperative's manioc field in Kok Key that Bong Son told me about.

Our camp is near the southern end of Kok Key. I have never entered this village, and I am unfamiliar with the ins-and-outs of the village's geography.

One day, after eating my midday porridge, I decide to take a walk to find the manioc field. I stop by the cooperative's dining pavilion near the south end of the village. The villagers have all finished eating. They eat porridge like the mobile units, but they mix manioc pieces in with their porridge. It appears that they have so much to eat that some bits of manioc have spilled onto the ground and been left there. I pick up two bits of manioc slightly larger than my big toe. I use the hem of my shirt to wipe the dirt off them and then hide them in my mouth. Nobody sees, as the villagers have all gone home now, and all is quiet.

I walk westward toward the riverside, where there are sparse trees growing. It is late September, and the Rumduol River is flowing heavily, the color of dirt, flooded to the tops of the banks. I stand watching the water flow, staring at the manioc field on the opposite side of the river.

Some maniocs have already been pulled. The field is clear, and manioc plants have been heaped into piles. I don't see anybody in the manioc field.

The river is about thirty meters wide. Along the riverbanks reeds grow here and there, half submerged in the water. I stand thinking, *Am I strong enough to swim across this river?* I take off my shirt and hide it in a clump of grass, leaving only my shorts. I wrap up a long cloth sack with the small hatchet that I use to drive the plow hitch pin and hold them over my head with my right hand. I swim across the river. It is a little bit difficult, as the water flows rapidly, but I make it to the other bank. I climb out and walk across the part of the field where the maniocs have already been pulled and head toward the piles of manioc plants. I inspect the stumps where the tubers were attached to the stalk of the plant, but it is hopeless, as the tuber stumps have a hard rind like wood. These maniocs plants appear to have been pulled four or five days ago.

I have come here with the intent of salvaging the stumps of the tubers, not to steal maniocs themselves. But now there is nothing to salvage. Should I steal some maniocs? No! I don't dare! I am too afraid of dying. I circle around the piled-up manioc plants, from one pile to another. I encounter a pile of manioc peels. Due to the heat of the sun, the hard outer peels have separated and curled back away from the thick inner peels. I sit down and open the mouth of the sack and scrape manioc peels into it, packing them tight, and then pick a vine and tie it around the sack's mouth.

I slink away from this place. I swim across the river with my right arm, my left arm holding the sack in the water. At the middle of the river, I turn over and swim on my back, floating with only my face emerging from the surface of the water. I float with the current, the sack getting heavier and pulling me down under the water. I choke on water, I kick my legs hard, I paddle hard with my right arm. I am so tired! My head goes under and comes back up repeatedly, but I refuse to let go of the sack. Now I am swimming under water. My hand touches a reed, and my feelings surge with excitement. I have escaped death! I am near the bank. I clutch a bundle of three or four reeds and cling to them for support while I collect my strength. I kick my legs and swim through the reeds to the riverbank. I lie face-down on the bank with half of my body out of the water. I am so tired!

After resting and recovering my strength, I get up and dump out the manioc peels and clean them off, rinsing them in water, then head back to camp. I boil the peels, then lay them out to dry on the eaves of the shelter about a meter above the ground. Once they dry, if you roast and eat them, they taste a bit like crackers. When I have finished, I go out to do my evening plowing.

When I return from the fields, I hurry to check on my manioc peels. My God! Half my manioc peels are gone. I am extremely disappointed, deeply regretting my lost manioc peels, regretting my wrong-headed thinking. I had thought that nobody is as hungry as I am, nobody would eat manioc peels as I would. This is why I was careless and made no effort to hide my manioc peels but laid them out openly and boastfully for all to see.

Why did somebody have to be so free and loose with their hands, taking my manioc peels, without any consideration or compassion for me, who spent so much effort, nearly dying, to obtain those manioc peels? If they are hungry, if they want some, why don't they go collect some like I did? Or do they think they are such worthless objects that it would only denigrate them if they were to collect them? If collecting them denigrates a person, then how dignified is it to steal and eat such worthless things?

It is true: Some people are so afraid of abasing themselves, and yet commit base acts. They are afraid of sin, and yet they commit sin. *I won't beg. I'd rather steal*, they think. Is this the behavior of dignified people?

I am filled with regret! I regret the strength that I spent, and I regret the peels that were lost! I am so angry I can't restrain myself, and I cry out, complaining out loud to myself, "Damn it! Who took and ate my manioc peels?"

Mea Chout, lying on a hammock inside the shelter, hears me and calls out, "What is it, Tuch?"

"Somebody took and ate most of my manioc peels, Mea!" I reply to Mea Chout with a drawn-out whiney voice to illicit sympathy.

But Mea Chout has no sympathy and scolds me instead. "I don't know what you're on about, Tuch. Something that people just throw away, and you're complaining about it!"

Good Lord! Those who are full do not understand the hungry, and the rich truly do not understand the feelings of the poor. Or they pretend not to know, anyway. Do they not know that I have nothing to eat? Do they not know that I am hungry? As leaders, they should know, they must know, but somehow they don't know because they are tyrants. They know only about using people, forcing us to work, making us exert ourselves; but they take no thought and pay no attention to whether we have enough to eat or not, or whether we live or die.

Is this what they call the revolution to eliminate poverty, to eradicate exploitation from human society?

CHAPTER 52

Cattle Unit Economy Worker

Among the thirty members of the cattle unit, I am the thinnest and frailest. I begin to deteriorate again for the second time. Faced with such fragile health, the leaders of the unit either take pity on me, or they fear wasting my strength by allowing me to rest outright, as on the 15th of October they decide to send me to work as an economy worker at the Or Kambot camp, and they remove the cattle unit's economy worker from there and send him to manage cattle in my stead at the Kok Key camp.

The word *economy* has a meaning not unlike that under a free-market regime. That is, it is something that governs the sources of life of the unit and the society. But it differs in that in the economy of a free-market regime, they manage a currency with paper money, whereas *economy* in the communist regime of this damned Democratic Kampuchea refers to the cooks—the people who govern rice, salt, and *prahok*. (We have no fish sauce, MSG, sugar, pepper, or garlic.)

The economy team of the Fourth Brigade keeps its supplies and does its cooking in a kitchen shed roofed with thatch grass, about four by six meters, only half of which (four by three meters) is enclosed by walls, on the east, south, and west. The economy team has four members: Comrade Kun, team leader; Comrade Da,[1] economy worker for the fertilizer unit; Bong Et,[2] economy worker for the paddy-dike unit; and me.

The economy team works in the shade and avoids direct sunlight but endures heat from the cookfires. There are no pans; all we have to cook with are big iron pots resting on cookfires supported by stones. We must cook food to support more than one hundred people.

Whether cooking rice or porridge, we must cook and then dump each batch out into large metal bowls over and over to free up the pot to cook another batch. Dumping out the cooked rice is a little bit easier than the porridge, as the crust doesn't stick to the bottom of the pot. When we knock the pot it all falls

---

[1] Author's note: "Currently Dr. Ket Lysottha at the Japanese hospital." *Japanese hospital* is a reference to the National Maternal and Child Health Center, run by the Japan International Cooperation Agency in Phnom Penh.

[2] Author's note: "now a comedian called Neay Haeum"

out, as long as we soak the bottom of the pot in water briefly after removing it from the cookfire. The porridge is easy to pour out, but it's hard to scrub the bottom of the pot before we start to cook the next batch.

As for soup, we cook only two pots and then divide it between the three units, reckoned according to the number of people in each unit. Generally, we mostly cook sour soup with *trakuon*, sour soup with water lily, or sour soup with gourds and tomatoes. Occasionally, we get turnips to boil.

The four of us work together to prepare the vegetables and cook the soup, but Comrade Kun, the leader, mostly does easier jobs than the other three of us. We don't have to bother to go out looking for vegetables, as the oxcart driver brings them to us, but our work is very busy, with no spare time.

In the mornings, the workers go to the fields, while the economy team begins preparations for cooking. We have to rush to cook the soup in time to be ready by nine or nine-thirty. Then we get ready to distribute the porridge and soup to each unit. Comrade Kun is in charge of measuring the porridge and dividing up the soup. We use a metal soup bowl with a diameter of eighteen centimeters and a depth of five centimeters as a measuring device to dish out the porridge and rice. As the porridge is thick, we measure it by dipping the metal soup bowl in and dishing out the porridge. Then we take a ladle or piece of bamboo and scrape around the mouth of the bowl. If after we have divided up the porridge for all three units there is any porridge left, we add one additional bowlful for every five or six people, depending on how much porridge is left. But before we divide it up for the units, Comrade Kun dishes up porridge into slightly larger bowls and sets them aside for the ten cadres, who get three to four rations apiece (on these, we don't scrape the mouth of the bowl), as well as our own rations. Those of us on the economy team get full just from all the tasting here and there. But we are prepared to eat and renew our strength later, after we have returned from carrying the porridge on shoulder yokes out to the workers in the rice fields.

In the evenings, the fertilizer unit and the paddy-dike unit mostly return to camp to eat their porridge, so the economy workers don't have to bother to carry the porridge out to the fields. The cattle unit, on the other hand, has to have their porridge brought to them at the Kok Key camp every day, both morning and evening. At about ten o'clock, we carry the porridge and soup out of the economy kitchen shed and head off in separate directions. At about twelve o'clock or twelve-thirty, we return to camp. After eating our own porridge, we divide up our tasks: some go out to find firewood, while others go fetch water and wash the dishes and pots and then set up the pots to start cooking the rice and soup for the evening.

We have to finish cooking the food by three o'clock or three thirty and then get ready to distribute it to the units. The rice must be stirred and fluffed thoroughly so that it doesn't congeal into lumps before we divide it up. When measuring the rice, we only scrape the bowl level with our hands without having to use a ladle handle. After dividing it up, the economy men assigned to the fertilizer unit and paddy-dike unit each have time to rest and wait for the workers to return from work in the evening. For the cattle unit, their economy worker has to carry rice and soup on a shoulder yoke out to the Kok Key camp all over again.

The work of the economy team is easier than that of the workers out in the fields. In addition to this, the economy team gets plenty to eat, unlike the workers. All of us want to be economy workers. But this job cannot be demanded or requested; it must be assigned by the leadership. My friends must be envious or admiring of my fate to have become an economy worker. For my part, I sit around with a pathetic face, feeling depressed over the job. If I told my friends this, they would laugh and say I was crazy because if I can't keep up with this job, there is nothing left for me but bed rest and half-rations.

As for the work of cooking in the economy shed, I can do this as well as the others. But carrying porridge and soup weighing about fifteen kilograms on a shoulder yoke, walking along narrow paths and paddy dikes, is not easy for me right now. I used to easily carry a shoulder yoke with two or three *bangky* baskets full of dirt on each side, but then I was stronger and fitter. But now I am thin; I am so thin!

On the first day, I struggle to carry my load, stopping frequently, until I finally reach the Kok Key camp at about noon. The members of the cattle unit are all there sitting and waiting for me. Bong Sary, the former economy worker who has just traded places with me, stands there with his hands behind his back and his head tipped to the side, glaring at me as I slowly, haltingly carry the porridge.

The next day, my shoulder, which is nothing but skin and bone, has become very swollen and sensitive. Like Thunchey,[3] who rigged up a sail and poled with a long pole to drive the old elephant, I find a small cushion and tie it to my yoke pole to cushion my shoulder and prevent it from hurting. But the swollen shoulder still hurts. After carrying the porridge about half a kilometer outside of camp, I sit down, and tears fall from my eyes. I am disappointed in myself for being unable to fulfill my duties on time, and disappointed that I finally got an easy job but continue to struggle anyway, and I'm worried that they will think that "keeping me is no gain and removing me is no loss."

It just so happens that today Comrade Chuch has an errand to come fetch some things at the Or Kambot camp. When I meet Comrade Chuch, I am overjoyed and beg him to help me. Comrade Chuch feels sorry for me and carries the porridge for me all the way to Kok Key.

One day there is heavy rain in the morning, causing the ground to become wet and slippery. My body is weak, the porridge is heavy, the path is slippery, and I struggle greatly to carry my load. About half a kilometer out of camp, I have to carry my load up onto the levee road that runs alongside the north-south canal and then come back down off of it a hundred meters later. Climbing up the slope onto the levee is difficult, but by digging in my toes I am able to make it without slipping. Coming back down off the levee is twice as hard, and I struggle so much to slow my descent that my knees shake, making the loads swing on their hooks, and suddenly I slip down the slope. I try not to fall forward and end up falling backward and land on my butt, slamming the bottoms of the porridge and soup pots onto the dirt. The thick porridge adheres to the pot, but about half of the soup sloshes out of the pot and spills onto the ground. With fear and anxiety, I pick up bits of fish, winter melon, and tomatoes scattered in the dirt and toss them back into the soup pot. I scrape dirt over the spill to cover it up so that if anybody travels this way, they won't know that soup was spilled here.

---

[3] Refers to *The Tale of Thunchey*, a traditional Khmer legend of unknown authorship and date of origin, known for promoting resourcefulness and perseverance. In the story, the title character Thunchey is required by the king to make a timely journey on an old elephant, set up to fail; but he attaches a sail to the elephant and poles with a long pole, like a boat, which wins the king's admiration despite his extreme lateness.

I am late bringing the porridge to the camp. The members of the cattle unit have each brought their porridge bowls and laid them out in a line on the ground, waiting for me. They stand with their arms folded, staring at me with great agitation. They are very hungry! They are starving! Some of them scold me. I don't dare talk back. I begin to dish up the porridge into the bowls and distribute them right away. They all stand around watching me measure out the porridge, scarcely daring to blink. Then I divide up the soup into three medium-sized bowls for the three teams. Each man takes his bowl of porridge, the soup bowls are set out in three spots on the ground, and each team crouches around its own soup bowl and eats. How fortunate! Because they are so hungry and angry at my lateness, they don't even notice that there is less soup than usual.

Early November 1978

Even though my younger brother is working nearby, I have never had time to visit him, and I don't even know for sure which camp he is at.

One day, at about two o'clock in the afternoon, I am washing the *trakuon,* preparing the vegetables for the soup, when suddenly my brother walks up and stands near the economy shed. He is very thin, wearing black clothing, and wearing a *krama* wrapped around his head and covering his face.

I ask him, "M'orn! Where have you come from?"

"I'm carrying bundles of seedlings to Kok Key, Bong."

Samorn sits down across from me and starts to grab stalks of *trakuon* and ball them up and stuff them into his mouth. He is eating *trakuon* straight without any salt. I feel so sorry for him, but I don't dare hand him anything to eat for fear of violating revolutionary discipline, for fear that they will remove me and not allow me to work on the economy team anymore, as I've only just started to recover my strength a little bit.

Samorn pulls the *krama* from his head and says quietly, "Bong, I shaved my head."

"Why did you shave your head, M'orn? Too many lice?"

"No. I went and snuck some beans from the cooperative's field and the *chhlops* caught me."[4]

---

[4] i.e., he was required to shave his head as a punishment

My brother speaks slowly while looking down and chewing *trakuon*. I feel like I am watching them march my sister away to be killed, and I am shocked and afraid, worried that my brother will be killed like my sister was. I try to control my emotions and rein in my panic, and I say softly to my brother, "Our sister just died. Why would you dare risk your life like that?"

"I'm so hungry, Bong!"

This short answer devastates me and moves me with compassion for my brother. He is now dealing with weight loss, frailty, and exhaustion like I was. He must be very hungry indeed. Besides, in the young men's unit, the discipline is very strict, and they are not allowed to do private cooking as in the middle-aged unit. I have no capacity to help him as his older brother. Though we are brothers, we live alone and die alone. What is even the use of having a brother?

"M'orn! We are the only two left. We have to be patient so that we can survive and return to our ancestral village and perform merit[5] for Mom and Dad! If you die, what will I have left?" Tears fall from my eyes.

My brother says softly, "Goodbye, Bong."

He stands up, wraps his *krama* around his neck, lifts his yoke onto his shoulder, and walks away. Hot tears continue to flow as I quietly watch my brother walk away. He is so thin; he must be so hungry. He knew that his brother works on the economy team, so he went out of his way to meet me, supposing that he would get something to eat. But instead, all he got was a scolding.

I am not angry at my brother. Like everybody else, he is facing hunger, extreme hunger. He is facing death by starvation. He has to follow his instincts, which say that if you are hungry you must eat, you must find something to eat, you must steal to eat. But still, I am afraid that my brother will die and leave me!

---

[5] refers to religious ceremonies performed for departed souls

Chapter 53

Flight

Our daily lives get more and more difficult and more and more miserable, sliding closer to death. Death by starvation, death by execution for stealing, death by execution under charges of being an enemy of the Revolution. Everyone sees more and more clearly that they are far from the Glory of the Revolution, and that they have no hope of seeing what they call the "Glory of the Revolution."

If you live without hope, awaiting your day of death, what point is there to living? It is a question without an answer. We never ask this question to ourselves. We only think that if we die, it is fate. But we must fight to keep living. It's like we have handed ourselves over to the Organization to decide our fates, as we have no hope of twisting free from the claws of this blood-sucking demon.

Most of us are thin and overworked. If we were to sneak away, we would have to travel to the Thai border, which takes three or four days for a regular journey, and even longer if you are sneaking. None of us knows the way. And we have absolutely no provisions. We have no uncooked rice or salt to take with us. Nevertheless, despite living in these dead-end circumstances, some people do try their luck, refusing to surrender to a fate of death. They attempt to break free from the iron yoke of the demonic regime.

As November arrives, some of the rice in the fields has become ripe enough to harvest. At the same time, we hear that there are groups of bandits in the forest. Some people have run away from a mobile unit or cooperative. But because they can't seem to find a path for escape, they remain in hiding in the jungle along the Rumduol River, in the area of the former Spean Thom subdistrict. They survive by stripping paddy rice grains from stalks in the fields, pounding them, and roasting them to eat. But we don't know what they do to obtain salt. Salt is an essential thing for our survival these days, and it is not as easy to find as rice is. It is only found in the economy sheds of the mobile units or in the cooperative offices.

In mid-November, the plowing and harrowing work at the Veal Saen Khyal rice-farming worksite slows down. Bong No's plowing team is given orders to deploy with their oxen to plow at the Daeum Ko Bey Daeum[1] worksite. (This worksite is along the road between Prey Moan and Kok Rumchek, but I'm not familiar with it.) Comrade Dy and Comrade Mang's teams continue to work here in Veal Saen Khyal. Bong No's team is a strong team, a team of people with strong, sturdy bodies, and mostly decently educated. Many of the members of this team are bold enough to talk in a sort of pretend-joking manner with the cadres. For example, one morning Bong Pav dared to take Mea Pov's spoon and eat his own porridge with it, pretending to be oblivious.

Bong Pav has a large sturdy frame and is about thirty years old. He is a man who is accustomed to a dignified manner of living. Even during these times, he still maintains the habit of speaking with his wife using the words *oun* and *bong*.[2] This couple appears to be childless, as they are both deployed on mobile units. His wife stays with the women's brigade. Like other members of the Fourth Brigade with wives working on mobile units here in Veal Saen Khyal, Bong Pav has constructed a small hut for himself to live in apart from the rest of us, east of the common shelter.

One night, during the waxing moon, at about eight o'clock, before the moon has risen, Bong Pav wakes me by whispering to me and calling me to come to his little hut.

The two of us sit in his little hut, and I ask him, "Where are you coming from, Bong?"

"I've just come from my wife's camp."

"Why have you come back in the middle of the night?"

"Tuch, there is something I want to ask of you."

"What is it, Bong?"

"We are planning on running away."

"Running away? Where will you run to?"

"We plan to run to Thailand."

"How many of you will go?"

"There are nine of us."

"Where are the others?"

"We have agreed to meet up near Kok Rumchek when the moon crests the treetops."

---

[1] "Three Kapok Trees"

[2] as opposed to "comrade"

"Do you know the way?"

"We don't know the way, but we have a guide."

"So how did you want me to help you, Bong?"

"I want to ask your help to find salt for our journey because we don't know where to find any."

"Damn Bong, this is kind of short notice! Why didn't you let me know sooner? I could have stolen a little bit at a time and kept it for you. Now where will I get my hands on it?"

"Tuch, you work on the economy team, you know the nooks and crannies where they keep the salt; you can steal it easier than I can!"

"But it's very hard to steal at night, Bong! A-Kun ties his hammock up and sleeps right there in the kitchen hut!"

"We have no options. Please help us a little, Tuch!"

It is a hard favor to satisfy. I have never stolen, and it is not a good opportunity. But they have no choice; if I don't help, they will be stuck. If they are able to get away, then there can be opportunities for others of us to follow after.

"Bong, you wait for me here!" I decide to steal the salt to help my friend. The waxing moon will rise soon with its faint light in the eastern sky. Being accustomed to living in the dark, my eyes are able to easily discern the things around me. Everyone in camp is sleeping quietly. I creep carefully, placing my footsteps very gently in the darkness, toward the economy shed.

I sit down in front of the shed and peer inside to ascertain the situation. Comrade Kun has tied up his hammock to the center pole and the main roof support pole on the south side. He sleeps with his head pointed south, wide open, with no mosquito net. My heart pounds and my hands and legs shake in fear. Should I steal? Comrade Kun is very cautious and very stern! He is sleeping with his face toward the entrance, with his head directly over the sacks of rice and salt. If I get near the salt sack, my breath will be near his ear. Both the rice sack and the salt sack have their mouths tied shut; if I approach them, I will have to take time to untie the sack, and then tie it back up again after taking the salt.

I crawl very cautiously near Comrade Kun's feet. At that moment, Comrade Kun turns over. Dear God! I am petrified and freeze instantly. Comrade Kun is still not deeply asleep, and it is hazardous to risk it. I remain still for a time while my heart thumps. Without any hope of advancing forward, I slowly withdraw.

A faintly lit moon peeks out above the horizon and Bong Pav departs without hope. I feel bad and regret that I was unable to help out in these impoverished times. I am not brave enough to sneak away, but I am sympathetic and supportive of rebellion. Only rebellion can change the situation. Only a revolution can transform society.

But the possibility of uprising for those of us living here is almost nonexistent. I have traveled to the mountains before, and I am aware that there are many obstacles:

- Now is the cool season, and there is no rain. The lack of water along the roads could kill you.

- During the rainy season, you absolutely could not run because there is no ripe rice in the fields to strip from the stalks for food. Being soaked by rain and shivering from the cold in the jungle, as well as being bitten by mosquitos, could kill you by malaria.

Many days later we find out that they were ill-fated. Bong Pav could not make it from Or Kambot to his appointed meeting place near Kok Rumchek by the time the moon rose over the trees. They got lost and separated, and some of them were caught by the Organization and taken to the prison at Phnom Liep. I never hear any further word of Bong Pav or Bong No.

After I have worked for the economy team for one month and somewhat regained some weight and strength, the Organization removes me from economy work on 27 November 1978.

CHAPTER 54
Tomorrow We Part

By the end of November 1978, the plowing work becomes infrequent as rice farming draws to an end. After leaving the economy team, I receive orders to go cut trees to make fish enclosures[1] for three days. After that I am tasked with herding oxen at Kok Key for a week.

On the 7th of December, I don't know how the situation has changed, but suddenly the Organization decides to disband the general-population units to return to the cooperatives, and the young men of Phnom Srok district are all combined into a single brigade. For me, there is nothing in the cooperative to entice me to return and live there. My sisters are both dead now, and all I have left is a brother-in-law, which is not much to hope for. In a way, I feel that these changes in direction by the Organization are noteworthy:

- When they were first gathering the general-population forces to construct Trapeang Thmor Reservoir, Ta Lam said that this force would never be disbanded back to the cooperatives. But now that's what is happening.
- According to the Prophecy of the Buddha, the final plain is Veal Saen Khyal, Or Ta Phal, and Phnom Tralok. Now we are crossing this plain. Are the current changes an omen of the end of our misery?

My brother is a young man and cannot be permitted to return to the village. So if I go back to the village, I will surely be separated from my brother. After eating our morning porridge, the middle-aged workers depart for their villages. I, however, make a request to join the young men's brigade to stay with my brother.

On the afternoon of the 7th of December, at four o'clock, the chairman of the young men's brigade summons all of the members to a meeting to reorganize the brigade, as many additional members have now joined. We all sit in our own units in a circle on the threshing floor at the young men's camp, which is out in the open east of Kok Key and Ta Khek villages (the area between them). My brother sits with his unit, far from me.

---

[1] fence-like structures for containing fish in the shallows of a body of water

The comrade chairman of the brigade stands in the middle of the circle and proclaims the opening of the meeting:

"Today our brigade has received many new members who have come to join us, which has necessitated the reorganization of the teams and units. At the same time, the region has given our brigade two new responsibilities: harvesting rattan[2] and making *bangky* baskets and yoke poles in preparation for maintaining the Trapeang Thmor Reservoir dams according to the plan for 1979; and gathering in the harvest for the rice that we have planted at this worksite. Therefore, we must organize into two regiments: the rattan collecting regiment, and the rice harvesting regiment.

"Because Region Five lacks rattan, the Organization has allowed us to make a rattan collection camp in the Northern Zone. So that the Organization and people of the Northern Zone don't look down on the forces of the Northwestern Zone, we will choose 170 people with strong, fit bodies to form the rattan-collection regiment. The remaining workers will form the rice-harvesting regiment."

When he finishes speaking, the comrade chairman stands and points one by one to people considered fit to join the young men's rattan-collection unit, asking them to rise and sit off to the side. I am chosen by the brigade chairman to rise and sit in the new area. My brother, who has already been involved in this work for a long time, is not included on this unit. The comrade chairman of the brigade stops pointing to people. Then the unit leader counts the number of people and gets a total of 160. There are still ten people needed. I resolve to stand and speak.

"Comrade Chairman! I request that my brother also join the rattan-collection unit!"

The brigade chairman asks me, "Who?"

"Comrade 'Orn, Comrade!"

"Oh, the bald one? No, he cannot! Let him grow his hair out a bit first."

I sit back down in despair. The unit leader takes some long-handled *phkeak* knives with smallish blades, all old, and distributes them to us, one apiece. Then the comrade brigade chairman organizes the rice-harvesting regiment, dividing

---

[2] specifically, *ropeak* (*Calamus salicifolius*), a species of rattan native to Cambodia and Vietnam, used to weave baskets

it into the rice-transport battalion and the rice-threshing battalion. The meeting is adjourned at about 5:30 p.m.

The sky begins to darken. After they distribute the evening porridge (the young men's brigade cooks porridge both morning and evening), my brother and I take our bowls of porridge and go to sit away from the others. Neither of us shares with the other; we each eat our own porridge. But this is a shared meal between two brothers who haven't been together in two years (since moving to Paoy Snuol; we have been apart ever since). It is a shared meal between brothers to express the joy of being together this evening, and it is a goodbye party for our separation again in the morning.

I did not return to the village for fear of being separated from my brother, but it turns out we are to be separated far from one another after all, and I lose hope. Tomorrow we part ways. Will it be only for a time, or will it be forever? The song "Tomorrow We Part,"[3] which I used to belt out with my friends on the last day of school (primary school) and around the campfire on the final evening of youth camp, echoes melodiously in my mind...

Tomorrow We Part

1. Tomorrow we part, farewell, my friend,
we shall not meet from this day on.

2. This time of parting, my friend, will it be our last
or do we have hope of meeting another day?

3. This time of parting, my friend, it is only for a time
don't worry, my friend, we shall surely meet again.

4. May Indra, Brahma, and all the angels in Tusita[4] of the six heavens
bless us to be well and happy, each and every one.

---

[3] published by the Ministry of Education to be sung by school children at the end of each school year
[4] the fourth heaven in Hindu cosmology, where sensual passions are still enjoyed

Do I have hope of meeting my brother again, as expressed in this song? Will this be an evil fate? What shall we talk about on this night of togetherness before we part? We are each filled with sadness and worry. We sit eating our porridge silently, our heads down. We eat together like mute people, without speaking. We want to express the pain that tightens our chests, but it won't come out. In former times, we ate our porridge together as four siblings; but now our circle has diminished to two, and tomorrow our porridge circle will be no more.

It is true: those who talk a lot feel little pain, while those who feel much pain speak little. In plays and novels, the characters expound profound truths, expressing great, poignant sorrows. But real life is dreary and stressful and inexpressible. I say goodbye and impart my parting message to my brother.

"M'orn! Tomorrow I will be leaving. Take care of yourself, and be very careful, all right?"

"Yes, Bong."

8 December 1978

The sun rises bright and clear, and the young workers depart from the camp toward their various destinations. Meanwhile, the rattan-collection unit busily gathers our clothing bundles and hammocks into one place and begin to take down the shelters to salvage the thatch grass.

At about nine o'clock, the economy team has finished cooking the porridge, and we eat it, then receive orders to depart. No longer carrying hoes and *bangky* baskets, nor pulling plows and harrows, we each carry our bundles of clothing and hammocks on poles over our shoulders, along with three thatch panels apiece. We march in a long single-file line along the footpath leading from Kok Key to Lao Te, Bat Trang, and other villages along the east bank of the Rumduol River whose names we don't know, heading toward Highway Six.

Behind my back are the rice fields where the grains of rice ripen and turn golden, covering the face of the land. And even further behind me is the land of Phnom Srok district, the place where my younger brother, my cousin, my two sisters, my uncle, and my nieces were killed or lost their lives, their bones littering the earth and the woods. My body walks forward, but my feelings run backward, as though pining for the land that took the lives of my family, the place that left me and my brother orphaned and aimless young men. No! I do not pine for that blood-soaked land. But I miss my brother, my sisters, and my uncle, who carried and supported me, allowing me to come here and become acquainted with this land. And now I am walking away from them, leaving behind their corpses, victims of unnatural deaths, left in woods without graves, without relatives or friends.

If we had never left Kien Svay, it is not certain that we ever would have met such destruction. All of these losses are my fault, they are the results of my decision. I was the leader of the family; I was the one who brought them here to die in droves in this place.

It's true, the mistakes of leaders carry a price of death for their followers! What leader ever feels unaffected by their many followers who sacrifice their lives? I am filled with remorse, feeling like I am an officer defeated in war, abandoning the bodies of his soldiers on the battlefield. Oh, Phnom Srok! Phnom Tuk![5] Karma Prison!

Prisoners of Class

1. Spean Thom, Phnom Srok, karma prison   we live three years in a wordless land
prisoners of class awaiting the day   they butcher us like beasts.

2. Working night and day without rest   tired and wasted, yet we dare not shirk
laboring as cattle, a dish of porridge   our bodies wasting and frail.

3. My body, oh, how thin you are   battered and pale, swollen and numb
ears ringing, limbs weak   strength nearly drained to oblivion.

4. Nights asleep on the earth, beneath the sky   rain or heat, trembling in pain
struggling to endure our fate, wondering   whether they will declare our demise.

5. Oh God, look down on animal man   parents dispersed, children lost
husbandless wife, monkless temple   come, Oh Lord, and redeem mankind.

penned on 6 March 1980[6]

---

[5] "Mountain of Suffering"

[6] Author's note: "These lyrics were sung by the students at the Trade Union Cadre School on the occasion of the class Singing and Arts Competition in March 1981 and received First Prize."

At about one o'clock, we arrive at Highway Six where a bridge crosses the Rumduol River, called Spean Rumduol by the locals. We rest here for the night, waiting for vehicles to take us onward toward the Northern Zone.

At night on the following day, after about eleven o'clock, six tractors pulling trailers arrive to pick us up. It is only the start of the waxing moon, and the sky has little light. The tractors drive along the highway toward Siem Reap province. After a long while, the tractors turn left, driving along a red-gravel road northward. After another long while, the tractors stop and drop us off, then turn around and go back the way they came.

We don't know exactly where we are or what time it is when we finally clear places to lie down on the side of the road and go back to sleep.

CHAPTER 55
The Last Camp

10 December 1978

We awake at dawn. The place where we spent the night is a section of Route 68, which leads to the town of Samraong, Oddar Mean Chey province. We are in Srey Snom district, Siem Reap province. East of the road is a forested rise of land that follows the road continuously. West of the road is a depression with scattered trees, thinly forested along the road itself, but far from the road the land has the aspect of a grassy plain with scattered trees here and there. This place appears to be the old campsite of Region Five's rattan-collection unit that came to this area in previous years.

We work clearing the land for the campsite along the east side of the road, where there are skeletons of three shelters already constructed, awaiting only to be covered with thatch grass (apparently a workforce came to prepare the site beforehand). Then, the brigade chairman holds a meeting to divide our forces up to go and carry out the work. This includes: the rattan-collection battalion; the basket-weaving and rope-twisting battalion; and the battalion in charge of cutting small trees to making the *bangky* frames and wild bamboo to make yoke poles. I am assigned to the rattan-collection battalion.

After organizing the forces, the brigade chairman makes remarks about the work: "The basket making unit will work in camp, while the rattan-collection unit and the yoke-pole cutting unit will go work in the forest east of here. Comrades, you can reach the site by two routes.

"The first is through Moung Thmey[1] village about 200 meters south of our camp here, walking eastward from there along the cart path until Kok Lvea.[2] You will enter the forest north of that village, comrades.

"Or you can walk along this red-gravel road[3] northward toward Kambaor and Khvaek villages. About a kilometer from camp, there is a cart path that turns off to the right. If you follow this cart path, it will take you into the big forest.

---

[1] "New Moung"; *Moung* on official maps and records
[2] *Lvea* on official maps and records
[3] Route 68

"Those of you comrades who are new here should accompany those who came last year, as they know the geography of the forest. It is especially important to remember the path that you take. Do not tarry long in the forest. At about two or three o'clock in the afternoon, you must make your way out of the forest and back to open ground. If you get lost and are unable to find your way out of the forest, then at night you must climb a tree and sleep there, and don't forget to bring your *krama* and tie yourself to the tree.

"When passing through the local villages, you must maintain dignified behavior and preserve the honor of the Northwestern Zone. Whatever you do, don't give the people of the Northern Zone any opportunities to accuse us of lacking morality or living inappropriately. You should especially not enter the dining pavilion or homes of the villagers and ask for this or that, and you must not pick up and eat any scraps of food that they have discarded. Any comrades who do not follow the discipline of the Revolution will be sent back to Region Five.

"The daily rations will be one can of uncooked rice per person. We will eat porridge in the morning before leaving camp, and again in the evening after returning to camp. This morning, after we eat our porridge, the rattan-collection unit and the yoke-pole cutting unit will go into the forest, while the basket-weaving unit will finish covering the shelters."

The meeting is adjourned. We eat our porridge and head off into the forest at about 8 a.m.

I don't know anybody in this brigade apart from Comrade Set, a Cham[4] who had been in the same brigade as me while constructing Trapeang Thmor Reservoir. Most of the people on my team are young men. Even though the brigade chairman told us to travel with people who had been here before, most of them walk only with their own friends and the people they already know and trust. Because of this, newcomers who don't know the forest are forced to walk with other newcomers.

Collecting rattan follows a daily quota that increases steadily from 100, to 150, to 200 rattan stems per day. On the first three or four days, I don't dare go far or penetrate deeply into the forest. I stick to the sparse parts of the forest and collect rattan from the smaller bushes with soft, young fronds that are only

---

[4] member of the Cham people, a Muslim ethnic minority in Cambodia and Vietnam

about two or three meters long. Collecting these young, fresh rattan stems is very difficult. We have to creep in and cut the rattan fronds that grow in large unruly bushes and then drag them away from the bush into the open and then start to peel them from tip to base. We risk being punctured by the spines, and the work is slow because we have to peel them one at a time. Those who penetrate deeper into the forest collect long rattan stems five or six meters long, which they tie into bundles and carry on their shoulders, the ends dangling loosely and dragging in the dirt. These long rattan fronds grow in bushes of only six to eight fronds beneath large trees, which the fronds climb. We cut all the leaves off, leaving the bare, dry frond stems clinging to the tree trunk. After hacking them off at the base, we pull four or five stems off at a time by wrapping them around a stick. When we do this, the stems peel away from the tree trunk. Then we just cut off the tips, then take a knife and peel them from tip to base in one motion. The work is easy and fast, but it is somewhat difficult to minimize the walking. We have to go deep into the forest to find many sites, many plants, in order to fulfill the daily quota.

Every morning we set out walking along one of the two routes, as directed by the brigade chairman, one to the north and one to the south. On the northern route, we follow the red-gravel road for more than a kilometer, then turn right and follow an oxcart path that passes through the forest for more than another kilometer, where we encounter a village of locals in the forest called Damrey Slap.[5] Leaving this village, the path passes through more forest for another two or three kilometers, and then we come to a large open field, which the locals call Field Thirty. There are many cart tracks crisscrossing this field, from east to west, from north to south, and we must pay close attention to remember which one is the path that we take. In this field, we encounter a lovely carpet of purple, yellow, red, and white, made up of grass flowers and *krachip* flowers, as described by the author of *The Wilted Flower*.[6] In the later afternoon, when coming out of the forest, we often take time to rest and recover our strength here in this field, breathing in the lovely fragrance of the beautiful wildflowers. We must pass through this field for another kilometer before entering the forest where we are to search for rattan.

---

[5] "Dead Elephant"
[6] see page 38

On the southern route, we follow the red-gravel road for about 200 meters to Moung Thmey on the east side of the road. It is a somewhat sizeable village, with about forty or fifty houses, both large and small. We pass through to the east side of the village where we encounter a plain of rice fields four or five kilometers long. But the width is not very wide, only about a kilometer. We walk along a cart path that bisects this plain eastward. At the end of the rice fields, we reach a spot of higher ground with trees, such as mango and coconut, growing here and there (apparently an old village site). After this we pass through another kilometer of rice fields before reaching a small village of locals with about twenty houses called Kok Lvea. The cart path we follow hugs the north side of this village. Beyond the village, rice fields continue eastward, but we mostly leave the path and enter the forest north of this village.

Between following the cart paths and searching for rattan in the forest, we walk an average of about twenty to twenty-five kilometers per day. The ground in this region is sandy; firm when wet, when flooded; but loose when dry.

When walking into the forest, having just eaten porridge and carrying nothing, we walk quickly. But when we come back out of the forest, we walk so slowly it seems as though we are unconcerned whether we ever make it back to camp or not. Our bodies are tired, and we carry on our shoulders bundles of 200 rattan stems, so long that they drag on the ground behind us, wading through water and sometimes walking over loose, dry sand. Now we know how hard it is to walk on loose, dry sand. We struggle to push our bodies forward, but our steps are more rigid and sluggish than normal. It feels as though we are walking without moving forward, or only with great difficulty.

Now we choose wading through water as preferable to walking on dry sand. We prefer the southern route, which has both wet and dry land, as preferable to the northern route, which is dry all the way.

Though we live in a communist regime led by a single party, governance and leadership differ from cooperative to cooperative, from district to district, from region to region, and from zone to zone. In Phnom Srok district, the people living in the Ponley and Srah Chik cooperatives received a better living than the people living in the Paoy Char cooperative. The people living in Preah Netr Preah district were better provided for than the people in Phnom Srok district.

When we reached the Northern Zone, we saw that the people living in this zone are not as miserable as those in the Northwestern Zone. The region where we are now did not have any evacuees brought to live here. All the people in the villages are base people, the original masters of the land and the villages. While they do have cooperatives and eat their meals in common, they eat freely, with plenty to eat and no shortages. They have fit bodies and robust strength. They stare at us with an attitude of puzzlement and compassion. With kindness, they sometimes covertly pass us cakes and snacks as we pass through their villages.

One day at about five o'clock in the evening, we carry our bundles of rattan out of the forest and pass through Damrey Slap. In the village, four or five children, about seven or eight years old, stand holding boiled Khmer arrowroot which they hand to us, one apiece, as we walk in single file past them, like giving alms to monks. Why are these children giving us gifts? Because they and their parents feel sorry for us. The older folks don't dare come out and give us the gifts directly; perhaps they are under restriction of some kind.

We encountered such giving of gifts, with great value for our lives, once before, when passing through Kok Lvea in the evening. Small children stood holding pieces of sugar cane, each about forty centimeters long, and quietly handed one to each of us.

Apart from their daily food rations, which routinely include fish, chicken, and duck meat, on the 10th, 20th, and 30th of each month they receive another special ration: a feast with *ansam* and *kom* cakes, desserts, and *banhchok* noodles,[7] and sometimes they even slaughter a pig or cow to cook. These days are also special holidays for us, the damned spirits of this world. Those among us who are less inclined to obey the rules often sneak over and surround the dining pavilion of the villagers, and the women often take pity on them and give them cakes. In particular, they hand them pieces of *banhchok* dough that they have rolled out, flattened, and roasted. I am too afraid to go near the dining pavilions; I just stand off staring at them out of the corner of my eye and swallowing my spit. Sometimes I covertly pick up the end of a stalk of sugar cane or piece of fruit that somebody has discarded and eat it. But I don't really profit much from this, as I am so scared.

---

[7] a kind of Cambodian noodles made from rice flour

Faced with hunger, people get bold in disobeying orders. After only four or five days, most of us frequently leave the group to find opportunities to sneak into the local villages and raise our hands, palms together, to beg for cakes, snacks, rice, and porridge.

Noticing that there are rule violations and disorder, the brigade chairman takes new measures that are stricter than before. Every morning, the battalion leaders walk along behind us as far as Damrey Slap or Kok Lvea. They herd us closely, like herding cattle, so that we don't deviate right or left from the path or stop to pick something up off the ground to eat. In the afternoon at about three thirty, they have already come and stand waiting for us at Damrey Slap or Kok Lvea.

One day a comrade emerges from the forest before everyone else. When he reaches Kok Lvea, he doesn't see the unit leader, so he takes advantage of the opportunity to visit the homes of the villagers. This comrade emerges just as the unit leader arrives, who calls out to him, "Comrade, what were you doing in the village?"

Taken by surprise, and not having time to think, he answers, "I was just asking for a drink of water, Comrade!"

"You just waded through water in the fields, why didn't you drink then?"

Cornered, he doesn't dare say anything else, but just stands there hemming and hawing, and the unit leader "builds" him. "Don't go into the homes of the villagers anymore, you hear, Comrade?"

"Yes, Comrade!"

On the 10th, 20th, and 30th of the month, the mobile forces are now forbidden from entering the forest. Rather, they remain and work in camp, each person required to weave two sets of *bangky* baskets and twist two pairs of *bangky* ropes. Once we have fulfilled our quota, we are allowed to leave camp and forage for wild fruits and edible plants, but we are not allowed to go near the local villages.

Having entered the cool season, it gets cold in the wilderness area where we are camped. But natural obstacles cannot impede the pace of labor or the work activities that we are required to perform.

When the morning star rises, the economy workers rise and start to cook the porridge. When the sky begins to turn faintly red in the east, they wake us and call us to eat the porridge. Now I know that living with the young men's unit has different challenges from living in the middle-aged unit. They rarely have soup to eat, but mostly eat boiled *prahok* broth, and sometimes they give us each a pinch of rock salt to hold in our hand and eat with our porridge. Our daily rice ration remains one can per day, but the porridge in the young men's unit is more abundant because the unit leaders and brigade chairman don't embezzle so much of it. The Organization brings milled rice once per week when the tractor arrives to take the *bangky* baskets back to Region Five.

Once we have finished eating our porridge, the sky has brightened enough that we can clearly see everything around us. We put away our bowls and dishes and pick up our knives, one apiece, and head out. Though it is full daylight, there are still layers of thick fog drifting through the air, making it hard to make out anything more than a hundred meters away. We take our *kramas* or our sheets of cloth (the two-meter sheets of white cloth) and wrap them around our heads to protect our ears, which are most susceptible to the cold. But we have nothing to protect our fingers and toes, and they become so cold they are nearly numb.

A Khmer proverb says, "Enter the forest while it is morning; start school while you are young." We take long strides in a hurry to reach the forest. The sun, which appears unusually large, is a dark red color as it crests the treetops. We draw closer to the mouth of the forest. The line of humans marching in single file splits up little by little.

The old folks often say, "Look up while walking in the forest." But we look up, down, left, and right. Our eyes search not only for rattan plants, but for anything edible that can be put into our mouths.

Cheas lizards are very quick. The moment they hear human footfalls, they vanish into their holes immediately. But they are the stupidest animal. If we see one enter its hole, we find a thin vine and tie a snare loop in front of its hole and walk away. When we return a little while later, the lizard is caught in the snare loop and thrashing about.

Some people watch closely for bees and *mrom*.[8] They cut up their mounds and eat the *mrom* hives. I have never seen these. Some wild fruits are edible, like *triel sva*,[9] *triel dah krabey*,[10] and *tromung*, but some are not.

When I was young, my father used to tell me, "When you go into the forest, watch the animals. If animals are eating some fruit, then humans can eat that fruit too." One day, I come across an overgrown tree with round fruits, smaller than lemons, growing densely all over the tree, with shiny yellow rinds. Myna birds are happily jostling each other to peck the fruits, dropping the rinds all over the ground below. The flesh of this fruit is clear and white like the flesh of a longan berry, and it looks delicious. If animals can eat it, then humans can too! I walk under the tree and reach out to pick one of these fruits. I hold it and wipe it off, then put it in my mouth and bite through the rind. Dear God! So bitter! I quickly spit it out, for fear of being poisoned. I don't know what kind of fruit it is, but the flavor is so bitter that I become afraid of it. The villagers later tell me it is *slaeng voa*[11] fruit. I'm very fortunate that I spat it out so quickly.

We are very ignorant about unfamiliar things! I have experienced this matter of eating fruit without consideration before. It happened once after we were evacuated to Paoy Snuol in late 1976. When I was young, my brother Leang told me that "the seeds of a castor-oil tree help chickens become disease resistant if they eat them." When we got to Paoy Snuol, I saw that there were many castor-oil trees, as the villagers planted them as a kind of fence around the village. Remembering my brother's words, I took Samorn to pick castor-oil seeds to eat. In addition, Samorn also roasted and ate these seeds. Because my brother ate so many of them, he became very ill, vomiting and unable to get up.

I ran to ask for some sugar from the cooperative, and the cadre asked me, "What do you need sugar for?"

"To neutralize poison!"

"Who was poisoned by what?"

"My brother was poisoned from eating castor-oil seeds!"

---

[8] a type of small stingless bee
[9] a type of tree with small red fruit
[10] a type of tough vine with large red fruit
[11] a type of strychnine plant (vine-like; possibly growing over a tree)

"What kind of moron dies from eating something without knowing what it is? Don't just feel sorry for the little guy; if his big brother is sick too, might as well let him die, with a big brother who is so stupid!"

He didn't know that my little brother was a grown-up man like me, and he didn't know that, in fact, I was starting to feel a bit shaky myself. He gave me three spoonfuls of palm sugar, which I cooked until it was burnt and then boiled it in water, and then we both drank it to escape death.

His ridicule of me was not wrong. I truly was ignorant, but this is the effect of hunger: it compels us to do all kinds of things to satisfy its ambitions through the demands of the stomach. The stomach controls our thoughts and feelings all the time. There is never a time that it forgets or takes a break, so we are required to constantly be on the lookout to satisfy its demands.

Along the road, near Moung Thmey, there is a pond with *snao* trees growing beside it. Every evening when we reach this pond, the Sun has entered his hole, leaving only a dark red light across the sky. I drop my bundle of rattan and climb into the pond and collect the seeds from ripe *snao* fruit and wrap them in a fold of cloth. After eating my evening porridge, I roast the *snao* seeds and then lie chewing on them in my hammock until I fall asleep. They aren't particularly delicious, but my mouth just wants something to chew on.

Though our hearts desire only to look for things to eat, we first work hard to collect our daily quota of rattan before foraging for edible things, as the time available for working in the forest is very short. Once the sun passes overhead, at about one o'clock, we start to edge toward the exit of the forest. I don't dare delay for long, as I am afraid of getting lost. At just after three o'clock, I emerge from the forest into the open. Some others, however, are not so hasty.

Generally, I go to the forest from the south because along the way there are rice paddies and water for bathing and drinking to alleviate my fatigue.

Even if we leave the forest before the others, we cannot walk back to camp before the others. The cadres require us to stop and wait for the others at the old village site west of Kok Lvea. There we take the opportunity to sit and weave rattan fibers into cordage, which we bundle and save to twist into rope on the day of rest when we will work in camp. At nearly four o'clock, we are permitted to resume walking.

After having had only one bowl of porridge to eat and then spending twelve hours working and wandering around, we are very tired. We plod along, dragging our feet on the sandy path, feeling with each step like our foot is stuck in the sand. It is the same distance, but it is not the same amount of time as in the morning. We walk for a long time. We usually reach camp after dark when there is barely enough light left to see. We are so tired our ears ring.

Once we are all together, we take our bowls and go to collect our porridge by unit. But even before we have collected our porridge, we start to light small cookfires and begin the continuous cooking and roasting, making scattered red light all around the shelters. (Here the Organization is not so strict with us when it comes to adding ingredients and doing private cooking.) It is these small cookfires that produce the light by which we eat our porridge in the darkness of the cool-season nights.

When all the cookfires have gone out, a silence covers the camp, which is sprinkled by a cold dew, along with a night breeze that rustles the leaves with a whooshing sound.

Late December 1978

One night, after eating porridge, the brigade chairman calls us to a common meeting. We gather and sit in a circle west of the shelters by the side of Route 68 in a darkness devoid of firelight.

The brigade chairman stands in the middle of the circle and starts the meeting. "It has been half a month since you comrades have come here to wage a labor offensive in the forest! The Organization is very pleased with your conscientious efforts to fulfill your revolutionary duty, as well as your obedience to the Organization's discipline. But at the same time, some comrades have committed errors which the Organization considers to be a bad example that can have a bad influence on other comrades!"

The brigade chairman stops speaking for a moment, and then calls out, "Where is Comrade Set?"

Comrade Set stands and responds, "Yes, Comrade Brother!"

"Where did you wander off to yesterday?"

"When I came out of the forest, I was dizzy and got mixed up about the cart paths and didn't know which one led to camp. I followed a path but didn't run into anybody else. The sun was about to set, and I met some villagers who invited me to ride their cart and brought me to their place near the Kralanh district reservoir. There are a lot of fish there. They cooked some rice and

roasted and boiled some fish to eat. Then in the morning they brought me back
to camp."

Comrade Set finishes speaking, and the comrade brigade chairman continues, "That's good! You got lost and hit the jackpot! You got lost and found
roasted fish and small-pot rice! Would any of you other comrades like to get lost
as well?"

At first, we admired the good fortune of Comrade Set, who got lost and
ended up with delicious food. But now we are worried instead, each of us
sitting in silence.

The comrade brigade chairman continues, saying, "I instructed you to keep
together, and to hurry out of the forest, but you did not listen, Comrade, and
you took the opportunity to meet villagers and pretend to be lost and ride a cart
and go for an outing and act like it's no big deal. Getting lost like this is not
good! You other comrades, don't you want to get lost too, lest the Organization
is not inclined to forgive! As for Comrade Set, the Organization is merciful, but
do not let it happen a second time!"

"Yes, Comrade!"

The comrade brigade chairman tells Comrade Set to sit down. Then he asks
loudly, "Where is the group of people who dug up a dead water buffalo for
meat?"

These words stun and surprise those of us who did not know about this.
Seven people stand and present themselves. (I don't know their names, as they
are in another unit and sleep in the north shelter, while I sleep in the south
shelter.)

The comrade brigade chairman asks, "Where did you go to dig up a water
buffalo corpse?"

"Near Kambaor, Comrade Brother!" one of them replies.

"Perhaps you stole somebody's water buffalo and ate it?"

"No. The water buffalo died, and the villagers buried it, Comrade Brother!"

"You ghouls dug up a dead water buffalo to eat, and aren't afraid of dying?"

The comrade brigade chairman stops speaking and nobody dares to open
his mouth. They stand in silence.

The comrade brigade chairman continues, saying, "If a water buffalo died,
and they buried it, then that water buffalo must have had a disease! Why were
you not afraid to die, to do such a thing? Are all of those who *didn't* eat a water
buffalo corpse not still alive? Why are you so much hungrier than the others? If

the villagers were to hear about this, would not the reputation of Region Five, Northwestern Zone become as foul-smelling as a water buffalo corpse? This is a very serious matter and cannot be overlooked. Tomorrow morning, you seven comrades must return to Region Five!"

That was truly bold of the seven men. They brought the meat back and hid it in camp without any salt to preserve it with. The meat turned rotten, and that's how they were found out.

I am not so bold as they are: on the third day collecting rattan here, I didn't dare go far into the forest yet. That day I went to collect rattan along the northern route. In the afternoon, after the sun had passed overhead, at about one o'clock, I came across an ox calf about a year old lying dead in the forest. Its abdominal organs had been devoured by wild animals. The head, legs, and torso were still in good shape. In the place where the calf had died, there were drag marks in the shape of a circle with a diameter of about two meters. The flesh of the calf was still fresh, and it appeared as though the calf had become separated from its mother and was caught by a wild animal and eaten in the night.

I stood staring at the corpse of the calf and pondering its cause of death, wondering what could be done to be able to eat it. But I couldn't think of anything and felt at a dead end, as I had no fire. And I didn't dare to cut and take the meat with me, as I was afraid of bringing danger upon myself. I thought, *The villagers must be missing a calf. If I take veal and go off and eat it, I will surely be accused of killing their calf. If they were to believe that wild animals killed the calf, I'm not certain that I could lead them back to the place where the calf died. And unless I stay and stand guard, I'm not certain that tonight some wild animal won't come and drag the calf away either. In that case, I would face accusations. I would face death.* I walked away and left the veal with regret.

Two or three days later, I told this story to some of the others. They concluded that a pack of wild dogs must have caught and eaten that calf.

_____

The Ansam Stub

In all circumstances the poor face hunger.

After 1970, amidst the fires of war, some rural areas became battlefields, and the people were forced to flee their villages and homes and come to live in the city, one after another.

1972

One morning, at six-thirty, I rode my bike to high school along Street 484 up to Monivong Boulevard. When I reached the football pitch at the College of Law, I saw a slice of soft bread lying on the asphalt, and I saw a man of about forty wearing loose black *kong mov*[12] trousers and a white Chinese shirt stop his bike and walk it over and lean it against a small milk-fruit tree near the side of the boulevard. I thought to myself that he must have stopped to pick up the slice of bread, and I rode past him and stopped at the street corner near the Baby Rabbit Center (an orphanage) and watched him. The man looked both ways and walked over and picked up the slice of bread and stuffed it into his mouth.

Nobody paid any attention to that little slice of bread. But for this man, it had value. He must have been very hungry!

I had fifteen riels in my pocket. I took out five riels and held them in my hand. When the man rode near me on his bike, I got on my bike and rode up beside him and passed the money to him.

"Uncle! I want to give you five riels."

The man was puzzled and turned to ask me, "Why are you giving me money, Nephew?"

"I saw you pick up that bread to eat. You must be very hungry!"

His countenance changed. He was ashamed to think that somebody had seen him pick up and eat the slice of bread. He said slowly, "I really am hungry. I fled from my home village, and I have no money! Last night I spent the night at my relatives' house at Boeng Trabek. They are also poor, and I didn't dare ask to eat any of their rice, so I went to bed hungry until morning."

"Where is your home village?"

"My home is in Me Mut. My house was burned down."

_____

[12] a traditional style of loose trousers with a wide, loose waist that is fastened by wrapping and tucking, like the waist of a sarong

"Where are you going now?"

"I borrowed my relatives' bicycle to go looking for work."

The man was riding the bicycle very slowly, and his hands were shaking. Because it was nearly time for school to start, I took my leave from him.

"With these five riels, you can buy a piece of bread with sugar sprinkled on top. Goodbye, Uncle!"

Who could have known that the person giving an offering then would become the starving man now?

31 December 1978

Yesterday was a feast day for the villagers, and for the Region Five mobile rattan-collection unit, it was also a day to rest and work in camp. This morning we hurry into the forest like every other time, though our mood is unusual. Generally, the poor don't get enough to eat, while the rich have so much that they can't eat all of it. For this reason, this morning our mood is on edge, as we are imagining and hoping that we might get some bit of leftover food that the villagers didn't eat and discarded.

We walk with rapid steps and quick eyes. Along the path we cast our eyes about, left and right, especially when near a village, in hopes that we will have some good fortune. But the rules are stricter here than in Region Five, Northwestern Zone. In Region Five, we never picked up anything off the ground to eat because there never was anything to pick up. Here, there is occasionally something to pick up and eat, but we don't have the right to pick it up. All we can do is stare at it, swallow our spit, and then walk away filled with regret. The unit leader accompanies us until we have passed all the villages, and then watches until we have entered the forest before turning back.

This morning, as soon as we have left Kok Lvea, I glance down and notice the stub of an *ansam* cake very recently discarded by a villager, hiding in a clump of grass. It is not very big, probably only a mouthful. It is a leftover that the wealthy leave after eating the rest and then discard as an honor, to signify that they have plenty to eat. This tiny little *ansam* stub makes my feelings jump with elation, a secret and solitary smile of hope in my heart. I can't bend over and pick it up because the unit leader is watching from behind. But I think that it belongs to me, and it will be mine.

In the forest my feelings dwell entirely on that *ansam* stub. I see it smiling at me. I see it waiting for me! I work hard to find rattan to fill my quota as fast as possible so that I can leave the forest before the others, before the unit leader arrives at Kok Lvea.

At about three o'clock, while the sun is still high in the sky, I emerge from the forest and arrive at the rice fields. Feeling giddy, I walk toward the clump of grass where the *ansam* stub is waiting for me. Nobody has picked it up; it's still in the same place, though the color has turned somewhat redder. I bend down and part the grass, about to pick it up. Good Lord! Fire ants are devouring the *ansam* so that now it is almost completely gone. All that remains is the bit of banana leaf that was used to wrap it.

I am not destined to be as fortunate as the man with the bread slice. An obstacle I had not even anticipated destroys my hopes.

———

This evening, as I am returning to the nest, suddenly a figure comes running toward me.

"Bong!" It is my little brother.

"M'orn! Have you been here long?"

"I just arrived this afternoon, Bong!"

"How many came with you?"

"There are seven of us. The Organization sent us to replace the seven men who were sent back to Region Five."

It is extremely fortunate that those men made that mistake and were sent back to Region Five. Otherwise, I would not have been reunited with my brother. Is this fate or destiny, or is it intervention by the spirit of someone to whom we owe much?

I never imagined that such coincidences could happen. We are reunited at the most crucial moment, a moment which could well determine our fate, whether we will be together or apart. We are in different battalions, and sleep in separate shelters, and go out to fulfill different duties, but we live together in the same camp.

9 January 1979

Normally returning to camp is not very orderly or coordinated, but happens in waves, by unit, mostly in groups and clumps. This is because some people are strong and can take long, rapid strides, while others are weak and drag their feet one by one, like an old ox. Besides, gathering to wait at the old village site slows down those who leave the forest before the others, and delays the opportunity to bathe and get clean along the road in the rice paddies between the old village site and Moung Thmey, so the unit leader relaxes the rules and permits us to depart from the old village site in groups of six or seven at a time.

The sun has set over the horizon, leaving behind scattered patches of light in the gaps between the trees, and a red light in the western sky. As we walk along, dragging our feet, carrying our bundles of rattan on our shoulders, trudging sluggishly along the sandy path, we are still about a kilometer away from Moung Thmey. Suddenly a cloud of dust rises before us and moves closer, growing larger and blocking out the rays of light from the sun. It is a group of several oxcarts galloping and racing one another, as though celebrating some joyous occasion.

The riders cry out, "Hooray! We are free! Hooray! We are free! Hooray! Hooray!"

When the oxcarts draw near to us, some motherly women shout out, "Boys! The Front[13] has liberated us! Drop your rattan, boys, and go back to your home villages! We are free!"

This is an odd message that we have never heard before, that we have never even imagined. These several oxcarts appear to be returning from the rice-harvesting worksite. They drive past us with sounds of laughter, while we are left puzzled, wondering if there is really anything to be happy about. We return to camp, eat our food, and go to bed quietly. Nobody seems to know anything about freedom as the villagers seemed to.

---

[13] The Kampuchean United Front for National Salvation (a.k.a. Salvation Front), a politico-military organization formed of Khmer Rouge defectors that united with the Vietnamese army to overthrow the Khmer Rouge regime. The Vietnamese army, along with the Salvation Front, invaded Cambodia on 25 December 1978, reaching Phnom Penh and driving out senior Khmer Rouge leaders on 7 January 1979 (a day now celebrated as a day of national liberation.) These forces continued to advance through the rest of the country in the following days, gradually taking over the country and driving the Khmer Rouge out of populated areas and into the jungles along the Thai frontier. The Salvation Front's members would form the core of the post-Khmer-Rouge government in Phnom Penh, and the Vietnamese army would continue to occupy Cambodia for another decade.

10 January 1979

Today we have to remain in camp and work, twisting ropes and weaving *bangky* baskets. Starting at dawn, on Route 68, a strange thing happens that we have never seen since arriving here: a sporadic stream of vehicles is driving north, sometimes one, sometimes two or three, at fairly slow speeds. As we weave baskets, we glance at the vehicles driving along the road. I see a bus painted red from the windows down and white from the windows up, which I used to ride from Phsar Daeum Thkov to Phsar Thmey.[14] Men and women dressed in black sit quietly on the bus with serious, somber faces. Where are they going? Perhaps they are going to attend a meeting in Samraong.

After one o'clock, I have fulfilled my daily quota: weaving two sets of *bangky* baskets and twisting two pairs of *bangky* ropes. I leave camp and walk off to pick some jujube fruit and gather some *samraong*[15] tree seeds in the forest near Damrey Slap to bring back to roast and eat. Other people head off one by one to forage for their own food. At about three o'clock, I am returning from the forest with some other young men who walk spread out ahead and behind me. On Route 68 automobiles continue to drive by now and then, single vehicles hundreds of kilometers apart. A truck for hauling dirt, painted blue, with rails around the bed made of blue-painted boards, comes from the south at a medium speed. Only two people ride in the cabin of the truck. The surface of the road is not very smooth, and the truck jostles back and forth and occasionally lurches with a loud rickety sound. As the truck passes in front of me, a dried snakehead fish falls out onto the dirt. Overjoyed, I lurch forward to pick up the dried fish, then I cut it in half and split it with the young man walking along behind me.

This truck had been transporting dried fish, and there was a broken board on the bottom of the truck's tailgate, and dried fish had fallen out, one by one, every four or five hundred meters. I could see that there were only about fifty or sixty fish left in the truck bed.

---

[14] "New Market," the large, dome-shaped, art-deco central market in Phnom Penh (which is not actually new, as it was completed in 1937)

[15] *Sterculia lychnophora*

Tonight we rest quietly, nobody feeling particularly suspicious about the events of the day.

11 January 1979

We rise in the dark and eat our porridge, as usual. After eating, the economy team informs us that the situation is tense, and the unit leaders and brigade chairman have all fled the camp. We all divide up the remaining uncooked rice, salt, and *prahok* to go our own separate ways.

The sun rises over the trees, and we have finished dividing up the food supplies, and now we pack up our clothing bundles to leave camp. We walk to Moung Thmey, then suddenly we hear the sounds of gunfire. The villagers conclude that there must be fighting at Spean Moung. I am not familiar with the place, but by the sound of the gunfire, it is maybe only two or three hundred meters from the village.

The sound of gunfire increases in frequency and volume. The villagers run in panic to find hiding places. We start to scatter. Some of us are trying to find a way back to Region Five because their parents and siblings are there. Some seek refuge with the villagers to await an opportunity to continue their journey to Region Five. I have no doubts: we will not be returning to Region Five; my brother and I are going to get away. Four or five young men from the mobile brigade travel with us. We escape into the forest area, toward the villages in the forest, where surely there is no fighting going on.

Farewell, Moung Thmey, Srey Snom! Farewell, collecting camp!

Farewell, criminal prison! Farewell! Farewell!

The Last Camp

1. Moung Thmey, Srey Snom, the last camp   I bid you farewell, criminal prison
captive three years, swollen and wasting away   Life Slaves living as beasts of burden.

2. Eating frogs, tadpoles, geckos,   worms, lizards, cicadas, grasshoppers,
tarantulas, snails, scorpions, mice,   toads, centipedes, and snakes.

chorus:
phek, phty, anao, skun, kantolet   *trakuon, kanhchhaet, chrach, kamping puoy,*
water lilies, bamboo shoots, bits of rice   if you get a manioc—even better

3. This is the life of a Life Slave   we live, but our hearts fret
struggling to survive, daydreaming   bound to be killed like beasts.

                                            penned on 25 September 1979

CHAPTER 56

Freedom

At about nine o'clock, we reach Kok Lvea and pitch in to help the villagers harvest the rice. Here we don't hear much gunfire, but everybody is in an agitated mood: rejoicing and trepidation mingled together. They harvest in a state of urgency.

At noon we eat rice with the villagers and then go out to continue harvesting in the paddies east of the village, while the young men who came here with us continue their journey onward. My brother and I don't go with them, as we think that we ate the villagers' rice, so we should stay for a while and help them work.

Here we harvest alongside villagers from Kok Chas (a village east of Kok Lvea about two kilometers). The village chief of Kok Chas is a man in his thirties. He leads the work enthusiastically and cheerfully. While he works, he shows his excitement and cheer by singing boisterously. It is a song that he makes up himself, using the *roam vong*[1] rhythm with a chorus that says, "O Na, O Na, my friends!" The villagers, men and women, sing along and shout the chorus in unison along with the comrade village chief.

Like birds released from their cage, the villagers are overjoyed. But my brother and I somehow don't feel very cheerful. It is because we are people without a destination. Where should we go? Where should we live? Every now and then, the comrade village chief comes over to ask how we are doing and where we are from.

Later in the afternoon, there is a commotion and cry of alarm from Kok Lvea, about a kilometer from where we are harvesting: the Khmer Rouge are rounding people up. The villagers drop their sickles and bundles of rice and harness up their oxen and buffalo and head for Kok Chas. As we have no possessions, we start running ahead of everybody else, but my brother is skinny and can't run very fast.

It is every man for himself, and nobody wants to help anybody else. We run along behind the others. Some carts drive into the village, while others drive around the west side of the village and go past it. My brother and I run into the

---

[1] a traditional Khmer social dance in which participants dance in a circle

village and pass by the dining pavilion. Some motherly ladies cooking there see us and call out to us, "Boys! Take some rice with you before you go!"

The rice is done cooking, but we don't have time to wait to dish it up. The ladies take some rice crusts and dump them into a mess tin for us. We continue running.

We don't have the strength to keep up with the oxcarts. They drive off and leave us behind. Once past the village, my brother and I go and hide in the forest directly north of the village, the big forest. The Khmer Rouge ride by on horses chasing after the carts. They don't pursue us, as we have run on foot and taken cover in the thick woods.

We hide in the forest for a long time. The sun begins to set, and the atmosphere is still. We emerge from the forest. East of the village, and stretching southward, is a vast and open grassy field with no trees and no rice paddies. The villagers drove their carts down a path that cuts across this field to the south. Not daring to return to the village, my brother and I follow this cart path. But despairing of finding out where the villagers have driven off to, and afraid of running into the Khmer Rouge, my brother and I hide in a thicket of rattan on the side of the road.

It is very dark, and we begin to get hungry. I creep out of the rattan thicket and fetch some water from a paddy west of the cart path. We soak the rice crusts in water and eat them.

The moon starts to rise—a full moon, appearing large, her round face peeking above the treetops. We start to worry about wild animals: wild dogs, snakes, wild boars, tigers. We must not sleep here. Without options, we walk back toward the village.

We walk into the dining pavilion and sit on the chairs where the villagers sit to eat their meals. The village is completely still; perhaps all of the villagers have run away.

The village's economy shed has a floor made of boards, about forty centimeters above the ground, and is divided by a wall to create a supply storage room. I am worried about the movements of the Khmer Rouge at night and afraid that they will come across us. I try to persuade my brother. "M'orn! Let's go sleep in the economy shed supply room!"

"If I sleep on the floor, my back hurts so much, Bong! Let's just tie up our hammocks and sleep here."

My brother is very thin, and his back must really hurt, like when I was sick and had to sleep on the bamboo-slatted sleeping platform. I can't just go hide by myself; I have to stay near my brother. We tie up our hammocks and sleep in the space between the dining tables. Because we are so exhausted, we fall asleep without any effort.

"Hey! Where have you jungle bandits come from, tying up your hammocks and sleeping here?"

The sound of somebody's voice shouting loudly wakes us. I struggle to open my eyes. Three Khmer Rouge soldiers, all holding guns, surround and question Samorn. He is too scared to speak.

I get up from my hammock and go sit beside him and plead with them. "We are young men from the mobile rattan-collection unit, Comrades!"

"What mobile rattan-collection unit comes to sleep here? You must be jungle bandits!"

"No, Comrades! We really are from the mobile rattan-collection unit. There are our knives!" I say, pointing to our knives used for harvesting rattan.

"If you're with the mobile rattan-collection unit, why have you come to sleep in the village?"

"Yesterday we received orders to retreat to Region Five. But because there was fighting at Spean Moung, we all scattered into the local villages."

"All right. In that case, in the morning you should head back to Region Five. Your unit leader is waiting to gather over in Moung Thmey!"

"Yes, Comrade!"

"Hey! Tomorrow you better go to Moung Thmey, you hear? Don't you dare go anywhere else, or you'll be shot!"

"Yes Comrade!"

The soldiers walk away.

The moon, directly overhead, casts a soft light on the village. Four or five village women mill and pound rice and winnow the polished grains near a house a good distance west of the economy shed. The soldiers walk toward the women and stand conversing with them. Then they turn and head toward a house south of there about twenty meters.

Our fear subsides and we go back to bed. But I am still worried. If these soldiers are going to talk to their commander, and their commander orders them to come back and arrest us and take us to be killed, then we are dead. My brother seems unconcerned; he has already fallen back asleep. In fact, my brother is in a state where he doesn't care whether he lives or dies. He is very thin and has lost the will to live. Although, he does become very frightened directly in the face of death.

The soldiers menaced us to go back to Moung Thmey. This must be a trick. There is no unit leader waiting to gather us there; they all ran away to save themselves last night. I will not follow their instructions. Lying there thinking and worrying and unable to sleep, I pray for dawn to come quickly so we can get away from this village.

When the eastern sky starts to brighten, I creep over and cut two sugar cane stalks near the economy shed, cut them into sections, and stuff them into my clothing bag. I ask the villagers about other villages away from this one. They tell us to walk through the forest eastward and we will find another village called Kok Knang.

My brother and I leave while the light is still faint and walk along the cart path across the fields east of the village for about a kilometer before we start to enter the forest. It is a large, thick forest, and there are trees along both sides of the cart path. It is an unfamiliar path, and we have to follow its twists and turns, not daring to leave the path or take any shortcuts. Our speed is not fast because my brother is so thin, but we walk without stopping to rest.

At about nine o'clock we hear a rooster crow ahead of us. We feel hope that perhaps we are near a village, but we see none; we are still walking through the forest. It was just the crowing of a wild rooster after all.

At about ten o'clock, we emerge from the forest and enter Kok Knang. The villagers who have not gone off to work, mostly women and children, surround and welcome us. They take us to rest in the dining pavilion and ask us about our journey. They inform us that two of our companions, Comrade Tan and Comrade La, arrived in the village yesterday evening. We ask them if we can live in the village. They agree and promise to bring Comrade Tan and Comrade La to see us after lunch.

The villagers prepare rice for us to eat. As we are eating, two oxcarts drive rapidly into the village. The villagers hold a discussion with the cart drivers, and then come to see us.

"The situation is not good. We don't dare let you stay here in the village," a man says to us, as though encouraging and pleading with us to leave.

I am curious about their change in attitude, and I ask him, "Is something the matter, Bong?"

"Last night the Khmer Rouge arrested Comrade Chaok, village chief in Kok Chas, and took him away to be killed, accusing him of providing shelter to mobile workers from Region Five. We are afraid the same thing will happen in this village!"

Something like this must have really happened for them to have driven their carts so quickly to the village. Last night the Khmer Rouge soldiers who menaced us must have gone to the home of the village chief. Are we truly responsible for bringing such sorrow upon the villagers? Why didn't they arrest the two of us last night and take us to be killed? Where should we go now?

The villagers comfort us, saying, "We feel so sorry for you, comrades! But our village is not liberated yet. The Khmer Rouge still come and go. You can't live here, Comrades. You two should go to Kralanh district. They have been liberated there. After we have been liberated, if you want to come live here in this village, we wait to welcome you!"

"Is Kralanh district far?" I ask the villagers.

"It's not very far. If you leave now and walk quickly you can arrive before sunset. You can follow the cart path south of the village, or just cut across straight south and a little bit south-west, and you will come to some villages of locals."

We don't understand why they allowed Comrade Tan and Comrade La to stay but they don't dare accept us. We can't force them to explain, or refuse their wishes, so right away my brother and I set out in the direction they advised.

When we are about 200 meters outside the village, Samorn tells me, "Bong, we shouldn't follow the cart path." My brother has been on the battlefield before, and he knows tactics: following the cart path could lead to an encounter with the Khmer Rouge. We leave the path and cut through sparse trees, thick woods, and fields. The woods south of Kok Knang are not so thick as those we passed through this morning.

The sun is about to set, and we reach a grassy field, where we meet a boy herding cows. I ask the boy, "Little Brother, is there a village up ahead?"

"Yes. Just follow the cart path."

"Thank you!"

The young cowherd boy stares after us as though puzzled and raises his hand to point the way for us to follow. Feeling relieved, we walk slowly along the oxcart path headed southward, and after about a kilometer the path starts to curve westward.

The sun has set, leaving only a faint red glow in the western sky. To our right are wide-open fields of grass. To our left are trees and bamboo—an unruly but not particularly dense forest.

We stumble and drag our feet like lethargic people. Suddenly, there is the sound of panic and shouting some distance ahead of us. A cloud of dust rises into the air. It is an oxcart fleeing from the Khmer Rouge, who are trying to round people up.

The cart heads straight toward us. Another emergency is upon us. We have no strength to run. We grab each other by the hand and leave the road, creeping into the unruly woods, into a thicket of bamboo to the left. We pass over a dry streambed and scramble up a slope, groping in the dark. The darkness prevents us from being able to tell where we have ended up. But many people have arrived here before us. They are lighting fires and starting to cook. No longer afraid, we prepare to cook some rice and eat along with them.

13 January 1979

The sound of a dog barking near my ear wakes me from my slumber. Good Lord, the sun has already risen quite high. The people who slept here with us last night have all gone. A tall man, about fifty years old, wearing *kong mov* shorts down to his knees and a dingy-white long-sleeved shirt and holding a small *phkeak* knife in his hand, comes walking toward us, following the barking of his dog. The man stops near us and says, "Nephews, where have you come from, sleeping here in my yam field?"

"Father, my brother and I are running away from the Khmer Rouge who are rounding people up."

We both raise our hands together before us in respectful greeting to this man and tell him about our journey, starting from the beginning. With concern, he leads us away from the yam fields of Kok Pongro to the village not very far away.

As though witnessing beings from another planet, the people in the village—men and women, old and young—put down whatever they are working on and run over to surround us and stare at us. They must not have ever encountered such shabby and frail people as the two of us. They jostle to ask us endless questions. Though we live in the same society, they have never tasted such abuse as we have endured. They are surprised and filled with compassion for us.

"Gee! What have the Khmer Rouge been using you for that you are so thin?"

"Where is your home village, youngsters?"

"Never mind! No need to go anywhere else."

"That's right! You just stay here with us."

"Don't you be going anywhere else! Stay here with us and rest and get some rice in you and put some meat on your bones."

"That's right! You stay here with us, youngsters. We don't lack for rice to eat. Our village has an ample rice crop."

"With your parents and siblings all gone, I don't reckon why you should bother going back home. Why don't you live here in our village and take local wives..."

The village we have come to is called Ta Toy village, Cha Chhuk subdistrict, Puok (present-day Angkor Chum) district, Siem Reap province. The village is on the border of Kralanh and Puok districts. The cart path we abandoned last night was located in Kralanh district. And the cart driver who drove past us was a villager from Prey Khyang village, Kralanh district. The women of this district mostly walk around without shirts, wearing only small brassieres to cover their breasts.

The welcome we receive from these people makes me realize that THE POOR FOLK OF THE COUNTRYSIDE ARE A PEOPLE FULL OF COMPASSION AND MERCIFUL KINDNESS.

THE END

Author's Note[1]

After publishing Parts One, Two, Three, and Four, I received numerous comments and opinions from readers via letter, phone call, and personal meeting. Generally, readers praised my efforts to compile this bitter history and my accomplishments as an author in drawing readers emotionally into my story and making them want to keep reading. Some readers felt that the content depicted therein was mild, and not sufficiently reflective of the level of misery which Cambodians suffered. Some people commented that I only described my own personal story.

I wish to express my deepest gratitude for all efforts by readers to provide feedback and comments. This was a tremendous moral support from all of you to me. Every assessment of this publication confirmed that people were reading and analyzing it. This is the pride of the author, as the chief concern of an author is the interest of the public: Are people reading and paying attention to my work?

At the same time, I wish to expound on some of these latter comments:

1. *Prisoners of Class* is mild
2. *Prisoners of Class* only tells my personal story

During that period, Cambodia was the stage of a great human tragedy (see "Journey to Spean Sreng," page 252). Everywhere, people were being hurt, tortured, and killed. *Prisoners of Class* is only one story among millions that played themselves out on the stage of Cambodia. *Prisoners of Class* cannot reflect all of the events that occurred throughout Cambodia.

In 1981 I accompanied a specialist from the FAO[2] to inspect livestock in Pursat province. A member of provincial administrative staff accompanied us to Phnom Kravanh town. Along the way I pointed out to him the stretch of railroad where I had lain sick waiting for the train to Battambang during the Pol Pot era. This man told me about his own history during the Pol Pot era on the way to Phnom Kravanh.

---

[1] published with Part Five of the first Khmer edition
[2] the Food and Agriculture Organization, a UN agency focused on food security and nutrition

"One night there was a meeting in the cooperative. After giving instructions about the work, the comrade chairman of the unit said, 'Thank you, mothers and fathers, brothers and sisters, for all of your hard work. Now, finally, I wish to submit myself to the collective for criticism of any of my shortcomings so that I can correct myself to become a true revolutionary!'

"A young women stood to speak. 'I think that the fact that you, comrade chairman, dragged a comrade sister from the rice field and beat her for transplanting too slowly, and then raped her in the open, was an inappropriate act.'

"The comrade chairman of the unit became very heated and stood up and screamed, 'How dare you, you bitch! I will split your chest open and see just how big your liver[3] is!' The comrade chairman picked up a hatchet and hacked open the abdomen of that young woman, as she stood before the assembly in the hall, and ripped out her liver then and there."

This was an act of extreme viciousness and cruelty! But this incident did not occur where I lived, and I did not witness it personally.

In order to preserve the value of truth, I have no intention of writing about events or circumstances which my eyes did not witness, and my ears did not hear. It is in this context that I had to use my own name as the main character of the story, and preserved the true names of the other characters, along with the actual dates and places. For if I were to invent a fictional main character, anything else could be fictional or made-up, and then this book would be a novel.

As for the second opinion: in fact, this was my own initial thought before publishing this book. I felt shy and hesitant to write about my own story for others to read. I felt that other Cambodians would likely have the same sentiment, for in Khmer society there are very few books in which authors talk about themselves.

However, after reading the book *A Story About a Real Man*,[4] recounting the personal history of a Soviet pilot; and after seeing the television series *Oshin*, about the terribly sad life of a Japanese woman; and after reading the book *Beyond the Horizon*[5] by Laurence Picq, which was translated into Khmer by His

---

[3] In Khmer, "big liver" is an idiom for insolence.
[4] *Повесть о настоящем человеке*, 1946, by Boris Polevoi (1908–1981)
[5] *Au-delà du ciel*, 1984

Excellency Khieu Kanharith;[6] and after reading *Prisoner of the Khmer Rouge*[7] by Prince Norodom Sihanouk, I became emboldened to prepare this book, *Prisoners of Class*, for publication.

Besides, I also wanted to remind people that during that dark period of Khmer history we were inmates of a prison without walls. Inmates of prisons with actual walls have the right to receive visits from family members and to be asked about the conditions inside their prison. We, on the other hand, had no rights at all. It was extremely difficult to receive any news whatsoever from beyond the place where we slept at night! Even my younger brother and older sister, who were taken away and executed—I have had great difficulty finding any information about them. The only things we could know about with any certainty were the things occurring immediately around us.

I hope that you, the readers, will be satisfied with this explanation. I am ready and delighted to receive any additional comments and opinions.

Thanks to my wife who worked hard to sustain the family and make it possible for me to compile this book for publication within seventeen months.

Thanks to my foster parents (the "Iron Rod" family) and my family members, friends from the period, friends from outside the period, and colleagues who helped provide financial support for the publication and helped to facilitate related tasks.

May this book inspire thought, promote awareness, and be of benefit to young Cambodians and Khmer society in subsequent generations.

Phnom Penh, 20 July 2000
Chan Samoeun

---

[6] 1951–present; Cambodian minister of information, 2004–2023
[7] *Prisonnier des Khmers Rouges*, 1986

Afterword

A few months after my exchange of letters with Chan Samoeun in early 2022, I found myself face to face with him in his home office in Phnom Penh, a small, air-conditioned room with a low ceiling, packed to the gills with books. Unlike the pictures I had seen of him from the Khmer editions, with dark hair and a plump face, now his hair was long and gray, and he had grown thin from a recent bout with COVID-19. We chatted for hours and then had the first of several lunches together in his small kitchen. In that first meeting, the first time he spoke of his early years, he became choked up and had to collect his feelings before he could continue. "I can't even talk about my childhood," he finally said, "without tearing up." He showed me the original handwritten manuscripts of *Prisoners of Class,* now more than forty years old, inscribed in a stack of small, yellowing school composition books. I was awed in the presence of these artifacts and honored to be handling them after so many years. He showed me on his laptop computer the electronic manuscript of a prequel book that he was working on, describing his childhood and youth growing up in poverty in the Phnom Penh of Sihanouk and Lon Nol.

The big news that day, by far, was that he had recently renewed contact with Comrade Ly, the tragic love of his youth, after believing for two decades that she was dead. This was a stunning revelation! The second edition of *Prisoners of Class* contained a short epilogue noting that he had been informed by a first-edition reader about Comrade Ly's execution in Thmor Puok district back in 1978. But now, he had recently learned that this was a case of mistaken identity, a different Comrade Ly altogether. He learned that *his* Comrade Ly was alive and well after all and still living in Thmor Puok, and he had recently been re-united with her, as well as Comrade Dy. In fact, when I phoned him on my arrival in Phnom Penh, the day before I met him, he happened to be enjoying a reunion dinner in town with Comrade Ly and her family at that very moment, he said, which struck me as a case of strange and serendipitous timing. Though both Comrade Tuch and Comrade Ly had long been married to other people, with their own children and grandchildren, in distant parts of the country, their friendship and deep connection was quickly rekindled, and during my time with him over the following few weeks, they would chat almost daily via Facebook messenger. It would become obvious to me that they enjoy an unusually strong connection and a naturally warm affinity for one another, even now these forty-four years later, almost as though no time has passed.

In that first meeting he explained something I had wondered about for twenty years. Though the protagonist's name in *Prisoners of Class* is Samoeun, the book cover cited the author's name as "Engineer Oum Sambath," with only a short mention on the back cover, without elaboration, that his "former name" was Chan Samoeun. He now told me the story of how he came to be called Oum Sambath, a typically Cambodian kind of story: When seeking an education in post-revolutionary Phnom Penh in 1980, an acquaintance offered him his coveted place on a three-month veterinary medicine course being offered by the Russians. That other young man's name was Oum Sambath, and Samoeun adopted his name in order to attend the course in his stead. Since the name on the completion certificate was Oum Sambath, he opted to continue using the name in his subsequent courses and employment. He eventually obtained a civil engineering degree in 1987 and went on to fulfill a career as an engineer in the Cambodian civil service, still under the pseudonym Oum Sambath. When he finally published his memoir, he used that name on the cover for the sake of the lifelong prestige and reputation he had, by then, built behind it. He has no idea what ever became of the original Oum Sambath.

When I told him of my plans to visit Phnom Srok district and do research for the English edition, he asked whether I would mind if he came along and told me that his brother Samorn in Siem Reap province has a car we could use. (Samorn had indeed married a local young woman and remained in Siem Reap province after the liberation, while Samoeun made his way back to Phnom Penh in 1980, alone, to seek an education.) Of course I was delighted and honored by this proposal and readily accepted. He got on the phone with Samorn straight away and started to make plans.

———

The landscape of Phnom Srok district, as described in *Prisoners of Class*, is notable for its many *koks*—the local term for spots of wooded high ground peppering the vast, flat plains of rice fields, often home to either villages or graveyards. Most of the local placenames contain the word *kok*, or sometimes the synonymous *paoy*, as civilization in this region was necessarily built on high ground in order to remain dry during seasonal flooding.

But by June 2022, when Chan Samoeun and I travelled to the region to-gether (first by bus to Siem Reap and then by car), many of the *koks* that were not already occupied by villages had since been erased to make way for yet more rice fields. Some of these lost *koks* were on my list of places to find and visit. For instance, I had hoped to see Kok Kakah, setting of the revolutionary farm with the little haunted hut by the chicken pen, backdrop of the women's sleeping-shelter inferno, and site of the arrests of both Bong Yong and Bong Tith. But there remain now no signs of the former location of this *kok* where it had once been situated, north of Kok Rumchek beside the main road that passes between Highway Six and Phnom Srok town. Between the established human settle-ments, there remain only endless green rice fields stretching along the road and beyond. (It is hard to overstate how vast and flat the landscape is here, or how green in the rainy season.)

On a sweltering tropical day, I sat at a table in the noontime heat beneath the front awning of a combination metal shop, lunch café, and house along the main road of the small town of Phnom Srok. Across from me sat the brothers Samorn and Samoeun, and to my right the fourth member of our expedition, their friend Prak Chanthoeun. Chanthoeun, an elected member of the Siem Reap Provincial Council, had also spent the revolution in Phnom Srok district as an evacuated new person. He had become friends with the author much later because of *Prisoners of Class*, as he had read the book and reached out to him. He had driven us there from Siem Reap in his own Prius, which was in better shape than Samorn's old Rav4. We ate rice, fried eggs, and soup while we planned the rest of our afternoon.

Of the various sites I wished to find, Paoy Trach was near the top of my list. The site, a grove of trees in the middle of an expanse of rice fields, was notorious in the region as the favored execution grounds for the local Khmer Rouge *chhlops* during the revolution, but none of my companions that day had ever actually been there or seen it up close with their own eyes (though the author had spoken with people who saw it and lived to describe it; see page 271). We doubted whether it was even locatable anymore, as it must have gone the way of the other *koks* and *paoys* long since effaced by rice paddies. Beside me, Chanthoeun chatted with an elderly man, residing at the house, who had spent his whole life in Phnom Srok. He asked him about Paoy Trach, and the old man said, "Sure, I know where Paoy Trach is." When asked if it might be possible to drive there, he said, to our surprise, "Yes, you can drive right to it." He told us that if we take the dirt track branching off the southwest corner[1] of town and follow it west across the rice fields, after a couple of kilometers we would come to a solitary Bodhi tree beside the road. That tree, he said, marks the spot where Paoy Trach had once been.

Samoeun, listening silently, suddenly became choked up, his face contorted with emotion, unable to speak. After blinking back the tears and collecting himself, he looked up and said, "Today I will finally visit the place where my brother and sister died." Samorn had stepped away for a moment, and when he returned just then, Samoeun turned to him and said, "M'orn, go and buy some incense sticks. We are going to visit the place where Samat and Oun died."

We found the road, and then the tree, just as promised. There was no longer a wooded *kok* at the site; only the dirt road and the rice fields on both sides and a pond with a low structure (a hut, or perhaps a shed) behind it. And of course the Bodhi tree, a holy symbol of Buddhism—representing the tree beneath which the Buddha attained enlightenment—with a stone bench beside it. The brothers lit incense sticks and inserted them into the ground at the base of the tree. Samoeun held a few more of the smoking sticks between his hands, palms together in prayer position, as he stood in the shade of the tree and prayed aloud to his departed brother and sister, wishing their souls wellbeing and peace in the hereafter. I felt honored to be present for this solemn event.

While they performed their rites, I looked around in vain for any sign of a mass grave. It was uncertain exactly where the victims' remains lay buried, or the precise location of any execution site, apparently now long obscured by paddies, the pond, the hut, the road, even the tree. (The following year, I would obtain from the Documentation Center of Cambodia, an organization dedicated to documenting Khmer Rouge crimes, a 1998 "mapping report" that described the "Kok Trach woods" as a killing site for hundreds if not thousands of victims. The report notes that the site did not contain a mass grave; rather, the

---

[1] One can see on a map that Phnom Srok is surrounded on four sides by an ancient rectangular moat. Interestingly, the author was unaware of this feature while living in the area or writing the book; he only recently realized this, with surprise, when looking at a map. He only knew, he said, that one crosses a bridge over water when entering the town and another when leaving, but it never occurred to him that this water formed a moat like those around ancient Khmer temples. He was very interested in this feature on our trip there together, his first time since learning of it, as he had come to believe that Phnom Srok must have been built on an ancient temple site. (As there are no known ruins there, I wonder if a more likely explanation is that the moat was dug long ago to control flooding, as the town lies in a floodplain.)

Khmer Rouge killed people here and left the bodies scattered on the ground in the woods, just as the book describes. Human remains from here and elsewhere in the district had since been collected and stored in a memorial in Wat Kandal, Phnom Srok.)

Just west of Paoy Trach, the dirt lane comes to the easternmost and largest of the three canals emerging from Trapeang Thmor Reservoir, flowing across the fields from the first water gate. It was while digging this canal by hand, and while sleeping on its levees and in the fields beside it and gazing wearily into the night sky, that Tuch and his comrades spotted a glowing spacecraft traversing the field of stars overhead, and he silently prayed to it, imploring it to look down and see them and send for help, recounting to it the horrors of Paoy Trach. (This passage touched my heart more than almost any other in the book. Something about the poignancy of that desperate, silent pleading with the spacecraft—intruding, incongruous and semi-godlike, into their isolated prison world from the modern world outside—moved me almost to tears.)

Earlier that morning, we had driven east along the causeway linking Kok Rumchek and Char Kok Team villages, through the twin villages of Char and Smach on the Rumduol River. We had stopped and gazed at the plain of Veal Saen Khyal, still covered by the grid of verdant rice paddies that the Life Slaves had constructed and plowed forty-four years prior, stretching southward past Or Ta Phal toward Highway Six and Phnom Tralok in the distance. We stopped in Smach, Char Kok Team, Pongro, and Rok villages and chatted with elderly locals about the past and the changes that had come with the passage of time. We visited the ruins of Prasat Pram and the ancient stone bridges of Spean Thom and Spean Kmeng, still standing as they have for hundreds of years.

As we explored and spoke with the locals, the bitterness formerly expressed by Samoeun for the Khmer Rouge cadres within the pages of *Prisoners of Class* seemed to have softened considerably with age, apparently tempered by a desire for friendship with all the people we met. On a couple of occasions, while riding in the car from one place to another, one of our traveling companions expressed a cautious but cynical distrust of one or another of the local old men we had just chatted with, former base people, speculating that he might have been a former cooperative chairman or other Khmer Rouge cadre, now hiding this fact from us out of shame. After the second such instance, Samoeun launched into a moralizing lecture as we drove, surprisingly passionate and reproving. He urged his companions that they cannot hold it against those men even if it were true; that not all of the cadres were malicious and were themselves under tremendous pressure; that some of them even tried to help people the best they could but were under orders from the Organization, and if they had not followed their orders they and their own families' lives would have been in peril; and that they cannot live their lives being mistrustful and nursing resentment for the past, or the nation would never find peace, unity, and happiness. (If any of our traveling companions had further reservations after this lecture, they did not say so.)

Though the ancient ruins are still intact, and the villages and subdistricts remain, some landmarks from the book are gone or transformed. The old wooden hospital house in Phnom Srok with the dirt floor, where Comrade Tuch had lain sick on his sheet of warped corrugated iron, and which had been intact back in 2006 when the two brothers had last visited and photographed it, had been torn down and replaced with something more modern. The site of the main building and former patients' dining hall just around the corner is now the location of the district health center.

Later in the afternoon, we visited Paoy Char subdistrict, where our first stop was Paoy Snuol village. There we found that the former site of the ramshackle hut where Ol had died, and toward which Comrade Tuch had later hurried, hoping beyond hope to find Oun still alive, only to confirm what he already knew, was now an empty plot of land just before the road from Phnom Srok turns north toward the reservoir through the villages of Paoy Char. (Only a smallish red stupa, memorializing someone else's lost loved one, stands on the lot near the road.)

A little further north, the road passes the lot where the wooden Khmer-style house of Father Suk and Mother Lam once stood high on stilts,[2] beneath which the brothers' family had slept in late 1976. That house, too, has since been dismantled and replaced with a more modern house of bricks and cement and

---

[2] In photographs of the author taken in front of this house in 2006 (see page 513), the house is considerably lower than his memories of it from 1976. He told me before our visit there, when chatting about these photographs, how baffled he was by this strange fact, trying to understand how or why the house had apparently been lowered, while otherwise appearing the same as before. Later, chatting with local villagers about this mystery during our visit, he discovered the answer: when the road through Paoy Char was paved, the elevation of the road had been raised considerably, and some of the homeowners along the road had brought in dirt and filled their yards to match the height of the road. Thus, the house had not been lowered, but rather the ground beneath it had been raised.

tiles, now flush with the ground; though a small wooden outbuilding in the corner of the lot is constructed of wood from the original house, the current residents (descendants of Suk and Lam) informed us.

But in Trapeang Thmor village, we found that the large rectangular "brick-kiln pond" west of Wat Trapeang Thmor was still there and full of water, though the kiln itself and the brickmaking shed are long gone. Where the first vegetable field had been is now the Trapeang Thmor Market. At the north end of the pond, a younger Bodhi tree grows in the same spot where the former one had been, marking the former site of the mobile workers' dining pavilion beside the pond, where Comrade Tuch first met Comrades Ly and Dy. Standing there by the pond in the midafternoon, it was not hard to imagine a young Comrade Tuch fetching water for his vegetables with his shoulder yoke while a young Comrade Ly looked on admiringly.

Trapeang Thmor Reservoir is surprisingly vast in person. Standing on the east-west dam road in the afternoon, the mirror-like water appears to extend almost to the horizon, faint trees and tiny hills barely visible on the far side. It is staggering to think that not so long ago, the vast dams creating this massive body of water were constructed by hand, by thirty thousand starving slaves with nothing but hoes and bamboo shoulder poles and baskets. Total mastery of water and irrigation had been the hallmark of the ancient Khmer civilization at Angkor, and by creating such large-scale, ambitious irrigation works, the Khmer Rouge had intentionally invoked ancient Khmer power.

With the passage of time, beauty and unexpected utility have emerged from the suffering that created this place. Now the reservoir serves as a habitat for an endangered species, the sarus crane, and there is a wildlife reserve at the site. Young people sit on their motorcycles beside the dirt road running along the top of the dam and watch the waves lapping the shore and the water flowing over the gates on its way to irrigate the plain of rice fields southward. Between the ancient stone bridge of Spean Reap and the first water gate, at the place where the east-west dam begins to branch northward, near where the Organization's regional mobile-committee office had once been located, I saw rows of huts with colorful umbrellas and large signs featuring beer logos, where visitors can enjoy drinks and snacks, and heard the sounds of a Khmer rap song coming from unseen speakers. To me, at that moment, the time of mass labor mobilization, starvation, and revolutionary fervor felt very distant; but for the three older Cambodian uncles traveling with me, I sensed that the events of those years were still in some ways very near and very vivid, the reservoir itself a permanent and tangible proof of the labors they had once performed under such travail.

I later asked Samoeun what he feels when he looks at Trapeang Thmor Reservoir now, if he still feels the pride of accomplishment that he mentioned briefly in his book (see page 213); and if so, whether it outweighs the bitterness. He told me that despite the terrible price of suffering paid, he does feel a sort of pride of national accomplishment when he looks at the results of all that work in which he played a part. The feelings of bitterness have faded, he said, because "as long as you insist on dwelling on suffering, you can't build a new life. You can't build happiness."

———

On another sweltering day, now much closer to Phnom Penh, I stood alone on the eastern shore of Don Duong lake in Kien Svay district, Kandal province, now swollen with water in the rainy season, and looked across at Tuol Ampil village on the other side. I had just come from visiting and photographing the beautiful Wat Chroy Ampil and its spacious grounds where so many refugees had camped back in April 1975. My taxi had parked just inside Wat Slaket off Highway 1, and I had walked through that *wat* to get here, just as Samoeun's mother had done seventy years before, and as the three brothers had done twenty-three years after that with their long *phkeak* knives over their shoulders. I found that the lake's eastern shore had crept considerably westward by means of dirt and gravel fill, dumped and smoothed behind the *wat* to create additional real estate for the construction of stupas memorializing the deceased family members of *wat* patrons, some of which were presently under construction. But the lake is still there, as is the original rectangular lotus pond just behind the *wat*.

I took my taxi clear around to reach the villages on the other side. It seemed that most of the side roads there in Koki subdistrict, Kien Svay district, off of Highway 1, are now paved with concrete, smooth and accommodating and modern; but the dirt track that runs along the rise west of Don Duong lake was somehow still untouched by concrete or asphalt, like a setting plucked from the past. The villages strung along the dirt track, the locals confirmed, are still called Ta Riep, Tuol Ampil, and Tuol Tnaot. There was a whiff of wood smoke and an air of poverty in these villages to match the state of the road, reminiscent of the poverty of the region as I remembered it from twenty-five years before.

I hadn't dragged Samoeun out with me on this day trip out of Phnom Penh, so I was on my own. (I wished to spare him the exertion of tramping around in the scorching heat as I collected photographs and GPS readings for a map.) The villagers were friendly and accommodating, though. Referring to a single sentence in Chapter Four of *Prisoners of Class*, I sought the location of Kor Ko, the burial site of Comrade Tuch's father somewhere behind Wat Tamol. I wondered if it was even possible to find this spot among all that vegetation, let alone a grave marker.

The locals were familiar with the name Kor Ko, and each person I asked helpfully directed me steadily closer. Finally, as I tramped, sweating, down a muddy side road, I asked another man standing in front of his home, and he pointed to the dead end of that lane and said, "Kor Ko, right there."

"By the way, what is Kor Ko?" I asked him. "Not the name of a village..."

"No, not a village, just that place right there," he said, pointing again.

I could see a solitary stupa erected there in a clearing and thought it a good sign that it appeared to be a graveyard of some kind, better marked than I had feared. The phrase *kor ko* literally means "ox's neck." Samoeun would later speculate, when he called me that evening at my hotel to chat about my day's adventure, that perhaps at some point in the past, a spot of land jutting into the lake had reminded someone of an ox's neck, and the moniker had stuck.

I walked to the end of the lane and over to the stupa perched above the edge of the water, which was choked with aquatic vegetation here at the north end of the lake, and read the plaque on the front of the stupa, facing the water. I was startled to find the words "Oum Sambath (Chan Samoeun)" engraved there in Khmer script. The possibility that this imposing stupa might mark the very grave I was seeking had not even occurred to me until that moment, as his father's burial had been done in poverty and desperation, and I was imagining something much humbler. The plaque informed me that the author had erected the stupa over his father's gravesite in 2002, and inside were grave markers not only for his father, Pen Doeuk, but another for his mother, Chan Ith, as well. Along the banks beside the lone stupa there were a handful of ground-level, Chinese-style cement graves.

In the wake of this unexpectedly successful discovery, I was feeling suddenly more optimistic about the prospect of finding additional landmarks from the book intact. I directed my taxi to yet another *wat*, Wat Kien Svay Krau, to photograph the elevated monks' dining pavilion, setting of that vivid scene where the family anxiously wait to collect their rice rations after having raced up the highway in the darkness, hoping I would find it still there and photographable. But alas, inside the *wat*, the old, traditional, elevated dining pavilion with double stairs had been torn down and the site paved over with concrete, and a newer ground-level brick-and-tile dining hall for the monks had been constructed adjacent to the site. I had to content myself with photographing the concrete slab instead.

As my taxi took me back into the city, we passed through Chbar Ampov and over the Monivong Bridge, the evacuees' former means of egress from the city, actually now two twin bridges instead of one. We drove through the tangled traffic interchange on the Phnom Penh side of the river, with elevated overpasses, that was once (in my own youth, even) a much simpler intersection with a roundabout called Kbal Thnal (the "Highway Head"), starting point for Highway One, Highway Two, Monivong Boulevard, and Norodom Boulevard. The final battle for Phnom Penh that Tuch and his family had heard on the morning of April 17th was fought at and around this place.

My last two stops on this outing were the playing fields of Boeng Trabek High School and the roundabout at Phsar Daeum Thkov in the south of the city. I wanted to get photographs. This is the part of the story that intersects with my own life. As a young man in the nineties, I had ridden my bicycle across the soccer fields of Boeng Trabek High School many times, often in the golden hour of evening, taking a shortcut to Monivong Boulevard from the neighborhood eastward. Later I had felt a jolt of historic connection to read in *Prisoners of Class* about Tuch's family camping, along with countless other evacuees, on those very same fields, at dusk on 18 April 1975 (see Chapter 2).

Between the 1979 liberation and 1999, Phnom Penh developed comparatively little, as the struggling country was preoccupied with recovery, poverty, and ongoing civil war and political strife. Like most sites in the city, Boeng Trabek High School and its grounds probably looked much the same in the late nineties, when I knew it, as it had in April 1975. But after the 1998 elections and the surrender of the last Khmer Rouge rebels in 1999 (the same year that

Prisoners of Class was finally published), things began to modernize dramatically in Phnom Penh and elsewhere; fairly slowly at first, but then at an exponentially accelerating pace. Foreign money and investments have been pouring into Cambodia ever since.

So when I entered the grounds of Boeng Trabek High School through the front gate on Monivong Boulevard in 2022, I found that the several smallish soccer pitches with patchy grass and bare goals that had once filled the large yard, flanked by palm trees, had been mostly replaced with a single, full-sized, ultra-modern playing field, complete with a high net fence, spectators' bleachers, manicured turf, white painted lines, and even field lights high on poles. Such modernity was absolutely unthinkable only twenty years prior, especially for a state school. A skyline of dozens of high-rise condominiums and hotels rose up behind and around the school yard. (Until 2010, the number of high-rise buildings in Cambodia was exactly zero; now it is probably closer to a thousand and growing rapidly.) But I was relieved to find that one of the original, humble soccer pitches, with original, white-painted iron goal, had been left intact near the front gate, and that the original pre-war school building had, somewhat surprisingly, not yet been torn down to make way for something more modern. At least I had *something* to photograph to capture the past as it had been.

Likewise, the Phsar Daeum Thkov neighborhood, due west from those school gates, had changed a great deal as well, but remained recognizable from its familiar geometry: five roads converge here at a roundabout with a golden mermaid statue, described in the first chapter of *Prisoners of Class*. This is where Tuch had stood, not far from his house, and watched the columns of Khmer Rouge soldiers marching northward into the city on April 17th. Just north of the circle, on a triangular sliver nestled between two spoke roads, is the Phsar Daeum Thkov Health Center, where Tuch's brother-in-law *Nho* had worked. Designed and built by the legendary Khmer architect Vann Molyvann in 1961 as the Preah Suramarit Dispensary, the building remains intact and is still a public health clinic to this day. The school remains but is now a high school instead of a primary school. Not far north of the roundabout, along one of those roads, is Tuol Tumpung Market, where Samoeun and his sister used to go sell snails and *trakuon* harvested from the lake (and where I first discovered *Prisoners of Class),* largely untouched by the passage of time.

But where this neighborhood had previously been a gateway to the city's rural outskirts, now the whole area has since been subsumed into the modern, expanding metropolis. Traffic streams past the roundabout on smooth, paved roads, flanked by shops. The large circle features a garden with grass and paving stones surrounding a pond with the golden mermaid in the center.

Accounts of the roundabout after its construction in the early 60's describe it as paved with asphalt and featuring a lotus pond and fountain around a golden mermaid statue, lit at night by underwater spotlights, surrounded by a larger garden with paving stones. The mermaid was a likeness of Sovann Maccha from the *Reamker*, the ancient Khmer version of the *Ramayana* epic.[3] In those days, the circle garden was a popular neighborhood gathering spot in the evenings.

As a young man, more than two decades after that fateful day in 1975, I rode my bicycle past this roundabout countless times. But I knew nothing then about any of this history and would never have guessed it. For the roundabout by then was unpaved, and the circle was only a small ring of reddish stone or cement surrounded by dirt, with nothing inside but more dirt and weeds. That ring, I now realize, was merely the remnants of the original pond enclosure and not the full circle that once existed there. There was no sign that a garden, paving stones, fountain, lights, asphalt, or statue had ever existed at all.

Then one day, in late 1998 or early 1999, as I pedaled past the circle, I noticed with interest that someone had placed a small gold-painted mermaid statue on a plinth inside the stone ring, a small sign at its base reading "Sovann Maccha" in Khmer. I would not realize until I read the first chapter of *Prisoners of Class* a few years later—again with an electrifying sense of historical connection—that this was not an innovation, but an attempt to restore something that had existed in a former time. Subsequent restorations have brought the circle closer to its original grandeur and size. In hindsight, the history of this landmark is emblematic of how the post–Khmer Rouge Cambodia of the eighties and nineties remained, in many ways, a wounded and degraded version

---

[3] By all accounts, the artistry of that original statue, her arms and hands frozen in a pose taken from the classical Khmer *Apsara* dance depicting the *Reamke,* her tail stretched out behind her—not to mention the fountain and lights—was more impressive than the comparatively lackluster design of the current version. According to a personal interview with Ms. Khieu Sophal, present-day custodian at the clinic, whose late father Pin Chhuon was instrumental in constructing the clinic and roundabout in her youth, the original circle and statue were also designed by Vann Molyvann himself.

of its pre-war self, struggling to retain its former glory, and how the turn of the millennium was an inflection point in that progression.

Just to the south of the roundabout is Street 490, the little road where Samoeun had lived growing up. Once a sleepy dirt lane near the swampy Boeng Trabek ("Guava Lake," the namesake of the high school), it is now just another urban side street, and the lake has been all but shrunk to nothing to make way for more urban sprawl. Forty-seven years before, on this lane, in a modest, wooden Khmer house elevated on stilts, built by his family, a young Chan Samoeun had left his prized photographs spread out on his bed, thinking he would return for them in a few days, not realizing until it was too late that he would never see them again. During our first meeting, he told me about the regret he still feels for those lost photos from his youth. Today the only things connecting this street to its past self are its location on the map and its name.

———

I still have a special affinity for the early chapters of *Prisoners of Class*, which capture so many details of 1975 Phnom Penh at the moment of Khmer Rouge victory. I feel almost greedy for those details; I collect any photograph, map, or description from the city's past that I can find. I feel a deeply personal connection with and nostalgia for what I am now coming to think of as "Old Phnom Penh," and very fortunate that I got to know it well in the last years before it began to change dramatically. With the breakneck pace of economic investment and development, seemingly devoid of coherent urban planning, increasingly little of Old Phnom Penh remains now, at least on the surface. I have been taken completely off guard by the speed and scope of the transformation in recent years, which is hard to overstate. (This has been a common topic of conversation with Samoeun, as he feels a similar disorientation.) The city had changed so little during my first several years there, and still looked so much like it had in pictures and film from before the revolution, like an insect trapped in amber, that I never imagined I wouldn't be able to just continue revisiting old haunts or exploring landmarks whenever I liked, finding them much as they had always been, or that everything was about to become so different, so quickly.

It is truly the passing of an era.

Passing, too, is the generation of people who lived through the most turbulent, defining, and transformational eras of modern Cambodian history in the twentieth century—the post-colonial years of Sihanouk and the *Sangkum* (1954–70); the Khmer Republic and civil war (1970–75); and the Khmer Rouge regime (1975–79). It is a generation now grown unexpectedly gray-haired and frail. In my early years in Cambodia, including when I first discovered *Prisoners of Class*, this generation constituted the backbone of Cambodian society. They were the parents, the shopkeepers, the maids, the farmers, the doctors and nurses, the taxi and *cyclo* drivers, the policemen, the politicians—all of the aunties and uncles of Cambodia. At that time, only the youngest Cambodians, those about my age and younger (I was born in 1977), had no memories of Khmer Rouge rule. For everyone else, virtually the entire adult population of the country, the Khmer Rouge era was fairly recent memory, and the effects of it were pervasive. (And in rural areas, especially, a sizable percentage of that population had themselves once *been* Khmer Rouge in some form or other.) I somehow don't know that I ever truly appreciated that this would change.

But now, the vast majority of people in Cambodia have no memory of those events. Nobody younger than about their late forties or so—and current demographics skew overwhelmingly young—has even so much as an early childhood memory of the realities of Democratic Kampuchea, and nobody under their late fifties or so has any memory of life in pre-war Cambodia. And those numbers keep going up every year from this writing. And now many of those who do remember, especially those who were grown when the Khmer Rouge captured power, are dying out slowly, soon to be quickly. Samoeun's thick black mop of black hair has now turned silver. Before long there will be nobody at all left who remembers what happened, and the country that they knew will have finally passed, transformed, to an entirely different cohort of forward-looking Cambodians. It will all belong to the past, to the history books.

Thus *Prisoners of Class* is and will remain a precious link to history, a priceless document to remind later generations of the now almost unthinkable things that occurred, to memorialize the heroic travails and losses (and crimes, lest we forget) of the now-passing generation. In the preface to *Prisoners of Class*, the author laments that "in Cambodian society we have very few articles or books describing the real lives of people who lived in any era of our history." How fortunate indeed that that young man felt compelled to write down everything that he and his family saw and experienced while the memories were so fresh. How fortunate that he thought to include so many details! And how fortunate that he had the heart of both a chronicler and a poet. Though he almost certainly did not appreciate it at the time, that labor of personal writing would become a historical treasure memorializing, for all time, not just him and his family, but his entire generation, a whole era, a whole country, for future generations of Cambodians—and now for the world outside of Cambodia as well.

So now, with this translation, it is my hope and aspiration to give this important historical document an even wider distribution, a stronger foothold, a larger audience, to preserve and propagate a witness of a not-so-distant but rapidly receding past, for many more people in many more generations to come. May it become an essential and immortal resource for all those who seek to understand Cambodia's turbulent twentieth-century past.

Matthew Madden, 17 September 2023

Translator's Acknowledgements

I acknowledge with gratitude the contributions of the following people in bringing this translation to print: author Chan Samoeun, first and foremost, for his generous friendship and invaluable cooperation; my wife, CarrieAnn Madden, without whose patience and support this project could not have been possible; Lek Chumnor of the Khmer Writers Association in Phnom Penh for his valuable assistance in connecting me with the author and facilitating our meetings and communications from afar; Chan Samorn and Prak Chanthoeun for their companionship, assistance, and added perspectives; Lachlan Peters, Cambodian-history podcaster extraordinaire, for being my first reader and enthusiastic supporter; Andrew Moscrop, for his eager willingness to be an early reader and for his priceless encouragement and feedback; Michael Madden, for his keen eye and valuable feedback; Ros Sampeou of the Documentation Center of Cambodia for his research assistance; Sebastian Strangio and Craig Etcheson for their attention and generous words; and my daughters Beatrice and Julia Madden, my wells of motivation and delight.

Appendices

Glossary

The following is a summary of non-English words referenced in this book, as well as unique English terms representing particular Cambodian or Khmer-Rouge concepts.

English

base people — a Khmer Rouge term denoting those Cambodians who already lived in the liberated zones prior to 17 April 1975; a relatively favored class; opposite: new people

build — a term commonly employed by the Khmer Rouge to refer to revolutionary indoctrination and discipline, usually in the context of correcting incorrect behavior; Khmer: *kasang*

cadre — a term used to refer to leaders or officials within the communist party; though used commonly as a collective noun, referring to a core group or cell of leaders, it can be used to refer to a single individual, a member of such a group. The word is used in this latter sense throughout this book to refer to individual Khmer Rouge party officials and leaders. Khmer: *kammaphibal*

coining — a traditional remedy (for dizziness, headaches, fatigue, insomnia, stomachaches, and all manner of ailments) in which the patient's skin is scraped with a coin, producing dark red stripes of subcutaneous blood, on which ointment (if available) may be applied

consciousness sickness — a phrase often used by the Khmer Rouge to imply sickness that is only in the mind, psychosomatic (or even faked) illness caused by an unrevolutionary mindset or by dwelling excessively on the past.

Day of Ceremony — a Khmer Rouge euphemism for a mass wedding

economy team — mess unit; the Khmer Rouge term for a team tasked with supplying communal food and water (cooking the food and managing supplies) for a unit or cooperative

liberated zones — a term denoting those regions secured and administered by the Khmer Rouge during the war (1970-1975) prior to the capture of Phnom Penh and other major cities on 17 April 1975

new people — a Khmer Rouge term denoting those Cambodians evacuated from the cities on or after 17 April 1975; an underclass targeted for destruction; opposite: base people

Life Masters	an epithet coined by the author to denote Khmer Rouge cadres and "base people"; opposite: Life Slaves
Life Slaves	an epithet coined by the author to denote the "new people," the class of people treated most harshly by the Khmer Rouge (though sometimes defined as everyone except the cadres); opposite: Life Masters
The (Revolutionary) Organization	the term by which the Communist Party of Kampuchea, a.k.a. the Khmer Rouge, commonly referred to itself. Khmer: *Angkar (Pakdevoat)*
PC motorbike	nickname for a Honda PC50 moped
sleeping platform	a low platform attached to hut walls, topped with loosely spaced slats of bamboo strips or wood, used for sleeping on (as well as sitting, eating, or working); Khmer: *rean*

Pali

anichang, tukkhang, anata	"uncertainty, misery, immateriality"
attahek attanao neathao	"one must be self-reliant"
cheatek, chorea, pyeathik, moranak	"birth, old age, illness, death"
sokatao sokata	to give comfort to others and receive comfort in return

French/Khmer

cyclo	from the French *cyclopousse*, a classic Cambodian pedicab/ trishaw common in cities like Phnom Penh, in which the driver pedals behind while the passenger rides in front (*/see-klo/*); see photograph on page 508
diplôme	a junior high school completion certificate
bac un	from the French *baccalauréat un:* first baccalaureate exam, the first of two rounds of Cambodian high school completion exams, this one taken after the penultimate year
bac double	From the French *baccalauréat double*: second baccalaureate exam, taken after the final year, conferring the equivalent of a high-school diploma or A-Level

Khmer

achko a type of frog (scientific name unknown)

ambaeng a kind of thin pancake

ambah changkeh a traditional protective amulet made from a cotton string, worn tied around the waist

aeut to stick one's head in or out; to pop in/by; by extension, to visit briefly

anao a kind of wild plant (scientific name unknown)

andaeng a type of fish *(Clarias batracius)*

angkam a species of duck (scientific name unknown)

angkunh a type of vine with large, woody seeds that are used to play the traditional game *bah angkunh*

anlung kong a type of poisonous mushroom; also called *chungkung kreal* (scientific name unknown)

ansam a kind of dense traditional Khmer cake eaten at holidays, made from sticky rice, coconut milk, and other ingredients, steamed inside banana-leaf wraps; see photograph on page 517

apaong a gambling game in which a die is spun and covered with a coconut shell

baboh a kind of cake

bah angkunh a traditional game ("toss the *angkunh* seed") in which *angkunh* seeds are placed upright in a triangle formation and players attempt to knock them down by tossing other *angkunh* seeds; see *angkunh*

bangkuoy a general term for a broad category of lizards (multiple genera)

bangky a kind of scoop-shaped earth-moving basket with handle loops on two sides, used primarily by attaching to the two ends of a shoulder yoke for hauling, and dumping dirt; see photograph on page 517

barang a type of grass (scientific name unknown)

bhikkhu senior monk

bong	older brother or older sister; also a polite term of address for someone somewhat older than the speaker, and an affectionate term of address for a romantic male partner
bot	a type of cake made from sticky rice flour and salted mung beans, wrapped in banana leaves
chae kach	a small elephant tusk left embedded in a tree, believed to have great magical power and used as an amulet of protection
chambak	a type of tree (*Irvingia malayana*)
chan srak	a set of stacking, cylindrical metal dishes with a frame and handle on top, for carrying food; see photograph on page 518
chang'er	a kind of large, flat basket
chaol chhung	a traditional game ("throw the cushion") involving two sides (typically boys vs. girls) singing songs and throwing a cushion back and forth at one another until one side has eliminated the other
chap kon khlaeng	a traditional game ("catch the kite")
cheas	a type of lizard (*Acanthosaura*)
Chetr	lunar calendar month from mid-March to mid-April
chhlonh	a type of fish (*Macrognathus siamensis*)
chhlop	spy; a Khmer Rouge officer, combination intelligence officer and enforcer, who monitors the behavior of community members and enforces punishments, including executions; a role often filled by young people, including children
chhveng	"left"; a type of climbing vine that spirals up a tree trunk from left to right
choar	a type of edible mushroom (scientific name unknown)
chrach	a type of edible aquatic plant (*Monochoria vaginalis*)
chungkung kreal	another term for *anlung kong*; see *anlung kong*
dah kun	a type of vine (*Tetracera scandens*)
dangraek	a type of vine (scientific name unknown)

duong	a type of worm (*Calandra palmarum*)
hing	a type of toad (*Callula pulchra*)
kakah	a type of tree (*Sindora cochinchinensis*)
kamphlang	a type of edible aquatic plant (*Polygonum tomentosum*)
kamping puoy	a type of edible aquatic plant (*Ludwigia adscendens*)
Kampuchea	Cambodia
kandaol	a type of tree (*Careya sphaerica)*
kanh	a type of fish (scientific name unknown)
kanhchae	a type of dark-red beetle (scientific name unknown)
kanhchanh chek	a type of tree frog (scientific name unknown)
kanhcheak sla	a type of edible mushroom (scientific name unknown)
kanhcheu	a kind of medium-sized round basket
kanhchhet cromoh	a type of fish with white scales (scientific name unknown)
kanhchou	a type of edible mushroom (scientific name unknown)
kanhchraeng	a kind of shallow basket
kantolet	a type of edible aquatic grass (scientific name unknown)
kantraeuy	a type of grass (*Chrysopogon aciculatus*)
kantuot	a type of tree with small edible fruit (*Phyllanthus acidus*)
katha	a magic charm made of a rolled-up gold or silver scroll with an inscribed prayer, used as a protective amulet
kathen tean	an annual festival in which clothing and supplies are donated to the Buddhist monks
Katdek	lunar calendar month from mid-October to mid-November
kbal lan	a type of fish with white scales (scientific name unknown)
kben	a skirt or sarong worn passed between the legs and tucked in at the waist on the other side to make a sort of rudimentary short trousers

khlong	a type of tree (*Dipterocarpus tuberculatus*)
khlouk	a type of gourd (*Lagenaria siceraria*)
Khmer Serei	the "Free Khmer," a dissident guerrilla movement led by nationalist Son Ngoc Thanh that opposed both communism and the monarchy through the late 50's and 60's
khnay tan	a wild boar's tusk believed to have magical power and used as a protective amulet
kho	to cook meat in a kind of dark stew with caramelized sugar, soy sauce, and spices; or meat stew that has been cooked this way
khvaev	a long-handled knife similar to a *phkeak;* see *phkeak*
kingkuok	a type of toad (*Bufo melanosticus*)
knhyong	a type of beetle (scientific name unknown)
kok	in the dialect of northwestern Cambodia, a spot of relative high ground (Central Khmer: *tuol)* in the plains of rice fields, which stays dry during flooding; villages and cemeteries tend to be located on these. This word, as well as the synonymous *paoy,* is found in many place names in the region.
kray	krait (*Bungarus*), a genus of highly venomous snake
l'ey	a kind of small round basket
leak kansaeng	a traditional game ("hide the handkerchief") involving hiding a handkerchief behind one of several players in a circle
lenh	a type of fish with white scales (*Dangila siamensis*)
lngieng	a type of tree (*Cratoxylon cochinchinensis*)
lveang	a type of tree (*Rhamnus tinctorius*)
Mara	the Buddha's demonic enemy; the Destroyer
maong dop	a type of flower (*Portulaca grandiflora*), the "ten o'clock flower"
mchey	a type of tree (scientific name unknown)
me smel	weaver-ant princess; large, greenish, winged type of weaver ant, a proto-queen, considered edible

mea	same as *pu;* also, an honorific, egalitarian term of address for mid-level cadres under the Khmer Rouge
memut	a kind of witch
Mikaser	lunar calendar month from mid-November to mid-December
mrom	a type of small stingless bee (scientific name unknown)
neak ta	guardian spirit; ancestral spirit (usually represented as a statue)
nirasar	an aide who serves as a messenger, bodyguard, and/or liaison officer to a Khmer Rouge cadre; a Khmer Rouge–coined term
nonoung	a type of gourd (*Luffa*)
om	uncle/aunt (older than one's parents); polite term of address for an older man or woman older than one's parents
Or Ta Phal	"Grandfather Phal's Stream"
oun	a diminutive form of *p'oun* ("younger sibling"), used as an affectionate term of address for a romantic female partner; also, the personal name of the author's sister
paoy	similar to *kok* (possibly from Thai)
ph'ak	a kind of seasoned, fermented fish kept in earthen jars
phchoek	a type of tree (*Shorea obtusa*)
Phchum Ben	a traditional Cambodian festival honoring the spirits of the deceased, who are believed to visit the earth during the festival, during which food offerings are left out for them
phdiek	a type of tree (*Anisoptera scaphula*)
phek	a colloquial term meaning porridge mixed with leaves
phkeak	a kind of traditional utility knife used for cutting vegetation, with a blade on the end of a long handle meant to be wielded with two hands; see photograph on page 518
phneang	see *phnom phneng*
phnom	mountain; hill

phnom phneng	a type of shrub (*Hymenocardia wallichii*)
Photrabot	lunar calendar month from mid-August to mid-September
phty	a category of edible greens including amaranth and purslane
Pisakh	lunar calendar month from mid-April to mid-May (also called Visakh)
poat seima	a protective ritual in which a monk recites Pali incantations while walking in circuits around the boundary of something, e.g. a house, often with a string, for a prescribed number of circuits
pongro	a type of tree (*Schleicheria oleosa*)
poun	a type of tree with edible fruit (*Spondias*)
prae rup	a traditional ceremony involving washing the bone fragments of a cremated individual
prahok	a paste made of salted fermented fish, and a key component in Cambodian cooking
prasva	a type of tree (scientific name unknown)
Preah Phirun	Varuna, the Hindu god of rain
preal	a type of shrub (*Columbia auriculata*) whose bark is used to make ropes
prech	a smallish species of wild bamboo (scientific name unknown)
preng	a type of vine (*Derris scandens*)
prich	a type of wild edible plant (scientific name unknown)
pring	a type of tree with edible fruit (*Syzygium jambos*)
pring bay	a type of tree with edible fruit (*Syzygium cinereum*)
pu	uncle (younger than one's parents); a polite term of address for an older man younger than one's parents
puk bangkang	a type of grass (possibly *Alternanthera sessilis*)
reang	a type of tree (*Barringtonia acutangula*)

roneam	a region of seasonally flooded forest, particularly the one along the shores of the Tonle Sap lake
riel	1. the currency of Cambodia 2. a type of fish (*Dangila cuvieri*)
roam vong	a traditional Khmer social dance in which participants dance in a circle
ropeak	a type of rattan (*Calamus salicifolius*) used to weave baskets
sakhu	a colloquial pronunciation of *saku* in Phnom Srok district
saku	arrowroot (*Maranta arundinacea*)
sala chortean	a traditional open-sided pavilion-like structure used for distributing alms
Samdech	a Khmer title of high honor; all instances in the book refer to Prince Norodom Sihanouk
samraong	a type of tree (*Sterculia lychnophora*)
sangkae	a type of tree (*Combretum lacriferum*)
Sangkum	see *Sangkum Reastr Niyum*
Sangkum Reastr Niyum	Sihanouk's political movement ("Popular Socialist Community") that held power from 1955 to 1970
sdau	a type of tree (*Azadirachta indica*)
sdoksdol	a type of tree (scientific name unknown)
skun	a type of edible aquatic plant (*Limnanthemum hydrophyllum*)
slaeng voa	a type of poisonous strychnine vine (scientific name unknown)
slap chravar	a type of edible aquatic plant (*Ottelia alismoides*)
snao	a type of edible aquatic plant (*Sesbania javanica*)
snuol	a type of tree (*Dalbergia nigrescens*)
sokram	a type of tree (*Xylia xylocarpa*)
spean	bridge
Srapn	lunar calendar month from roughly mid-July to mid-August

srot	to sink down
t'aeuk	a kind of vine (*Merremia hederacea*)
ta	grandfather; a polite term of address for older men around the age of one's grandparents; also, an honorific, egalitarian term of address for senior cadres under the Khmer Rouge
tau	a unit of dry measure equivalent to about half a bushel (18 liters, 4 gallons)
tbaeng	a type of tree (*Dipterocarpus obtusifolius*)
thkov	a type of tree (*Neolamarckia cadamba*)
thnang ampov	"sugar cane joint"; another name for the *kray* or krait snake; see *kray*
thnoeng	a type of vine (*Aganonerion polymorphum*)
thnuong	a type of tree (*Pterocarpus cambodianus* or *Pterocarpus pedatus*)
tong	a large square tin (for holding oil)
trabaek prey	a type of tree (*Lagerstroemia rigina*)
trach	a type of tree (*Dipterocarpus intricatus*)
trah	a type of tree (*Combretum trifoliatum*)
trakuon	an edible green plant that grows in still water, very commonly eaten as a vegetable (both cultivated and foraged) in Cambodian cooking; bindweed; water convolvulus (*Ipomoea aquatica*)
traok	a type of earthworm (scientific name unknown)
treas	a type of tree with poisonous leaves (*Caesalpinia digyna*)
triel dah krabey	a type of tough vine with large red fruit (scientific name unknown)
triel sva	a type of tree with small red fruit (scientific name unknown)
tro	a traditional Khmer stringed instrument with one string, played with a bow
tromung	a type of tree with edible fruit (*Garcinia oliveri*)
Veal Saen Khyal	"Plain of Great Wind"

wat	a Buddhist monastery and temple complex, consisting of the grounds, the temple itself, stupas, monks' dormitories, and other buildings
Yama	lord of Hell and judge of the dead in Buddhist scripture
yeav	a type of vine (*Nephroia sarmentosa*)
yoant	a magical drawing inscribed on paper, cloth, or skin, used as a protective amulet

Maps

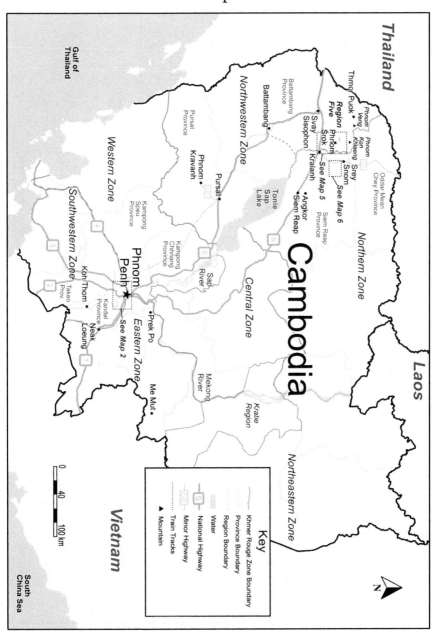

Map 1: Cambodia 1977–79

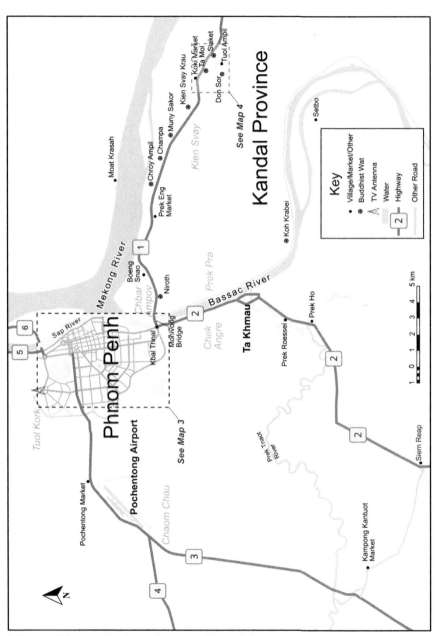

Map 2: Phnom Penh and Parts of Kandal Province, 1975

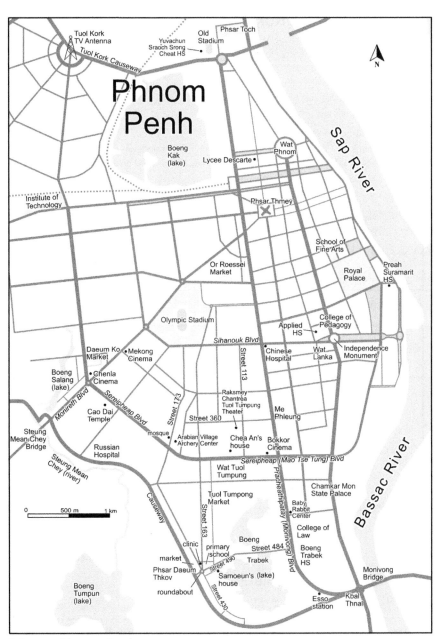

Map 3: Phnom Penh, 1975

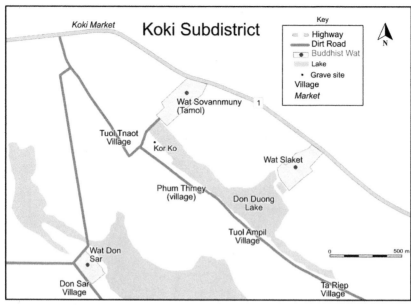

Map 4: Koki Subdistrict, Kien Svay District, Kandal Province, 1975

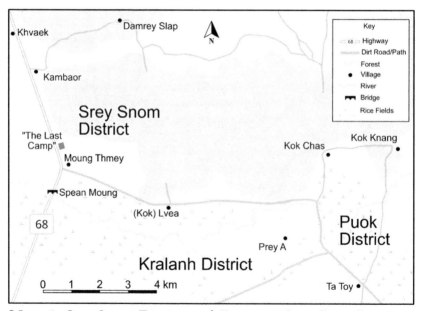

Map 6: Srey Snom District and Environs, Siem Reap Province, 1978–79

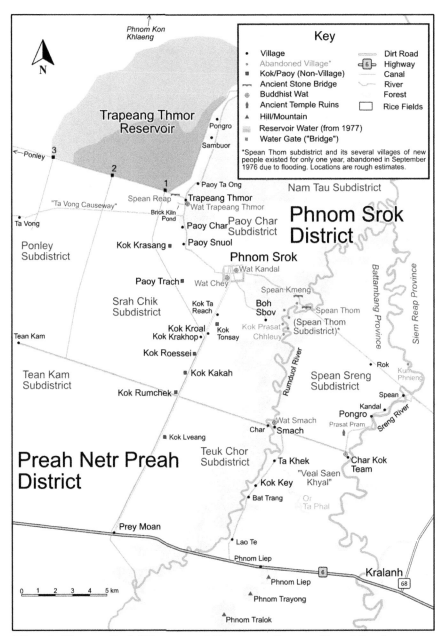

Map 5: Phnom Srok District and Environs, Region Five, Northwestern Zone, 1975–78

Photographs

Pen Doeuk and Chan Ith, the author's parents

Applied High School class of 1973. Chan Samoeun: bottom row, second from the left; Chea An: bottom row, second from the right; But Bunroat: back row, middle

A cyclo driver takes a rest in Phnom Penh, ca 1998.[†]

photo credit key: * DC Cam † Matthew Madden ‡ Chan Samoeun § Chan Samorn

Phsar Daeum Thkov roundabout with pond and mermaid statue in 2022, looking northwest [†]

Phsar Daeum Thkov Health Center, formerly called the Preah Suramarit Dispensary, immediately north of the roundabout, still extant in 2023 [†]

Khmer Rouge revolutionaries march down a Phnom Penh boulevard on the morning of 17 April 1975. [*]

the exodus from Phnom Penh in April 1975 *

evacuees carry their things by any means available, April 1975 *

Last of the old football fields on the grounds of Boeng Trabek High School in 2022. The author's family camped here on the night of 18 April 1975. The original school building, extant, is partially visible through the trees. †

The temple at Wat Chroy Ampil in 2022. Many refugees camped on the spacious grounds here, including the author's family, in April 1975. [†]

Koki Market on Highway 1 in 2022 [†]

Don Duong Lake with Tuol Ampil Village on the other side, from behind Wat Slaket, in 2022 [†]

Pursat train tracks (photographed in the dry season, 2006) where the evacuees camped waiting for the train heading northwest in October 1975 [‡]

Chan Samoeun in front of the hospital house where he convalesced in Phnom Srok in 1976, still extant in 2006 [§]

Spean Kmeng in 2022. (Spean Thom, a kilometer away, is larger and made from similar stones, but almost totally obscured by foliage.) [†]

Ancient stone railing of Spean Reap in 2006. The southern dam of Trapeang Thmor Reservoir stretches directly ahead (due west), and the beginning of the eastern dam is visible on the right. [‡]

Chan Samoeun in front of Father Suk and Mother Lam's traditional Khmer-style house in Paoy Snuol village, still extant in 2006 [§]

workers digging at a Khmer Rouge canal site [*]

workers hauling dirt with shoulder yokes and *bangky* baskets at a Khmer Rouge reservoir site *

looking south along the canal flowing from the first water gate at Trapeang Thmor Reservoir in 2022 †

the second water gate at Trapeang Thmor Reservoir in 2022 †

Trapeang Thmor Reservoir in 2022, looking northeast toward the eastern dam from the second water gate. Comrade Tuch inspected Comrade Ly's cheek in a hut near this spot. [†]

A Bodhi tree marks the location of Paoy Trach, former Khmer Rouge execution grove in Phnom Srok district, now largely erased by rice fields in 2022. Samorn and Oun were likely killed here, as well as countless others. [†]

Chan Samoeun at the ruins of Prasat Pram in 2022 [†]

Bodhi tree north of the brick-kiln pond in 2022; former site of the dining pavilion where Comrade Tuch first met Comrade Ly[†]

Chan Samoeun at the brick-kiln pond, Trapeang Thmor, in the dry season of 2006. The brick kiln was formerly located approximately in the immediate foreground of this picture, but it is no longer extant. [§]

Veal Saen Khyal in 2022, from the causeway looking south, with the trees of Highway 6 and the three mountains visible on the horizon. Phnom Tralok is the smaller-looking one on the right among the trees. [†]

Brothers Chan Samorn and Chan Samoeun in 2022, the only two members of their whole family to have survived the Khmer Rouge Revolution. They are wearing *krama* scarves. [†]

ansam cake [†]

water buffalo [†]

bangky baskets [†]

phkeak and khvaev knives [†]

chan srak [†]

some of the original school notebooks in which Chan Samoeun wrote the original text of *Prisoners of Class* in 1979-80 [†]

a sample of the original manuscript of *Prisoners of Class*, written in 1979 or 1980 [†]

the five volumes of the first Khmer edition of *Prisoners of Class* (1999-2000) with the single-volume second edition (2006) [†]